W9-BBZ-705

Marshall Loeb's Lifetime Financial Strategies
Little, Brown

# Marshall Loeb's Lifetime Financial Strategies

# Marshall Loeb's Lifetime Financial Strategies

YOUR ULTIMATE GUIDE TO FUTURE WEALTH AND SECURITY

Marshall Loeb

LITTLE, BROWN AND COMPANY
Boston New York Toronto London

First Edition

Library of Congress Cataloging-in-Publication Data

Loeb, Marshall.
Marshall Loeb's lifetime financial strategies : your ultimate guide to future wealth and security / Marshall Loeb. — 1st ed.
p. cm.
Includes bibliographical references and index.
ISBN 0-316-53075-1
1. Finance, Personal. 2. Investments. 3. Financial security.
I. Title.
HG179.L552 1996
332.024—dc20 95-17011

10 9 8 7 6 5 4 3 2 1

RRD—VA

Published simultaneously in Canada by Little, Brown & Company (Canada) Limited

Printed in the United States of America

For my family

# Contents

# Preface

Welcome to *Lifetime Financial Strategies.* My hope has been to produce the one book that you will turn to for useful information and advice—now, and well into the future.

Many talented and dedicated people have helped me in this work.

Let me express my gratitude to Little, Brown's CEO Charles Hayward, who suggested that I write this book, and Editorial Director Roger Donald, who edited it with great skill. Both of them offered wise counsel and steady support.

Special thanks to my team of researchers, who chased down and checked facts and didn't hesitate to challenge the author. Excellent young journalists all, they include Ann Sample, Patricia Lynch, Jordanna Fraiberg, Leslie Brenner, Lauren Long, Joseph McGowan, Karen Oberbrunner, Erica Pereira, Victoria Rainert and Melanie Warner.

Art directors Linda Eckstein and Beth Power, assisted by Mark Rosenthal, created the design and the colorful charts. Jennifer Y. Brown, aided by Leslie Dickstein, Charlotte Faltermayer and the other researchers, was in charge of checking them.

I'm also deeply appreciative for the major editorial contributions made by Glenn S. Daily on insurance, Emily Andren on computers, Helen O'Guinn on travel, Janice Castro and Edmund Faltermayer on health-care costs, Monci J. Williams on small business, Charles Burck on housing and investments, Alex Taylor and Jack R. Nerad on cars, and John Elbare and Randy Siller on retirement and wills, trusts and estates. Special thanks also to Richard Van Waalwijk and Marvin Strauss on insurance.

Warren M. Bergstein, Certified Public Accountant and professor of accounting and taxation at the Brooklyn campus of Long Island University, and his assistant, Monica Young, were sure-footed guides through the maze of tax law. Warren gracefully fielded our endless questions, and I am very grateful for his expert insights and suggestions.

John Macklin and Lu Anne Morrison at Mark McCormack's Investors Advisors International of Cleveland, Ohio, reviewed large portions of the manuscript and provided excellent advice on a number of investment issues.

At Little, Brown, Mary Tondorf-Dick worked logistical wonders to get the book into production, Steve Lamont was a superior and thoughtful copyeditor, Amanda Murray provided many editorial services, Caroline Hagen produced the handsome basic design of the book, and Donna Peterson, in Little, Brown's production department, went beyond the call of duty to keep this project on schedule.

My deepest appreciation to Nancy La Porte, my highly talented executive assistant, and to her predecessor, Shirley Nelowet, both of whom helped in so many ways.

Let me express my gratitude to John Huey, *Fortune*'s Managing Editor, and to Norman Pearlstine, Editor-in-Chief of Time Warner Inc., both superlative journalists, who have been sources of inspiration, and to Edward L. Jamieson, longtime Executive Editor of *Time,* my friend and colleague for many years, who offered numerous valuable editorial suggestions.

New York City — M. L.
October 1995

# Marshall Loeb's Lifetime Financial Strategies

CHAPTER I

# Getting It All Together

*America's economy has changed. But have you? Here are 10 basic steps to help secure your financial future.*

▼

The time has come. It is *now.*

The decision to secure your financial future is here. It is *yours.*

It may be the most important decision of your life.

Do you sit back, wait anxiously, watch helplessly while the waves of the New Economy's revolutionary changes wash over you and your dreams, pushing you back financially, leaving you stranded?

Or do you surmount your fears, seize the moment, grab your opportunities — opportunities not only to survive the upheavals ahead but also to use them to succeed and prosper?

Which do *you* choose?

This book speaks to your opportunities. It exposes your real risks and examines your potential rewards. It prepares you to act to your best advantage regardless of what the economic future may hold: deep recession, continued moderate growth or inflationary boom. It shows how you can confidently create a secure future for yourself — and your family.

To do that, it answers five specific questions:

How can I *earn* more money?

How can I *invest* it more profitably?
How can I *save* it more prudently?
How can I *spend* it more sensibly?
How can I enhance my *career?*

If you wonder whether you need answers to these questions, consider this cold-splash fact: Towers Perrin, one of the leading benefits consulting firms in the nation, calculates that if a 45-year-old married person with a household income of $50,000 wishes to retire at age 62 with an undiminished standard of living, he or she will then need $1.3 million. If that same person has a household income of $100,000, he or she will then need $2.1 million! Yes, Towers Perrin factors in expected inflation and figures that more than 70% of that startling sum will come from the assumed future value of your 401(k) plan and other benefits accrued on the job if you contribute consistently. But where will the *remaining* money come from?

That's up to you — and increasingly you alone — because more than ever before both the government and your employer are counting on you to provide for your own future and your ultimate retirement. If you cannot produce that money from your savings and investments, then retirement will be something of a squeeze.

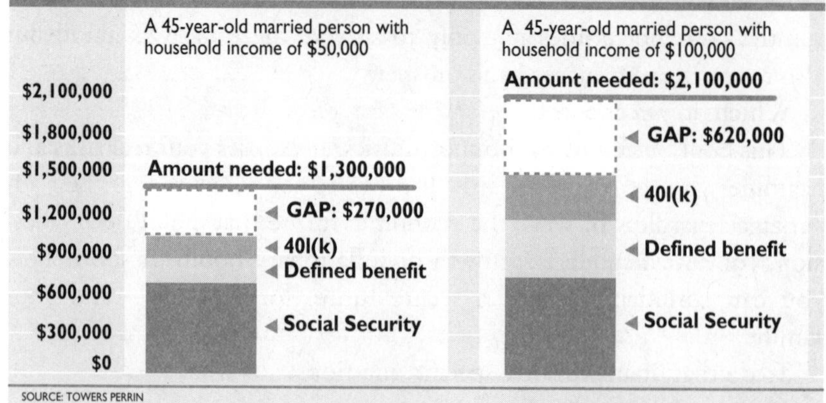

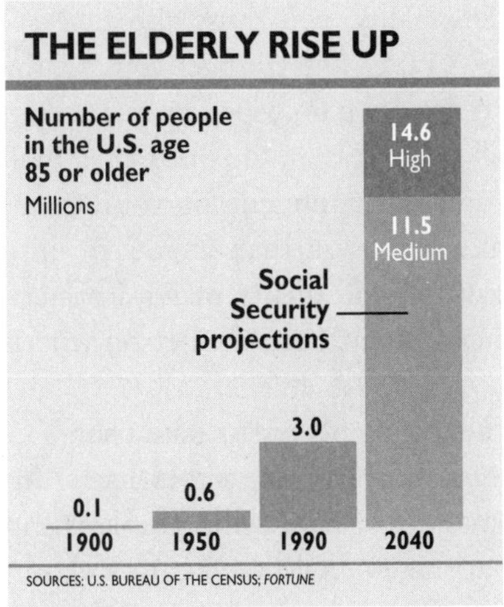


Good news: You stand to live much longer than your forebears.

Bad news: You stand to live much longer than your forebears.

Many people who quit work at age 62 can look forward to *30* years, or more, of life. Where will all the money come from to pay for your comfortable retirement — and well before that, to pay for raising your children, buying your dream home (or improving the one you have), taking that perfect vacation and generally living the good life?

For the answer — the *only* answer — look in the mirror.

You *can* accumulate money, and you don't have to be a financial genius. What you need is common sense, determination, dedication and reliable information. First, however, you must overcome your greatest obstacle: fear — and the inertia it engenders. Fears come in many forms, and they afflict almost all of us.

Some people fear *risk.* Because they are afraid of doing the wrong thing with their money, they are paralyzed into doing nothing. But the worst thing that you can do with your money is nothing: Keep it in a low-yielding bank account, and inflation will gnaw it into a fraction of its value.

Are you a highly risk-averse person? If so, face up to that reality, but also recognize that *everybody* makes mistakes sometimes. Think seriously about how much risk you can handle. Is your fear of losing money stronger than your desire to pile up profits? In that case, lay out a conservative strategy that will let you sleep at night. (No one can put a price on your ability to sleep soundly at night.)

Conservative people aim for safe and steady returns. They favor savings over investments, bonds over stocks, blue-chip shares over risky high-fliers. More adventurous types put the accent on growth. Either way, if you stick to a sensible strategy for handling your money, even in spite of occasional loss, you can make the most of what you have. The most important rule: Know thyself.

Aside from knowing your own personality, you must also take account of your age, your job, your stage in life. The younger you are, the more risk you can reasonably accept. If you have no dependents, you can obviously spend more on growth stocks, and less on life insurance, than parents of young children can. If you are confident of your career prospects for the future, you can take more risk than if you are in a chancy field. If you have a high net worth and plenty of liquid assets, you can be more aggressive in your investments than the person who is still accumulating a cash cushion.

Some people fear *responsibility.* They want others to take charge of their money, so they fall prey to tipsters and hustlers, or they listen unquestioningly and credulously to all manner of hard-selling brokers and self-professed financial planners. What these people need is to seek out the best professional advice — but then to weigh it and make their own decisions.

Some people even fear *wealth.* They feel undeserving, guilty of greed, worried that they may become worth more than their parents or peers. Their guilt translates into immobility. They should recognize that affluence carries no stigma, that poverty brings no moral superiority.

In fact, people enjoy more personal freedom and can make better choices about their lives if they have money and learn to handle it wisely. Just as a financially sound company has more opportunity to do great things than a strapped and worried organization does, so a financially sound person has more opportunity to act imaginatively and expansively. Certainly, money is not an end but a means — a means to help make the most out of ourselves by being able to pay for education, travel, medical care and a worry-free retirement. The more we earn, quite obviously, the more we can spend to enhance and secure our lives and those of our families, to enrich our communities, to benefit our favorite causes. The more we save and invest, the more we also provide the seed capital that helps create new enterprises and jobs.

Each and every one of us has the opportunity — and the obligation — to preserve and protect our money and make it grow. We have better chances than any other people at any other time to do all that. Chances to put our money into forms of investments, savings, insurance, that did not exist just a few years ago. Chances to build our careers or start businesses in fresh forms of industry, services or commerce, in newly expanding regions of the country. Chances to borrow capital through rather novel means.

The trouble is that chances mean choices, and making choices is hard. We have new freedoms to decide whether, when, how and how much to invest, save, spend. Tough choices. Too many people dodge such decisions. They take life as it comes and then lament their missed opportunities. That is practically always a mistake. Almost invariably, it is better to make some decision than no decision. A bad decision can be reversed; making no decision leaves you in limbo, uneasy, frustrated.

Thus, my aim is to outline your money choices and to urge you to seize your opportunities. Let me start by explaining 10 ways in which you can act immediately to preserve and protect what you have and help it to grow. Many of these steps will sound familiar, but few people have taken advantage of all of them; they provide a sound base on which to begin. All of them — and many more — are elaborated upon in later chapters of this book.

*Step one:* Build up a cash cushion to protect yourself against emergencies.

That way, if you unexpectedly need money, you will not have to borrow cash at exorbitant interest rates or sell off investments at what may be fire-sale prices. Try to accumulate and maintain easily tapped liquid savings equal to at least three months of your after-tax income. Six months' worth is even better. If you are retired, aim for a minimum of 12 months' worth.

Put that cash into a money-market deposit account or a certificate of deposit at a *federally* insured bank or savings institution. Another sound choice is to place your savings in a money-market fund at a solid, well-known mutual-fund company. It will be virtually as secure as in an insured bank account, and you will earn a fraction more in interest.

Your safe, liquid savings are the bedrock of your whole financial plan. They give you the security and confidence that come from knowing that you will always have funds to take care of yourself. With savings securely in place, you can move on to the next steps in your plan.

One of the surest and simplest ways to increase your savings and investments is to have a regular amount *automatically* deducted from each paycheck. If your employer offers an automatic deduction-and-deposit plan, grab it. If not, look for similar plans at most banks and many mutual-fund companies. As a bank depositor, you can often arrange for a regular transfer of a fixed amount from your checking account to your savings account. As a mutual-fund customer, you can arrange automatic deposits from your paycheck into a money-market fund.

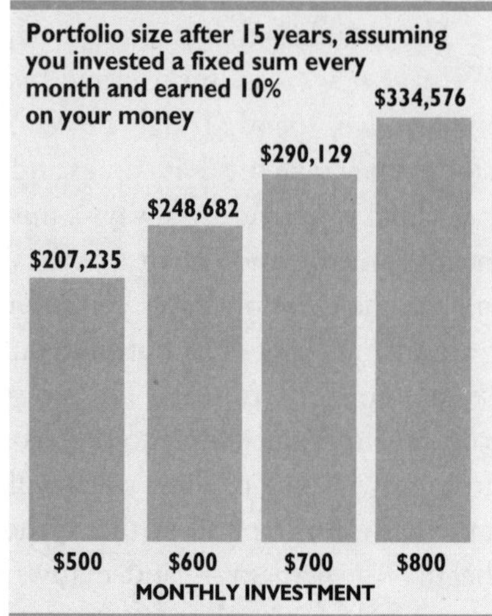


Another way to save is to bank each pay raise until the next one comes along. Or sock away any minor windfalls, such as bonuses, gifts, tax refunds, profits from your investments or free-lance fees.

*Step two:* After you have established your necessary liquid savings, start investing regularly and faithfully, come rain, come shine. Your insured savings are secure; you can tap into them at any time, and they grow at a measured pace. Your investments carry some risk; their value moves up and down, but they can grow at a faster rate than your savings.

Reduce your risks by diversifying. Markets have become so volatile that you can no longer buy only one stock or bond and confidently hold it for a lifetime. Thus, it is wise to start investing by buying into one or two diversified, professionally managed mutual funds. Over the last 10 years, the funds that invest in growth stocks have had total returns averaging slightly under 12.9% a year.

Once you have built up some profits in mutual funds, and you have done enough day-to-day studying of the market to feel confident in making your own choices, branch out into some individual stocks and bonds. Keep in place all the money that you have in well-performing mutual funds; simply channel some of your new investments into stocks and bonds. If you want to know what a powerful wealth-builder the stock market can be, consider this: If on March 31, 1980, you had put $1,000 in the stocks that make up Standard & Poor's 500 and had reinvested all the dividends, then your money on August 1, 1995, would have grown to $9,903.03. (I chose the March 31, 1980, date as a base

## PRECIOUS METALS MUTUAL FUNDS

These funds invest in equities of precious metals mining companies. They have not done nearly as well as other stock mutual funds.

| Fund name | One-year total return | Three-year annualized return | Five-year annualized return |
|---|---|---|---|
| **Smith Barney Precious Metals and Minerals A** | **–12.17** | **12.21** | **2.22** |
| **Blanchard Precious Metals** | **–12.36** | **15.43** | **3.35** |
| **Cappiello–Rushmore Gold** | **–8.60** | **NA** | **NA** |
| **Dean Witter Precious Metals and Minerals** | **–9.83** | **10.80** | **NA** |
| **Oppenheimer Gold and Special Minerals** | **–8.12** | **10.27** | **1.82** |
| **Fidelity Select American Gold** | **–8.36** | **19.13** | **4.50** |
| **Scudder Gold** | **–10.65** | **12.98** | **2.18** |
| **Fidelity Select Precious Metals and Minerals** | **3.66** | **18.69** | **5.72** |
| **Bull & Bear Gold Investors** | **–14.42** | **8.32** | **–0.06** |
| **Pioneer Gold Shares A** | **–8.18** | **15.33** | **NA** |
| **Franklin Gold** | **–0.70** | **11.43** | **3.54** |
| **Invesco Strategic Gold** | **–29.28** | **6.93** | **–3.27** |
| **IDS Precious Metals A** | **–4.90** | **16.31** | **3.80** |
| **Keystone Precious Metals Holdings** | **–14.08** | **13.04** | **4.22** |
| **Lexington Goldfund** | **–6.62** | **11.52** | **0.99** |

SOURCE: MORNINGSTAR

for a rather sentimental reason; it was then that I became Managing Editor of *Money* magazine.) Next, after you have become still more knowledgeable about investments beyond stocks and bonds, you can diversify further. Move perhaps into some real estate investment trusts (REITs) or shift a small amount into precious metals, in the form of gold bullion or a mutual fund that invests in gold- and silver-mining companies. Precious metals are volatile and have underperformed the stock market in general, but they have some minor virtue as a potential hedge, in case the stock market crashes.

No matter what stage of investment you're at, resolve to invest the same amount of money every month or from every paycheck. That's known as dollar-cost averaging, but you can think of it as investing on the installment plan. When your investments rise in value, you can congratulate yourself for having earned some paper profit. When they fall, at least you can take advantage of your new opportunity to pick up some bargains: A short while ago, your regular monthly investment could buy perhaps only two shares of your favorite mutual fund, but now it can buy three!

Above all, don't despair; all investments decline sometimes. Wise investors position themselves for the long term. If you believe that the country and its economy will do well over the long term, then your investments will do well. That is, they will do well if you don't become greedy and rush to buy when markets surge to their tops, and if you don't panic and rush to sell out when markets plunge to their bottoms. The discipline of dollar-cost averaging helps you avoid those two common errors.

*Step three:* Act now to reduce your taxes for this year and future years. For money earned in 1995, higher-income people face federal income tax rates of 36% and 39.6%. In addition, many states have income taxes that increase this burden by as much as 10%. And with the potential cost of a national health-insurance program still to be reckoned with, more federal tax increases may lie ahead.

Probably nobody takes all the deductions to which he or she is legitimately entitled. So resolve now to use your tax-saving opportunities and to keep better records of all your deductible expenses.

Here are a few of the many tax-saving steps you can take:

- Buy municipal bonds. The federal government does not tax the interest you collect on most of them, and if the bonds are from your home state, you will probably escape state and local taxes, too. Also invest in supersafe U.S. Treasury securities or U.S. savings bonds, the yields on which are exempt from state and local taxes, or in U.S. government bond funds if your state exempts their yields from its taxes.

## 1995 INDIVIDUAL FEDERAL INCOME TAX RATES

| | Base taxable income* | Tax on base | Percent on excess over base |
|---|---|---|---|
| **MARRIED, FILING JOINTLY** | **$0** | **$0** | **15%** |
| | **39,000** | **5,850** | **28** |
| | **94,250** | **21,320** | **31** |
| | **143,600** | **36,619** | **36** |
| | **256,500** | **77,263** | **39.6** |
| **SINGLE** | **$0** | **$0** | **15%** |
| | **23,350** | **3,503** | **28** |
| | **56,550** | **12,799** | **31** |
| | **117,950** | **31,833** | **36** |
| | **256,500** | **81,711** | **39.6** |

*Income after all deductions and exclusions.
SOURCE: JACK W. EVERETT, CFP, AIMC

## WHAT MUNICIPAL BONDS PAY

| Bond | Rate | July '95 yield | Equivalent rate at: 31% bracket | 39.6% bracket |
|---|---|---|---|---|
| Triborough Bridge/Tunnel Authority, NYC | **5.00%** | **5.90%** | **8.55%** | **9.77%** |
| San Francisco County Sewer Authority | **5.38** | **6.00** | **8.69** | **9.93** |
| Anne Arundel County, MD, Pollution Control Revenue | **6.00** | **6.15** | **8.91** | **10.18** |
| Orange County, FL, Tourism Board | **6.00** | **6.07** | **8.80** | **10.05** |
| Florida State Board of Education | **5.80** | **6.03** | **8.74** | **9.98** |
| NYC Industrial Development Authority | **6.13** | **6.54** | **9.48** | **10.83** |
| NYC Industrial Development Authority | **6.00** | **6.38** | **9.25** | **10.56** |
| Salem County, NJ, Pollution Control Finance Authority | **6.25** | **6.22** | **9.01** | **10.30** |
| Portland, OR, Sewer Authority | **6.25** | **6.15** | **8.91** | **10.18** |
| Douglas County, CO, Sanitation District | **6.50** | **6.26** | **9.07** | **10.36** |
| Cleveland, OH, Public Power Authority | **7.00** | **6.46** | **9.36** | **10.70** |
| Illinois Development Finance Authority | **6.75** | **6.44** | **9.33** | **10.66** |

SOURCES: *THE BOND BUYER*; INCOME SECURITIES ADVISOR

- Deposit money in your company's profit-sharing or stock purchase plans; taxes are deferred on any contributions made by your employer and on any earnings made by those contributions and by your own deposits.

  Take advantage of a 401(k) salary-reduction plan if your company offers one; of the income you earned in 1995, you can contribute up to $9,240 tax-deferred. The saving for someone in the top tax bracket is more than $3,659. And many big corporations add 50 cents for each dollar of employee contributions, up to a maximum of 6% of pay.
- Expand your dollars by using flexible spending

### GE's vs. IBM's 401(k)

General Electric's 401(k) beat IBM's from 1990 through 1992—because GE allowed employees to put in more and then matched more of that contribution. Here's how an employee who earned $60,000 in 1990 and $70,000 by the end of 1992 and kept roughly 75% of his or her retirement money in stocks and the rest in fixed-income investments would have fared at each company over three years.

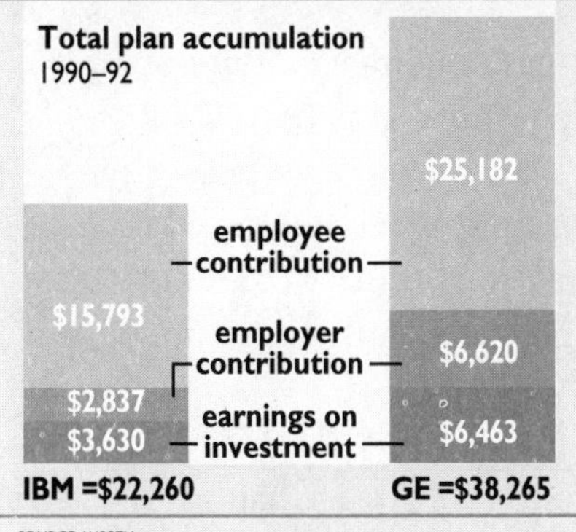


SOURCE: *WORTH*

accounts (FSAs) if your employer offers them. With FSAs, you tell your employer to set aside part of your *pretax* earnings that you may then use to pay up to a set limit — $5,000 a year for child-care or health-care benefits. (You can set side pretax earnings for both child-care *and* health benefits up to a total of $10,000.) The FSA money is not taxed — as long as you spend it for these purposes. But you *must* spend all the funds within the year you set them aside. In short, use it or lose it.

According to a study by the benefit and compensation consulting firm of Hewitt Associates that tracked 1,035 large employers, 80% of companies offer a dependent-care spending account for child-care expenses and 47% for elder-care expenses. The money generally can be spent on the care of any dependent child or aged relative. But usually the person must live with you and be financially dependent on you. With health-care FSAs, employers have the most discretion as to what they will allow to be covered. The Internal Revenue Service says no to cosmetic surgery, but generally allows coverage for insurance deductibles, prescription and over-the-counter medicines, dental work, glasses and many other medical costs.

- Deduct expenses incurred for charitable work, such as making phone calls or driving your car to and from the place where you do volunteer work. The allowance for your taxes on 1995 income is 12 cents a mile. Give your old clothes, books or furnishings to charities and collect receipts for the gifts' estimated value. You can also donate shares of stock or other securities. Note: You must itemize your income tax return in order to take charitable deductions.
- If you own a house or apartment, use a home-equity line of credit instead of a bank loan when you need to borrow substantial sums of money. You can deduct from your taxable income the interest you pay on real estate loans of up to $1 million. But your interest payments on ordinary consumer loans — including bank loans and credit cards — are not deductible.

For other ways to hold down your taxes, see Chapter 9, "Saving Money on Your Taxes."

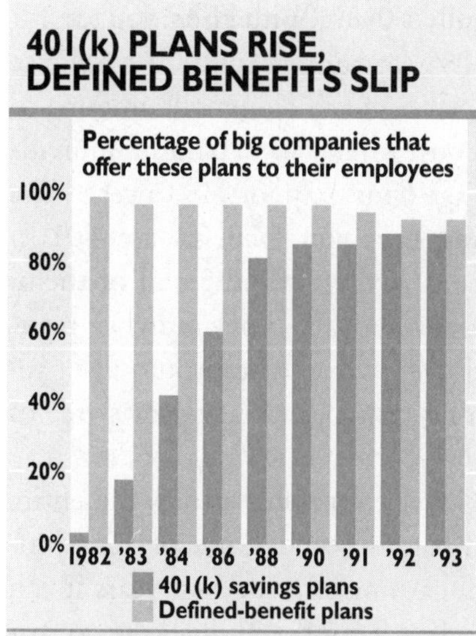

SOURCE: TOWERS PERRIN

*Step four:* If you are employed, take advantage of all the liberal employee-benefit plans offered by many corporations. Job-hopping from company to company is not the way to build a reserve of capital. Most programs go into effect only after you have been with a company for at least a year. But an employee earning $50,000 who stays with the same generous firm for 20 years can amass over half a million dollars from a combination of 401(k), profit-sharing, stock purchase, and other plans. And if that same employee stays with a firm for 30 years, he or she may amass close to $1.5 million from the same benefit plans.

This is important because, as noted earlier, Americans are being asked to take on more of the burden and responsibility of saving for their own retirement. Many employers have switched from a straight defined-benefit plan to a combination of both defined-benefit and defined-contribution plans. The defined-contribution plans put the responsibility on you — the employee — to invest your own money in company-sponsored, tax-deferred savings or investment programs, such as 401(k) plans. A 1994 study by Hewitt Associates concludes that 81% of employers offer both a defined-benefit plan and one or more defined-contribution plans to their employees.

Hewitt also calculates that if a person retires at age 65 after working at a company for 30 years, Social Security and a pension from a

**WHAT SOCIAL SECURITY PAYS TO RECIPIENTS**

| | | Maximum per month | Maximum per year |
|---|---|---|---|
| 1990 | | $975 | $11,700 |
| 1991 | | 1,022 | 12,264 |
| 1992 | | 1,088 | 13,056 |
| 1993 | | 1,128 | 13,536 |
| 1994 | | 1,147 | 13,764 |
| 1995 | | 1,199 | 14,388 |
| 1996 | PROJECTIONS | 1,252 | 15,024 |
| 1997 | PROJECTIONS | 1,320 | 15,840 |
| 1998 | PROJECTIONS | 1,388 | 16,656 |
| 1999 | PROJECTIONS | 1,458 | 17,496 |
| 2000 | PROJECTIONS | 1,533 | 18,396 |

SOURCE: SOCIAL SECURITY ADMINISTRATION

defined-benefit plan will replace roughly 60% of preretirement pay for today's $100,000-a-year employee, 70% for today's $50,000 employee and 85% for the $25,000 earner. Social Security alone will amount to only a small slice of pre-retirement income; the 1995 maximum individual payout for a person who retired at age 65 is only $14,388 a year. The three most significant capital-building corporate benefits are 401(k) plans, profit-sharing plans and company savings plans. In all of them, your employer usually contributes money above and beyond your regular salary to an account that is turned over to you when you quit or retire. All three are tax-deferred, meaning that the money grows free of taxes until you withdraw it.

In a profit-sharing plan, your employer commonly makes the entire contribution, often in the form of company stock. The size of this windfall depends on the company's annual earnings. In the best years it can amount to about 10% of your salary. But if profits plunge, the contribution may be zero, so you cannot count on a profit-sharing plan or stock-granting plan as a key ingredient of your savings-and-investment strategy. Look upon it as a significant extra: nice to have, but don't rely on it.

In a company savings program, you make the contributions, and your employer typically matches each dollar you invest with 50 cents of its own (in some cases more, in others, less). And remember: Everything the company tosses into the pot, plus all the earnings on both your own and the company's contributions, grows free of taxes until you withdraw the money.

In the increasingly popular 401(k) plan, you get a terrific tax break. You elect to put part of each paycheck into the plan. The money that you contribute is not considered immediate income, so it is tax-deferred and can grow with extra speed. Access Research, a benefits consulting firm, reports that about 240,000 corporations now sponsor 401(k) plans, and these have total assets of $525 billion. Of the 24.7 million employees eligible to take part, 18.5 million have 401(k) plans; 20% of them have balances over $50,000.

The biggest mistake that people make when building their 401(k) and other retirement plans is being too conservative. Participants tend to put too much in low-yielding investments like money funds and GICs (guaranteed investment contracts) and too little into stocks. That's why individuals often get returns on their 401(k) investments that are two to three percentage points below what professional money managers achieve.

*Fortune* has cited a case that sums up the power of wisely invested 401(k) plans:

Karen Schafer, 24, who does cost analysis for the catering division of Nordstrom's in Seattle, puts 10% of her $25,000 income into her 401(k). If she continues to contribute 10%, her salary goes up 5% a year, and she earns 11% a year on the money, then by the age of 59½ she will have accumulated some $1.6 million *before* adjusting for inflation. If she continues contributing till age 65, she will have $3 million.

You may think that earning 11% annually is beyond reach. Well, that approaches the 10.2% historical average return — from dividends and capital gains — of Standard & Poor's 500 stock index.

One drawback to 401(k) and other company savings plans: You generally cannot take out any of your money before you reach age 59½, or else you'll pay full income taxes plus a 10% penalty on all but the after-tax contributions you may have made. If you withdraw early to pay for certain allowable medical expenses or if you retire because of disability, you will have to pay ordinary income taxes on the money but not the 10% penalty.

Most employers let you borrow against your 401(k) plan. A Hewitt Associates survey in 1993 showed that 67% of companies offering 401(k)s had loan provisions, and an additional 3% were considering them. It is possible to borrow at least some of your contributions and often the employer's contributions as well. You can borrow up to $10,000 on a balance of $20,000 or less; on higher balances, you can borrow up to $50,000 or 50% of the amount that is vested, whichever is less. The interest rate is likely to be lower than you would pay to a bank or other commercial lender. It is a fixed rate based on a money-market measure such as the prime rate or the five-year U.S. Treasury note. You repay the loan with payroll deductions that can be spread over five years — or longer in some instances.

Another advantage of 401(k) loans is that they ultimately do not reduce the balance in your retirement fund. You restock it by repaying your loan. Meanwhile, all of your money not on loan keeps earning tax-sheltered income.

*Step five:* Open an Individual Retirement Account. One of the smartest ways to begin your financial plan is to put the $2,000 maximum each year into an IRA. Even though one of its most important tax-saving features has been limited or eliminated for many people, an IRA can be a valuable device both for reducing your taxes and for increasing your capital.

Everyone who earns money from a job can have an Individual Retirement Account, and almost everyone should. The dividends, interest and capital gains on your investment compound tax-free until you withdraw the money, probably after you retire. When that time comes, you can arrange for gradual withdrawals over the course of many years.

If you are not covered by an employee pension plan, you can deduct your full IRA deposits from your taxable income. So can anyone who meets certain income limits. The Congressional Joint Committee on Taxation projects that in 1995, 66% of all taxpayers filing individually will be eligible for the maximum deductible IRA contribution, as will 54% of households with two earners.

If you *are* covered by an employee pension plan — whether or not you are vested — you can still deduct your full contribution if you are a single person earning $25,000 or less annually in adjusted gross income. Married couples filing jointly keep the full deduction if their combined income is $40,000 or less. Singles who earn between $25,000 and $35,000 and joint filers who earn between $40,000 and $50,000 can deduct part of their contribution. The deduction tapers off as you earn more money. It vanishes altogether when your income tops $35,000 for singles or $50,000 for joint filers.

Even if you cannot deduct your contribution from your taxable income, an IRA can still be an excellent tax saver. That's because your money grows without being diluted by annual tax bills. And it grows at compound rates, meaning that you earn returns not only on your original stake but on your accumulated gains as well. It's remarkable how fast money accumulates when it rises at compound rates and is unencumbered by taxes. If you put away $2,000 every January and it grows 8% annually, you will have some $31,291 after 10 years, $98,845 after 20 years, $244,690 after 30 years and $559,562 after 40 years. And at a 10% rate of return, which is slightly less than the average for stocks over the past 70 years, your investment would double in seven years and reach $126,005 in 20 years.

Of course, withdrawals and taxes on them are inevitable. You may begin withdrawing your money at age 59½ and you must start withdraw-

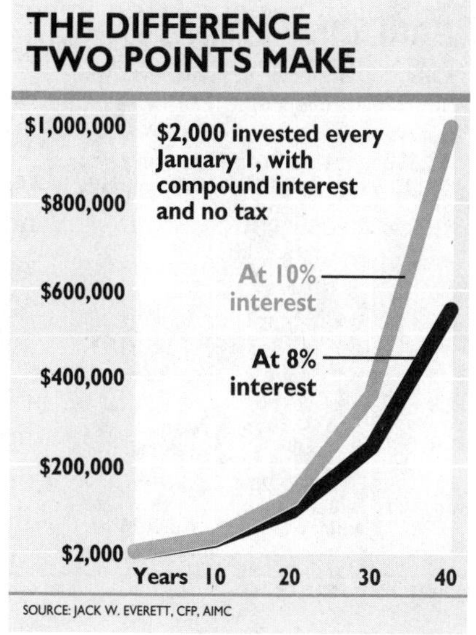


ing no later than at age 70½, but you still stand to come out way ahead.

You can put your IRA money into almost any form of savings or investment except for art and other collectibles. My own favorite repository for an IRA, particularly for young people who are confident of the future and willing to take sensible risk, is a no-load growth mutual fund that invests in stocks and other securities. Over the past 10 years, the growth funds have had total returns averaging 13.2% a year. Funds with the best performance records are named in Chapter 6, "A Sensible Strategy for Investing in Stocks," and you can get an updated list of the top performers in the monthly "Fund Watch" column of *Money* magazine.

*Step six:* If you are eligible, also open a Keogh plan account or a Simplified Employee Pension, known as a SEP. Keogh plans and SEPs work much like IRAs, but you can put much more money into them and deduct it all from your taxable income.

It's surprising how many people are eligible for Keoghs or SEPs but don't know it — or don't take advantage of these large and liberal tax shelters. You qualify just so long as you work for yourself. You can work full-time, part-time or free-lance. You can work at one job for an employer but still contribute your earnings from a second, self-employed moonlighting job. Among those eligible for Keoghs and SEPs are most small-business people and many lawyers, doctors, dentists, carpenters, plumbers, actors and directors, free-lance writers, waiters, taxi drivers and the like.

**SOME JOBS ELIGIBLE FOR KEOGHS AND SEPs**

- lawyers
- doctors
- dentists
- carpenters
- plumbers
- actors
- theater directors
- taxi drivers
- waiters
- free-lance writers
- self-employed and other small-business people

SOURCE: JACK W. EVERETT, CFP, AIMC

You can contribute slightly less than 13.5% of your income from self-employment to a Keogh or 15% of your income to a SEP, up to a maximum contribution of $30,000 a year. Also, you can have both an IRA and a Keogh (although most probably you may not be able to deduct your IRA contribution). Between these two plans, some high-income individuals can put away as much as $32,000 a year. If both spouses are self-employed, they can shelter up to $64,000 annually. There's even a special kind of Keogh, a form of defined-benefit plan, to which older high-income professionals can contribute much more than $30,000 a year.

**EARLY INVESTING PAYS...**

Contributions made in January vs. April of the following year

**$2,000 invested in an IRA every year for 10 years at 10% growth annually**

| January 1 | April 15 of following year |
|---|---|
| $35,062 | $29,087 |

SOURCE: JACK W. EVERETT, CFP, AIMC

*A warning:* Unlike an IRA, which you can open as late as April 15 of *next* year, you have to open a Keogh plan by December 31 of *this* year in order to contribute any of this year's earnings to it. However, you can make those contributions up to the time you file your income taxes — as late as April 15 of next year, or August 15 if you get an automatic extension. Or you can open a SEP, which follows the rules for IRAs.

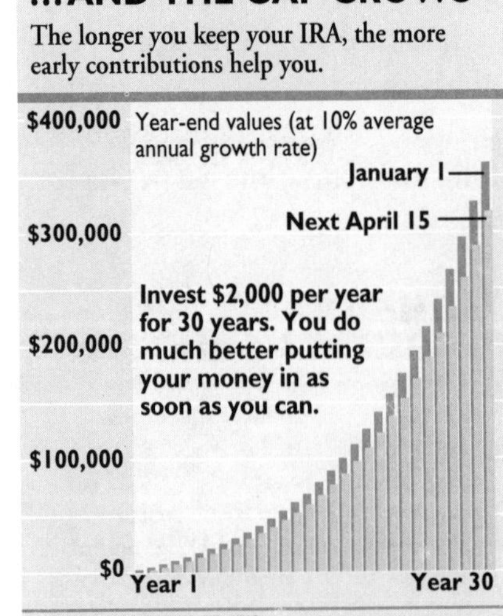


In any case, it is wise to make your annual contribution to any of these plans as early in the year as possible. Let's say you deposit $2,000 every year for 10 years and earn 10% annually on it. Put that money in every January 2, and in 10 years you will have $35,000. But if you regularly wait until April 15 of the *following* year,

## WHAT $100,000 OF LIFE INSURANCE CAN COST*

| ISSUE AGE | MEN whole life | MEN term | WOMEN whole life | WOMEN term |
|---|---|---|---|---|
| 30 | $840 | $130 | $714 | $120 |
| 40 | 1,365 | 150 | 1,155 | 140 |
| 50 | 2,310 | 210 | 1,890 | 180 |
| 60 | 4,032 | 400 | 3,192 | 310 |

*Per year, for preferred risks. Term policies are annual renewable term.
SOURCE: GLENN S. DAILY

your money will have grown to only $29,000. Over a period of 20 to 30 years, the compounding of tax-deferred earnings on early contributions can add tens of thousands of dollars to your account.

*Step seven:* Be certain you have a will — a sound, valid, hard-to-shake and up-to-date will. There is no way without a will to make sure that whatever you leave goes to whomever you wish. If you do not have a will, your heirs could be clobbered by taxes and your children could be raised by someone you don't want to. Yet it is shocking how many adult Americans do not have this basic document — almost two-thirds of them do not.

Estate laws change fairly often and sometimes radically, so it is important to review your will regularly. Check right now to see if your will is current. If it is not, make an appointment with a lawyer to prepare a new one as soon as possible. It is best to have your will drafted by an attorney and updated at least once every three years.

*Step eight:* Save money on your life insurance and make sure you have the right kind of policies. For basic insurance protection, the least expensive policy is still annual renewable term. If you are a nonsmoking man, say, 40 years old, $100,000 of coverage is likely to cost you some $150 for annual renewable term and $1,365 for traditional whole life. But if you want to protect your family and simultaneously build up tax-deferred savings, your best means may well be whole life. And if you are age 55 or older, the premiums for annual renewable term will approach or equal those for whole life bought when you were younger. Another strategy: You might be wise to buy term insurance and then put the

## FEDERAL ESTATE TAXES

| Base taxable amount* | Tax on base | % on excess over base |
|---|---|---|
| Under $600,000 | $0 | 0% |
| $600,000 | 0 | 37 |
| $750,000 | 55,500 | 39 |
| $1,000,000 | 153,000 | 41 |
| $1,250,000 | 255,500 | 43 |
| $1,500,000 | 363,000 | 45 |
| $2,000,000 | 588,000 | 49 |
| $2,500,000 | 833,000 | 53 |
| $3,000,000 | 1,098,000 | 55 |

*After all deductions and exclusions
SOURCE: JACK W. EVERETT, CFP, AIMC

money you save into mutual funds or some other sound investment. You can save still more by buying only the life insurance you need.

How much do you need? The answers are in Chapter 13, "Insuring Yourself." For now, remember this: If no one is relying on you for financial support, you probably don't need any life insurance at all.

*Step nine:* Save money by giving it away. If you think income taxes are high, you should look at death taxes. They start at 37% on the federal level and go all the way up to 55%. State taxes and excise taxes on large pension plans can easily raise your total estate taxes above 75%. Instead of leaving all that to Uncle Sam, give it away — while you're alive — to those whom you want to have it. You don't have to pay tax on gifts of money paid directly to a college to help cover your children's or grandchildren's tuition and fees, nor on payments made directly to hospitals or nursing homes to pay the bills of less fortunate family members or friends.

Generous donations to your favorite charity or cultural institution, whether the local symphony or your alma mater, can also help to save you money now. (Don't forget to get receipts. Starting in 1994, the IRS no longer considers your canceled check as sufficient documentation for charitable contributions over $250.) It often pays to make the gift to a charitable trust. While endowing a worthy cause, you can reduce your current income taxes on gifts of appreciated stocks. In one form of charitable trust, you get the investment income from your gift for the rest of your life. For more on trusts, see Chapter 23.

*Step ten:* Buy a personal computer and learn to use it. If you invest your money — and, more important, your time — in purchasing and mastering a computer, it will pay you dividends many, many times over. With the vast range of new and sophisticated programs available, the computer has become an essential household and business tool. The tasks it can help you with include storing (and easily retrieving) huge amounts of information and picking out the best stocks. For example, from the thousands of issues, you can segregate those few that are priced well below their book value or that have especially modest price/earnings ratios or that are selling far beneath their recent peaks. A computer also can help you chart and graph the movements of specific stocks. It can keep track of the investments you have and alert you to any that are starting to go sour. Not least, new programs that employ simple question-and-answer procedures can help you mightily to plan your tax strategy, keep the records that will simplify the chore of paying taxes and legitimately reduce what you have to pay. These programs will also help you fill out your tax forms faster and more accurately, to file electronically and to get any refunds sooner.

And there is yet *one more step:* Keep up with the news that affects your money. The world changes rapidly, and almost every event of consequence close to home or in some distant corner of the world influences your investments, your savings, your personal balance sheet. A further dramatic move toward peace in the Middle East, continued regional conflict in the former Soviet Union, an election in South America, a coup in Africa — not to mention events at home, such as urban unrest, the passing of a bill in Congress or a policy shift by the Federal Reserve Board — can alter the price of everything from chocolate bars to new cars. Such events can also lead to sharp gyrations in the values of your investments and the levels of the interest rates you pay or collect. It is important, then, to become an avid reader of the daily financial pages and of business magazines. One rather immodest but heartfelt comment: I think you will find *Fortune* to be particularly valuable and enjoyable.

So there you have the 10 initial steps. All of them are discussed in detail in the following pages. And there are more steps, many more, that each of us can take in order to seize the moment, make the right choices and take advantage of our opportunities. For an explanation of them, read on.

CHAPTER 2

# Planning to Achieve Your Goals

Your long-term goal, above all, is to achieve financial independence. That means having enough to say to yourself, "If I wanted to, I could quit what I'm doing today and live comfortably for the rest of my life."

Millions of Americans *can* reach that goal, but as we have seen in Chapter 1, you cannot count on your employer to do it for you; and you also cannot count on Social Security. For every $1 that today's retirees have paid into the Social Security trust fund, they collect an average of $4. The fund will not be so flush in the future, and what you can hope for is probably just $1 for every $1 you contribute.

Nor can you bank on a real estate boom lifting the value of the house you paid $100,000 for to $1 million when you sell it. Property values are generally expected to rise only moderately in the years ahead.

No, it's up to you. Small wonder that the Gallup organization reported that the most popular New Year's resolution among Americans was no longer losing weight or quitting smoking, as it had been for the previous 12

### HOW INFLATION DEVALUES YOUR MONEY

**Value of $1,000 at various inflation rates**

| | Average annual rate of inflation | | |
|---|---|---|---|
| | 4% | 6% | 8% |
| **5 years** | **$815** | **$734** | **$659** |
| **15 years** | **542** | **395** | **286** |
| **25 years** | **360** | **213** | **124** |

**Capital needed to maintain $20,000 in annual purchasing power over 20 years**

| If inflation is: | You need: |
|---|---|
| **4%** | **$286,145** |
| **5** | **310,133** |
| **6** | **336,868** |
| **7** | **366,695** |

SOURCE: MUTUAL FUND EDUCATION ALLIANCE

years, but managing their personal finances better. There are two initial steps to that:

First, you have to know what you're worth.

Second, you have to know how to budget.

## Calculate How Much You Are Worth Now

A primary step toward taking control of your financial life is to calculate your net worth. That is what you own minus what you owe. Once you figure out what you are really worth, you can set your financial goals — for example, to take a vacation, buy a house or secure a comfortable retirement. Then you can devise strategies to reach those goals.

Most people who calculate their net worth are surprised to find out that they are worth more than they thought. Just get a simple pocket calculator and add up the current value of all your assets. Start with your checking and savings accounts and money-market funds. Don't forget the current market value of any stocks, bonds or other securities you may own. Your insurance agent can supply the current cash value of your life insurance if it is not stated in the policy itself.

To find out what your house or condo is worth, consult a real estate broker or note the asking prices of similar homes for sale in your neighborhood. Also, add in the current worth of your employee benefits, such as profit-sharing and thrift plans and unexercised stock options. Often these assets are second in value only to your house.

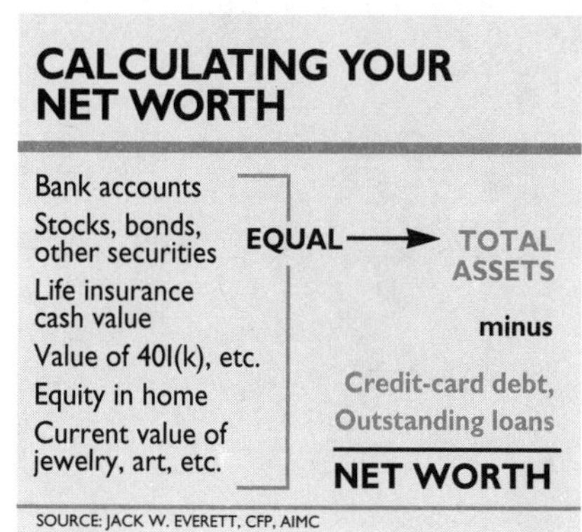


If you own art, antiques, jewelry or other collectibles, estimate their current resale price; you may need to call in an appraiser. Expect to pay an expert appraiser $100 to $300 an hour. If you have only a few collectibles, you do not need an appraiser. Just ask a knowing dealer what he or she thinks you could sell them for.

You should recalculate your net worth at least once a year. Some debt counselors urge their clients to take their financial reading immediately before they start Christmas shopping.

## Make a Budget You Can Really Keep

After having determined your net worth, your next move to financial security is to create — and stick to — a budget. Maintaining a real budget — not one that you pretend to keep in your head — allows you to sleep at night without agonizing over how you are going to keep up with ordinary expenses and pay for the unexpected. If you do not have this all-important personal balance sheet, start one now.

In just three months' time you can win the battle of the budget. If you devote only a few hours during each of those months to considering and correcting your income and outgo, you can reduce overspending, free up money for savings and investments and build a cash reserve for that sudden urge — or need — to splurge. Investing just a few hundred dollars more every month can make a tremendous difference in your net worth over time. At an 8% rate of growth, money doubles in 10 years, triples in 15 years, quadruples in 19 years and quintuples in 21 years.

Here's your three-month budget scenario:

*Month one:* During this first month, figure out precisely what you earn and what you spend. There are many products on the market — ledgers at stationery stores and computer software programs — that can help you to organize your expenses. Add up your salary and any other money you've received in the past year, such as dividends, interest, rents, bonuses, allowances or child support. Your 1040 income tax form for the past year can help you find the figures.

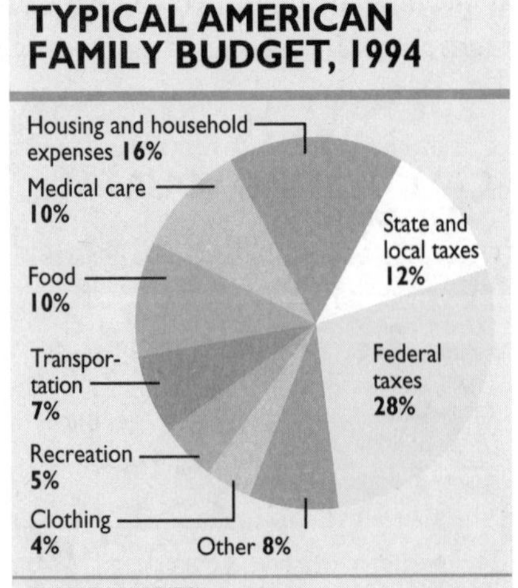


Then examine how you have spent your money. You don't have to exhume all records dating back for years. It is more than enough to analyze your expenses and your income for, say, the last 12 months. This will enable you to determine routine monthly expenses as well as sums that you must pay at irregular intervals, such as insurance premiums, school tuition and gifts. One purpose of your analysis is to help you plan for these irregular but necessary expenses so that you will never again have to invade your investments to pay for unexpected bills. If you cannot account for a large share of your spending, keep a journal and jot down all expenses as they hit you, day by day, for one week.

*Month two:* Devote the second month to figuring out how you can trim any excesses in your spending so that you can build savings and investments. Calculate what percentage of your income goes to each expenditure, from clothing to commuting costs to mortgage payments.

Allocate no more than 65% of your take-home pay for regular monthly expenses, including food, utilities, and rent or mortgage payments. Of course, that can be hard for young people living in expensive urban areas. But, ideally, try to find a way to stick to that two-thirds-of-monthly-income figure.

Allow another 20% for occasional outlays, such as for clothes, household repairs and recreation. Put aside 10% for necessary expenses that hit at different but predictable intervals, such as insurance premiums and property taxes, and the last 5% — or more, if possible — for savings and investments.

Take a close look at your monthly installment debt. You are in good shape if you spend 10% or less of your after-tax income on car payments, department-store and credit-card installments or bills for furniture and appliances that you bought on time. Particularly during periods of economic recession, you may be tempted to buy more items on installment, and to keep big, one-time expenditures to a minimum. But beware: The last thing you want is to be laid off and to find yourself saddled with many bills. If the amount of those monthly installment bills is 10% to 15% of your income, you are creeping toward the danger zone. If they stretch beyond 15% to 20%, you are in trouble.

To correct that, allocate a set amount of money each month for debt repayments. Pay as much as you can possibly afford. Figure out what indulgences and luxuries you can sacrifice — temporarily. It may be sensible even to raid your savings to pay your debt. You will never get rich keeping cash in a statement savings account paying less than 3% while your credit-card or other installment debts cost you 15% to 18% and, in some cases, even more.

Particularly if you have a checking account that pays interest, you may be inclined to wait till the last minute to pay your ordinary bills. After all, the longer you delay, the more interest you earn. But be careful! If you cut it too close, you could end up paying finance charges. They probably would cost you far more than the interest you would earn on your checking account. Interest-bearing checking accounts in mid-1995 paid about 2.5% annual interest, but credit-card charges average 16% and often exceed 18% annually. Despite recent "wars" among credit-card companies to win customers, the charges have not fallen significantly.

*Month three:* In the third month, carefully re-evaluate your income-and-outgo statement and make changes so that you can live on your budget — realistically. Don't get carried away. Everybody needs some luxuries, so you and each person in your family should be allowed to keep at least one indulgence. If you are passionate about movies and want to see three or four films a week, then adjust your spending in some other area. Successful budgeting depends on being neither too rigid nor too loose. If your budget is too lean, you will not stick to it. Your purpose is to make a budget that you can keep.

Once you have created a workable budget and conquered any debt problems, start saving a fixed amount each month. Deposit that sum in a money-market fund, a bank money-market deposit account, short-term bank certificates of deposit, U.S. Treasury bills or other liquid savings. Put that cash away as regularly and as faithfully as you meet your mortgage payments or rent.

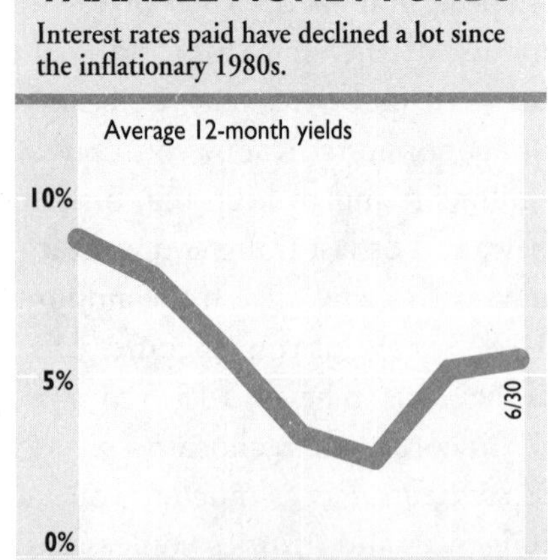


As noted earlier, among the surest and simplest ways to save is to have a regular amount automatically deducted from each paycheck. To find out how you can best accomplish that, just ask an official of the payroll department where you work or the bank, mutual-fund company or other financial institution where you want your money deposited.

Sticking to a budget requires work. You have to keep sound records. You can do that by paying for all items over $25 with checks and letting them serve as your expense ledger. Put an asterisk on a corner of each check that you might later charge off as a tax deduction. If your bank doesn't return your canceled checks, fill out your checkbook registers or stubs as if they were your expense ledger, which indeed they should be. Of course, a much simpler, surer and quicker way is to use a computer and a personal finance program.

You will also have to keep working to hold your spending in line. Probably your biggest expenditures are your income taxes. As we saw earlier, you may be able to cut them by setting up an IRA — or a Keogh plan or a Simplified Employee Pension if you have any self-employment income — and by switching from some taxable investments to tax-free ones, such as municipal bonds.

Your second major expense is housing. If you are spending as much as 40% of your take-home pay on your home loan, check with a banker or some other mortgage lender to see if it makes sense to renegotiate your loan. Usually it pays to do so if you do not plan to sell your property soon and can get a longer-term mortgage or one with a rate one or more percentage points below the loan you now have. With a favorable new mortgage, you may be able to recoup the closing costs in a year or two and reduce your monthly expenses by more than $100.

## Set Your Financial Goals

Few people know what they really want their money to do. Several years' accumulation of savings or a sudden inheritance or windfall leaves them with money to invest and no idea of how to make it work best for them.

What is *your* financial goal? For example, are you saving for a specific, short-term goal such as paying college tuition, or a broader, long-term goal such as achieving future security? Determine just what you want your money to do and how much you will need to do it. Then figure out how much to put away each week — or each month — to reach your goal.

## 10 Steps to Save Money Now

Save a few dollars here, a few more there: It all adds up. Just think of how much money your parents would have now had they saved up and invested just $100 in Warren Buffett's Berkshire Hathaway Co. in 1975. (Answer: $50,000.) To further help you with your budget, here are 10 random steps that you can take to save money immediately:

- Get a home-equity loan and use it to pay off your consumer loans. The interest you pay on a home-equity loan is tax-deductible; the interest on consumer loans is not.
- Trim your interest charges still more by using a bank loan or a home-equity loan to pay off all your credit-card bills (on which the interest averages 16%).
- Switch to a lower-cost long-distance phone carrier. For a comparison of rates, services and the features of eight of the largest carriers and 28 calling plans, send $3 and a self-addressed, stamped envelope to Telecommunications Research and Action Center (TRAC), P.O. Box 12038, Washington, D.C. 20005.
- Reduce your electricity bills as much as 40% by buying a load controller that shuts down or lowers power sent to certain appliances. Example: The load controller may turn your water heater off at times during the day when rates are highest.
- Cut your auto insurance bills more than 10% by increasing your collision deductible from $200 to $500.
- Ask your doctor or pharmacist if you can use generic versions of name-brand pharmaceuticals.
- Get free companion air travel by asking your travel agent and checking airlines about what buy-one-get-one-free deals are available.
- Save on brokerage commissions by using discount brokers (unless you need a lot of research and hand-holding from full-service brokers).
- Save still more by favoring no-load or low-load mutual funds over load funds.
- Use dividend-reinvestment plans, which allow you to plow back your quarterly payments into shares without paying commissions and sometimes at slightly discounted prices.

## The High Cost of Delay

Don't put it off. The cost of not making investment moves immediately can add up. Say you decide to shift some money from a lower-paying savings account into higher-yielding U.S. Treasury bond mutual funds. If you delay just a few months, your procrastination can cost you a bundle.

For example, if in January 1985 you had invested $10,000 in a Treasury bond mutual fund, by December 1994 it would have been worth $26,487. But if you had waited and invested the $10,133 (the additional $133 would have been made in the savings account earning 5.5% interest) in April 1985, then by December 1994 the dollar amount would have been a full $880 less.

The sooner you start saving, the easier and faster you will be able to achieve independence. If you're young, you can begin modestly: Put the $2,000 maximum each year into a tax-deferring Individual Retirement Account. Start doing that in 1996 and earn 10% compounded annually on the money, and in the year 2016, you will have $101,924; in 2026, you will have $277,359. At a compounded 10% rate of return, your investment would double in seven years.

Here are three worthwhile rules to help you achieve your financial goals:

- *Don't be tax-greedy.* Yes, some investments still carry nice tax benefits, and we will examine them in detail in later chapters. But many people are so obsessed with making tax-exempt or tax-deferred investments that they often miss much more lucrative, if taxable, investments. You should look for good, sound economics in an investment before you weigh the tax benefits. This is especially true now that changes in the law have eliminated or reduced the tax advantages of quite a few investments. Remember: The key is not how much you reduce your taxes but how much you increase your income.

- *Keep an open mind.* Many people invest in just one thing and stick with it. Huge sums of money are still locked away in statement savings accounts, which these days typically pay interest of less than 3%. They could earn much more from other forms of savings and investments — for example, tax-deferred annuities from the strongest insurance companies. But many people are — in the words of one savings bank president — too lazy or afraid to move their money.

And you probably won't reach your goals with money funds, certificates of deposit and other forms of savings alone — not when they are paying barely more than inflation. You will need help from stocks. They are risky in the short term but still your best means to achieve security over the longer run.

- *Get advice from professionals.* Beware of advice from people who are not qualified to give it. Amateurs — like your next-door neighbor or your cousin's son-in-law — can do more damage than good. You are better off soliciting and then carefully considering professional advice from brokers, bankers, attorneys, accountants or certified financial planners. Fees should be agreed on in advance, but sometimes the advice is free. Don't be afraid to ask questions. Additional help in getting your finances together ranges from books, which can motivate and educate you, to public seminars in personal finance given by brokerage houses and financial planners.

Courses on personal finance are offered by more and more community colleges, universities, community service organizations and other sponsors of adult education programs. The charge is often $75 or less, and some courses are free for senior citizens and others. The chance you take is that your teacher may be merely a salesperson in the guise of an educator, so check his or her credentials closely. Avoid instructors whose expertise is limited to selling stocks, bonds, insurance or other so-called investment products. Finally, you can get an inexpensive education by enrolling in one of the thousands of investment clubs.

## What a Financial Planner Can Do for You

A good financial planner can be hard to find, but we'll tell you how to hire the right one. He or she can save you a ton of time, make you a pot of money and help considerably to meet your goals. What can you reasonably expect from a professional planner? More or less in this sequence, he or she should (1) calculate your net worth; (2) help you devise a workable budget; (3) make sure you are properly insured against sickness, disability and death; (4) check that you, your cars and your house are well protected against damage and injury and lawsuits; (5) help you create a strategy for holding down your taxes; (6) prepare a retirement plan for you; and (7) review your will and help you prepare an estate plan for passing along your wealth.

Most practitioners write a comprehensive plan diagnosing your financial ailments and prescribing monetary medications. The plan generally costs from $500 all the way up to $10,000, depending on three factors: your net worth or income, the planner's reputation and whether the planner also collects commissions on any investments you buy from him or her.

If a basic plan is all you want — and not any face-to-face, ongoing advice — there is a less-expensive alternative in "plans-by-mail." You fill out a questionnaire and back comes a report with some recommendations. Price Waterhouse is one of the accounting firms that sells to people who want a plan without the expense of ongoing counsel. For generic strategic advice, but not specific investment recommendations, the Personal Financial Products Division of Price Waterhouse (55 East Monroe Street, 30th Floor, Chicago, Illinois 60603; 800-752-6234) charges from $45 to $285 for paper-based reports and software applications. Major brokerage houses and some large banks and insurance companies also offer these basic plans.

You probably will want more than that, notably guidance in implementing your plan and continuing advice. In that case, you would be best served by engaging a real-life planner, and the two of you should review your finances at least once a year. This will cost you 30% to 50% of your original bill. However much you pay a planner, the cost is relatively modest compared with the potential long-term rewards — and risks — of following his or her recommendations. Planners' fees are usually tax-deductible. As a rule, don't spend more than 1% of your investment assets on a plan — unless you have complications caused by divorce, multiple pensions, tax shelters that make the IRS gasp or the like.

A planner should coordinate the specialized help you will need from such other professionals as your broker, accountant, insurance agent and lawyer. For a fee, some planners will even take responsibility for running your everyday finances. But that's usually still your job.

Further, a planner will advise you to direct your investments into broad areas according to a strategy that meets your needs — and your nerves. He or she may suggest, for example, that you put half of your capital into stock mutual funds, one quarter into bond funds and one

## Before You See a Planner, Ask Yourself:

1. What are my financial goals? How do I rank them? Does my spouse have the same goals?
2. Am I willing to spend less and save more to reach my goals?
3. What do I want my planner to do? Check out my existing arrangements? Set up a plan that includes creating a monthly budget, reviewing insurance and taxes, building and overseeing an investment portfolio?
4. What kind of investor am I? How much risk can I live with comfortably?

Source: *Fortune,* May 16, 1994

quarter into secure and predictable savings certificates. Because most planners are not stockbrokers, they rarely recommend individual stocks.

Before recommending what you should do, a planner should first ask you several questions. How much risk are you willing to take? Are you more interested in maximizing gains or in minimizing taxes? How do you feel about borrowing to invest? As you answer, you often begin to realize that your attitudes about money may not square with the way you actually spend and invest it.

Once the planner has a fix on your goals, he or she begins to make recommendations. At that point, you are free to head for your nearest insurance agent or mutual-fund dealer to do your own buying. Or you can allow the planner to sell you the financial "products" he or she thinks you need. On such sales, the planner collects commissions of 1% to 10%, and sometimes more.

Anyone can hang out a shingle and call himself or herself a financial planner regardless of education, experience or ethics. There are almost no licensing regulations. The Securities and Exchange Commission (SEC) requires financial planners to register as investment advisers, referred to as RIAs, and can put them out of business for breaking securities laws. But almost anybody can register by filling out a form and sending the SEC a $150 fee. A few self-professed planners are charlatans, and too many are simply salespeople of financial products, worried more about their own commissions than about your wealth. However, first-rate financial planners are increasingly available.

When selecting a planner, assemble a short list of prospects and interview each one, asking the questions listed on page 35. Most planners work independently but some are on the staffs of accounting firms, brokerage houses, banks, insurance companies or mutual-fund companies. You can find a planner by asking for recommendations from an accountant or lawyer, by attending the free seminars that planners hold to recruit clients and by requesting names from planners' professional societies or trade associations. See pages 38–39 for a list of sources.

Good practitioners usually have credentials as Certified Financial Planners (CFPs) from the Certified Financial Planner Board of Standards Inc. Most CFPs have taken correspondence courses from the College for Financial Planning (4695 South Monaco Street, Denver, Colorado 80237-3403; 303-220-1200), a division of the National Endowment for Financial Education. These courses are offered in preparation for examinations designed, administered and graded by the CFP Board (1660 Lincoln Street, Suite 3050, Denver, Colorado 80264; 303-830-7543). The exams cover taxes, estate planning, investments and other subjects. Many accredited colleges also give courses that prepare planners for the exam. Roughly 200,000 people purport to be financial planners, but only 30,866 have passed the exams and are CFPs.

Another respected certification is that of Chartered Financial Consultant (ChFC), awarded by the American College (270 Bryn Mawr Avenue, Bryn Mawr, Pennsylvania 19010; 800-392-6900). Cross off any candidates who have not bothered to get at least the CFP or ChFC designations. And check the planner's credentials with the organization that issued them. Sometimes the planners' organizations are less than ferocious watchdogs in policing standards.

The Institute of Certified Financial Planners (ICFP), in Denver, and the International Association for Financial Planning (IAFP), in Atlanta, run referral services that list planners who have met the organizations' rather similar requirements. These include appropriate professional training, the passing of an exam in the case of the ICFP, and full-time experience in planning or a related profession. To retain membership in either group, planners must put in a prescribed number of hours for continuing education each year. Call the ICFP (800-282-7526) or the IAFP (800-945-4237) to find out whether any of their members work in your area.

If you want more information about financial planners, call any or all of the organizations listed above. They will be happy to send you pamphlets and other valuable documents.

Before you hire a planner, ask some tough questions. That's the best way to separate the crack advisers from the quack advisers. Start by inquiring how the planner earns his or her money. In fact, the SEC says that any registered investment adviser must initiate disclosure of his or her fees and other compensation.

Members of the National Association of Personal Financial Advisors (NAPFA) accept no commissions for recommending that you buy mutual funds, life insurance and other financial products. Instead they charge you flat fees of $75 to $200 an hour, and thus are known as fee-only planners. The advantage is that you know the planner will not recommend an investment with an eye to collecting a commission. But fee-only planners are commonly costlier than those who accept commissions. For more information on fee-only planners and a list of those in your area, write or call NAPFA (1130 Lake Cook Road, Buffalo Grove, Illinois 60089; 800-366-2732).

Most planners combine fees and commissions. As a compromise, some planners charge fees but subtract from them the commissions earned selling products to you. Always ask how much money a planner makes on everything he or she tries to sell you. If you know that your adviser stands to pocket a 10% commission on a certain investment and only 3% on a less-expensive alternative, you will have reason to ask why you are being steered toward the costlier one.

Consumer complaints about planners usually involve those who earn their keep solely by commissions, especially those who sell just one line of goods. A conscientious planner should channel your assets into a variety of investments so that your returns will be reasonably stable despite market or interest-rate fluctuations. Ask your planner to draw up a pie chart of his or her recommendations. If one type of investment swallows more than a quarter of your pie, request an explanation.

Ask the planner how much wealth you can reasonably accumulate in five years. Most investors do well if their returns consistently outpace inflation by four or five percentage points a year. If your planner claims to be able to top those rates, he or she may be misleading you or guiding you into high-risk ventures.

Ask how much time the planner will spend with you, and who will write your plan. In large firms your case may be consigned to junior staffers, and you may not get the experience you want. Expect a planner to spend three or four hours with you, gathering facts and discussing ideas. Take time to consider the planner's recommendations before you buy any financial products. And do not feel you have to buy anything. What you need may well be insights instead of new investments.

Here are some other questions you should ask a planner:

1. What is your educational background? What were your areas of study in college and what degrees did you earn?
2. What financial-planning designations have you earned? Have you qualified as a Certified Financial Planner or a Chartered Financial Consultant, or are you a member of a registry of financial planning practitioners?
3. Are you a member of any professional financial-planning

associations, such as the Institute of Certified Financial Planners, the National Association of Personal Financial Advisors, or the International Association for Financial Planning?
4. How long have you been offering financial-planning services?
5. What continuing education in financial planning do you pursue to keep up-to-date?
6. Will you give me references from clients?
7. How many clients in my financial circumstances do you have? May I see a copy of a plan you have prepared for a client like me (with the name removed, of course)?
8. Who will work on my plan — you or a junior employee of your firm? And what ongoing help will you give me to put the plan into practice?
9. Have you ever been cited by a professional or regulatory governing body for disciplinary reasons?
10. How are you paid? If by fees only, what are your charges, and what do you do to earn them?

If you are within 10 years of retirement, you have special needs. Ask your planner to calculate how much money you will require to meet your retirement goals. He or she will get estimates of how much you can expect from Social Security and company pensions, from your own savings and from investments. Then the planner will factor in an expected inflation rate so that your living expenses will not outrun your means. With this information in hand, he or she should tell you whether you will need to save more or work longer to meet your objectives, and what rate of return your nest egg should earn to keep you ahead of inflation. He or she should also show you the sources from which your income will flow — interest, dividends or the sale of assets.

Again, if you are nearing retirement, a planner should help plan your estate — largely a euphemism for reducing death taxes. He or she should total up your net worth and ask to see your last will and testament. The heirs of people who leave assets in excess of $600,000 must share 37% to 55% or even more of that excess with federal tax collectors, unless something is done to head them off. The federal estate tax moves up in steps. The tax on any sums between $2.5 and $3 million is 53%

after the federal government takes an initial $1,025,800; above $3 million, it's 55% and an initial $1,290,800. State taxes, plus certain federal excise taxes, can lift the total beyond 75%. (For more, see Chapter 23, "Dealing with Wills, Trusts and Estates.")

The final clue to a financial planner's caliber is commitment. Your planner should be ready to work over the long term with other professionals you may hire, such as a lawyer or tax accountant. No one person can master all of the technical information that goes into preparing a well-designed financial plan. Have your planner arrange for you and all your advisers to sit down together at least once. That way everyone will know what everyone else is supposed to do.

### Using Your Accountant as a Financial Planner

More and more accountants are expanding into financial planning. It makes some sense. Who else knows your financial situation as well as your CPA does? Your stockbroker certainly doesn't pore over your financial records as much. Your financial planner doesn't know as much about your taxes — and the impact that various investments might have on them. Accountants dissect your finances every year, and if you are a small-business person or entrepreneur, they dissect them quarterly.

You must ask yourself, "Should I get investment advice from a person or firm that I also rely on for help with taxes? Is it ever safe to listen to only one source?" Another potential problem: Your accountant may not be as widely trained as a Certified Financial Planner in such matters as stocks, bonds, annuities, insurance and estate planning — and he or she may learn at your expense.

Here are some questions to ask your accountant if you are considering him or her as a broader financial planner:

- What kind of financial-planning education do you have?
- Are you trained as a Personal Financial Specialist, or PFS? (The American Institute of Certified Public Accountants offers the required education to gain the designation.)
- What financial services do you offer?
- On what basis do you charge? Do you charge hourly fees (as

you do when doing accounting), or commissions or fees based on dollar amount of assets in my account?

- Are you a member of any financial-planning, trade or business organizations that will enable you to associate with other financial planners and keep you abreast of related news?

Here are some sources of help:

Institute of Certified Financial Planners
7600 East Eastman Avenue
Suite 301
Denver, Colorado 80231
800-282-7526

International Association for Financial Planning
2 Concourse Parkway
Suite 800
Atlanta, Georgia 30328
800-945-4237

National Association of Personal Financial Advisors
1130 Lake Kood Road
Suite 150
Buffalo Grove, Illinois 60089
800-366-2732

Certified Financial Planner Board of Standards
1660 Lincoln Street
Suite 3050
Denver, Colorado 80264
303-830-7543

National Endowment for Financial Education
4695 South Monaco Street
Denver, Colorado 80237-3403
303-220-1200

American Society of Chartered Life Underwriters and Chartered Financial Consultants
270 Bryn Mawr Avenue
Bryn Mawr, Pennsylvania 19010
800-392-6900

Note: For a discussion on picking a stockbroker, see Chapter 6, "A Sensible Strategy for Investing in Stocks."

## The Separate Role of the Investment Adviser

Some people, particularly active investors and recipients of six-figure rollovers from retirement accounts, find it pays to hire an investment adviser. This professional may be either a specialized financial planner, a money manager recommended by a planner or broker, or an expert whom you find on your own.

An investment adviser goes beyond a planner: He or she recommends specific stocks, bonds or mutual funds that, in his or her judgment, are suitable to your goals and taste for risk. With a discretionary account, you may give this adviser the power to buy and sell securities for you without first consulting you. Or you may give him or her discretion only to sell your holdings, or to do nothing without your permission.

Until recently investment advisers wouldn't even look at you unless you could give them custody of $250,000 or more. Competition has forced many advisers to accept smaller accounts, fairly often $100,000 but sometimes starting at $10,000. Annual fees generally run 1.5% to 2% of assets up to $500,000 but move lower as the account rises in size. An adviser might charge from 0.75% to 1.5% of a million-dollar stock portfolio, 0.5% to 0.75% for a more easily managed portfolio of bonds. Many firms charge a minimum of $1,000, which can be prohibitive if you have $25,000 or less to invest. Clients also pay brokerage costs.

Financial planners and brokers often use talent scout services to match you with the right investment adviser. Firms such as CDA Investment Technologies of Rockville, Maryland (301-975-9600), Mobius Group (800-662-4874), and Stolper & Co. of San Diego (619-231-9102) calculate the total returns, risk factors and other gauges of performance for hundreds of advisers. This information is updated quarterly — or, in Mobius's case, for some clients twice quarterly — and sent to investment consultants on CD-ROM disks. Stolper & Co. is the only talent scout that deals mainly with individuals. It will choose a manager for you from among 1,500 in its files for a sliding fee starting at $5,000. Then, for $1,500 a year, it will monitor your results.

It's not easy to determine whether an adviser measures up to your needs. The performance statistics that money managers hand out may be more inflated than the Goodyear blimp. Nevertheless, ask for figures going back at least 10 years. If the numbers have been audited by an outside accounting firm, so much the better. Check the results in years when stocks fell as well as when they soared. A first-rate manager preserves your capital in bad years. You can't expect him or her to beat Standard & Poor's 500 stock average every time, but he or she should have turned in a superior long-term record.

Before making your choice, find out an adviser's investment philosophy. It should harmonize with your own. A growth-oriented manager tries for capital gains by picking companies whose earnings are expected to go up more than the average for their industry. A pursuer of aggressive growth leans toward riskier small-capitalization stocks. A conservative growth seeker looks for blue-chip shares. A market timer tries to get you into the market near the bottom of the price cycle and out near the top. A value investor ignores market trends but buys neglected and depressed stocks of well-managed companies and often holds them indefinitely. A contrarian takes the same approach but doesn't make long-term commitments to the stocks he or she buys. A value or contrarian adviser tends to buy stocks with low price/earnings ratios (P/Es); a growth-inclined adviser often buys shares with high P/Es.

Once you have contracted with an adviser, be patient. In general, wait at least a year before you judge the record — but sometimes less than that. If the value of your holdings drops 20% while the market is rising or holding steady, the adviser should take corrective action. If he or she does not, it may well be time to fire him or her. (For information on how to pick a broker, see Chapter 6, "A Sensible Strategy for Investing in Stocks.")

# Know the Charms of Asset Management Accounts

To pull your personal finances together and make the most of what you have, you can get considerable aid from a service offered by brokers, bankers and mutual funds: an asset management account. It acts like your personal financial supermarket and goes by many names, such as Merrill Lynch's Cash Management Account, Citibank's Citigold and Smith Barney's Financial Management Account. By any name, it is a combination money-market and brokerage account that usually lets you earn interest on your spare cash, buy and sell securities, borrow more money than you otherwise could and write an unlimited number of checks at no extra charge. You also get a single monthly statement listing all your financial transactions, and that can be a convenience.

So what's the catch? You generally need cash or securities worth $10,000 or more to get into the tent. And you have to pay an annual fee of $80 to $125. But here are two notable exceptions: The Schwab One Asset Management Account at the Charles Schwab & Co. discount brokerage doesn't charge any fee as long as you maintain a balance of $5,000 in cash or securities or make at least two trades in a 12-month period. The Fidelity Ultra Service Account, at the Fidelity mutual-fund and discount brokerage house, also asks for a $10,000 opening deposit and requires no annual fee.

Your first decision is to choose where you want your asset management account to be. A broker and a banker are equally safe: They offer plenty of insurance for your assets. Choose a full-service broker if you are primarily interested in investing, you want a broker's advice and you see the account as a way to simplify your investing paperwork. Choose a discount broker if you pick your own stocks and bonds or if you prefer no-load mutual funds. Choose a bank if you want mainly to organize your savings and checking transactions.

Look carefully at the standard features these accounts offer. One of their best is the so-called sweep. It automatically takes any dividends and bond income you receive and deposits it in a money-market account. So your cash earns interest from the day or week you get it until the day you spend it. When selecting an asset management account, find out whether the sweep is done daily or weekly, and whether it includes all your cash or just the amount above a certain minimum.

Asset accounts let you write checks against your money-market deposits. Checking typically is free, and you can write as many drafts as you wish with no minimum checking amount. The big issue here is whether or not you will get your canceled checks at the end of the month. Banks generally return asset-account checks, but most brokers simply note the payee, amount and date on your monthly statement.

Most asset accounts provide a MasterCard, Visa, or American Express card at no added charge. Generally, this plastic works like a debit card, immediately deducting your charges from the cash in your account. Otherwise, you receive a monthly bill, and your money is automatically deducted soon after.

You can borrow against your securities in an asset management account. Shop around to see where you can get loans with the lowest interest rate. Often that is from a broker. With a brokerage asset management account, you can borrow as much as half the value of your listed stocks at the so-called margin rate, which is usually much less than consumer loan rates charged by banks.

When picking an asset management account, also study the kind of brokerage service you can expect. An asset account with a bank or a mutual fund gives you access to discount brokerage service, with commissions as much as 90% lower than the fees charged by full-line stockbrokers. But traditional brokers will give you something for their extra charge: investment advice.

Take a close look at the monthly financial statement you will get with your asset management account. Some are jumbles. Make sure you can understand the statement.

Also find out exactly who will service your account. Many banks promise that if you open an asset management account with them, you will be assigned a personal banker. With a brokerage asset account, you will be assigned an account executive to handle securities trading. But he or she most likely will be underjoyed when you call about a lost check or a statement error, since an account executive doesn't earn commissions by solving such problems.

In sum, a bank may offer you better personal service and lower brokerage commissions, but a broker may offer you lower interest rates on loans and more investment advice.

CHAPTER 3

# Building Your Nest Egg

It's almost never too early — or too late — to start creating, and adding to, your nest egg.

But it sure pays to start early, if possible as soon as you begin working. Let's say that at age 25 you start investing $2,000 a year in a tax-deferred retirement savings account, like an IRA or 401(k) plan. And say you earn 8% on that money, which is a not unrealistic goal. When you turn 65, you'll have almost $560,000.

However, what if you wait just 10 years and don't start saving until age 35? Then your nest egg by age 65 will total only $244,000. In short, by beginning at 25 instead of 35, you more than *double* your savings by retirement age.

Begin storing money away for *specific* goals. Keep your hands off money that you save and invest for *long-term* goals, such as retirement. But you may withdraw money that you put away for *short-term* goals, and often you will shift this money from one form of savings or investment to another. For example: Your children's college fund. You'll want to regularly set aside and invest money for college. Place the funds in a so-called custodial account in your child's name at a bank or brokerage house.

If your child is under the age of 14, the first $650 in annual investment earnings is nontaxable, and the next $650 is taxed at the child's rate, presumably 15%. Anything above $1,300 is taxed at the parents' rate. The savings, as the Institute of Certified Financial Planners (ICFP) reports, can be significant. On $1,300 of interest income, a parent in the 28% bracket would pay $274 in federal taxes, and a parent in the 39.6% bracket would pay $515. (This assumes that the income is not long-term capital gains, which are taxable at a maximum 28%.) But a child in the 15% bracket would pay only $97 in federal taxes.

It gets better if your child is older than 14. Then *all* of his or her interest, dividend income and capital gains are taxed at the child's rate, not yours.

A potential disadvantage is that you lose control of the money. As the ICFP notes, your gifts to a custodial account are irrevocable, and you have to spend all the money on the child's behalf. Upon turning 18 or 21, depending on the state, your child can spend the money as he or she wishes — even for a car or a cult instead of college.

Also, a big custodial account in your child's name may reduce the college financial aid he or she will be eligible for. The aid formula used by most colleges requires a dependent child to contribute at least 35% of his or her assets to college costs each year, while parents need contribute only 5.6% of their assets. On balance, however, custodial accounts make sense for most families.

Consider buying U.S. savings bonds for young kids. The interest you collect on them may be tax-free — if you use it to pay for your child's education — and if your income is below a certain level.

Americans are not great savers. In 1994 they put aside an average 4.2% of their disposable income, way down from a peak of 7.5% in 1981. Comparisons with people in other countries are difficult because methods of measuring savings vary, but according to their statistics, the Germans save 11% and the Japanese 14.9% of their incomes. By any gauge, they bank much more than Americans do. Surveys show that about 40% of all employed Americans save or invest nothing for *retirement* beyond what's already in their company retirement plans.

**U.S. vs. FOREIGN SAVINGS**

Individual savings as a percentage of disposable household income

| Italy | Japan | France | Germany | U.K. | Canada | U.S. |
|---|---|---|---|---|---|---|
| 15.0% | 14.9% | 13.5% | 11.0% | 10.4% | 7.6% | 4.2% |

SOURCE: ORGANIZATION FOR ECONOMIC COOPERATION AND DEVELOPMENT

*Saving*, of course, means putting your cash in an absolutely secure place in order to accumulate money for a specific purpose — a down payment on a house, a college education, a comfortable retirement — or for use in an emergency. You deposit your savings in rock-solid repositories that promise both to preserve your capital and to pay you steady income.

*Investing*, by contrast, involves accepting the risk of losing at least some of your money in exchange for a chance to earn richer gains.

When you save, you are basically limited to a few choices, and your yields do not differ very much regardless of what choice you make. But when you invest, you have an infinity of choices, and the results can vary sharply. Thus, it is wise to diversify among your investments. If some of them should drop, others may climb. Similarly, you're smart to diversify within particular classes of investments. When picking stocks, for example, don't limit yourself to big blue chips, but spread out also to shares of smaller companies and foreign firms.

The amount that you should be saving depends on your age, your family responsibilities and your outlook on life. If you are reasonably young, have few or no family responsibilities and face strong earnings prospects in the future, you can afford to save relatively less and invest relatively more. But if you have children to educate or are rapidly approaching retirement, you should save more and invest less. You should also follow this course if you are basically a risk-averse, conservative person or if you believe that future prospects for America and its economy are not ebullient.

How much should you put away? One good but *bare-minimum* plan is this:

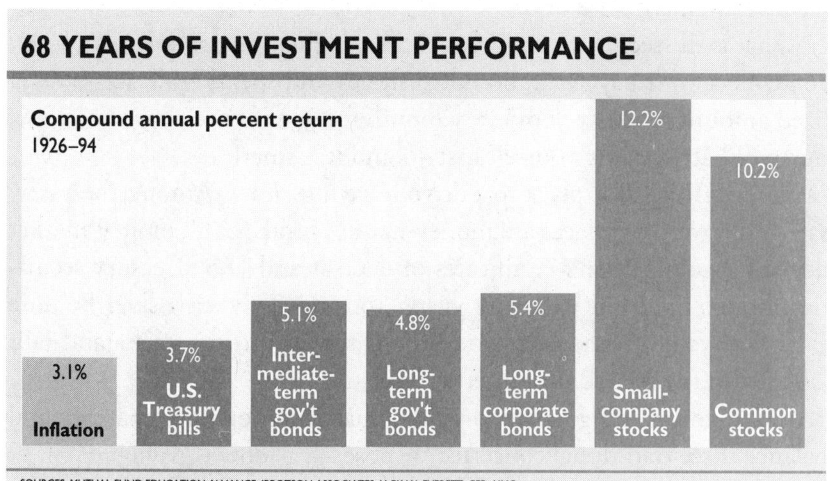

- Between the ages of 25 and 40, save or invest at least 5% of your *pretax* income.
- Then increase that amount by one percentage point a year between the ages of 40 and 45.
- After you are 45, aim to put away 10% a year — and preferably more.

Far too many Americans think they just cannot afford to save at all. If you are one of those who never seem to have anything left from your paycheck, go back to Chapter 2, read the section on budgeting and examine your expenditures to see where you can cut back.

*A tip:* You can enhance your savings by lengthening your home mortgage. A 30-year mortgage may well be a better choice than a 15-year loan because your monthly payments will be lower, and you can invest the money you save each month in order to build up your nest egg.

The best way to increase your savings is to treat them as a necessity, aiming to build an emergency cash reserve. As discussed, it should equal at least three months' worth of living expenses.

Once you have provided for emergencies, start saving for specific purposes. Saving is like dieting: It's tough to do unless you set goals. So set short-, medium- and long-range goals. Short-term objectives could include saving for a summer holiday or for Christmas. A three- to five-year target might be buying a vacation house or paying cash for a new car. The major long-term goals are educating the children and saving for a secure retirement.

What is the secret of saving more? Simply this: *Pay yourself first.* When you collect your paycheck, do not rush out and spend it all. Lay away a fixed amount every week or every month for your own savings or investments. That is paying yourself first — and it is smart.

Where is the best place to put your savings now? Among the many safe and rewarding places are money-market funds, bank money-market deposit accounts, bank certificates of deposit and U.S. Treasury securities. Bonds hold out tempting yields, too, but they are riskier because their face value — the price you buy or sell them for — rises and falls along with the gyrations of interest rates.

When determining where to put your savings, you have to weigh and balance three traditional concerns:

*Yield:* How much am I earning on my money?
*Liquidity:* How quickly can I withdraw my money if I need it?
*Safety:* Am I sure to get back every penny that I put in?

Weighing all these, the best all-around place to put short-term savings is in one of the money-market funds offered by mutual-fund companies and brokerage firms. They usually give you slightly higher yields than banks, as well as instant liquidity and strong safety.

If you prefer the convenience of a nearby bank, you can place your money in a bank money-market deposit account — but make sure that the bank is *federally* insured. You give up some advantage in yield, but the difference is quite small — particularly when interest rates in general

## PICKING FUNDS TO MEET YOUR GOALS

The chart below helps identify the types of funds best suited to your investment objectives.

| If your objective is: | You want these fund types: | They invest primarily in: | Capital appreciation potential | Current income potential | Stability of principal |
|---|---|---|---|---|---|
| Maximum capital growth | Aggressive growth | Common stocks with potential for very rapid growth. May employ certain aggressive strategies | Very high | Very low | Low to very low |
| High capital growth | Growth, specialty | Common stocks with long-term growth potential | High to very high | Very low | Low |
| Current income and capital growth | Growth and income | Common stocks with potential for high dividends and capital appreciation | Moderate | Moderate | Low to moderate |
| High current income | Fixed income, equity income | High-dividend-paying stocks and bonds | Very low | High to very high | Low to moderate |
| Current income and protection of principal | General money-market | Money-market instruments | None | Moderate to high | Very high |
| Tax-free income and protection of principal | Tax-exempt money market | Short-term municipal notes and bonds | None | Moderate to high | Very high |
| Current income and maximum safety of principal | U.S. government money market | U.S. Treasury and agency issues guaranteed by the U.S. government | None | Moderate to high | Very high |
| Tax-exempt income | Municipal bonds double and triple tax-exempt | A broad range of municipal bonds | Low to moderate | Moderate to high | Moderate |

SOURCE: MUTUAL FUND EDUCATION ALLIANCE

are low. There's some advantage in being able to deal face-to-face with neighborhood bankers. Also, it's often easier to get a loan if you have some money on deposit in a bank.

For still more safety, consider a money-market fund that invests solely in securities of the U.S. government and its agencies, such as the GIT Money Market Fund (1655 Fort Myer Drive, Arlington, Virginia 22209; 800-336-3063). Government money-market funds yield about one-third of a percentage point less than money funds that buy commercial paper and other non-Treasury issues. Even so, they are a smarter bet. The interest on Treasury bills, as well as on some federal agency securities, is exempt from state and local taxes. Although you draw a lower pretax yield from government-only money funds, the after-tax yield can be as much as a full percentage point higher, depending upon how steep your state tax rate is.

The interest rate on government-only funds is adjusted daily to equal the average rate that the securities are yielding that day. In late 1995 that rate was about 4.67%. Bear in mind that since all the securities are backed by the U.S. government, the fund cannot default, and your money is safe.

If you are in a high tax bracket, you are probably best off in one of the tax-free money-market funds. They are offered by mutual-fund companies and in late 1995 were paying about 2.41% — free of federal income taxes.

It does not make much sense to put considerable savings into an ordinary statement savings account. These days you would get only 3.51% interest on it — all taxable — at a commercial bank, savings bank, or savings and loan (S&L) association. You can earn a bit more at the very same institution merely by switching to other forms of savings. With $1,000 or less, you can open a money-market deposit account. And you can buy a bank certificate of deposit for $500 or less. Some banks hold out for higher minimum deposits, however, so shop around. And remember: Healthy S&Ls often pay slightly more than banks do.

Traditionally, the longer you were willing to tie up your money, the higher the yield you would get. That's another tradition that barely holds in the current environment. As of late 1995, six-month certificates yielded an average 4.88%. If you put some savings on ice for a full year, you would have earned an average 5.12%.

In 1992 new Federal Deposit Insurance Corporation rules placed limits on the rates weaker banks can offer customers, while allowing well-capitalized banks — which, happily, means nearly three-quarters of the country's commercial banks — to set their own rates. Such regulations spelled the end of the upward-spiraling rates of the 1980s, when small, undercapitalized institutions offered ever-higher premiums and made ever-riskier loans — contributing greatly to the S&L crisis of the early 1990s. Though it's now a waste of time to go looking for sky-high rates at your neighborhood bank, you can feel more confident about the safety of your funds in a top-rated bank. Yet there are still differences among banks — in the variety of their services and the size of their fees. So the commonsense advice still applies: Shop around for your best deals in banking.

The neighborhood bank is probably still the best place for your checking account, but not necessarily for your savings. You can sometimes earn more at no risk by putting your money into certificates of deposit sold not by banks but by stockbrokers. And you might be able to earn still higher interest by using the mail to put your savings in an out-of-state bank. In late 1995, for example, MBNA America of Wilmington, Delaware, was paying 5.45% on money-market funds, while the national average was closer to 3.65%.

On the other hand, it often makes sense to give all your banking business to one institution. This is called "relationship banking," and in return for it, you can get higher interest on your savings or lower fees on your checking or better terms on a loan than the bank usually offers. When all your banking business is lumped together, you can become a fairly big customer. For example, if your balance in a money-market deposit account or an interest-bearing checking account exceeds $5,000, you may earn a fraction of a percentage point more interest than do customers with smaller accounts. *A tip:* If you do a lot of business with a bank, then negotiate to collect higher rates. Bankers can be surprisingly flexible and give bonus rates to their best customers.

But relationship banking does cost you something. If instead you use many different financial institutions, each for a different service, you might get still better deals. Bottom line: Talk to your banker and see what kind of deals he or she can make if you do *all* your transactions with the bank. The convenience alone might well make it worthwhile for you, even if you could get fractionally more favorable rates by splitting your business.

# Your Best Deals in Checking Accounts

The most convenient place to put your money is in a checking account that also earns interest. Money-market mutual-fund accounts allow you to write checks, but with limits. Other interest-bearing checking accounts have their own restrictions, and some can be downright tricky when it comes to figuring minimum balances and interest rates.

While the minimum deposit for opening an account varies from institution to institution, here's how some of the basic highly liquid interest-paying devices compare:

| | *Minimum opening balance* | *Minimum monthly balance* | *Interest yield (late 1995)* |
|---|---|---|---|
| Bank interest-paying checking account | Can be as low as $10 | $500–$1,000 | 1.52% |
| Bank money-market deposit account | $2,500 | $2,500 | 2.85% |
| Money-market mutual funds | $2,500 | $2,500 | 5.29% |

Sources: *Bank Rate Monitor;* IBC's Money Fund Report Average

## Cut-Price Checks

Here's one sure way to save a bit of money on your checking account: Have your checks printed elsewhere. You can knock off about half the price of replacement checks by ordering checks over the phone from independent suppliers. A company called Checks in the Mail (800-733-4443) charges $4.95 plus $1 for shipping for 200 checks printed with the same name, address, account number and computer codes that appear on your existing checks. Current, Inc. (800-426-0822) charges $4.95 for your first 200-check order and $6.95 for reorders. It adds up.

*A tip:* Money funds sold by mutual-fund companies generally pay one or two percentage points more than bank money-market deposit accounts — and sometimes even better than that.

*A warning:* Most banks have monthly charges that can add up, especially if you keep only a small balance in your account.

The way to compare various banking offers is to find out exactly how much money you will have in your account at the end of the year if you deposit, say, $1,000 on the first of the year. Call half a dozen banks and S&Ls and compare their interest rates and fees. Ask how minimum balances are calculated and find out how much it costs if you slip under that minimum.

Your best buy in checking accounts depends on how much money you have and how many checks you write. Here are some of your choices:

*Economy checking.* If you write few checks, this may be for you. It costs $2 to $3 a month, plus 20 to 25 cents per check. It pays no interest, but it requires no minimum balance and may be opened with a deposit of $25.

*NOW account.* If you write many checks, this may be a better choice. On such accounts, some banks will allow 15 to 20 free checks a month and you pay interest of 1.5% or so. But you usually have to maintain a $1,000 minimum balance, and there can be a maintenance fee of $8 to $10 a month. That can easily wipe out the interest payments.

*Super NOW account.* This account gives you unlimited free checking. The interest it pays varies with market conditions, and in late 1995 was about 2%. You usually have to keep a minimum deposit of $2,500 or more, and you may have to pay a monthly maintenance fee of about $10 to $20.

*Bank money-market deposit account.* This is more of a savings account than a checking account. Typically, you need $2,500 to open the account. It pays an interest rate that can be about 1% higher than a Super NOW account but restricts the number of checks you may write to anyone except yourself to three a month. There are no restrictions on teller or ATM withdrawals. In late 1995 the interest rate was 2.85%.

### The Cost of Bouncers

Though you — of course — will probably never bounce a check in any of these accounts, you might be curious to know what the returned-check charges are for those unfortunate people who do. The cost varies from $15 to $25; the average is $15. An overdraft checking account will make your account bounce-proof, but you will pay interest, lately 19% or more, for at least one month, on overdrafts.

Another option is to join a credit union and open a checking account there. You can join through your place of work, through a club, even through a church. Call the Credit Union National Association (800-358-5710) to find out what you need to do. Credit unions pay slightly higher rates than banks on ordinary checking accounts (2.3% vs. 1.52% in late 1995). Fully 58% of credit unions, versus only 19% of banks, don't charge any fees for the privilege of holding a checking account. The average fee for those who do pay at credit unions is $2.90 a month. To be safe, make sure that any credit union where you put your money has federal insurance; fewer than 5% of them still have private, not government, insurance.

## How Safe Are Deposits in Banks and S&Ls?

The costly, scandalous crash of hundreds of savings and loans and banks in the late 1980s and early 1990s led to broad reforms. New regulations aim to guarantee that never again will financial institutions be guilty of such foolish investments — and outright fraud — with their customers' money. The federal government, not state governments or private companies, now insures almost all banks, S&Ls and credit unions.

For your own protection, find out what kind of insurance your institution has. The Federal Deposit Insurance Corporation guarantees up to $100,000 per depositor in almost 10,950 commercial and savings banks and about 1,512 S&Ls. The FDIC can ask for additional money from the U.S. Treasury if it ever needs to. Equal amounts of insurance coverage come with deposits in credit unions that belong to the National Credit Union Share Insurance Fund, which has a much higher ratio of reserves to deposits than does the FDIC.

If you had money in a federally insured institution and it should fail, you probably would not even feel the collapse. Government regulators can arrange a takeover or merger so quickly that your bank's doors would never have to be closed. At worst, you might have to wait a few days to collect your money and forgo interest payments during that period.

Remember: Insurance will cover your deposits — including certificates of deposit — only up to $100,000 in each account. *But* there are ways to expand the $100,000 limit. If you are married, you can have one account in your name, another in your spouse's name and a third joint account. Thus a married couple between them can have $300,000 in federally insured deposits in the same bank or savings institution. But you can have no more than $100,000 *under the same name* in the same institution even if you have more than one ordinary account. Say you have $70,000 in a money-market account and $40,000 in a CD, both under your name at the same bank. Your combined $110,000 exceeds the insurance limit by $10,000.

As with most regulatory matters, there are exceptions — and the first concerns your Individual Retirement Accounts. If you have an IRA at a bank or an S&L, any money-market deposit accounts or savings certificates in it will typically be insured separately. In this way, a married couple can have as much as $500,000 federally insured at the same institution: $100,000 in each of their two regular accounts, $100,000 in their joint account and $100,000 in each of their two IRAs.

The other exception concerns testamentary accounts, also known as irrevocable trusts. The money in them is paid directly to a beneficiary — or beneficiaries — upon the death of the grantor. When payable to a spouse, children or grandchildren, the account is insured up to $100,000 *per beneficiary.*

## Certificates of Deposit

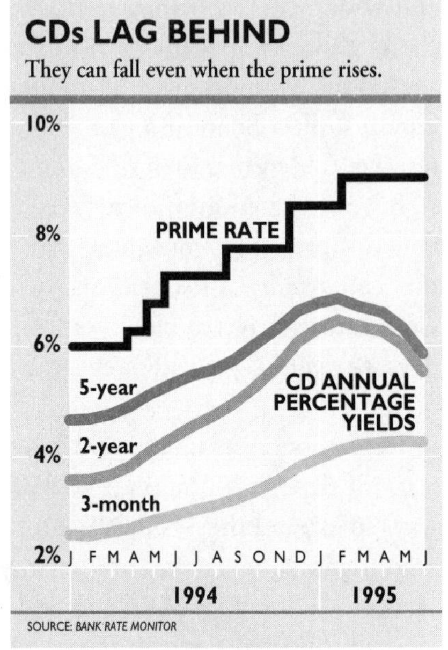


Sometimes it pays to tie your money up for several months in bank certificates of deposit. While ordinary statement savings accounts usually yield only 3% at best, one-year CDs in mid-1995 were paying a handsome 5.12%. In addition, you may be inclined — for reasons of convenience or safety — to invest in a CD. You'll be reassured to know that the truth-in-savings law of 1993 regulates how the bank figures the interest on your CD as well as on your interest-bearing checking account and your savings account. Banks must now calculate interest on the *full principal* in the account each day. Nevertheless, you should always check exactly which method your bank or savings institution uses to calculate interest, including whether it will pay you simple interest or compound interest.

The yield on a *simple-interest* CD is much lower than you might expect. Let's say you bought a $1,000 five-year simple-interest certificate paying 6%. It would pay you $60 interest every year, for a total of $300. Yet if that five-year CD paid the usual 6% *compounded quarterly,* then after five years you would end up with $347. And the bigger the CD, the greater the gap.

Often you should be more concerned about a CD's term than its interest rate. Reason: You may wish to lock in a slightly higher rate for a longer period of time than the lower rate for the shorter term. For example, back in mid-1989 the top six-month CD rate was around 10.70%, while the top five-year rate was closer to 10.25%. Then rates proceeded to decline. It turned out that investors who bought the five-year CDs locked in a rate that was nearly six full points higher than the rates that were offered in mid-1992. Generally, if rates are dropping, buy longer-term CDs; if they are rising and you expect them to continue to do so, keep your maturities short.

Be sure to find out what the bank's penalties are for early withdrawal. Many banks are afraid of losing their CD deposits, so they tack on stiff penalties to discourage early withdrawals. Others, eager to attract investors, ease restrictions to make the accounts more liquid.

Ask also how you will be notified when your CD comes due. The bank should send you a reminder a few weeks before you have to decide whether to withdraw or redeposit the money.

*A tip:* You can usually get a little more interest by putting your money into a certificate of deposit at a brokerage house instead of a bank. Many stockbrokers buy small-denomination CDs in bulk from banks. The brokers then offer the certificates to the public in $1,000 units. Just like the CDs you get at a bank or savings and loan, brokered CDs have the ironclad backing of the Federal Deposit Insurance Corporation.

But these CDs don't pay compound interest, so many brokerage clients take their interest each month. On the plus side, when you buy a CD through a broker, you can often sell it before it matures and not suffer any early-withdrawal penalty as you would at a bank. And you will not be charged a commission.

Brokers trade CDs the way they trade bonds. So if interest rates rise after you buy a CD, your certificate's value falls. But if rates drop, you can sell out early at a profit. All in all, brokered CDs are usually a better deal than bank or savings and loan CDs.

# Out-of-State Deposits

Even if banks and S&Ls in your state pay relatively low interest, you are free to get in on the highest rates wherever you can find them. Almost every bank or savings and loan accepts out-of-state deposits. Institutions in states other than your own may pay a point or two more on your savings. You will have to deal with them by mail, but for a 32-cent stamp, you might earn an extra $100 a year on a $10,000 deposit. Just make sure that you are dealing with a federally insured bank.

Depositing your savings out of state is easy. Most banks will assign you an account number by phone. You then start the account by mailing in a check made out to your new account number. Be sure to endorse the check and write "for deposit only" on the back. And by all means make sure you know how long the quoted rate will be in effect. Some banks change their rates daily.

Federally insured banks in some parts of the country have been offering above-market rates. For example, in late 1995, 5.7%. You can find out where the highest yields are now by looking in financial newspapers and magazines, such as *Money*, the *Wall Street Journal* and *Barron's*.

Two weekly banking newsletters can help you search for the steepest returns. One is *100 Highest Yields* (P.O. Box 088888, North Palm Beach, Florida 33408-8888; 800-327-7717). It ranks only federally insured institutions, and it costs $124 for one year. Another is *Rate Watch* (P.O. Drawer 145510, Coral Gables, Florida 33114; 800-388-6686). It rates federally insured institutions that its publisher considers sound, and it costs $39 for three months, $59 for six months or $99 a year. Also, an information-and-money-broker service that quotes the highest yields at federally insured banks across the country is *BanxQuote Online* by MasterFund, Inc. (45 Essex Street, Milburn, New Jersey 07041; 800-666-2000). You can call and speak directly to brokers who will offer the highest savings and jumbo CD and money-market rates in the country. There is no charge for this service.

Once you have selected several banks to explore, write or phone each of them for an application form and information on rates, minimum deposits and withdrawal penalties. To be on the safe side, request a copy of the institution's most recent financial statement.

Also ask about credit-card policies for nonresidents. Many banks offer no-fee Visa and MasterCards nationally, sparing you the usual annual fee of $16. Others charge a fee but keep interest rates on their cards at below the national average of 18.2%.

## Money-Market Mutual Funds

Money-market funds that are sold by mutual-fund companies and brokerage firms have been a bonanza for small savers. They have usually returned comfortably more than the inflation rate. In mid-1995 the seven-day compound rate on money-market funds averaged 5.29%, while inflation was running at around 3.2%.

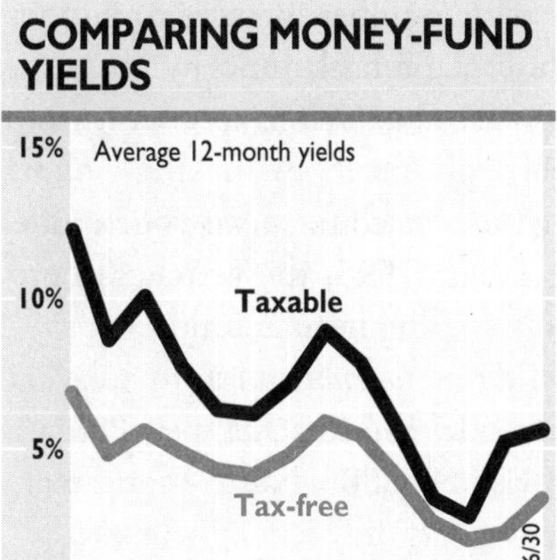

SOURCE: *MONEY FUND REPORT*, IBC/DONOGHUE, INC.

The chief measure of a money fund's safety is the quality of the investments that its managers make with your cash. Under rules of the Securities and Exchange Commission (SEC), all general-purpose funds take similar low risks. In effect, the funds make short-term loans to federal, state and local governments as well as to corporations and U.S. and foreign banks. Generally, the funds that tack on the lowest charge for management expenses pay the highest yields.

Some safety-first investors have flocked to money-market funds that buy only government securities, such as Capital Preservation Fund and Dreyfus 100% U.S. Treasury. These often pay you one-sixth of a point to a full point less than ordinary money funds. Almost invariably, you feel quite secure investing in a regular money fund, particularly if it is run by a well-established mutual-fund group or brokerage firm. But to sleep even more soundly at night, check that the average maturity of the fund's securities is 60 days or less by asking the fund or looking at IBC/Donoghue's Money Fund Tables, published in more than 40 newspapers. Longer maturities do not give fund managers enough flexibility. If interest rates rise and the fund is locked into securities that pay lower rates, disgruntled shareholders might start a drastic withdrawal of their funds.

Choosing a money-market fund only because of its high yield can be a mistake. Since most ordinary money funds make the same kind of investments, their returns are usually within a fraction of one percentage point of each other. You might be wiser to seek out a money fund on the basis of the size and success of its parent company. How varied and successful are the other mutual funds in its family? These families also have funds that invest in stocks, and usually in corporate, government and tax-exempt bonds. You may well want to shift more of your assets into those funds when you think interest rates are nosing down and the stock and bond markets are heading up. Some money funds have such exchange agreements with independent mutual funds, but many others belong to the convenient, one-stop-shopping fund families.

Once you invest in a family, as a rule you can shift your cash from, say, a money fund into a stock mutual fund merely by making a phone call. Often the transfer costs nothing, and you can move your money around as often as you like. But a few families limit the switches to protect themselves against a sudden loss of assets in any one fund.

A number of companies have good reputations for performance and offer a variety of funds. A sampling includes Fidelity, Kemper, Putnam, T. Rowe Price, Scudder, Stein Roe & Farnham, Vanguard — and many more.

Your own selection of a fund family should be based chiefly on how well its stock funds have performed over the past decade. If you have chosen your fund group carefully, you will be able to transfer assets from a money fund to a stock fund — and keep it all in the family.

One newsletter that covers money-market funds as well as their mutual-fund families is *Donoghue's Money Letter* (P.O. Box 9104, 290 Eliot Street, Ashland, Massachusetts 01721-9104; 800-445-5900). The newsletter is published twice a month, and a one-year subscription is $127. Free sample issues are also available.

## How Safe Are the Money Funds?

The answer: very safe. Almost always, you can take out, dollar for dollar, what you have put in, plus interest. The interest is usually declared daily and automatically credited to your account once a month.

However, there are some risks. Although they were paying 5.29% in mid-1995, they can plummet. In 1989 two big funds, Value Line Cash Fund and Unified Management's Liquid Green Trust, were clobbered by losses in their holdings of commercial paper, a form of corporate IOU. Each had lent several million dollars to Integrated Resources, a major dealer in limited partnerships. Integrated Resources defaulted when its partnership business went into a tailspin, the victim of tax reform and the real estate recession. Fortunately for shareholders, both funds' sponsors bailed them out by absorbing the loss.

Similarly, in 1990 half a dozen funds, including T. Rowe Price Prime Reserve and Prudential-Bache's Money-Mart Assets, took losses on the commercial paper of Mortgage & Realty Trust, a real estate investment trust, after rating services downgraded the firm's credit rating. Again, the sponsor absorbed the losses. In the summer of 1994, Community Bankers U.S. Government Money-Market Fund, a fund serving big institutions, ran into trouble and paid off only 94 cents on the dollar. But the fact that remains is that no individual investor has ever lost a penny on a money fund.

Since 1990 government regulations have limited money funds' purchases of commercial paper — which are among their riskiest holdings — to issues in the top two rating levels, AAA and AA, and to unrated paper of equal quality. Even so, no law says that financial institutions that sponsor money funds must make good on shareholders' losses. The lesson for investors is not to abandon money funds but rather to choose them with care.

Here are three guidelines:

- First, know the manager or sponsor. You need not entrust your money to complete strangers. You may already do business with a firm that sponsors a money fund — say, a brokerage house, a life insurance company or a mutual-fund group. A sponsor with an established reputation for financial responsibility will not jeopardize that reputation by abandoning its customers. Strong sponsorship can give you more peace of mind.
- Second, choose funds whose securities have a low average maturity. The temptation of money-fund managers is to extend their maturities and lock in high returns when they think interest rates are about to fall. The SEC compels most funds to stay to an average maturity of 60 days or less. By going longer, the funds risk having to report sharp cuts in daily dividends if they guess wrong and rates rise. That could cause their shareholders to switch to higher-paying funds. You should favor a fund that doesn't stray far from the pack. When other funds are hovering around the 35-day mark, be wary of those with average maturities in the 40s or 50s. You can get updated reports on a fund's average maturities by calling the fund or checking the fund's listing in the *Wall Street Journal* or your local newspaper.
- Third — and to repeat — don't chase after the highest possible yields, or the hottest fund of the month. Over a year's time, the

difference in interest payments between one fund and another may be modest. Don't be greedy; settle for a reasonable rate of return.

You can find a rating of your money-market fund in a monthly newsletter called *Income Fund Outlook.* It ranks the 149 largest funds from AAA+ through BBB on the basis of the diversification, maturity and quality of their investments. It also cites the 10 highest yields for money markets and the 70 best yields for CDs and rates the banks for safety. For a free copy, write to *Income Fund Outlook,* 3471 North Federal Highway, Fort Lauderdale, Florida 33306 (800-442-9000). An annual subscription costs $100 and includes free access to the Income Fund Outlook hotline, a weekly update of the money-market fund sector.

# Treasury Securities

For the safest place in the world to park your money, look to the federal government. Uncle Sam borrows more than $200 billion a year, and if he cannot pay his debts, he can always print more dollars.

The government securities with the most appeal for individual investors are Treasury bills, notes and bonds. As long as you hold these federally backed issues until they mature — as with all Treasury secur-

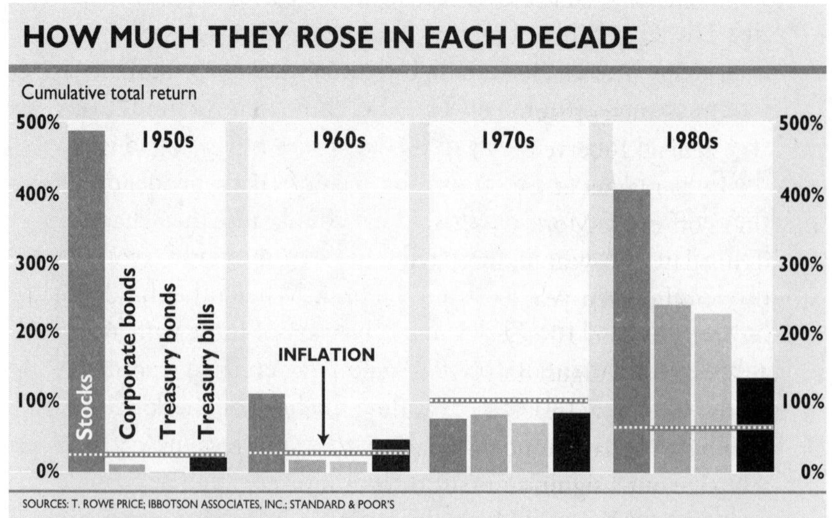

ities — you will get back your entire principal. The interest, which is paid in advance, is exempt from state and local taxes.

That advance payment of interest is a nifty extra. Let's take one example with round numbers for easy calculation: If you buy, say, a $10,000 10% one-year bill, it will cost you only $9,000 — that is, $10,000 minus 10%. A year later you will be paid the full $10,000. The real interest that you will collect is your $1,000 profit divided by your $9,000 investment. In fact, that's not 10% but 11.1%.

Some basics:

- *Bills* are sold in minimum denominations of $10,000, and they come in three-, six- and 12-month maturities. They are the safest short-term investments. The trouble is, that $10,000 price of admission is steep.
- *Notes* are sold in minimum denominations of $5,000 when they have maturities of less than five years — and a minimum of $1,000 when they have maturities of five years or more. You can get them in maturities ranging from two years to 10 years.
- *Treasury bonds* also sell in minimums of $1,000 but have maturities of 10 years to 30 years. They pay less than a percentage point below similar debt issues of top-rated corporations. In late 1995 a 30-year Treasury bond was paying 6.91%, and an AAA-rated 30-year corporate, 7.5%. But all government securities rate an AAA+ for safety.

You can buy Treasury issues through any of the 12 Federal Reserve banks or 25 branch offices. Or order them by mail, using forms that you get from Federal Reserve banks or the Bureau of Public Debt. The securities come to market at various intervals. Three- and six-month bills are auctioned off every Monday; 12-month bills are sold every four weeks, on a Thursday; two-year and five-year notes are generally sold at the end of each month; seven-year notes are sold in January, April, July and October; three-year and 10-year notes and 30-year bonds are generally sold in February, May, August and November.

You can also buy Treasuries from a commercial bank or from your broker. This eliminates much of the hassle but can cost from $30 to $60 and can wipe out a significant part of your return.

One problem: You will pay a rather stiff penalty if you ever want to sell your government securities before they mature. Just as brokers will charge a small investor substantially more than the market price if he or she is buying, so they will pay him or her substantially less if he or she is selling. Thus you are best off sticking to new government issues and holding them until they mature.

Series EE U.S. savings bonds remain an attractive option for investors when compared with other guaranteed investments. Series EE bonds pay interest equal to 85% of the average of six-month Treasury security yields. In mid-1995 they were paying a short-term rate of 5.25%. Bonds held for more than five years earn long-term rates equal to 85% of the five-year Treasury yields. In mid-1995 the long-term rate was 6.31%. In both cases the interest is changed twice a year, on May 1 and November 1, to adjust to market rates.

These rules apply to EE bonds issued after May 1, 1995. Bonds that were issued earlier will continue to earn interest under the terms that were then in effect; notably, they had a guaranteed minimum that ranged between 4.0% and 7.5%. You don't collect the interest in the form of periodic checks but in a lump sum when you cash in the bond. Like Treasury bonds, notes and bills, U.S. savings bonds are exempt from state and local taxes.

## Rolling Them Over

You can save a bundle of taxes on the lump sum of cash or stock that you collect from your company 401(k) or other qualified retirement plans when you leave the firm. You do that by opening a special tax-deferred Individual Retirement Account, called a rollover account, at any bank, brokerage firm or mutual-fund company. Then you instruct your company to transfer the proceeds directly to that account. You thus postpone paying taxes on your contributions and earnings in these company plans, and on your employer's contributions, until you start withdrawing the money from the IRA.

The direct transfer is imperative because of a change in the law. Previously, employers always paid out the money. You then had 60 days to put it in an IRA rollover account. Later, if you joined another company that offered a 401(k) salary-reduction plan, you could move your rollover account into that plan.

But starting in 1993, employers were authorized to transfer these retirement savings accounts directly to your IRA or into the retirement plan of your new employer, enabling you to avoid immediate income taxes. If they issue you a check instead, employers must withhold for tax purposes 20% of previously tax-deferred lump-sum payments. You can still roll over the whole lump sum within 60 days, but first you will have to scrounge up an amount equal to the 20% that has been withheld. On $500,000 worth of retirement money, that's a staggering $100,000. Later, when you file your tax return, you can apply for a refund of the amount withheld. Or you can roll over the 80% and pay tax on the rest. Check with your employer, who is required by law to give you a written explanation of your choices at least 30 days before you take the money.

Another caution: The taxman won't let you roll over any after-tax contributions that you made to the company plan, since these are not subject to income tax when you leave the company. Be sure to have your employee benefits consultant or your tax adviser spell out your tax liability before you accept any lump sum subject to withholding tax.

## Some Better Alternatives

Although IRAs are a worthy way of saving money and reducing your taxes, they are not the only way. You might do better not only with a company savings plan but also with a nonprofit-group annuity, a 401(k) salary-reduction plan or a Keogh plan.

If you are self-employed and don't earn too much, you can have both a Keogh plan and an IRA, so you need to decide which to contribute to if you cannot afford both. The Keogh wins hands down because you can shelter much more income in it than in an IRA.

Another nice shelter is the 403(b) nonprofit-group annuity. It can be bought by teachers, hospital nurses, social workers and other employees of charitable or educational nonprofit organizations. If you work for an eligible group, you can tell your employer to put as much as 20% of your pay into an untaxed annuity or mutual-fund custodial account. You get all the advantages of an IRA but usually can shelter up to $9,500

## WAYS TO REACH YOUR RETIREMENT GOALS

| Type of Plan | Sponsor | Limit on annual contribution | Pros and cons |
|---|---|---|---|
| **401(k)** | **Corporations** | **$9,240** | The ability to contribute pretax income from your paycheck, along with the possible money match from your employer, makes this a dynamite option to maximize. Although hardship withdrawals are limited, loans are widely available. |
| **403(b)** | **Tax-exempt institutions** | **$9,500**[1] | Another nice pretax salary-deferral plan, although fee-heavy annuities are common investment options. A bonus: Employees who have failed to contribute in the past may make up the difference by putting in a lump sum. |
| **Keogh or SEP** | **Small businesses** | **$22,500**[2] | It's well worth starting one of these plans if you run your own show. Either is a great way to put aside piles of money, and there is a lot of flexibility if your business suffers a bad year. |
| **Variable annuity** | **Individuals** | **None** | Beware the hot insurance product: High fees and limited investment options may make taxable alternatives more valuable. Surrender penalties hit investors who cash out early. |
| **IRA** | **Individuals** | **$2,000** | Without the tax deduction most folks once enjoyed, they aren't as attractive as they used to be. But IRAs are great holding cells for money rolled over from a 401(k), and there's no one to argue with if you want to take the money out. |

[1]Or 16⅔% of gross income, whichever is less. [2]Or 15% of earnings, whichever is less. Contributions to a money-purchase Keogh plan could be as high as $30,000 per year.

SOURCE: *FORTUNE*

of your salary per year. All withdrawals are taxed, and there is an additional 10% penalty tax for early withdrawals before age 59½.

As noted earlier, many companies are offering their employees 401(k) plans. Again, a portion of your salary is withheld — untaxed — and the money is invested in your choice of a CD-like guaranteed-investment contract, in the company's stock or in some type of mutual fund.

To repeat: If your employer has a savings plan that matches at least some of your contributions, chances are you will be able to accumulate more money, after taxes, by contributing to it than by opening an IRA.

C H A P T E R 4

# Investing Profitably

Just as war is too important to be left to generals, so investing is too important to be left to stockbrokers, mutual-fund salesmen and financial planners. Of course, in the battle for investment success, it's smart to get all the four-star professional advice you can. But ultimately *you* have to determine how much money you want to commit and where you want to deploy it; which filigreed certificates, shiny bars of gold or cold steel bank vaults you want to place it in, and what objectives you want to achieve.

What you need most — move over, General — is an investment *strategy.* Start by analyzing yourself. Do you prefer moderate risk with a chance for high capital growth, or minimal risk with a promise of slower growth? Define your financial goals and how you plan to reach them. Is your goal to pay for college, for a condo or for a comfortable retirement — or all of the above — and just how much money will you need? And it cannot be repeated too often: Before you put cash into anything that has the slightest risk, be sure you have enough life, health and disability insurance and sufficient federally insured savings to protect yourself in case of an emergency.

To repeat, there is a basic difference between investing and saving. Saving means putting your cash in an absolutely secure place in order to accumulate money for a specific purpose — a down payment on a house, a college education, a comfortable retirement — or for use in an emergency. You deposit your savings in rock-solid repositories that promise both to preserve your capital and to pay you steady income. Investing, by contrast, involves accepting the risk of losing your money in exchange for a chance to earn richer gains.

* * *

The single most important determinant of your success as an investor will not be which individual stocks or bonds or mutual funds you choose, nor even which gems or precious metals or antique ceramics you select. No, it will be your choice of asset allocation — how you divide and distribute your assets among the various classes of investments, what percentage you put into stocks, bonds, mutual funds, real estate, gold and myriad other investments. Ibbotson Associates, the investment consulting firm, and Brinson Partners, the global investment management company, both in Chicago, conducted an elaborate study of asset allocation, based on the performance of 91 huge pension funds over time. They concluded that asset allocation accounted for — get ready for this — 91.5% of the difference in returns among various portfolios. Selection of particular assets within classes accounted for a wimpy 8.5%. Other analysts agree. The chart below gives the various weights of factors that account for total return.

## Starting with a Small Stake

What if you have only a small stake to start investing, say $100? At least 150 mutual funds accept an initial investment of $100 or less — and some have no minimum at all. Unlike mutual funds, many stock brokerage firms have such large minimum commissions — sometimes as much as $39 every time that you buy or sell — that it does not make sense to open an account with just $100. As an alternative, you can try Merrill Lynch's Blueprint Program. It charges $12.50 on trades up to $125, and 10% on trades to $200. After that, commissions decrease on a sliding scale. Trades exceeding $7,500 are charged at Merrill's regular rates. Another way to begin is to join an investment club (for more on investment clubs, see Chapter 6).

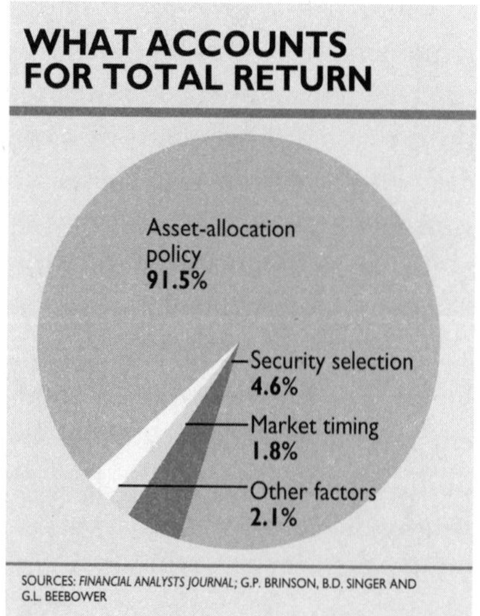

SOURCES: *FINANCIAL ANALYSTS JOURNAL*; G.P. BRINSON, B.D. SINGER AND G.L. BEEBOWER

It's a good idea, as discussed earlier, to arrange with your employer to transfer a fixed amount from every paycheck into an investment plan, or to arrange with a mutual fund to shift a fixed amount each month from your checking account or money-market fund into the stock fund of your choice. Or the fund company will send you 12 postage-paid envelopes, each printed with a different month of the year.

Another way, proposed by financial planner Dennis Kelly of New York's Janney Montgomery Scott, is to put money into U.S. Treasury bills and invest the interest payments in a highly diversified portfolio of stocks, which you can get through mutual funds. Since most of your money is in T-bills, your principal is safe no matter which way the market moves. If you had followed Kelly's advice for the five years up to the start of 1995, your average annual return would have been 8.42%. That's not as high as the 8.84% you would have earned on an index fund invested in Standard & Poor's index of 500 stocks, but it is better than the 5% you would have earned on T-bills alone.

## Reducing Your Risks

An investor by definition is a person who takes risks — but there are ways you can reduce them. Remember: The first aim of safe investing, even in good times, is to hold on to your principal. Money lost is not so easily regained. The example is an old one, but if your stock or bond declines 50% in value, it will have to double in price just to get you back to where you started.

All investors must contend with the risk of down markets, which reduce the value of securities, and the risk of inflation, which diminishes buying power. Shorter-term investors — those who will need their money in five years or less — should worry more about down markets. Longer-term investors should worry more about inflation.

Shorter-term money should go to work in instruments that guarantee (or implicitly guarantee) all of your money back when you're going to need it. These include bank accounts, certificates of deposit, money-market mutual funds, Treasury bills and Treasury notes or tax-free municipal bonds maturing in less than five years. The best all-around place to put shorter-term savings is one of the money-market funds offered by mutual-fund companies and brokerage firms. They usually give you higher yields than banks, as well as instant liquidity and durable safety. If you prefer the convenience of a nearby bank, you can place your money in a federally insured bank money-market deposit account. You give up some advantage in yield, but the difference is quite small.

To defeat future inflation, however, longer-term investors should put some money into investments that come with no guarantee but can grow in value. Primarily, growth calls for stocks and real estate. Over the years, both will surely fall as well as rise, but their general direction throughout modern times has been up.

## A Smart System of Regular Investing

It never fails. You start investing, and find yourself buying in at the top. Then, mutual funds and stocks or bonds stumble and you sell — precisely at the bottom. You can avoid these expensive errors and reduce your risks by investing a set amount of money each month — regardless of whether the market is heading up or down. This is a canny and often profitable investment strategy called dollar-cost averaging.

A strong case can be made for it: You regularly invest, say, $100 or $200 month after month. If stock and mutual-fund prices then go up, you can congratulate yourself for having earned some profits. But what if prices go down? Well, you congratulate yourself on your new opportunity to pick up some bargains. Several months ago, your $200 monthly investment could buy, say, only four shares in your mutual fund; now it can buy five!

A sound means of practicing dollar-cost averaging is to buy shares of a mutual fund at regular monthly intervals, particularly a no-load fund that has done better than the broad market averages over the last several years. No-load mutual funds give you professional management of a diversified portfolio of securities without having to pay a commission.

Even if you dollar-cost average into a so-called index fund — a mutual fund that clones the 500 stocks in Standard & Poor's index — your results could be terrific. For example, in the 18 years up to January 1, 1991, a stock fund that duplicated the S&P 500 would have rewarded semi-annual purchases with an 11.5% average annual return. Investments of $1,000 made every six months over that period totaling $36,000 would have grown to more than $104,000. The market value of the account would have fallen only three times.

## MONTHLY vs. LUMP-SUM INVESTING

| Years to invest | Regular investments $50 | Regular investments $200 | Regular investments $500 | One-time investment $10,000 | One-time investment $25,000 | One-time investment $50,000 |
|---|---|---|---|---|---|---|
| 3 | $2,027 | $8,107 | $20,268 | $12,597 | $31,493 | $62,986 |
| 6 | 4,601 | 18,405 | 46,013 | 15,869 | 39,672 | 79,344 |
| 12 | 12,025 | 48,102 | 120,254 | 25,182 | 62,954 | 125,908 |
| 18 | 24,004 | 96,017 | 240,043 | 39,960 | 99,900 | 199,801 |

SOURCE: MUTUAL FUND EDUCATION ALLIANCE

Assumes 8% yield compounded annually

Dollar-cost averaging also can be used to buy individual stocks, but brokerage fees on small transactions can be prohibitive. And because mutual funds have diversified portfolios, they tend to bounce back from market disasters — when the market ultimately recovers. But an individual stock can fall through the floor and stay in the cellar for years.

Investing a fixed amount each month or each quarter is the traditional form of dollar-cost averaging, but a lesser-known version called value averaging lowers the cost even more, according to Michael Edleson, finance professor at the Harvard Business School. Value averaging works best with a no-load fund. Each month you invest only enough money to increase your fund's total value to a set amount. In months when your fund has risen, you add only enough to round out the market gain to your preset monthly target. In months of sharp price rises, you might actually sell shares.

For example, if you are value-averaging at the rate of $100 a month, and the market during the previous month has lifted your holdings by $60, you add only $40. But if your fund has lost $30, you invest $130. And if your fund has gained $150, you sell shares worth $50. In historical analysis and thousands of computer simulations using Vanguard's S&P 500 Index Fund, Edleson found that value averaging outperformed dollar-cost averaging 90% of the time.

True enough, if you sink all of your money into the stock market in a lump sum, and then the market proceeds to rise like a rocket and continue climbing for many years, you will do better than if you put in your money bit by bit, month after month. But look at dollar-cost averaging as a defensive strategy. It will keep you from getting crushed in the wild up-and-down market swings. The discipline of investing fixed amounts in regular installments helps you to avoid two common errors: shifting all your money into the stock market at a time when it might be getting ready for a sharp tumble, and selling out at big losses when stocks are deeply depressed.

## Making Smart Asset Allocations

The "classic" division of investments often recommended by advisers is:

- 55% in stocks
- 35% in bonds
- 10% in cash — that is, money-market funds, Treasury bills and other safe and liquid short-term savings

But no single division of assets is the right one for all investors. Your allocation of funds hinges on your strategy, your attitudes, your age, your needs.

If you are a conservative investor looking for a place to put money you may need some years from now, you might divide your investment cash into three equal parts:

- 33% in two- to five-year Treasury notes
- 33% in mutual funds that buy U.S. and foreign stocks
- 33% in short-term corporate bond funds and adjustable-rate mortgage funds

But what if you are less conservative and more willing to accept moderate risk in hopes of earning more profits? Then you might put:

- 50% in growth stocks or the mutual funds that buy them
- 10% in two- to five-year Treasury notes
- 10% in a money-market fund
- 20% in intermediate-term corporate bonds rated AA or higher
- 10% in real estate, which is a sound hedge against inflation

If you want high yields with some tax protection and you've already made your maximum contributions to your tax-sheltered IRA, Keogh or 401(k) account, you might carve up your money this way:

- 40% in short- to intermediate-term municipal bonds that are exempt from federal taxes
- 50% in no-load municipal bond funds and short- to intermediate-term (three to 10 years) bonds and tax-exempt municipal bonds
- 10% in real estate

To some extent you can have it both ways: the stock market's superior return without all the price gyrations. The Neuberger & Berman money managers of New York City looked at capital market returns to calculate the performance of various asset-allocation strategies from 1960 to1993. Neuberger found that if you had put half your money in five-year Treasury notes and the other half in S&P 500 stocks, you would have achieved 91% of the equity market return with only 59.1% of its price volatility. While the S&P 500 has yielded a compound average annual return of 10.2% since 1926, this 50-50 mix would have grown at a very respectable 9.35% rate.

In any event, you need different strategies for investing at different stages of your life:

*Young singles.* Say you are in your 20s and unmarried, with all your money tied up in a savings account paying only 2% or 3%. Shift some of it into a higher-yielding certificate of deposit. You can get a federally insured CD for a minimum of $500 at most banks, savings and loan associations, and stock brokerage firms. After you have accumulated savings equal to three months' worth of your after-tax living expenses, you can take some measured risks and begin investing. Most people still have far too much wealth tied up in relatively low-return investments like cash, money funds, certificates of deposit or U.S. Treasury securities.

More and more young people are setting aside part of their paycheck to invest in the stock market. They also recognize that when you invest while young, you can afford to take some risks in search of rich profits. Unlike people in or nearing retirement, you have time to make up for any stumbles.

When starting in the market, your first decision is whether to aim for income (that is, for high dividends) or for growth (that is, for stocks that pay little or no dividends but have good reason to rise in price). Most investment counselors agree that young people should choose a strategy that shoots for capital growth. The younger you are, the more of your income you should invest in stocks.

*Young marrieds.* If you are a working couple in your mid-20s, much depends on whether you own your own home. If you don't, many advisers still suggest applying your money toward the down payment on a house or condominium. Real estate values are not expected to rise as fast as in the 1980s, but they should keep pace with inflation. In many cities and suburbs, real estate prices are still below their peaks of a few years ago, creating a rare buying opportunity. And switching from rent to house payments will remain a good deal, since you get a tax deduction for your mortgage payments and property taxes.

Dual-income couples should try to put $4,000 every year into his-and-her Individual Retirement Accounts, even if not all of it is deductible from your taxable income. (It *will* be deductible if you have no tax-sheltered pension plan on your job or if your income is below certain ceilings; see Chapter 1.) A sensible buy for your IRA or any other investment might be a growth-stock mutual fund. To cite just one example, the Twentieth Century Select Investors fund, headquartered in Kansas City, gained an average 13.3% a year from 1983 to mid-1995.

If you do not have children, you have a special opportunity to build up some savings and investments. Financially, a married couple can be more than the sum of their parts. When you have only each other to look after, you have an obvious edge over singles and parents. One spouse can work steadily while the other goes for a college degree or launches a promising business. Or if both spouses hold jobs, you can try to live on the income from one and save or invest the other paycheck.

But couples do face special financial hurdles. While you have more investment opportunities, you also confront more complex choices than ever before. Above all, avoid making devastating mistakes. The worst disasters often involve high-risk investments that crash. If you want to be safe, don't put too much reliance on any one investment. Here's a list of financial dos and don'ts for married couples:

- Do buy life insurance and disability policies to protect both spouses in case anything happens to one of you. But don't buy more insurance than either mate will really need; your employers may already provide enough. If you do buy, your best choice is probably term insurance.

- Do build up your savings. But don't keep money in a low-yielding statement savings account. As mentioned above, you are better off with a money-market fund, which you can find through a mutual-fund company or a brokerage house, or with a certificate of deposit, which you can get at a bank or savings and loan association.
- Do put money away in savings or investment plans that your employer offers. Not only do such programs give you tax breaks, but often the employer kicks in 50 cents or so for every dollar you put in, and that's "found money."
- Do be financially nimble enough to change course suddenly when baby makes three.

*Married with children.* Financial planning and investing for parenthood is a bit like preparing for a long siege. As parents, you may have to stretch your budget to accommodate pediatrician bills, piano lessons and pilgrimages to summer camp. For a middle-income couple, the cost of rearing a child until the age of 18 will be over $100,000. And that estimate does not include the special parenting costs faced by two-income couples: They must choose either to pay for day care or to lose a paycheck while one parent stays at home with the child.

Nor does that figure include the towering burden of college. In the 1994–95 school year, the average cost of tuition and fees for a student at a four-year private university was $11,709, up from $11,007 the prior year, while room and board averaged $4,976, up from $4,788. The price has risen an average 8% annually since the 1987–88 school year. The College Board estimates that, including books, supplies, transportation and other expenses, the total bill for a resident student at a four-year private university averaged $18,261 in the 1994–95 school year. Prestigious schools such as Stanford, Chicago, Sarah Lawrence, Tufts, Harvard, Bennington, Princeton, and Brown cost an average $27,000 a year. For more particulars, see the *College Costs and Financial Aid Handbook 1995,* published by The College Board ($16). It is a comprehensive guide to paying for postsecondary education and compares over 3,000 schools. Two good computer discs produced by The College Board are the College Cost Explorer FUND FINDER ($495) and ExPAN ($750).

Couples with children should aim to build up a major sum for college

## AVERAGE COLLEGE COSTS 1994–95

One academic year

| Four-year college or university | Tuition and fees | Room and board | Books and supplies | Other expenses | Total expenses |
|---|---|---|---|---|---|
| **PUBLIC** | **$ 2,686** | **$3,826** | **$578** | **$1,308** | **$8,398** |
| **PRIVATE** | **11,709** | **4,976** | **585** | **991** | **18,261** |

SOURCES: THE COLLEGE BOARD; MUTUAL FUND EDUCATION ALLIANCE

tuition. Two possibilities are to buy (1) tax-exempt securities or (2) stocks in fast-growing companies or a mutual fund that focuses on such shares. Until a child is within five years of entering college, investing in a well-managed stock mutual fund gives you the best chance for high returns without excessive risk.

Above all, don't put money that you will need into highly speculative investments. Some people sank their children's college money into oil and real estate tax shelters in the 1980s. The shelters collapsed and consequently the children had the character-building experience of working their way through college.

For the safest possible investment for college, consider Series EE U.S. savings bonds. Any EE bonds that you bought in 1990 or later may be redeemed tax-free after six months to pay college or vocational-school tuition for you, your spouse or your child. To qualify, you must be at least 24 years old when you buy the bond. Parents must buy the bond in their own name. And when you redeem it, you must have a modified adjusted gross income below a certain total, or else the amount of interest that you can collect tax-free starts to decline.

For money earned in 1995, the decline starts for couples filing jointly with incomes above $63,450, and $42,300 for singles

## ELITE COLLEGE COSTS

| | Est. total expenses for 1995–96 | Increase since 1989–90 |
|---|---|---|
| Harvard | **$29,750** | **40%** |
| Yale | **29,020** | **36** |
| Princeton | **28,455** | **33** |
| Sarah Lawrence | **27,933** | **33** |
| Brown | **27,740** | **30** |
| Tufts | **27,700** | **33** |
| Stanford | **27,594** | **31** |
| Middlebury | **27,300** | **33** |
| Bennington | **26,900** | **24** |
| U. of Chicago | **26,870** | **31** |
| Northwestern | **23,793** | **26** |

SOURCE: THE COLLEGE BOARD

and heads of households. There is no tax benefit at all for people filing jointly who earn $93,450 or more, or for singles and heads of households who earn $57,300 or more. But these brackets will rise in step with the Consumer Price Index, so even if you earn, say, $70,000 today, your EE bond interest may be tax-free by the time your child enters college.

If you don't qualify for the federal tax exemption, you can still save on taxes with EE bonds. Their income is exempt from state and local income taxes. And you need not pay federal taxes on their interest until you cash in the bonds. (For more on savings bonds, see Chapter 7.)

*Older couples.* If you are over age 50, you will probably want to put a large share of your spare cash into safe, income-producing assets, notably Treasury and top-grade corporate bonds. You can get instant diversification by investing in a bond mutual fund or unit trust. But inflation is no respecter of age, and you will probably need some stocks to stay ahead of rising prices. Even after your retirement, your money must last 20 or more years — perhaps many more. So plan on having at least some money in stocks all your life.

Retired couples should invest around half their money conservatively for income. Depending on current yield, they might consider Treasury notes as well as CDs. In mid-1995, 10-year Treasury notes yielded 6.5%; two-and-a-half-year CDs, 6.1%.

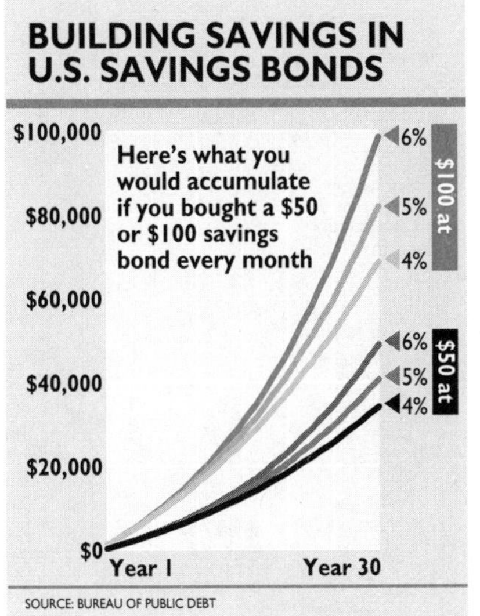


What if you have already put away enough money for emergencies, your children's education has been taken care of, and you have funded your retirement? Congratulations! Now you have a bit of excess cash you want to invest.

But where to invest it? As discussed in later chapters, not only mutual funds and stocks, but also bonds, should be a reasonably sound investment in the long term, provided inflation remains moderate. Real estate will most likely be an iffy buy in 1995, if you are thinking in terms of making money. But if you are looking for a good deal on a home, the real estate market will be attractive.

One lesson of the 1980s and early 1990s will continue to hold true: Technological developments will most likely drive growth. Investments in such industries as fiber optics and computer imaging, biogenetics and other emerging technologies may well lift any wisely chosen portfolio.

CHAPTER 5

# The Many Attractions of Mutual Funds

## How to Make Money in Them

Just as there is no perfect person or painting or poem, so there is no perfect investment. But the one that comes closest for many people is the mutual fund. Never before have mutual funds been so popular. From 1980 to the end of 1994, investment in the funds increased 16 times. During 1994 investors put nearly $1.3 billion a day into them, according to the Investment Company Institute. Sales of funds more than tripled from $150 billion in 1990 to $474 billion in 1994. In mid-1995, more than $2.4 trillion was invested in funds.

The reason for this broad ownership is simple: Funds give you the double-barreled advantages of instant diversification of your investments and professional management of your money. Your investments are handled by people who devote their full time and attention to them. A fund buys a wide variety of securities and then sells its own shares to the public. The price of a share rises or falls every day, along with the ups and downs of the total value of the securities the fund owns. And you can sell your shares back to the mutual fund at any time. These characteristics are particularly valuable for the beginning investor or one who does not have the time or inclination to follow individual stocks and bonds closely, day after day.

Funds offer you an increasingly wide range of investment choices to meet your personal strategy and objectives, indeed to mesh with your own temperament, mentality and view of the world. You can buy anything from aggressive but risky funds that aim for maximum capital

## READING THE FUND LISTINGS

Although they may look rather cryptic, fund listings in newspapers are very easy to read and can tell you a lot about the fund in a small amount of space.

Funds are listed alphabetically by fund company, with specific funds listed under each company.

NAV means "net asset value" and is the value of stocks held in the portfolio divided by the number of the shares of the fund held by the shareholders. The NAV shows how much each share in the fund is worth.

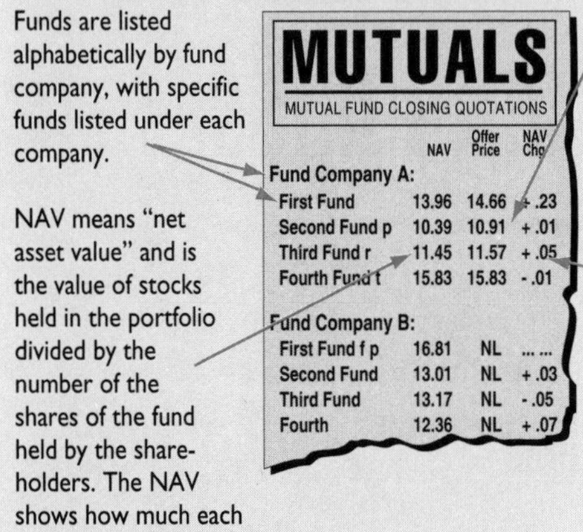

**MUTUALS**

MUTUAL FUND CLOSING QUOTATIONS

| | NAV | Offer Price | NAV Chg |
|---|---|---|---|
| **Fund Company A:** | | | |
| First Fund | 13.96 | 14.66 | + .23 |
| Second Fund p | 10.39 | 10.91 | + .01 |
| Third Fund r | 11.45 | 11.57 | + .05 |
| Fourth Fund t | 15.83 | 15.83 | - .01 |
| **Fund Company B:** | | | |
| First Fund f p | 16.81 | NL | ... ... |
| Second Fund | 13.01 | NL | + .03 |
| Third Fund | 13.17 | NL | - .05 |
| Fourth | 12.36 | NL | + .07 |

Offer Price is the amount you would pay if you wanted to buy the shares and is the same as the NAV, plus any sales charges. NL means it is a no-load fund and you would pay the same price per share to buy it as you would receive if you were to sell it.

This tells how much the net asset value of the fund has changed since the previous trading day. A plus (+) means your shares have increased in value by the amount indicated since the close of the last trading day, and a minus (-) means each of your shares has fallen by that amount.

SOURCE: MUTUAL FUND EDUCATION ALLIANCE

gains to more conservative funds that hold bonds or tax-exempt securities and aim to pay you high regular interest.

As discussed in Chapter 3, there are money-market mutual funds, which give you an escape hatch once readily available only to the rich and professional investors. If you think that trouble is ahead for stocks, you can switch out of the stock market and into the safe money market

## SOME MUTUAL FUND CHOICES

**HIGH-RISK** investments offer the greatest potential for capital growth or income or both. They are often volatile and involve steeper risk, but with the higher likelihood of providing above-average return.

- **Aggressive-growth funds**
- **Growth funds**
- **Small-capitalization stock funds ($100 million or less)**
- **Specialty funds**

**MEDIUM-RISK** investments are generally high-quality investments offering reasonably good potential for capital growth or income or both. They offer greater safety than high-risk investments.

- **Growth-and-income funds**
- **Growth funds**
- **Balanced/equity-income funds**
- **Municipal bond funds**

**LOW-RISK** investments generally offer a high degree of safety and stability, with minimal risk.

- **Money-market funds**
- **U.S. Government money-market funds**
- **Fixed-income funds**
- **Tax-exempt funds**

SOURCE: MUTUAL FUND EDUCATION ALLIANCE

by making a phone call to the mutual-fund company. To have this flexibility, just be sure that the company you choose offers a variety of stock, money-market and other mutual funds.

But mutual funds as a group often don't keep pace with the broad market indexes. Lipper Analytical Services reports that from 1969 to 1994 Standard & Poor's (S&P) 500 stock index outgained the average stock fund, rising 1,251% versus 1,174%. That means $10,000 invested in a portfolio that matched the S&P 500 would have grown to $125,085 by January 1, 1995, while the same amount in the average stock fund would have grown to about $117,400. The expense of running a mutual fund accounts for much of the difference. Another problem: Short-term investments in mutual funds can be very risky, especially in declining markets. Too many people learned that lesson in the crash of 1987, when most funds — though by no means all — plunged. Like stocks themselves, mutual funds are for the *long-term* investor.

Once you invest in a fund, you may receive dividends every quarter and capital-gains distributions semi-annually or annually, if the fund has earned either. A fund earns and distributes capital gains if and when it sells securities at a profit. Almost all mutual funds offer to reinvest your earnings automatically in additional shares. You can also use mutual funds for your Individual Retirement Account and Keogh plan.

What kind of mutual funds should you choose and how should you choose them? The choice depends on your objectives and on how much time you are prepared to spend regularly studying the stock market.

*Income funds* are favorites of conservative investors. The emphasis is on generating dividend income while also increasing capital gains by investing in common or preferred stocks.

Perhaps you follow the financial news but certainly do not want to reexamine and make changes in your investments as often as every week. What you need is a mutual fund that over the years *consistently* climbs at least as much as the stock market averages during good times while not falling much more than the averages in bad times. Quite possibly that will be one of the so-called *growth-and-income funds,* which also favor stocks and bonds of large, high-dividend-yielding companies but put somewhat more emphasis on growth than income funds do.

Another category, *growth funds,* invests in the stocks of expansive but generally well-established companies. Still, growth funds are sufficiently chancy that you would want to avoid putting too many chips on them if

## HOW MUTUAL FUNDS HAVE GROWN

| Type of fund | AVERAGE ANNUAL TOTAL RETURN* One year | Three years | Five years |
|---|---|---|---|
| **Aggressive-growth** | **25.57%** | **16.65%** | **13.34%** |
| **Growth** | **22.22** | **12.80** | **11.50** |
| **Growth-and-income** | **19.62** | **11.51** | **10.58** |
| **Balanced** | **14.65** | **9.53** | **9.82** |
| **Income** | **10.62** | **8.00** | **10.39** |
| **Corporate-bond** | **10.30** | **6.72** | **8.65** |
| **Government-bond** | **8.73** | **5.31** | **8.00** |
| **Municipal-bond** | **7.17** | **6.02** | **7.49** |
| **International** | **2.34** | **9.85** | **5.64** |
| **Gold** | **–0.13** | **12.00** | **3.63** |

*As of June 30, 1995.
SOURCE: MORNINGSTAR

you are risk-averse. If you choose to add them to your well-diversified portfolio, you can expect them to surpass the S&P 500 during bull markets, but do slightly less well than the market averages during bear markets. Growth funds that have performed best are usually managed by people whose records of success go back five or 10 years. So make sure that funds which claim outstanding records still have the same managers who built those gains.

If you are willing to pay really close attention to your investments, have a high tolerance for risk and would like to try for spectacular gains during bull markets, you are a candidate for *aggressive-* or *maximum-capital-gains funds.* They search for the fast-moving stocks of small, potentially rapidly rising companies. But be ready to bail out of such a high-flier quickly. Maximum-capital-gains funds tend to climb fast — and then tumble fast when the market starts to turn down.

You can specialize — and hedge your bets — by buying *sector funds,* which concentrate on specific areas of the economy. Let's say you are essentially optimistic about stocks but also a bit wary about a possible resurgence of inflation. In that case, you can invest part of your assets in a technology-stock fund, which buys into promising though risky technology companies. But simultaneously you would keep another part of your money in a natural-resources fund that buys into mining, forest-products and energy companies, which tend to rise when inflation strikes. But because sector funds concentrate on just one economic area,

## SOME TOP-PERFORMING INTERNATIONAL FUNDS

Funds that buy foreign securities are chancy, but many have done so well in recent years that it may pay to put part of your stock investments into them—say, 10% or so.

| | % RETURN TO MAY 31, 1995 | | | | |
|---|---|---|---|---|---|
| FUND | One year | Three years | Five years | Maximum % sales charge | Telephone (800) |
| M Stanley Institutional: Asian Eq | 7.65% | 91.20% | NA | 0.0% | 548-7786 |
| Colonial Newport Tiger/T | 7.86 | 75.34 | 115.59 | 5.0 | 248-2828 |
| Merrill Lynch Dragon/D | 1.75 | 69.50 | NA | 6.5 | 637-3863 |
| Merrill Lynch Dragon/B | 0.09 | 64.09 | NA | 5.0 | 637-3863 |
| GAM Funds: International | 26.90 | 96.56 | 118.52 | 5.0 | 426-4685 |
| M Stanley Institutional: Intl Equity | 8.18 | 53.01 | 60.58 | 0.0 | 548-7786 |
| MetLife Port: Intl Equity/C | –2.89 | 52.05 | NA | 0.0 | 882-3302 |
| ALL PACIFIC FUNDS | –3.16 | 50.01 | 43.64 | 3.42 | |
| ALL INTERNATIONAL FUNDS | 0.59 | 30.53 | 37.24 | 2.33 | |
| ALL U.S. STOCK FUNDS | 9.88 | 35.04 | 63.17 | 2.87 | |

SOURCE: MICROPAL

don't put more than 10% of your assets into any one of them. That way you will not be hurt too badly if that sector turns down.

*International funds* are managed by U.S. companies but consist wholly or largely of foreign securities. They are much too risky, at least in large doses, for the conservative investor. Foreign companies release far less — and less timely — information than U.S. companies do. When trouble strikes, it often comes with little warning. Investors in Mexican stocks were caught off guard by the devaluation of the peso in early 1995, and they lost big-time. With almost any foreign investment, there is always currency risk; when local currencies decline, the value of your investment drops. That said, some foreign markets have outperformed the U.S. market in the last 10 years or so, and many experts argue that the well-diversified stock portfolio should contain about 10% foreign securities or international mutual funds.

## The Various Types of Mutual Funds

### AGGRESSIVE-GROWTH FUNDS

The investment objective of these funds is to maximize capital gains by investing aggressively in speculative stocks and tending to stay fully invested at all times. Some funds use financial leverage (stock market margin) in an attempt to enhance returns; others invest in small-equity-capitalization firms; still others aim to purchase common stocks of the fastest-growing companies regardless of whether they are large or small. The prices of these funds are quite volatile, performing very well in bull markets and faring very poorly in bear markets. After underperforming the S&P 500 index between 1986 and 1990, aggressive-growth returns exploded to the upside from mid-1990 through mid-1995. A few of the top performers in mid-1995 were Crabbe Huson Special, with a 19.61% average annual return through the end of May 1995; Twentieth Century Ultra Investors, with a 19.48% return; Keystone Small Company Growth (S-4), with an 18.16% return; and Kaufmann Fund, with an 18.03% return.

#### GROWTH FUNDS

These funds aim for long-term growth of investment capital. Growth funds tend to invest in the common stock of larger, established companies that generally pay a cash dividend and provide a modest amount of current income. During the past five years, these funds have provided an average annual compound rate of return of 8.9%, versus an 8.7% compound annual rate of return for the S&P 500.

#### GROWTH-AND-INCOME FUNDS

If you long for a high level of current income, some capital appreciation and preservation of capital during tough times, choose growth-and-income funds. They combine balanced funds, which concentrate on a relatively fixed combination of stocks and bonds, and equity-income funds, which buy stocks with above-average yields. Additionally, they tend to be suited for conservative investors who are not willing to assume the full risk associated with equity investments. On average, growth-and-income funds are about three-fourths as volatile as the market as a whole.

#### INTERNATIONAL FUNDS

These "foreign" funds can be divided into four groups: global funds, which invest in both U.S. and foreign securities; international funds, which invest only in companies outside the U.S.; regional funds that invest in countries in a specific geographic region, such as Europe or the Pacific Basin; and country-specific funds that limit their investment to the issuers of a single country. Investment risk tends to parallel a fund's degree of diversification, with the most diversified (global funds) possessing the least risk and the most concentrated (single-country funds) possessing the most risk.

#### PRECIOUS METALS FUNDS

These funds, of course, invest in gold bullion, silver, platinum and the shares of various mining companies. Given the depression in the gold and silver bullion markets, precious metals funds were among the industry's poorest performers from 1988 to 1992. But in 1993 world demand for gold outstripped supply, and inflation fears sparked one of the best gold rallies in years, with precious metals funds producing returns of 85%. Shares of these funds languished in 1994, dropping 11.6%. In the first six months of 1995, they rose 1.18%.

#### ASSET-ALLOCATION FUNDS

These funds invest in a wide spectrum of assets, such as domestic stocks, gold, international equities, real estate and money-market instruments. The funds' goal is to produce a combination of capital appreciation and current income while reducing risk. In theory, asset-allocation funds should provide a greater rate of return than the S&P 500 index, and at the same time be less volatile. Unfortunately, asset-allocation funds are relatively new additions to the investment world, and there is insufficient data to tell how investment fact measures up to theory. What is known is that these funds are not always winners but shine during periods marked by adverse conditions in the financial markets.

#### BOND FUNDS

Designed for income-oriented investors, they invest in bonds issued by corporations, the U.S. government, government agencies, and state and local governments. Their risk depends on the types of bonds held and their average maturity. For example, in recent years, "high yield" bond funds introduced a considerable amount of risk because they invest in corporate junk bonds.

Some funds try to increase income by speculating in financial futures.

Long-term bonds have traditionally been the haven for investors requiring current income and a high degree of safety, but over the entire period from 1926 to 1994 long-term corporate bonds provided investors with a compound annual rate of return of only 5.38%.

INCOME FUNDS

Otherwise known as equity-income funds, income funds provide about 50% more current yield than the S&P 500 index and are half as volatile. Portfolios generally consist half of high-yielding common stocks and half of bonds and preferred stocks. They are well suited for conservative investors who want both current income and growth of capital.

Source: *The Mutual Fund Encyclopedia*

Two major decisions: Do you buy directly from a mutual-fund company — or from a stockbroker or a financial planner? And which type of fund do you want to buy: load or no-load? You buy no-load funds by mail, over the telephone or through some discount brokers, and you pay no commission for them. You buy load funds from a broker or planner, and you pay a commission, usually 3.5% to 8.5%, which is the legal limit. In return for the load, this professional should give you expert, ongoing investment advice and explain to you in detail the fund's objectives, what it invests in and how it has performed in both up and down markets. If he or she does not know or refers you to the prospectus instead, find another salesperson.

For a description of nearly 4,000 funds, look in your public library for *CDA/Wiesenberger's Investment Companies Yearbook.* Another source is *Winning with Mutual Funds* by the editors of *Money.* Check, too, the performance rankings by Lipper Analytical Services and its weekly roundups of the top-yielding funds in the *Wall Street Journal* and *Barron's. Money* magazine's "Fund Watch" is updated monthly. Listings appear annually (and sometimes more often) in business magazines and *U.S. News & World Report.*

## MUTUAL FUND LEADERS AND LAGGARDS

Here are the highest- and lowest-ranking funds that invest in single industries, according to Lipper Analytical. Rankings are in terms of total returns for the 12 months through June 30, 1995.

| | One-year | Five-years | Assets June 30, 1995 (in millions) |
|---|---|---|---|
| **TOP 10 PERFORMERS** | | | |
| **Seligman Communication; A[4]** | **107.85%** | **289.06%** | **$1,673.3** |
| **Seligman Communication; D[2]** | **106.16** | **NA** | **582.9** |
| **Alliance Technology; A[3]** | **82.40** | **201.01** | **292.9** |
| **Alliance Technology; B[2]** | **81.09** | **NA** | **121.3** |
| **Alliance Technology; C[1]** | **81.09** | **NA** | **20.1** |
| **Fidelity Select Electronic[3]** | **80.91** | **232.10** | **1,005.2** |
| **First American: Tech; C[1]** | **79.02** | **NA** | **22.4** |
| **First American: Tech; A[3]** | **78.79** | **NA** | **0.6** |
| **Fidelity Select Computer[3]** | **70.32** | **219.93** | **466.4** |
| **Fidelity Select Software[3]** | **68.71** | **191.35** | **291.9** |
| **BOTTOM 10 PERFORMERS** | | | |
| **Evergreen Global Real Estate; Y[2]** | **–6.16%** | **27.03%** | **$75.0** |
| **Progressive: Environment[3]** | **–3.71** | **–29.36** | **1.6** |
| **GT Global Financial Services; B[2]** | **–1.84** | **NA** | **3.6** |
| **GT Global Financial Services; A[4]** | **–1.31** | **NA** | **4.6** |
| **PRA: Real Estate[1]** | **–1.07** | **44.21** | **92.9** |
| **Crabbe Huson Real Estate[1]** | **0.27** | **NA** | **21.2** |
| **US: Real Estate[1]** | **1.09** | **32.40** | **9.2** |
| **Retire Plan: Real Estate Secs; A[4]** | **1.09** | **NA** | **26.3** |
| **Fidelity Real Estate[1]** | **1.17** | **81.66** | **513.7** |
| **Templeton Real Estate; I[4]** | **1.22** | **52.76** | **130.9** |

[1] No load [3] Low initial load of 4.5% or less
[2] Redemption load [4] Full initial load of over 4.5%

Loads and fees have not been deducted.

SOURCE: LIPPER ANALYTICAL SERVICES

Of the 6,468 U.S. mutual funds, 2,515 are no-load and 3,953 carry loads. The average one-time load is 4.34%. Loads on new purchases often decline as your assets grow. An 8.5% load on $1,000 might become 4.5% on $50,000 and 3.5% on $100,000.

Instead of a load up-front, many funds charge an exit or redemption fee of 1% to 5%. There are two kinds of back-end loads, one for early withdrawal and one simply for redemption no matter what the timing. In addition, to cover their operating expenses, stock funds charge an average *annual* fee of 1.4%, taxable bond funds charge 1.02% and municipal funds .78%.

The most popular new charge, tacked on by more than 1,000 funds, is made under the so-called 12b-1 plan. Fund managers take money each year directly from shareholders' assets to pay for advertising, marketing and distribution. Funds charge anywhere from .001% to a recently established limit of 1% — set by the National Association of Securities Dealers. (Morningstar, Inc., the mutual-fund rating service in Chicago, reports that annual fees of diversified U.S. equity funds in 1994 averaged 1.37% — almost exactly the same as in 1980. Asset growth over that period should have lowered costs, but a surge in promotional expenses pushed fees up.)

You can expect 12b-1 fees to proliferate despite the new cap. The nature and full amounts of all the fees and other charges should be laid out explicitly in the prospectus, in the front section under the heading of "expenses." Be sure to read it, and if you have any questions, write or call the fund and get a response in writing. Fund companies sometimes waive the fees for brief periods, temporarily increasing your returns to lure new money. A few funds, such as Fidelity Spartan Government Income Fund (10.1% return for year ended June 30, 1995) have high gains in part because they boast zero fees. But be forewarned that the deal may not last forever. Footnotes in the fund's prospectus should tell you the amount likely to be tacked on once the promotion ends.

If you feel that you need investment counsel, it makes sense to buy a load fund. The broker or banker or financial planner who sells it to you should always be available to answer your questions about the fund, to explain changes that it makes in its investments and to advise you when to buy more — or to sell out. But if you feel you don't need handholding from a broker or planner, buy directly from a fund company and save the commission.

## DISCOUNT BROKERS THAT SELL NO-LOAD FUNDS

These discount brokers offer no-load, no-transaction-fee funds from a variety of fund families.

| **BROKER** (Mutual-fund program name) | Number of funds | Number of fund families | Telephone (800) |
|---|---|---|---|
| **Jack White & Co. (NoFeeNetwork)** | **541** | **80** | **323-3263** |
| **AccuTrade, Inc. (AccuFunds)** | **420** | **76** | **582-5534** |
| **Fidelity Investments (FundsNetwork)** | **370** | **46** | **544-9697** |
| **Muriel Siebert & Co. (FundExchange)** | **360+** | **~45** | **872-0666** |
| **Charles Schwab & Co. (OneSource)** | **350** | **43** | **2NO-LOAD** |
| **Waterhouse Securities (Waterhouse Mutual Fund Connection)** | **175** | **30** | **934-4443** |

A load fund's sterling performance over time can make up for the commission. But there is no evidence that load funds *as a group* outperform no-loads. With the commission taken into account, the strong long-term performers tend to be split fairly evenly between load and no-load funds. Above all, remember this: A far more important consideration than the size of the commission, if any, is how well the fund has performed compared with others in its class in the past three to five years.

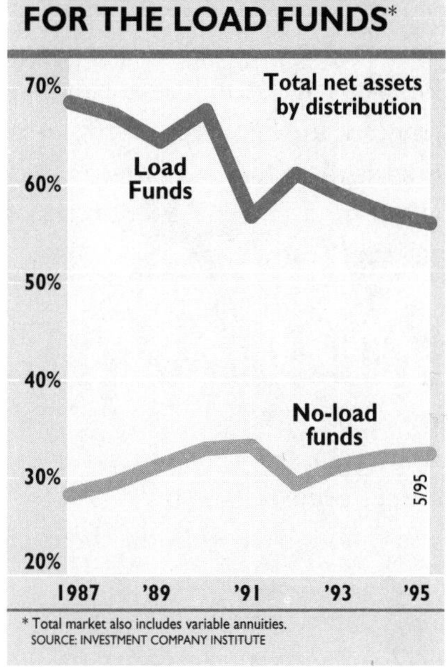

* Total market also includes variable annuities.
SOURCE: INVESTMENT COMPANY INSTITUTE

But if you want to put your money in a mutual fund for only a short time — three years or less — then follow the no-load road. A load fund always has to earn a higher total return to perform as well as a no-load. And three years is seldom long enough.

For a directory of 850 no-load and low-load funds, send $7 to the Mutual Fund Education Alliance, 1900 Erie Street, Suite 120, Kansas City, Missouri 64116.

Whether you choose load or no-load, don't necessarily buy the hottest fund of the moment. Funds that surge like fighter jets when the market is rising often crash when it falls. This year's heroes can easily turn into next year's bums — and often do.

Funds that are on a roll are sometimes swamped with new shareholders and more money than they can wisely invest. Check the size of a fund's total assets. Smaller funds are nimbler than larger ones. Funds managing less than $100 million of capital are better able to invest a significant portion of it in a promising company that has only a slim amount of outstanding stock. The larger a fund, the more difficulty it has investing an important share of its assets in those thinly traded stocks. If the fund's assets have risen to $500 million or more, chances are it will move away from emerging growth companies.

So, to repeat, it is wise to look for funds that have been *consistently* profitable over the years, that have outperformed the broad stock indexes in both up and down market cycles. This provides the best test of fund managers' ability to handle money for the long term. Funds that replicate the S&P 500 portfolio outperform most managers. One such fund is the Vanguard Group's Index Trust 500 Portfolio. Both the Vanguard fund and the S&P index have beaten most of the human managers for years.

## Eight Top Long-Term Performers

In its February 1995 issue, *Money* magazine identified eight funds that outperformed Standard & Poor's 500 stock index over the previous 10 years and topped both the three- and five-year gains of the S&P 500 and the average equity fund. Here they are in order of their gains for the five years ended January 1, 1995.

*Twentieth Century Giftrust* (800-345-2021) is an aggressive fund that invests in small-cap stocks (those with total market values under $1 billion) and companies with rapidly rising earnings. For the five years ended January 1, 1995, it returned an annual average of 22%. The fund has no initial sales charge, and the minimum initial investment is $250.

*FPA Capital* (800-982-4372) is an aggressive fund that looks for small-cap stocks that are inexpensive in relation to assets and earnings. The fund's five-year return averaged 17.3% annually. The initial sales charge is 6.5%, with a minimum initial investment of $1,500.

*Fidelity Destiny 1* (800-752-2347), a growth fund, buys stocks that blend growth and value characteristics and have total market values of more than $5 billion. Its five-year annual return was 15.4%. Though the initial minimum investment is only $50, investors must agree to continue contributing at least $50 a month for 10 years or longer.

*Vanguard Primecap* (800-851-4999), a growth fund, seeks stocks with growth and value characteristics and market values of $1 billion to $5 billion. With a five-year return of 13.2%, it has no initial sales charge but requires a minimum investment of $3,000.

*Mutual Qualified* (800-533-3014), a growth-and-income fund, buys stocks that have total market values of more than $5 billion and are considered inexpensive in relation to assets or earnings. The five-year return was 11.6%. The fund has no initial sales charge, and the minimum initial investment is $1,000.

*EuroPacific Growth* (800-421-4120), the only international fund among the eight, emphasizes stocks that have market values of more than $5 billion and are deemed by the fund's managers to be inexpensive in relation to assets and earnings. The fund's investments are spread among nearly 36 countries. For the five years ended January 1, 1995, its return was 10.7%. The fund carries an initial sales charge of 5.75% and a minimum initial investment of $500.

*Dodge & Cox Stock* (800-621-3979), a growth-and-income fund, looks for the securities of large companies that are underpriced relative to their intrinsic value. With a five-year return of 9.7%, it has no initial sales charge and requires a minimum initial investment of $2,500.

*United Income* (800-366-5465) buys large stocks with growth and value characteristics. Its five-year average annual return was 9.1%. There is no initial sales charge, but the minimum initial investment is $3,000.

## Choosing the Best Ones for You

Before you invest in a mutual fund, write or phone the fund for both its prospectus and its latest financial report. You can find the addresses and toll-free phone numbers of most widely sold funds in the ads in financial magazines or the business pages of newspapers. Read the financial report to learn how much the fund has gained — or lost — not only over the past year but also over the past five or 10 years, and how well it has held up over periods of major market downturns. The report also lists the securities that the fund holds.

The prospectus should clearly define the fund's investment objectives. Make sure you are comfortable with them. Look also for the section that says whether the fund's managers are allowed to shift out of stocks and into, say, U.S. Treasury bills or bank certificates of deposit as market conditions change. This flexibility to switch into fixed-income investments gives you added protection against losses when stocks turn down.

Many mutual-fund firms manage a family of funds. They let you switch your money from one type of fund to another, usually just by making a phone call. This convenience can be important if you buy into a fund that invests aggressively for maximum capital gains. If you anticipate that the fund will be rocked by a declining market ahead, you can quickly switch to a steadier, income-oriented fund.

Whichever types of funds you choose, it's sensible to pursue a strategy of dollar-cost averaging. You simply put an equal amount of money into the same fund at regular intervals. That way, you buy many of your shares when prices are down, and you avoid the temptation to throw in too much money near a market peak.

The choices you make among funds will depend on your financial and family situations. Ask yourself what your financial commitments will be in the future for college costs, retirement or other necessities. Can you afford to take some risks now, or is preserving your money overwhelmingly important to you?

Once you have answered such questions, look for a *package* of different mutual funds that suits your needs. Many strategists recommend putting 20% to 40% of your investment money into corporate or tax-exempt bond funds. Bond funds tend to perform better than stock funds during recessions; on the other hand, bond funds were clobbered when interest rates were kicked up in 1994. Consequently, investors stopped pouring money into them. It's a bit of a comfort to know that

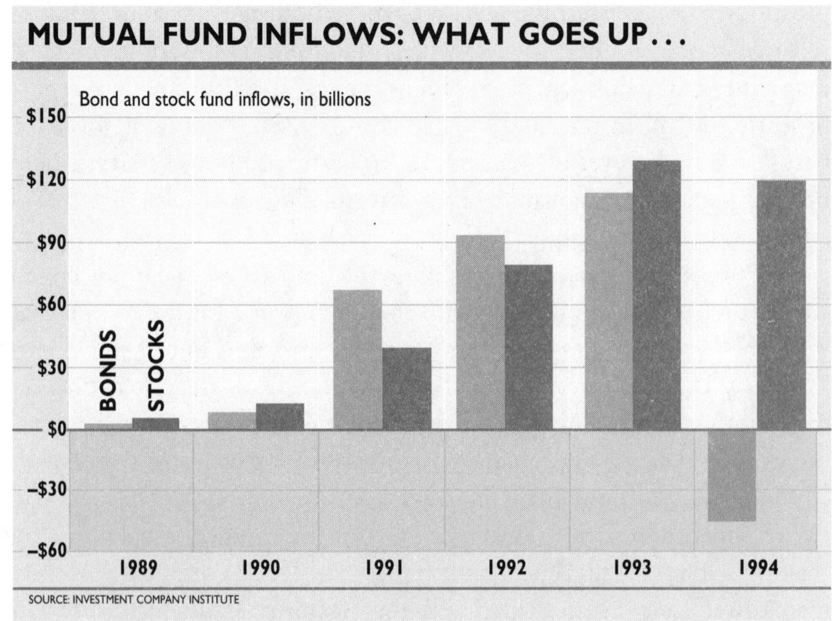

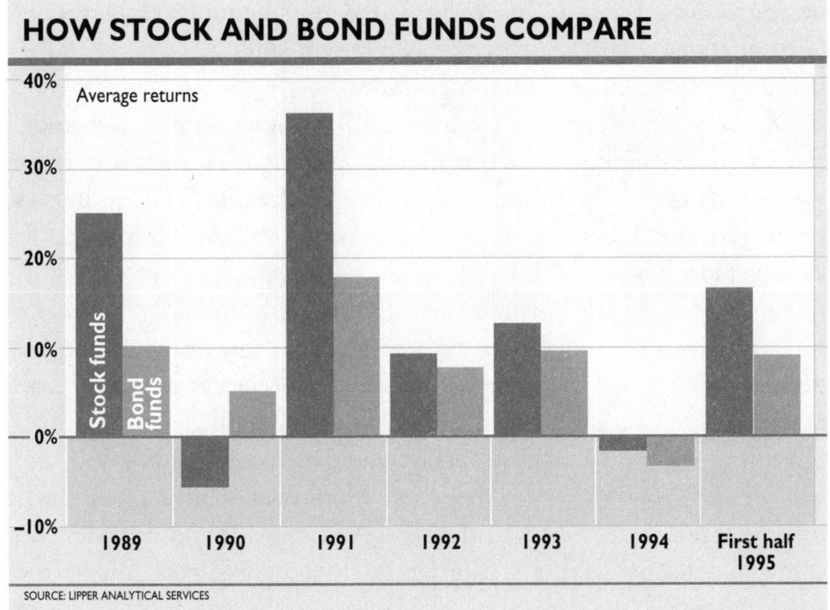


temporary losses in bonds' market value show up only on paper — eventually, when they mature, the bonds pay back 100 cents on the dollar — while the interest income that bonds pay continues to flow steadily and unchanged to the people who must depend on it.

Among the top-performing corporate bond funds in mid-1995 were Smith Barney Investment A Shares (20.32% gain over the preceding 12 months), Smith Barney Investment B Shares (20.05% gain) and Sierra Corporate Income (15.82% gain).

If you are in a high tax bracket, municipal bond funds may be the right choice for investments that are made outside of retirement accounts and are therefore exposed to current taxes. Municipal bond funds' dividends are exempt from federal taxes. For a list of the top-performing high-yield tax-exempt funds for the year ended December 1, 1994, see Chapter 7.

Four outstanding stock funds that have had average annual returns of more than 15% over the past 10 years are Fidelity Magellan with an annual return of 17.8% (800-544-8888); New York Venture Fund with 17.2% (800-279-0271); United Income Fund with 15.5% (800-366-5465); and AIM Weingarten with 15.1% (800-347-1919).

Three stock mutual funds that had average total returns of 15% or more a year over the past five years are Fidelity Contra (800-544-8888), Oppenheimer Mainstreet Income & Growth (800-525-7048) and Fidelity Blue Chip Growth (800-544-8888).

One way for a fund to minimize risk is to move its money between the securities markets and the money market as the economy goes through its cycles. Two funds that successfully employ this flexible approach are the Phoenix Capital Appreciation (800-243-4361) and the Crabbe Huson Special (800-541-9732).

You have to decide how much cash to put into the different types of funds. If you are young and confident and have few obligations or dependents, you might want to emphasize aggressive funds that aim for maximum capital gains. But if you are saving for college bills or an approaching retirement, you probably would be more comfortable with less-volatile growth funds, or the still more conservative growth-and-income funds. You will make the wisest selections if you consider such changing personal factors as your family situation and your financial responsibilities.

*A fairly young couple,* earning comfortable salaries from their two jobs, would be smart to aim for long-term growth of capital. They might put one-third of their mutual-fund assets into aggressive-growth or long-term growth funds. Another third would go into a growth-and-income fund, and the last third into a bond fund.

*A couple with two or more teenage children* would have college costs on their minds. They would want to start moving some of that tuition money from stock or bond funds into a money-market fund, where they could withdraw it swiftly and without fear that their shares had lost value. This midlife couple would also be concerned about building a nest egg for retirement. Thus, after covering the college costs, they probably would want to put half of their remaining money into growth and growth-and-income funds, a third or more into bond funds and perhaps 5% in a gold fund as a hedge against inflation.

*Older couples* intent on preserving whatever wealth they have built for retirement might put 20% of their fund assets into growth funds with strong records even during periods of weak stock markets. Another 35% might go into growth-and-income funds, and still another 35% would be put into bond funds, including one that invests in tax-exempt bonds. The remaining 10% should go into a money-market fund.

# Managing a Team of Funds

A wise way to invest is to buy the shares of not just one but several mutual funds, in several different categories. This increases your chances of scoring consistent gains. For example, over the five years through 1993, you would have done well if you had divided your money among international funds, growth-and-income funds and capital-appreciation funds. Those that specialize in foreign companies showed impressive gains while the dollar was decreasing in value relative to foreign currencies. In 1993 many international funds surged, lifting diversified portfolios. Later these funds tumbled, in part because of the strengthening of the dollar. But growth-and-income funds remained sound, and capital-appreciation funds tracked the continuing strong economy. By mid-1995 growth-and-income funds were doing extremely well, while high-tech funds were jumping over the moon.

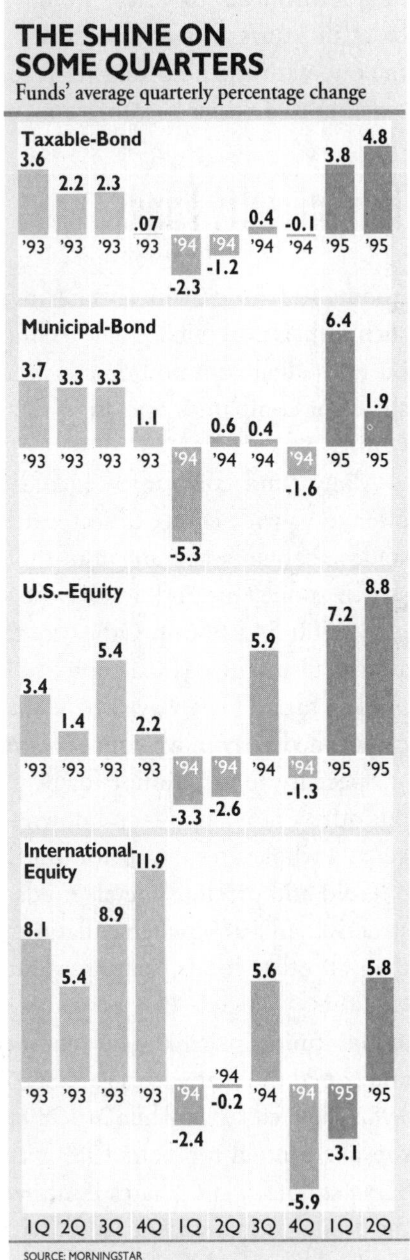


It is often wise to put money in several mutual funds whose managers excel in different investment specialties. You would want one champion at picking growth companies, for instance, *and* another who has done well at identifying undervalued companies. You would want a specialist in finding large corporations and a wizard at spotting small companies. Your job, says Thomas Ebright, comanager of Pennsylvania Mutual Fund (average annual return over 10 years through mid-1995: 11.42%), is like that of a baseball team's manager. You find the best player for every position — the one with the best long-term record — and you let all the stars work together to do their best for you.

## The Specialty Funds

About 400 funds concentrate investors' money in specific industries, such as health services, high technology or banking. Or they may focus on individual commodities, such as gold or oil and gas. They may buy shares of companies operating in a particular region of the U.S. or the world.

Many fund companies, including Fidelity, Vanguard and Franklin, offer you a wide choice of sector funds. Fidelity's Select portfolios, for instance, contain separate mini-funds for 35 different sectors. You can switch money around among the sectors simply by phoning the company (800-544-6666). Other companies may offer only one sector, but almost all will give you a choice of switching out of it and into a money-market fund. That way, whenever you sense danger in the sector, you can immediately move your investment to a safe money fund.

Specialty funds are not for beginners. Some tend to be quite stable, but others move up — and down — much more sharply than the market as a whole. In sum, sector funds can be highly volatile and risky.

Gold and precious metals funds are mercurial. A historical look is instructive. In 1980, when inflation was in double digits, they rose faster than all other funds, soaring as much as 64%. Later, when gold prices fell, they plunged. But they rose again and were the biggest gainers among funds in 1987: They climbed 75% during the first nine months and ended the year with a gain of 37% despite the stock market crash. In 1988 they fell 17%, while in 1989 they climbed 29%. In fact, two of the top five mutual funds in 1989 were gold funds. They were the United Services' U.S. Gold Shares Fund, with a return of 65% for the year, and the Strategic Investment Fund, with a return of 61%. But in 1991 gold funds plummeted again. In the first five months of 1995, while the rest of the market was surging, they rose a bare .34%. Talk about a roller coaster!

If you think the inflation genie will get out of the bottle once again, and you are willing to take big risks for the possibility of high gains, you might put some money into gold funds. On the other hand, if you believe that inflation will not run away and that the economy and the stock market will do well for the next few years, it would be logical for you to invest instead in growth or even aggressive-growth funds.

While aggressive-growth funds are not specialty funds, they tend to concentrate on a particularly incendiary area: small companies that have large potential, often in high-tech, biotech, and health care and other services. Like the companies they invest in, the funds usually jump — and tumble — faster than the market itself. Two aggressive-growth funds that buy into small companies are Kaufmann Fund, with a gain of 16.8% for the 12 months ended June 30, 1995 (and 19.3% annual average over the five years from 1990 through 1994), and MFS Emerging Growth Fund Class B, with a gain of 16.5% for the year through June 30, 1995 (24.96% from 1990 through 1994). You can reach Kaufmann at 800-237-0132 and MFS Emerging Growth Fund Class B at 800-637-2929. But even the most optimistic analysts stress that you must be prepared to move out of highly speculative aggressive-growth funds at the first sniff of decline.

Risky opportunities offering potential outsized rewards are available in the mutual funds that specialize in stocks sold over-the-counter (OTC). These are generally shares of companies too small and too new to be listed on the major exchanges. One fund that concentrates in them is Fidelity's OTC Portfolio (82 Devonshire Street, Boston, Massachusetts 02109; 800-544-8888). It started in December 1984; by December 1994 it had gained a total 410%, adjusted for a 3% load. In the 12 months through June 30, 1995, it gained 30%.

## Tax-Exempt Bond Mutual Funds

You get a free ride from Uncle Sam on the interest payments from municipal bond funds. But you will be hit with state income taxes on at least part of the interest, unless the fund invests only in bonds issued by state or municipal agencies in the state where you live. Muni bond funds

## HOW MUNI-BOND FUNDS HAVE PERFORMED

These tax-free issues did not do brilliantly in the year through mid-1995, as these examples from The Vanguard Group show.

| FUND | YIELD June 30, 1994 | YIELD June 30, 1995 | Share price change |
|---|---|---|---|
| **Short-term (1–2 yrs.)** | **3.60%** | **3.77%** | **0.7%** |
| **Limited-term (2–5 yrs.)** | **4.09** | **4.13** | **1.2** |
| **Intermediate-term (7–12 yrs.)** | **5.02** | **4.78** | **0.5** |
| **Long-term (15–25 yrs.)** | **5.65** | **5.40** | **1.1** |

SOURCE: THE VANGUARD GROUP

are becoming exceedingly popular; since 1980 their assets have jumped from $1.9 billion to $94.9 billion.

The managers of these funds invest in a large variety of tax-free bonds, and this diversification helps protect you against loss. They watch their holdings closely, aiming to unload any bonds that may be going sour. And they can make gains through trading. The risk, as with all bonds, is that the price of your shares will decline when interest rates rise. That is exactly what happened after the Federal Reserve kicked up interest rates in 1994 and 1995.

The top tax-exempt bond funds ranked by 10-year average annual return up to the period ended mid-1995 were Smith Barney Managed Municipals (10.33% gain), United Municipal Bond (10.22% gain) and Vanguard Muni–High Yield (10.02% gain). The phone numbers are Smith Barney, 800-544-7835; United Municipal Bond, 800-366-5465; and Vanguard, 800-662-7447.

## "Humanistic" and Environmental Funds

If you are concerned about social issues, such as the spread of armaments or pollution, should you apply your ethical standards to your investments? That's your decision, of course. Many people think that trying to do good with your investments will keep you from doing well. In fact, you can profit both financially and spiritually. Self-professed "socially responsible" investment managers were in charge of $650 billion in stocks, bonds and mutual funds in 1995, up from only $100 billion in 1985. Over the past 10 years, some of the funds that are guided by their own ethical criteria have performed better than stocks in general. Other such funds have not done as well, so you have to be particularly selective.

Picking investments to match your ethics limits your choice. If you want to avoid arms makers, as well as alcohol, tobacco and gambling enterprises, you will not be able to invest in 60% to 70% of the issues listed on the New York Stock Exchange. You can achieve reasonable results, but you may not get the highest return possible.

The first question to ask yourself is what you really hope to achieve. If you want to influence corporate or government policy, you may be disappointed. Chances are your investments will just not be big enough. You would probably be better off investing for maximum returns and donating some money to an action group. But if your goal is to keep a clear conscience, social investing can work for you.

If you want advice, contact a membership and trade organization called the Social Investment Forum (P.O. Box 2234, Boston, Massachusetts 02107; 617-451-3369). For $35 it will send you its annual directory listing more than 1,000 financial professionals and firms that use social criteria when deciding upon investments. The Forum estimates that there are 35 mutual funds dedicated to making only investments that the group deems to be socially responsible, and the Forum will provide a free list of these funds.

For example, the Dreyfus Third Century Fund (800-645-6561) favors companies that have exceptional records on environmental protection, occupational health and safety, purity of consumer products and equal employment opportunity. Dreyfus Third Century rose 18% in the 12 months through June 30, 1995. Both the Calvert World Value Fund and the Calvert Serial Investment Growth Fund (800-368-2748) keep their money away from companies involved in nuclear power or weapons systems. For the year through June 1995, these funds rose 4.8% and 14.5%, respectively.

If you are concerned about energy development, you might want to try the New Alternatives Fund (800-423-8383). It searches for firms that conserve and produce alternative sources of energy, excluding nuclear power, and will not invest in arms makers or companies with poor environmental records. The fund gained 12.5% for the year through June 1995.

The Pax World Fund (603-431-8022) also avoids arms makers; companies with gambling, alcohol or tobacco interests; and those that it believes discriminate against minorities and women. It was the first fund to adopt social criteria. A so-called balanced fund, Pax World puts about two-thirds of its money in stocks and one-third in bonds. Its annual return over the past 10 years averaged 11.4%, and 12.2% for the year ended June 1995.

The Parnassus Fund (415-362-3505) is both a socially conscious and a contrarian fund. It invests in out-of-favor companies that its managers believe make quality products, treat their employees well and are community-minded. It returned 27% in price appreciation and dividends for the year through June 1995.

A money-market fund that applies very strict rules is the Working Assets Money Fund (800-223-7010). It even shuns U.S. Treasury securities as part of its antiweapons policy. The fund also searches for firms that have waste-reduction and recycling programs, do not violate Environmental Protection Agency regulations or show a pattern of discrimination and do have a record of good labor relations. Its return for the 12 months through June 1995 was 4.42%.

To find out about more such funds, you may subscribe to *Investing for a Better World* (monthly; $29.95 a year; 617-423-6655).

The 1990s have been called the Green Decade, and that is only tangentially a reference to the color of money. Our earth has become the focus of soaring public concern, and the waste-management industry seems destined to clean up — eventually. Several major mutual-fund companies are riding along. Fidelity was the first to devise a sector fund that invests in waste-management, toxic-waste-disposal and pollution-control firms. From its start on June 29, 1989, until December 31, 1994, Fidelity Select Environmental Services (800-544-6666) earned only 1.03% after adjusting for a 3% load for its investors, while Standard & Poor's 500 stock index rose 59.6%. Three other funds begun since 1989 are Alliance Global Environmental Fund (800-227-4618), Freedom Environmental Fund (800-225-6258) and Oppenheimer Global Environmental Fund (800-525-7048). Kemper's Environmental Services Fund (800-621-1048) has been around since 1990.

Another, smaller group of mutual funds avoids waste-management and -disposal companies, citing their waste-disposal and water-pollution violations and voicing concern over toxic-ash disposal. *Investing for a Better World* recommends two of these funds:

The New Alternatives Fund, known as the greenest of the green, was started in 1982 and is devoted exclusively to investing in companies with positive records in environmental protection and energy conservation. For the year ended June 30, 1995, New Alternatives produced a total return of 12.5%.

The Progressive Environmental Fund (800-826-8154), launched in February 1990, also has tight environmental screens and will donate a portion of its marketing fees to environmental groups. Its total return for the year through June 1995 was 9%.

## Switching Among the Funds

Since today's fast-rising mutual fund can easily turn into tomorrow's loser, one strategy is to be a fair-weather friend. You get out of the losers and into the winners by switching from fund to fund in an ongoing effort to be in the groups or sectors offering the best returns. When the market is advancing rapidly, you invest in growth funds. Then at the merest flutter of danger, you can switch to the safety of a more secure conservative fund or a money-market fund. Investors can also move to tax-free municipal bond funds or corporate bond funds within the same fund company.

For guidance on when and where to switch, you can subscribe to a monthly newsletter that tracks the performance of the various funds and that may recommend the best buys or timely sells. Such newsletters include *Growth Fund Guide* (P.O. Box 6600, Rapid City, South Dakota 57709; $89 a year); *NoLOAD FUND*X* (235 Montgomery Street, San Francisco, California 94104; $140 a year); *Mutual Fund Strategist* (P.O. Box 446, Burlington, Vermont 05402; $149 a year); *NoLOAD FUND*Investor* (P.O. Box 318, 1 Bridge Street, Irvington-on-Hudson, New York 10533, $119 a year); and *No-Load Fund Analyst* (800-776-9555; $195 a year).

The newsletters rank the funds by how much their shares rise or fall over one-month, three-month, six-month or one-year periods. One strategy of switching is to (1) buy into the fund that is on top of the rankings for performance over the past year and (2) keep your money in that fund as long as the advisory service tells you it is among the top five in its category for the past year. When your fund falls out of this circle, replace it with the new number one. But since this strategy calls for frequent switching, confine it to no-load or low-load funds.

You must be willing to go to the trouble of closing your account with one mutual-fund company and opening a new account with another company that offers the currently best-performing fund in its category. Leapfrogging from fund to fund does require a bit of work. The first step is to call the toll-free number of the new fund you want to invest in. You can get these numbers from mutual-fund newsletters or fund companies' ads or merely by dialing toll-free information at 800-555-1212. When you reach the fund company, ask for shareholder services. Announce that you want to open an account and then request an account number for yourself.

Next, write to the head of the shareholder services at your old fund, that is, the one you are currently invested in. Your letter should state, "Please sell all full and fractional shares in the account of . . ." with your name and your old account number. Ask that the redemption check be made payable to, and sent to, the new fund you are moving to. And be sure to request that the words "for the benefit of" appear on the check, followed by your name and your new account number.

Probably it will take one to two weeks for your money to arrive at your new mutual fund. You can short-circuit this process if you have a money-market account with the mutual fund that you are leaving. Tell that fund to switch all your assets to your money-market account. Then write a check for the full amount you have in the account and mail it to your new mutual fund.

Fortunately, there is one way to skip that paperwork. Just open an account at any office of Charles Schwab & Co., the San Francisco–based discount broker. Then, by making a single toll-free phone call to Schwab, you can switch in and out of over 500 no-load mutual funds. Schwab will charge a fee based on the size of your order — for example, $39 on a $1,000 swap or $70 on a $10,000 swap. So this will cost you more than if you shift assets on your own.

## Borrowing Against Your Mutual Funds

The Securities and Exchange Commission has repealed an old rule on using mutual-fund shares as collateral when you borrow money from a stockbroker. That means you now can use your mutual funds to get a personal loan from your broker or to buy securities on margin.

Should you take advantage of this opportunity? Probably not — if you are a conservative investor who likes to buy steady and sound securities and just put them away in a safe-deposit box without trading them. But if you have a high tolerance for risk, margin buying can increase your potential rewards.

Federal rules limit borrowing against securities and funds. To borrow $4,000 as a personal loan, you would have to put up $8,000 in fund shares. You would also pay a variable interest rate, usually one-half to two and a half percentage points above so-called broker loan rates. As with broker loans, the interest rate decreases as your account balance increases. You do not have to make regular payments on the interest or the principal. You can repay whenever you want, just as long as the market value of the fund shares you pledge as collateral remains above a certain percentage of the loan amount. Usually the loans can be for no more than 65% to 70% of the market value of the fund shares.

As a margin buyer you will be at greatest risk when interest rates are rising. That means you will have to pay higher rates on your loan. Also the value of securities tends to fall at such times, so you may get a margin call from your broker and thus have to put up additional collateral. The good news is that mutual funds are less volatile than many stocks and bonds. When markets turn down, fund shares are not likely to drop dramatically in price and trigger a margin call.

CHAPTER 6

# A Sensible Strategy for Investing in Stocks

No investment has performed better for more people than stocks. Look at the record: Almost 70 years of carefully documented financial-market performance reveals their long-term superiority over any other type of investment. From 1926 through 1994, the 500 stocks in Standard & Poor's index have produced an average return — from price rises plus dividends — of 10.2% a year, almost double the average 5.4% annual return from long-term corporate bonds and well over double the 4.8% from U.S. Treasury bonds. One dollar — a single dollar! — invested in the S&P 500 stock index in 1925 would have grown to $974 by mid-

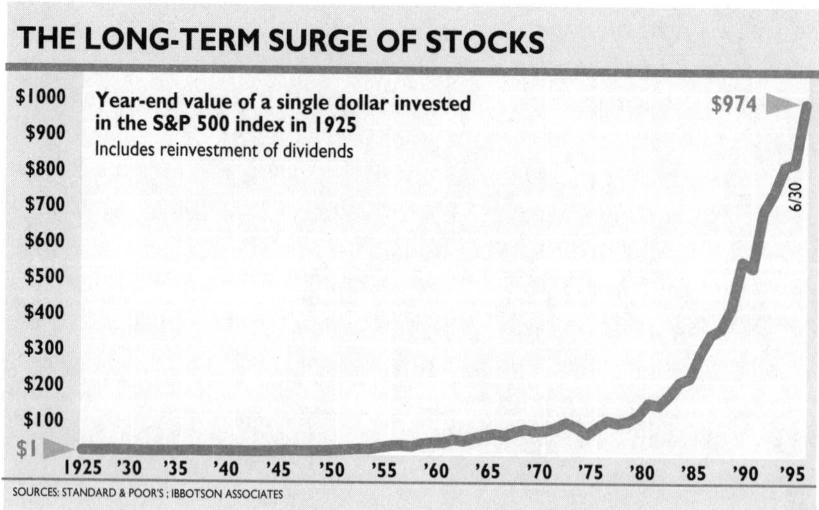

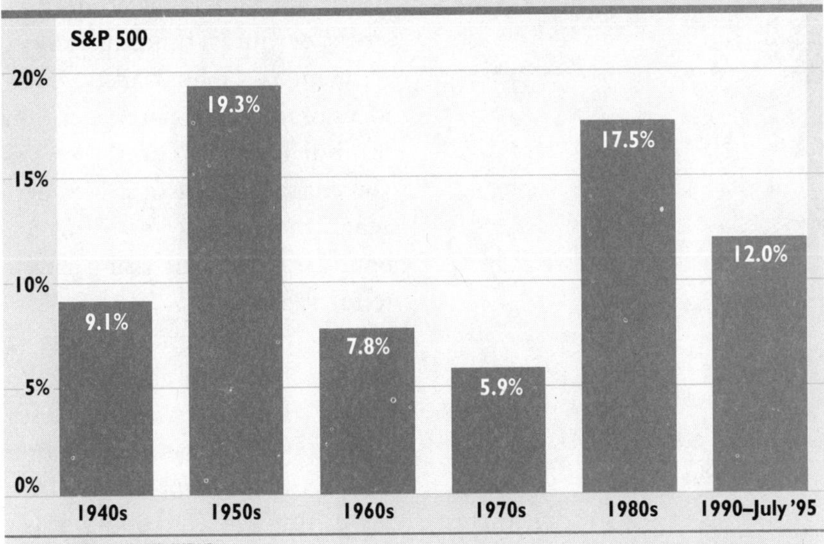


SOURCE: STANDARD & POOR'S, *FORTUNE*

1995, assuming no taxes and the reinvestment of all dividends. Under the same assumptions, a dollar invested in intermediate-term U.S. government bonds would have grown to only $22, and in Treasury bills to a meager $10, barely enough to beat inflation. (Inflation since 1926 has been 771.4%.)

The performance of stocks is even better if you take away the time of the Great Depression and measure only the years from 1940 through 1994. In that period the S&P 500 returned an average of 11.7% a year. The *total* compounded returns for stocks over 10-year periods were 486% in the 1950s, 112% in the 1960s, 77% in the hyper-inflationary 1970s and 403% in the 1980s.

Certainly, there are many years when the market heads *down.* Given the historical record, you can expect a severe drop of 15% or more about every three years, and a bear market with a decline of more than 20% every five years. But it doesn't bascially matter whether the market is sinking fast, just treading water or hitting new highs: Any time can be the right time to invest in stocks, provided you're committed for the long term.

History teaches that you take a worse risk by staying out of the market than by getting — and staying — in. That lesson is just as true whether you are young, middle-aged, nearing retirement or already

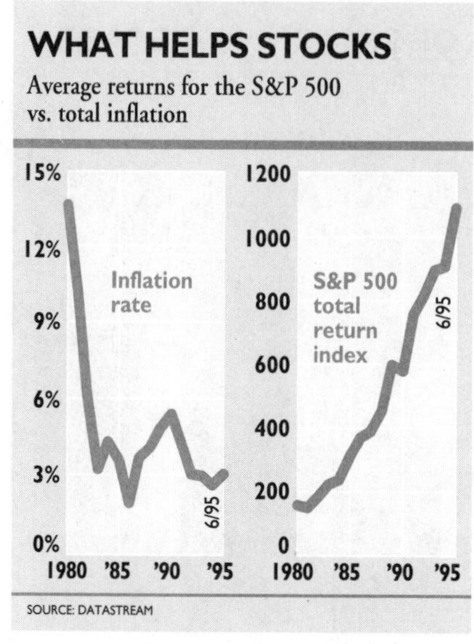


retired. You probably would benefit from a substantial position in stocks or mutual funds that invest in them. Says John Markese, president of the American Association of Individual Investors, "Unless you maintain at least a fifty percent stock allocation, you are bound to lose purchasing power to inflation."

But this lesson — almost a proven rule — applies only to money that you won't need for the next five years. No matter how good the long-term record, stocks can kill you in the short run. According to Chicago's Ibbotson Associates, from 1926 to 1992 the S&P 500 index lost as much as 43% of its value in its worst year (1931) and recorded a sobering total of 20 losing years during that period. By contrast, long-term government bonds (20-year maturity) lost no more than 9% in their worst year (1967). So remember: Time is the ally of the investor in stocks.

The longer you hold stocks, the more favorable the odds become. Ibbotson reports that over 63 successive five-year periods (1926 through 1930, 1927 through 1931, etc.) — in spite of the Depression, periodic recessions, wars and political upheavals — stocks were winners all but seven times and at worst were down no more than 12.5%. Over 58 successive 10-year periods, stocks had only two down periods, never gave up more than 1% and always beat inflation. Finally, over 25-year periods, stocks *never* showed a loss.

So, while from September 5 through October 11, 1990, the Dow Jones industrial average plunged a frightening 10% and fell to 2365, it bounded back and broke the 3000 barrier by April 1991; by January 1992 it passed the 3200 mark and in mid-1995 the market was at 4556 — almost double where it was five years before. The secret to investing wisely in stocks is to chant the market mantra over and over again: "Think long-term, think long-term."

Many people go into a panic and dump stocks whenever the market

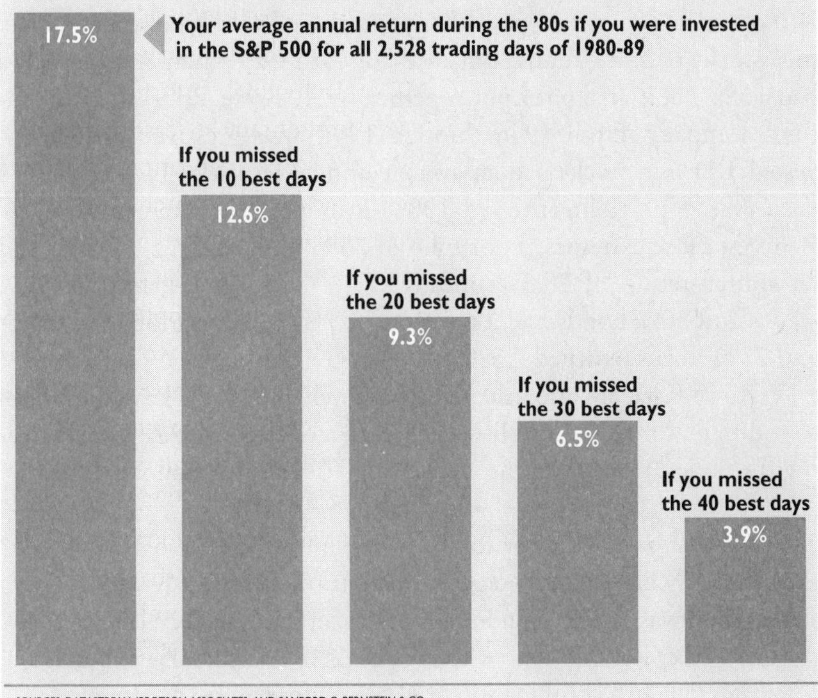


swoons. That is an Olympic-grade blunder. Markets often make their sharpest gains after deep or lengthy slumps. If you had stayed invested in an index of the S&P 500 stocks for all 2,528 trading days from 1980 through 1989, your average annual return would have been 17.5%. But had you pulled out and missed only the 10 best trading days in those 10 years, your average annual return would have dropped to 12.6%. Had you missed the 40 best days, it would have fallen to 3.9%. Lesson: It doesn't pay to try to "time" the market, to guess what its immediate next moves will be, and then to pull out or put yourself back into the game. You're much better off getting in and staying in.

This does not mean that *you* should do the stock picking. Unless you are willing to spend hours each month studying markets and individual equities, you may be better off putting a substantial share of your investment money into mutual funds, whose professional managers invest in a diversity of stocks. Indeed, I believe that mutual funds that have strong long-term records are the best all-around investments for most people (see Chapter 5).

No sensible person suggests that you place all your investment money into stocks or stock funds. But in theory at least, it may not be such a bad idea. Look at figures put together by T. Rowe Price, the mutual-fund company. From 1946 through 1994 an aggressive portfolio invested 100% in stocks had an average annual return of 11.5%, while a conservative portfolio invested 100% in bonds had a return of 5.7%. Between those extremes, a portfolio of 75% stocks and 25% bonds had an annual return of 10.2%; meanwhile, a balanced portfolio of 50% stocks and 50% bonds had a return of 8.8%, and a split of 75% bonds and 25% stocks returned 7.3%.

T. Rowe Price has also calculated how well you would have done with four different model portfolios, each with a different degree of risk, during the period from 1974 through 1994. The four portfolios are:

- *Minimal risk* This portfolio was committed 100% to 30-day Treasury bills. The average annual return over the 20-year period was 7.3%. Even in its worst year, it gained 2.9%.
- *Low risk* This portfolio was invested 35% in cash, 40% in bonds and 25% in a combination of U.S. and foreign stocks. Its average annual growth was 11.2%. In its worst year, it gained 3.2%.
- *Moderate risk* This portfolio was invested 20% in cash, 40% in bonds and 40% in U.S. and foreign stocks. Its average annualized return was 12.4%. But in its worst year, it gained only 1.7%. (Although there have been some market declines since 1974, the past two decades have been a generally bullish period in the market. Were you to look back to 1950, the picture would not be as ebullient. For example, a similar moderate-risk portfolio, but without foreign stocks, was down 6.7% in its worst year.)
- *High risk* This portfolio was invested 10% in cash, 30% in bonds and 60% in U.S. and foreign stocks. Its average annualized return was 13.5%. In its worst year, it lost 1.8%.

Whatever strategy you adopt — from minimal risk to high risk — it pays to (1) continue putting in a fixed amount of money at regular inter-

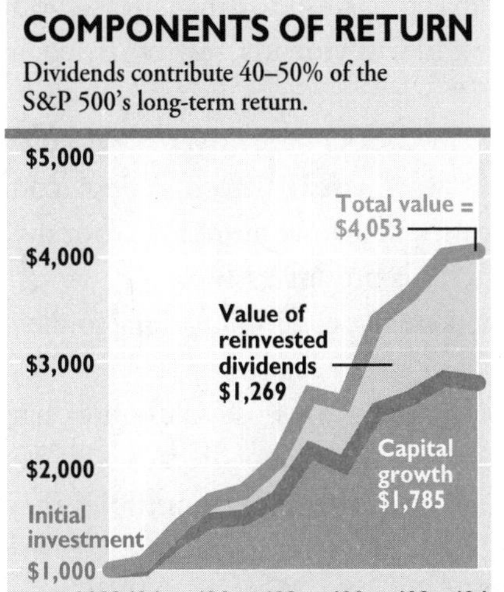


vals, (2) diversify, and (3) reinvest your dividends and capital gains. The last point mentioned — reinvestment — is not often remarked upon, but it is a powerful weapon for investment success. The nonprofit National Association of Investors Corporation puts it this way, "If you reinvest your earnings, your money grows faster. In seven or eight years, if you earn five or six percent on your investments, the return on accumulated earnings will be about as big as your monthly investment. And your new money invested each month will be almost twice as much as when you first began."

Diversification is also basic to your strategy, and Brinson Partners has provided some evidence of its virtues. If you had allocated your money over the 20 years from December 31, 1974, to December 31, 1994, into 60% U.S. stocks (from the Wilshire 5000 index) and 40% U.S. bonds (from Salomon Brothers' Big Bond index), you would have gained an average annual return of 13.2%. Had you initially put up $100,000, it would have grown to $1,202,000. But you would have earned six-tenths of a percentage point *more* if you had spread your money more widely: 40% in U.S. stocks, 15% in foreign stocks, 20% in U.S. corporate bonds, 5% in foreign bonds and 20% spread among real estate, venture capital funds and junk bonds. With that foreign-salted mix, your $100,000 stake would have grown to $1,323,000.

You'll be interested to know that billionaire Warren Buffett, who may well be America's most successful investor, disagrees with what he calls the "diversification dogma." Buffett, whose famous Berkshire Hathaway company has major interests in only nine stocks, says, "We believe that a policy of portfolio concentration may well *decrease* risk if it raises, as it should, both the intensity with which an investor thinks about a business and the comfort level he must feel with its economic characteristics before buying into it."

When you buy stocks, even with much less of a stake than Buffett has, you become part owner of a company. A stock can increase your wealth in two ways: by paying you regular dividends and by rising in price. If it does indeed rise, you can sell out at a profit. It is this growth, even more than the dividends, that gives stocks their investment edge. Besides, if you hold your stock for at least a year before selling, your profits are taxed as long-term capital gains, at a maximum 28%. But dividends are taxed as ordinary income, at a maximum 39.6%.

Though there are thousands of listed stocks, your choices narrow basically to two types: growth or value.

GROWTH SHARES are those of companies whose sales and earnings often sprint ahead faster than the overall economy. Because of their hormonal growth rates, they sell at higher price/earnings multiples than the average share even though they pay little or no dividends. Growth stocks are often found among young companies concentrated in such areas of the economy as technology, medicine, communications and entertainment. In rising markets, their stocks tend to perform at least one-third better than the broad stock indexes. The trouble is, when the market falls, they are also likely to plunge faster. In a word, growth stocks are volatile.

Before buying, examine growth shares by five important measures:

- *Earnings* Ideally, profits should have increased an average 20% or more a year for the past five years and should be expected to grow that fast over the next five years.
- *Capitalization* That's the marketplace value of all the common shares. If capitalization is below $100 million, the stock may be selling at a bargain price.
- *Price/earnings ratio* A stock selling for more than 20 times its earnings per share is expensive. A stock selling for less than 10 times earnings is a bargain.
- *Return on equity* This shows how effectively management is using the money it received from shareholders. A return of 15% on equity is good; 30% is extraordinary.
- *Debt-to-equity ratio* A company's long-term debt usually should be no higher than the total value of its common stock.

You can get these figures from your broker or by reading *The Value Line Investment Survey,* available in most libraries.

VALUE SHARES are like some people you know: good at heart and basically strong but going through some problems right now. You're sure that they will come back someday.

Many of the professional stock pickers who have done best in fair and foul markets alike are value hunters, searching for intrinsically strong companies whose earnings are temporarily off key. Fear has driven the price down more than the fundamentals would justify. Value investors believe that the soundest strategy is to buy a stock when it is selling at prices irrationally below the company's true value, when it's undervalued and unloved.

The company should have low debt and a return on equity of more than 15%. Before value hunters become interested, both the price/earnings ratio and the price-to-book ratio should be below the market. Then they wait patiently — perhaps for years — for other investors to recognize this value and bid up the price. For example, value hunters went after depressed bank and other financial stocks in 1992, defense and automobile stocks in 1993 and pharmaceutical stocks in 1994 — and did well on all of them.

To succeed with such a strategy, you need discipline and a willingness to buck the lemmings of Wall Street. But value stocks are so cheap to begin with that they have less distance to fall — and while you are waiting for them to rebound, you can collect some dividends. You won't be able to put your child through Stanford on those dividends, but they are above average.

Among other kinds of shares are the so-called income stocks. They emphasize dividends today over capital gains tomorrow, and their prices are more stable than those of growth stocks. In a prolonged market rise, they do not climb as fast as growth stocks and may even fall. Electric-utility shares are a foremost example. Lately their dividends have averaged a steep 7.3%, compared with the S&P index average of 2.8%. But their stock prices have not kept up with the market because deregulation by the states has sparked competition among power producers. It is quite possible that in the future a number of utilities will cut their dividends.

In the past, if you were shopping for utility stocks, you might have been advised to avoid companies with plans to build nuclear plants. The plants too often become bogged down in costly lawsuits and construction delays. Today construction of nearly all power plants has halted, the victim of overcapacity at both nuclear and fossil-fuel plants and of the stiff regulations and high costs of building and maintaining nuclear facilities. Even though the last order to build such a plant in the U.S. was placed in 1978, many power companies have at least some nuclear facilities. Among those that do *not* and thus may be good buys are Sierra Pacific, Citizens Utility, Cincinnati Gas and Electric, PSI Resources, Allegheny Power, Teco, DPL and Idaho Power. Other utilities have already built nuclear plants and operate them safely and conscientiously. They include FPL Group, Scana Corporation, Pennsylvania Power and Light, and Union Electric.

Beyond utilities, you can find high dividends among shares of real estate investment trusts (average: 7.8%), telephone companies (4.75%) and oil companies (3.9%). More important than a large dividend is a rising dividend. In the first half of 1995 a rather high number of companies — 500 — raised their dividends. Indeed, over the past half dozen years a number of companies have steadily increased their dividends by an annual average of anywhere from 10% to 20%. Among them are Conagra, H&R Block, Johnson & Johnson and Procter & Gamble.

*A tip:* Standard & Poor's *Stock Guide,* a monthly, gives letter grades from A+ to D to stocks; the grades reward companies that have consistently raised their earnings and dividends over the last 10 years. Surprisingly, stocks in the A+ group tend to be overpriced. Over time, stocks graded A and A– give the best return to investors. The *Stock Guide* is available in many libraries, or you can subscribe for $135 a year (800-221-5277).

What if you have never invested before? How do you start investing and do it right?

Many people find it wise to begin with mutual funds. But after you have had some experience with them, the time will come when you will want to branch out into individual stocks. You may be able to gain more from individual issues than from the broad range of shares in a fund.

You probably will be able to afford only one or two stocks at first. But anyone with more than $2,000 to invest in stocks should spread it among two or more companies. You will want to diversify among industries, too. That will help protect you. If, for example, mortgage rates rise and you own nothing but housing stocks, your roof will cave in. Countless academic studies larded with complicated formulas have shown that diversification lowers your risk without crimping returns. Warren Buffett notwithstanding, the three U.S. economists who established the importance of diversification as an investing tool won the 1990 Nobel Prize.

Ultimately, you should aim to own five or more stocks. That is a small enough number to be manageable and large enough for diversity. When you reach that point — and you wish to strike a balance somewhere between the young, daring investor and the older, conservative investor — you may want to consider the following division of the money you invest in the market:

- A quarter of your stock portfolio might consist of small and promising companies producing goods and services that are unique or stand to be in strong demand even in periods of recession.
- Another quarter might be invested in the largest, most conservative companies that can offer stable growth.
- The remaining half might be in medium-sized concerns that are growing faster than the economy as a whole.

In every case, try to spot companies whose share prices are relatively low given their current earnings and future prospects. Also, learn to watch for companies whose earnings surpass research analysts' expectations. Wall Street falls in love with their shares. In the three months through mid-August 1995, fully 234 of the companies in the S&P 500 reported earnings higher than predicted; and their shares rose an average 9.8% during the period, while the S&P itself gained 6.8%.

Business conditions affect various stock groups differently. In the depths of a recession, shares of banks and other financial companies often get a lift in anticipation that the Federal Reserve will cut interest rates to stimulate business. At the beginning of a recovery, interest rates tend to be low, and so consumers go out and buy houses and cars; homebuilding and automobile stocks benefit. In the midst of a recovery, cyclical stocks that move in sync with the economy tend to do well. These include companies in basic industries and industrial commodities, such as steel, paper, chemicals and nonferrous metals.

Keep your eye on investing's early-warning system. The market as a whole usually moves about three to six months ahead of changes in the economy. On average, stocks begin to rise about six months before a recession ends. Typically, the new climb lasts two and a half years, followed by about one and a half years of downturn or sluggish markets.

If you buy individual stocks, you will have an advantage over big institutional investors. They tend to buy conservatively for bank trust departments, corporate investment plans and pension programs. Because so many of them concentrate on safety and the ability to sell out quickly if they have to, the institutions' managers generally stick to the shares of 500 or so of the biggest and best-known companies. But you can choose from over 8,000 stocks that most of the institutions ignore. It is easier for small investors to buy shares in young, unproven, rapidly growing firms that historically have produced the best earnings. If the business becomes large enough to attract big investors, the stock's price — and your profits — may jump dramatically. Look in Standard & Poor's *Stock Guide* for shares that are owned by five or fewer institutions. They may not offer as much safety as the institutional favorites, but they tend to rise faster.

But don't get too caught up in the race for quick profits. Investors often do best by picking several stocks as a way of cushioning the loss of one flier that takes a dive. And be prepared to live with the rule of five. It says that out of every five stocks you own, probably one will be a loser, three will do nicely and one will do much better than you expected.

Don't become overly zealous about saving on taxes. A single-minded pursuit of holding down your tax bill can lock you into some investments that won't grow enough to keep you ahead of inflation.

Before buying a stock, you can look up its record in *The Value Line Investment Survey*, *Standard & Poor's Corporation Records* or *Moody's* manuals, available in many public libraries. You also can ask a broker to send you a copy of the company's annual report and the even more detailed 10-K statement that must be filed every year with the Securities and Exchange Commission.

In sum, these are three sensible rules for investors, beginners and veterans alike:

First, put aside a fixed amount of money each week or each month, no matter how small. Then save or invest it regularly, in both rising and falling markets.

Second, diversify. Even if your investments are modest, spread out to several kinds of stocks — or into a widely diversified mutual fund.

Third, don't wait to buy in at the very bottom of the market and do not try to sell out at the very top. Nobody — but nobody — is smart enough to do that. Remember: Bulls make money and bears make money, but hogs never make money.

Finally, sit back and let the power of compounding work for you. A nice, sedate 9% annual rate of return will double your money in eight years.

Here are some stock-buying strategies for different kinds of people:

- Let's suppose you are young and have saved enough for an emergency. You might start with stocks in small companies. They're riskier than large-company stocks from year to year, but over decades they have outperformed the bigs. Small-capitalization stocks ("small caps") are those whose market capitalization (the price per share multiplied by the number of shares) is $750 million or less. From late 1990 to mid-1995 small caps on average more than doubled in price, while Standard & Poor's stock index went up 61.5%. Says investment guru Peter Lynch, "Small stocks make big moves, whereas big stocks make smaller moves."

  Or invest in depressed industries. Some of the most successful investors do just that, figuring that stocks in battered businesses have nowhere to go but up. For example, shares of many pharmaceutical companies, which had plunged deeply in 1992 and early 1993, made a remarkable recovery in 1994 and 1995.

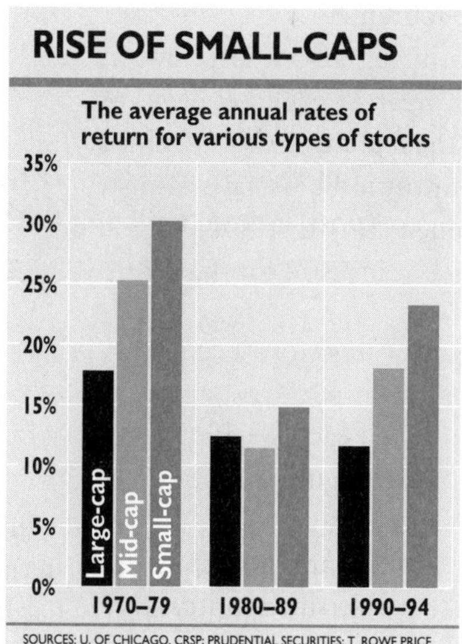


  If you are willing to take a bit more risk in hopes of getting more reward, consider buying shares in a real estate investment trust, a REIT (pronounced "reet"). These trusts invest in buildings, land and mortgages and are like mutual funds of real estate. Their shares trade just as

## HOW TAXES CRACK YOUR NEST EGG

| 25 YEARS: 1969–93 | AVERAGE ANNUAL RATE OF RETURN* Pretax | After-tax |
|---|---|---|
| **Common stocks** | **10.52%** | **7.42%** |
| **Treasury** | | |
| **20-year bonds** | **8.23%** | **3.48%** |
| **5-year notes** | **8.18** | **3.69** |
| **30-day bills** | **7.12** | **3.10** |
| **Municipal** | | |
| **20-year bonds** | **6.64%** | **6.62%** |
| **5-year bonds** | **5.60** | **5.60** |

*Maximum applicable federal income and capital-gains tax rates applied, assuming 33% turnover annually for stocks and 10% for bonds.
SOURCES: BROWN BROTHERS HARRIMAN; IBBOTSON ASSOCIATES; DELPHIS HANOVER; *FORTUNE*

stocks do — you buy them from a stockbroker — and they pay dividends.

- Let's say that you are middle-aged, and your children have fairly recently finished school and have struck out on their own. You are rather suddenly relieved of a great financial load. Your immediate temptation may be to spend all your new extra money on yourself, on the many things you have been waiting so many years for. Purge that urge to splurge! Now is the time to put money away in a savings-and-investment plan. You will need it soon enough for a secure retirement.

  To help you achieve that security, figure out just how much those tuition bills and other child-rearing expenses have cost you. Then aim to save and invest just about that much for at least the next several years. If your tuition bills have come to, say, $20,000 a year, try to continue taking that $20,000 out of your ordinary living expenses — but invest it for the future.

## Strategies for Selling

Anyone can buy a stock, but the real test of smart investing is knowing when to sell. Certainly, do not rush to sell a stock with strong long-term growth prospects just because it hits a temporary sinking spell. That is when smart investors consider buying even more shares — at bargain prices. But almost from the moment you purchase a stock, you should be thinking about when will be the right time to unload.

For many investors, selling a losing stock is like shaking some bad habit. It's a painful step you know is good for you, but you keep putting it off. In fact, deciding when to sell a stock is harder — and more important — than deciding when to buy. If you do not buy a stock and the price rises, all you lose is an opportunity. But if you fail to sell a stock and the price falls, you lose real money.

Here are some guidelines to help you decide what to do when the stock you love no longer loves you back:

*Set a goal.* You might aim to sell if a stock rises 50% above the price you paid — unless you have sound reason to believe it will climb a lot more.

*Cut your losses.* Never hesitate to sell because you are behind. You could wind up farther behind. Consider dumping a New York Stock Exchange issue if it declines 15% from the price at which you bought it. NASDAQ and American Stock Exchange stocks are more volatile, so give them more rope: Sell if they decline 20% to 25%.

You can instruct your broker ahead of time to sell a stock automatically if and when it falls to a certain price. You do this by placing a "stop-loss order" every time you buy a stock. But a stop-loss order isn't a guarantee, because the stock price can drop still farther from the time it reaches the stop-loss level to when your broker actually executes the sale.

*Face up to disappointments.* If you bought a stock expecting favorable developments that then do not occur within a reasonable time, dump it. And if the expected does happen, but the price of the stock does not move, unload promptly.

*Beware of price spurts.* A sudden jump in the price/earnings (P/E) ratio of a stock often means that buyers are becoming too wildly optimistic. In falling markets, stocks with P/E ratios that have soared are likely to come tumbling down if earnings are at all disappointing. Consider selling if a stock's P/E ratio rises more than 30% above its annual average for the past 10 years. For example, if the price historically is about 10 times earnings per share but suddenly climbs to 13, that may be the time to retreat. You can get these figures from a broker or from *The Value Line Investment Survey.*

If you learn of a significant deterioration in a company's sales growth or profitability or financial health, then it is time to kick the stock out.

The same applies if the prospects for the industry that the company is in no longer seem so bright, or if the company itself loses its competitive edge.

It pays to read through the proxy statements that clog your mailbox just before annual shareholders' meetings. While the proxies' purpose is to explain proposals to be voted on at the meeting, including such routine items as reappointing a company's accounting firm, they often disclose a wealth of information, including how much top management is paid as well as any special deals benefiting management and directors.

Sometimes the behavior of the stock itself will tell you that your love affair with it is getting too hot not to cool down. One sign is if the market is rising and trading volume in the issue is heavy, but still it fails to advance in price. Another is when a stock is not making gains similar to those of others in its industry.

Many people put off selling when it's time to sell because they don't like the idea of paying taxes on their gains. But it's much wiser to take a taxable short-term gain than wait and suffer a long-term loss.

Losing some money is inevitable. No investor buys only winners. But as Martin Zweig, a top investment adviser, says, "You can be right on your stocks only forty percent of the time and still do fine — if you cut your losses short."

## Managing the Different Kinds of Risk

When you invest, as the late Wall Street writer Charles Rolo observed, there are seasons for courage as well as for caution. So a strategy for all seasons must be one that decreases or increases your exposure to risk, depending on what kind of investment weather you expect. Managing risk does not mean dumping all stocks or other investments when you see storm clouds — or rushing in to buy at the glimpse of a rainbow. Controlling risk usually calls for making a few adjustments in your investments rather than for effecting a sweeping change.

To develop a strategy for all seasons, first ask yourself, "Am I more interested in seeing my investments grow in value for the long term or in collecting immediate income from dividends and interest?" The degree of risk that you choose to take should be determined by your family situation, current and prospective earning power, net worth, tax bracket —

and temperament. A single person with bright career prospects may be more inclined to take large risks than a couple with children or retired persons living on their savings.

When calculating how to manage risks, it pays to bear in mind that, as Rolo concluded, there are three kinds of investment risk:

First, the risk that is related to the overall behavior of the securities market is called, not surprisingly, *market risk.* The standard yardstick of a stock's market risk is its volatility — that is, the extent of its price fluctuations in relation to those of Standard & Poor's 500 stock index. A stock that historically has risen or fallen more sharply than Standard & Poor's index is considered riskier than the market as a whole. To find out a stock's historic record of volatility, ask your broker to look it up in *The Value Line Investment Survey.* If you think it's time to be cautious, you can cut your market risk by reducing the portion of your assets that is invested in common stocks, eliminating the most volatile issues.

Second, stock prices also fluctuate because of industry and company developments. This type of risk is called *diversifiable risk* because you can reduce it if you diversify your investments. Small investors can achieve good diversification by owning only five stocks, provided they are in different industries that are exposed to different types of economic and political risk. For example, some stock groups that are not likely to behave in the same way at the same time are airlines, banks, computers, cosmetics, energy exploration, gold mining and hospital management.

Third, investors also face *interest-rate risk.* It stems from changes in interest rates and applies primarily to bonds. But it can also affect the shares of corporations whose earnings are hurt when interest rates rise — and helped when they fall. The stock market often sinks when interest rates soar, because stocks must then compete with high bond yields. Companies in some industries are especially sensitive to changing interest rates: utilities, banks, finance companies, and savings and loans, among others. Ideally, you would buy interest-sensitive stocks just before interest rates started to turn down — and then switch into money funds or Treasury bills just before the next uptrend began. Calling the precise turns on interest rates is an impossible dream, but if you read the financial pages carefully, you should be able to get a handle on which way rates are likely to head.

Before you make any investment decisions, watch the relationship between short-term and long-term interest rates. The stock market always has trouble making headway when short-term rates, such as those available on Treasury bills, are higher than long-term rates, the kind offered on bonds. When short-term rates fall significantly below long-term ones, a bull market quite often follows in a few months.

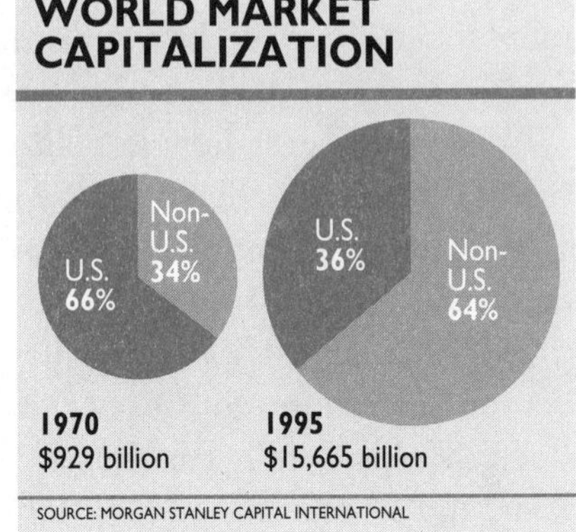


If unexpected bad economic news sends the market down, avoid companies with big debts. Look instead for stocks of large growth companies with low price/earnings ratios. Because of their low base, even a modest rise in price would mean a big percentage gain for you.

## Your Safest Strategy

The safest strategy is to put your money in a variety of investments. If some of them tumble, the others may well stand up — and you won't lose everything. As a rule, place no more than 10% of your investment money into the stock of any one company, and no more than 20% into stocks in any one industry. That way, trouble in a single stock or industry won't derail your holdings.

Base your choice of stocks on their value, not on their price alone. Begin by comparing a stock's price against a measure known as its book value per share. (This is the company's net asset value — its assets minus liabilities — divided by its number of outstanding shares.) You can find that figure in the firm's annual report, or ask a broker. Stocks that sell below their book value may well be bargains.

Next, check the stock's price/earnings ratio. You can find this number in the financial pages of most major newspapers. If the P/E ratio is below 10 to 1, and the company's earnings are rising, you may have found solid value. (In mid-1995 the P/E ratio of the 30 stocks in the Dow Jones industrial average was 15.9 — that is, they were selling for 15.9 times their earnings per share over the previous 12 months.)

Other relatively safe stock market strategies include buying so-called

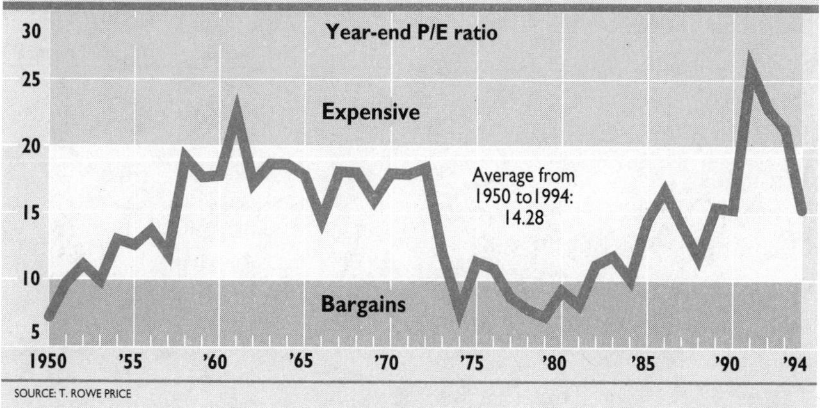


convertibles. These are hybrids — part stock, part bond. They offer higher profit potential than is typical with conventional bonds. They are also less risky than common stocks.

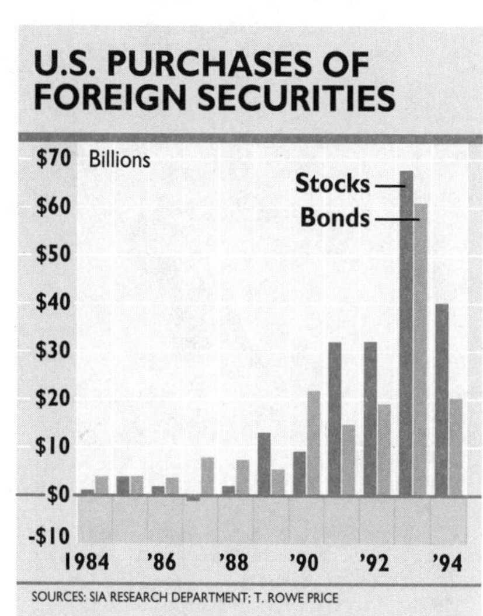


## Fortunes and Failures in Foreign Shares

As business becomes increasingly global, more and more Americans are investing in stocks overseas. American purchases of foreign shares surged from less than $10 billion in 1970 to almost $70 billion in 1993 and $40 billion in 1994. The reason: Foreign stocks often rise faster than U.S. shares.

Since records of the world's 22 largest markets began to be kept in 1983, the U.S. through 1994 has never ranked better than fifth, and once — in 1993 — was dead last. The best-performing markets included those of Malaysia (in 1993), Hong Kong (in 1992 and 1984), Mexico (in 1991 and 1990) and Austria (in 1989 and 1985).

### THE WORLD'S BEST-PERFORMING STOCK MARKETS

Out of the 22 largest markets

| Year | Best market | U.S. rank out of 22 markets |
|---|---|---|
| 1983 | Australia | 14 |
| 1984 | Hong Kong | 7 |
| 1985 | Austria | 16 |
| 1986 | Spain | 18 |
| 1987 | Japan | 12 |
| 1988 | Belgium | 15 |
| 1989 | Austria | 13 |
| 1990 | Mexico | 8 |
| 1991 | Mexico | 5 |
| 1992 | Hong Kong | 5 |
| 1993 | Malaysia | 22 |
| 1994 | South Africa | 14 |

SOURCES: COUNTY NATWEST WOODMAC/ T. ROWE PRICE

From December 1984 through December 1994, a $20,000 investment in a Standard & Poor's 500 stock index mutual fund would have risen to $76,741; but T. Rowe Price calculates that had it been invested in a typical diversified portfolio that included some foreign stocks, it would have jumped to $83,356.

Of course, domestic stocks sometimes perform even better than foreign shares. In the year through mid-1995, U.S. stocks produced a total return of 20.2%. That was much higher than most foreign shares. Japanese stocks had a negative return of 5.5%, Latin American stocks returned a negative 17.8%, Asian stocks not counting Japan returned 5.1% and European stocks had a return of 16.2%.

### U.S. AND FOREIGN STOCK PORTFOLIO vs. 100% U.S. STOCKS

*80% U.S. stocks, 20% foreign stocks.
SOURCES: IBBOTSON ASSOCIATES, T. ROWE PRICE

Foreign shares stand to do well if the dollar remains relatively weak against the currencies of Japan, Germany, Britain, Switzerland, the Netherlands and other countries. Even if the stock you pick doesn't rise but the dollar declines against the currency of that

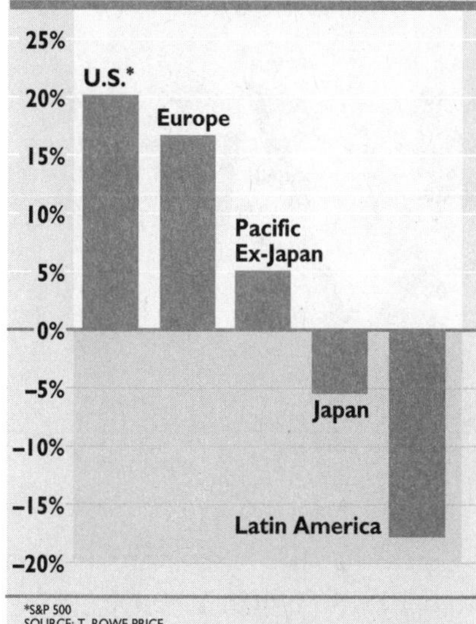


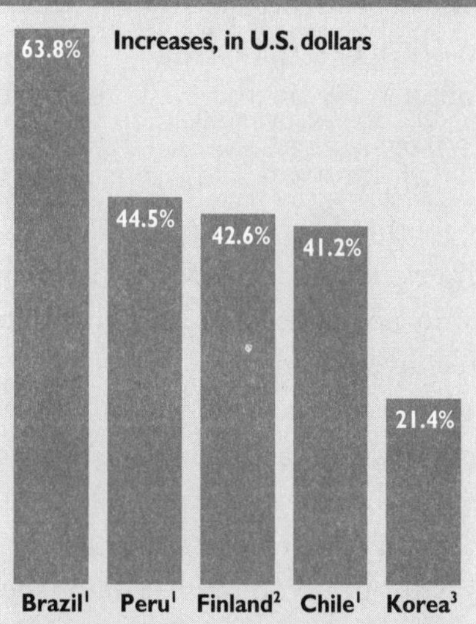


country, you will come out ahead when you sell. The foreign currency you collect from the sale will convert into more dollars than it cost you to buy the stock. And if the stock rises, you will get a double lift.

The downside is that Americans who invest in foreign stocks run the risk that a foreign-currency decline will cut into any stock gains. In the case of Japan, the yen rose so fast against the dollar and Japanese stocks soared so high relative to corporate earnings that they were destined to crash, as they did early in 1992. Also, different accounting standards make it hard to evaluate foreign companies, and information is not as quickly or easily available as it is for U.S. stocks.

Foreign markets can be highly volatile. In the first four months of 1994, the high-flying Hong Kong market (which is basically a play on the emerging China market) plunged 24% and the Mexican market, 22%; the Hong Kong market then stabilized and started to recover, but later the Mexican market fell even farther, devastated by the unexpected devaluation of the peso. Unanticipated political eruptions can also cut into some foreign markets, as they did in Mexico, which suffered from uprisings among poor Indians in the south of the country and political assassinations as well as general instability. Given all that, unless you are a professional in the market, you probably should limit your international investments to *at most* 15% of your stock holdings — and probably more like 10%.

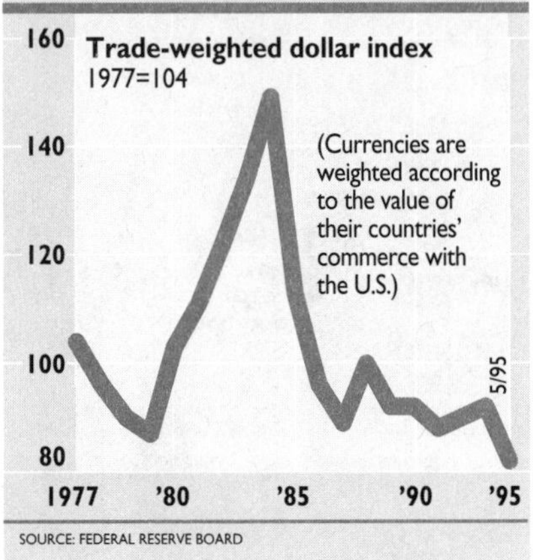


One important reason for investing part of your money abroad is — here's that word again — diversification. Further, while the U.S. stock market did very well for investors in the 1980s, with a total return of just over 400%, eight overseas markets substantially topped that figure. Britain's market returned 431% for the decade, and Sweden's, more than 1,100%.

You can buy individual foreign stocks yourself. Most Canadian shares are traded in the U.S. just like American securities. So are about 1,200 other foreign stocks, largely from Japan and Britain. They are sold in the form of American Depositary Receipts, or ADRs. Each ADR is issued by a U.S. bank and represents one to 10 shares of a foreign stock held abroad at a custodian bank. ADRs often trade on the New York and American stock exchanges and the NASDAQ.

Look for ADRs that have been "sponsored" by their foreign companies; about one-third are. They meet specific U.S. accounting and disclosure standards, which are generally tighter than standards in their home countries. Unsponsored ADRs do not have to provide investors with more information than they would give at home.

Experienced investors seeking a wider choice can buy and sell shares directly on foreign stock markets. Your U.S. broker should be able to handle the trades. But don't expect him or her to offer expert advice on which foreign stocks or ADRs look particularly attractive.

An easy way to get your feet wet is with American mutual funds specializing in foreign stocks. Among them are Smith Barney International, GAM International, Warburg Pincus International and Price International Stock Fund. Meanwhile, Merrill Lynch Pacific, G. T. Pacific, Price New Asia and GAM Pacific concentrate on Far Eastern stocks, while Scudder's Japan Fund invests in that country. Scudder Latin America focuses on Mexico and other countries to the south. For stocks of companies in Europe and elsewhere, you might consider Alliance International, T. Rowe Price International, Scudder International and EuroPacific Growth.

Investors willing to take high risks may look into the small-cap overseas funds, which buy stocks with market capitalizations generally between $100 million and $1 billion. They include Acorn International, Montgomery International Small Cap, Scudder Global Small Company, Seligman Henderson Global Emerging Companies, T. Rowe Price International Discovery and Templeton Small Companies Growth.

You also can invest indirectly by buying the stocks of American companies that have large operations overseas. *Fortune* has pointed out that a number of U.S. companies get much of their revenues from Europe, including Compaq Computer, Emerson Electric, Ferro, Hewlett-Packard, 3M, York International and Loctite. And *Money* has noted that Ford, Caterpillar, Mattel, Beckman Instruments, Vishay Intertechnology,

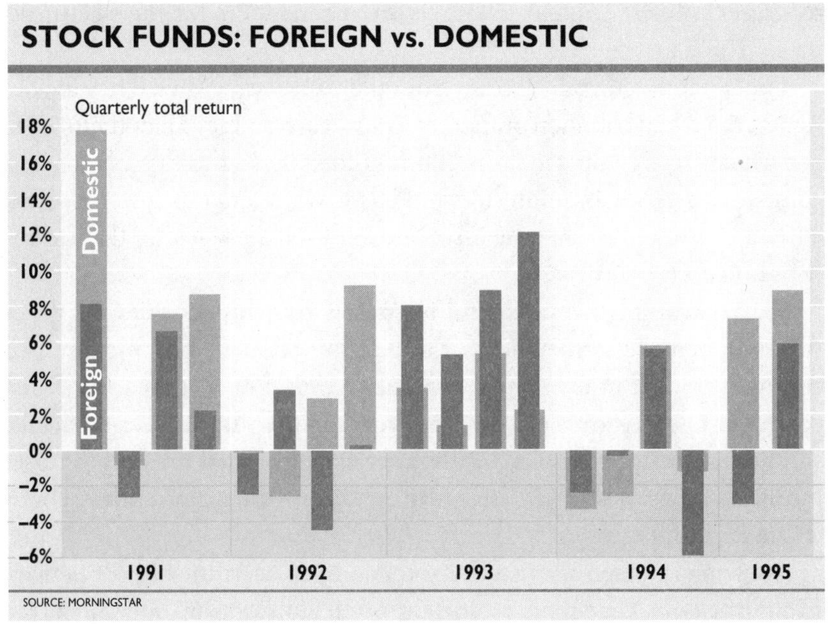

American International Group, Duracell International, Foster Wheeler, Boeing and Kellogg draw 30% to 68% of their sales from abroad.

Also, it might be worthwhile to troll among the many previously state-owned foreign telephone, transport, steel, oil, utility and other companies that are being — or are about to be — privatized. Historically, many of those have risen fast. The new managers typically reduce bloated, bureaucratic staffs and sharply increase productivity and profitability. According to Henry Gibbon, editor of the London newsletter *Privatisation International,* "a composite of 150 privatised stocks gained 94% over the last five years, compared with a rise of about 65% for the S&P 500."

## Buying Shares of Bankrupt Firms

Business failures do happen, and that's a shame. But many investors are finding bargains in bankruptcies. They buy up the stocks and bonds of big, bankrupt corporations at distress prices. These speculators hope that the companies will come out of their court-directed reorganizations slimmed down, propped up and comparatively debt-free, and that their securities will rise enough to amply reward investors for the steep risks they are taking.

The potential for gain springs from the bankruptcy laws. They are designed to give moribund companies a new lease on life, to let them work out a plan to pay off creditors. Bondholders have the first claim on a company's assets. Common stockholders' rewards are much less assured. They are entitled to whatever assets are left — if any — after the various debt holders are paid.

So, bankruptcy investors tend to stick with debt securities. At times they will venture farther down the pecking order to buy preferred or common stock. But usually they will do so only after a company has just come out of reorganization, shining with such virtues as a clean balance sheet, an accumulation of tax losses that can be carried forward to offset future earnings, and a talented management with definite ideas about where it's heading.

Investing in bankrupts is not for the faint of heart or short of pocket. Even situations that look promising often do not pan out. Since the bankruptcy investment game is dominated by the professionals, it would be foolhardy to sit in without coaching. One mutual-fund manager with a flair for profiting from bankruptcies is Michael Price, head of Mutual Series Fund Inc. (51 John F. Kennedy Parkway, Short Hills, New Jersey 07078; 800-448-3863, 201-912-2100). Its four funds performed as follows for the 12 months from June 30, 1994, through June 30, 1995: Mutual Shares was up 20.6%; Mutual Qualified rose 19.9%; Mutual Beacon climbed 16.3%; and Mutual Discovery gained 15.8%.

For help in picking your own stocks on the rocks, you might consult the experts at Bear Stearns, a brokerage firm that invests in bankrupts. Another source of advice is the *Turnaround Letter,* edited by bankruptcy investment specialist George Putnam III (225 Friend Street, Suite 801, Boston, Massachusetts 02114; 617-573-9550; $195 a year). It reports on the prospects for securities of companies in trouble and has monthly buy-and-sell recommendations.

## Buying on Margin

Brokers are only too happy to lend you money to buy stocks and bonds if you open a so-called margin account. You have to put up only part of the securities' price, and your broker lends you the rest. You just sign a couple of forms, and your broker runs a routine credit check on you. Brokers are eager to approve your application because margin accounts lead to more business and higher profits for them.

You can come out ahead in rising markets because you put up only 50% of the cost of your stocks, and 25% of the cost of your bonds. So your money works at least twice as hard for you. The interest that you pay on your margin loan is not only relatively low but is also deductible from your taxable income, up to the amount of your net investment income for the year. In mid-1995 interest rates on margin loans ranged from 9% to 11%, compared with about 9% for personal secured loans at a bank.

Sound easy? Maybe too easy. Margin accounts can be a lot riskier than you might expect. Let's say you want to buy 100 shares of a $40 stock. Normally you would pay $4,000 plus commissions. But with a margin account, you must put up only 50% of the price, or $2,000. Your broker lends you the remaining $2,000, and the stock that you bought acts as the collateral for your loan.

If your stock rises — great! If it rises enough, you could sell some shares, pay off the loan and come out ahead. But if the gains in your stock do not cover your interest payments, you lose money. And if the stock price falls, you could suffer in two ways. Not only would your investment dwindle, but you could receive a call from your broker — a so-called margin call — to put up more cash.

A margin call occurs when the value of your collateral falls below a certain percentage of your total purchase price — usually 30% to 35%. If the worth of your holdings drops under that level, your broker will demand that you deliver enough cash or other securities to bring your collateral back up to the required amount. If you can't deliver — sometimes by the next day — the broker will sell your stock, take back what he or she lent you and collect interest.

Before you decide to borrow on margin, ask yourself this key question: "Do I believe in the shares so wholeheartedly that I would be willing to borrow money even from a bank in order to own them?" If not, a margin account is not for you.

If you do invest on margin, keep a close eye on your stocks. Check the prices at least twice a week, or more often if the shares tend to fluctuate widely. You don't want a margin call to take you by surprise.

To protect yourself if you think the market is heading for a fall, you can buy what's called a put option. It is the right to sell a stock at a specified price within a set period of time, usually up to eight months, to the seller of the put. If the price of your stock drops enough, the put option will become more valuable. Then you can sell the option to offset the losses on your stock. Example: In January 1996 the stock of ABC Steel is up to $80, and you believe that is too high. So you buy a put on 100 shares of ABC at $80, coming due on September 1, 1996. Lo and behold, the stock does drop to $60 on September 1. You cash in your put and collect $80 per share, or a total $8,000 for the 100 shares. But those shares are worth only $6,000 in the market, so you have gained $2,000 — minus whatever you paid for the put. And those costs are highly negotiable.

For extra insurance, you can instruct your broker to sell your shares automatically if they fall to a certain price; this is a so-called stop order. Choose the price at which you would no longer want to own the stock and advise your broker to sell at that level. Then, if your shares fall without your noticing, your broker will sell them anyway to prevent you from losing more money.

*A tip:* You can use margin loans to buy more than stocks or bonds. Say you want to buy a house or condo that costs $200,000. If you are fortunate enough to own $400,000 worth of stocks, your broker will lend you $200,000 against them. You continue to own those securities, and you avoid much of the up-front costs that you would have to pay on a mortgage loan. For a $200,000 mortgage, those so-called closing costs — for taxes, origination fees, lawyers' fees, title search and the like — can easily run $6,000 to $10,000. Just remember that you ultimately have to pay off your margin loan, and you will have to pony up more securities if their price drops in a falling market. And check with your tax adviser: Margin interest has limited tax deductibility.

# How to Act When Interest Rates Move

Nothing affects the prices of your investments more than changes in interest rates. Just look at how the market fell in early 1994 as a result of repeated interest-rate raises by the Federal Reserve Board. Here are answers to some common questions about consequences of those changes — and how to act on them.

► Can you make profits on bonds when interest rates fall?

Yes, you can. Since bond prices rise when interest rates decline, and vice versa, a skillful trader can earn money by buying bonds at the top of the interest-rate cycle — and then selling at the bottom. The trouble is, those once-steady interest rates now bounce down and up quite quickly — and this new volatility makes bond trading riskier than ever.

► When interest rates fall, does it make sense to buy stocks?

Yes, it often does. Lower interest rates reduce a company's costs and thus lift its profits — and frequently its stock price.

► What stocks do best when rates fall?

Many stocks do well at those times. Among them are the shares of banks and savings and loan associations, because they can pay lower interest rates to depositors. Utilities are big borrowers, and so they stand to gain when their interest costs decline. Lower rates also help boost the housing market, so real estate investment trusts, lumber companies and appliance manufacturers also prosper.

▸ Do any stocks perform well despite high interest rates?

High rates reflect expectations of steep inflation, and investors turn to natural resources as inflation hedges. So oil-, gas- and mining-company stocks tend to rise.

▸ Should you buy stock on margin when rates are high?

Not unless it's a very promising stock. The interest you pay is tax-deductible up to the amount of net income you earn from your investments. But when rates are high, your stock still would have to rise quite a bit for you to break even.

▸ If you want to play it absolutely safe, where can you invest your money for the short term when rates are high?

Three financial instruments offer a safe return at close to top interest rates: money-market funds, six-month certificates of deposit and U.S. Treasury bills with maturities of 90 days to a year.

▸ But do these three have any disadvantages?

Yes, they do. Since these investments are short-term, you can't lock in high rates for very long. Also, remember that the minimum investment for Treasury bills is $10,000.

▸ Should you borrow on your life insurance to invest when rates are high?

Probably not. Even if you have an old whole life policy that you can borrow against at a rate between 5% and 6%, you would not earn more than that after taxes unless short-term financial instruments were yielding 9% or more.

## Which Economic Indicators to Watch

We're always hearing about the latest change in this or that economic indicator. Unemployment is up, say. Or, the prime rate is down. But which economic weather vanes really help you understand the direction of the economy?

An excellent indicator is the payroll employment figure. This counts the number of employees on company payrolls around the country. As this figure rises, so probably will consumer spending. That may well send the stock market up.

The unemployment rate is an important indicator. If it falls below 6%, that's good for the country, but it may lead to an increase in inflation. And when inflation picks up, interest rates stand to rise. That, of course, is bad for the stock market.

To see how interest rates are trending, watch three-month Treasury bills. This rate is especially sensitive, and it can give you some clues to the direction of the Federal Reserve monetary policy. Rising rates lead to tighter conditions, so you might want to become a bit more conservative in your investments. On the other hand, declining rates usually lead to a stronger economy — and a stronger stock market.

One of the most significant measures of the strength of the economy is the gross domestic product. When the GDP rises at a nice, steady rate of 2.5% to 3.5%, that usually means corporate profits will be strong, and inflation won't get out of hand. That, of course, is good for the stock market. Conversely, when the GDP declines for two straight quarters, we're in a recession.

To predict the future direction of *interest rates,* watch the interest rate on three-month Treasury bills. It's especially sensitive because it is based on the rate that investors demand in return for putting up their own money — and on the direction of Federal Reserve monetary policy.

To figure out whether *inflation* will rise or fall, keep a close watch on major labor contracts. Steep increases in wages are, of course, a signal that inflation could soon reignite.

An excellent indicator of whether the economy will go up or down is payroll employment. This counts the number of employees currently on company payrolls around the country. As this figure rises, so probably will consumer spending. But the much-discussed unemployment rate can be a misleading indicator. It can go up just because more people become hopeful of finding a job and resume looking for one.

Probably no statistic is more closely watched as an indicator of the financial future than the stock market itself. When the market rallies, it's an optimistic sign for the economy. People and companies become more willing to invest and create jobs. To read the market, Standard & Poor's 500 stock index, which samples 500 companies, is a better gauge than the Dow Jones industrial average, which embraces only 30.

# Starting an Investment Club

Investment clubs are becoming more popular than ever among people who want to learn about the stock market — and make a little money while they are at it. New clubs are being formed in college classrooms, corporate offices, condominium living rooms and even church basements. The National Association of Investors Corporation (NAIC), which helps new clubs get started, estimates that there may be well over 25,000 of them across the country, with around 275,000 members. Some 2,000 new clubs a year join the NAIC.

Over the past 42 years, 3.5 million investors have been members of clubs. Typically clubs have about 17 members, split almost evenly between men and women, and for them the monthly meetings are an opportunity to learn about investing and dabble in stocks at an affordable price. No one seriously expects to grow rich solely through a club. On average, members invest $40 to $50 each a month, and clubs in 1994 had an annual return of 10.6%. According to the NAIC, the average club's portfolio contains 15 to 20 stocks with a total value of less than $95,000 — meaning about $5,600 a member. But some clubs have impressive growth rates on their investments, and the clubs and their members hold an estimated $50 billion in stock.

At some meetings the atmosphere is relaxed and informal; at others it's almost as intense as a session of a billion-dollar mutual fund's portfolio committee. In successful clubs, members usually do their own research rather than rely on brokers or investment analysts. The members spend hours poring over annual reports and such resources as *Standard & Poor's Corporation Records* and *The Value Line Investment Survey.* Both are often available free in public libraries. Some clubs even send members to interview the chief executives of local firms that look like promising investments.

Because most investment clubs are partnerships, individual members must pay capital-gains taxes on their share of any profits. New clubs with only small amounts to invest may find brokerage costs running more than 10% of their trades. So some of them use discount brokers, who charge considerably less but give you no advice on where to put your money. There is a trend toward using corporate dividend-reinvestment plans to save on commission fees.

Sometimes clubs are so popular that they reach their maximum membership limits, and you are better off starting a new one than trying to join an existing group. The majority begin simply, with two friends deciding to launch a club; then they each sign up two or three other friends, and the chain grows. If you want to create a club of your own, you can get valuable help from the NAIC. It will send you a handbook with advice on organizing a club and, for $18, a primer on the fundamentals of stock analysis. Write to the NAIC, 711 West Thirteen Mile Road, Madison Heights, Michigan 48071 (810-583-6242). The NAIC's annual dues are a modest $35 per club, plus $11 for each member. This includes a free subscription to the NAIC's monthly magazine, *Better Investing,* and a copy of the primer.

The NAIC recommends that all clubs, especially new ones, follow the fairly basic conservative principles:

- Invest regularly, preferably monthly, no matter where you think the stock market is heading — because a club that tries to predict broad stock trends is often wrong.
- Reinvest all earnings so that your club's portfolio can rise faster through compounding.
- Invest in growth companies. The association defines them as firms with both earnings and dividends outperforming their industry average.

From May 1994 through April 1995, reports the NAIC, clubs had an annual return of 12.27%. Clubs should aim for 15% annual growth in their investments. The NAIC provides worksheets to help members analyze stocks on their own.

Investment clubs tend to do well, but when they fail it is often because they allow a trading attitude to sweep away the more reliable accumulation attitude. When the market moves sideways or down, impatient members often urge the club to follow an in-and-out strategy. It is much wiser — and more profitable — to hold on to sound investments for long-term growth.

# Beware of Boiler-Room Scams

Did you ever get a phone call from a smooth-talking salesman who promised you could win a license in a federal lottery for new business opportunities? Or perhaps he gave you a once-in-a-lifetime chance to invest in a gold mine, with a promise to sell you the gold at two-thirds the market price? Watch out. You could be getting a snow job straight from America's sunny capitals of fraud.

Much of the selling that goes on over the telephone is legitimate, but be wary of get-rich-quick schemes, a remarkable number of which originate in California and Nevada. Florida has its share, too. These operations generally depend on a corps of salespeople working out of a cramped office — a "boiler room." They may reach you on specially rigged phones that filter out the background din to give you the impression of someone calling from a quiet suite. Sometimes the voice seems to come from Davy Jones's underwater locker. And when you hear it say, "Hi there in Philadelphia, we have a great investment for you from here in Los Angeles," you should know that this is a caller you can hang up on without feeling impolite.

The pitch is always smooth and grabby and sounds as though it's read from a carefully prepared script. You may be offered certain profits with no risk of loss. Often the salesperson will falsely claim that you'll be able to deduct the entire investment from your income taxes. Sadly, this last claim might come true. If you lose your entire investment, you may be able to deduct that amount as a capital loss.

You wouldn't be alone. The Alliance Against Fraud in Telemarketing estimates that such scams rob Americans of as much as $40 billion a year. The Alliance publishes a free brochure, "Schemes, Scams and Flim-Flams," that offers advice on how to avoid being taken by con artists. Write to the Alliance, c/o National Consumers League, P.O. Box 65868, Washington, D.C. 20035 (202-835-0618).

Boiler-room victims rarely get their money back. So never buy any investment that is pitched to you over the phone unless and until you carefully — very carefully — check out the company making the offer. The place to begin checking is with your own state government securities department or Attorney General's office. If you have been defrauded, call the National Fraud Information Center (800-876-7060) to file a complaint and receive free information and assistance. The center, a service provided by the National Consumers League, refers complaints to law-enforcement and regulatory agencies.

Watch out also for investment scams on radio talk shows. Though most financial shows are legitimate, a distressing number are used by buyers of radio time to tout questionable investments. If you have doubts, call the station to find out if the broadcast is an infomercial paid for by a promoter. Or phone the disciplinary hotline of the National Association of Securities Dealers (800-289-9999); if the host or his or her "guest" are members, you can check if either has a record. Be suspicious if the host or "guest" is always giving out a toll-free number.

Another possible scam may involve penny stocks. They are high-risk securities that are issued at $1 a share, or much less. Sometimes they quadruple in price on the first day of trading, possibly because they have been manipulated by unscrupulous securities firms. Penny stocks usually trade not on an exchange but in markets made by some 300 regional brokerage houses. Many penny-stock brokerages use fraudulent sales pitches to promise gains that don't materialize.

The Securities and Exchange Commission lists three warning signs of penny-stock fraud: unsolicited phone calls, high-pressure sales tactics and the investor's inability to sell the stock and receive cash. If you want to report any of these, contact your state's division of securities regulation or write to the Securities and Exchange Commission, Office of Consumer Affairs, Mail Stop 2-6, 450 Fifth Street NW, Washington, D.C. 20549.

If you buy penny stocks, make sure your brokerage is registered by the National Association of Securities Dealers. Then if it should be liquidated, you can get back whatever money is in your account and the stock you bought, whatever it is worth. Trying to recover the money you originally paid for the stock is another matter.

## Where to Hold Your Certificates

When you buy stocks or bonds, you can choose to either hold the certificates yourself or keep them in so-called street name. That means they are held by your broker. Which is better for you?

Holding your stocks in street name has one clear disadvantage. If the brokerage firm runs into severe financial troubles, your holdings could be tied up for months. You will get them back eventually, because they are insured by the Securities Investor Protection Corporation.

But keeping your securities in street name also has many advantages. It is certainly convenient. You do not have to worry about losing your certificates or sending them through the mail. If you want to borrow on margin — take out a loan from your broker — your securities in street name easily serve as collateral. In addition, brokerage houses maintain up-to-date records on the value of your holdings and will reinvest your dividends automatically in, say, a money-market account.

## How to Pick Them

Before you make your stock selections, learn what investment analysts — those among them who have the best records of forecasting and picking winners — think will happen in the market. You can get a reasonable idea of that by reading the financial press and investment advisory newsletters.

You probably will benefit from reading sophisticated market guides, notably Standard & Poor's *Stock Guide* and *The Value Line Investment Survey,* both described in some detail later in this chapter. They can help you find stocks with certain promising characteristics:

- Scout for stocks owned by fewer than five big institutional investors. These shares, while risky, often tend to rise faster than others. You can find out how many institutions hold an issue by looking it up in Standard & Poor's *Stock Guide.*
- Look for shares of well-established firms that have high dividends relative to stocks in general, notably relative to stocks of companies in the same industry.
- Search also for stocks whose prices are low relative to their earnings. Newspaper stock tables show the price/earnings ratios based on the previous 12 months' earnings. For a better guide, use the ratio based on analysts' estimates of future earnings, published in *The Value Line Investment Survey.* Or ask your broker to send you Standard & Poor's stock reports for specific companies.

- Try to catch a fallen star, a stock that has fallen victim to bad news. You can spot these unfortunates in daily newspaper lists of stocks reaching 52-week lows. To find out whether the company is reeling from only a temporary setback instead of a terminal problem, look for long-term debt that is not greater than 40% of the company's total capitalization and less than 10% of annual sales. Aggressive new management, significant cost reductions and the introduction of potentially profitable products are other signs of a potential comeback.

Remember, however, that low stock prices don't automatically mean value, as buyers of commercial bank stocks in 1990 learned to their sorrow. The median decline in 1990 of the shares of the 50 largest banks was 36%, despite the fact they began the year at depressed levels. Your margin of safety will come from buying healthy companies at attractive prices. "Healthy" means low debt with returns on equity of more than 15%. "Attractive" means that the stocks are selling at or below the market's average price/earnings multiple, and at a 25% to 50% discount to book value.

Sometimes you can find hot stocks on Wall Street by making a cool evaluation of the people, products and services you encounter on Main Street. Many successful small investors discover that personal experience leads them to stock market winners. Your children might direct you to a new fast-food chain that is packed with hungry youngsters. Perhaps the firm's stock is worth a nibble. Or you might detect a changing pattern in sales at your job. An investment opportunity may be behind it.

Investing in what you know firsthand lets you exploit two of your best assets: your experience and your own good judgment. But do not invest without first finding out more facts. Superb products and services can come from poorly run, unprofitable companies. And a close encounter with a single product tells you nothing about a firm's other lines of business. They may not be so terrific. In other words, use your experience but do not let it overimpress you.

You should do the same kind of research you would do with any investment. For example, does the company have cash hoards, real estate, oil reserves or other assets that might catch the eye of a takeover artist or make the market take a second look? Again, the most convenient source of answers is usually *The Value Line Investment Survey*.

Ask a stockbroker for a copy of the firm's latest annual report, or write to the company for one. Look for steady growth in revenues and net income over a five-year period. See how current assets compare with current liabilities, and hold out for close to a two-to-one ratio in favor of assets. Also see how the company measures up to others in the same industry. You can find reliable comparative data in Standard & Poor's annual industry surveys. One of the key figures to compare is return on equity. If your firm's return is lower than that of its competitors, beware. The company probably is not being managed as well as it could be.

## Strategies for Buying

The safest strategy, as discussed earlier, is to put a fixed amount of money into the stock market, month after month. That is the surest course for beginners and for people who are not prepared to spend time studying the market. But if you do gather some experience and expertise, and if you are willing to invest some time, you probably can earn more by aiming to recognize in advance — and act upon — the few really major, long-term turning points in the market, such as the huge rebounds that began in August 1982 and after the crash of October 1987.

Stocks generally move in expectation of changes in the economy and in corporate profits. The market is always looking ahead. If both inflation and interest rates are heading down, that's bullish news, of course. But when the consumer price index and interest rates on Treasury bills show sustained increases, that's a clear and present danger signal.

Fortunately, your own decisions about the stock market do not have to be perfect to be profitable. Just watch for those major turns in the market. You can buy somewhere above the bottom and sell out sometime after the market has hit its peak — and still make more money than the investor who ignores the market's long-term gyrations.

One old belief about the stock market is called the "efficient market theory." It holds that all new information about any stock spreads too quickly for ordinary investors to profit from the news before the stock rises. But that's not really so, according to a study by the Institutional Brokers Estimate System. It found that after several stock market analysts sharply increase their earnings estimates for a company, its stock probably will do better than the major market averages for the *next six months.* In other words, you can benefit from good news, even if you're not the first person to hear it.

Over the period from January 1980 to July 1995, if you put money into the 50 stocks with the highest upward revisions of earnings estimates and then sold them a year after you bought them, you would have earned 40% a year. That's far more than the 15.3% annual rise during the same period in Standard & Poor's 500 stock index. The moral: It pays to shop around for stocks of companies on which several stock market analysts have recently increased their future earnings estimates.

At the other extreme, you can also do well buying stocks that recently have plunged as a result of disappointing earnings or other sour news. A number of them become good bargains. In fact, some of the shrewdest investment professionals study each day's stock market tables just to find shares that have hit new lows. They figure that if these stocks have intrinsic value, they may have nowhere to go but up.

When you buy stocks, you must determine their basic values. To help you gauge that, look at four measures (a full-service broker can give you assistance with these):

1. *Historic trading range* You should consider buying on bad news when a stock nears its lowest price in the last three to five years.
2. *Earnings* For an idea of what a company is capable of earning, look at how well it has done over the last 10 years. If the most recent results are at the low end of the range, ask a broker for his or her firm's estimate of earnings for the next six or 12 months. If a turnaround is expected, you may consider buying the stock.
3. *Book value per share* That is the company's net assets divided by the number of shares. If the stock is selling for less than book value per share, it may be underpriced — and thus a good buy. If the price is less than half the book value, you have little to lose.
4. *Balance sheet* Be suspicious of an unusually large amount of long-term debt. The ratio of a firm's debt to the market value of its stock should not be significantly above the average for its industry.

Once you have picked out some undervalued stocks, don't buy right away. Turnarounds are like marriage proposals: They generally take longer to materialize than anyone expects. So spend some time watching those stocks. But also don't plan to wait until a stock hits its very bottom. Nobody is smart enough to know when a stock has gone down as far as it will go. Instead, set target prices, and buy if and when the stock reaches them. By doing that, you might well make good money buying bad-news stocks.

## How Technicians Spot Trends

Some professionals called technical analysts have several theories worth knowing about. To judge when the market is ready to make a major move, technicians study a number of objective indicators.

One is called *momentum.* This is the speed with which market averages, such as Standard & Poor's 500 stock index, rise or fall. If the index continues rising, but at a slower and slower rate every day, it may be heading for a fall.

Another is *trading volume,* the number of shares changing hands. It is a good sign when volume is large on days that the market rises, and small on days that it sags.

Yet another measure is *on-balance volume.* If the market rises on a volume of 100 million shares one day and then falls the next day on only 60 million, the on-balance volume is plus-40. That means there were 40 million more shares traded when the market was rising than when it was falling, and that is a bullish omen. But when the on-balance volume turns down, it could be a signal that the pent-up buying power is nearly exhausted and that stocks are about to decline.

Then there is the *advance/decline line,* the number of stocks that rise and the number that fall each day. When gainers outnumber losers, the advance/decline line goes up; that is a sign that the market is getting stronger. When losers predominate, the advance/decline line goes down. That is a sign of market weakness.

One sign that a climbing market could be about to drop is when different stock market indexes say conflicting things. If the Dow Jones industrials are rising at the same time Standard & Poor's 500 are falling, that is a warning sign. Another technical indicator is how much money mutual-fund managers are keeping in cash instead of in stocks. If they have more than 7% of their assets in cash, it usually is a favorable sign for the market: The money might go into stocks.

Market peaks are marked by clear signs of speculation. Two of the surest occur when small investors start borrowing heavily to buy on margin and when small-company stocks all seem to be scoring huge gains.

## Watch the Insiders

Do you want an inside tip on the market? Then watch for those times when high executives buy or sell shares in their own company. Information on such insider trading is easy to find and simple to use.

When the officers of a company trade its stock, they often know something you don't know, and their deals have to be reported to the Securities and Exchange Commission. When they *buy* a lot of their own stock, it usually does much better than the market averages. But when insiders *sell,* consider bailing out yourself. Heavy sales by insiders preceded many a market debacle. The situation is particularly dangerous when insider selling suddenly increases after a stock has started to decline. You can protect yourself with a stop-loss order. That way, if disaster does strike, you can escape with limited damage. That doesn't mean you have to stay out of the market entirely. It's a good time to look at the stocks those knowing insiders have been buying.

You can follow insider trading by subscribing to newsletters that follow the subject. A top letter is *The Insiders,* a biweekly (2200 Southwest 10th Street, Deerfield Beach, Florida 33442; 800-442-9000; $49 a year, or less for multiple-year subscriptions).

And have you ever heard of a 13D filing? No, it is not something that you would find in a dentist's office or on a clerk's desk. It is one of those obscure government reports that might give you a clue to making money in the market. For that clue, recall what Damon Runyon used to say: "If you rub up against money long enough, some of it might rub up against you."

Some of it might rub off on you — if you follow the purchases of the handful of billionaire investors who make audacious bids in the stock market to take over whole companies. Their names are often in the headlines, names like Warren Buffett, Kirk Kerkorian, Robert Bass and others. You can follow the trades of these highest rollers fairly easily. Many of their deals are a matter of public record because of the size of their purchases. By law, any investor who acquires more than 5% of a company's shares must report that transaction to the SEC within 10 days on a form called a 13D. The SEC publishes a daily summary of these 13D filings in the *SEC News Digest,* which you can study at the SEC's public reference rooms in New York and Washington, D.C., as well as at libraries of universities with strong business departments. Or, for a fee, you can get this information more conveniently from several computer services and newsletters. Two such newsletters are *SEC Today* (655 15th Street NW, Washington, D.C. 20005; 202-783-1928; $665 a year), a daily service provided by the Washington Service Bureau, and *Special Situation Report and Stock Market Forecast* (P.O. Box 167, Rochester, New York 14601; 800-836-4330; $230 a year). *SEC Today* includes the entire *SEC News Digest.*

## The Best Market Newsletters and Services

More than 400 newsletters claim to tell you which stocks to buy to make money, and the editors of some of them have done amazingly well over long periods. Such advice does not come cheaply. Newsletters typically cost about $150 a year, though the price ranges from $18 to $895 or even more. If you don't know much about the market and have a few hundred or few thousand dollars to invest, you would be better off letting mutual funds manage your money. But a good service might be helpful if you have, say, $25,000 or more to invest.

Of course, many letters have flopped. Anybody can do some research and put one out. The Supreme Court has ruled that newsletter publishers no longer must register with the SEC as investment advisers. They can publish anything as long as it is not misleading or fraudulent information. Indeed, the publishers have included high-school dropouts, an electrician and a hairdresser.

Some of the investment services are addicted to self-congratulation, often making ambiguous forecasts and then boasting that they have been "right on target." Published performance records, as Charles Rolo has pointed out, often overstate gains and understate losses because they don't take buying-and-selling commissions into account. If a service advises buying a stock at $10 and then decides it should be sold at $11, the service credits itself with a 10% gain. After brokerage commissions on a trade of 100 shares, the investor's real gain might be closer to 3%.

To find the best newsletters, you can read services that keep score on them. *The Hulbert Financial Digest* (316 Commerce Street, Alexandria, Virginia 22314; 703-683-5905; 12 issues a year at $67.50 for first-time subscribers and $135 a year for regular subscribers) rates about 150 advisory services on their performance. Another service, *Timer Digest* (P.O. Box 1688, Greenwich, Connecticut 06836; 18 issues a year for $225), monitors 80 to 100 newsletters that claim to call the major turning points in the market and reports on the 10 best.

It's wise to sample as many advisory services as you can before committing yourself. Most offer a one- to six-month trial subscription for a low price; some will send you a free copy, or you can see one at a stockbroker's office. The best way of getting to know a variety of services is to write for the free catalog published by Select Information Exchange (244 West 54th Street, Suite 614, New York, New York 10019; 212-247-7123). It describes hundreds of services and offers a trial subscription to 20 of your choice for $11.95.

The major advisory services that focus mainly on fundamentals are often the most useful. They provide earnings estimates, industry and company analyses, investment strategies, stock recommendations and model portfolios — a package of investment materials that you cannot find assembled elsewhere.

One of the largest is *The Value Line Investment Survey* (220 East 42d Street, New York, New York 10017; 800-833-0046). This weekly service costs $525 the first year, or you can try 10 issues for $55 and pay $460 a year thereafter. For those who learn to use the vast amount of information and guidance it offers, *Value Line* can be very helpful. Every week its staff of about 100 analysts, economists and statisticians evaluates 1,700 stocks. Each issue also includes a comprehensive overview of the market.

Standard & Poor's *Stock Guide* (800-221-5277, or 212-208-8572 if you're in New York) gives the vital statistics on over 5,300 common and preferred stocks and more than 500 mutual funds. The monthly guide costs $135 a year. There is sometimes a special for first-time subscribers.

Another major service is *The Outlook,* published weekly by Standard & Poor's (25 Broadway, New York, New York 10004; 800-852-1641); a one-year subscription costs $217 for first-time subscribers and $298 for regular subscribers. *The Outlook* is cautious. It's easy to read and digest, does not encourage taking great risks and is backed by Standard & Poor's large analytical staff. It lists the best- and worst-acting stock groups and gives a weekly update on some 1,100 issues, with buy-and-sell recommendations graded on year-ahead appreciation potential.

For a quick scan of economic and market indicators plus computer-based forecasts and a lot more, a popular publication is the twice-monthly *Market Logic* (2200 Southwest 10th Street, Deerfield Beach, Florida 33442; 800-442-9000; $95 a year). It counsels subscribers on almost every aspect of investing, from stocks and mutual funds to options and gold.

Charles Allmon, noted for finding growth stocks ahead of the crowd, publishes the twice-monthly *Growth Stock Outlook* (4405 East-West Highway, Suite 305, Bethesda, Maryland 20814; $195 a year). His is one of a handful of publications whose recommended stocks have made money every year since 1975. Allmon also produces *Bank Stock Analyst,* which follows more than 100 U.S. banks — most of them smaller regional banks — selected for their financial strength. It comes out twice a year and is available only to *Growth Stock Outlook* subscribers, free of charge.

The biweekly *Dick Davis Digest* (P.O. Box 350630, Fort Lauderdale, Florida 33335-0630; 305-467-8500; $140 a year) reprints excerpts, including specific recommendations, from 450 market letters.

In addition, the American Association of Individual Investors (312-280-0170) publishes a monthly journal with advice and sponsors seminars for beginners in 50 chapters across the U.S. Membership costs $49.

On-line databases are an even richer resource. With a personal computer and a modem, you can

**GROWTH-STOCK CHARACTERISTICS**

- **Above-average earnings growth**
- **Above-average potential for returns**
- **Low dividend yield**
- **Higher volatility than market**
- **Higher price/earnings ratios**

SOURCE: T. ROWE PRICE

tap a variety of services that provide financial information on corporations and mutual funds and news reports that might affect their shares. The most comprehensive of these is Dow Jones News/Retrieval (P.O. Box 300, Princeton, New Jersey 08543-0300; 800-522-3567). It provides stock quotes and trading volumes of shares on all major exchanges and a full text of the *Wall Street Journal* and *Barron's.* It even lets you buy and sell securities through electronic hookups with discount brokerage houses. Dow Jones News/Retrieval charges a start-up fee of $29.95 plus $18 a year; the real costs are the minute-by-minute fees for using the service, which vary according to the time of day.

Other services include America Online (8919 Westwood Center Drive, Vienna, Virginia 22182; 800-827-6364; $9.95 a month, which includes five free hours a month; each additional hour is $2.95); CompuServe (5000 Arlington Center Boulevard, Columbus, Ohio 43220; 800-848-8199; $9.95 a month, including five free hours a month; $2.95 per additional hour), owned by H&R Block; GEnie (401 North Washington Street, Rockville, Maryland 20850; 800-638-9636; $8.95 a month); Prodigy (445 Hamilton Avenue, White Plains, New York 10601; 800-776-3449; $9.95 a month for basic services); and Signal (1900 South Norfolk Street, San Mateo, California 94403; 800-367-4670; $420 start-up fee and monthly fees of $125 or more depending on the type of service).

For all the electronic razzle-dazzle, you will still profit from reading several books on investment. Among the best are *The Intelligent Investor* by Benjamin Graham ($30, HarperCollins); *The Battle for Investment Survival* by Gerald M. Loeb, who was no kin, alas ($18, Fraser Publishing Company); *The Mutual Fund Buyer's Guide* by Norman Fossback ($17.95, Probus); and *Gaining on the Market* by Charles Rolo and Robert Klein ($18.95, Little, Brown and Company).

Also, for information on specific stocks, you can call almost any corporation's shareholder-relations department. Ask for the annual report, the 10-K form that public corporations file with the Securities and Exchange Commission, all recent corporate reports to shareholders and transcripts of presentations that the firm has made to brokerage societies or analysts' groups. For the phone numbers of major corporations and the names of their chief executives, see the *Fortune 500* issue, published every May.

# The Merger Market

Merger mania is staging a comeback, and it's not just a Mickey Mouse game. Suppose a company in which you own stock is reported to be a takeover target. What should you do?

Don't believe mere rumors. There are far more phony stories out there than real deals. But if the company does become an active and announced target, your choices are many. Remember that more than nine out of 10 of these proposed deals ultimately go through. In the first seven months of 1994, the offering price was an average 53% higher than the stock's price on the day before the announcement.

Should you hold on to your shares — or sell out? The primary advice: Don't get greedy. The buy-or-sell decision is particularly difficult in a hostile takeover bid. If you're an aggressive investor, you might hang on to your shares in hopes that another bidder will jump in and offer still more. If you're conservative, you might immediately want to sell all — or at least half — of your stock. As the battle wears on, sell out if the stock rises to within 10% of the price the raider proposes to pay.

But say the shares have not risen quite that high yet. Then you still might consider selling and taking whatever profits you have earned as a result of the takeover bid — if the management seems to stand a fighting chance of beating back the offer. It often does so if top managers and directors own more than 10% of the stock. If management seems too weak to resist, you would be wise to hold on to your stock, wait for the raider's last offer, and then get out.

You also want to delay selling if the target firm actively seeks a friendly White Knight to pay a still higher price or if it announces an offer to buy its own shares. A bidding war could result and kick up the price of your stock. Of course, do not sell if you think the price of your shares will eventually rise anyway, with or without the takeover.

Another corporate maneuver is the leveraged buyout (LBO). The firm's own management or an independent investor proposes to buy up the shares owned by the public and take the company private. If an LBO proposal comes your way, do nothing until you have read the official offering statement. Then see what you are really getting for your shares. Be especially wary of offers in which you will be paid in low-quality junk bonds and other wallpaper as well as cash. Often the bonds in these deals are riskier than the stocks you are holding. Many LBOs have come to grief. On the other hand, if you're offered real money — and a premium price — you're probably wise to sell.

If a company whose stock you own decides to spin off one of its divisions, you have to ask yourself a couple of questions. First, should you hold on to your shares in the parent firm, or perhaps even buy more? The best answer is that the parent is often worth keeping — if the spin-off rids it of unprofitable, debt-laden divisions or if the deal unloads businesses that the parent lacks the expertise to manage. Second, should you dispose of the stock you receive in the spun-off enterprise? The best answer: Don't automatically sell those shares. Give the company a year or so to prove itself. If it does not do well within that period, then sell.

It's worth scouting for firms that you think might be candidates for takeovers. According to Charles Rolo, here are some guidelines for finding them:

First, look where the bargain-hunting corporations shop. Acquirers prefer companies that have large cash holdings. The buying company then can recover part of the purchase price by using the selling company's very own cash. Acquisition-minded corporations also look for stocks selling appreciably below book value — that is, total assets minus total liabilities per share.

Second, look where owners may want to sell. Dealmakers often search out companies whose principal owners have reasons to wish to be acquired — for example, they are elderly, own the controlling interest and have most of their eggs in that one corporate basket. A sellout would enable them to diversify their holdings and perhaps get some stock that is more readily marketable.

Third, look where takeover and merger activity is already strong. It has been intense in the entertainment, cable, insurance, banking, health-care and software industries.

## Investing in Tomorrow's Products

The classic way to grow rich is to get in on the ground floor of a new product — not necessarily by making it or selling it, but by investing in it. You do not have to be an Eli Whitney or an Alexander Graham Bell to invest profitably in the products that will create the fortunes of the future. What you do need is information, patience and an eye for the products, processes and services that can make life easier, more efficient, longer or more enjoyable.

Which fields are most likely to produce the next generation of successful new companies? If you ask venture capitalists, business school professors, bankers and owners of small enterprises, they most likely will recommend the following:

*Data processing:* Bruising competition has brought a series of failures, but many survivors should do splendidly. The future looks bright for those companies that manufacture or service computers and software — provided they bring unique products or special capabilities to this crowded field.

*Genetics:* Some of the best possibilities for smaller firms in this area are in support fields — for example, making lab equipment or producing enzymes for use in genetic research.

*Communications:* Opportunities can be profound for entrepreneurs who make, sell or service cable TV and satellite transmission equipment.

Beware of being seduced by hot tips from unknowing in-laws and friends. As one top mutual-fund manager warns, there is no faster way to the poorhouse, other than pursuing slow horses and fast women, than following tips in the new technologies.

Shares in the exciting but highly speculative and volatile health-technology industry, for example, aren't for people who need Tagamet or Xanax. They rise and fall with amazing speed. Often, profits are a long time coming because years of clinical testing are required before a medical product can be sold. Ask a stockbroker for firms whose products are well along in the clinical-testing phase.

A sober and sensible way to invest is to first pick out an emerging field in the new technology and then follow it carefully. Subscribe to specialty magazines and trade journals. Some good ones are *Electronic News* (P.O. Box 1978, Danbury, Connecticut 06813-1978; 800-722-2346; $69 a year); *Electronic Business Buyer* (275 Washington Street, Newton, Massachusetts 02158; 800-662-7776; $70 a year); and *California Technology Stock Letter* (P.O. Box 308, Half Moon Bay, California 94019; 800-998-CTSL; $295 a year, plus tax for California residents).

Once you have done your homework, you can consider putting cash into those companies that are most effectively pioneering new products.

Conservative people might wager 10% or so of their investment money on such ventures; more aggressive types might put in 30% or even 40%.

## The Pleasures and Pitfalls of New Issues

You also can try to buy the shares of new companies when they first go public. It is not always easy to get on the train before it leaves the station. Supplies of shares are often limited, and so most promising and popular new issues are offered first to a broker's best clients. The price may shoot up when all the people who could not buy it try to pick it up from those who could. But within a year or less, many new issues slip back to their offering price — or go even lower. Investors who wait for such a decline in order to buy in usually have gains as big as those who got in early.

Lured by the stunning success of a few new issues, investors seem to be passionately eager to get in on them. But offering prices are often inflated, and companies that are too questionable to win the financial support of blue-ribbon underwriters have little trouble finding unexacting sponsors. As one long-established underwriter warns, "Anyone who ventures into new issues needs to be rigorously selective. A lot of junk is being brought to market, and that's scary." On the other hand, quite a few companies of real substance are selling their issues to the public for the first time. Getting information is not hard. Some brokerage houses publish weekly calendars of offerings. Most brokers subscribe to *Investment Dealers' Digest,* a weekly that covers the new-issues market.

If you're considering buying into an issue, ask your broker for the stock's prospectus, the so-called red herring, and scrutinize it carefully. Look for the passage that lays bare the holdings of the company's top officers. If they are unloading a lot of their own shares, you should shun the issue.

Check the prospectus to see that the underwriter of the issue is a well-established firm. Even the best underwriters make errors of judgment, but they will not knowingly market the stock of a company that is likely to damage their reputation. Some of the highest-quality new issues are brought to market by such blue-chip investment firms as Ladenburg, Thalmann, Alex. Brown & Sons and Morgan Stanley. Yet these companies, too, can fall victim to cyclical downturns in the market or unexpected competition from lesser-known firms and suddenly find their deals and reputations souring. The bottom line is to be careful not to depend too heavily on issues from any one underwriter.

See who is providing the venture capital financing. Strong backing by venture capital entrepreneurs suggests that the new company has been well groomed to go public and probably has genuine promise. You can breathe easier if the prospectus lists such respected venture capital firms as Kleiner Perkins Caufield & Byers, Sutter Hill Ventures, Venrock Associates, Accel Partners or New Enterprise Associates.

Examine the balance sheet in the prospectus. Are the new company's finances strong enough to keep it going even if profits do not meet expectations — or, if profit growth is on target, to provide capital for continued expansion? If you don't trust your own judgment on these matters, don't invest in new issues without reliable professional guidance.

Before you buy, learn all you can about a company that is going public. Ask your broker for copies of newsletters that discuss new issues. Among the leaders are two monthlies, *New Issues* (2200 Southwest 10th Street, Deerfield Beach, Florida 33442; 800-442-9000; $95 a year) and Standard & Poor's *Emerging & Special Situations* (25 Broadway, New York, New York 10004; 212-208-8786; $249 a year, or $60 for a three-month trial).

Look to see if responsible analysts say the company's product has the potential for capturing a 20% share of a market that itself could grow very large within a decade. Favor concerns that have 20% to 30% annual growth in both sales and earnings over the past several years and that are plowing 10% to 15% of annual revenues into research and development.

Above all, read the prospectus. You owe it to yourself to slog through it before you put up a penny. Check out who the company's officers are — they're listed in the prospectus — and how much experience they have had marketing other products in the same or related fields. Make sure that the underwriters and the venture capitalists who are backing the firm have sound records of success. If the venture capitalists are not selling their entire stock holdings in the offering, it could be a favorable sign that they think the company has a strong future.

On the other hand, if all the original backers are now backing out, beware. The public offering of stock may be rescuing them from a bad investment. But if the original investors are hanging on to their shares, it could be another positive sign.

You can also invest in tomorrow's products by buying shares of mutual funds that concentrate on stocks of small, promising companies. Get a subscription to one of the many newsletters that rate mutual-fund performance. One of the best is the monthly *NoLoad FUND*X* (235 Montgomery Street, Suite 662, San Francisco, California 94104; $140).

Among the most successful funds that invest in small stocks that have big growth prospects are the Twentieth Century Ultra Investors, Kaufmann, Brandywine, Acorn, and Baron Asset funds. If you want funds that specialize in high-tech issues, you might look at Alliance Technology Fund or Kemper Technology Fund.

Another way to invest is to buy into publicly traded venture capital companies and small-business investment companies. Their shares are traded on the NASDAQ or other exchanges, and these companies use the money to invest in enticing new ventures. The best measure of their performance is their net asset value per share — which, of course, should be rising.

## Investing in NASDAQ Stocks

If you are willing to buy stocks that are risky but may offer some outsized rewards, you might want to shop on the over-the-counter (OTC) market. OTC shares tend to be those of companies that are too small and too new to be listed on the major exchanges. These companies have fewer shares on the market than big corporations do, so even a small amount of buying or selling can cause sharp moves, up or down.

Thousands of smaller companies are listed on the NASDAQ, the National Association of Securities Dealers Automated Quotations system. That's a computer-linked network of about 500 competing broker-dealers who electronically post the prices at which each of them will buy or sell certain OTC stocks. The NASDAQ listings are loaded with small, glamourless companies, some of them selling for a bargain price of only 10 times earnings — or even less. They may be undervalued simply because few people have bothered to look at their financial statements.

For guidance, you can turn to newsletters. One with a high batting average is *OTC Insight* (1656 North California Boulevard, Suite 300,

Walnut Creek, California, 94596; 510-274-5000). It costs $69 for a trial of three monthly issues, or $295 a year.

Among the mutual funds that specialize in these stocks, one of the best is Fidelity's OTC Portfolio (82 Devonshire Street, Boston, Massachusetts 02109; 800-544-8888 outside the state). It started in December 1984; as of the end of August 1995 it had gained 582%, adjusted for a 3% load, and in the 12 months through June 30, 1995, it gained 30%.

## Venture Capital Shares

Only rich people used to be able to ante up the venture capital that launched new companies. Now you, too, can put some funds into a promising start-up. In exchange, you will be given some of that company's stock, and you can call yourself a venture capitalist.

The trouble is, these opportunities are rarely publicized. Your best leads will come from local bankers. Ask them what ventures are just beginning and need some cash. Look for companies in businesses you know something about. Preferably start with ventures that are near your home so that you can keep close contact with the people running the company.

But let's face it: Most investors in start-ups will lose money at least sometimes. Even successful ventures rarely show a payoff within five years.

You can improve your odds by buying shares in small-business investment companies (SBICs) that are open to public investment. They raise capital and invest it in businesses with a net worth of $6 million or less. There are 268 all-purpose SBICs and another 133 that specialize in enterprises run by what they define as socially or economically disadvantaged people. Most are owned by banks or groups of private investors, but a few have public shares that you can buy or sell over-the-counter or on the American Stock Exchange.

SBICs concentrate on small businesses that create jobs and are licensed by the Small Business Administration, which guarantees repayment of up to 90% of their loans. Some of the money is invested in start-ups that offer little more than potentially workable concepts. The rest is in second- and third-round financings to help spur the growth of companies that are already marketing a product or have moved solidly into the black. A number of SBICs prefer to cut out as much risk as possible. They invest only in companies that are mature enough to pay them some current income, which they in turn distribute to their shareholders in dividends.

What kind of SBIC you invest in depends on whether you want immediate income or longer-term capital gains. But whatever kind you select, ask yourself two questions, "Do I think that the companies supported by the SBIC are sound businesses? And what is the investment record of the SBIC's manager?" You can draw much of this information from the SBIC's quarterly and annual reports.

Another way to get in on start-up businesses is through a venture capital company. This is essentially a mutual fund that invests in nonpublic concerns. Venture capital firms tend to put their money in riskier enterprises. But some of them have produced memorable winners. For example, Boston's Nautilus Fund is best known for its investment in Apple Computer back in 1979, on which it made a ton. One of Kleiner Perkins Caufield & Byers' huge recent successes was investing $5 million in Netscape, a company that produces software for accessing the Internet. The firm purchased the stock at $1 a share in September 1994 before the company's public offering in August 1995, when the stock shot up to $50 a share. Kleiner Perkins made a proverbial killing.

Venture capital companies are traded over-the-counter or on the American Stock Exchange. Before you buy shares in a venture capital firm, read carefully the annual and quarterly reports. You want to know what new companies it is financing and how well — or how poorly — the firm's investment manager has performed in the past.

# How to Choose a Broker

*There's no free lunch.*

— Milton Friedman

Yes, somebody has to pay for all that butter and baloney. Guess who. And who pays for all the research reports, hand-holding and nifty offices provided by your friendly full-service broker? Often all the advice is well worth the price, particularly if you're a novice or need an expert second opinion. But, as *Fortune* has pointed out, dealing with a no-frills discount broker instead of a full-service broker gives you many kinds of savings.

The commissions on buying 500 shares of a $20 stock could run $252 at a full-service broker like Prudential Securities, but only $110 at Charles Schwab. If you sell the stock a year later and realize a 25% profit from capital gains and dividends, your *real* gains net of round-trip commissions would be only 20% at a full-service broker, versus 22.8% at Schwab. If you haven't traded in a year, a full-service outfit like Smith Barney will hit you with a $50 inactive-account fee. If you open an IRA, Merrill Lynch might charge you up to $100 a year to maintain a large account. Every time you trade at Merrill Lynch, you'll pay $4.85 to cover postage, handling and miscellaneous expenses. Most discounters, including Schwab, charge lower IRA fees and don't have any inactive-account fees.

In sum, if you follow the market very closely yourself and feel you do not need regular, professional advice, you're better off using discount brokers. They generally offer you no coaching but often charge commissions of less than 1%, which is less than what full-service brokers charge. (See page 157 for more detailed information on discount brokers.)

Choosing the right broker is not quite as important as selecting the right spouse or the best boss; but since the broker will do much to determine whether you are affluent or financially uncomfortable in the future, it is a serious decision. And it isn't easy, particularly for small investors. Some firms don't want to bother with accounts of less than $15,000. Not many will turn you down flat, but your account is likely to get serious attention only if it can generate sizable commissions.

If you are a small investor, you will find that big, national brokerage houses generally are more hospitable than lesser outfits. These large firms stand to make a bit of profit from the sheer volume of their small accounts. Look for the major firms that offer special services, such as cut-rate commissions along with some research advice.

But if you want to concentrate on investing in companies located in your own area, you might do better with one of the well-established regional brokerages. Their strength has been in spotting small local companies that have gone on to become home-run hitters. True, they also have a disadvantage: They are often less familiar with companies located far away, and with complex stock strategies, than are the larger national houses.

*A tip:* If you build a fairly large account, divide it between two brokers — one national, the other regional. That way, you diversify and get the benefit of two investing styles.

Once you have picked the brokerage house, how do you select the salesperson in that firm who is just right for you? First, solicit recommendations. Ask friends who are successful investors. Ask accountants and tax preparers. They have inside knowledge of how well their clients are doing in the market, and legally and ethically they can tell you who some of the winning brokers are.

If referrals don't produce enough candidates, write or fax the branch managers of some brokerage firms listed in the Yellow Pages. Set forth your financial situation and investment goals. When replies come in, interview not just one but several brokers. Ask each one:

How long have you been a broker? Where do you get your information? In what areas have your greatest successes been? At the time you suggest buying a stock, do you also prudently recommend a price at which I should sell out in the future?

Don't be shy about asking him or her for the names of people whose accounts he or she handles. Then call up at least two or three of them. You might uncover some unexpected blemishes, such as a tendency to overtrade. Too much trading may produce high commissions for your broker, but very small returns for you.

You are generally better off with a veteran, well-experienced broker — who has been through a few market reverses, who knows that stocks go down as well as up — than with an eager newcomer who will learn his or her lessons with your money. Instead of looking for a broker who will tell you what to do, search for one who can use his or her knowledge and experience to help you make your own decisions. Read financial publications and perhaps subscribe to an investment advisory service. Get research reports from your brokerage house. Use them to learn the factors that professional analysts employ to evaluate stocks.

▾ ▾ ▾

# How to Deal with Your Broker

Stockbrokers are salespeople, and so they can sell hard. If you feel uncomfortable when a broker urges you to buy a stock, be sure to ask some further pointed questions:

- How has that stock done lately? A more important question, particularly if you are a long-term investor who plans to buy and hold: What are the long-range earnings forecasts for the stock? If your broker doesn't have the answers immediately, tell him or her that's all right — that he or she can call you back when he or she gets them. Patience pays.
- Is the stock undervalued? One sign that a stock could be a buy is that its price is near the bottom of its trading range of the past few months. But a stock could be cheap because the company faces serious problems. Ask what makes the stock such a bargain.
- What is the company's profit margin? If it is above its industry average, the company is probably well run.
- Why should you buy this stock now? Obviously you don't want to bother with a concern when its business cycle is about to turn down. Most industries have predictable cycles of earnings declines and recoveries. Ask when to expect the next longer-term upswing or downswing and when the stock price is likely to reflect that change.
- What are the chances that, near-term, the stock will go down instead of up? Ask if the company faces strong competition, is involved in expensive litigation or is laden with debt. Heavy interest payments may cut into earnings. Get your broker to help you set a price at which you might be wise to sell and cut your losses. The price he or she chooses will help you gauge the risk that your broker sees in the investment.
- How does this stock fit in with your overall strategy? Make sure that your broker knows whether your investment objective is long-term growth, high-dividend income or a quick killing. Tell him or her how much risk you are willing to shoulder to achieve your aims. If you are a buy-and-hold investor and your broker keeps suggesting ideas suited to frequent traders, then

trade brokers. Don't forget: A buy-and-hold strategy will limit commissions and let your gains grow for a long while before the taxman takes his share.

- Who are the large shareholders in this company? What you would like to hear is that some wealthy private investors have just bought a lot of the stock and are thinking of attempting a takeover. Or that the firm's management owns a sizable portion of the shares. Top managers who are also substantial stockholders have an added incentive to see that a firm does well.
- Is this stock better than the one the same broker urged you to buy last week? Most brokers have several stocks to sell, so get your broker to compare some of the other issues on his or her list with the ones he or she is flogging now.
- Did your broker or an analyst at his or her firm do the research on the stock? If it was an analyst, ask to see his or her report on the company. And find out how well other stocks recommended by this analyst have performed.

Many analysts are too often bullish on the wrong stocks. Michael O'Higgins, president of his own investment counseling firm in Albany, New York, and author of the book *Beating the Dow,* compared the records of professional analysts. He checked their forecasts from 1973 to 1989 of the 30 stocks in the Dow Jones industrial average. O'Higgins found that you would have earned almost three times as much money investing in the 10 firms that analysts predicted would have only slow earnings growth as you would have if you had taken their recommendations of the 10 that they expected to have faster earnings increases.

Analysts often fall in love with their stocks and fear that gloomy forecasts will cut them off from the managements of the companies they follow. Many analysts rarely rate a stock as a "sell"; instead a recommendation of "hold" is a code for "sell." Sometimes an analyst is under pressure to give a company a good report because the analyst's parent firm is acting as the well-paid underwriter for that company's new stock issues. When a broker recommends a stock to you, ask if his or her firm has an investment-banking relationship with the company he or she is pushing. If it has, be extra careful.

Some analysts tend to pass news along first to big, institutional customers and then to the retail brokers who do business with smaller investors. This puts you at the rear of the information line and, in many cases, that is too far back to take any profitable action. In general, it is wise to patronize brokerage houses that freely publish their analysts' recommendations and keep track of the resulting profits or losses in those stocks.

Remember: If you invest in a stock and its price plummets, you will lose money but your broker will still pocket a commission. Unlike you, he or she is guaranteed to profit if you follow his or her advice.

Your brokerage firm should send you a statement of your account every month. It may look a little forbidding, but it can tip you to problems with your investments — or your broker. Zero in on the dollar figure showing your account's equity or net worth. This figure may tell you that your portfolio is being depleted by excessive commissions or high-risk investments that are underperforming the market. If so, call or visit your broker immediately.

Do you see on your statement a record of a sale or purchase that you don't remember discussing? That could be an unauthorized trade, one of the worst offenses in the brokerage business. Complain immediately, in writing. Brokerage firms sometimes defend themselves against delayed claims of unauthorized trading on the grounds that the customer ratified the trade by seeing how it turned out — before complaining.

Chances are your broker will be a well-trained, honest professional. After an extensive, two-year investigation, the Securities and Exchange Commission concluded that "bad brokers are not widespread." But, just to protect yourself, put any important communication with your broker in writing. If you have conservative, risk-averse goals, express those aims in a letter to your broker. Then he or she will not be able to claim at a later date that you really wanted a more aggressive strategy. If you are thinking of making an investment on the strength of an oral assurance from your broker, write a letter to him or her confirming what he or she told you about it.

And don't *automatically* sign agreements that give your broker the power to buy on margin or buy options for you. Some investors make the mistake of thinking that these documents are just part of the initial paperwork for opening a brokerage account. But options and buying on margin magnify your potential for gains and losses by raising your risk.

What happens if you get bad or even fraudulent advice from a broker?

To avoid costly litigation, many brokerage firms now require customers to sign an agreement to resolve disputes through arbitration. That's not necessarily bad. Arbitration has advantages over a jury trial. Complaints are resolved faster; the process is less expensive than litigation; and arbitrators, unlike jurors, are usually experienced in the securities industry.

If you feel your broker has steered you in a ridiculously wrong direction, you can always take him or her to arbitration. According to the Hearings Department of the American Stock Exchange, investors who went before an arbitration panel of any of the exchanges — the panels consist of one securities representative and one or two public arbitrators — won awards on 35% of their claims in 1992. And securities attorney Lloyd S. Clareman wrote in *Fortune* that investors brought some 6,464 arbitration claims against U.S. brokerage firms in the 18 months through mid-1990, complaining of misrepresentation, negligence or unauthorized trading. One-third of them settled, and half of the rest were awarded damages averaging 60% of what they claimed. In another study, by the U.S. General Accounting Office, 60% of the complainants received an award through arbitration.

A final note: After you have been with a broker for six months, coolly evaluate your total market performance. And then do it yearly. Compare your gains and losses with Standard & Poor's index of 500 stocks. If your portfolio's performance, before commissions, falls below the S&P's index, don't hesitate to take your money and run — to another broker.

## The Discounters

Should you use a discount broker? You can save as much as 95% on commissions. But you pay some penalties for those price cuts.

Discounters are found through ads in newspapers and financial magazines, and can be reached over toll-free phone lines. The choice is vast: There are more than 100 independent discount brokerage firms, plus perhaps 3,000 discount offices associated with banks. The field is dominated by Charles Schwab, Quick & Reilly and Fidelity.

The appeal of discounters goes well beyond thrift. More and more of them offer special customer services, and a few even supply that most touted of full-commission services — stock market research. But don't assume that all discounters are alike. Mercer Inc., which publishes *The*

*Discount Brokerage Survey* ($34.95; 379 West Broadway, Room 400, New York, New York 10012; 800-582-9854), points out that there is a surprising range in commission prices among the discount firms. In a trade of 500 shares at $10 a share, the average discounter would charge $65, but the most expensive discount rate would be $100, possibly more. That fee is still much less than the $160 an average full-commission brokerage would charge.

In mid-1994 a fee war broke out among the so-called deep discounters, the very cheap brokers who handle about 20% of the discount market. Among them, prices for trading, say, 500 shares of a $30 over-the-counter stock dropped to between $25 and $35 at such firms as Brown, E-Trade, Forbes and National Discount.

Whether or not you use a discount broker should depend on your investment behavior. If you are fairly new at investing and don't know your way around the markets, a traditional broker is the right choice. He or she will advise you what to buy, what to sell and when to buy or sell it. Just one winning stock recommendation from a full-service broker's research staff could more than make up for his or her higher commissions. If you want cut-rate commissions but feel hesitant to end your relationship with a full-service broker, try asking for a discount. Your broker probably can offer as much as 30% off the full fee on any substantial transaction. Most trading continues to be handled by full-service firms.

Move to a discount broker if you feel confident enough to make your own stock market decisions. In choosing a discounter, select a firm that can weather precipitous ups and downs in the market. If a company has at least eight years of service, then it already has survived two market downturns, and you are probably safe. (See below for what happens when a broker goes broke.)

Discount commission rates vary with the kind of trading you do. So-called value brokers charge rates that are a percentage of the dollar value of each transaction. This usually works best for you if you deal in low-priced stocks. So-called share brokers offer bigger discounts when you trade large numbers of shares. They work to your advantage if you buy or sell 500 shares or more and if you deal in high-priced stocks.

To cite a couple of examples of the wide variances in discounters' commissions:

If you wanted to buy 100 shares of a $10 stock, Quick & Reilly

## COMPARING THE DISCOUNT BROKERS

Here are the commissions charged by three large discount brokers and three of the deep discount brokers, along with the full-service brokers' typical charges.

| | | CHARGES | TELEPHONE (800) |
|---|---|---|---|
| **SAMPLE TRADE A: Buy 100 shares at $50 each** | **LARGE DISCOUNT BROKERS** | | |
| | Quick & Reilly, New York | $49 | 368-0446 |
| | Fidelity Investments, Boston | 54 | 544-9797 |
| | Charles Schwab, San Francisco | 55 | 435-4000 |
| | **DEEP DISCOUNT BROKERS: THREE OF THE CHEAPEST** | | |
| | Wall Street Equities, Omaha | $15 | 447-8625 |
| | K. Aufhauser, New York | 25 | 368-3668 |
| | Pacific Brokerage Services, Los Angeles | 25 | 421-8395 |
| | **FULL-SERVICE BROKERS** | | |
| | Typical charge | $106 | |
| **SAMPLE TRADE B: Buy 1,000 shares at $10 each** | **LARGE DISCOUNT BROKERS** | **CHARGES** | **TELEPHONE (800)** |
| | Quick & Reilly, New York | $84 | 368-0446 |
| | Fidelity Investments, Boston | 110 | 544-9797 |
| | Charles Schwab, San Francisco | 110 | 435-4000 |
| | **DEEP DISCOUNT BROKERS: THREE OF THE CHEAPEST** | | |
| | Wall Street Equities, Omaha | $15 | 447-8625 |
| | Pacific Brokerage Services, Los Angeles | 25 | 421-8395 |
| | Lombard Institutional, San Francisco | 34 | 566-2273 |
| | **FULL-SERVICE BROKERS** | | |
| | Typical charge | $290 | |

Figures exclude administrative charges, discounts for unlisted-stock trades and other special deals. Not listed are brokers in business for less than a year and those limited to computer trading.

SOURCE: *THE DISCOUNT BROKERAGE SURVEY*, MERCER INC.

would charge you $37.50. But Whitehall Securities in New York City would charge $50. That's about the same as a full-commission broker.

If you wanted to buy 500 shares of a $50 stock, Whitehall's commission of $62.50 would be about half the fee charged by Quick & Reilly. And a full-service broker might charge about $400.

The major discount brokers are licensed to do business in most states and have nationwide toll-free numbers that you can find in newspapers and business or financial magazines. All have Securities Investor Protection Corporation insurance of $500,000 per client and usually additional commercial insurance. They are subject to the same regulations as traditional brokers. In sum, discounters are safe.

Many offer specialized services that set them apart. Charles Schwab insures the value of your securities up to $2.5 million. And when you phone in an order to buy or sell, Schwab will execute it immediately. Before you hang up, you will learn the price you paid or received. That is information you normally don't get as fast from regular brokers.

When picking a discounter, choose on the basis of not only the size of the commissions but also the scope of the services. You should be free to trade more than just stocks and to buy stocks on margin — that is, to borrow up to 50% of the cost from your broker. You also should expect a discounter, like a full-service broker, to pay you interest on cash in your account and to give you stock quotes during market hours.

In the past, discounters provided impersonal service. Now they increasingly offer you the choice of dealing with one representative or a team of them. Many discounters will take custody of your Individual Retirement Account or Keogh plan. A few — like Charles Schwab and Fidelity Investments — offer the combination of debit-card service, margin trading, free checking and 24-hour toll-free phone numbers available in a full-fledged asset management account. So read the financial press closely to see the various deals and extras, and shop around.

While national firms like Schwab and Fidelity can charge you less than half the rate of a full-service shop, you could save even more — up to half again as much — at several dozen smaller firms around the country. These deep discounters can offer such low rates because they have found ways to cut costs even more than the well-known discounters. They spend far less on advertising and marketing and offer fewer services. Such brokers include K. Aufhauser, which charges $36.50 for 500 shares at $20 per share, and Pacific Brokerage Services, which charges $25 for the same kind of transaction.

## Using Your Bank as a Broker

Can your banker also be your stockbroker? Well, not until the government began to allow such double duty several years ago. Now some 3,000 bank holding companies and savings and loan associations have either bought or linked up with discount stockbrokers. Just about every large bank in the country has brokerage operations. And it's almost impossible to find a city where some bank doesn't sell stocks. So, the one-stop financial shop may be right down your block.

At some banks, the brokerage is nothing more than a self-service computer terminal with a telephone. Or it's a counter with a bank clerk to help you fill out applications and phone in orders. At other banks, it's a fully staffed mini–brokerage office, complete with trained broker.

Most banks sell stock through their own or an affiliated discount broker. So their commissions are usually lower than those at full-service brokers. But the banks' discounters often are 10% to 20% more expensive than independent discounters are. In a 1990 study by Mercer, banks charged an average of $88 on a $9,000 trade, while discount brokers charged an average of $73 for the same trade. The reason for the higher commission is that only a handful of banks execute their own trades. The rest just take your order and must hire — and pay — another company to do the buying and selling of securities.

Still, banks are more likely than independent discounters to offer a wide range of so-called financial products. Bank-affiliated discounters often sell everything from bonds to gold bullion, while some independents confine themselves to stocks and stock options. On other counts, bank-affiliated brokerages score well, too. They can execute trades almost as swiftly as any discounter — and perhaps get the money to you even faster. But if you want detailed investment research or advice, a full-service broker is best. Most banks will give you only current stock quotes and basic investment information.

## Regional Brokers

Regional brokerage houses can, early on, get you into the stocks of local companies that are among the fastest growing in the country. These firms often specialize in fairly small companies with strong managements. Some limit their bailiwick to a single city; others concentrate in regions — for example, growth companies of the Midwest or Southwest. Analysts read the local papers, understand the local economy and continue to follow local companies even if they temporarily fall out of favor with investors. These brokerages tend to have strong and deep ties to their region. Many began as municipal bond houses handling underwritings for towns and small cities too insignificant to be noticed by national firms. Gradually, the regionals branched out into selling stocks as well.

If you think prospects are bright for companies in a specific part of the country, a call to a regional broker will get you a sampling of research reports. If you like what you see, you can open an account, also by phone, and start receiving monthly market newsletters with regional economic forecasts and lists of recommended stocks.

Many regional brokerage houses have notable performance records. In the East are Advest in Hartford and Alex. Brown & Sons in Baltimore. In the South are J. C. Bradford in Nashville and Robinson-Humphrey in Atlanta. In the Midwest are David A. Noyes & Co. in Chicago and Milwaukee's Robert W. Baird & Co. In the West and Southwest are Rauscher Pierce Refsnes of Dallas, Sutro & Co., Inc., in San Francisco and Rocky Mountain Securities & Investments, Inc., in Denver.

To find others, a Standard & Poor's guide called *Security Dealers of North America* lists securities firms by city and state, with their addresses and phone numbers. The two-volume set for spring and fall costs $540, and is available in most libraries. When these firms venture out of their regions, it usually is to cover the competitors of local companies. Their analysts keep turning up small companies that have fast-expanding markets and earnings. Gradually the glitter of these little stars will attract attention by national firms — or so they hope. That is the regional analyst's dream: finding stocks, getting clients into them early, then waiting until a big national firm discovers them, recommends them — and sends the price up.

## How Safe Is Your Brokerage Account?

Whenever a brokerage fails, investors start wondering, "What happens if *my* broker goes broke?" Since the market collapse of 1987, 48 brokerage firms have failed — out of 7,600 in the nation. So it is very unlikely that your brokerage will go bust. But if it does, your stocks, bonds and money-fund shares are protected by the Securities Investor Protection Corporation (SIPC) against losses up to $500,000. This government-chartered private corporation — nicknamed "Sipic" — oversees liquidations of brokerages and restores securities to clients. To do this, SIPC has a fund of more than $700 million, raised by assessing the brokerage firms. It also can tap a $1 billion line of credit at the U.S. Treasury and a $1 billion credit line with private banks.

Commodity futures contracts are not covered by SIPC, nor is cash left with a broker specifically to earn interest. Options are covered; but when a firm fails, they are closed out as of the date SIPC files for trusteeship in court.

One problem is that providing customers with access to their accounts usually takes from one to six months. In the meantime, customers cannot sell any securities in their accounts. Customers first receive any securities held in their own names. If their stocks or bonds are in the firm's name — that is, in "street name" — clients will be given a pro-rated share of any such securities the firm can produce. SIPC then will make up the difference between what the clients got and what they are owed, up to the limit of the statute.

If you are worried about your broker's financial health, watch for signs of trouble. Does it take a long time for your broker to execute your orders to buy and sell? Do confirmation slips fail to square with transactions? Are your monthly statements inaccurate? Problems like these suggest the firm could be having back-office snarls, and it might be time to move your account.

Even if you are confident of your broker's stability, you should take steps to protect yourself. Certainly, don't hold more than $500,000 worth of securities at any single brokerage house that you have the slightest doubt about. If you are really skittish, hold your securities in your name instead of the firm's name or even keep the certificates at home or in a safe-deposit box.

## Dividend-Reinvestment Plans

You rarely get something for nothing, particularly when buying stocks. One exception is the dividend-reinvestment plan (DRIP). It lets you buy shares without paying a broker's commission — and sometimes at a discount price.

Some 800 companies offer these DRIPs to their shareholders, and 90 of them — mostly utilities and banks — also give you discounts of between 2% and 10% on the price of the stock. Among the biggest sponsors of DRIPs are large blue chips such as McDonald's and Philip Morris. McDonald's has the highest participation rates of any company — 52% of its stockholders.

## Selling Without a Broker

Did you know that you can sell stock that you own without using a broker — and thus save the sales commission? You can also buy and sell Treasury bills without a broker, although the actual transfer of funds must go through a bank or a brokerage. The procedure for transferring ownership of stock is not all that hard. First, sign the back of your stock certificate and have your bank guarantee your signature. That is to protect you against forgeries. Then, fill in the new owner's full name, as well as his or her Social Security number and address. Next, get the name and address of the transfer agent of the company in which you own stock. To do so, simply write to the corporate secretary of the company. Finally, send the stock certificate by registered mail to the transfer agent. Attach a letter explaining that you are selling the shares. The transfer agent then will issue a new certificate in the new owner's name. And what is the charge for this? Nothing at all.

Once you are on record as a shareholder, you simply sign a form authorizing the company to convert all your dividends into additional shares. But to qualify, your shares must be registered in your own name — not held by your broker in street name. If you reinvest, say, $100 of dividends in a company that also offers a 5% discount, you get $105 worth of stock. When you don't have enough to buy a full share, the company credits you with a fractional share. You can also buy additional shares for cash, thus sidestepping a broker's commission. A few companies even permit you to buy the initial shares directly from them, without commission.

Dividend reinvestment is an easy, money-saving way to build a portfolio. A broker can give you the names of companies that offer reinvestment plans, or you can get a list of more than 700 by sending $39.95 to Standard & Poor's Direct Marketing Department, Directory of Dividend-Reinvestment Plans, 25 Broadway, New York, New York 10004. The directory is updated annually.

Keep accurate records of the prices at which you bought shares through dividend reinvestment. When you ultimately sell the stock, you will need to know its original cost basis in order to determine your taxable gain or loss.

## Index Options

When you invest in only one or two stocks, you are taking the chance that they might not go up when the market does. Many people cannot afford to buy a variety of stocks wide enough to fluctuate with the entire market. But, in addition to index mutual funds, there is an investment that lets you profit from the rise or fall of the total market: index options.

They give you the right to buy or sell an index of securities at a predetermined price anytime before the option expires. An option to buy is a call; the right to sell is a put.

When you buy such an option from a broker, you place a bet that some broad index of stocks will rise or fall, usually within the next 90 days. An index option usually costs only a few hundred dollars for some 1,000 shares, but you could reap the same profits as if you had invested $15,000 to $20,000. That is because a small move up or down in the index can cause a much bigger change in the value of the option. This enormous leverage accounts for the thrills of index-options trading. And the chills: If you wager wrongly you lose everything you had invested — as happened to many sad investors in the crash of October 1987.

The most popular index option is the Standard & Poor's 100. It is a weighted average of the current market value of 100 blue-chip stocks selected by the Chicago Board Options Exchange. Twelve other stock indexes are also used for options trading, including the New York Stock Exchange composite and the American Stock Exchange's major market index.

If you are optimistic about the market, you buy a call option. It surges in value when the market rises. If you are pessimistic, you buy a put option. It surges when the market goes down.

Remember, investing in stock index options is very chancy. One top brokerage officer recommends this strategy: First, determine how much capital you are willing to put up. Then, invest it all in supersafe one-year Treasury bills — except for an amount equal to the interest that you will collect on your Treasuries. Next, place that amount into stock index options. Even if you lose it all, the interest you collect on your Treasuries will cover your options losses.

You can also use puts to protect any profits you already have made on the stocks that you own but do not want to sell just now. If the market should fall, your stocks also would probably fall, but your put option would rise. That gain would offset at least part of the losses on your stocks.

## Consistent Winners

In its March 1994 issue, *Money* listed four stocks and four funds that had posted gains every year since 1980. They are (with their 14-year cumulative total returns in parentheses):

Gillette (3,020%)
Hershey (1,799%)
Unilever NV (1,697%)
Dominion Resources, a Virginia electric utility (1,367%)

All of those stocks also showed gains in 1994.

CGM Mutual Fund (737%; 800-345-4048)
Investment Company of America Growth-and-Income Fund (697%; 800-421-0180)
Merrill Lynch Capital A Fund (683%; 800-637-3863)
Sentinel Balanced Fund (510%; 800-282-3863)

A final point: Several firms, including Merrill Lynch and Smith Barney, Inc., offer "wrap" accounts. Instead of charging a commission each time a trade is made, the broker charges a flat annual fee of 3%, which is shared by the broker and an independent money manager who handles the account. Brokers justify the high commission by noting that in-house analysts' research is part of the package and that a lot of time is spent monitoring the account — in short, they are engaged in customized money management. The fee, they contend, is a fair price to pay for getting a number of big-name money managers to handle your relatively modest nest egg. This is a weak argument. A 3% fee is too steep; management expenses and brokerage costs for the average stock mutual fund are only 1.6%.

CHAPTER 7

# Branching into Other Investments

What about other investments? Bonds should be a reasonably sound buy in the long term, provided inflation remains moderate. Real estate will most likely be an iffy investment in the late 1990s, if your primary goal is to make money. But if you are looking for a good deal on your first home, the real estate market will be attractive. Here are insights into those investments and many more.

## Buying into the Bond Market

Bonds used to offer secure income from interest, a safe harbor for your money, easy employment for the friends of Jay Gatsby — and no excitement whatever. Oh, how that has changed: Witness 1994, the year of the worst bond market loss in history. By some estimates the massacre wiped out $1.5 trillion in bond values worldwide.

Few experts look for such a drastic replay soon. Thank goodness. The bond market has grown tremendously and has become mystifyingly complex even to professionals. Wall Street's wizards have invented new ways — including the now-infamous derivatives — to speculate on tiny changes in interest rates or to hedge against risks. Traders play the leverage game, buying bonds on margin for as little as one or two cents on the dollar. Markets are linked electronically around the globe; an earthquake in Japan can instantaneously rattle prices from Manhattan to Capetown.

Result: Interest rates now fluctuate more in a day than they once did in a year. Since bond prices move as fast as interest rates, but in the opposite direction, the jagged rises and falls in rates send them plunging and leaping like a bronco with a burr under its saddle.

Quite clearly the bond market is no longer a calm haven for the fainthearted. One sign is that bond newsletters — which purport to give you insiders' information on tomorrow's big gainers — are a disaster area. Says Mark Hulbert of the *Hulbert Financial Digest,* which measures these newsletters: "Cumulatively, over the past five years, none of the bond newsletters beat the index."

Does all this mean you should avoid bonds? Pondering the debacle of 1994, some advisers have told investors to forgo them entirely, and instead stick to a mix of stocks and cash. But nothing compares with a well-constructed bond portfolio for ensuring a fixed cash flow over time and hedging against deflation. The key, more than ever, is to know what you are doing.

Let's review the basics. A bond is a long-term IOU, and it pays a fixed rate of interest — the longer the term, the higher the interest rate. Usually, you collect your interest checks every six months. Then when the bond comes due, your capital is repaid in full. You can choose to tuck your bond away in a safe-deposit box and collect regular interest payments until the bond matures.

But it is precisely those far-off maturity dates and the fixed interest

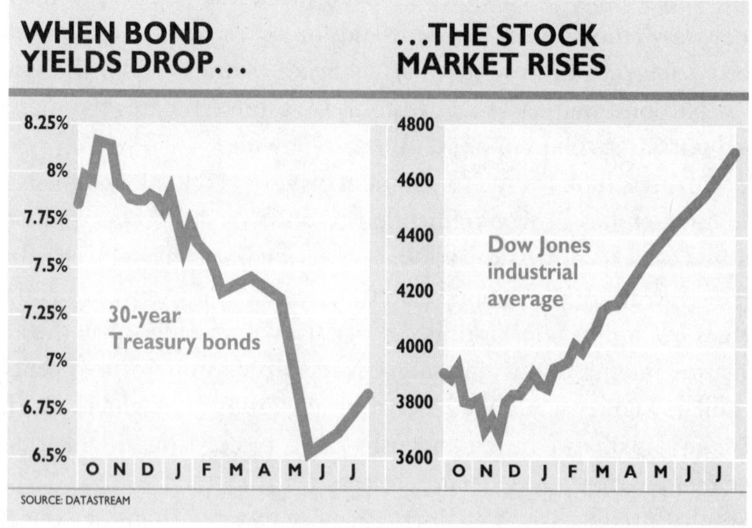

rates that can make bonds speculative. That is why longer-term bonds pay higher rates — investors expect richer rewards in return for the extra risk.

Why do bond prices fall when rates rise, and vice versa? Take an example: Say you buy a new 30-year corporate bond at its face value of $1,000. Say also that it pays 7% interest, so you collect $70 a year every year until the date when the bond matures, or comes due. But if long-term interest rates in the meantime rise — say, to 14% — your bond will fall in value. It will be worth only about $538 in the open market, because that is the amount that makes your $70 annual return equal a 14% yield. The bond is said to have a 13% yield to maturity. If you had to sell it to raise cash before it matured, you would lose money. And while you owned it, your $1,000 would be tied up earning only 7% when it might have been yielding 14% in another bond.

On the brighter side, however, if interest rates fall below 7%, your fixed-interest bond is obviously worth more than $1,000. That is because an investor would have to pay more than $1,000 in the market to buy a bond that would yield the guaranteed $70 a year that you collect. You may want to speculate in bonds if you think that interest rates will fall, thus pushing bond prices up.

The principles of bond trading are simple: To get the highest yields, you should invest for as short a term as possible when rates are rising. Then, once you are convinced that rates have peaked and will turn down, you should move into longer-term securities — to lock in those high yields and to reap any capital gains.

When investing in bonds, you have a vast smorgasbord of choices. You can buy ordinary, individual bonds (just like Mom and Dad did) or whole portfolios in the form of a bond fund or a unit trust. You can do well if you mind the risks. For in-and-out speculators seeking quick capital gains, trading can be as attractive in bonds as in stocks. But if you seek steady income, you can still find that old-time safety, perhaps by buying the bonds of reliable, major corporations that are selling at deep discounts from their face values. For $740 in mid-1995, you could buy bonds of Norfolk & Western Railroad that would return $1,000 in 2015, and for $775, you could get International Paper bonds returning $1,000 in 2012.

Most investors should stay with bonds that have a quality rating of AAA or AA. Treasury securities, which are guaranteed by the federal government, are even safer than AAA corporate or municipal bonds. No corporate calamity can downgrade their quality.

But adventurous buyers might consider lower-quality issues. A bond rated BBB offers a yield one and a half to two percentage points higher than one rated AAA. And yields for so-called junk bonds — those rated BB+ or lower by Standard & Poor's — are still richer. These low-rated bonds have higher risks. Interest payments could be deferred or the bond's quality rating could be lowered further, thereby depressing the price.

Business cycles often create bond profit opportunities. When investors sense the onset of a recession, they begin bidding up bond prices in expectation that the Federal Reserve Board will start pumping money into the economy. Boosting the money supply forces down interest rates. At the other end of the seesaw, bond prices rise.

Conversely, when the economy warms up, the Federal Reserve is inclined to raise interest rates to hold off demand-inspired inflation. Just that happened in 1994, when the Fed raised short-term rates six times, and a seventh time in February 1995. They jumped from 3% in February to 5.5% in November. This was the first time the Fed had lifted short-term rates in five years; it was also the largest increase since 1981. Consequently, prices of 30-year Treasury bonds plummeted. So much for stability.

If you are aware of the risks, if you have sound professional advice and if you have enough capital to weather some losses, you can profit nicely. The problem is that it's nearly impossible to *consistently* predict interest rates with accuracy, and many top professionals occasionally guess wrong. Almost none of them expected the Federal Reserve to kick up interest rates seven times in the 12 months beginning in February 1994 — causing bond investors to rush for Tagamet.

*A tip:* Your most prudent course is to spread your bond money over a range of maturities, from as short as two years to no longer than 10 years or, at most, 15 years. You seldom earn much extra income for tying up funds longer than 10 or 15 years. This is called "laddering" your maturities. If and when interest rates rise, you will soon have money coming due that you can reinvest. If and when interest rates fall, your 10-year and 15-year bonds will have locked in higher yields than the market offers; thus, their face value will go up.

Whatever your strategy, you should consider seven factors when buying bonds:

- *The coupon rate* This is the fixed dollar amount of interest you collect at regular intervals.
- *The maturity date* This is the date when you will be paid back the face value of the bond, usually in multiples of $1,000.
- *The current yield* This is the coupon rate divided by the current market price. For example, if the rate on the face of the bond is 7% and the bond is selling for $700, the current yield is 10%.
- *The yield to maturity* This combines the current yield with the price you pay. It tells you the real return you will get from income plus capital gain if you hold the bond to maturity.
- *The yield to call* This applies to bonds whose issuers have the right to call, or pay off, the bond at the first call date before it matures. You will get the face value, or a bit more. The calculation is similar to the yield to maturity in that the principal value at maturity is replaced by the first call price, and the maturity date is replaced by the first call date.
- *The tax status* The interest paid on bonds issued by government bodies is usually exempt from certain taxes.
- *The quality rating* A bond's rating — AAA or B–, for example — tells you the financial soundness of the issuer. Bonds represent the debt of a company or government agency, which is the issuer. When you buy a bond, you lend money to the company or government agency, and become one of its creditors. The stronger the company or agency, the higher its quality rating.

Keep an eye on a measure called "effective duration." It takes into account a bond's maturity date as well as varying coupons, payment schedules and call features. The longer a bond's duration, the greater the risk from fluctuating interest rates. A bond fund's managers can tell you the average duration of the bonds in the fund.

Cautious investors should buy bond funds with short average durations — say, two to three years. These funds tend to be less volatile than others. The Neuberger & Berman Ultra Short Bond fund in mid-1995 had an average duration of only 10 months and was yielding 5.48%. For people willing to take on slightly more credit and interest-rate risk, the T. Rowe Price Short-Term Bond fund had an average duration of 2.2 years and was yielding 6.42%.

You can do well buying U.S. Treasury issues (T-bonds) or perhaps

## EFFECTS OF CHANGES IN INTEREST RATES

Impact of rate changes on the total return over one year of three Treasury issues, e.g., a two-point drop in rates would cause the total return on a 30-year Treasury bond yielding 6.9% to rise to over 33%; a two-point rate rise would cause this bond's return to fall to minus 15.2%. (The chart assumes the two-year note has an original yield of 6.1%, and the 5.5-year note one of 6.4%.)

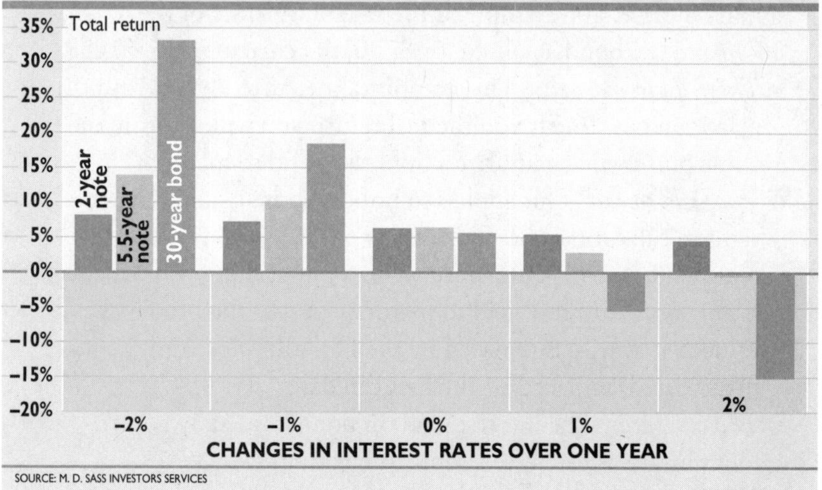


SOURCE: M. D. SASS INVESTORS SERVICES

AAA-rated corporate bonds. Yields on 10-year Treasuries in mid-1995 were about 6.6%, and on top-rated corporates, 6.86%. This was a spread that made T-bonds the wiser choice of the two because they offer greater liquidity and are, of course, free from state and local taxes. Corporate bonds yield more because you take a chance that the company issuing the bond might get into trouble and be unable to pay the interest or principal when it comes due. Not only are Treasuries safer — the U.S. government would have to fall before they default — but also the interest they pay is exempt from state and local taxes. Sorry, you do have to pay federal taxes on it.

There is another important difference between Treasury and corporate bonds: When interest rates drop, private companies and state and local government agencies often "call" — that is, buy back — their high-yielding bonds. And the investor is obliged to sell them back. By contrast, 30-year Treasury bonds are "noncallable" for at least 25 years, and some for the full 30 years; all other, shorter-term Treasury bonds are totally "noncallable." So you can hold on to these high-yielding bonds for a long time — usually until they mature — without fear that the government will force you to sell out.

## Save on Brokerage Commissions

When buying new issues of U.S. Treasury bills, bonds or notes, you may wish to use the Treasury Direct purchasing program. It avoids the fees and commissions charged by banks and brokers. Interest payments are made by direct deposit into the bank or financial institution you designate, allowing you to have immediate access to the funds and to start earning more interest on them right away. The minimum purchase for a Treasury bill is $10,000. For more information, call the Treasury's Bureau of the Public Debt (202-874-4000).

If you're buying Treasuries already in circulation through a brokerage, you can pay a full point or more on the spread between the price at which the broker buys ("bid") and sells ("ask"), plus commission. Early in 1995 the American Stock Exchange introduced a market for Treasury notes and bonds that guarantees spreads of just a quarter point. On a $20,000 purchase, a quarter-point spread could save you $150 over full-point spread. The exchange was also planning to provide similar markets for Treasury bills and strips, Ginnie Maes, Fannie Maes and Freddie Macs. Just ask your broker to execute your order on the American Stock Exchange.

When you buy any kind of corporate or municipal bond, check how soon it can be called in by the issuer. Some corporate bonds guarantee against calls for up to 10 years.

As for municipal bonds, they are hard to buy in units smaller than $5,000. They are equally tough to sell without paying a high commission if you own fewer than 25 bonds. So the best way for most people to buy them is through a tax-free municipal bond fund.

Speculators who aim for maximum capital gains — but are willing to take maximum risk — might consider convertible bonds. They can be swapped for a stated number of shares of the issuer's common stock when that stock rises to a prestated price. A convertible's price swings not only with interest rates but also with the issuing company's shares. When share prices rise or fall, so do convertible prices.

## Fear and Loathing: The "D" Word

Many bond funds have pumped up their returns in recent years with derivatives, those securities whose payments are based on, or derived from, the performance of underlying assets such as bonds or mortgages. Properly and responsibly used, derivatives can be valuable financial tools and rewarding investments. Futures contracts and put-and-call options are derivatives.

The problem is that derivatives are almost irresistible for speculators to abuse. Because derivatives have earned such a bad name, many fund managers are now avoiding them, or disguising them under such names as "complex securities."

As an investor, you're most likely to encounter derivatives in the form of mutual-fund holdings of zero coupon bonds or Collateralized Mortgage Obligations (CMOs). Underwriting firms create high-yielding CMOs by slicing the cash flows from traditional mortgage pass-through securities, such as Fannie Maes, into dozens of new securities.

Should you shun funds with significant CMO holdings, or flee from any you now own before they slip into trouble? Not necessarily. In fact, many experts in mid-1995 were making a plausible case for buying. The biggest risk to CMOs is that homeowners will prepay their mortgages. That's what many did in 1994. As a result, holders of CMOs that were based on high-yielding, short-term securities instantly saw them become low-yielding, long-term ones.

That risk has greatly diminished since then. In mid-1995 most CMOs were backed by mortgages paying rates far below current mortgage-lending rates, so a rush to prepay those loans was most unlikely.

## Bond Funds and Unit Trusts

With prices of individual bonds so unsteady, investors are turning to bond mutual funds to spread their risk. Funds and unit trusts give you a small share in a large number of bonds and thus reduce the risk of default by any one or two bonds. Professional managers also relieve you of worries about which bonds to buy and sell, and when. They decide for you.

A bond fund will always redeem your shares at the present worth of the underlying bonds. If the prices of bonds in the fund's portfolio go up, your shares go up. Of course, if prices decline, your shares decline, too. Brokers sell bond funds and collect commissions of 4% to 6% from you, but you easily can buy commission-free, no-load bond funds by mail. As an alternative, of course, you can buy individual bonds. And you can sell them back in the market at any time. But you will usually take a beating on the price because commissions are high unless you are trading very large amounts. Here are examples, using corporate bonds:

| *Amount* | *Typical Charges* |
|---|---|
| Individual bond, $1,000 face value | $35 |
| Ten bonds, $10,000 face value | $50 |
| $10,000 of load bond funds | $400 to $500 |
| $10,000 of no-load bond funds | $0 |

Here are typical commissions for Treasury bonds and Treasury bond funds:

| *Amount* | *Typical Charges* |
|---|---|
| Individual bond, $1,000 face value | $50 |
| Individual bond, $10,000 face value* | $50 |
| $10,000 of load bond funds | $200 to $500 |
| $10,000 of no-load bond funds | $0 |

*Short-term Treasury bills are sold only in denominations of $10,000 and more, with maturity dates of three months, six months, nine months or a year.

Individual bonds do have one big advantage over funds. If interest rates rise and a bond's price drops, you know that your bond eventually will be paid off at its face value — when it matures, or comes due. But bond funds never mature. So, if interest rates surge and stay high, your bond-fund shares may never again be worth what you paid for them.

*Another warning:* Be wary of bond funds with terrific records. Says Ken Gregory, editor of the *No-Load Fund Analyst* newsletter, "If returns are way out of line with other funds, that means the manager is most likely taking risks that others aren't." Risks include loading up on volatile financial derivatives or junk bonds, or betting on currencies.

Unit trusts are usually huge fixed bond portfolios assembled by brokerage houses, not mutual funds, and sold in slices of $1,000 to $5,000. They give you the dual benefits of diversification and fairly good prices. After paying commissions, you generally get $950 to $960 worth of securities for each $1,000 you invest. The yields are slightly bigger than those of bond funds because there is no management fee.

The trust's sponsor almost always will buy units back from you at a price equal to their net asset value. The advantages of liquidity and diversification, however, come at some cost; you run a risk that interest rates will rise, and the price of your units will decline. Also, the big difference between a bond fund and a unit trust is that the sponsors of the trust don't try to beat the market by doing a lot of in-and-out trading. They usually buy 30-year bonds and don't sell them unless the issuer is revealed to be in imminent danger of default. By then, of course, it is usually too late.

True, you will not be too badly clobbered, because the trust owns many different bonds, and it is highly unlikely that more than a few bond issuers would default at any one time. Still, the way to safeguard yourself against turkeys in your trust — before you send in your money — is to read the trust's prospectus. It lists each bond in the portfolio along with its credit rating and tells you whether the issuers can call in the bonds early if interest rates fall.

*A tip:* To reduce the risk of

**VIEWING VOLATILITY**

Some investments tend to rise—and fall—much more sharply than others. Gold funds, for example, are almost seven times as volatile as those that buy Ginnie Mae securities.

Standard deviation from the mean, 1990-1995

HIGH RISK

| | |
|---|---|
| 7.99 | Japan funds |
| 7.17 | Gold funds |
| 5.32 | Health/biotechnology funds |
| 4.91 | Emerging-market funds |
| 4.30 | International funds |
| 3.82 | Growth funds |
| 3.27 | S&P 500 funds |
| 2.85 | Equity-income funds |
| 2.58 | T. Rowe Price int'l bond fund |
| 2.42 | Balanced funds |
| 2.17 | Junk-bond funds |
| 2.03 | World income funds |
| 1.09 | Ginnie Mae funds |

LOW RISK

SOURCE: LIPPER ANALYTICAL SERVICES

credit downgrades, buy only those funds that invest in bonds rated AA or better by Standard & Poor's.

You can also buy *tax-exempt* unit trusts, which invest in an almost unchanging portfolio of municipal bonds. And for extra safety, you can put some money into an *insured tax-exempt* trust. The bonds are backed by an insurance company guarantee that interest and principal will be paid on schedule. But the cost of the insurance may reduce the yield.

*Conclusion:* Taking all the factors together, the easiest and safest way for most people of moderate means to buy a diversity of bonds is via a no-load bond mutual fund. The interest income is reasonably steady, there are no commissions when you buy or sell, and the annual fees are modest. Unlike unit trusts, bond-fund portfolios are actively managed. The issues in them are constantly being traded in search of higher profit and greater safety. Presumably the managers know enough to escape from a troubled situation and sell out well before a bond encounters the danger of default.

# Tax-Exempt Municipals

Municipal bonds, or munis, have become the tax shelter for everyone. The federal government does not tax the interest you collect on most of them, and if the bonds are from your home state, you probably will escape state and local taxes, too. (When you sell munis, however, you do pay federal taxes on the difference between the face value and discounted price of a muni bought in a secondary market.)

Tax breaks are not the only reason to buy munis. They often yield high interest. They tend to pay about 80% to 85% as much as 30-year U.S. Treasury bonds, but your income from Treasuries is *not* exempt from federal income taxes, although it is exempt from state and local taxes. In mid-1995 AAA general obligation municipals were paying around 5.75%, which was 87% as much as 30-year Treasury bonds and substantially higher than the 3% to 3.5% inflation rate.

You can do even better with a *single-state* municipal bond fund or unit trust. You usually pay no federal, state or local income taxes on the interest from this investment — provided you are a resident of the state in which the securities are issued. For example, residents of high-tax New York and California have been buying single-state funds of those states

## WHY A $100,000-A-YEAR FAMILY NEEDS MUNIS

The combined effect of federal, state and local taxes, especially in places like New York, Boston, Los Angeles, Atlanta and Phoenix, makes munis tough to beat.

| If you live in . . . | Your cumulative tax rate is . . . | So you'd need a taxable bond yielding . . . |
|---|---|---|
| New York City | 39.47% | 10.26% |
| Boston | 39.28 | 10.23 |
| Los Angeles | 37.42 | 9.92 |
| Phoenix | 35.49 | 9.63 |
| Atlanta | 35.00 | 9.55 |
| Chicago | 33.07 | 9.28 |
| Houston | 31.00 | 9.00 |

. . .TO MATCH THE 6.21% NATIONAL AVG. YIELD* ON MUNIS

SOURCES: JOHN NUVEEN & CO.; *THE BOND BUYER*; *FORTUNE*

*Bond Buyer 40 Yield to maturity, July 25, 1995.

for years, and demand has been rising throughout the country. Arkansas, Maine, New Mexico and Washington are some of the latest states among the 42 where you can get single-state funds or trusts. Both the funds and the trusts give you diversification; you get a variety of bonds, all issued by government and agencies within the state. The higher your tax bracket, of course, the more you can benefit.

To love tax-free bonds, merely compare the interest rates with those of other bonds after taxes. For example, if you were in the 31% federal tax bracket for your 1995 income, an uninsured AAA-rated municipal yielding 5.75% would have paid you the equivalent of an 8.33% taxable yield. If you were in the 28% tax bracket, your taxable equivalent yield would have been 7.99%, and in the top 39.6% bracket, 9.52%. If you're in the 39.6% tax bracket, a 6% return on a municipal bond free of federal, state and local income taxes would be worth al-

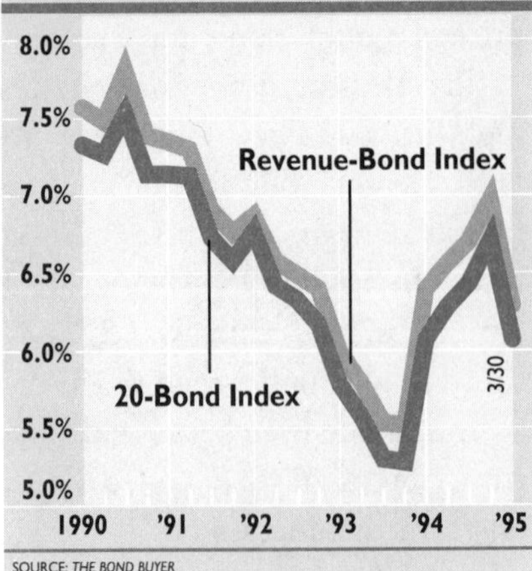

most as much as a 10% yield on a taxable investment. In doing these calculations remember to adjust for the exemption of U.S. Treasury interest from state and local income taxes.

The income that you collect from municipal bonds *must* be reported to the government, even though it is tax-exempt. Early in the year financial institutions that pay you interest — whether tax-exempt or not — should send you statements that contain all of your interest information. These are Forms 1099-INT or 1099-OID. Sometimes a bank, savings and loan, or brokerage house will put this information on its end-of-the-year statement to you. The financial institution makes the same report to the IRS. And the IRS matches the information that it receives from the institution with the information that it receives from you. So it is important that you report to the IRS exactly the same data that is reported to the IRS by all financial institutions that you deal with.

Municipals have the usual risk: If interest rates climb, their prices fall. Then if you had to sell the bonds to raise money, you would get less than you paid for them. Another risk is that the state or city agency that issued the bond could go broke and default on its payments of principal and interest, as Orange County, California, did with some $800 million of its short-term debt. It cannot be repeated enough: To guard against such danger, small investors should stick with the highest-quality bonds — those rated AAA or AA by Moody's or Standard & Poor's. (This is no perfect protection; Orange County's bonds were rated AA by both Moody's and S&P just before its troubles erupted.)

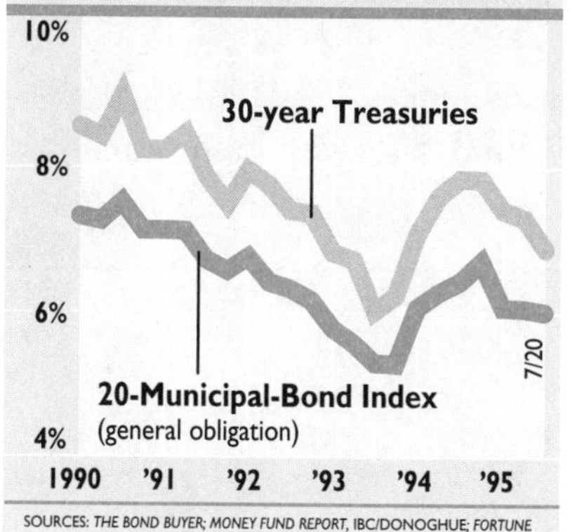


You can get muni bonds from a stockbroker; he or she usually will require you to buy at least $5,000 worth. But it is unwise to buy them unless you plan to hold them until they mature and the issuer pays you back the full face value. If you sell out earlier, you could lose as much as 5% of the value of your bond just on the spread between the higher "asked" price at which the broker sells you the bond and the "bid" price at which he or she will buy it from you. You are at the broker's mercy for what he or she will pay because the vast majority of municipal bond prices are not even published in newspapers.

## Who Needs Paper?

You can get a municipal bond that has no certificate. Buying or selling the bond through a broker is merely a computer transaction, and your record of ownership is a monthly brokerage statement. An advantage is that the interest is paid directly into your brokerage account on the day it is due. You do not have to wait for a check to arrive or clear. Nor do you need to worry about certificates being lost or stolen.

You can reduce your risks as well as your costs by buying shares in a municipal bond fund or a unit trust, whether single-state or not. Bear in mind that you will have to pay state taxes on your earnings from multistate funds.

Probably the best *tax-exempt* investments for most people are the shares of *no-load* tax-exempt bond mutual funds. For annual management fees and expenses of only about one-half of 1% of your investment, the funds give you a share of a professionally managed portfolio of bonds that you can sell at any time.

Based on total returns for the *five years* ended May 31, 1995, the best-performing no-load municipal bond funds listed by Lipper Analytical Services include:

| *Fund name* | *Five-year annualized yield* | *Phone (800)* |
|---|---|---|
| Dreyfus General Muni Fund | 9.02% | 782-6620 |
| SAFECO Muni Bond Fund | 8.87% | 624-5711 |
| Scudder Managed Muni Bond Fund | 8.64% | 225-2470 |
| USAA Tax-Exempt: Long-Term Fund | 8.12% | 382-8722 |

The funds with the highest total returns for the *12 months* through May 31, 1995, were:

| *Fund name* | *Total 12-month return* | *Phone (800)* |
|---|---|---|
| Smith Barney Managed Muni; A | 10.55% | 451-2010 |
| UST Master Tax Exempt, Long-Term | 10.16% | 233-1136 |
| Vista Tax-Free Income; A | 9.91% | 648-4782 |
| United Municipal Bond | 9.40% | 366-5465 |
| Flagship All-American; A | 9.39% | 227-4648 |

You can buy funds directly from mutual-fund companies. Just find their toll-free numbers and addresses in ads in the financial press.

Worried that many states and localities are severely troubled by federal budget cutbacks and shrinking tax revenues? You can insure yourself against any losses from defaults. Portfolios of *insured bond funds and trusts* are backed by a number of private insurance companies, and all are rated AAA by Standard & Poor's. Though prices still fluctuate, the insurance guarantees that you will receive full payment of interest and principal when due; the insurance costs about $1.25 a year for every $1,000 worth of bonds. This has the effect of reducing your annual yield by only one-eighth of 1%.

Many brokerage firms sponsor insured funds and trusts. You can buy units through your broker, who will deduct a sales commission of roughly 5%. For $1,000 you get about $950 worth of bonds. Example: Merrill Lynch's Municipal Bond Fund Insured Portfolio is insured principally by AMBAC Indemnity Corporation and Bond Investors Guaranty Insurance Company. The fund offers an extra: You can write checks of $500 or more against your money. Bond insurance is a major marketing tool and is important to investors. The Public Securities Association reports that insured munis accounted for 37% of the $163 billion of long-term tax-exempt issues sold in 1994.

▾ ▾ ▾

# Beware of Unwelcome Calls

To elaborate on an earlier point: You may have an unpleasant surprise in store if you own high-paying, long-term bonds originally issued years ago. They could soon be called in and paid off. Yes, you would get back all the money you paid for them, but you would lose those nice, regular, high interest payments.

Interest rates on municipal bonds, for example, hit their high of more than 13% back in 1982. When yields later fell, state and local government agencies paying those 13% rates redeemed their older bonds as soon as they could and sold new bonds at lower rates. Investors generally are protected from these premature payoffs for at least 10 years after the bond is issued. But some bonds may be redeemed within five years, or even earlier. A stockbroker or a financial planner can tell you whether your bond is at risk of an early redemption.

*A tip:* Be sure that any new bond you buy offers you call protection for at least 10 years.

You also have to watch call provisions in bond unit trusts, especially if they tout extraordinarily steep yields. Such trusts often are invested in many of the older high-interest bonds, which may be called. Check the call dates on bonds listed in the trust prospectus to see if you are adequately protected. Otherwise, in a few years you could end up with most of your money back — and the need to find another high-yield investment.

One investment that allows you to earn tax-free income without tying up your money for more than a year is the *variable-rate option bond.* It is a long-term municipal bond, but the rates it pays are adjusted annually — up or down — to whatever the current market rate is for munis. The advantage of this bond is that, after holding it a year, you have the option to cash it in at any time and collect what you originally paid for it.

According to Kenny S&P Evaluation Service, one-year variable-rate option bonds, sold by many brokerage firms, were paying approximately 3.75% in mid-1995. True, the variable-rate yield was significantly below the 6% rate available on AAA long-term municipal bonds. But if investors in those regular bonds sell out early, they have no assurance of getting back the full amount they have invested. If you plan to hold on to your tax-free bond for many years, you are probably best off buying a regular municipal bond. But if you think you may need your money back in a year, you would be well advised to consider variable-rate option bonds.

## The Glories and Dangers of Junk

Junk bonds have gone through more collapses than an oven full of soufflés in an earthquake — only to come back every time. Many of these low-rated, high-yield securities defaulted in 1989 and 1990, their treasuries emptied by bankruptcies of companies that had used junk bonds to finance leveraged buyouts (LBOs) and by the demise of the Drexel Burnham Lambert investment banking firm that engineered so many LBOs. Soon the junk market was virtually nonexistent. But then the marvelous levitation act resumed: Junk rebounded.

Investors busily bought up junk bonds and junk funds, feeling that the yields were enough to make up for the risk: a big 4.25 points over Treasuries. Consequently, there were some spectacular gains. The default rate on these high-risk bonds dropped from 10.3% in 1991 to 3.4% in 1992, to 3.1% in 1993, and to 1.7% in 1994.

Junk bonds either have no rating or are graded low by the rating services: BB+ or lower by Standard & Poor's, BA1 or lower by Moody's. If you are eager to get into junk, there is a somewhat higher road to take. In the last four years a new market began to emerge: "near junk" bonds, rated a slightly more solid BBB by Standard & Poor's. More than 88 such bonds were issued in 1994, with a volume of $12.1 billion. They offer better yields than higher-rated fixed-income securities.

When you shop for junk, you should distinguish between two types: genuine trash and quality junk. With a little more polish, some quality junk bonds may be diamonds in the rough. The companies that issue them may simply be too young to have a long and favorable credit history. Or they may be in lines of business that are temporarily out of favor. Or the rating services may not have yet recognized turnarounds in the issuing companies. So you may do well by scouting for glitter amid the junk.

To be safe, avoid junk bonds issued for use in takeovers and buyouts.

Some may be sound, but that's almost impossible for non-professionals to evaluate. Also, reduce your risk by diversifying. The best way to do so is investing in a corporate bond mutual fund that actively manages 70 to 140 issues. Look for a fund that has the term "high-yield" in its name — that's polite language for junk. In 1993 junk funds tracked by Lipper Analytical returned an average 18.95% in price appreciation and interest payments, and 13.85% in 1994. Some of the top performers in mid-1995 were:

| *Fund name* | *Total 12-month return* | *Phone (800)* |
|---|---|---|
| MAS Funds: High Yield | 17.69% | 354-8185 |
| Morgan Stanley Institutional: High Yield | 16.56% | 223-2440 |
| IDS Extra Income | 15.98% | 437-4332 |

# Convertible Securities

Part bond and part stock, a convertible can be a sensible buy for the experienced investor. A convertible is a bond or preferred stock that pays a fixed rate of interest or a preset dividend. And it has a unique advantage: It can be exchanged for the issuing company's common shares — if and when they rise to a certain price, known as the "conversion price." So the investor collects interest or dividend income now — and maybe he or she pockets big profits later on by converting into the stock.

This flexibility comes at a price. The cost of a convertible is higher than the present value of the stock you can exchange it for. That's why the stock has to climb before your investment becomes exciting. Also, the interest or dividends that a convertible pays are usually two or three percentage points below what you could get on the same company's bonds.

Another shortcoming is that almost all convertibles can be called back by the issuer within five years of their offering date. If you buy on a bet that the underlying shares will rise, you may not be able to keep your convertible long enough to make the conversion worthwhile.

And what if the stock market goes down? The convertible is attractive because it usually holds its value better than the common stock. That is, it will go down less than the stock.

To many investors, the ideal convertible is one that sells for $1,000, pays you 4% to 6% interest and costs you only 10% to 12% more than the value of the common stock that you can switch it into. Such a convertible will tend to keep pace with the common stock in an up market and fall only half as fast as that stock will in a down market.

You might also consider convertible bond funds. They pay about as much interest as money-market funds do. But since funds can trade in their bonds for stocks, you can also reap gains when stocks rise. Convertible bond funds are less risky than stock mutual funds, in part because bonds are safer than stocks. The total returns of convertible bond funds for the year ended July 31, 1995, as tracked by Lipper Analytical Services, averaged 14.60%.

Three low-load or no-load convertible funds that did well were:

| *Fund name* | *Total return* | *Phone* |
|---|---|---|
| Rochester Bond Fund for Growth | 20.8% | 800-955-3863 |
| Pacific Horizon Capital Income Fund | 16.28% | 800-332-3863 |
| Fidelity Convertible Securities Fund | 14.62% | 800-544-8888 |

# U.S. Savings Bonds

United States Savings Bonds may just be the most underappreciated investment of all. The Treasury Department has overhauled them to make these standbys more enticing. Are the bonds better investments than before? They certainly are. They are the Miss America of fixed-income securities.

In mid-1995 Treasury bills and money-market accounts and funds were paying 5.25% and 5.53%, while Series EE bonds paid 5.25%. Their interest rates rise — and fall — with rates in general. The return on EE bonds held five years is fixed at 85% of the average of six-month Treasury security yields for the preceding three months. A new rate is announced each May 1 and November 1.

You can buy EE bonds with face amounts of $50 to $10,000. You pay

50% of the face amount — a $50 bond will cost you $25, a $5,000 bond will run you $2,500. The time it takes to collect the face amount on an EE bond depends on current interest rates. In mid-1995, when short-term rates were at 5.25%, bonds would mature in 13.7 years. You buy savings bonds from local banks or a Federal Reserve bank. They are also good investments for payroll savings plans offered by your employer, who will automatically deduct the amount you choose from your paycheck and send you the bonds.

The interest is exempt from state and local taxes. And you pay no federal tax until you cash in the bonds when they mature. Even then, you can defer the tax by swapping Series EE issues for Series HH bonds, which you can get in denominations of anywhere from $500 all the way up to $10,000. The interest on Series HH bonds — 4% paid twice a year — is taxable annually, but you are still postponing payment of taxes on your Series EE bonds' interest and using tax-deferred dollars to earn interest on Series HH bonds.

## Zero-Coupon Bonds

You might think that zero-coupon bonds are the real nothings of the investment world. They pay you no interest now, nor will they do so for years to come. Worse, you are liable for income taxes on the interest you have not even received. What kind of an odd investment is this — and who would want to buy it? Well, you might.

Zeros, like aging oil tycoons, are not without their assets. You can invest as little as $50 and be assured that it will grow to a specific sum when the bond comes due. The term ranges from six months to 30 years. These securities sell at discounts that can be as deep as a canyon. Example: For only $781 you could buy a U.S. Treasury zero-coupon bond in mid-1995 that would pay you $1,000 in 1999; for $350 you could get one that would pay you $1,000 in 2010.

When the bonds mature, you collect all the accrued interest. If you own a zero-coupon bond, you are not confronted every six months with the problem of reinvesting the interest income — at unpredictable rates — in a struggle to maintain the high yield. That is the zeros' strong point: They eliminate reinvestment risk.

And you can escape the necessity to pay taxes on the phantom interest year by year. Just buy zero-coupon Treasury or corporate bonds for your Individual Retirement Account or your Keogh plan or some other tax-sheltered account. Or invest in municipal zero-coupon bonds; they are tax-free, so you do not have to put them into a sheltered account.

Watch out for brokers' hidden markups. They can cause the zeros' prices — and yields — to vary. Many brokers don't disclose the commissions you pay. Take a AAA-rated, insured $1,000 zero-coupon bond maturing in the year 2011. One regional broker, A. G. Edwards & Sons in St. Louis, quoted the bond in 1995 to sell for $318. Another broker, Wheat First Butcher Singer in Philadelphia, charged $310. In the former case, you would get a yield of 7.8%; in the latter, 7.4%. So shop around among brokers to make sure you get your very best deal.

## Ginnie Maes

Meet my friend Ginnie Mae. She's quite comely, not a racy type at all, but trustworthy and most rewarding for those who know and love her.

Ginnie Mae is really a security, issued by the Government National Mortgage Association and backed by the mortgages that this U.S. government corporation holds. When you invest in a Ginnie Mae, you are buying a share in a pool of fixed-rate home mortgages insured by the Federal Housing Administration (FHA) or the Department of Veterans Affairs (DVA) (the successor agency in 1989 to the Veterans Administration). You also get your principal returned in monthly installments because homeowners pay off their mortgages monthly. You will probably want to reinvest that principal right away so you do not deplete your capital. Since you get both interest *and* principal paid in monthly installments, you collect higher regular payments from a Ginnie Mae than from a bond or certificate of deposit (CD) or some other interest-bearing security.

The government does give you a limited guarantee with Ginnie Maes, but it is a guarantee only against late payments and losses from foreclosures on the loans backing the securities. You can never be certain how much money you will receive each month and how long these installments will last. That's because homeowners often pay off their mortgages ahead of schedule. Prepayments are so common that Ginnie Maes backed by 30-year mortgages have an average life of only 10 to 12 years.

To compensate investors for the uncertainty, Ginnie Maes offer a higher interest rate than Treasury issues. For example, in mid-1995, the current coupon 30-year Ginnie Mae mortgage yielded 1% more than the corresponding Treasury benchmark. So a 10-year Treasury yielding 6.5% may be equated with a 7% Ginnie Mae mortgage yielding 7.5%. The bond equivalent tells you how much you would have to get from other bonds that pay interest only twice a year in order to equal the yield of a Ginnie Mae.

Ginnie Maes will give you only about a point or two more yield than comparable Treasuries. Many investors find that such a narrow spread is not enough to compensate for the risk that homeowners will prepay the mortgages if interest rates fall. Another trouble is that Ginnie Maes cost a bundle — $25,000 each.

But for $1,000, and sometimes as little as $100, you can buy Ginnie Mae mutual funds or unit trusts from stockbrokers or fund companies. The funds produced an average total return of 10.22% for the year ended June 30, 1995. Beware: If mortgage rates fall a point or two, Ginnie Maes won't shoot up in price as much as bonds will. Instead, more homeowners will prepay their mortgages, and you will have to reinvest your capital at the lower rates.

Some Ginnie Mae mutual funds let you write an unlimited number of checks against your money; the minimum check is usually $500. Another advantage is that you can reinvest your monthly payments of interest and principal, allowing your money to compound and to keep continually working for you. And you can cash in your shares at any time, without fees or penalties.

## Fannie Maes and Freddie Macs

Another way to park a good bit of money in mortgages that earn safe, high yields is to invest in securities known as Fannie Maes and Freddie Macs.

Fannie Mae is the Federal National Mortgage Association, and Freddie Mac stands for the Federal Home Loan Mortgage Corporation. Both issue mortgage-backed securities similar to the more famous Ginnie Maes. The difference is that when you buy a Fannie Mae or a Freddie Mac, you invest in a pool of conventional home loans, and not the FHA and VA mortgages that you get with Ginnie Maes.

Like Ginnie Maes, both Freddie Macs and Fannie Maes pass along to investors on a monthly basis the mortgage interest and principal payments made by homeowners. Even if homeowners do not meet their obligations, Fannie Mae and Freddie Mac guarantee that you will receive your fair share of interest and principal every month. Fannie Maes and Freddie Macs tend to pay back the investor's principal at a faster rate than Ginnie Maes do.

Newly issued Freddie Mac and Fannie Mae securities require a minimum investment of $1,000. You can buy into a mutual fund that invests in them. One is USAA Income Fund of San Antonio, which in mid-1995 yielded 6.85%.

Both Freddie Mac and Fannie Mae are agencies chartered by Congress but owned by private stockholders. They are publicly traded on the New York Stock Exchange. Ginnie Mae is a government-owned agency within the U.S. Department of Housing and Urban Development, which buys and pools mortgages and sells them to investors. In mid-1995 Fannie Maes and Freddie Macs were both yielding about 7.5%.

## SONYMAs and Sallie Maes

If you are in a high tax bracket, SONYMA can help you. It stands for the State of New York Mortgage Agency, which issues bonds that are backed by fixed-rate mortgages. It uses the proceeds to subsidize housing loans at below-market interest rates for first-time homebuyers.

SONYMA bonds are exempt from federal income taxes for most investors; but you will have to pay taxes on them if you are subject to the alternative minimum tax. For New York State residents, these bonds are also exempt from state and local taxes. They are not guaranteed, but it would take billions of dollars of losses for the State of New York to default on payments. In mid-1995 a SONYMA maturing in 2015 was yielding 6.45%.

Many other state housing agencies issue similar mortgage-revenue bonds. Check to see whether your state offers double- or triple-tax-exempt issues at a nice price, selling at or below face value. And find out what kind of guarantee or insurance backs those securities.

Then there is Sallie Mae — the Student Loan Marketing Association, a government-chartered, publicly owned corporation that buys and otherwise finances education loans, primarily federally sponsored student loans. To bankroll these activities, the corporation issues debt securities. For steady income, you might consider buying Sallie Mae bonds. They are rated AAA by Standard & Poor's and Moody's, and the interest you earn on them is exempt from state and local taxes. Minimum investments are $1,000. You might prefer Sallie Mae stock, traded on the New York Stock Exchange. Sallie Mae shares were first issued in September 1983 at $20; in mid-1995 they were trading at the equivalent of $135 — in fact, $54, after a two-and-a-half-for-one split in 1989.

## Annuities: The Lure of the Tax Shelter

The Scottish businessman was beaming when his friend walked into the office. "What are you so happy about, Jock?" asked the friend. "Ah, laddie," said Jock, "it's a grand day. I've just gone over my year-end accounts and I've lost money. I will have no taxes to pay!"

Many people who have invested in annuities are also smiling for the wrong reason. These savings plans seem seductive, offering up to 7% interest, all of it tax-deferred, plus monthly checks for life. They can be useful for some people under some conditions. But compared with other investments that offer higher returns, the tax advantages may be elusive, especially for the highly popular variable annuities.

Until recently only insurance companies sponsored annuities. Early in 1995 the Supreme Court gave banks the power to produce them. It is too soon to know how the bank offerings will compare, but the competition will probably put pressure on the insurers to lower the high fees that they have been charging for their variable annuities.

An annuity is two things at once. First, it is a contract promising to pay you income for a specified time, usually from the day you retire to the end of your life and perhaps your spouse's, too. Second, it is an investment that pays either a fixed return (as a CD does) or a variable return (as a mutual fund does). In either case, the earnings are tax-deferred. You don't pay income or capital gains taxes on the earnings until you withdraw them. Consequently, they grow at an extra-fast rate.

Annuities are sold by brokers, bankers, financial planners and insurance agents. Contracts called single-premium annuities generally require a deposit of \$5,000 to \$10,000 or even more, but others called flexible-premium annuities allow you to start with as little as \$250.

The earnings on the money grow until some specified time in the future. Then you can either take one lump sum or "annuitize" — that is, start collecting monthly payments. Each payment is considered to be partly a return of principal that will not be taxed, and partly taxable earnings or income. If you should die before you can begin collecting, your heirs may be able to collect the money you put in. They may get it either in a lump sum or stretched out in payments over a period of time, depending on your type of annuity. Your heirs will have to pay income taxes on the accumulated earnings, but the proceeds of the annuity will not be subject to probate. But the value of the annuity at the date of death is part of your taxable estate. (For more, see Chapter 22, "Securing Your Retirement.")

After you buy a contract, the insurance company or bank may let you withdraw up to 10% of the value of your annuity each year without penalties. But if you want to take out more than 10%, the company will exact a surrender charge in the early years. Often it starts at 5% to 10% of the amount you are withdrawing and declines each year until it disappears after five to 10 years. You also pay income taxes on your withdrawals, under a last-in, first-out rule that all withdrawals are considered interest until no more earnings are left. And the IRS imposes an additional 10% penalty if you withdraw money before age 59½.

Because of these penalties, along with the fees the sponsors charge, annuities are not for you if you're seeking a convenient place to park your spare money for a short time or if you figure you may have to cash out early — say, to pay a child's college tuition. Nor are annuities sensible for young adults who cannot afford to tie up capital. They are most likely to be useful for middle-aged people who won't need the money for many years and can realistically expect their tax rates to fall after retirement.

For such investors, the best choice is a fixed annuity. It is similar to a CD, except that the interest rate is readjusted periodically. The sponsor guarantees to pay you a certain rate on the money for a fixed period —

one, three, five or sometimes up to 10 years. After that, the rate moves up or down at the sponsor's discretion. Most insurers guarantee a return of 3.5% to 5% a year, even if rates dip below that in the future.

Some insurance companies have been guaranteeing relatively high, effective one-year yields on fixed annuities, after management fees. But watch out: A number of insurers have guaranteed a rate on your contributions each new year but say nothing about the rate that they will pay on your deposits and reinvested earnings from previous years. Make sure you ask the insurance agent which rate he or she is quoting: the new money rate or the so-called portfolio rate, which applies to your past contributions and all the money in your account.

The disadvantages of annuity plans are the high charges you will face if you want to withdraw more than 10% of your funds during the first few years, and the IRS penalties for early withdrawal. Also, yearly management fees on variable annuities can run high. But annuities offer you the largest choice of payout plans once you do retire, including a lump sum. Just be sure to pick an insurance company with a high rating for its ability to keep its promises.

Before you buy, consider the alternatives. Make sure you've first taken full advantage of your Keogh plan and IRA. Municipal bonds are tax-exempt; you could wait 15 years or more to get the same returns from an annuity with comparable yields.

Don't necessarily buy the annuity that promises the highest interest. Many contractors dangle high rates before first-time buyers but cut the interest in later years. Before you buy any fixed-rate annuity, ask to see the rates the sponsor has paid over the past 10 years. You can compare the interest rates of the top 100 by reading the *Comparative Annuity Reports Newsletter,* P.O. Box 1268, Fair Oaks, California 95628 ( 916-487-7863; $10 a month or $80 a year).

Deal with only the most reliable insurers. Look for the ones rated highest by the rating services: Standard & Poor's, Moody's, A. M. Best and Duff & Phelps. Their publications are available in public libraries and sometimes at insurance agents' offices.

Look for a so-called bailout clause. This can help you if you want to withdraw your money because you think your renewal interest rate is too low. Most companies offer an option that lets you do so without paying an early-withdrawal penalty, provided the new rate is, say, one or two percentage points lower than the previous one. The bailout clause usually comes at the cost of an initial interest rate of one-half to one full percentage point below annuities that do not have it. If you bail out, you can transfer the money to another company and avoid paying taxes. But you're generally better off choosing a no-bailout annuity from a company that has paid consistently high rates.

*Variable annuities* offer you the chance to place your money in a range of stocks, bond and money-market investments — think of them as tax-sheltered mutual funds. They fluctuate along with the ups and downs of the stock or bond market. You can earn higher returns than with fixed annuities if you choose wisely. Unlike with fixed annuities, you get a crack at capital gains. Of course, you can also suffer capital losses.

There are other drawbacks. Your principal is not guaranteed. Fees and expenses are complex — and high. Added together, they average more than 2% a year, according to the *Morningstar Variable Annuity/Life Peformance Report.* Often these fees will offset any tax savings unless you hold your annuity and let its value grow for 15 years or more. Even then, the benefits may not be as great as the sales pitches and prospectus promise. These often make the assumption that you will be in a significantly

## SOME CAUTIONS ON VARIABLE ANNUITIES

Annuities can be worthwhile investments for retirement, but they're not for everyone. Before you put money into them, consider this advice:

STAY FOR THE LONG TERM.
**Don't buy a variable annuity unless you won't need to withdraw your money before age 59½. Otherwise, you might face stiff tax penalties. You'll also want to keep up the investment for at least 10 years, the usual time required for the benefits of an annuity to exceed expenses.**

CONTRIBUTE TO OTHER TAX SHELTERS.
**Don't buy until you have already put the maximum amount into your 401(k), IRA and other tax-advantaged plans. They may be more efficient shelters than annuities are.**

INVEST IN AGGRESSIVE FUNDS.
**Don't buy conservative money-market funds for your variable annuity; they will not give you rich enough yields to balance out costs. You're probably better off selecting more aggressive funds that have strong records of growth.**

BEWARE OF HIGH EXPENSES.
**Don't be drawn into an annuity that has excessively steep fees. The higher they are, the longer you must wait before you enjoy net gains.**

lower tax bracket when you retire. But many moderately affluent Americans will not, unless tax rates are lowered in the years ahead. Finally, few variable annuities match the performance of top stock mutual funds.

So shop with care. Look for ratings of variable annuities in consumer-finance magazines or go directly to the research services that compare them. Among these are the monthly Morningstar report mentioned above ( 800-876-5005; $195 if ordered monthly, $95 for a quarterly subscription and $45 for a single issue) and U.S. Annuities (98 Hoffman Road, Englishtown, New Jersey 07726; 800-872-6684), which provides free quotes by phone and publishes the quarterly *Annuity & Life Insurance Shopper* (single issue, $20 plus $4 shipping and handling; one-year subscription, $65).

## The Rewards of Real Estate

Real estate has been the source of more great fortunes than almost any other investment, but its future is clouded because of overbuilding and reductions in once-lavish tax benefits. The roof caved in on the market in the late 1980s and early 1990s; then it recovered in 1993 and 1994 — until the Federal Reserve aggressively pushed up interest rates and the market leveled off.

Despite such volatility, real estate in general remains a sound *long-term* investment. The key is to acquire property that offers value beyond tax benefits, because of location or other attributes. Invest in real estate for income and capital appreciation, but don't insist that every nickel you spend bring a deduction.

Investments in rental real estate are considered passive investments unless you are a real estate professional, working as, say, a broker or a real estate lawyer. You can no longer deduct passive losses from other income, such as your salary or earnings from stocks and bonds. You can use passive losses only to offset income from passive investments. Thus, if you own rental property, you will be allowed to deduct your mortgage interest, property taxes and expenses only up to the amount of your rental income plus any other passive income, such as income from limited partnerships. But if you have net losses above this amount, you can carry them forward to next year.

The key to success is patience, with an eye toward long-term gains and consistent annual income. This advice holds true whether the investment you are considering is part of an office building, a shopping center or an apartment house or even your own home. But novice investors should avoid buying entire parcels of commercial properties such as stores and office buildings. Managing them requires special expertise: for example, knowing how to handle business leases. Stick with residential properties; they are easier to handle.

If you are buying a house or condo now for your own use, don't count on making a profit if you are likely to move within three or four years. The increase you can expect in the value of your home probably will not offset the cost of borrowing and the real estate commissions you will have to pay when you sell. The increase in property values is expected to average 5% or so annually, though it will be much higher — or lower — in some regions and neighborhoods than in others.

If you are buying with a view to renting out, then particularly desirable investments are three-bedroom, two-bath houses. They are large enough for small families, which tend to be the most stable tenants. Demand for these structures is strong in many communities. That means they usually can pay you enough in rents to cover your mortgage and maintenance costs — and give you a nice profit. They are also relatively easy to sell if you need to cash in your investment in a hurry.

If you are a first-time investor, stick close to your own community. The market will be familiar, and the travel time will be less than if you buy a far-off building. By investing in your backyard, you are in a good position to anticipate what will happen to real estate prices. Wherever you buy, talk with other owners and visit many properties to get a feel for real estate values. Make sure the neighborhood is economically stable. There is no quicker way to lose your money than to buy a house on a block that is about to be engulfed by crime. Look for solid construction and sturdy appliances before you worry about charm.

If you do not have much time to spend on repairs, buy real estate that is in ready-to-rent condition. But if you do have hours to spare and are handy with a saw and paintbrush, look for structurally sound houses in less-than-sterling condition that can profit from a moderate amount of fixing up. One sensible rule is to buy the worst house on the best block. A property that can be pulled into rentable condition with a fresh coat of exterior paint could be an excellent investment. Bringing this home up to par with its neighbors by later adding a room or doing some landscaping can pay large dividends in rental profits. It also can produce a plump gain when the property is sold.

Another choice is to look for a deteriorating house in a turnaround neighborhood. You will stand your best chance of locating such a property by searching in a community that you know well.

Being a landlord is surely not for everyone. Many busy people simply do not have the time or temperament to cope with tenant complaints and broken boilers. For a lot less money, you could become a limited partner in a real estate syndication or a shareholder in a real estate investment trust, or REIT. But if you do want to own and manage property directly, your best investment today would be either the single-family house or, if you can afford it, a multi-unit apartment building.

Landlords can deduct from their real estate income not only mortgage interest and property taxes but also fire and liability insurance premiums, expenses for finding and screening tenants, commissions for collecting rents, the cost of traveling to and from the property and, best of all, depreciation. You depreciate residential real estate on a straight-line basis over 27½ years. Put simply, to calculate your annual deduction for depreciation, divide the cost of the property by 27½.

Investors who fix up old buildings can do well. But use caution. Such investments require rehabilitation skills and a sharp sense of timing. If you get into a deteriorating market before it is ready for turnaround, you will not get enough rent to pay for the upgrading.

You can get a federal tax credit for rehabilitation expenditures on buildings that were constructed before 1936. The credit is equal to 10% of your cost of renovation, subject to some limitations. To qualify for the tax benefits, you must sell or rent out the building for nonresidential commercial or industrial use, which does not include apartment rentals. The improvements must cost at least $5,000, or more than the so-called adjusted tax basis (often it's practically zero) for the building, whichever is greater. If the building is a federally certified historic structure or is located in a historic district, you get a tax credit for 20% of the renovation costs, again subject to limitations. In this case you can also take the credit for apartment buildings.

To find out whether a building qualifies, check with the U.S. Department of the Interior or your state's or city's historic-preservation office. And to learn what your tax credit might amount to, consult your tax adviser.

Once you decide to invest in rental property, you probably will be eager to buy something quickly and put your money to work. Resist the temptation. Many new real estate investors underestimate the complexity of the field and overestimate how much they know. Immerse yourself in a study of real estate as you would any new business venture. Talk with other investors and brokers; that will help you pinpoint the neighborhoods with the best potential. Seek out areas that have begun to gain favor among young householders as an alternative to more expensive established neighborhoods. Look for good transportation, shopping and schools and a strong, diversified employment base.

Then you can narrow your search to specific properties. Your best ally is likely to be a broker who is knowledgeable about your chosen area. Check his or her reputation with local bankers and attorneys. Discuss with the broker your debt limits and investment standards. Other obvious sources of sale properties are newspaper real estate sections, posted FOR SALE signs and auctions of buildings in arrears. Plan to inspect dozens of buildings before you make a bid.

If you find a property that approaches your standards, investigate it thoroughly. Unless you are versed in building construction and mechanics, take along a construction engineer whose judgment you trust. The $175 to $400 fee will be worth it. You can also use the engineer's report to negotiate a better deal.

Look for a modern furnace and a water heater that has a capacity of at least 40 gallons for each family. Ask when that water heater was purchased. Be alert for signs of trouble; stains on ceilings might mean plumbing or roof leaks and sagging floors could indicate structural defects. Your biggest worry will be the condition of the roof — replacement costs are high. Particularly with a large building, check the condition of the central air-conditioning plant and that of the asphalt parking lot, if there is one.

Before investing in a rental house or apartment building, always ask yourself, "Does it make financial sense for me? Can I really afford the initial cash outlay?" Rental units may cost about $100,000 — and, of course, many are much costlier. You will have to put 10% to 25% of that down — or $10,000 to $25,000. Legal fees, advance property taxes and mortgage surcharges will add another $3,000 to $5,000 on the medium-priced home. Make sure the property can pay you enough in rents to cover mortgage payments, taxes, utilities and maintenance costs. A property that does not is especially risky in low-inflation periods. You cannot count on its price to rise steeply enough to make up the losses.

When calculating the economics of a property, pay particular attention to your financing. Shop around among several banks and other lenders to get the largest possible mortgage at the lowest interest rate. Often the best source of financing is the seller. If the owner is eager to unload the property, he or she may offer terms that are far more attractive than those at the banks. Many real estate ads will mention the availability of owner financing.

If the price is more than you can afford, look into a type of cost splitting called a shared-equity financing agreement. With it, you will not buy the entire property for yourself, but you will share the ownership — and the cost — with the occupant.

## Learn How to Be a Landlord

Possible tax breaks and potential capital gains might well tempt you to consider becoming a landlord. But be warned: The migraines are multiple, and the investment is not the instant winner it once was. This is true whether the property you rent to outsiders is a vacation cottage, the home you have lived in or a multi-family apartment building.

Before you leap into landlording, be sure you can afford to tie up your money for as long as it will take for the investment to become profitable. The restrictions on deducting losses virtually require that the building you buy produce a positive cash flow — that is, its rents must exceed your maintenance and financing costs. If it does not do so immediately or at most within a year, the property will merely wring cash out of you. For this reason, when you are stalking the positive-cash-flow property, look for a tight rental market where the vacancy rate is 6% or less and rents can reasonably be increased.

Now consider the troubles of being a landlord. Do you really want to hunt for tenants? How do you feel about being roused out of bed by a midnight phone call telling you that a pipe has burst? Do you possess grace under pressure, and can you count on yourself to deal firmly but fairly with your tenants when the inevitable disagreements arise?

If so, take a couple of tips from experienced landlords. Use great caution in screening tenants. The hours you spend can save days of grief later. Check each applicant's references. Call his or her employer to confirm job tenure. Ask the applicant's present landlord if he or she would gladly continue renting to the applicant. You may want to run a credit check, and you would be wise to get a security deposit of two months' rent.

Once the tenant has moved in, inspect the premises often, looking for little problems that could cause big troubles in the future. Then fix them. If you do not want to be bothered by frequent minor repairs, you can offer the tenant a rent break to do his or her own maintenance. Your periodic checks will let you know whether the work is being done properly.

Of course, you can hire a management firm to take care of those chores. That will cost you 4% to 6% of the rent and could go as high as 20% if you have a single-family house. But you can deduct this fee on your tax return as part of your rental costs, so long as you're still involved in key active management decisions. This means that you, not the management company, must approve new tenants and decide on rental terms and capital or repair spending.

## Rent to Your Parents or Grown Children

If you have older parents, there is a superb way for you to help them and at the same time enjoy the tax benefits of being a landlord. You can buy a condo or house, lease it to your elderly parents and take deductions for maintenance, mortgage interest and depreciation — provided that your deductions are within the limits set by the tax laws. The IRS insists that you charge your kin a fair market rent. You can easily document that by asking a local real estate broker for a written estimate of what rent the property should command.

If your parents are age 55 or older, you may want to buy *their* house. That way, you both can get tax breaks. Your folks do not have to pay any federal income taxes on their profits from the sale — up to $125,000. And now that you own the house, you can deduct the property taxes, mortgage interest payments and depreciation from your rental income and perhaps as much as $25,000 of your net losses, if any, from your ordinary income.

Your same tax breaks apply when you buy a house in a college town and rent it out to your son or daughter, the student. Many parents are managing to make money on their children's college education by buying houses for them — and perhaps a few classmates — to live in. Again, be sure you charge a fair market rent to get a passing grade from the IRS. But if you hire your child as the building superintendent, you can give him or her a 10% rent rebate.

Buying a house in a college town can be an excellent investment, but it does present risks. Some students are too immature to be property managers, or may see their parents' real estate venture as an opportunity to shelter friends. These youngsters may be reluctant to collect rent from their pals. Besides, owning a house requires constant attention. The student landlord occasionally has to make a tough choice between mopping up a flooded basement and studying for an exam.

If you like the idea of buying a house or condo for your college-bound youngster, you may be wise to let your child spend freshman year getting used to his or her surroundings before you commit your money. If you then decide to buy, choose a larger, five-bedroom house over a smaller, two-bedroom one; the extra rental income is often worth the additional expense.

Some other tips:

- Avoid a rattletrap house that needs a lot of work — unless you are prepared to spend considerable money to fix it.
- Pick a property as close to the campus as possible. But if housing demand is really high, do not rule out anything up to five miles away.
- Think twice about buying in a small town that does not have many year-round residents. Remember, you have to find people who will be temporary tenants during the summer vacation.

## Buying — and Selling — Condominiums

Owning a condo — a dwelling unit in a group-owned building or on group-owned land — has all the advantages of investing in real estate, and then some. Most condos require less capital to buy and have fewer maintenance problems than single-family houses do.

You can start by buying a unit for your personal use. Condo owners who live in their own units can deduct mortgage interest and real estate taxes from their taxable income. People who rent out units to others can also deduct monthly maintenance and depreciation — up to the limits set by tax laws. About 15% of the condos in the U.S. are held as investments.

Some investors convert whole apartment houses into condos. Others participate indirectly in these deals, acting as limited partners who supply some of the capital but stay on the sidelines. Either way, you will be able to use any losses only to offset income from passive-activity investments.

If you are a tenant in a rental building that is being converted, you often will have to pay twice as much per square foot to buy your apartment as the converter did. Even so, that "insider's" price may be well below the market value of similar homes. Some tenants make a profit by immediately reselling. That's known as flipping. Tenants who buy and stay on commonly have to pay more per month in maintenance fees and mortgage expenses than their previous rent was, but much of that extra cost may be offset by tax deductions.

What do you do if you own a condo and want to sell in a slow market? Above all, don't panic. In mid-1995 the National Association of Realtors (NAR) reported that condo sales dropped 8 percent in the first quarter of 1995, but this was coming off a record year in 1994 — when sales of condos peaked at 437,000 units. According to the NAR, the national median price for existing units rose only slightly, from $84,900 in 1993 to $85,700 in 1994. If you're selling, you should not just sell your condo but market it. John Tuccillo, chief economist at the NAR, recommends focusing on the two primary buyers of condos, young first-timers looking for affordable starter units and people older than 65 who want housing that doesn't require a lot of maintenance. Put yourself in the buyer's shoes and figure out how to make your condo unique.

Besides waiting for the market to strengthen, another choice for a condo owner is to move and rent out the unit. You might consider offering a tenant a lease with an option to buy at a prearranged price in, say, 12 months. That way, if real estate values rise, the tenant will be delighted to buy your condo at what will then be a discount.

If you must sell now, list your condominium for 10% to 20% less than the price of a single-family house in a comparable location.

Historically, that's the difference needed to draw buyers to condos. Also, put some buzzwords in your newspaper classified ads. The words "overlooking pool" appeal to singles. Young couples might be lured by the opener "Can't Afford a House?" And phrases such as "carefree living" may attract empty-nester parents in their 50s or older.

Vacation homes also can be profitable investments, though they are bought primarily for recreation, relaxation and retirement. You have the best chance of getting a good price when you sell if your second home has two characteristics.

First, it has to be fairly easy to get to. The choicest turf is no more than a gas tank away from a big population area. If you can afford it, buy on or near the water. This is the surest bet for both high rentals and capital appreciation.

Second, the land surrounding the property should have only limited potential for development. That automatically holds down the supply of houses. Environmental laws that put a lid on construction have made waterfront properties especially attractive, though costly, investments. The state of New Jersey, for example, stopped a developer from filling in and building on some wetlands. In the three years after that ruling, prices of second-home plots in the area surged 300%.

Stay away from idiosyncratic vacation homes. The dwellings that hold their value best are those with exteriors that are in keeping with the area. And look for communities that have stable growth, strong zoning and a distaste for go-go construction projects.

If you are considering a development that is under construction, ask the developer and the real estate agent about the timetable for installing recreational facilities, community water supplies and sewage disposal. Get guarantees in writing. Check with the local real estate commission or with an office of the federal Department of Housing and Urban Development to see if the developer has registered for interstate land sales and has posted a substantial bond to pay for anything he or she inadvertently omits.

When you have located a property that interests you, bargain vigorously. Bid at least 20% less than the asking price — especially in areas where the market is sluggish. Timing is critical in both the purchase and sale of vacation real estate. Because it is a discretionary purchase, prices fluctuate more widely in economic booms and busts than the prices of other houses do. Lately, buyers with cash in hand have been finding tremendous bargains in some overbuilt areas.

Finding a mortgage should not be a problem. Both the Federal Home Loan Mortgage Corporation (Freddie Mac) and the Federal National Mortgage Association (Fannie Mae) now buy vacation-home mortgages held by banks. That helps make credit readily available. Also, many sellers will take back the mortgages themselves. This means they, in effect, agree to receive payment for the house over a period of 10 years or so.

But it is important to shop around for financing. Many banks demand not only a 0.5% premium for vacation home loans but also 20% down, plus points and fees that can amount to at least 3.5% of the total mortgage. Check with a local real estate agent or title company to find which banks grant the best vacation-home mortgages.

One way to beat the cost of second houses is to divide the ownership — and expenses — with several families. For example, four couples share a $100,000 ski condominium in Keystone, Colorado. Each couple arranged their own financing and borrowed from private sources, since banks do not give mortgages on a quarter of a house. Under a legal agreement, if one couple wants out, the others get first crack at buying their share.

To help pay for the mortgage, taxes and upkeep, more and more owners are renting out their second homes. Before renting your property to others, check with your mortgage lender. Some lenders define properties that are rented as "investor properties," and the terms of loans on them may be different from those for properties that are not rented. Local real estate agents find tenants and keep an eye on the property once it is rented. The agents' fees range from 10% to 20% of the rent. For higher fees, managers of some resort communities not only find tenants but also collect the rent and take care of repairs.

Like owners of any house, you can deduct the mortgage interest and property taxes on your vacation home, so long as the IRS deems it a second home. If you do not use it for more than 14 days a year, the house may qualify as rental real estate. Then you must meet the requirements of any rental real estate owner in order to deduct up to the maximum $25,000 allowed beyond the amount of any passive income you may have.

# REITs and Limited Partnerships

So you're not Donald Trump or Al Taubman. Few small investors can afford to spring for a towering office building, a large apartment house or a crowded shopping center. Yet you can fairly easily get in on these potentially lucrative investments. Just buy shares in a REIT — a real estate investment trust. They have become increasingly popular with the recovery of real estate in the past couple of years. If you buy, ideally you should diversify with a half-dozen or more REITs; and they should account for no more than 10% or 15% of your investments.

A REIT operates somewhat like a closed-end mutual fund that invests in a diversified portfolio of real estate or mortgages instead of in stocks and bonds. The properties may include apartment buildings, shopping centers and malls, office structures, industrial parks, hotels, hospitals, warehouses and even mobile-home parks. Shares of REITs are traded on the New York or American stock exchanges or the NASDAQ just like

**A SAMPLER OF REITs**

| Name | Price* | 52-week range | Dividend yield | Description |
|---|---|---|---|---|
| **Equity Residential Properties** | **$29.38** | **$24.88–33.50** | **7.2%** | Owns and operates more than 100 apartment properties in 29 states |
| **Kranzco Realty Trust** | **18.13** | **16.63–21.63** | **10.6** | Owns and operates neighborhood and community shopping centers in the mid-Atlantic states |
| **National Golf Properties** | **21.50** | **17.00–22.50** | **7.3** | Owns nearly 70 golf courses across the country |
| **Oasis Residential** | **22.13** | **18.75–25.63** | **7.4** | Develops and operates apartment complexes in greater Las Vegas metro area |
| **Post Properties** | **30.63** | **28.25–32.88** | **6.4** | Develops and operates upscale apartment complexes in Southeastern states |
| **Spieker Properties** | **22.50** | **19.13–22.88** | **7.5** | Develops and operates industrial, office and some retail properties in California and the Northwest |
| **Tanger Factory Outlet Centers** | **26.75** | **20.25–28.88** | **7.5** | Develops and operates factory outlet centers across the country |

*8/10/95 close
SOURCE: *FORTUNE*

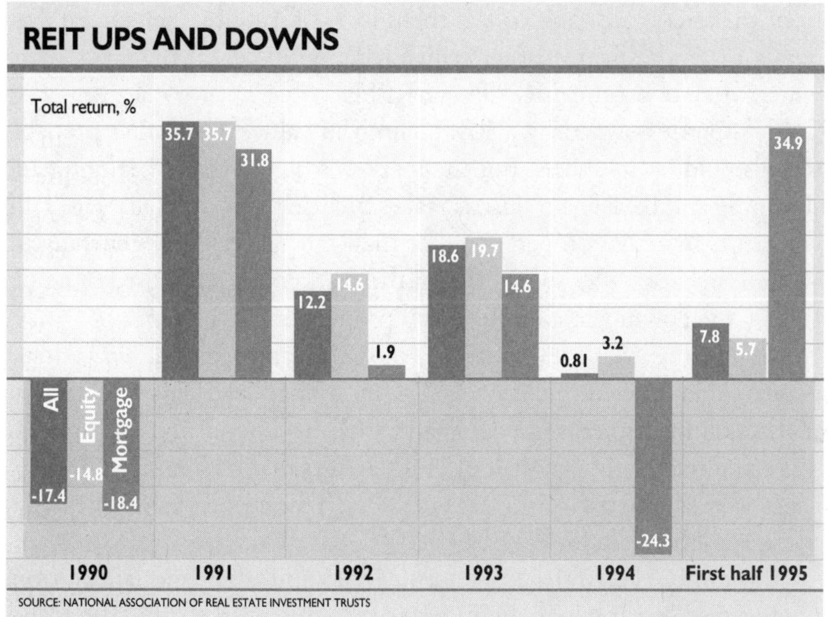


those of closed-end funds or common stocks. So you can sell your shares in the open market. REITs thus offer the advantage of being a liquid form of investment in real estate, which is usually an illiquid asset. They can also be an inflation hedge because owners can raise rents when prices in general rise.

You can buy REIT shares from stockbrokers and financial planners, commonly for $15 to $30, with no minimum purchase required. You then collect the income that the trust earns from rent and other sources. The more than 230 REITs in the U.S. are required by law to distribute at least 95% of their taxable income as dividends to shareholders. Because they pay out so much of their earnings, they pay no corporate income tax; most states do not require them to pay state income tax — meaning that their earnings, unlike those of companies that issue stock, are not taxed before they are distributed. Thus, investors get a bigger share of the profits than they do with stock.

REITs typically generate dividends of 6% to 9%. When you collect those dividends, you also may be able to defer paying taxes on a portion of them. As much as half of a REIT's cash distributions may be sheltered.

When the trust sells off the properties it owns, you also get the profits from the sale, if any. You collect them in the form of either special dividends or, if the proceeds are reinvested, increased earnings per share, which often boost the price of your REIT.

If properties owned by a REIT climb in value, the market probably will also bid up its shares. But the market is highly volatile, surging and slumping and back again, just as real estate itself rises and falls. REIT investments in actual property (rather than mortgages) have generally increased; in early 1995 some 90% of the market was composed of equity REITs, each owning about 30 to 100 properties.

Despite a year-end slump, plenty of REITs prospered in 1993, largely because they offered higher yields — an average 18.55% — than other traditional investments like CDs and stock and bond mutual funds. In 1994 and during the first half of 1995, REITs that had invested in mortgages were clobbered as interest rates rose. This cut the value of existing mortgages that paid lower rates.

The most successful REITs are regional and often specialize in one type of property, such as shopping centers or apartment buildings. Example: In the Southwest demand for apartments is fairly brisk, occupancy rates are high and rents are rising by 8% to 10% annually.

Some of the best REIT companies thrive on buying rundown properties and revitalizing them, says Kenneth Gregory, president of Litman/Gregory & Co., San Francisco investment managers. He cites as an example New Plan Realty Trust, which buys poorly managed strip shopping centers in small mid-Atlantic cities with no competing malls. It fixes them up, improves the mix of tenants and finds ways to attract shoppers. Many analysts also recommend health-care REITs: They are recession-resistant and are expected to benefit from the aging population.

In picking REITS, as in selecting mutual funds, caution is especially important today because they have grown so popular. As always, when demand calls forth new supplies of a financial product, quality is likely to suffer. Don't be snowed by current dividend yield or cash flow, since these numbers can easily be manipulated.

The value of the underlying properties is a surer indicator — one argument for investing in local REITs, since you can better judge those values. Most important, hitch yourself to skilled managers with long records of success. Prospectuses of REITs aren't perfect sources of information, but they are sufficiently revealing so that you should read them before investing. Or make sure that your broker has studied the prospectuses.

If you want to be safe, let professionals do the picking. Three no-load funds specialize in REITs and other real estate stocks:

- Fidelity Real Estate Investment Portfolio (800-544-8888) was yielding 3.37% in mid-1995.
- United Service Real Estate Fund (800-873-8637) was yielding 3.12%.
- Evergreen U.S. Real Estate Fund (800-235-0064) was yielding 3.40%.

For more information, you can get the *REIT Basics* book from the National Association of Real Estate Investment Trusts, 1129 20th Street, NW, Suite 305, Washington, D.C. 20036 (202-785-8717). The cost is $25.

## Buying into Second Mortgages

Almost everybody complains whenever mortgage rates climb to daunting levels, but rising rates are a cause for rejoicing for one kind of person: the sophisticated investor willing to take the risk of putting his or her cash into second mortgages. If you are prospecting for high returns, these investments may be for you.

Second mortgages are loans made to homebuyers whose down payments and primary mortgages still don't add up to the appraised value. Anyone with a fairly large sum to invest can grant such second-mortgage loans and earn an annual return of 10% or more. With most second mortgages, the borrower makes monthly payments only on the interest. The investor — that is, the lender — gets his or her principal back in a lump sum when the loan expires, typically in three years. The interest rate is negotiated by the lender and borrower. As a rule, it is about two percentage points above the rate local banks charge on first mortgages.

One alternative to the second-mortgage formula is a shared-equity financing. Here an investor puts up part of the down payment on the house. Technically, this is not a loan; the investor becomes a co-owner.

Say that you want to invest in a second mortgage or a shared-equity deal. You can get leads to people who need such financing by asking builders, real estate agents or mortgage loan brokers. Beware, however, of shady brokers luring investors with promises of suspiciously high returns of 18% to 24%. In New Mexico two mortgage brokers were sentenced to prison for, among other things, failing to tell investors that one-third of their borrowers defaulted.

With either a second mortgage or a shared-equity investment, it is easier to get in than to get out. If the investor in a second mortgage needs his or her money before the term of the loan is up, he or she can sell the note. But if interest rates are higher than at the time the loan was made, he or she will have to sell it at a discount. So be prepared to keep your money locked up for the length of the loan.

## Make Tax-Free Swaps

When the day comes that you want to sell out for a profit, you may get a better deal if you swap for another piece of property. That way, you delay paying any taxes on your capital gains; you do not pay until you ultimately make a sale. This rule applies to all kinds of real property, so long as you use it as an investment. It could be a house or a condo, a plot on which you plan to build or even barren land that you are holding for possible future development.

Say that you live in Colorado but own 100 acres of idle farmland way off in Georgia. Because you bought it many years ago, when prices were cheap, you would face a big profit — and large capital-gains taxes — if you sell it. But you can avoid that if you find someone with whom to make a tax-free exchange for other property, maybe closer to home in Colorado.

The properties you exchange do not have to be identical or even of the same value. You can swap farmland for an apartment building or a condo. But you will be taxed on any additional cash you receive at the time of the deal. And the swap has to be almost simultaneous. You have to receive your new property no later than 45 days after you transfer ownership of your old property.

How do you find another property owner to swap with? Just write to your state Board of Realtors for a list of brokers who are certified commercial investment members. Certification means the brokers have received special training in real estate transactions and passed state exams. Be certain to seek the help of a tax attorney who is knowledgeable about real estate to ensure that your swap contract meets all the requirements of a tax-free exchange.

# The False Promise of Precious Metals

### Gold

Led by gold, precious metals have a historic role as security against inflation, economic collapse and civil disorder. But gold in particular has lost much of its gleam in recent years. Though its price rose 5.7% in 1994, it is hard to think of an investment that has performed worse in the last 15 years than gold.

How does it fail us? Let us count the ways.

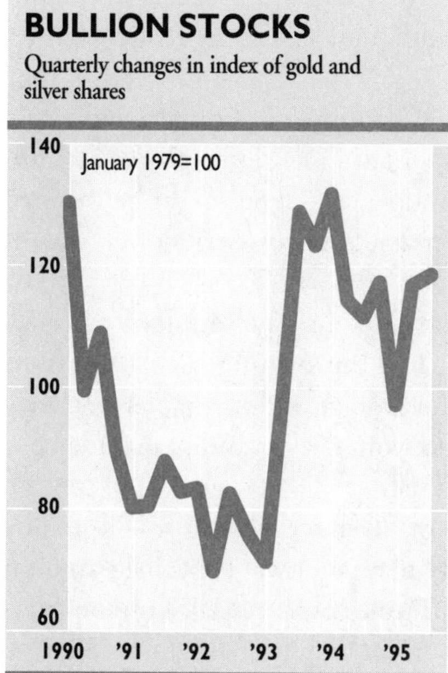


First, gold pays no dividends. That may seem trifling when its price is streaking ahead, but over many decades it matters a lot. Since 1926 dividends have accounted for almost one-half of the return from owning stocks.

Second, gold cannot compound investors' gains, as can a company when it retains earnings and uses that fuel to grow.

Third, gold has lost much of its allure as a safe-haven investment. It spiked and then declined after the stock market crash of 1987 and the junk bond collapse of 1990. Just after Iraq invaded Kuwait, the metal didn't even maintain a 10% price increase.

While some advisers say that an all-out war might have sent more investors scurrying for bars of bullion, others feel that different, higher-yielding and secure investments — such as U.S. Treasury securities — have become much more appealing.

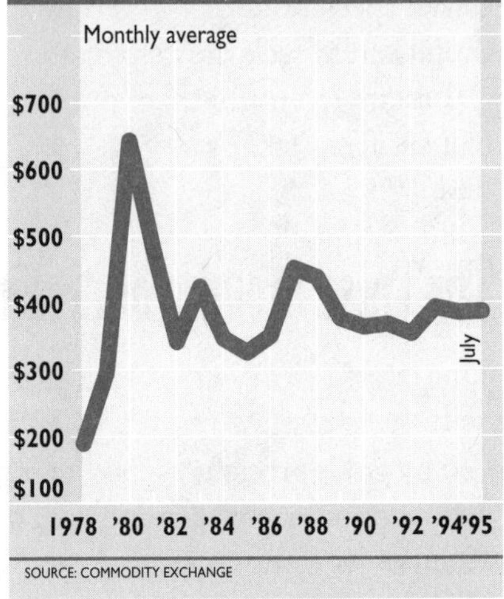


Even gold buyers who want to hedge against inflation may get less than they bargain for. Though an ounce of gold today has the same purchasing power as it did hundreds of years ago, its shorter-term record as protection against inflation is poor. Since 1980 inflation has reduced the purchasing power of a dollar by over 50%. Not only has gold failed to offset that loss, but its price during that period has actually fallen by more than half. It tumbled from a high of $850 an ounce in January 1980 to a low of $304 in February 1985. Silver has done even worse since 1980, although it, like gold, lately has recovered somewhat.

Still, if you believe that double-digit inflation, oil droughts and world monetary crises will strike yet again — not to mention a plague or a nuclear attack by a desperate Third World force — you might be inclined to invest in precious metals. You then would have a series of choices of what and how to buy.

Hard-core pessimists who have no faith in any country's currency would prefer gold bars. Ingot they trust. But owning such hard assets can be a nuisance. You have to pay for storage and insurance; you may also have to transport the metal to and from dealers and perhaps lay out more money for assay costs when you sell.

A simpler way to invest in gold — or silver and platinum — is to buy certificates of ownership. They signify that you own a specified amount of the metal stored in vaults. When the time comes to sell, a phone call is all that is necessary. Your minimum initial purchase might be $2,500.

After that, you make investments of as little as $100. Commissions range from 1% to roughly 3% when you buy, depending on the quantity, and 1% to 2% when you sell. You also pay an annual storage charge based on weight. Choose your dealer carefully: Some metals certificate programs have been exposed as scams.

Instead of certificates, many people prefer to buy one-ounce gold coins, such as South African Krugerrands, Canadian Maple Leafs, Chinese Pandas and American Eagles, which the U.S. Mint introduced in 1986. Though you pay 3% to 6% more than their gold content is worth, and sales tax on top of that, coins are easier to resell than gold certificates or bars. The easy portability and worldwide acceptance of coins appeal to the so-called refugee mentality. Again, bear in mind that neither coins nor bars nor certificates pay any dividends.

Shares of high-quality South African mining companies do offer high dividends and a chance at capital appreciation. The free elections of 1994, producing a multiracial government under President Nelson Mandela, have removed considerable risk from South African stocks. But mining stocks of all nationalities are typically more volatile than bullion. That's because mining profits balloon once the price of the metal moves above the cost of extracting and refining it. A price rise of a few percentage points can double the earnings of a mining company. The other side of the coin is that when gold prices decline, shares also drop more sharply than the metal itself.

This volatility partially carries over to the dividends that the companies pay. In mid-1995, when gold was selling for $384 an ounce, the dividends were roughly 5% to 10%. Were the price to rise to $450 an ounce, dividends would likely be 8% to 16%.

To minimize the risks of gold stocks, diversify. For example, you can balance South African mining shares with North American ones such as Placer Dome and Newmont Mining.

You can buy diversification for a small price by investing in gold mutual funds that acquire shares of gold-mining companies. But these funds are as unstable as nitroglycerin. They soared in the early 1980s, then slumped, recovered strongly and took a dive in the crash of 1987. They led other fund groups in gains for a brief period in 1989, only to slip again in 1990 and 1992.

During 1993 the price of gold rose 14%, to $383 an ounce, and gold funds were again big winners. Of the 10 best-performing funds, eight were gold funds, each gaining at least 93.36%. But even friends of gold were muting their pitches. Analysts considered the rally minor-league and risky because there was no widespread fear of inflation — a traditional catalyst for higher gold prices.

For the five years ended December 31, 1994, Lipper Analytical Services has identified the top four gold mutual funds:

- Fidelity Select Precious Metals (5.55% annualized return; 800-544-7558)
- Excel Midas Gold Shares (4.86%; 800-783-3444)
- Vanguard Specialized Portfolio-Gold and Precious Metals (4.27%; 800-851-4999)
- Keystone Precious Metals (3.82%; 800-633-4900)

The disparity in performance between these and the -0.17% average annualized return of gold funds indicates the risk in gold investment.

Whether you choose to buy gold stocks or funds or the metal itself, your total purchase should be only a relatively modest share — perhaps 5% — of a well-diversified investment portfolio.

### Platinum

When people think of investing in precious metals, platinum rarely comes to mind, although it is rarer than gold and has more industrial uses. Platinum's price rose from $350 an ounce in mid-1993 to $435 in mid-1995.

Platinum is used in catalytic converters, which reduce harmful emissions from cars and truck exhausts. Those devices should get a double lift — from increased sales of cars and from rising pressure by environmentalists; platinum's role as an anti-pollutant will expand as emission-control standards tighten around the world. In April 1995 the New Jersey–based Engelhard Corporation announced a deal with Ford to develop clean-air-catalyst systems using platinum as the primary component. The cars with the new systems are expected in 1998 and could double the amount of platinum in the U.S. market if all goes well.

Catalytic converters and jewelry jointly and equally account for 75% of all platinum sales. Of the jewelry, 85% to 95% is sold in Japan; some studies show that nearly every woman there owns at least one piece of platinum jewelry. The Japanese give platinum coins as graduation and birthday gifts, further buttressing demand.

As with gold, a rise in the metal's price leads to outsized gains in the price of the mining companies' stocks — and outsized losses when the metal's price declines. Two South African companies, Rustenburg Platinum Holdings and Impala Platinum Holdings, produce close to 60% of the world's supply, and their American Depository Receipts, or ADRs, are sold over the counter in the U.S.

Investors often choose to buy platinum futures, which bet on tomorrow's price trends. But futures are extremely risky; you can lose many times your stake if the market goes against you. It is much safer to buy the metal outright. The least expensive way is to buy one-ounce or 10-ounce bars from refiners such as Johnson Matthey of London. You can also get them from brokerage houses, bullion dealers and some banks.

One-ounce platinum coins sell for 3% to 8% over market value for the metal itself, because of both fabrication and distribution costs. In mid-1995 the limited-edition Australian Koala, which carries a different depiction of a koala bear every year, sold for 4% above market value, or $452; the Canadian Maple Leaf sold for 4.5% above market, or $454.

## Commodities: Playing the Riskiest Game

For those who yearn for the fastest, toughest, highest-risk financial game of all, there are commodities. As many as 90% of all amateur traders lose money and drop out within a year, and the only consistent winners are the brokers who charge you commissions. Still, if you crave excitement and have a gut of copper, commodities can offer impressive gains for that tiny portion of your investable funds that you are willing to put completely at risk — your mad money. But unless you are an expert, and have pockets as deep as an oil well, never put more than a nickel or dime out of every investment dollar into commodities.

The reason that commodities futures trading offers both exceptional losses and exceptional gains is leverage. You buy commodities contracts on margin. They give you the right to buy a specified commodity at a set price for a limited time.

Let's say the price of gold is $400 an ounce, and you think it will rise in the next six months. Then you can invest in a contract to buy 100 ounces of gold at $400 an ounce. That's $40,000 worth of gold. But speculating in gold futures requires you to put up less than 10% of the price of the metal. If gold goes up to, say, $450 an ounce by the time your contract expires six months from now, you win. On an investment of less than $4,000, your profit will be $50 an ounce, or $5,000 — minus commissions. That means your gross profit would be 125% or, on an annualized basis, 250%.

But if prices move strongly against you, your broker will demand that you put up still more money. Unless you produce the cash immediately, the broker will sell out your position, at a potentially bone-chilling loss. To avoid that, give your broker a stop-loss order on each futures contract. That way, you establish in advance a price at which you will automatically sell rather than take further losses. As in the case of stocks, however, the stop-loss order doesn't guarantee you will get the price that you set. The price of the stock — or the commodity — could change from the time it hits the stop-loss level to when your broker executes the sale.

It cannot be stressed too much that the commodities market is a casino. Small investors who speculate there make two major mistakes. Many of them operate on tips; they are often wrong, and the amateurs cannot hope to match the professional traders in access to updated, accurate information about markets. Small investors also tend to be undercapitalized. To stay in this game, you should have $5 in reserve, ready to commit, for every $1 you put up. You might also read one of the dozens of market newsletters on the subject. The weekly *Commodity Traders' Consumer Report* (1731 Howe Avenue, Suite 149, Sacramento, California 95825; 800-999-2827) tracks 26 commodity advisory services and provides helpful articles, interviews and trading tips. A subscription costs $198 a year.

You can make do with less money by buying mini-contracts on the MidAmerica Commodity Exchange in Chicago. Mini-contracts control smaller quantities of commodities than do regular futures, but they are just as volatile as full-size contracts, and you will still get margin calls. But because you put up proportionately less money, you have less to lose.

A reasonable way for some sophisticated small investors to get into the market is to invest in one of the 180 or so publicly traded commodity futures funds. They are professionally managed and diversify your investment among many types of commodities. More important, any losses are limited to the amount of money you put up; you are never subject to a margin call. But before you invest, you should know that average annual costs eat up 20% of the fund's equity. Also, you should make sure that the fund's trading advisers have proved that they can make money. Ask to see their records.

You can follow commodity funds in the *Managed Account Reports* monthly newsletter (220 Fifth Avenue, 19th Floor, New York, New York 10001; 800-638-2525). A subscription costs $345 a year.

There are also futures contracts for people who don't know beans about soybeans. Welcome to the fast and furious market for financial futures.

Financial futures include contracts in Treasury bills, bonds and notes, bank certificates of deposit and a variety of other interest-bearing securities. When you buy one of these contracts, you are betting that, for example, interest rates will go down in the future and thus the prices of the bills, bonds or notes covered by the contract will go up.

You can buy financial futures through commodity firms and brokers who specialize in commodities at large stock brokerage houses. But take a tip from the experts and do your trading on paper for a while, until you get your sea legs. If and when you are ready to start dealing for real, then pick active markets, such as those trading in Treasury bill and Treasury bond futures. The more trading that is going on, the more likely you are to find a buyer or a seller for your contract at the price you want. Again, don't forget to place stop orders with your broker. They instruct him or her to close out your position when the price reaches a certain level — and they can help you limit any losses.

Any way you play it, futures trading is a highly leveraged business. This kind of investment is not for people who aren't prepared to take substantial risks.

## Investing in Collectibles

Collectibles can and do appreciate, some greatly. But many more lose value over time or go nowhere. You will do best if you follow this simple rule: Acquire them because you can get joy from owning them, admiring them and showing them off. Then, because you have made a passion of them, you will become expert in their value and prospects.

Two general sources to help you get started are *Kovel's Know Your Collectibles* by Ralph and Terry Kovel (Crown Trade Paperbacks, $16), a comprehensive, illustrated guide to young antiques — collectibles less than 100 years old — which covers a wide range of collectibles, including furniture, ceramics, glass, jewelry, lamps and clocks, and *Lyle's What It's Worth* by Anthony Curtis (Perigee Books, $14.95), a sourcebook that helps novice collectors identify and assess the value of antiques and collectibles.

### Art

It requires artistry to invest intelligently in paintings, sculpture, photographs and prints. The key is to avoid fads and have patience. Even when you buy with extreme sensitivity — and with the close advice of a reliable dealer — you may not be able to sell for a profit for five years or more, unless you are able to afford one of the few sought-after masterpieces.

But this is a good time for newcomers to the art market, whether you want to collect for the sheer joy of it, or with an eye to future gain. The reason: Prices have been lower in the 1990s than in the previous decade. With the economy still shaky in a number of countries, fewer people are willing to spend top dollar on what could be considered frivolous items.

Three fields are particularly promising and reasonably inexpensive for beginning collectors: prints, photographs and contemporary paintings and sculpture by little-known contemporary artists. Some of them may become tomorrow's stars. Fine pieces may be had for as little as a few hundred dollars.

Buyers on limited budgets no longer have to settle for obscure artists. For example, you can acquire some of the 4,000-plus lithographs by 19th-century French social satirist Honoré Daumier for less than $100 each. Christie's Kathleen Guzman notes that you can find prints by a contemporary superstar such as Robert Rauschenberg for as little as $5,000, and photographs by a giant like Ansel Adams for $3,000 to $5,000. A caveat: Insist on top condition. A Rauschenberg in less-than-perfect shape won't increase in value.

A factor that has nothing to do with an image's beauty can lift the price of a print or photograph. People regularly pay 100% more for a work that bears the artist's signature. Only two of the 10 Andy Warhol works offered at Sotheby's 1993 spring auctions were sold; dealers said the pieces were doomed because, among other reasons, the works weren't signed. For less affluent collectors, the absence of a signature is a small price to pay for the opportunity to acquire a superb print for a pittance.

- Among the most reputable sources of prints are major auction houses and the galleries that belong to the Art Dealers Association of America. For their names and addresses, write to the Art Dealers Association at 575 Madison Avenue, New York, New York 10022 (212-940-8590).
- To find the best sources of photographs, write to the Association of International Photography Art Dealers (AIPAD), 1609 Connecticut Avenue NW, Suite 200, Washington, D.C. 20009 (202-986-0105). You can order its $5 booklet, *On Collecting Photographs,* or, for $25, its illustrated catalogue and membership directory.

In assembling a collection of contemporary paintings and sculpture, sometimes it is fun to try to discover new talent on your own. But the safest path for the neophyte is to develop long-term relationships with professional dealers who are closely associated with emerging artists. These dealers can offer much expertise and advice. When selecting a dealer, AIPAD suggests you consider the number of years he or she has been in business, his or her reputation among other gallery owners and collectors, and the dealer's sensitivity to specific collecting needs and tastes.

The major galleries and auction houses are concentrated in New York City, still the undisputed capital of the U.S. art trade. If you cannot make fairly regular trips to Manhattan, seek out local dealers as your agents to establish relationships with other dealers. The place not to buy works by lesser-known contemporary painters and sculptors is at an auction. Auction houses rarely offer such works anyway, because they sell poorly there.

But auction houses are often excellent sources of prints and photographs. First, go to dealers to see what the prices are. Then, if something you want comes up at an auction, you may be able to bid for a better price.

When you are ready to buy, deal only with galleries and auction houses whose directors and employees have well-established reputations for honesty. Make sure they're willing to disclose all the facts about the art they sell. No reputable dealer should object to your consulting other experts before you make a purchase. You can also consult *Mayer International Art Auction Records;* the 1995 edition costs $175 and is also available on CD-ROM for $1,500.

Another source is the *Art Sales Index,* which sells for $179 and, depending on the year, lists 80,000 to 120,000 auction results. Both sources date back to the sixties. *Fine Art: Identification and Price Guide* by Susan Theran (Avon Books, $20) is still another comprehensive reference and price guide to every piece of original art sold at U.S. auction houses within the past five years. These references will be of use in helping you determine what a piece of art should be selling for. Remember, too, that buying art is like seeking out the best doctor for an operation: Feel free to get a second, even a third, opinion.

When buying from a dealer, it's customary to negotiate the prices. Many dealers routinely add 10% to their asking prices for bargaining purposes. But don't badger a dealer who insists that his or her price is firm. Other factors may affect the price as well. If the market is going through a soft phase, or if the dealer got a terrific deal on the piece of art, he or she may be interested in a quick sale that will be advantageous to you as well. Many dealers will let you make a minimum down payment and take the print or painting, and then bill you quarterly during an agreed-upon period of time, usually a year, interest-free. Others will keep the painting until it's paid off. A lot depends on how well you know the dealer.

Even if you are buying art on a low budget, there are some so-called bargains you will want to avoid. Stay away from World War I and World War II posters that are more interesting as historical curiosities than as art. Also avoid any contemporary prints that were produced in huge numbers and photos that are neither rare nor of high quality. And remember: Nothing is a good buy unless you really want it and have a passion for it.

## Folk Art

Not even the experts agree on what domestic folk art is, and nobody can say for sure what it is worth. Generally, as writer Gus Hedberg has observed, American folk art can include any tangible rudiment of daily life in the 18th, 19th and 20th centuries that has been enhanced by a touch of art — everything from a gravestone to an old rag doll. Some 19th-century weather vanes can cost more than the average meteorologist earns in a year, and some patchwork quilts are so rare and valued that nobody would dream of sleeping under one. And there are folk art paintings, portraits and landscapes by talented individuals who, in many cases, lacked formal training.

You can find plenty of investment-grade American folk art for under $1,000 — and even more that is just fun to own for much less. Above all, the best folk art buy is something that delights you aesthetically and personally. It should figure as a wise investment only secondarily. A reliable guide to the shops, auctions and regions where a fledgling collector might begin looking is the monthly *Maine Antique Digest* (P.O. Box 1429, Waldoboro, Maine 04572-1429; $29 a year). You might check *Antiques and the Arts Weekly,* also known as the *Newtown Bee,* for the newspaper it once was part of (5 Church Hill Road, Newtown, Connecticut 06470; $45 for a 52-week subscription).

If you want to buy folk art, concentrate on a particular category. That will help you to establish a sense of confidence and expertise. Some guidelines when shopping:

- *Quilts.* Among the most enduring investments are quilts, partly because international demand for them has been growing. Look for a visually appealing quilt with small, disciplined stitches and unusual features, even a one-of-a-kind pattern. Top-quality old examples range all the way from $1,000 to $20,000, and the exceptionally beautiful and rare ones have gone at auction for $100,000 and more. But for less than $500, you also can get handsome contemporary quilts that you can actually sleep under without depreciating your investment.
- *Baskets.* When buying a basket, check the bottom to see if it is still strong. But if the rest of the basket looks well-worn, yet

the bottom has hardly been scuffed, that's a sure sign of a forgery. The best investments in baskets are those with unusual forms or with hand-painted decorations. It's hard to find one in sound condition for less than $150. To get bargains, avoid shops with expensive business cards, and head for stores and auctions in the back hills. There you sometimes can come across an oak splint basket from the late 19th century for as little as $75.

- *Weather vanes.* With a weather vane, older is better. If wood, it should be dulled and weathered; if gold leaf, it should have lost much of its gilt; if copper, it should be green. A vane with a beautifully aged patina is worth considerably more than one that has been repainted.
- *Paintings.* Be wary of heavy restoration. And an anonymous folk painting may be just as valuable as one by a recognized artist.
- *Furniture.* Rely on the eye of an experienced dealer to avoid counterfeits. Once you get home with your piece of furniture, stifle any ambitions that may arise in you to fix it up. One woman bought an 18th-century painted chest a few years ago for $25,000, then proceeded to refinish the piece. As a result, it's now worth no more than a few hundred dollars.

## Plates, Books and Medallions

Advertisements breathlessly proclaim that limited editions of porcelain plates, books, medallions and china dolls offer terrific investment opportunities. In fact, companies that make and sell these purportedly limited editions of collectibles tend to exaggerate their investment value. Still, a careful collector can come out ahead. If you are tempted to buy, you would be wise to follow four rules:

- Buy only what you love. If it takes 20 years to sell your four Finnish Christmas plates, at least you will enjoy looking at them in your china cabinet.
- Make sure that a manufacturer announces how many items constitute an edition before it begins taking orders. Avoid companies that will sell to anyone who orders within a fixed

period, usually six months or a year. That means everybody who wants the item will get it, thereby killing the potential for a resale market.

- Buy the finest material and craftsmanship that you can afford.
- Keep your collectibles in mint condition. You can't dine off collector's plates or let your children play with limited-edition porcelain dolls. If you eventually try to sell them, such factors as how clean they are or whether or not you can provide the original box they came in can make all the difference.

Each type of limited edition has its own characteristics and peculiarities. For example:

*Plates.* Over seven million Americans — more than for any other limited-edition item — collect plates made of porcelain, pewter, crystal and even silver. About 150 manufacturers, including Royal Doulton and Rosenthal, bring out some 500 new issues a year. Single plates range from $25 to $100, though some go for as much as $5,000. But if you ever try to sell, you may not get what you paid. Only about 30% of the bids ever find buyers.

The most publicized place to buy and sell plates is the Bradford Exchange at 9333 Milwaukee Avenue, Niles, Illinois 60714 (800-323-8078). Sellers phone in their asking prices and buyers call in bids. If a trade is made, sellers pay a 28.5% commission, and buyers pay a minimum of $4 if the plate is under $100, 4% over $100. All transactions are guaranteed by the Exchange. Should either party back out, either the buyer will get a mint-condition plate or the seller will get the cash agreed upon.

*Books.* With a complete set of Audubon's *Birds of America* bringing a record $4.07 million at Christie's in 1992, investors are learning the value of a good book. You don't have to pay seven-figure prices to get pleasure from buying books and profit from selling them a few years later. But be careful. Buy only top-quality volumes with handmade paper, hand-set type and illustrations commissioned for the book.

Bibliophiles scorn many mass-produced reprints of classics. Though they claim to be limited editions, thousands of such books are printed, and their quality is often mediocre. But serious collectors admire and have bid up the prices of volumes published by some quality limited-edition presses. Among them is the Limited Editions Club (980 Madison

Avenue, New York, New York 10021; 212-737-7600). For example, its edition of Joyce's *Ulysses* sold for $10 in 1935; recently it brought $2,200 at auction! In the early 1960s, a first edition of *Catcher in the Rye* was selling for $15 to $20. Today, a good-quality first edition brings $2,500. In all, a few hundred small presses irregularly publish well-crafted books in editions of fewer than 500 volumes.

A good reference on book collecting is *Book Collecting: A Comprehensive Guide* by Allen and Patricia Ahearn (Putnam, $35), which presents guidelines for finding and recognizing first and limited editions, and gives market values for first printings of first edition books for 5,000 authors.

*Medallions and commemorative coins.* Beware of buying gold and silver medallions that are minted not by governments but by private companies. Interest in these novelties peaked in the 1970s, when private mints rushed to capitalize on gold fever. Even in the best of times, such ceremonial wampum has been hard to resell. For example, one 12-medallion sterling set honoring the poet Robert Frost was issued in 1974 for $275; today, coin dealers will pay only about $55 for it.

Perhaps 10% of the medallions can be resold at more than the intrinsic value of the gold or silver in the piece or set. With very few exceptions, those issued by private companies in so-called limited editions are actually mass-marketed and thus are worthless as either investments or collectors' items. Unless you are an expert at evaluating the age of those issued by a government, it is also best to stay away from them as investments. They are rarely dated, and thus the buyer has no way of knowing whether the piece was minted in the early 1920s or 1990 — the government often uses the same mold over and over again, perhaps with time lapses between mints.

Many of us first became captivated by coin collecting when we were children. While helping to count up all the pennies and nickels in the kitchen cookie jar, we hoped to find a valuable old coin among them, or, at the very least, an Indian-head penny. The Professional Coin Grading Service (P.O. Box 9458, Newport Beach, California 92658; 800-447-8848) has started "slabbing" graded coins. That is, once the condition of a coin has been graded, the coin is encased in a grade-labeled tamper-resistant plastic holder called a slab. Investment-graded coins are judged on a scale from MS-60 to MS-70, the highest mint-state grade. Until slabbing began, few dealers would buy a coin sight unseen. Many current investors in the numismatic market haven't ever seen — and probably won't ever lay hands on — a rare coin.

Some independent dealers still won't buy a coin sight unseen, and many will de-slab a coin in order to submit it for another shot at a higher grading. The grading of a coin depends in part on its age. But condition is even more important: An 1892-S silver dollar in good condition is worth about $13, but the same coin in uncirculated, "gem" condition can be valued at $65,000.

Grading alone doesn't mean that a coin will attract high prices; the rare coin market, just like other art-related markets, is fickle and subject to the rapidly changing whims of investors. For example, in the mid- to late 1980s Morgan silver dollars (graded about MS-65 or higher) were hot. These coins, minted between 1878 and 1904 and again in 1921, could command more than $1,500 each in 1989. But that market has since taken a dive, high grading or not.

If you are new to the game, find a dealer you can trust, one who has been in business at least 10 years and belongs to the Professional Numismatics Guild or the American Numismatic Association. Ask him or her for references from customers and from a local bank. Be particularly wary of mail-order offers and telemarketers.

Dealer markups range from 10% to 15%, depending upon the dollar value of the coin. So if you try to sell a coin back, expect to get about 15% less than its stated market value at the time. Usually, you will have to hold a coin at least five years, and possibly 10 years, before turning a profit. That's why dealers and financial planners recommend that you commit no more than 10% to 15% of your investment money — and usually much less than that — to your collection.

You will stand a better chance to profit if you concentrate on coins of a particular period or country. U.S. government mintages are the only reasonable choices for novices because they have the broadest appeal to investors and collectors. With experience, you can reach for the exotic. For example, so-called ancient coins — those minted before the fall of the Roman Empire in the fifth century — have appreciated about 10% to 20% annually in recent years. You can still get some bargains on ancient coins sold in the U.S. and Europe. Prices span from about $10 to $20 for common, fourth-century bronze coins to many thousands of dollars for rare gold or silver pieces. Two magazines that publish current prices are *Coin World* (911 Vandemark Road, Sidney,

Ohio 45365; 800-673-8311) and *Numismatic News* (700 East State Street, Iola, Wisconsin 54990; 800-258-0929), available at larger newsstands.

The IRS says that coin dealers must report purchases of South African Krugerrands, Canadian Maple Leafs and other government-minted gold coins. The tax collector wants to be sure that any profits that collectors make on them will not go unreported and untaxed. But the rule generally does not include numismatic coins — that is, scarce or rare coins that usually are worth far more than the gold, silver or bronze they contain. Consequently, some goldbugs have been trading in their Krugerrands for numismatics. A caveat: Sales tax is due on these purchases in some states, and capital gains have to be reported to the IRS when numismatic coins are resold.

Four good sources on coin collecting are *Coin Collectors Survival Manual* by Scott A. Travers (Bonus Books, $13.95), which includes information on grading coins and understanding the grading system, detecting counterfeit or altered coins and dealing with the tax laws of selling coins; *Coin World Guide to U.S. Coin Prices and Value Trends* by William Gibbs (Coin World Publishers, $5.99), which lists 22,000 values for U.S. coins in a range of conditions; and *Unusual World Coins* and *Standard Catalog of World Coins,* both by Colin R. Bruce III (Krause Publishers, $19.95).

### Gems

Diamonds, emeralds, rubies, sapphires — ah, what romance! But as investments, those luscious gems are quite chancy. They are terrific to look at, terrible to trade in for cash. Before you attempt to profit from your jewelry box, remember that gems which have been bought to wear are seldom of investment quality. When you buy them, the dealer takes a substantial markup — as much as 100%. And if you ever try to sell the stone, dealers will usually offer you even less than wholesale prices. There is no easily quoted market for gems because no two stones are identical in quality or value.

Diamonds are the only stones that are graded by specific criteria. They are evaluated by four measures: carat (or weight), color, clarity and cut. Even the color of white diamonds is graded from D for the most brilliant whites, to Z for dingy yellow. The difference of just one letter grade can change the price by thousands of dollars per carat. A D – flawless diamond, the highest grade, is extremely rare and costly. A one-carat D flawless stone sells for around $15,000 wholesale — or $20,000 to $22,000 retail at Tiffany's. The same stone would have sold for $60,000 in 1980. A two-carat ring of the same quality now retails for some $72,000 at Tiffany's. However, a very good ring with a moderate grade — I — sells for some $7,700 at one carat and $17,500 at two carats.

When buying diamonds, insist on receiving a certificate from an independent laboratory that has graded the stone within the last 12 months. Even with that, you also should get a recertification from the Gemological Institute of America. It has offices at 580 Fifth Avenue, New York, New York 10036; 212-221-5858 and 1630 Stewart Street, Santa Monica, California 90404; 310-828-3148.

The diamond market lost much of its luster during the recession of the early 1990s but has enjoyed a mild upturn lately. One third of the world's diamonds and diamond jewelry are sold in America, and polished diamond imports rose from $3.8 billion in 1989 to $4.9 billion in 1994. In 1995 diamond imports continued to advance, climbing 7.6% in the first quarter.

If you are acquiring jewelry for pleasure, fine. But don't deceive yourself into believing you are making a sure-fire investment. Unless you are an expert, gems are for buying, not for selling.

With occasional exceptions, colored stones are less costly than diamonds — but riskier. That's because a world diamond cartel usually keeps a floor under prices, but there are no cartels to hold the prices of the three most precious colored stones: emeralds, rubies and sapphires.

Among them, emeralds are the costliest, but fine rubies have risen the fastest lately. Supplies are short because few rubies are being exported by Burma, source of the richest and reddest stones. The next most valuable rubies come from Thailand, while the lighter Sri Lanka rubies are less coveted. Sapphires are almost as rare as rubies, and some of the best and the bluest are from Kashmir. Emeralds may be a safer investment because they are easier to resell than sapphires. The best emeralds, by far, come from Colombia.

The steep price of precious stones is stirring interest in much more speculative semi-precious stones, notably tanzanite, aquamarine and topaz. The finest opals are too fragile to be a solid long-term investment; they can crack fairly easily.

Before buying a colored stone, remember that although there is no universally accepted grading system for them, you should insist on independent written appraisal of the gem's quality, weight, color — and, of course, its dollar value.

## Toys

Toys of the 1950s and early 1960s aren't kid stuff anymore. Now they are called contemporary collectibles, and many command precious prices. Collectors are paying hundreds — and sometimes thousands — of dollars for toys that sold for a few dollars when new. The buying and selling is done at antique toy auctions. You can find auction locations and dates advertised in a monthly, *Antique Toy World* (P.O. Box 34509, Chicago, Illinois 60634; $25 for a year's subscription).

Collectors covet dolls of the 1950s and early 1960s for their beauty and wardrobes. Among those that have appreciated the most are the eight-inch Madame Alexander–brand Romeo and Juliet dolls. They cost $3.50 each when they came out in 1955; now a pair in mint condition can fetch up to $3,000. An original Barbie, first sold for $3 in 1959, can command as much as $2,500 in pristine condition and preserved in her original box. The 1965 "Side-part American Girl Barbie," originally $4.89, is now worth $3,500 in the same condition.

The 1950s-era techno-toys, such as robots and satellites, also fetch high prices at auction. Other valuable toys include small metal trucks and cars of the 1950s. Some of the tiny Matchbox vehicles that originally sold for 39 cents are now more than $40. And the Hot Wheels versions of America's muscle cars — Chevrolets of the late 1950s and Mustangs of the early 1960s — go for as much as $50. So-called character toys, often from cartoons or kids' TV shows, are popular. A wind-up tin Popeye doll from the 1930s brings nearly $550.

Before you buy, make sure that the toy is functioning properly, has no missing parts, peeling paint or other signs of corrosion. With toys, condition is everything. Top bids are reserved for toys in mint condition and with their original boxes. An excellent reference is *Schroeder's Collectible Toys: Antique-Modern Price Guide* by Sharon and Bob Muxford (Collector's Books, Schroeder Publishing Company, $17.95), which identifies and values over 20,000 collectible toys.

Where can you find toys that have more than nostalgic value? Garage sales are one source. But the best place to find toys worth a bundle is at home. Just think: The joys may be in your attic.

## Pop Collectibles: Rock 'n' Roll, Movie and Sports Stars

Some of the hottest collectors' items now are rock 'n' roll memorabilia, traded at auction houses that deal in collectibles or sold in stores. They include original recordings, posters, souvenirs, clothing and guitars. At a Sotheby's New York auction, an electric guitar that Roy Orbison played went for $8,800. Christie's in London sold five of Elvis Presley's bedsheets — plain white percale, but adorned with the King's laundry mark — for $1,200. Leonard Nimoy's blue brocade tunic from *Star Trek* sold for an astronomical $5,500, and Joan Crawford's 1945 *Mildred Pierce* Oscar — expected to fetch up to $12,000 at Christie's 1993 spring auction — went for $68,500. Also at Christie's, you could have bought John Belushi's bee antenna for a mere $320 or, at the other end of the scale, one of Marilyn Monroe's poured-on *Some Like It Hot* gowns for $35,000.

Gotta Have It! Collectibles, a memorabilia store in Manhattan, carries a variety of goods, including souvenirs from the sports and music world (153 East 57th Street, New York, New York 10022; 212-750-7900). Items can range from several hundreds to six figures. Babe Ruth's jersey from the 1938 World Series sold for over $100,000, and Rocky Marciano's boxing robe for $7,500.

If you want to collect such items, be disciplined. With rock 'n' roll, you should specialize in items related to a single band, or in a particular category of items, such as backstage passes. The most valuable collectibles are likely to be those associated with musicians who marked a turning point in rock history.

At Sotheby's auctions, a suit that John Lennon wore on concert tours fetched $3,575, and one of Jimi Hendrix's electric guitars went for over $300,000. For collectors who want a bit of Hendrix without tossing around a lot of notes, a poster might be the next best thing. Rock 'n' roll poster prices have been rising quickly. But keep in mind that assets like these are not very liquid. As with most collectibles, you are best off buying an item because you want to own it, not because you expect to make a profit.

References on pop collectibles include *The 40's and 50's — Designs and Memorabilia* by Anne Gilbert (Avon Books, $12.50), an identification and price guide to collecting posters, textiles, lighting designs, etc.; *The 60's and 70's — Design and Memorabilia* by Anne Gilbert (Avon Books, $12.50), covering ceramics, fashion, glass, rock 'n' roll, etc.; and *Miller's Rock and Pop Memorabilia* by Stephen Maycock (Reed International Books, Ltd., $24.95), which includes illustrated information on clothing, musical instruments, signed ephemera, presentation discs, etc.

CHAPTER 8

# How to Play Your IRA

If you were limited to just one savings-and-investment plan, what would you select? A sound choice would still be an Individual Retirement Account, even though Congress back in 1986 took away from many people the ability to deduct from their taxable income every dollar invested. But IRAs continue to offer what could be a more important benefit: You will pay no taxes on the interest, dividends and capital gains you earn on your money as long as it remains in your IRA. Therefore, your whole account can benefit from the marvels of compound interest and unfettered growth until you start making withdrawals, presumably after you retire. Then you will pay income tax at your ordinary rate — but only on the taxable part of the cash you remove. It is even possible that your tax rate at that time will be lower than it was when you were working — but don't count on it.

To repeat and expand on what we've said earlier: Employed people and their spouses who are *not* covered by a pension plan can deduct from their taxable income all contributions to an IRA. But if you *are* in a company plan — whether you are vested or not — you can deduct your contribution only if your income falls below certain income ceilings. Married couples who file jointly can deduct their full IRA deposit if their adjusted gross income is $40,000 or less a year, regardless of whether either spouse participates in a pension plan. Single filers can deduct up to $2,000 if they earn $25,000 or less. Couples who earn between $40,000 and $50,000, and singles who earn between $25,000 and $35,000, can write off part of their contributions. The amount you can deduct tapers off as you earn more money. Unfortunately, these amounts are not adjusted, as income tax brackets are, to account for rises in the cost of living.

Even if your earnings put you above the $35,000 to $50,000 ceilings, you may be able to claim at least part of an IRA deduction. One way is to take advantage of a 401(k) plan if your company offers it. With a 401(k) you can instruct your employer to put away part of your salary — up to $9,240 in 1995 — toward your retirement. For each dollar you contribute, many employers add 50 cents or more to your account, up to a predetermined maximum.

Because the money you invest under a 401(k) is *not* considered taxable income (although it is subject to Social Security taxes), your contributions lower your adjusted gross income. Say that you and your spouse earn $52,000 and thus are not eligible for an IRA deduction. But if in 1995 you put the maximum $9,240 into a 401(k) plan, your adjusted gross income would decline to $42,760. In that case you would be able to make a partially deductible contribution to your IRA. Similarly, you may qualify for a full or partial IRA deduction if you put money into a Keogh plan or a Simplified Employee Pension (SEP) and are within the income limitation.

The chart below gives you some indication of how you can build capital for future security by taking advantage of a whole variety of tax-deferring savings and investment plans. It may not seem like much to put away $2,000 a year in an IRA, but this can be an important building block for financing a comfortable retirement. The point is to use not only the IRA but also the 401(k) and just about all other plans at your disposal to enlarge your nest egg. You then can gain from a series of

## HOW THOSE PLANS BUILD CAPITAL

Here's what three different employees would save in their qualified plans—an IRA, a 401(k) plan, and profit sharing—assuming an annual employee contribution of 8% of salary, a 4% company match, 5% profit sharing and 8% growth. All salaries increase 4% annually.

| | 30-YEAR-OLD | 40-YEAR-OLD | 50-YEAR-OLD |
|---|---|---|---|
| Income: | **$40,000** | **$100,000** | **$130,000** |
| Amount in qualified plans now: | **$30,000** | **$100,000** | **$150,000** |
| Amount at age 65: | **$2,500,000** | **$2,700,000** | **$1,300,000** |

SOURCES: JOEL ISAACSON & CO.; *FORTUNE*

benefits: (1) you make regular contributions, (2) they enjoy tax-deferral, (3) your employer adds to your contributions in some instances, and (4) everything gets an extra lift from compound growth.

The fact that IRAs compound tax-free means that they are government subsidies to savers and investors. Examples:

- Assuming you put the maximum $2,000 a year into an IRA each January for 20 years and it earns 10% annually, your $40,000 in contributions will turn into $126,000.
- Assuming you put $2,000 a year into nonsheltered investments for 20 years and it earns 10% annually, but you withdraw the amount needed each year to pay taxes; using an average federal and state tax rate of 32%, your $40,000 in contributions will turn into only $85,000.

The farther you are from retirement, the more an IRA's tax-deferred compound earnings can do for you. If you are age 35 and start depositing $2,000 a year for the next 30 years and your money earns 10%, you will be richer by $362,000 when you turn 65.

IRAs don't have many drawbacks. Yes, you may have to pay between $10 and $50 a year in fees to the bank, savings and loan association, brokerage firm, or mutual-fund or insurance company where you keep your account. (Charles Schwab & Co., the discount broker, has free IRAs.) Plus, you cannot ordinarily withdraw the money before age 59½ without being assessed a 10% penalty by the tax collectors. But both are small prices to pay for what can be a really terrific tax shelter.

You have until the time you file your income taxes — as late as April 15 — to open or fund your IRA and put some of your previous year's pay into it. An extension to file your return does not help as it does in the case of a Keogh plan. For an IRA contribution to be deductible for the previous year, April 15 is the absolute deadline.

You can invest your money in bank certificates of deposit, stocks, bonds, mutual funds, annuities, limited partnerships, stock options, futures contracts, real estate, Ginnie Maes and U.S. Treasury securities. Off-limits are life insurance, precious metals, gems, art and other collectibles. But you are allowed to buy U.S. Treasury gold and silver coins as well as U.S. state-issued coins.

Your IRA will grow much faster if you put in your contributions as early each year as possible. Let's say you make the maximum $2,000 contribution, but you wait until the very last minute — that is, until every April 15 — to write the check for your contribution for the prior year. If your investment earns 10% annually, in 20 years you will have $114,500. But if you make that same contribution as soon as each new tax year begins, on January 1, you will end up with $11,450 more over the same amount of time. And after 30 years you will have $33,000 more than you would have if you had waited until the last minute.

Remember that you do not have to put the maximum $2,000 in your account every year. Legally you can open an IRA with as little as $1, but most banks require at least $25. Your contribution need not be made all at one time. You can make periodic deposits, as with any other bank or brokerage account — as long as you meet the April 15 deadline. You can even skip a year, but you cannot make up for it by putting in more than $2,000 the next time. You can also open as many IRAs as you please and divide deposits among them, just so long as your total contribution in one year does not exceed $2,000. Watch out, though, for multiple fees. You can also switch your IRAs from one financial institution to another without forfeiting the tax benefits. Note that you can no longer make deductible contributions to an IRA after you reach age 70½.

Once you make your initial contribution, you can leave your account at that level or build it up with weekly or monthly deposits. Even small deposits grow nicely. Put away just $9.60 a week and in 12 months you will have a tax-sheltered nest egg of $500 — plus whatever interest, dividends and capital gains you have earned on it.

Some employers offer payroll-deduction plans for IRA contributions. These periodic, direct transfers of cash into your IRA are a convenient method of forced savings. One disadvantage of installment-style pay-ins is that they do not let you accumulate the maximum amount possible in your IRA, because your total allowable contribution is not made in one lump sum on January 1 and is not working for you the entire year.

As mentioned above, your IRA money will be taxed as ordinary income at your regular rate when you start withdrawing it. One exception: If you made your annual contributions from nondeductible dollars, they obviously will not be taxed. To do otherwise would amount to double taxation.

Be careful about withdrawals. Unless you are disabled, you may face stiff consequences for permanently withdrawing any money too early in life. The IRS will claim as a penalty 10% of the funds you take out, on top of your ordinary income tax on the total withdrawal.

The youngest age at which you could avoid the penalty used to be 59½, but in 1988 that rule was liberalized. Under some circumstances, you can now start taking out money much sooner by scheduling annual withdrawals as lifetime income. At age 50, for example, a man can begin tapping a $100,000 IRA — without penalty — for as much as $11,000 a year or as little as $3,000, depending on a wide range of permissible assumptions about his life expectancy and the rate of return his money will earn. You can even change the assumptions from year to year.

The new rules also cover other retirement plans, such as Keoghs and SEPs. So parents can use tax-deferred retirement money to help pay for their children's college or even for a wedding. But once withdrawals start, you must continue withdrawing the same amount for at least five years or until you reach age 59½, whichever comes later. Stopping the withdrawals too soon will cost you retroactive 10% penalties on all the money previously taken out, plus interest. You'll need expert guidance from an accountant or financial planner on how much you can safely siphon off, and for how long.

There's one other escape hatch in the early-withdrawal rules. You can *temporarily* withdraw money from your IRA once a year without paying any tax or penalties. You just have to roll over the money and replace it within 60 days. So, if you are careful, you can use your IRA money for a *short-term* emergency loan. The only cost may be a fee imposed by some banks, S&Ls or mutual funds when you withdraw and replace your IRA funds this way.

You are allowed to start permanent withdrawals anytime after age 59½, but you must begin making them soon after you turn 70½ — to be precise, by April 1 of the next calendar year. Then you must take out at least the minimum amounts decreed by the IRS on the basis of life-expectancy tables. For instance, if you are a 70-year-old man, you are expected to live 12 more years, so you must withdraw at least one-twelfth of your funds in the first year. If you are dependent principally on the IRA income, it might be safest when you retire to transfer the entire sum into an annuity that provides lifetime payments for you and your spouse. Then at least you can't outlive your money.

When you leave this world, the money or annuity payments from an

IRA may go to any beneficiaries you have named. A surviving spouse may re-register the IRA in his or her name and continue enjoying tax deferrals. If the beneficiary is not a spouse, the money must be withdrawn and the tax paid in no more than five annual installments.

If only one spouse is employed or if one spouse has a very small income, the couple can contribute a total of $2,250 annually under the "spousal" IRA provision. But each partner must have a separate account. The $2,250 spousal IRA can be divided as the couple wishes, so long as no more than $2,000 goes into either account in any year. For example, one partner may contribute $2,000 and the other, $250; or each may put in $1,125. You can contribute the full $2,000 to your spouse's IRA even if you are older than 70½, as long as your spouse is younger than 70½. In case of divorce, the ex-spouses keep individual control of the funds already in their separate accounts — except for settlements in community-property states, where the IRAs must be divided 50-50.

If you own a small business, you can increase your nonworking spouse's IRA deduction. Just hire your beloved part-time. As long as the service he or she performs is legitimate and the compensation is reasonable, you can put up to $2,000 of the spouse's salary in the IRA every year. But you will also have to make some federally mandated tax payments for your spouse, such as for Social Security.

True enough, some people should not open IRAs. As a rule, children ought not to put earnings from summer or after-school jobs in an IRA, because they are already in a very low tax bracket or pay no taxes at all. And if you think you will need your savings in a few years to buy a house or start a business, that money should not go into an IRA. The penalty for early withdrawal may well exceed what you would gain in tax-sheltered earnings on several years of IRA contributions. But almost anyone else who has earned some income from a job, and can afford to put aside savings that he or she will not need anytime soon, should think seriously about opening an IRA.

## Where to Invest Your IRA Money

Investing your IRA cash is like shopping in a well-stocked financial supermarket. You can choose from many thousands of securities, bank certificates, mutual funds, annuities and income-producing limited partnerships. But your decision will be considerably easier if you answer these four questions:

*First, how old are you?* The closer you are to retirement, the less risk you may wish to take. The stock market might be a terrific investment for most of the savings of someone younger than 50 or even 60. But at age 63 you might be asking for trouble, since a market slump could leave you shortchanged at a critical time. Stock market investments are for the long term, for money you will not need immediately.

*Second, what other investments do you have?* You want to diversify. If your non-IRA assets are mostly in stocks or mutual funds that invest in them, you might balance them by filling your tax-deferred account with high-yielding fixed-income investments such as bond funds and bank certificates.

*Third, how daring are you?* If an investment is going to give you insomnia, it is not for you. One fairly painless way to learn your tolerance for risk is to put a small part of your IRA money into a growth stock or an aggressive-growth mutual fund. Aggressive funds often invest in small growth stocks, which have under $500 million in market capitalization. As the price swings, the lining of your stomach will tell you how much risk you feel comfortable with.

*Fourth, what do you know?* Don't invest in something you do not understand. Avoid limited partnerships in real estate or other areas unless you are expert enough in such investments to tell a good deal from a bad one. Other investments that demand extreme caution include options and commodities futures.

Over the years your IRA should grow — and change — just as you do. The younger you are, the more you should go for growth. Let's say you are 30 years old and have some safe investments outside your IRA. In that case, you might do well to place almost all of your IRA money in long-term growth mutual funds.

By contrast, if you are in your 50s and plan on dipping into your IRA within five years or so, you would be well advised to start moving out of stocks and into such safer staples as money-market funds and short-term bonds. Specifically, you might be wise to invest 50% of your money in certificates of deposit, U.S. Treasury securities, Ginnie Mae funds and short-term or intermediate-term corporate bonds. Another 10% might be in money-market funds. The remainder could comfortably stay in a portfolio of solid stocks with growth potential.

To repeat, if your IRA investment strategy emphasizes safety, fixed-income securities are hard to beat. Short-term CDs are the best-known type. But you should also look into other fixed-income investments that offer comparable returns, including Ginnie Maes, which are home-mortgage securities backed by the federal government, as well as short-term U.S. Treasury bills, which mature in one year, and Treasury notes and bonds that are close to maturity. For longer-term, high-quality fixed-income securities, try U.S. Treasury notes and bonds with farther-out maturity dates (over one year), federal agency obligations, Fannie Maes or Treasury STRIPS (separately trading registered principal securities, also known as zero-coupon bonds).

You can take more risk — and possibly earn a bigger return — by buying shares in a mutual fund. There are more than 6,400 stock and bond funds, and you can choose one whose strategy fits your own.

If you are undecided how to allocate your IRA funds between stocks and fixed-income investments, consider a new breed of mutual fund that will make the decision for you. Known as asset-allocation funds, they strive to get the best return by dividing their assets among stocks, bonds, foreign securities, gold and money-market securities. Several of the best-performing asset-allocation funds have been Quest For Value (with an average annual return of 15.36% in the three years ended mid-1995), SoGen International (13.02%) and Overland (12.01%).

If you have accumulated at least $10,000 in your IRA and are willing to do your own investment research, you may want to open a self-directed account at a bank, brokerage house or mutual-fund company. Such accounts let you trade stocks, bonds, funds, certificates of deposit (CDs) and other securities at will. Self-directed IRAs can cost about $25 to open, $25 a year to maintain and $50 to close.

Some investments are truly unsuitable for IRAs. You should question any rate of return that seems seductively high. Excessive risk may well be the reason for the steep yield. Be especially wary of CDs that offer split rates — a lofty one for 60 days and a lower one for the duration of the term. Insist on having the *annual yield* calculated for you. It is the best basis for comparison. The truth-in-savings law requires bankers to give it to you.

In evaluating an IRA investment, first consider how it scores for preservation of principal. Ask yourself how great a chance there is that you could lose some, or even all, of the money you invest. But remember that you generally pay for high safety by accepting relatively low returns.

Another key characteristic to watch for in your IRA account, once you reach age 59½, is liquidity. The quicker you can convert an investment into cash, the more liquid it is. The more liquid your IRA assets, the easier it is to plan cash withdrawals and adjust your investments in response to economic changes. You can always withdraw securities from an IRA without selling them. But whenever you withdraw, you have to pay taxes on your capital gains.

Also consider volatility. If investments that jump and fall sharply make you nervous, play it safe. But if you have a strong gut, go for growth and don't worry too much about volatility.

Consider also how well an investment will stand up to inflation. A locked-in 8% interest on a long-term Treasury bond looks nice enough when inflation is around 3%, but that unchanging rate loses much of its luster if inflation rises toward double digits. The message: Include in your IRA some investments, such as stocks, whose long-term growth can keep you ahead of inflation.

## Mutual-Fund Plans

Now, to elaborate on these points:

Considering everything, the most sensible place to invest your IRA money may well be in a large mutual-fund company, one that operates several kinds of funds. When you put your cash in one or more of these groups, your fees are low, your investment choices are numerous and you can move your money around from one fund to another simply by making a phone call. Several major fund companies now also offer discount brokerage services, including Fidelity, T. Rowe Price and Vanguard.

A great many companies have funds that invest in stocks, bonds and the money market — plus, in some fund families, an astonishing array of permutations and combinations of the three — and let you switch your money among them. Fidelity offers more than 100 choices, from a money-market fund that invests exclusively in federal government securities, to a fund that buys stocks of fast-growing high-tech companies, to highly specialized funds that buy into companies in specific lines of business or particular parts of the world. The primary advantage of such variety is that you are not locked in to one type of investment. That is important when you are putting money aside for a retirement that is possibly decades away.

The three discount brokerage firms of Charles Schwab & Co., Jack White & Company and Waterhouse Securities have a special deal. They let you use your IRA money to buy, sell and switch among some 500 no-load and low-load mutual funds as well as stocks, bonds, options and government securities. The brokerage fee at Schwab, for example, for a $2,000 IRA transaction is $39 for a mutual fund, $39 for a bond purchase and $64 for a stock purchase.

When you buy a load mutual fund, you pay a commission — as much as 8.5% — most of which goes to the salesperson or broker who sells it to you. But you can save a lot by investing instead in a no-load fund family. In that case you will generally pay only an annual IRA maintenance charge of $5 to $10 per fund. That can add up, however, if you spread a few thousand dollars over several funds. No-load funds, like load funds, also charge annual management fees, normally 0.5% to 1.5% of the value of your account. The difference is that you buy directly from the no-load fund group instead of from a broker. There is no evidence that either load or no-load funds outperform the other.

### Bank and S&L Plans

If what you want is a worry-free and very nearly decision-free Individual Retirement Account, you may be wise to open your IRA at a federally insured bank, savings and loan association, or credit union. An IRA at any of them has several advantages. You deal face-to-face with your banker, the fees are modest to nonexistent, you can get started by depositing as little as $25 at some institutions, and the federal government insures your CD and money-market account balances up to $100,000. When your account gets near the insurance limit, just open another IRA at a different banking institution. More and more banks also sell mutual funds, usually load funds.

But there are reasons why not everybody is beating a path to his or her local banker. One is the modest rates CDs have been paying. Also, if you need to withdraw your money for some emergency, you may have to forfeit at least three months' interest on bank certificates of more than a year, and one month's interest on those of a year or less. *A tip:* If you are

59½ or older, most banks will waive this penalty when you cash in certificates of deposit in your IRA.

The closest equivalent to a bank or credit union savings account is a money-market mutual fund. Money funds are considered quite safe, though they are not federally insured. Banks and S&Ls attempt to compete with money-market funds by offering money-market deposit accounts that have federal insurance up to $100,000. As noted earlier, in mid-1995 bank money-market deposit accounts were paying around 2.85%, while money-market funds were paying about 5.29%.

Banks and S&Ls also offer two types of longer-term IRA savings certificates:

First, there are fixed-rate certificates. They guarantee you both preservation of capital and predictable returns. This they do by locking you — and the bank — into the same interest rate for anywhere from three months to 10 years. The shorter a CD's life, the lower the rate, though rates have been dipping at the long end. You would want a short-term CD if you believe interest rates will rise in the future; then fairly soon you could cash in your CD and buy a new one that pays the higher rate. But if you think that interest rates will decline in the future, you would want a certificate with a fairly long-term fixed rate. That way you would continue to enjoy today's rates, which would be relatively higher. Better yet, divide your CDs into maturities from six months to 30 months or more. This is called "laddering," and it covers some of your money whichever direction rates go.

Second, there are variable-rate certificates. The initial yield is a percentage point or so lower than on fixed certificates, but the yield moves up or down every few weeks, in line with interest rates in general. Consequently, you would choose variable certificates if you think rates will rise.

Stock brokerage firms also sell — or, rather, resell — CDs that they have bought from a bank or savings and loan association. Most brokers don't charge a commission on them, and the interest rates they pay you are often higher than at banks and S&Ls. That's because brokers can scour the market for the steepest returns. In mid-1995 one-year CDs bought from a bank were paying some 5.12%, but brokerage CDs of the same duration were paying 5.61%. Then again, brokerage CDs don't reinvest your interest. It goes into a money-market fund, where it is likely to earn less than the CD was yielding.

The rates that banks and S&Ls pay on IRA accounts vary widely from plan to plan, from bank to bank and from state to state. So shop around. The only accurate rate comparison is between the compounded annual yields, also known as the effective annual yields.

When shopping for CDs, be wary of advertising hype. A "bonus of 2%," for example, may turn out to be exactly what it says it is — a premium of only 2% of the base rate, not a bonus of two percentage points above the base rate. Another lure is the split-rate CD. It pays an extraordinarily high rate for a millisecond or two before reverting to a rate that may be lower than prevailing ones.

## Bond Plans

Despite their plunge in 1994, it is easy to see why bonds have proved seductive to IRA investors. They offer steady, fixed rates of return. Plus, if you hold a high-quality bond until the day it matures and pays off, you are almost certain to get back every penny you put in.

Bonds are issued by corporations, by the federal government, and by state and local authorities. But for your IRA you should consider only bonds issued by Uncle Sam or by corporations. That is because interest on municipal bonds is tax-free. So if you spend your IRA money on a muni, you would be paying for tax breaks you cannot use. Worse, you would pay tax on the supposedly nontaxable interest when you withdrew it from the IRA. *All* withdrawals from IRAs are fully taxable by the federal government *and* — if they impose income taxes — by your state and city.

Unless you are willing to take chances with your money, you are best off picking bonds rated A or higher by the major bond-rating services. There is little risk that the borrowers will not be able to pay your interest and return your principal when the bonds mature.

The safest bonds, bar none, are issued by the U.S. Treasury and other federal agencies. If Uncle Sam gets into a pinch on his debts, the government simply raises taxes or prints new dollars or issues new securities. But safety has its price. Treasury bonds usually yield a percentage point or two less than do corporate bonds with comparable maturities.

You generally buy corporate bonds and government agency certificates from brokerage firms. Banks and brokers sell Treasury securities. Be sure to search around for the lowest commissions.

One investment to use as a base may well be zero-coupon U.S. Treasury bonds. With zeros, you don't collect your interest payments in semi-annual installments but in one big lump sum when the bond matures or comes due. (See Chapter 7.) A potential problem is that you are liable for income taxes on that interest even though you do not collect it right away. *So zeros belong only in a tax-deferred account such as an IRA.* You might put as much as 90% of your IRA money in them.

## Real Estate Plans

Real estate may not be the very top investment this year, but nearly everyone should have some real estate assets in his or her IRA. That's because tangibles such as land and buildings provide a good hedge if inflation roars up again. Their value will tend to jump, while such paper investments as stocks and bonds usually slump.

An easy way to get real property into your IRA is to invest in real estate investment trusts, or REITs. REIT shares are publicly traded, just like other stocks, and you can buy them from brokers. REITs own and operate such projects as apartment complexes, office buildings and shopping centers. A small number of REITs also make mortgage loans.

By law, REITs must distribute at least 95% of their taxable income to their shareholders. Consequently, shareholders can collect high regular payments if the trust performs well. From 1992 through 1994 investors in equity REITs — the kind that invest in property — received total average annual returns of 10.3%. But for REITs that exclusively make or invest in loans, the total average annual returns for that period were *minus* 4%. Equity REITs are usually best for IRA investors. Their value will grow as real estate climbs over the years.

Before you buy, study the annual financial statements of several equity REITs and look for those that actively try to improve their properties. Shares in such REITs are more likely to outperform inflation. For safety, lean toward REITs that have bought their properties outright with all cash or use low levels of debt. They will not be saddled with tough-to-meet mortgage payments in hard times. Stay away from REITs that own mainly urban office buildings in areas with vacancy rates of 17% or more. Too many of them have been thrown up, and a glut exists in the central areas of Chicago, Houston and Los Angeles.

Better yet, invest your IRA in no-load real estate mutual funds. Fidelity

Real Estate Investment Fund holds a diverse portfolio of REITs and in 1994 had a total return of 9.64%. Another good performer, Cohen & Steers Realty, had an 8.3% return.

### Self-Directed Plans

Some 42 million taxpayers have Individual Retirement Accounts, but only a quarter actively manage them. The rest just hand their IRA money over to banks or other financial institutions. But if you only tried, perhaps you could beat the big boys. Particularly if you read the business press and take the time to study markets, consider opening a self-directed IRA, for it will give you a nice variety of investment choices.

Of course, you can buy stocks for your IRA, selecting either shares that pay high, dependable dividends or growth stocks that offer the chance for fat profits — along with, alas, the risk of big losses. As stated earlier, you can also fill your account with mutual funds, ordinary bonds, zero-coupon bonds, Ginnie Mae unit trusts, commodity funds, promissory notes, certain kinds of options and income-producing limited partnerships. About the only investments you cannot put in a self-directed IRA are life insurance and such tangibles as gold, silver, Oriental rugs or diamonds. But remember: U.S. Treasury gold and silver coins are off the forbidden list, as are state commemorative coins.

You can open your self-directed IRA at almost any brokerage house. It usually costs at least $25 to start one, and you have to pay commissions on any trading. For example, they will run to $70 or so on a $2,000 transaction with a full-service broker. So if you plan on heavy trading, consider a discount broker who will trim a few dollars off relatively small transactions — and as much as 75% off the posted commission rate on trades of $10,000 or more. But some discounters limit their business to stocks and bonds. If you want to invest in, say, limited partnerships or commodities, you may have to go to a full-service broker.

When you open a self-directed account, consider how aggressive you want to be. If your strategy is conservative, look to ultra-safe corporate or government bonds. A-rated long-term industrial bonds in mid-1995 were paying 7.15%, and corporate bond unit trusts were yielding very nearly that much. But especially if you are in your 20s or 30s, you should consider that, over the long run, conservative investments such as bonds and bank CDs probably will not grow nearly as much as the stocks of well-managed companies. You stand to earn higher profits from such shares, even after taxes. Consequently, an investor who will not be needing cash for five or 10 years most likely will do better investing in a diversified portfolio of the shares of innovative companies than tying up money in fixed-interest securities. Almost anyone who feels optimistic about the future of the stock market should keep at least some IRA money in growth-oriented stocks or mutual funds that invest in them.

## Comparing the Fees

Depending on where you invest your IRA money, you can pay practically nothing in start-up fees and annual maintenance — or quite a lot. Banks and S&Ls generally charge the least — from nothing to only a few dollars a year. The banks often sell you a certificate of deposit for your IRA. If you decide to transfer your money to another kind of investment, there is only a modest charge, provided you do not switch out of your CD before it matures. At most banks, if you cash in your IRA certificate early, you will forfeit at least three months' interest.

No-load mutual funds — the kind you buy directly from the fund company or its salespeople — also charge minimal fees, usually $10 a year. But if you choose a load fund — the kind bought through brokers and some financial planners — plan to pay a large one-time 3% to 8.5% sales commission.

You can set up your own self-directed IRA not only at a brokerage house but also at a bank, a savings and loan association, or an insurance company. Both full-service and discount brokers may charge a small fee to start one, plus around $30 a year or more to maintain it. Charles Schwab & Co., which allows you to open an IRA at no charge, will bill you $29 annually to maintain the account if it has a balance below $10,000. Above $10,000 there is no annual fee. Wherever you open your IRA, you will have to pay commissions on all of your securities trades.

Annuities that you buy from insurance companies tend to have the heaviest fees. If you put $2,000 into an annuity, and then withdraw it in less than a year to switch to another form of IRA investment, the experience could cost you about $140.

**WHEN YOU CAN DEDUCT YOUR IRA PAYMENTS**

Based on adjusted gross income

| IRA deduction | Single and earning: | Married and earning: |
|---|---|---|
| **Full** | Under $25,000 | Under $40,000 |
| **Partial*** | $25,000–34,999 | $40,000–49,000 |
| **None*** | $35,000 or more | $50,000 or more |

*Whatever your income, if both you and your spouse are not covered by an employer-sponsored retirement plan, you may take a full deduction.

SOURCE: MUTUAL FUND EDUCATION ALLIANCE

Most institutions subtract your fees from your account. But if you do not want to drain assets from your IRA — and if you want the maximum tax deductions it offers — you can arrange to make separate payments of your fees. Then on your income tax return you can itemize them under "miscellaneous," and if your total miscellaneous deductions amount to more than 2% of your total adjusted income, Uncle Sam may share the cost with you.

## How to Switch Your Account

Just because you have put your IRA money in a bank, a brokerage firm or a mutual fund, don't think that you have to keep it there until you retire, many years from now. You can move your Individual Retirement Account from one financial institution — or one investment — to another quite easily.

Say you have your IRA invested in stocks but you figure that Wall Street is in for a walloping. What to do? Just tell your broker to sell the stocks. Then you can reinvest the money through the same broker, buying money-market funds or short-term Treasury securities or some other investment that pays a safe, fixed rate of interest. Or you can take all the proceeds and deposit them in a bank CD. This is called a rollover.

Similarly, if you already have your IRA money in a bank but figure the stock market will go up, you can switch your money into stocks or mutual funds. This is also a rollover. Usually, you can roll over an IRA only once a year. If, however, you have three or more separate IRAs in your name, you can make one rollover annually from each of the accounts.

To make a rollover, you can write for withdrawal instructions or go in person to the institution that now holds your IRA and just take out the funds. Then you deliver them to your new custodian.

One major caution: Be sure that you transfer all the money to your new account within 60 days of withdrawing it from your old account. Otherwise, the money will be taxable and you probably will have to pay a 10% penalty. To answer any future IRS challenge, always write "IRA rollover" on the back of the check or the security.

You can avoid this problem by making a so-called *direct transfer.* Just ask the institution to which you want to transfer your IRA money to have it sent directly from the institution that is now holding it. The new custodian will send you a transfer form to fill out and return. For example, if you have invested your IRA in a mutual fund, you can ask the fund to transfer it to a bank, or vice versa. A direct transfer is often the better means to handle the transaction. You can move your IRA this way as often as you wish.

Although major banks whisk millions around the globe in seconds, they typically require 30 days' prior notice for IRA transfers. Why so long? Chiefly because many financial institutions are inundated by more accounts than they can efficiently handle. Yet mutual funds manage to execute transfers smoothly and quickly.

## Rolling Over Into an IRA

You can save a bundle of taxes on the lump sum of cash or stock that you collect from your employer-sponsored 401(k) or other retirement plan when you leave your job. You do that by opening a special IRA, called a rollover account, at any bank, brokerage firm or mutual-fund company. Then you instruct your employer to transfer the proceeds directly to that account. You thus postpone paying taxes on your own contributions *and* your earnings in these company plans, *and* on your employer's contributions, until you start withdrawing the money from the IRA.

This direct transfer is imperative because of a change in the law. Previously, employers always paid out the money to you. Then you had 60 days to put it in an IRA rollover account. Later, if you joined another company that offered a 401(k) salary-reduction plan or another qualified plan, you could move your rollover account into that plan.

But starting in 1993 employers were authorized to transfer these retirement savings accounts directly to your IRA or into the retirement plan of your new employer, enabling you to avoid income taxes. If, however, they pay out your money directly to *you,* employers must withhold

**ROLLING OVER BEATS FIVE-YEAR AVERAGING**

When you collect your retirement money from a qualified pension plan, you are better off rolling it over into a tax-deferring IRA than taking five-year or 10-year averaging. Look at what happens to a $500,000 distribution to an unmarried retiree, age 62, who is in the 34% tax bracket and anticipates his money will grow at a 6½% rate.

| | Rollover | Five-year averaging | Ten-year averaging |
|---|---|---|---|
| **Immediate tax** | **None** | **$131,340** | **$143,682** |
| **Amount available for investment** | **$500,000** | **368,660** | **356,318** |
| **Accumulated assets at age 70½** | **881,285** | **649,789** | **628,036** |

SOURCE: MERRILL LYNCH

for tax purposes 20% of previously tax-deferred lump-sum payments. You can still roll over the whole lump sum within 60 days, but first you will have to scrounge up an amount equal to the 20% that has been withheld. On $500,000 worth of retirement money, that's a staggering $100,000. Or you can roll over the 80% and pay tax on the rest. Later, when you file your tax return, you can apply for a refund of the amount withheld. Check with your employer, who is required by law to give you a written explanation of your choices at least 30 days before you take the money.

Another caution: The taxman won't let you roll over any *after-tax* contributions that you made to a plan, since these are not subject to income tax when you leave your employer. For example, if your income is more than $35,000 (or more than $50,000 if married or filing jointly) and you are covered by a retirement plan at work, then you have made these contributions in after-tax dollars, which means no rollover. Be sure to have your employee-benefits consultant or your tax adviser spell out your tax liability before you accept any lump sum subject to withholding tax.

## Some Better Alternatives

Worthy though they are, IRAs are not the only way of saving money and reducing your taxes. Some employers sponsor special savings-and-investment plans that offer still more benefits. If you have only enough money to contribute to just one of them, you might also do better with a nonprofit-group annuity, a 401(k) or a Keogh plan.

If you are self-employed, you can have *both* a Keogh plan and an IRA, so you need to decide which to contribute to if you cannot afford both. The Keogh allows you to shelter much more income in it than in an IRA, but an IRA is much simpler and requires less paperwork.

Another nice shelter is the nonprofit-group annuity. It can be bought by teachers, hospital nurses, social workers and other employees of non-profit organizations. If you work for an eligible group, you can tell your employer to put as much as 20% of your pay into an untaxed annuity or some other investment. You get all the advantages of an IRA but usually can shelter up to $9,500 of your salary per year. There is no tax penalty for withdrawals.

As noted earlier, the 401(k) is a terrific plan. Again, a portion of your salary is withheld — untaxed — and the money is invested in your choice of a CD-like guaranteed-investment contract, in the company's stock or in a mutual fund. To repeat: Check all your options. Sometimes you can accumulate more money, after taxes, by contributing to plans other than the good old IRA.

## How to Hold Down Those Withdrawal Taxes

Your tax-deferred retirement plans will pile up more money than you think. But what the IRS giveth, the IRS taketh away.

Joel Isaacson, premier financial planner, looks out at the Manhattan skyline from his Fifth Avenue office and shares an ounce of wisdom that could save you a ton of money: "We spend our whole lives putting cash into retirement plans, and very little time thinking about taking it out. Every one of us should have an active strategy for withdrawal."

When and how to withdraw money from your tax-deferred retirement plans are among the most important financial decisions of your life. The way you do it could cost you, or spare you, huge sums.

Millions of Americans — probably including you — are heading toward punishing taxes on the money that is rapidly accumulating in their IRAs, 401(k)s, 403(b)s, Keoghs, SEPs, corporate profit-sharing, employee stock-ownership and all other plans that the IRS says are "qualified" for tax deferral. The money builds up in those qualified accounts, free of taxes. But taxes ultimately must be paid, when you pull out your money.

The trouble is, the IRS has a host of hurdles and penalties to make it tougher for us to do just that:

- In most cases, we cannot start withdrawing until we retire or reach age 59½. If we do, we'll have to pay an extra 10% penalty tax.
- We must start withdrawing when we reach age 70½. If we don't, we'll have to pay an extra 50% penalty tax.
- We cannot withdraw more than $150,000 a year — or a one-time lump sum of $750,000 — from any combination of our qualified plans after we reach 59½. If we do, we'll have to pay an extra 15% penalty.

Congress calls this last one the "excess distributions" tax. Like all the penalties, it is nondeductible from other taxes. So it lifts high earners from the 39.6% top bracket to a punitive 54.6% marginal tax rate, and propels upper-middle-income earners from the 31% bracket to a 46% rate. And that's before state and local taxes, which can easily add five to 10 percentage points to the total.

You don't have to be rich to be worried. Benefits counselors say that anyone who has accumulated $1 million or more in qualified plans is vulnerable to the 15% penalty tax. And many people who work 30 years for a company that generously offers a number of these plans, and who leave with a final salary of no more than $60,000, are now retiring with over $1 million.

You don't have to be old to be worried. In fact, the people who will be hurt most are young and middle-age adults, now building large sums in their qualified plans. Says the benefits chief of a *Fortune* 200 company, "This is another 'gotcha' for the baby boomers."

If you are 40 years old, and if the money in your 401(k), IRA and other qualified plans grows 6% a year, it will *quadruple* by the time you reach age 65 — even if you and your employer don't contribute another nickel to it.

A more realistic scenario is that you will continue contributing, and that your money will grow by more than 6% (Standard & Poor's 500 stock index since 1926 has returned an average 10.2% a year). If so, you may well be whacked by more than 50% in taxes. Here's the math:

Say you're a 30-year-old achiever earning $40,000 a year, and you expect your salary and other compensation will rise 6% annually. Assume that you now have a total $30,000 in your 401(k), IRA, profit-sharing and other qualified plans, and they grow 8% a year. Assume also that you and your employer together annually contribute an amount equal to 17% of your income. At that rate, you'll have this much in your plans in the future:

| *Age* | *Amount* |
|---|---|
| 45 | $ 366,782 |
| 55 | $1,007,951 |
| 65 | $2,495,966 |

If you start at age 65 to withdraw the maximum $150,000 a year, there's no way you can avoid the 15% penalty tax — unless your investments go into a tailspin. But if they continue to grow at an 8% annual rate, the net amount in your plans will rise, year after year.

By the time you reach age 70½, the total will hit some $3.8 million — and the law says you *have* to start withdrawing a certain percentage of the total each year, based on your expected longevity and marital status. In the first years, a single or widowed taxpayer would collect a minimum of 6.25%, or $237,500.

You would then have to pay federal income taxes on all that money at the maximum rate of 39.6% *plus* state and local taxes, *plus* 15% penalty tax. From your $237,500, you would pocket about $118,750. That may seem like a lot of money today, but it won't tomorrow, after inflation.

You say you're sailing past 50 and have too little in your qualified plans to be concerned? Then consider this:

- At an 8% growth rate, your money will more than double in 10 years.
- At a 10% growth rate, your money will more than quadruple in 15 years.

Surely, you say, the tax laws will change in the future. Yes, indeed. But all the changes since 1981 have *increased* taxes on retirement plans and *decreased* the amount of tax-deferred money you can put into them. When the top income tax rates fell to 28% in 1986, Congress enacted the 15% "excess distributions" penalty tax to get some money back from affluent people. But when the top tax bracket rose to 39.6% in 1993, Congress conveniently neglected to remove that penalty tax. And in 1993, Congress reduced the maximum amount you can withdraw each year without penalty from $230,000 to $150,000.

These moves have discouraged saving and impeded capital formation, and they contradict government pleas for Americans to put away more for their own retirement. But the government desperately needs all the money it can get, and a strong bloc on Capitol Hill feels that nobody should be allowed to accumulate too much money, particularly at the taxman's expense.

What, then, can you do to plan a sensible, tax-saving strategy for contributing to, and withdrawing from, your retirement funds? Your first step is to go both to a benefits counselor where you work *and* to your tax adviser, asking these key questions:

- How much money do I now have in my qualified plans?
- Given a reasonable growth rate, how much will I accumulate in all those plans in future years?
- How long, and how much, should I continue to contribute to those plans?
- When does it make sense for me to start withdrawing from those plans?
- Given my life expectancy, my tax situation, my expected pension and other retirement benefits, plus the amount of money I will need to live on, how much should I withdraw each year?

*A tip:* When doing this last calculation, draw up several scenarios, using different expected rates of growth in your income and in your plan's investments. In most cases, you'll probably find yourself earning more, and worth more, than you had expected.

Bear in mind that you most likely will have an 11-year window — between ages 59½ and 70½ — when you can choose to withdraw up to $150,000 a year without penalty. But if you pull out anything before that, you'll suffer major penalties. After age 70½, you have no choice: You *must* start withdrawing.

You may well conclude that it's wise to keep your money in the sheltered plans till the last possible moment, even though you'll be clobbered by the 15% penalty tax when you eventually withdraw. If stocks keep rising at anywhere near their historic rate of just over 10%, you'll gain more from stock appreciation over the years than you'll lose from higher taxation at some distant date. Also, financial planners have found that on fixed-income investments, you can earn as much as two percentage points more inside a qualified plan than outside a plan. For example, you can collect 6.5% on a Treasury bond inside a plan, versus only 4.5% on a comparable tax-free municipal bond outside a plan.

On the other hand, you may decide to start withdrawing the money as soon as you can to hold down taxes and avoid taking chances that the investment markets will tank. This is a very personal decision that only you — and your tax adviser — can make.

## Countering That Heavy Estate Tax

All those taxes on your IRAs and other qualified plans are pussycats compared with the real man-eating tiger: the estate tax. Anything above $600,000 that you leave to your heirs stands to be taxed at 37% or more. The tax rises steadily, to 55% at $3 million and above. Says John Elbare, an estate planning expert in Tampa, "You may think that your assets are far below $600,000, but you must add up the value of everything you own — your home, your vacation home, your savings and investments, your personal property and collectibles, your IRA, 401(k) and all other qualified plans, and the appraised value of any farm or small business that you own, among other things." To which former IRS commissioner Donald Alexander, now a Washington tax attorney, adds, "The $600,000 exemption is not enough to protect the typical middle-income person who has worked hard, accumulated some money and bought a home."

It surely is not enough to protect someone who has built a successful small business. The heirs may have to scrape up money to pay federal estate taxes that max out at 55% *plus* state death taxes that make the bill even higher in the states that charge taxes above and beyond the federal rate (for details, see Chapter 23, "Dealing with Wills, Trusts and Estates"). Small wonder that so few family businesses stay intact through the third generation.

Take the hair-raising case of a 65-year-old man who, through creating a small business and diligent saving and smart investing, builds an estate of $3 million. When he dies, this could be demolished by up to *five* taxes: federal estate, income and excess accumulations tax, as well as state inheritance and income tax. The total bill could range from a high of $2,369,300 if all assets were in qualified plans like 401(k)s, to a low of $784,000 if none of the money was in qualified plans and the man and his wife had established wills and trusts to take advantage of the $1.2 million that a married couple can pass on to their heirs free of federal taxes. (Note: A single person can pass on $600,000.)

Or consider the case of a 47-year-old self-employed woman — who has followed all those good rules about saving as much as you can — and has piled up $400,000 in her Keogh, IRA and other qualified plans. She adds $30,000 to them each year, and by following sound advice and investing prudently, she earns 8% on the money. When she reaches age 70, her qualified plans will total $2,524,729. If she then dies, the taxes on those plans will be $1,972,701, reducing their value to $552,028 — a 78% hit. And that doesn't even count state and local income and estate taxes, which vary in size, or additional taxes on other assets that she may own.

There are several things that you can do to soften the estate tax:

First, give away to your heirs during your lifetime as much as you legally can — and that you can afford. You can give up to $10,000 a year to each of as many individuals as you wish, free of federal gift tax. Your spouse can do the same. Together, you can give a maximum $20,000 a year to each of your children, or anyone else. In addition, you can give a total $600,000 during your lifetime to any person or combination of persons. Very few folks can — or want to — give that much. But if you see your estate creeping toward the $600,000 point where the estate taxes kick in, you would be wise to start a regular gifting program.

Second, if you're married, make sure that both you and your spouse use your separate $600,000 gift tax exemptions.

Third, if it looks as if your taxable estate will top $1.2 million, buy second-to-die life insurance. Because two people have to die before this pays off, it usually costs some 30% to 50% less than ordinary single-life insurance. Follow these steps, in this order, and the death benefit will flow to your heirs free of all taxes:

- Set up an irrevocable insurance trust, naming as beneficiaries your children or whomever else you want to be your heirs. "Irrevocable" means you can never change the beneficiaries or the terms of the trust, so be careful.
- Buy a second-to-die policy and put it in the trust. For safety's sake, you'll probably want to diversify and buy two or more policies from different, top-rated companies.
- Make sure that the annual premiums on the policies are paid either by your beneficiaries or by yourself in the form of *gifts* to your beneficiaries. You cannot pay the premiums yourself unless you declare them as gifts; you may even have to pay gift taxes on the insurance premiums if they exceed your gifting limits. If you violate this rule, the death benefits will become subject to estate taxes.

If you set up the trust properly and follow the narrow rules meticulously, you will not eliminate or reduce your estate taxes. But you will provide tax-free money to your heirs to offset the taxes.

Be absolutely sure that the lawyer who draws up the insurance trust knows exactly what you want, and exactly what he or she is doing. (Many don't.) Ask him or her to include in the trust such devices as Crummey powers, hanging powers and other arcane but super-important factors. To be sure that the trust is unassailable by the IRS, hire a second attorney and perhaps a third to vet it.

A solid insurance trust will be one of the three most important documents you will ever sign — along with your will and your marriage license.

There are other things you may do to leave more to your loved ones and less to the unloved tax collector. These include establishing a charitable lead trust (recently popularized by the late Jacqueline Kennedy Onassis in her wisely drawn will); a charitable remainder trust; a trust called a QPRT (by which you gift your house to one of your grown children, who takes ownership only after you live in it for another 10 to 12 years or so). Again, for more, see Chapter 23.

CHAPTER 9

# Saving Money on Your Taxes

The rich may or may not be different from you and me, but they no longer get all the tax breaks. Now that financial information is as common as sin, and just as cheap, almost anyone can reduce his or her taxes by using some fairly simple techniques that wealthy people have been employing — and enjoying — for years.

The biggest single tax mistake most of us make concerns our attitude. We treat taxes as an inevitable and irresistible force, a troublesome necessity over which we have no control. In fact, we can have considerable influence over the shape and size of our taxes.

But it pays to make a pre-emptive strike. Don't wait till the eve of April 15 to figure out how to take advantage of tax-sparing devices. Treat your taxes as a year-round issue. Start looking today for overarching strategies — as well as for specific deductions and credits — that will cut your tax bill for this year *and* well into the future. The earlier you act, the more time you have to consider strategies, and the more you stand to save.

As you read this chapter, you may recognize tax savings that you failed to consider when you filed your most recent tax return. Redemption may be at hand. If the omissions are large enough to really worry about, you can correct them by filing an amended return.

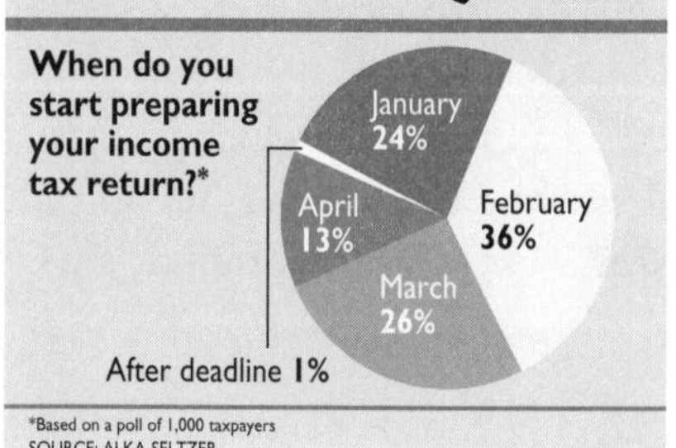

Re-examine whether you are taking full advantage of all your opportunities to reduce your tax bills. For example, you once may have put off opening an Individual Retirement Account because you felt pinched for money while you were still supporting your children. But if your children today are grown and paying their own way, consider starting an IRA now. It will help you build a tax-sheltered retirement account. No matter how big their income, employed people and their spouses who are *not* covered by a pension plan can deduct from their taxable income all contributions to an IRA.

Your income taxes are almost certainly higher now than before the draconian tax law of 1993 was passed. And while taxpayers earning over $100,000 a year have been hit hardest by the changes, more money is also extracted from the pockets and purses of the middle class.

What you have to pay depends upon your taxable income, that is, after all deductions and exemptions. Couples with gross incomes of less than $11,500 pay no income taxes. Nor do singles with gross incomes less than $6,400, and heads of households — typically single parents or other single people with at least one qualified dependent — with gross

## WORKING FOR TAXES

"Tax Freedom Day" is the last day the average American has to work each year to cover all his or her taxes. Here are past Tax Freedom Days and the number of calendar days needed to reach them.

| Year: Tax Freedom Day | Days |
|---|---|
| 1944*: March 30 | 90 days |
| 1949: March 24 | 83 |
| 1954: April 6 | 96 |
| 1959: April 13 | 103 |
| 1964*: April 13 | 104 |
| 1969: April 30 | 120 |
| 1974: May 2 | 122 |
| 1979: May 1 | 121 |
| 1984*: April 28 | 119 |
| 1989: May 3 | 124 |
| 1995: May 6 | 126 |

*Leap year makes Tax Freedom Day appear a day earlier.

SOURCE: TAX FOUNDATION

incomes below $10,750. But if you earn more than that, here are your tax rates, based on your taxable income earned during 1995:

| *Taxable income* | *Tax rate* |
|---|---|
| **COUPLES FILING JOINTLY** | |
| Under $39,000 | 15% |
| $39,000 to $94,250 | 28% on amount over $39,000 (plus all of the above) |
| $94,250 to 143,600 | 31% on amount over $94,250 (plus all of the above) |
| $143,600 to $256,500 | 36% on amount over $143,600 (plus all of the above) |
| Above $256,500 | 39.6% on amount over $256,500 (plus all of the above) |
| **SINGLES** | |
| Under $23,350 | 15% |
| $23,350 to $56,550 | 28% on amount over $23,350 (plus all of the above) |
| $56,550 to $117,950 | 31% on amount over $56,550 (plus all of the above) |
| $117,950 to $256,500 | 36% on amount over $117,950 (plus all of the above) |
| Above $256,500 | 39.6% on amount over $256,500 (plus all of the above) |
| **HEADS OF HOUSEHOLDS** | |
| Under $31,250 | 15% |
| $31,250 to $80,750 | 28% on amount over $31,250 (plus all of the above) |
| $80,750 to 130,800 | 31% on amount over $80,750 (plus all of the above) |
| $130,800 to $256,500 | 36% on amount over $130,800 (plus all of the above) |
| Above $256,500 | 39.6% on amount over $256,500 (plus all of the above) |

To elaborate a bit, say you are married and among the fortunate few with a taxable joint income of more than $256,500. You would then pay taxes at the following rates:

15% on your first $39,000 of income
28% on income from $39,000 to $94,250
31% on income from $94,250 to $143,600
36% on income from $143,600 to $256,500
39.6% on income above $256,500

What that all adds up to is this:

**Federal Taxes Due (estimated for 1995)**

| *Taxable income* | *Single* | *Married and filing jointly* |
|---|---|---|
| $25,000 | $3,964.50 | $3,750 |
| $50,000 | $10,964.50 | $8,930 |
| $100,000 | $26,268.00 | $23,102.50 |
| $300,000 | $98,936.50 | $94,488.50 |
| $1,000,000 | $376,136.50 | $371,688.50 |

The top tax rate on capital gains from investments held for a year or more remains 28%. Because that's so much less than the maximum tax rate of 39.6% on ordinary income, long-term capital gains are more valuable for wealthy people than they previously were. Also, the cap on the Medicare tax was scrapped in 1994. That means *all* your salary and self-employment income — without limit — is subject to the Medicare tax rate of 1.45% for salaried employees and 2.9% for the self-employed. So if you are in, say, the 39.6% bracket for income taxes, your *real* federal tax rate is closer to 41% or 42.5% for the self-employed, on your earned income. If you are in the 31% bracket, your real rate approximates 32.5% — 33.9% if you're self-employed. Your Social Security contributions, of course, come on top of that. For 1995, up to $61,200 of any earned income or wages is subject to Social Security tax.

Three out of four Americans now pay, directly and through their employers, more Social Security tax than federal income tax.

Payroll deductions for Social Security and Medicare, labeled "FICA" on most paychecks, have rocketed over the past 20 years. For income earned in 1995, the maximum Social Security tax for employees rose to $3,794.40. There are actually two taxes contained in your FICA figures. First, there is a flat rate of 6.20% on wages up to $61,200; that money goes to a fund to pay old-age, disability and retirement benefits. In addition, there is a 1.45% tax on all wages, salaries and self-employed earnings *without limit;* that money goes to pay for Medicare insurance. Matching employer taxes double the government's take for both Social Security and Medicare taxes.

If you have your own unincorporated business, you must pay *both* halves of the FICA tax out of your own pocket. This is known as the self-employment tax. But you can deduct one-half of it from your income on a special line on Form 1040 where you calculate your adjusted gross income.

The taxes on Social Security benefits received by retirees are heavier than they were just a few years ago. Retirees whose total income, including half of their Social Security, exceeds $34,000 for singles or $44,000 for couples now pay income tax on up to 85% of their benefits. Singles with incomes between $25,000 and $34,000 and couples with incomes between $32,000 and $44,000 pay federal taxes on up to 50% of their benefits.

What do Social Security beneficiaries get for the money? Pensions, life insurance to protect their dependents, disability insurance for themselves and their families, and help with hospital and other medical bills if they're disabled or over age 65. All told, more than 42 million people collect Social Security checks. The total they received in 1994 was about $318 billion. Quite a sum. Yet that sum is much *less* than what people paid in 1994. The result is that the annual surplus grew to over $50 billion, and by the turn of the century it is projected to hit $85 billion.

By the year 2015 the balance in the Social Security Trust Fund is expected to peak at the inconceivable total of $2.8 trillion. The fund will then start to decline as more and more baby boomers (born 1946–64) hit retirement age. In the meantime, by law, the Social Security Administration must invest the money in U.S. Treasury securities. So the $50 billion yearly surplus and the larger and larger surpluses to come are really helping to finance the federal budget deficit. Come 2030, our children or grandchildren will be paying still higher payroll taxes to help see the baby-boom generation through their lengthening old age.

## How to Get a Social Security Number

The IRS requires a Social Security number for every person listed on your return who is at least one year old. If you have a child who doesn't yet have a number, call or visit your local Social Security office and ask the people there to mail you Application Form SS-5. You should receive it within five to seven days. After sending in the form along with some necessary documents, you should get the Social Security card in another 10 to 15 days.

You can speed up the process if you apply in person at the Social Security office, which you have to do anyhow if your child was born outside the U.S. If you do make a personal visit, ask for a receipt showing that you have applied for the Social Security card. Then if you have not received your child's Social Security card by the time you file your tax return, simply enclose a copy of the receipt and write "applied for" where the number is supposed to go on the return.

Back to those documents that you will need to send in with the Form SS-5. They include an original or certified copy of a birth certificate and one additional identification with your child's name, such as a vaccination certificate, immunization record or doctor's bill. You'll also need an original or certified copy of one identification for yourself, such as your driver's license, marriage certificate or military ID. Documents must be originals or certified copies; regular or notarized copies are not acceptable. For certified copies, take the original documents to a public agency, like your city hall or the Social Security office. Don't mail original documents because they can get lost.

In addition to everything else, the top federal rates for estate and gift taxes are now 53% for estates valued at $2.5 million to $3 million and 55% for those above $3 million. Add to that stiff taxes levied by some states, plus the 15% special "excise" tax on any savings that you may have built up in 401(k), IRA and other tax-deferred "qualified" plans that the government considers excessive. It's possible that your estate will be paying 75% or more on your peak income. This laundering should remove any residual worry that your offspring will be spoiled by their rich inheritances.

Yet there are still ways to protect your hard-won earnings from taxes. You can save a ton by emphasizing tax-free and tax-deferred investments. *A warning:* Anyone mulling over investments that will save taxes is a little like a teenager pondering marriage. You had better be sure that the lust to avoid taxes is not leading you into a disastrous long-term commitment. Make certain that the investment is intrinsically sound, even without its tax benefits.

With that in mind, some strategies valuable for everyone are listed briefly here, and many of them are elaborated upon later in this chapter:

*Buy tax-exempt bonds.* Many of them are sound investments for almost anyone; but the more affluent you are, the more attractive they are. For example, a person earning more than $250,000 may find it worthwhile to *switch out* of Treasury bonds, the interest on which is taxable at the federal level up to 39.6%, and *switch into* tax-exempt bonds, which pay tax-free interest, or growth stocks, which could create future long-term capital gains that are taxable at a maximum 28%. For a fair reading, compare the interest rates on tax-free bonds with rates on other bonds before taxes. A top-rated muni paying 5.65% would be the equivalent of a corporate bond with a 7.1% taxable yield if you are in the 31% tax bracket or a 7.5% yield if you are in the 39.6% bracket.

*Buy supersafe U.S. Treasury bonds, notes or bills.* You will have to pay federal tax on your earnings, but states and localities cannot touch your income. To buy these securities, simply call the nearest Treasury Department regional office or a Federal Reserve Bank.

*Invest in reliable old U.S. savings bonds.* Your interest is exempt from state and local levies, and no federal tax is due until you redeem the bonds. Series EE bonds bought before May 1, 1995, and held five years or more will return at least 4% a year — or 85% of the average yield on Treasury securities with five years remaining to maturity, whichever is higher. In early 1995 this worked out to 6% for an EE bond that had been held for five years. Bonds bought after May 1, 1995, and held five years or more will earn 85% of the average five-year Treasury security yields.

If you use the money to pay higher-education tuition, you don't have to pay any federal taxes on the interest, provided that (1) you or your spouse bought the bonds, (2) you were at least 24 years old when you bought them and (3) you don't have too high an income. The break phases out gradually for couples reporting incomes between $63,450 and $93,450, and for single parents with incomes between $42,300 and $57,300. In short, this amounts to a nifty opportunity for middle-income and upper-middle-income parents of youngsters heading for college.

*Take deductions for capital losses.* You can deduct from your salary and other ordinary income up to $3,000 a year in net long-term or short-term losses that you have suffered from the sale of stocks, bonds or other assets. If you have had a larger loss than that in any previous tax year, you can save the excess, carry it over to later years and then use it to offset future capital-gains income.

To determine the size of your capital gain or loss, you should be keeping track of your "basis" price for all your investments. Remember, basis can mean more than your original purchase price. For stocks, any dividend reinvestments you make add to your cost basis — and reduce your capital gain. On the other hand, returns of capital reduce your basis — and raise your capital gain. Real estate investment trusts and utility stocks sometimes pay "dividends" that are untaxable returns of capital.

*Take deductions for charities and charitable work.* Do you do volunteer work for a church, a synagogue or other charitable organization? Then you can deduct from your taxable income the costs of traveling to meetings, fund-raisers and other events. The IRS permits you to write off 12 cents for every mile you drive to or from such events and to charitable volunteer work, plus parking, fees and tolls. Bus, taxi and train fares are

## CHARITIES THAT PUT YOUR MONEY TO WORK

Five charity leaders based on efficiency

| Category | Charity | Program spending as a percentage of income |
|---|---|---|
| **Health** | **Americares Foundation** | **98%** |
| **Social services** | **United Jewish Appeal** | **92** |
| **Relief and development** | **International Rescue Committee** | **91** |
| **Religion** | **World Opportunity International** | **95** |
| **Conservation** | **World Wildlife Fund** | **79** |

SOURCE: COUNCIL OF BETTER BUSINESS BUREAUS PHILANTHROPIC ADVICE SERVICE

also deductible — if you have receipts for them. You also can deduct out-of-pocket expenses, such as the cost of phone calls, stationery, stamps and uniforms. As for your contributions, you can deduct not only your cash gifts but also the property that you donate, including clothing, books and magazine subscriptions. But you generally cannot deduct contributions to foreign charities.

*Fund your retirement plans to the max.* Individual Retirement Accounts, 401(k)s and other plans are excellent devices that allow you to defer paying taxes — and thus enable the income from your savings and investments to compound even faster. Your money is locked up until you retire, and your earnings over time are not taxed until withdrawal.

An important warning: There are limits on how much you can accumulate and take out of such tax-sheltered retirement plans. Check with your accountant or tax attorney to be sure that you're not in danger of exceeding those limits. If you are, you could be stuck with heavy tax penalties. You will be hit with the 15% excise tax on "excess" distributions from your IRA, Keogh, 401(k) and other "qualified" — i.e., tax-deferred — plans and annuities. After you reach age 59½, you can withdraw up to $150,000 a year from all the plans that you hold. (For more, see Chapter 8, "How to Play Your IRA.")

*Use Keogh plans and Simplified Employee Pensions (SEPs) if you are self-employed.* They allow you to shelter a considerable amount of your earnings, with some limits. You can shelter up to 13% in profit-sharing plans and SEPs, and up to 20% in a "money-purchase" defined-contribution Keogh plan. Altogether, you can usually contribute up to $30,000 of compensation with a mix of plans. For plans beginning in 1994, the maximum that people were allowed to contribute to Keoghs and SEPs was capped at $22,500 a year. If you want to save more, consider setting up a money-purchase Keogh, to which you are required to contribute a fixed percentage of your earnings each year. You can choose any percentage up to 20%, to a maximum $30,000 a year.

Simplified Employee Pensions can be established by employers. Keoghs can be set up by just about any sole proprietor. You probably qualify if you are an entrepreneur or a self-employed lawyer, doctor, writer, entertainer or the like. Keoghs can also be opened by a business partnership. If you are an employer and set up a pension plan for yourself, you must establish pensions for your employees, too.

*Save money by giving it away.* You can give each child or grandchild —

or any other individual — up to $10,000 a year without incurring federal gift taxes. Couples can give $20,000 a year to each child or grandchild. In fact, you can give up to $10,000 each year to an unlimited number of individuals, even if they are not related to you, without incurring federal gift taxes. You may not, however, give your "gift" as compensation: Employees are not eligible to receive such gifts, though they can still receive noncompensatory gifts.

In the case of your family, you might, for example, want to give away $10,000 to each of three children, $10,000 to each of four grandchildren, and $10,000 to each of two daughters-in-law and one son-in-law — or $100,000 in all. If your spouse matches your gifts, the total would be $200,000.

This certainly would be an unusual burst of generosity. But, for very affluent people, such *annual* gifts can make sense, because they reduce the size of estate taxes later on — and those taxes can be punishing.

*An important note:* You can give $10,000 per person per year. You cannot skip one year and double up the next. If you did not give somebody up to $10,000 in 1995, you cannot give him or her $20,000 in 1996 — only $10,000. In short, use it or lose it.

*Shift assets to your children.* Unless your child is a rock star, his or her tax bracket is lower than yours. So it pays to shift assets from your name to your minor child's, where the income will be taxed less harshly.

An adult who owns stocks or bonds that have appreciated in value and sells them to pay for a child's education is just plain foolish. Instead, *give* the securities to the child over age 14, and let him or her sell them. Profits from the sale will be taxed at the child's rate instead of your presumably much higher one. (Naturally, you'll want to limit your gifts to $10,000 per child per year — or $20,000 if both parents are giving — to avoid the federal gift tax.)

*Open a custodial account for each child.* All you need is a Social Security number for the child in order to set up such an account at a bank, brokerage house or mutual fund. This is where you park your gifts for the child, plus any of his or her earnings. Much or all of the income from the account — dividends, interest and capital gains — will be taxed at favorable rates. So it makes much more sense to start a college fund in your child's name in a custodial account rather than in your own name.

Name yourself as the custodian, which means you control the account.

You can then spend the money and the earnings on it for any purpose that benefits the youngster. This can include private school, summer camp or violin lessons — but not some frivolous activity like a trip to Disney World. You also lose the tax break if you spend the child's money on anything that constitutes an ordinary parental obligation, such as clothing or food or shelter, except in the case of college room and board.

To reiterate what was said in Chapter 3: If your child is younger than 14, the first $650 of income in his or her name is not taxed at all. The next $650 is taxed at the child's rate, usually 15%. Anything above $1,300 is taxed at the parents' rate. That means the total federal tax on $1,300 of income is only $96. But if you are in the 39.6% tax bracket, and you had invested the money *in your own name,* the federal taxes on that $1,300 would have been $514.80.

Once your child turns 14, the tax break gets really attractive: *All* the dividends, interest and capital gains earned in the custodial account are taxed at your child's rate. This custodial arrangement continues until the child reaches maturity, which varies from age 18 to 21, depending on what state you live in.

*Make moonlighting pay.* If you have self-employment income from free-lance work, you can usually write off most business expenses — including tools like computers and software. And if you use a room in your home *exclusively* for business purposes, you are entitled to a deduction. But beware: The IRS, backed by a recent Supreme Court ruling, has written a strict set of restrictions for this break.

*Buy a house or condo.* Even though real estate prices haven't been going through the roof, a home usually remains a solid investment. It also leaves you up to your eaves in tax benefits. You can write off 100% of the interest on your mortgage, provided the loan is for $1 million or less. And, within limits, you can deduct from your taxable income the interest you pay on a home-equity loan or line of credit.

*Pay attention to frequently overlooked write-offs.* If you are itching to change jobs within your current field, you can deduct most travel and other expenses connected with your job search. Also, you can deduct this year any previous years' capital losses that exceeded the $3,000 annual limit, but only up to $3,000 per year.

Of course, it will not pay to increase your write-offs unless you itemize them or unless you have a business of your own that allows you to take the deductions as a direct offset against income. So add up any expenses that you are entitled to write off for the year. If your total tops the so-called standard deduction, then it pays for you to itemize. You probably will find it worthwhile to itemize, particularly if you own your own home, have a lot of medical bills or unreimbursed casualty losses, aren't reimbursed for job-related expenses like travel or union dues, or make contributions to charities. You will need appropriate records and receipts to support any of these claims.

Affluent people, however, have a tougher time taking deductions. As explained later in this chapter, the Revenue Reconciliation Act of 1991 reduced the size of itemized deductions they can claim.

The standard deduction is indexed to the consumer price index, and it rises with inflation. For income earned in 1995, the deduction is $3,900 for single individuals, $5,750 for heads of households (such as single parents) and $6,550 for married couples filing jointly. If you are 65 or older, or blind, your standard deduction is increased by $750 if you are married or are a surviving spouse, and by $950 if you are single or the head of a household.

It's smart to start thinking *now* about how to save on the taxes you will pay *next* year and in many future years. You do this by long-term *planning*. And you begin planning by estimating whether three things will be higher or lower in the future than they are today: (1) your own income, (2) your own tax bracket and (3) federal, state and local taxes in general.

If you think your own income or tax rates will *increase* next year, see if you can lighten your tax bill by collecting some of *next* year's income *this* year. That's harder to do if you earn a salary than if you're self-employed.

Conversely, if you think tax rates and your tax bracket will be the same or lower, try to push some of *this* year's income into *next* year. If you're self-employed, delay sending out some December billings until January 1. And bring some of next year's deductions into this year, when they may be worth more.

For example:

- Send in your January mortgage payment in December.
- Make next year's charitable contributions in December, perhaps on your credit card (they will be billed in December but you need not pay them until January).
- Make early payments of some real estate taxes, state taxes and quarterly estimated taxes.

- Renew next year's subscriptions to business and professional magazines this year.
- Pay next year's professional dues this year.
- Consider selling mutual funds on which you have losses, or swap bonds that aren't performing well.

Three notes:

1. Don't rush to make prepayments if you have to take money out of an interest-bearing account. Compare the interest you would earn by holding on to that money longer with the benefit of the tax deduction. It's usually better to take the deduction, but not always.
2. If your miscellaneous itemized deductions already add up to 2% of your adjusted gross income, look for any other expenses that fall into this category which you can prepay. These will be 100% deductible.
3. If you take enough deductions this year, you may get the added advantage of dropping into a lower tax bracket.

## Beware the AMT

The tax law of 1993 widened that old tar pit, the alternative minimum tax (AMT). If you earn a six-figure income and have extensive deductions, call your accountant to see if you are vulnerable to the AMT and if you can take any steps to avoid it. The top AMT rate is 28%, and it does not allow deductions for state or city taxes or miscellaneous itemized deductions. If you already know that you will be paying an AMT for this tax year, don't shift more deductions into this year. They will be gone forever.

Warren Bergstein, CPA and professor of accounting and taxation at Long Island University, warns, "Although this complex tax was adopted to make sure that wealthy people did not take too many deductions and would pay at least something, the AMT can apply to almost any taxpayer who has high itemized deductions. You need really good planning to avoid a surprise hit by the AMT."

Some retirement-plan contributions that you make *next* year can also help you reduce *this* year's taxes. If you qualify to take deductions for an IRA, you have through April 15 of *next* year to make a contribution that is deductible from income earned *this* year. Similarly, you can make contributions through next April 15 to Keogh plans or SEPs and deduct them from this year's taxes. But in order to do that, your Keogh plan needs to have been set up before December 31 of this year.

You can no longer take deductions for medical expenses unless they exceed a stiff 7.5% of your adjusted gross income. As a result, if you have a year with unusually high medical expenses, you may want to speed up other medical spending so that you qualify for the deduction. Similarly, you can use miscellaneous itemized deductions, like union dues and tax preparation fees, only if they amount to 2% of your adjusted gross income. So, if you're close to that threshold, look for other expenses that you can pay this year which might put you over the top.

If you want a tax loss and are willing to boot out a few dogs among your investments, there is a way to do it without altering your basic investment strategy. Sell the bonds that have been doing poorly and replace them with others in the same investment category. You can do the same with stocks, but it's harder to find shares that are almost identical to the ones you already hold. Generally you carry out the swaps late in the year. But do not wait until late December to make these exchanges. It may be difficult then to find just what you want.

Mutual-fund investors can consider taking a few losses as well. What you do is redeem only those shares that are worth less than you paid for them. You will need to review carefully your records of purchase, with their dates and prices, and it is drudgery. Pick out the losers and send a list of them to the bank that serves as the fund's transfer agent, instructing the bank to redeem only those particular shares.

In sum, if you have losses on stocks, bonds or mutual funds, ask your broker whether it makes sense to (1) sell them this year in order to deduct the loss from your taxable income and (2) replace them by buying back *similar* but presumably better stocks, bonds or mutual funds. When doing this, be sure to consider which year would be most beneficial to deduct the loss: this year or next.

*A warning:* Don't sell a stock in late December because its price has dropped below what you paid for it and then quickly buy back that *same* stock. This is called a wash sale, and some investors used to make such a wash so that they could painlessly claim a big stock loss. Of course, the IRS caught on. Now, if you're trading the same stock or a substantially identical bond, you have to wait at least 30 days between the date you sell and the date you make a new purchase in order to claim a deduction for any loss.

## File Electronically and Get an Early Refund

If you have a tax refund coming, you will collect it two to four weeks earlier if you file electronically with the IRS. This you can do when you have a computer and modem and use a tax software program. You send your data by telephone lines to the IRS. Returns filed electronically are processed much sooner than conventional returns — because IRS employees avoid keying in a lot of your data by hand — and you can instruct the IRS to deposit your refund directly into your bank account.

One thing seems clear: Electronic filing, despite some early glitches, is the wave of the future. Already, the IRS calculates, those who file electronically make only one-tenth of the mistakes made by the average manual filer.

*Here is an elaboration of some of the tax-saving devices we discussed earlier:*

*Take advantage of long-term capital-gains rates.* Capital gains and losses refer to the money you earn or lose when you sell capital assets. A capital asset is property you personally own or use, like stocks and bonds, or jewelry held for investment. Items that you make yourself, like pictures you paint, are not classified as capital assets. And neither are business assets, such as desks, computers or inventory.

If you own a capital asset for one year or less before you sell it, any profit you make is a *short-term* capital gain and is taxed at your regular income tax rate. But if you sell the asset more than one year after the date that you bought it, any profit is a *long-term* capital gain and is taxed at a maximum rate of 28%. If you're in a tax bracket higher than 28%, it benefits you to hold on to some assets long enough to take advantage of the long-term capital-gains rate.

Say you bought 100 shares of a company at $38 each and paid a brokerage commission of $200. Your total cost would be $4,000 ($38 × 100 + $200 = $4,000). Then you sold the stock for $52 a share and paid a brokerage commission of $200. You would collect $5,000 ($52 × 100 – $200 = $5,000). And your profit would be $1,000 ($5,000 – $4,000 = $1,000).

If you had owned the stock for one year or less, your profit would be taxed at your ordinary income tax rate; if you are in the top 39.6% bracket, your after-tax profit would be $604 ($1,000 × 39.6% = $396; $1,000 – $396 = $604).

But if you held on to the stock for more than one year, you would be taxed at a maximum rate of 28%, and your after-tax profit would be a much nicer $720 ($1,000 × 28% = $280; $1,000 – $280 = $720).

The next time you're contemplating selling a stock, consider the benefits of long-term capital gains versus the penalties of short-term capital gains.

You can deduct capital losses up to the full amount of your capital gains. Any additional losses, up to a total of $3,000, can be deducted against ordinary income. Any additional losses beyond the $3,000 can be deducted in future years, indefinitely. For example, say that this year you have $10,000 in capital losses and $5,000 in capital gains. Your net loss is $5,000. You can deduct $3,000 this year, and $2,000 in future years. Losses are deductible if they stem from investments, business transactions, or theft or casualty. You cannot deduct losses on the sale of a home.

*Take full advantage of tax-sheltered plans.* When bureaucratic-sounding memos come around your office explaining your employer's savings, stock purchase or 401(k) plans, do you just toss them? If so, you are making a money-wasting mistake. If your employer offers you a chance to get into such a program, seize it.

You get two big tax breaks from such company thrift plans. Taxes are deferred on all contributions your employer makes to your account and on all the earnings generated by the money put in by both you and your employer. You do not pay any taxes on the dividends, interest or capital gains until that income is distributed to you. But when it *is* distributed, you pay ordinary income taxes on it, not special, lower capital-gains taxes.

Two major corporate plans are:

- *The profit-sharing program.* In this form of thrift plan, the employer makes annual cash deposits in employee accounts. The amount may depend on the size of each year's corporate earnings, but it doesn't have to. On top of these contributions, employees may be able to add voluntary contributions of their own.

  Usually you have a choice of investing the money in stocks or bonds and perhaps an interest-paying savings account. Happily, some companies also offer a family of mutual funds as an alternative, giving employees a wider choice of investments. You can divide your stock money, for example, among mutual funds specializing in the stocks of large companies and small companies, respectively, or aggressive-growth stocks or conservative stocks.
- *The stock purchase program.* In this type of plan, you might have the option of contributing between 3% and 6% of your pretax salary. Often the company will kick in $1 for every $2 that you put up. All that money goes to buy stock in the company itself. You may have to wait three years or more to become vested — that is, to have title to the stock bought by the company-matching funds.

  If you have a choice of several company plans, the best place to park your voluntary contributions is where the company puts in the highest proportion of matching funds. That is "found money." But how much you want to contribute to a company stock plan will also depend on how optimistic you are about your employer's future. Beware of buying your company stock so heavily that most of your assets wind up in that one issue. A reverse in the firm's fortunes could leave you with nest egg on your face.

Whichever plans you select, you generally cannot withdraw your money until you quit or retire or reach age 59½ and you must start withdrawing at 70½. Otherwise, you may have to pay a 10% tax penalty to

Uncle Sam on top of the ordinary income tax you will pay. But many plans allow you to borrow against your accumulated balances at market interest rates.

When you leave the firm, you may be able to use a tax-saving maneuver on your lump-sum distribution, provided that you participated in the plan for at least five years. Instead of paying the tax on the lump sum, you can forward-average it over five years or, in some cases, 10 years. That is, you can divide the lump sum into five equal portions or 10 equal portions and pay the taxes, according to the special rate schedule, on each portion. Check it out both ways; this may lower your taxes. On lump sums of around $377,000 or more, five-year averaging is more advantageous than 10-year averaging.

Usually, you can do this kind of averaging only after you reach age 59½, and only once in your life. Or you can roll over your lump-sum distribution into an IRA and postpone any tax until you are 70½. Your IRA funds won't be eligible for averaging, but that seldom matters, because your earnings can keep on compounding with no tax to drag down their growth.

Remember: A rollover must be made within 60 days after you receive a lump-sum distribution from a retirement plan, and you must put the money into another qualified plan such as an IRA, a qualified employee retirement plan or a qualified annuity plan. If you change jobs and your new employer has a qualified plan, you can put into it all or part of your money from the qualified plans you had at your previous place of employment. If you put only part of your money into the new plan, only that portion will be tax-deferred. The rest of your money — that is, the amount you do not roll over into a new plan — will be taxed at your ordinary income tax rate.

*Take full advantage of 401(k) plans.* If you like your Individual Retirement Account, you'll love your 401(k) plan. It's like a super IRA. It reduces your income tax bill while helping you save and invest some salary for retirement.

Yes, you can have both an IRA and a 401(k). But the IRA contributions may not be deductible, depending on your income level, whereas your 401(k) contributions are taken from pretax earnings. That is, this money is not taxed until you withdraw it, usually many years from now. And you can put more into a 401(k) — up to $9,240 of 1995 income. All the dividends, interest and capital gains that you earn on the money grow untaxed until withdrawal.

More and more companies offer these plans to their employees. Instead of collecting all your pay, you can choose to put part of it into a 401(k). Often, for every dollar that you ante up, your employer chips in another 50 cents — and that is a bonus nobody should forgo.

A similar but more generous plan is usually available to employees of schools, colleges, hospitals and other nonprofit institutions. It goes by various names — tax-sheltered annuity, supplementary retirement annuity and 403(b) plan, among others. Whatever it's called, its upper limit is a $9,500 yearly contribution.

As with an IRA, you must pay income taxes on any amounts you withdraw prematurely from a 401(k), plus a 10% penalty in most cases if you are younger than 59½. Employers must deduct 20% for income tax on all withdrawals, unless you transfer the money directly into another tax-sheltered account. So if you are leaving one job for another, make sure that your old employer transfers your 401(k) money straight to your IRA or to your 401(k) account at your new place of employment. Get the counsel of a tax expert there to ensure that this so-called rollover is done properly.

You can't borrow from an IRA. But you can often borrow from your 401(k) or 403(b) to pay for education or medical expenses, or to buy a home. You can generally borrow as much as 50% of your vested account balance up to $50,000. You do, however, pay interest on the loan. And in some rare hardship cases, you can make permanent withdrawals from these plans. The usual penalty on an early withdrawal is waived if you become permanently disabled.

Don't be too conservative. The trouble with 401(k) and 403(b) plans is that most participants choose overly cautious investments. One survey of more than 400 large companies found that employees put 60% of their contributions into bonds, money-market funds and guaranteed investment contracts, or GICs. Stocks are riskier, but over the long run they have far greater growth potential.

The pity is that many employees have little choice but to be cautious. Ideally, a 401(k) plan should have at least half a dozen investment options. Some employers limit you to three or fewer. In addition to GICs and bond funds, a 401(k) should offer large-company and small-company stock funds and an international stock fund. Small stocks have outperformed large-company stocks over the years, while foreign markets beat the U.S. markets in some periods. There should also be a stock index fund, which mirrors the performance of the total stock market.

If your plan falls short, complain to your benefits department. Meanwhile, get as much information as possible about the investment options your company does offer. Employees have the right to examine the annual reports of their 401(k) plans. Such reports list the assets and investments in the plan, some of the expenses, and the performance figures for each fund.

Use this information to allocate some of your money to the highest-performing fund. Unless you expect to retire in the next seven years or so, you'd do well to put just about all your 401(k) money into stocks or stock funds. If that strategy seems risky to you, remember that you may already have one low-risk nest egg in Social Security, and perhaps a second in your company pension plan.

*Take full advantage, too, of your IRA.* It's worth repeating that the surest and simplest way for many people to reduce taxes is to contribute to an Individual Retirement Account. You can deduct the full amount of your contribution from your taxable income if (1) neither you nor your spouse is eligible for coverage by an employer retirement plan or (2) your adjusted gross income is under $40,000 if you are married, or under $25,000 if you are single. Take, for example, a couple who are both employed, but their employers have no established tax-deferred retirement plan. So, they set up IRAs at $2,000 each for themselves. If they're in the 28% tax bracket, for example, their $4,000 annual contribution translates into a tax savings of $1,120 a year.

But here's the point that so many people overlook: Even if you don't qualify for a deduction, you can still set up your own IRA and watch your investments grow *tax-deferred* over the years.

If you want to open an IRA for last year's income, you can do so any time before you file your tax return this year — that is, as late as April 15 of the current year. By contrast, self-employed people who want to establish a tax-saving Keogh plan have to set it up by December 31 of the year in which they earn the money — or their Keogh contributions will not be tax-deductible. Unlike IRAs, where contributions have to be made by April 15, you can contribute to your Keogh plan as late as the day you file your taxes, whether that is on April 15 or as late as October

15 if you get an extension. In either case, the earlier you make the contribution, the earlier you start collecting tax-deferred interest.

*Take full advantage of Keogh plans and SEPs.* Two marvelous tax-saving devices are available to most doctors, plumbers, movie directors, taxi drivers, lawyers, architects, actors, artists, authors and self-employed people of all kinds. The money-sparing pair are the Keogh plan and the Simplified Employee Pension, known as a SEP. Many people who are eligible to start a Keogh or SEP do not even know it. If you own a business or work for yourself, or just do some moonlighting as an independent contractor, you may be eligible.

If so, then by starting a pension plan and funding it with as much money as you can afford or the law allows, you can postpone taxes for decades on *both* your pension contributions and their investment earnings. People whose tax return includes Schedule C, "Profit or (Loss) from Business or Profession," are almost universally eligible for a Keogh or SEP.

Most Keoghs and all SEPs are defined-contribution plans. That is, you can take a defined amount of money out of your net earnings each year, untaxed, and invest it in a retirement account.

There are two kinds of defined-contribution Keoghs: profit-sharing Keogh plans and money-purchase Keogh plans. The maximum contributions to a profit-sharing plan are the lesser of $22,500 or 15% of net earnings less the self-employment tax deduction; this limit works out to be 13.04% of your net earnings. The maximum contributions to a money-purchase plan are generally the lesser of $30,000 or 20% of your earned income. Profit-sharing-plan contributions can vary from year to year, but money-purchase-plan contributions must be the same percentage every year.

In another kind of Keogh — called a defined-benefit Keogh — the limit can be much higher. This plan allows some people the flexibility to put away just about all the income generated by their enterprise. Under a defined-benefit plan, you promise yourself a retirement benefit of some fixed amount each month beginning between the ages of 59½ and 70½ and continuing for the rest of your life. The annual contributions are based on the amount necessary to provide you with that sized pension at normal retirement age.

If you die before you have started to receive benefits, the distribution will be made directly to your beneficiary, who can elect either to take the full distribution within five years or to take distributions over his or her lifetime. If you have already begun to receive benefits, your beneficiaries will continue to receive payments on the same schedule. You should be sure to choose a term-certain distribution to ensure that you get the full benefit out of the plan. Otherwise, the government will take the remainder when you or your survivor dies.

Obviously, this is a plan for people with lots of surplus income. They are likely to be folks in their 50s and 60s. And if they employ others, they must put enough money away to finance a pension for anyone who has been on the payroll for a year or longer (except their own spouses). But the decision to contribute each year to your defined-benefit Keogh is not discretionary. If you miss contributions for two years, your plan can be terminated. Also, if you have employees in the plan, you must insure the plan with the Pension Benefit Guaranty Corporation (PBGC).

A Simplified Employee Pension plan is so named because it is easy to set up and administer. A SEP resembles an oversized IRA. Instead of $2,000, the maximum allowable yearly tax-deferred contribution to a SEP is the lesser of 13% of self-employment income or $22,500. Simplified Employee Pensions have a special appeal for procrastinators. In contrast to the deadline for a Keogh, the last date for starting a SEP in time to make deductible contributions is the same as the tax-filing deadline, including extensions, for that year.

In choosing the right self-employment pension plan, ask yourself how much of your earnings you really can spare. If 13% or less is a comfortable limit, open a SEP. It does the least to complicate life. Keogh plans are more potent, but also more complex, and have more reporting requirements.

But, of course, nothing is truly simple where taxes are involved. The wrong kind of Keogh plan can put you in a financial bind by requiring larger contributions than you can afford in a tough year. To repeat: Up to the set limits, you can vary the size of your contributions each year to a profit-sharing Keogh plan. But you must always kick in the same percentage to a money-purchase Keogh plan.

The solution: Open one plan of each kind. Commit yourself to only 7% contributions to the money-purchase plan. And whenever possible, also put the full 13% in your profit-sharing plan.

How should you invest your Keogh money? Your strategy should mesh with your needs and goals. If you are a professional or an entrepreneur and you figure that your Keogh funds will be a main part of your retirement income, you will put a premium on safety. So, diversify to reduce your risk, and stick to top-rated bonds and stocks. If you are financially secure and willing to take some risks in hopes of higher gains, you might buy speculative growth stocks or funds and perhaps some high-yielding, lower-quality bonds.

If you eventually plan to take all the money out of your retirement fund in a lump sum, your Keogh may be less heavily taxed than your IRA or SEP because only the Keogh is eligible for forward-averaging. You can divide the lump-sum distribution into either five or 10 equal portions and apply the special tax rates on these smaller portions. This can result in lower than normal taxes on the lump-sum distribution. But it does not always work out to be a saving, and the calculations need to be done both ways to see which is more advantageous.

After you reach age 70½, you must start withdrawing funds from your Keogh. But you can continue to contribute to your Keogh or SEP for as long as you earn self-employment income — even after you begin mandatory withdrawals at 70½. You can't do that with an IRA.

*Buy Series EE savings bonds.* They are a conservative investment — there is *no* risk that you will ever lose your money — and they also offer little-known tax advantages. When you invest in Series EE U.S. savings bonds, you buy them at a discount and then earn interest on them until they mature. At that time, you collect in one lump sum both your initial investment plus your accumulated interest income. For example, you can buy a Series EE $50 bond for $25 and it is guaranteed to reach its face value after 17 years. If it has not matured at that time, the Treasury will make an adjustment to bring it up to its face value. You can continue to earn tax-deferred interest on the bonds for 30 years. Interest is earned at a variable rate, based on 85% of the average yield on five-year Treasury securities. If you cash it in before five years, the rate is 85% of the average yield of six-month Treasury securities. You do not have to pay taxes on your interest until you collect it — that is, until the bonds mature. So EE bonds are good investments for many people who are nearing retirement; if the bonds mature after you retire, you probably will be in a lower tax bracket than you are today. And you never have to pay state or local taxes on your savings bond interest.

The bonds may also be a sensible investment if you are saving for your children's, your spouse's or your own college education. Some or all of the interest you receive on Series EE bonds may be free from federal taxes if (1) you are at least 24 years old when you buy the bond, (2) your income is below certain levels of affluence and (3) you redeem the bond to pay for undergraduate, graduate or postgraduate college expenses for you, your spouse or your children.

*Buy SSBIC securities.* If you own some publicly traded stocks and bonds that you want to sell for another investment, consider investing in a Specialized Small Business Investment Company, or SSBIC. This may enable you to defer some capital-gains taxes. SSBICs are corporations or partnerships licensed by the Small Business Administration. They are organized to invest in small businesses run by people who are considered economically or socially disadvantaged. They are risky investments.

Here's the tax advantage: When you sell publicly traded securities, you normally are taxed on the gains in the year of the sale. But if you take all the money you receive in the sale and roll it into an SSBIC within 60 days, the taxes on your gains will then be deferred until you sell the SSBIC stock. The best way to find out about SSBICs in your area is through your local chamber of commerce or economic development board or a brokerage house.

*Consider starting a sideline business from scratch or turning your hobby into a business.* Particularly if you are a young adult, you should be looking for ways to increase your income rather than merely avoiding taxes. One familiar way in our highly entrepreneurial country is to start a small, part-time business of your own. Such a sideline endeavor can be both a tax haven and a nice investment that eventually may turn into a profitable full-time enterprise. You might even look to your hobby for something you really enjoy doing — and turn it into a spare-time occupation.

If you have your own business — or a part-time business — you can take some of the juiciest tax deductions the IRS will allow. You may be able to deduct all business expenses for your car, equipment, travel — even any magazines or books that you could demonstrate were necessary for research in your field of business, or the expense of attending out-of-town seminars directly related to your enterprise. You also may deduct 50% of your business-entertainment expenses.

A sideline business has another major tax advantage. If it loses money, the loss may be deductible from income that you earn elsewhere, say from your full-time salaried job, as long as you were an active participant in the business. The IRS will let you deduct such losses if you report a profit in three out of five consecutive years. For the breeding, training, showing or racing of horses, the activity must result in a profit in at least two out of seven consecutive years.

Many people have money-making hobbies that they would like to claim as businesses to take richer deductions, but there are some important distinctions you must keep in mind. You can deduct *hobby* expenses only up to the amount of income your hobby yields. But you can claim *business* expenses — and deductions — above and beyond the total income that your business produces. If you can make a very strong case that shows a relationship between your business and your so-called hobby, then you may be able to circumvent the hobby loss rules.

The IRS says the difference between a business and a hobby is the *primary intent* of your activity. Example: You have a backyard garden that you want to claim as a business because you sell your excess produce to a local health food store. The IRS declares that if your intent in gardening is primarily to gain pleasure, then gardening is a hobby. But if your intent is primarily to make money, then your gardening can qualify as a farming business. In that case, you can deduct all the expenses necessary for operating a farm for profit.

Whatever the origin of your business, the IRS first determines your intent by its profitability. If your farming — that is, gardening — shows a profit three out of five years, the IRS assumes that farming is your business. Even if you fail to make money in three of five years, the IRS may still recognize your gardening as a business *if* you can provide records to show that your primary intent was to earn money. These records include profit-and-loss statements, logs of your work, and any brochures or advertisements that show you were making a sincere effort to sell your farm products or services. Use a separate business checking account and separate charge cards. Get business licenses that are mandated by your city or county. Keep logs of your business uses of certain personal-type assets, like cars and computers. Get a separate telephone for the business, even if it's in your own home.

So, let's say that you own a small farm or big garden that qualifies as a business *and* you have a full-time job in town, working either for yourself or for a company. Let's also assume that you spent $40,000 on your farm business (for seed, tools, advertisements, etc.) but earned only

## STATE TAXES

| State | Corporate income tax (%) | Personal income tax (%) | General sales and use tax (%) | Gasoline tax (cents per gallon) | Cigarette tax (cents per pack of 20) |
|---|---|---|---|---|---|
| Alabama | 5% | 2–5% | 4% | 18¢ | 16.5¢ |
| Alaska | 1–9.4 | None | None | 8 | 29 |
| Arizona | 9 | 3.25–6.9 | 5 | 18 | 58 |
| Arkansas | 1–6.5 | 1–7 | 4.5 | 18.5 | 31.5 |
| California | 9.3 | 1–11 | 6 | 18 | 37 |
| Colorado | 5 | 5* | 3 | 22 | 20 |
| Connecticut | 11.5 | 4.5 | 6 | 33 | 50 |
| Delaware | 8.7 | 3.2–7.7 | None | 23 | 24 |
| Florida | 5.5 | None | 6 | 4 | 33.9 |
| Georgia | 6 | 1–6 | 4 | 7.5 | 12 |
| Hawaii | 4.4–6.4 | 2–10 | 4 | 16 | 60 |
| Idaho | 8 | 2–8.2 | 5 | 22 | 28 |
| Illinois | 4.8 | 3 | 6.25 | 19 | 44 |
| Indiana | 3.4 | 3.4 | 5 | 15 | 15.5 |
| Iowa | 6–12 | 0.4–9.98 | 5 | 20 | 36 |
| Kansas | 4 | 4.4–7.75 | 4.9 | 18 | 24 |
| Kentucky | 4–8.25 | 2–6 | 6 | 15 | 3 |
| Louisiana | 4–8 | 2–6 | 4 | 20 | 20 |
| Maine | 3.5–8.93 | 2–8.5 | 6 | 19 | 37 |
| Maryland | 7 | 2–6 | 5 | 23.5 | 36 |
| Massachusetts | 9.5 | 5.95–12†† | 5 | 21 | 51 |
| Michigan | 0–2.3 | 4.4 | 6 | 15 | 75 |
| Minnesota | 9.8 | 6–8.5 | 6 | 20 | 48 |
| Mississippi | 3–5 | 3–5 | 7 | 18 | 18 |
| Missouri | 6.25 | 1.5–6 | 4.225 | 15 | 17 |
| Montana | 6.75–7.25 | 2–11 | None | 27 | 18 |
| Nebraska | 5.58–7.81 | 2.62–6.99 | 5 | 24 | 34 |
| Nevada | None | None | 6.5 | 22.5 | 35 |
| New Hampshire | 8 | 5† | None | 18 | 25 |
| New Jersey | 9 | 1.9–6.65 | 6 | 10.5 | 40 |
| New Mexico | 4.8–7.6 | 1.7–8.5 | 5 | 17 | 21 |
| New York | 9 | 4.55–7.5 | 4 | 8 | 56 |
| North Carolina | 7.75 | 6–7.75 | 4 | 22 | 5 |
| North Dakota | 3–10.5 | 14* | 5 | 18 | 44 |
| Ohio | 5.1–8.9 | 0.743–7.5 | 5 | 22 | 24 |
| Oklahoma | 6 | 0.5–7 | 4.5 | 17 | 23 |
| Oregon | 6.6 | 5–9 | None | 24 | 28 |
| Pennsylvania | 10.99 | 2.8 | 6 | 22.35 | 31 |
| Rhode Island | 9 | 27.5* | 7 | 28 | 56 |
| South Carolina | 5 | 2.5–7 | 5 | 16 | 7 |
| South Dakota | None | None | 4 | 18 | 23 |
| Tennessee | 6 | 6† | 6 | 22.4 | 13 |
| Texas | None | None | 6.25 | 21 | 41 |
| Utah | 5 | 2.55–7.2 | 4.875 | 19.5 | 26.5 |
| Vermont | 5.5–8.25 | 25* | 4 | 16 | 20 |
| Virginia | 6 | 2–5.75 | 3.5 | 17.5 | 2.5 |
| Washington | None | None | 6.5 | 23 | 81.5 |
| Washington, D.C. | 9.975 | 6–9.5 | 5.75 | 20 | 65 |
| West Virginia | 9 | 3–6.5 | 6 | 20.5 | 17 |
| Wisconsin | 7.9 | 4.9–6.93 | 5 | 23.4 | 38 |
| Wyoming | None | None | 4 | 9 | 12 |

* % of federal income tax liability
† Interest and dividend income only
†† 12% applies to interest, capital gains, dividends and state business income earned by non-residents

SOURCE: TAX FOUNDATION

$30,000. You can then deduct your $10,000 net loss from the income you earned from your job in town.

You can also take some deductions for the purchase of office supplies, phone bills, utilities, repairs, and even maid service and other operating expenses in conjunction with your business. You can depreciate such tangible assets as file cabinets, desks and typewriters. Or instead of depreciating property, you can elect to treat all or part of the cost of it as a currently deductible expense — for example, the purchase of an automobile.

If you have a personal computer that you use at least one-half or more of the time for your business, you can either deduct that proportion of the cost from your taxable income in one year or depreciate it in installments over five years. Your business software and other expenses of an office at home may also be deductible.

Under current tax law, you are allowed to deduct, up to a total $17,500, the cost of tangible personal property the year you acquire it for use in your business. If you can't use the entire $17,500 deduction because you don't have enough taxable income, you can then use the remaining deduction next year. For example, if your taxable income is $10,000, you can carry over $7,500 to the next year. Alternatively, you can choose to take depreciation over the life of the assets. Expenses and losses of your business, as mentioned above, are fully deductible.

But be careful. If you report only minuscule earnings for your business, the IRS could assume that you are not serious about making it succeed. So keep meticulous records that document the place and purpose of all business expenses. Such records will help show that you spent considerable time and effort looking for clients and making the business work.

Unfortunately, the IRS audits the owners of small businesses more than any other taxpayers. Don't get carried away and deduct too much for your sideline. Deductions for what the IRS deems unnecessary or unreasonable business, travel and entertainment expenses come in for close examination. And the taxmen are especially watchful for such cardinal sins as failing to report income or neglecting to pay withholding taxes.

*Deduct your miscellaneous expenses.* You can lump together and deduct a number of unreimbursed business and job-related expenses as "miscellaneous" expenses. These include union or professional dues, tax preparation and investment advisory fees, legal and accounting fees, job uniforms and tools, job-related educational expenses and the cost of business publications — including this book. Alas, the "miscellaneous" category is a tricky one: The impecunious IRS allows you to write off only the amount by which the total exceeds 2% of your adjusted gross income. So, if you have a taxable income of $50,000 and miscellaneous expenses of $2,000 you may deduct only $1,000.

*See if you qualify for a home office deduction.* This is chancier than the sure tax-saving procedures we have discussed so far. Many people have offices in their homes, but few meet the tight IRS qualifications for a deduction. It's almost impossible if you're employed by anyone other than yourself, even if you do some of your work at home. The IRS agents scrutinize home office claims very carefully, and they have computer programs to help them. Claiming a home office deduction often invites an IRS audit.

To qualify for a deduction, you have to use your home office for the *most important* activities of your business *and* spend *most of your business time* in that office. In addition, the part of your home that you're claiming has to be used *regularly* and *exclusively* for your business, unless you're a day-care provider for children. If you work at your dining table during the day and serve family meals on it at night, that space is not used exclusively for business.

Clients don't need to visit your home for you to claim a home office deduction; you just need to conduct the main part of your service or create the product you sell in your home office. But if you provide most of the hands-on service for your clients or customers *outside* your home, you cannot claim a home office deduction, no matter how essential the office is to your business. If you're a free-lance writer and do your writing in your office, that's where your principal business is conducted. But if you're an electrician, a surgeon or an interior designer, most of your hands-on work is done out of the office — and you do not qualify for a deduction.

So, even if you have an office at home that's used exclusively for business — and you keep all your records there, plus your computer, your phone and your fax machine, and your business could not survive without this office — the IRS will still disallow your claim if, despite all this, your principal work is out in the field.

On the other hand, if you do qualify, you don't have to use an entire room to claim a portion of your home for business. The square footage of the area that's used exclusively for your business is the size of your home office. The kinds of professionals who should have no problems qualifying include writers, free-lance computer programmers and architects who do most of their hands-on work at home.

A fairly recent Supreme Court decision backed the IRS's tough stand on deductions and depreciation write-offs for home offices. If you want to set up a home office that the IRS can live with, you should do so for business-related reasons first and tax benefits second.

But once your home office passes the tests detailed above, you can start counting your deductions. In fact, you can claim deductions for a part-time business operated out of your house even if you work full-time somewhere else in another job. A deduction is also allowed if the taxpayer maintains a separate structure used exclusively and regularly in a trade or business. Not surprisingly, there is a limit to the generosity of the IRS in becoming your silent business partner. You cannot deduct more than your net income. And you usually are not entitled to deductions if you use your home office just to manage your investments.

You must include the actual square footage of your workspace and the total area of your home. Dividing total space into workspace gives you the percentage of maintenance costs you can deduct.

Your list of allowable deductions should begin with your direct business costs — those solely attributable to your workspace. They include expenses as diverse as painting or repairs and supplies that have a useful life of less than a year. If you rent an apartment and use one room as an office, you can deduct the portion of the rent that is equivalent to the size of the work area.

Homeowners and renters can deduct a pro-rated portion of their utility bills, including electricity, gas, oil, telephone, water and trash collection. Also deductible are insurance premiums paid to protect your home office from a casualty loss or theft. But you cannot deduct the cost of landscaping around your house.

Your juiciest write-off may be depreciation. If you own your house or condo or co-op apartment, you can depreciate the part used as an office over 15 to 39 years, depending on when you first started using that office for business. If you bought it between January 1, 1987, and May 12, 1993, you can depreciate the office over 31½ years; for a purchase after May 12, 1993, it's 39 years. Better yet, you can depreciate over five to seven years any office equipment and furniture, from a personal computer to a coffee table, or write off up to $17,500 in one year within net-income limitations.

The IRS does not give any guidance on how lavish a home office can be and still be deductible. As a rule, however, writing off a Persian carpet or a crystal chandelier is out. But you can depreciate, say, a $15,000 computer system if it is necessary for your business.

*Take deductions for your job-related car expenses.* If you use your car while on the job, and you are not fully reimbursed for it by your employer, you can write off your operating expenses as part of your miscellaneous deductions. We are not talking about your regular commuting costs to and from work; they are not deductible. But if you drive your car on business — say, to make sales calls — the IRS lets you deduct 30 cents a mile for all business use.

The trouble is, this can fall far short of what it costs to keep your car running. Fortunately, there is a better way: You can deduct your actual auto expenses — as long as you have the proper documentation. In short, you can fatten your deductions by maintaining thorough records.

Start by keeping a log of all the miles you drive for *business* purposes, and note separately your *total* mileage for the year. Also keep track of your total outlays for gas, repairs, insurance and other related expenses. Then figure out what proportion of your driving is for business. You can deduct that percentage of your total costs. For example, if you drove 25,000 miles last year and 14,000 of them were for business, that meant 56% of your use of the car was for business. Your standard mileage rate deduction would be 14,000 miles × 30 cents per mile — or $4,200. You could also deduct 56% of your parking fees, tolls and automobile taxes.

Keep records of the miles you drive in the course of volunteer work for charities, and to and from doctor's offices or hospitals for medical treatment. You get a lesser deduction — 12 cents per mile for charitable purposes and 9 cents per mile for medical purposes — but a deduction is always valuable.

In all matters, if the IRS doesn't understand something on your return, it will want substantiation in the form of a written record or receipt. For example, if you claim 30,000 miles of business travel in your car, and you do most of your work at home, the IRS may want to look at your business mileage log.

*Take deductions for your job-hunting expenses.* While any unemployment compensation payments that you may collect are taxable, your expenses in searching for a new job may well be deductible. You probably can write off some expenses if you meet two tests: (1) your search isn't for your first job and (2) you're looking in the same line of work as your old job. Expenses that you can deduct include typing, printing and mailing related to your job search, along with mileage and other expenses for traveling to and from job interviews. If the interviews are out of town, you can deduct 100% of transportation, lodging, and some other expenses, and 50% of meals. To back up your deduction claims, keep a personal diary and receipts and other records from your job search.

*Get a tax break on the sale of your house.* When you sell your principal residence — that's the house or apartment where you live most of the time — you can delay paying taxes on any profit you make *and* you may get a free ride on taxes altogether. You have *two years* to buy a replacement home, and if you pay at least as much for it as you sold your old home for, you don't have to pay any taxes for now. (But if you know you're not going to replace your old house for one that costs at least as much, you had better file Form 2119 in the year of sale. Form 2119 will calculate the tax on any gain, and you should include it in your return.)

Let's say that you bought your original home for $100,000. Over the years, you added another $100,000 in capital improvements. These have to be *long-term* improvements that increase the value of your house, like remodeling the kitchen, adding a bedroom or bath, and so on. And you have to keep reliable receipts and records of all such expenditures. Your total investment is $200,000. Now let's say you sell your house. One or more of four things can happen:

*1. You sell your house for no profit.* If you sell for $200,000 or less, you have not made any profit, so you pay *no* taxes.

*2. You sell your house for a profit.* Example: If you sell your home for $300,000, you make a profit of $100,000. You do not have to pay taxes on this profit for two years, *provided* you think that you will replace the home with one costing at least as much *and* that you will do it within two years. In that case, all you need do is file a Form 2119 that documents your sale.

*3. You buy or build another home within two years and move into it.* Example: If within two years of the sale for $300,000, you buy another principal residence for $300,000 or more *and actually start living in it,* you pay *no* taxes now on your $100,000 profit. If you buy a home for, say, $250,000, you pay taxes on $50,000 of your profit ($300,000 – $250,000 = $50,000).

*4. You are age 55 or older.* If you're at least 55 years old when you sell your principal residence, the IRS allows you a *one-time* exclusion of taxes for up to $125,000 of capital gains. Example: You have that house in which you've invested a total of $200,000, and you sell it for $350,000. You have a capital gain of $150,000. But $125,000 is excluded. So you pay capital-gains taxes on only $25,000. Naturally, if you owned your old house for more than one year, you pay a *long-term* capital-gains tax, at a maximum rate of 28% and often less than that.

Still another thing can happen: You can sell your house for a loss. Until a few years ago, it seemed unthinkable that homeowners might face a capital loss when the time came to sell. But in the 1990s, with real estate prices no longer booming, losses are no longer uncommon. Unfortunately, Uncle Sam refuses to share the pain. If you suffer a loss on the sale of your personal residence, you cannot deduct that loss from your ordinary income. But if you turn your house or apartment into rental property before you sell it, you may be able to deduct the loss.

*Get bigger deductions on rental property.* If you rent out residential property that you own, you have to deduct *remodeling* expenses over many years, but you can deduct *maintenance* expenses in full the year that you pay them. In short, maintenance expenses give you a better tax break. If you do repairs at the same time you do the remodeling, those repair costs may well be considered part of the remodeling. That is *not* to your best tax advantage, because then you have to stretch out your deductions for those repairs for many years instead of taking them immediately.

Here's the distinction between remodeling and maintenance:

Remodeling work adds to the value of your rental property for more than one year and thus enhances its resale value. This work includes major projects such as redoing a kitchen or bathroom, and putting on a new roof or floor. Substantial improvements like these are considered capital expenses, and you depreciate them over 27½ years.

Repair and maintenance, on the other hand, merely preserve the value of your property. They include everyday fixes like patching a screen or painting a door. You deduct these expenses in the immediate tax year.

If you hire a contractor to do both kinds of work, make sure that he or she does remodeling work on different days than the repair and maintenance work. To keep your tax records straight, ask for separate invoices and write separate checks for each kind of work. Again, you can take these deductions only if you rent out the residential property.

*Make your loan-interest payments deductible.* You no longer can deduct your interest payments on consumer loans such as auto or college loans. Nor can you deduct credit-card finance charges or interest you pay the government on tax deficiencies. Ah, but interest payments on home mortgages with a face value up to $1 million and interest payments on home equity loans with a face value of up to $100,000 are deductible. So consider restructuring your debt by taking out a home-equity loan.

*Get deductions for gambling losses.* If you gamble for pleasure, be sure to hold on to your *losing* tickets from the racetrack or the lottery or any other records that show when you lost money. You can deduct those losses from your gambling or lottery winnings, but only up to the amount of your winnings. You cannot deduct more than you won.

Don't expect to beat the house on this one: The IRS may well know when, where and how much you won, and it will expect you to pay taxes on your winnings. When you win a lot of money, whoever pays you off is supposed to ask for your Social Security number, report your number and the size of your take to the IRS and send you a Form W-2G (the "G" is for "gambling").

*Use medical and dental deductions.* The government has taken the teeth out of these deductions. In order to get them, your medical bills have to total more than 7.5% of your adjusted gross income for the year. That is quite a lot, of course, but you may have more deductible medical expenses than you realize.

Are you paying to support a child in college? Then your medical costs include any portion of college fees that covers his or her group health care. Among other often-overlooked expenses are your travel costs on your way to visit a doctor, a hospital or just about any place you go to get medical services. If you buy or rent equipment that your doctor prescribes, such as a whirlpool or dehumidifier, those costs are also deductible expenses (as long as they exceed 7.5% of your adjusted gross income). So are your expenses for insurance premiums on policies covering medical and dental care, and your expenses for replacement contact lenses. Deduct only expenses for which your insurance plan does not reimburse you.

Your medical expenses include those you pay for adult dependents, such as elderly parents or relatives. You can claim these bills if you provide more than half of the dependent's support. A lump-sum payment for lifetime medical care of a dependent can be claimed in the year you made it. The annual cost of institutional care for a mentally or physically handicapped dependent qualifies — so long as the care is medically necessary. By this measure, nursing-home fees can qualify as deductible expenses.

The 1990 tax act eliminated the deduction for unnecessary cosmetic surgery. Such procedures are deductible only if they are necessary to ameliorate a congenital abnormality, personal injury or disfiguring disease.

Some procedures and programs that improve your well-being can be claimed as medical expenses, especially if your doctor prescribes them. Paying for them in one year will enhance your chances of exceeding the 7.5% medical-deduction threshold. But that doesn't meany *every* medical-related expense is deductible. Weight-reduction and stop-smoking programs, for example, aren't deductible. Under current laws, they're not recognized as cures for disease, like alcohol or drug addiction.

You may increase your tax benefits by participating in a cafeteria plan offered by your employer. Also referred to as flexible benefit plans, they allow you to select from a number of qualified benefits, making contributions to your chosen plan in pretax dollars. An example is a flexible spending account (FSA) in which you can set aside pretax earnings to pay up to $5,000 a year in medical costs and $5,000 a year in child care. After making contributions to your plan in pretax dollars, you can then be reimbursed by the plan for specified medical costs without that reimbursement being taxed. Cafeteria plans can also be used to pay for dependent care.

In addition, a self-employed person can deduct 25% of his or her health-insurance premiums without regard to the 7.5% threshold. The remaining 75% of premium costs are considered part of total medical expenses, which then have to exceed the 7.5% threshold.

*Look for some last-minute deductions.* As a year's end approaches, taxpayers eagerly if belatedly start shopping for deductions to take before the year draws to a close. So long as tax rates are stable or decreasing, there are two golden rules of such year-end tax maneuvering. One is to claim all the sensible exemptions, credits and deductions you can in the current year. The other is to delay receiving as much income as you can until next year. That way, you quite legitimately can put off paying taxes on it for a full 12 months.

Self-employed people often delay billing their customers or patients until the very end of December so that the money will not arrive until early the following year. Companies put off paying their year-end executive bonuses until January. If you make estimated payments of state income or local property taxes, send in your final installment in December, instead of January when it usually is due, and you will normally be able to deduct it from your tax bill for the current year. For the same reason send in your January home-mortgage payment before January 1.

You might consider squeezing two years' worth of charitable contributions into this year to increase your deductions. Watch out, however, for maneuvers that may make you eligible for the alternative minimum tax.

You can get extra write-offs for business expenses by prepaying next year's subscriptions to business publications and dues to professional groups. But unless you run your own business, the IRS counts these as miscellaneous expenses — not deductible until they top 2% of your adjusted gross income.

## Getting the Tax Adviser Who Is Best for You

Once you are ready for your actual tax preparation, you may decide to go it alone or, like 51% of Americans, turn to a tax adviser or preparer to help you through the shoals.

Suppose you are salaried, earn less than $40,000 a year, perhaps own a little stock and pay a mortgage. Chances are your tax profile is simple. Then you should be able to handle your own forms with the help of a do-it-yourself tax preparation book. Or you can take your forms to one of the national storefront chains such as H&R Block or Beneficial Income Tax Service. They all charge set fees, depending on the complexity of your form. In 1994 the average price of an H&R Block preparation came to $58.44.

If your personal finances are more complex — say that in the past year you have sold a house, started a business or had active stock trades — you will find that no professional is better trained to handle your taxes than a certified public accountant. It is best to hire a CPA who specializes in taxes, rather than one who does general accounting. Accountants charge $70 an hour and up. Merely having your forms filled out probably will cost at least $300.

If your income is large enough to warrant an accountant's help, you probably will need tax planning, too. At one of the major accounting firms, that could include estate planning, several meetings with a personal adviser on tax strategies and shelters, updates on relevant IRS rulings, quarterly projections of your taxes, and an array of tax reports. The cost is generally more than $3,500. But an experienced CPA in a small firm should be able to approximate this royal treatment for $1,000 to $1,500.

A group of professionals who offer expertise in areas where even accountants fear to tread are tax attorneys. They are great for handling specialized tax problems such as those related to divorce and the sale, purchase or start-up of a business. These lawyers usually work for taxpayers in, or close to, the top tax bracket who want to shelter part of their income. Tax lawyers can argue your case before the IRS and into the U.S. Tax Court. Their rates can be $250 an hour or more.

Whomever you choose to prepare your taxes, he or she should sign your return and should be willing — unequivocally willing — to appear with you at the IRS in the event you are audited.

Before you sign the completed return yourself, read over each line and check to see that the figures correspond with your records. When you do not understand how your preparer arrived at a certain figure, ask. If the IRS finds an error, it is you who will have to pay any back taxes, interest and penalties. So do not just dump your financial records on your accountant's desk and run.

Also make sure your return will be completed before April 15. Recently, one taxpayer's attorney had prepared his forms but sent them in three months late because of a clerical oversight. The Supreme Court ruled that the taxpayer was indeed liable for a late-filing penalty. You should ask your preparer "early and often" how work is coming along on your return. If you think there is a chance he or she will not finish on time, file for an extension.

How can you evaluate the quality of help you will get from an accountant or tax lawyer or storefront tax preparer whom you are contemplating hiring? Start by asking what kind of clients his or her firm handles. See if its members are experienced with people in your situation. Beware of firms that operate on a "pool arrangement," in which your tax forms float among a number of accountants, each of whom handles a few lines. Listen to the questions the tax adviser asks you. If he or she neglects to inquire about the basics of your tax situation — whether you own a home, have a pension plan or contribute to an IRA — you have drawn a dud.

The vast majority of tax professionals are competent and honest, but the number who are incompetent, negligent or fraudulent is probably much higher than the Internal Revenue Service's estimate of only a few thousand out of roughly 200,000 in the country. The government's General Accounting Office has charged that the IRS is not doing enough to find or penalize the wrongdoers.

How can you tell if your tax preparer might be a problem? Watch out for one who demands a percentage of your tax refund as payment. Especially steer away from a preparer who guarantees you a refund. Also, avoid anyone who says he or she will give you a refund right away and will later cash your endorsed IRS check. That is illegal — and subject to a $500 penalty.

If you choose to prepare your forms yourself, there are many good books and software programs to guide you. Full-disclosure note: I have some vested interests in this area since I appear as an on-screen adviser in the TurboTax Multimedia CD-ROM computer program. Among many fine books are the *Consumer Reports Guide to Income Tax* (Consumer Reports Books, $13.99), *The Ernst & Young Tax Guide 1996* (Wiley, $14.95) and *J. K. Lasser's Your Income Tax 1996* (Macmillan Publishing, $14 paperback). Among the highly recommended software programs on CD-ROM are TurboTax Deluxe and MacInTax Deluxe (Intuit, each $44.95), Personal Tax Edge Deluxe (Parsons Technology, $29) and Kiplinger Tax Cut Multimedia (Block Financial Corporation, $29.95).

Whether you prepare your own taxes or get professional help, *here are some basic pitfalls to avoid and warnings to heed.*

Beware of IRA withdrawal penalties. If you have an IRA, a 401(k) or another tax-sheltered retirement plan, you can start making regular withdrawals from it as soon as you turn 59½. But if you take out money at an earlier age, you probably will be hit with a 10% penalty for early

## A SHOPPING BAG OF TAX AND FINANCIAL SOFTWARE

Here are leading personal finance software tools for home use. (Prices may vary.)

| Product/company | PLATFORM WINDOWS | DOS | MAC | List price | Street price |
|---|---|---|---|---|---|
| **Simply Money** Computer Associates, Islandia, NY | ● | | | $69.95 | $32.60 |
| **Managing Your Money** MECA, Fairfield, CT | ● | ● | ● | 35.45 | 34.95 |
| **Quicken Deluxe** Intuit, Palo Alto, CA | ● | | ● | 59.95** | 57.00 |
| **Microsoft Money** Microsoft, Redmond, WA | ● | | | 24.95 | 15.95 |
| **Retirement Planner** Vanguard, Valley Forge, PA | ● | ● | | 18.00 | 18.00* |
| **Prosper** Ernst & Young, New York City, NY | ● | | | 59.95 | 59.95* |
| **TurboTax/MacInTax Deluxe** Intuit, Palo Alto, CA | ● | | ● | 44.95 | 39.00 |
| **Kiplinger TaxCut Multimedia** Black Financial, Kansas City, MO | ● | | ● | 29.95 | 32.50 |
| **Simply Tax** Computer Associates, Islandia, NY | ● | | | 69.99 | 29.95 |
| **Personal Tax Edge Deluxe** Parsons Technology, Hiawatha, IA | ● | ● | ● | 29.00 | 29.00 |
| **TaxSaver** Novell, Orem, UT | ● | ● | | 34.95 | 23.70 |
| **U.S. Equities On Floppy** Morningstar, Chicago, IL | | ● | | 55.00 | 55.00* |
| **Value/Screen III** Value Line Publishing, New York City, NY | | ● | ● | 59.00 | 59.00* |
| **MetaStock** Equis International, Salt Lake City, UT | ● | ● | | 349.00 | 349.00* |
| **SuperCharts** Omega Research, Miami, FL | ● | | | 249.95 | 249.95* |
| **Windows on WallStreet 2.1** MarketArts, Richardson, TX | ● | | | 74.95 | 49.99 |

*Not available through retail stores, only through company

**Minus $10 rebate for resubscribers.

SOURCE: *FORTUNE*

withdrawal. There are some exemptions: You will not be penalized if you withdraw money early if you become disabled before age 59½ and can no longer work. After age 70½ you must begin to take a minimum distribution from the plan or you will pay a 50% penalty plus income tax on the distribution.

There are also no penalties if you take early distributions from your

IRA that are part of a series of equal payments over your lifetime as calculated by the IRS tables. This may be the only way that you can get to your money without paying the early-withdrawal penalty. You receive a yearly distribution for the balance of your life, as calculated by the IRS tables — like an annuity. In all cases, if you die before age 59½, your beneficiaries can collect your IRA assets without penalty within five years of death.

Many early-withdrawal problems strike when you change jobs and move your retirement funds. If your old employer writes you a check for the money, the law requires the employer to withhold 20% for federal taxes and often an added amount for state taxes. You can avoid this deduction if you deposit the full amount of the old retirement money into a qualified new retirement fund. This is known as a direct transfer or a full rollover. Again, you have *only 60* days to make this transaction.

If you take longer than 60 days, three bad things happen: The total amount of your old retirement money is added to your regular income for the year, you have to pay income taxes on the entire amount, and you may well have an additional tax penalty for early withdrawal.

To repeat a supremely important point: Avoiding these costly migraines is easy. Simply have your old employer deposit *all* your retirement fund money *directly* into a qualified tax-deferred fund with your new employer. This direct transfer is the safest and best way to move retirement funds because they are free from withholding taxes and early-withdrawal penalties.

*Beware of overlooking deductions.* It's smart to compare this year's tax returns with last year's — to make sure you don't forget to take any deductions, losses or credits. The claim that people most commonly miss is the state tax payment they make between January and April. If you cut a check to the state between January and April, then that is claimed as a deduction in the return you file the following year. But you can estimate those taxes and cut a check in December. In this way you can claim the deduction sooner and are less likely to forget about it in next year's return.

People also forget to carry forward claims from previous years. These claims are usually deductions *above* the limit you could take the previous year. They include charitable contributions (which are generally limited to 50% of adjusted gross income), capital losses (which are limited to the amount of capital gain plus $3,000 claimed against ordinary income), investment interest (which is limited to net investment income in any one year), business rent or home office expenses (which is limited to the net income of the business in any one year) or real estate losses (limited to passive income under the passive-loss rules). Don't overlook business tax credits (e.g., foreign tax credits, building in an enterprise zone, research credit). Each of the business tax credits has its own set of rules and limitations.

*Beware of missing mail.* When you mail in your tax returns or other important information, it's wise to spend a few dollars for certified mail with a return receipt requested. That way you'll have a document proving that you sent your tax return on the day you said you did, and that someone on the other end received it. And, of course, be sure that you — and your spouse, if filing jointly — have signed and dated your return and that your Social Security numbers are correct. If you are filing any tax forms besides the 1040, be sure that they are also signed and dated in all the specified places.

*Beware of losing your job-related expenses.* If you spend money on expenses related to your job, try to get your employer to reimburse you whenever you can. Even though you are allowed to deduct job-related expenses — such as subscriptions to professional journals, education related to your job or required uniforms — you usually lose money when your company doesn't pay you back. One reason is that your so-called employee business expenses are itemized in the miscellaneous category, and so they are deductible only when they exceed 2% of your adjusted gross income. If, for example, you have an adjusted income of $50,000, the first $1,000 of miscellaneous deductions just doesn't count. But companies do not face this limitation. For them, reimbursed employee expenses are 100% deductible (except for entertainment expenses). Wherever possible, you should also try to obtain checks for the reimbursement of business expenses separately from your paychecks.

## Beware of Throwing Away Important Records

Accountants often complain that their clients' idea of record-keeping involves tossing all sorts of papers into a shoe box or shopping bag and handing over the unsorted mess at tax time. To save heaps of time when doing your taxes, or heaps of money when your tax preparer does them, emulate Brer Squirrel. Save everything.

## Giving to the Presidential Election Campaign Fund

You may have wondered about the question on your 1040 asking whether you want to contribute to the Presidential Election Campaign Fund. If you mark "yes" in this box, you dedicate $3 of your taxes — or up to $6 if filing jointly — toward presidential election campaigns. Nearly 14.5% of Americans did just that in 1993. This has no impact on your taxes. Whether you say yes or no or leave this box blank, the taxes you owe — or the refund you are due — will not change.

Congress established the fund in 1973. It helps pay for party nominating conventions and other general election expenses. In the primary elections, qualified candidates receive matching federal dollars from this fund for some of the money that they raised privately. The fund has three purposes: to help reduce presidential candidates' dependence on special interest contributions, to reduce the demands of fund-raising so candidates can devote more time to discussing issues, and to promote a more competitive field of candidates through a combination of public funding and expenditure limits.

The tax check-off box is the only source of public funding for presidential election campaigns. When the fund was close to insolvency in 1993, Congress raised the contribution from $1 to $3. The Federal Election Commission, which administers the fund, says that this should be enough to support the next two presidential elections.

As the late editor and Certified Financial Planner Robert Klein advised:

The best and safest place to keep tax records is a well-organized, fire-resistant filing cabinet. Set up several headings that make sense to you, but be sure to provide a place for any slip of paper that could conceivably save you tax money or headaches, either now or in the distant future.

There are a multitude of computer software programs that you can use to put together the numbers and save you or your tax preparer lots of time, but you will always need to retain the original supporting documentation for some years. A list of vital documents would include the W-2 and 1099 forms that arrive in your pay envelope or in the mail after the first of the year, brokerage records of capital gains and losses, records of retirement-plan payments and withdrawals, doctors' bills and health-insurance reimbursement statements.

If you earn enough from investments or moonlighting to require payment of estimated quarterly taxes, reserve a filing slot for your Form 1040-ES, its accompanying worksheets for the current year and a record of each quarterly payment made. Medical bills must equal 7.5% of your adjusted gross income before you can start deducting them, but you never know when your turn will come for an avalanche of surgical, dental or drug costs. So tuck away in their own special filing slot receipts for prescription and over-the-counter drugs, health-insurance premiums and notes on mileage driven to visit doctors, hospitals and other treatment centers. Also store there the reimbursement records that come with health-insurance checks.

The list of things to file goes on: receipts for real estate taxes, charitable donations, job-hunting expenses and relocation costs and child-care services; the Social Security numbers of nannies and other domestic employees; year-end pay stubs showing cumulative deductions for health insurance, retirement plans and charitable contributions. If you are divorced, keep records of alimony and child-care payments made or received, and also your ex-spouse's Social Security number and a copy of the divorce decree.

Label other manila folders for statements of interest on mortgages and home-equity loans; K-1 tax forms; and financial records for limited partnerships, S corporations, and estates and trusts. Keep a log of unreimbursed business expenses, such as mileage driven in your own car, along with receipts for car rentals and fares for public transportation, including taxis.

Canceled checks and old bank statements are essential documents for tax files. Keep the latest 12 months' worth handy and older batches in long-term storage on the remote chance of a tax audit. Save all mutual-fund monthly statements. They are vital when a mutual fund is redeemed. Past statements help determine the cost basis of the shares you redeem. This information is necessary to determine your capital gain or loss.

After you have sent in the year's tax returns — federal, state and perhaps city forms as well as small-business or corporate forms — there is more filing to be done. Stuff all the supporting documents and records in a large envelope or container and label it with the year. Keep last year's package in or near your current tax file in case you get a query about the contents from the IRS, the state taxing authority or your tax preparer. Find a storage place for earlier years' records — always keeping each year's data separate.

Keep all supporting income and tax documents for at least seven years. These include tax-related receipts, canceled checks, investment paperwork, W-2s, 1099s, end-of-the-year records from banks and brokerage houses, and doctors' bills. You might consider using a personal finance software program to help keep track of your income and expenses.

Some papers, however, should be held on to permanently. Among them are real estate records. The average single-family home is owned for only seven or eight years. That means you will probably have a capital gain to report, though not necessarily a tax to pay, at fairly frequent intervals. Each time you sell your principal residence and buy another for the same amount of money or more, you can postpone paying the tax. But to minimize the eventual taxable gain, you must accumulate records that trace the financial history of every house you have owned. For this purpose, store in a safe place, such as your bank vault, all the documents that were generated when you bought each home. These include the property survey, the closing statement or escrow statement, the real estate broker's itemized invoice showing the sales commissions and other selling costs, and the many receipts that changed hands at the title closing.

As a further aid to figuring eventual gains, keep a separate but permanent file at home, where you can conveniently add to it receipts for any work that might qualify as a capital improvement. Anything that adds to the value of your home or prolongs its life is an improvement, from a built-in barbecue grill to weather stripping, from shrubs to a new kitchen. When in doubt about a home-improvement expense, file the receipt.

Again, to protect these irreplaceable records, it's best to store them in a fireproof strongbox. Keep duplicate records in a ledger of home improvements in your bank vault. Once a year, and after major projects, update your capital-improvements ledger. When you sell your home, you will need a complete record of the improvements you have made to it and to earlier properties and, above all, the receipts from contractors, home-improvement stores, nurseries and such. By carrying forward these costs, you will cut down your eventual taxable gain. Remember, however, the burden of proof is on you, the taxpayer.

Also store the purchase prices of stock in a permanent file. These figures become important when stock is sold.

Resolve to keep better records of all your tax-deductible expenses this year. As mentioned, at tax time pack rats always pay less. Silly little deductions have a way of becoming impressive big ones. Hold on to even your grocery receipts when the purchases are for business entertaining.

Records are all the more important because deductions are harder to come by than they once were. Always eager to squelch too much of a good thing, Congress in 1990 began taking away deductions for high earners. Single or married, if you have gross income of more than $114,700 for 1995, you lose 3 cents' worth of deductions for every $1 of income in six figures. For example, if you have an adjusted gross income of $150,000, you lose $1,059 in deductions ($150,000 – $114,700 = $35,300 × .03 = $1,059). There is a limit to how much the government can reduce your deductions, however: The reductions can never total more than 80% of your allowable deductions. And each year, the base amount of income rises a bit due to cost-of-living adjustments.

The new tax-the-rich formula applies to all itemized deductions except medical expenses, theft and casualty losses, and interest payments you incur to earn income.

Tax credits — which you can get for child-care expenses and certain investments, among other things — are much better than tax deductions. Deductions reduce only the taxable income on which your taxes are calculated, but credits reduce your actual taxes, dollar for dollar. So if you have a chance to gain any credits, take it.

Keeping thorough records helps you remember all the deductions you're entitled to and can protect you in case of an audit. Remember, you need to keep your tax returns and all tax records for at least six years. These include receipts, canceled checks, investment documents, W-2 forms, 1099 forms, end-of-year records from banks and brokerage houses, loan documents, doctors' bills and health-insurance statements, and receipts ranging from child-care expenses to job-hunting costs. The IRS will also accept personal diaries that document out-of-pocket expenses, so keep a calendar, too. In any year that you received money you didn't report as income — no matter how legal the reason was for not reporting it — keep that year's return and your records supporting it *forever.* If the IRS discovers that you were paid this money, it may be able to claim that your return was fraudulent. There is *no* statute of limitations for tax fraud.

## Beware of Overpaying

It's just not smart to overpay your taxes in order to get a large refund. For one thing, you lose money; the IRS doesn't pay interest. And you may incite some IRS official to wonder why your refund is so large. One question can lead to another, and then another, and then to an audit — and another audit.

You are much better off to make a close estimate of what your tax bill is likely to add up to, and pay accordingly. You can get help in making an estimate from the payroll office where you work, or from a tax accountant, or from a computerized tax-software program. The software enables you to plug in estimates of your income, deductions and so forth, and then gives you an idea of what you probably will owe. When you know this, you can figure out the proper amount that your employer should be withholding from your gross income every payday, or you can prepare an estimated payment. This helps you avoid undue IRS scrutiny.

Once you figure out what you owe, pay that amount. Then put the rest of your funds in a place where you get interest in cash, not interest in auditing your tax returns.

In sum, if you get an income tax refund this year, don't feel smug. You just gave the government an interest-free loan last year. The average refund is about $900. Had you invested that yourself over the years, you could be hundreds or even thousands of dollars richer by now.

Some people prefer to overpay. They figure that building up an income tax refund acts like a forced savings plan. They reckon that had they collected that extra money instead as part of each paycheck, they just would have spent it. But here's a much better idea: Have that extra money withheld from your pay not for taxes but for either a 401(k) retirement-savings plan or the purchase of Series EE U.S. savings bonds in your company's payroll savings program.

You can reduce your withholding by instructing your payroll office to change the number of so-called allowances on your W-4 form, the Employee's Withholding Allowance Certificate. Each allowance exempts $2,500 of your 1995 pay from withholding.

The amount rises from year to year in step with inflation. You get an automatic exemption for yourself, for your spouse and for each child who is either younger than 19 years old or a full-time student under age 24. If your full-time student is 24 or older, he or she could earn no more than $2,500 in 1995 to count as an exemption. If you cannot claim the exemption, the child may claim the exemption on his or her own return.

*A caution:* Personal exemptions have been phased out for certain high-income taxpayers. The phase-out is 2% per $2,500 of adjusted gross income (or fraction thereof) over $114,700 for single taxpayers, $172,050 for couples filing jointly, and $143,350 for heads of households. The phase-out stops at adjusted gross incomes over $237,200 for singles, $294,550 for married couples filing jointly, and $265,850 for heads of households. In other words, if you earn that much, you cannot take any personal exemptions. Consult your tax preparer.

To find out how many exemptions you can claim, use your tax return for last year to estimate your deductions for the current year. Then check the table on the W-4 to calculate the number of allowances your deductions generate. But do not go overboard in claiming exemptions. Your withholding payments plus any estimated tax payments have to total at least as much as your actual tax liability *last* year, or 90% of your ultimate tax liability for the *current* year. Otherwise, you could get hit with an underpayment penalty.

Once you have made all your preparations for filing, there are still several important questions you need to address:

*What is the best time to file?* The answer is the earlier the better after January 1 — if you expect to get a refund. If you file by the end of February, you should receive your check in the mail within six weeks. But if you delay till April, when the IRS is deluged by forms from other last-minute taxpayers, you could face a 12-week wait for your refund.

If you have the money to pay but just cannot complete your tax return by the April 15 deadline, the IRS will extend your day of filing to August 15. But you must send in an extension form — IRS Form 4868 — and an estimated payment of your taxes by April 15. Just estimate your income for last year and subtract any deductions and credits you expect to take. Then refer to the tax tables in the Form 1040 instruction booklet for the amount you owe.

If you still cannot complete your tax return by August 15, you may apply for an additional extension by using IRS Form 2688. The IRS may extend your day of filing to October 15, if the agency agrees with your reason for requesting the extension. This is your last deadline. All of these deadlines change if the 15th falls on a Saturday or Sunday. The due date then becomes the Monday immediately after the 15th. As for delaying payment of state taxes: Some states require that you send in their own special extension forms, but others will accept a copy of the approved federal extension form. Check your state tax office.

If you underestimate your federal tax bill, you may have to pay a 0.5%-a-month penalty — plus interest — on your outstanding balance. But if you send in your return late *without* having filed for an extension, the IRS will be much less forgiving, and you will have to pay a "failure to file" penalty. For each month or part of a month past the due date that the taxes are not filed, the penalty is 5% of the tax liability, not to exceed 25%. You also may be charged annual interest, compounded daily.

Another matter to watch: Even if you file an extension form, you must make your past year's contribution to your IRA by April 15. But if you have a Keogh plan, you can make your contribution to it up until the extended due date. If you have a SEP plan, you may also take an extension.

If you have omitted information or would like to add information to your tax return after you have filed it, you may prepare amended federal and state returns. Generally, the IRS allows you up to three years from the original filing date to amend your return.

*What if you can't pay on time?* Almost one out of four people who owe taxes on April 15 cannot pay. What if you come to the cold discovery that you owe the government more than you can possibly raise in cash?

Don't panic. As noted, what you should do is file your tax return on time and send in whatever amount you can. Otherwise, you will be stuck with stiff penalties.

You need to tell the government about your inability to pay now. Under the law, the IRS can attach your paycheck and seize your bank accounts and house. But it almost never takes such drastic action — if you earnestly try to pay your debts.

The key is communication. If you do not enclose a check with at least a portion of what you owe when you file your return, you eventually will receive a letter demanding payment within 10 days. Do not ignore this notice: The IRS gets tougher with every passing day. Just be sure to phone or visit the IRS office listed on the delinquency notice. Do that immediately after receiving the first notice instead of waiting for the fourth and final one about three months later. If you have a professional tax adviser, bring him or her along to the tax office. Your adviser probably will charge you, but he or she can get the IRS to agree to better terms than you can.

Several hundred delinquent taxpayers each year manage to persuade the IRS to reduce the amounts they owe. But such deals are reserved for people who the tax collectors think will never be able to pay their bills in full. For example, an elderly person with little in the way of assets and small chance of earning much might be a candidate for such a compromise.

Once this ordeal is over, make a point of preventing it from happening again. If you are a wage-earner, take fewer withholding allowances at work so more tax money will be deducted from your pay. If you are self-employed, increase your quarterly estimated tax payments.

*How does the IRS size up your 1040?* It was always a bad idea to try to cheat on your income tax, and it is even worse now. Supercomputers enable the tax collectors to examine your income more intimately and thoroughly than ever before. Until recently about the only lines on your tax return that the IRS could check and verify without an audit were those for interest income, dividends, salaries and wages. But the list is growing fast.

The IRS corroborates against other sources such income as any state and local tax refunds you may have received, proceeds you collected from any sales of investments, your Social Security benefits, IRA and pension payouts, and your mortgage-interest deductions and alimony income. By law, companies, banks, brokerage firms and government agencies that pay you various types of income must fill out IRS forms stating the amounts distributed to you during the year. Banks and other institutions have to declare how much interest they collect and any IRA contributions they receive from you.

It may take about 18 months for the IRS to finish matching the information it gets from these sources with what you declare on your 1040 tax forms. When there is a discrepancy that does not look like a harmless error, an IRS computer will fire off a letter demanding that you explain the difference or pay up. If you under-report interest or dividend income, the letter also will say that you owe a 20% penalty. Other discrepancies do not produce an automatic fine, although the IRS could try to prove in court that you intentionally tried to misrepresent your earnings or deductions.

You should check any IRS notice that you receive before sending in the amount shown as due. You may have listed the income under another name on your tax return, or in a different income category. If so, write a letter to the IRS explaining the discrepancy and asking the agency to adjust its notice. The IRS is not always correct.

## How Do You Get Quick Answers?

Whom do you call when you have a question or two when preparing your tax forms? Try the IRS. It provides recorded tax information that is accurate, reasonably clear and free.

The 24-hour IRS Federal TeleTax Information number to call is 800-829-1040; or check your local office for a separate telephone listing. The national number provides recorded information divided into 18 main categories, with a total of 140 subjects listed and their corresponding three-digit codes. Once you place the call, you punch these codes on your Touch-Tone phone to get a recorded discussion of the selected subject. (If you have a rotary phone you may call 800-829-1040 during normal business hours.)

In most cases, the recordings also refer you to free IRS publications for more information. If you want to talk directly to an IRS staff member, you can call the IRS's headquarters in Washington, D.C., or the local office nearest you. The trouble is, according to tests by the General Accounting Office and *Money* magazine, the live answers are often wrong. You stand your best chance of getting through to IRS staffers if you phone early in the morning or late in the week. But you can get recorded help around the clock seven days a week with a Touch-Tone phone.

# How Do You Complain to the IRS?

Say that you are entitled to a tax refund but it does not arrive, or it is smaller than expected, or you receive a bill to pay additional tax. If you have a complaint about your taxes, there are a few secrets for getting action — and satisfaction — out of the IRS.

Taxpayers have the right to be treated fairly, promptly, professionally and courteously by IRS employees. To help ensure such treatment, the IRS has a publication, *Your Rights as a Taxpayer,* that explains these rights.

What if you have tried all the normal routes and failed? For example, you've called all the numbers listed on IRS notices sent to you and received little or no assistance with your problem. If you have an administrative problem — such as unanswered inquiries, a delayed refund, incorrect billing notices — then get in touch with one of the agency's problem-resolution officers, or PROs. There is one of these merciful missionaries in each IRS district office and service center. If you call a PRO, he or she usually can sweep away weeks or months of potential bureaucratic frustration. If your problem isn't settled in five working days, the PRO is supposed to advise you of the status of the case and give you the name and phone number of the person down the line who can solve it.

If you disagree with a specific IRS tax ruling, or even the constitutionality of the tax system, you can then take your case to an IRS appeals office. If you lose there, you have 90 days to take one of three further steps:

First, you can withhold payment on a claim of less than $10,000 and bring your case to the small-claims division of the U.S. Tax Court.

Second, you can pay a disputed tax of any amount and file for a refund with your IRS office. If it's disallowed, you then can sue in a U.S. District Court or the Claims Court. The odds are clearly not in your favor, but quite a few people do get satisfaction.

The Claims Court has several drawbacks for aggrieved taxpayers. Fighting a case there requires you to make a trip to Washington. Before your case is even heard, you must pay not only the taxes in dispute but also any interest and penalties. Yes, you do get a refund if you win. But only when you can afford the cost and inconvenience should you resort to the Claims Court.

Third, you can sue in the U.S. Tax Court without paying the tax in advance. But in the past several years taxpayers had full victories in only a small percentage of cases.

You probably can avoid the courts if you have a legitimate claim. Indeed, if an IRS problem-resolution officer cannot help you, go to your congressman instead of to the courts. Often, he or she or an aide can break a logjam in your case in a matter of hours.

# How Do You Deal with a Tax Audit?

If you become one of the million or so unfortunate taxpayers who are audited each year, keep cool. The damage probably will be minimal, unless you have engaged in outright fraud. Little more than 1% of all personal income tax returns are audited, so chances are that you are safe. But if you are called in by the IRS for one of those troubling and time-consuming procedures, you can take some comfort from these facts:

About one in nine or 10 audited taxpayers emerged from the process in 1993 owing no more than when he or she filed. Indeed, about five in 100 people who were audited came away with refunds averaging about $5,900. Many thousands of others negotiated settlements with the IRS that left them paying more taxes, but less than the agency originally had demanded.

Who gets audited? Anyone can, of course. Whether or not you will be audited depends mostly on how closely your tax data compare with the average deductions, exemptions and credits claimed by taxpayers with your income. The bigger your income, the more likely you will be audited. High-income people who make the greatest use of sophisticated tax breaks are the most likely to claim the kinds of debatable write-offs that the IRS likes to challenge. Also prime candidates for audits are people who are paid mostly in cash, such as waiters, taxi drivers and beauticians.

The IRS generally begins sending out audit notices in July of the year in which the returns in question are filed. If you receive a letter saying your return will be audited, you typically have up to six weeks to get ready for a meeting at a local IRS office. There is one exception: If the deductions in question can be easily documented, you can respond by mail.

Typically, you may get a letter from IRS officials asking about one of your deductions, or about some interest payment they think you should have reported. Don't panic. The IRS just wants clarification. What's usually happening is that a bank, a brokerage or some other company reported that it paid something to you, but the IRS computers can't find where you reported that payment on your tax return. The computers match the payments you say you have received with the payments that employers, banks, brokerages, government agencies and others say that they have paid to you. The tax collector can verify your interest income, dividends, salaries and wages, state and local tax refunds, Social Security benefits, IRA and pension payouts, mortgage-interest deductions, alimony income and just about everything else that you receive or deduct.

You may already have explained where you recorded the payment in question on your return, but the IRS missed your explanation or did not know where to look. In that case, just send a polite letter to the IRS pointing out where to look on your forms, or explaining the discrepancy. Address the letter to the IRS office that notified you of the problem.

But if the letter the IRS sent to you tells you to show up *in person* at an IRS office, *that* is an invitation to an audit.

After such a notice arrives, try to get some idea of how extensive the examination is going to be. One way is to phone the IRS and say you want to schedule an appointment on a day when no one will be rushed. If the IRS agent responds that the interview should not take longer than a couple of hours, relax. It is likely to be a hasty one-hour job. That is the kind most people get. But if you are told to set aside a week, then you know it will be a serious review — and you have trouble.

On the other hand, you may show up at the IRS office only to find that the audit has been called because you "won" the IRS random drawing — a sampling of taxpayers are automatically audited each year — or because the IRS is confused by one or two things on your return.

If you find that you are repeatedly audited for the same deductions — say, higher-than-average dental bills — and these deductions have been allowed in the past, have your tax preparer write to the IRS to ask that the latest audit be canceled. When he or she points out that in past years these deductions have been allowed, you have a better than 50% chance of avoiding an audit this year. Too bad, this is not the case with an audit of taxes on your business if you are self-employed and report on a Schedule C.

Before you go into any audit, be sure you are well briefed. Confer in advance with your tax preparer. You probably will have to pay his or her usual fee for the strategy session, but it's well worth the expense to have your preparer explain the reasoning behind any challenged deductions, exemptions or credits.

Always bring a tax professional along, if you can, to help explain your return. Your preparer can even appear instead of you, though only if he or she is a CPA, an attorney or someone who has passed a tough IRS test to become a so-called enrolled agent. That rules out most storefront preparers. Insist that the audit take place at the IRS or at the office of your preparer, but not at your own home or office. There is no point in giving the tax collector a more complete picture of your economic situation than he or she will get from your written return.

When you make your appearance, dress professionally, bring all your tax records, arrive on time, and be courteous and correct. As in any business situation, good manners are important. Your attitude will do a lot to determine how tough or lenient the auditor will be, so be polite.

Do not act belligerently toward your IRS examiner. Do not speak loudly. Do not smoke and do not wear clothing or jewelry that might cause the auditor to think that your income is higher than you reported.

The most important factor in deciding the audit's outcome will be the evidence you present to support your deductions. A dossier of receipts, bills and diaries will help you document your write-offs. You will do best if you offer a sound defense without appearing defensive. You might even ask for additional deductions at your audit. If you can document them, you may improve your overall bargaining position.

Whatever you're asked to explain, remain calm. Don't get defensive or angry with an IRS auditor. Answer the questions simply and directly, but never volunteer any information. And remember: You don't have to answer every question *immediately.* If there are questions you don't understand, write them down, then make an appointment to come back later with the answer.

As long as you are professional and courteous, your auditor should behave the same way. If he or she does not, then politely but insistently request a switch to another auditor. You have the right to demand another auditor if the one assigned to you is abusive. In short, you have the right to be treated well, even in an audit.

If you are not satisfied with the outcome of your audit, you can appeal on the spot to the examiner's supervisor. That person will come to his or her own conclusion. If you then are still dissatisfied, you have 30 days to ask that an IRS appeals officer hear your case. You might find him or her more willing to concede some or all of the issues than your auditor was. Unlike auditors, appeals officers are allowed to weigh the cost of a possible court battle in determining how much, if anything, you should pay.

You can appeal further to the U.S. Tax Court, District Court or Claims Court. But before you take that step, you should decide whether the battle is really worth it. Tax Court cases are typically long, often expensive and rarely successful.

*A final note: There is nothing wrong with employing legal tax-reduction strategies. Every one of them was put into the tax code by an act of Congress or a judicial decision for some purpose — at best to encourage Americans to save, invest and become homeowners, which in turn enables businesses to start, to grow and to expand employment. As the late Judge Learned Hand said in a 1947 tax decision, "Nobody owes any public duty to pay more than the law demands: Taxes are enforced exactions, not voluntary contributions."*

CHAPTER 10

# Using Credit Cards and Borrowing Intelligently

## Getting the Best Deals in Loans

Will Shakespeare had it wrong when he admonished, "Neither a borrower nor a lender be." In fact, borrowing can be like wine: good for you — in moderation.

Here's your basic guide to borrowing sensibly:

- Never borrow more than you can reasonably pay off.
- Never borrow for luxuries, such as sports cars or jewelry, if that means you will not be able to borrow for necessities, such as mortgage, medical or education expenses. After necessities, in order of importance, are loans to finance long-term assets such as home improvements, major appliances, and furniture.
- Be sure to reserve some borrowing capacity for emergencies, such as unforeseen medical bills.

It used to be that borrowing could actually save you money in the long run. When inflation was running wild, it made sense to avoid future price increases by buying on credit. No longer. Inflation has been moderate, so the real cost of borrowing in the mid-1990s has been at one of its highest points in years. In mid-1995 banks were charging an average 18.08% on your credit-card purchases. Well, subtract the 3.2% inflation rate from the 18.08% interest rate, and you see that you would be paying a real rate of nearly 15% on your credit-card loan. Compare that with the real rate in 1980. Back then it was only 4%!

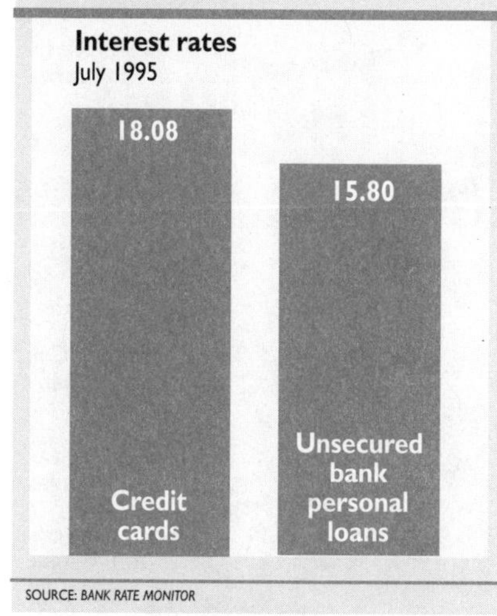


Another reason why borrowing is much costlier than some years ago: Your interest payments on car, college, credit-card and other consumer loans are no longer tax-deductible. That increases the pressure on you to consider carefully your many credit choices and to shop around for the most favorable rates and terms.

When looking for money, you should canvass several different kinds of lenders. That's because no bank, savings and loan, credit union or finance company will charge the lowest rate for every type of borrowing. Here are seven sources of loans:

*One:* The sensible place to start searching for a general-purpose loan is where you keep your checking and savings accounts. Many banks charge as much as two percentage points less for loans to current customers than they do for loans to new customers. In mid-1995 major banks in New York City were charging about 10.5% for personal loans that you could secure with collateral such as a savings account, CDs, stocks or bonds. For unsecured loans — which you often can get if you have a good job or regular income and can afford the repayments — they were charging about 15.8%. The rates are sometimes a couple of points less than the average for your credit-card debts. So if you are paying interest on big credit-card balances, it may make sense to switch to an unsecured credit line and pay off your plastic.

Your own bank also may be a good starting point for financing for a new car. True, in recent years the finance arms of General Motors, Ford and Chrysler might have charged you less for a car loan than a bank would have. But banks have wised up and are offering more competitive rates, while the manufacturers have pulled back and are doing fewer and more limited deals. Be smart and investigate both sources of financing.

*Two:* When financing a house or apartment, you generally will get the most competitive rates and terms at savings and loan associations and at mortgage banking firms. Once again, it pays to scout around, because rates vary from lender to lender and the savings can be gigantic over the long life of a mortgage. In evaluating the terms of different loans, be sure to compare the points — one point equals 1% of the loan, and you pay it up front.

If you already own a home, you can turn it into a piggy bank by applying for either a second mortgage or a home-equity loan. The best place to get a second mortgage is a bank or savings and loan association. In mid-1995 the rate averaged 10.17%. You can get a home-equity credit line from banks, S&Ls and brokerage firms. The rate in mid-1995 averaged 10.57%.

*Three:* Another source of cheap credit may be your whole life insurance policy. Such policies written before 1980 permit borrowing at 6% or even less; policies written after that have either fixed or variable rates that in 1995 averaged around 8% to 9%.

**BIG DIFFERENCES IN INTEREST RATES**

20%
15%
10%
5%
0%
7/93
7/94
7/95
Credit cards
Car loans
30-year mortgages
15-year mortgages
1-year ARM
1-year Treasury bills
1-year CDs

SOURCES: *BANK RATE MONITOR*; TREASURY DEPARTMENT

The amount you can borrow depends on the number of years that the policy has been in effect, your age when it was issued, and the size of the policy's death benefit. You do not have to disclose the reason for the loan, and you can repay it at your own pace — or not at all. But the policy's death benefit declines along with the unpaid balance.

For more information, contact Insurance Information Inc., 23 Route 143, South Dennis, Massachusetts 02660; 800-472-5800. It's a database service, and for $50 it will send you the names of five companies offering the most advantageous loan rates. Should you find a better deal, you will not be charged. Another source: The Consumer Federation of America,

Insurance Division, 414 A Street SE, Washington, D.C. 20003; 202-547-6426. For $25 the federation will send you an analysis of the investment return of a variety of insurance policies, including annuities.

*Four:* Many companies also let vested employees borrow from their assets in corporate profit-sharing, 401(k), stock purchase and savings plans. Three-quarters of all companies offering 401(k)s enable you to borrow some of your own contributions and often your employer's contributions, too. The interest rate is likely to be lower than you would pay to a bank or other commercial lender. It's a fixed rate based on a money-market indicator such as the prime lending rate or the rate paid on five-year Treasury notes.

Typically you can borrow *all* of your vested benefit up to $10,000 in a company savings plan, and up to *one-half* of your vested benefit between $10,000 and $50,000. Federal restrictions limit the maximum loan to $50,000, and employers must charge the going market rate of interest, usually one or two percentage points above the prime rate. In mid-1995 that amounted to around 10.5%. You usually make your repayments through payroll deductions. Federal law requires you to repay the loan at least quarterly, and finish repayment within five years. One exception: If you are using the money to buy your primary residence, you can get a payback period of 10 to 25 years.

If you need some money for a short time, you can borrow it from your Individual Retirement Account once a year with impunity — just so long as you repay it all within 60 days. If you don't replace the funds by then, the IRS will claim as a penalty 10% of the money you take out *and* you will owe income tax at your regular rate on the total withdrawal. Just go to the bank or brokerage house or wherever you have your IRA on deposit and take out some or all of your assets. If your IRA is invested in stocks or mutual funds, you may sell them. You pay no interest on the loan because you are acting as your own banker. On the other hand, you will not collect any interest or dividends on your money until you repay it.

*Five:* If you borrow from your family, you can find terms of endearment. A relative can give you up to $10,000 every year without incurring any federal gift tax; or he or she can lend you an unlimited amount, without running into the tax, provided you pay him or her a market rate of interest.

Of course, in exchange for cheap credit, you run the risk of straining a family relationship. To lessen that possibility, draw up a promissory note; many stationery stores sell preprinted forms. The agreement should include a repayment schedule. If the loan is large and interest is charged, you should agree to an annual rate that is high enough to compensate your relatives for their forgone income.

*Six:* Credit unions are another source, but few of them make unsecured personal loans larger than $5,000. (By contrast, many banks give their customers $10,000 credit lines secured only by a signature, though you will have to satisfy a series of income, net worth and length-of-employment requirements.)

You can join a credit union by depositing only a nominal sum — typically $5 to $25. Joining is a lot easier than it used to be; membership now tops 66 million people. You may be eligible and not even know it. You may not have to work for the same company or belong to the same union or community organization as other members. For example, the First Community Credit Union in St. Louis, once open only to Monsanto employees, now accepts residents of three communities near the Monsanto headquarters, as well as employees of more than 200 other companies in the area. Some credit unions even permit members' relatives to join. For more information about credit unions in your area, write to Credit Union National Association, Box 431, Madison, Wisconsin 53701.

*Seven:* If you own publicly traded stocks or bonds or mutual funds, you can take out a margin loan from a stockbroker, commonly for half the value of your securities. They act as your collateral. You'll generally pay interest at 0.5% to 2.5% above a base lending rate determined by the brokerage firm itself. The interest rates as of mid-1995 were 9% to 11%. Interest is usually charged to your account and compounded once a month. This interest will be tax-deductible, provided that the securities are not themselves tax-exempt and you have investment income against which to offset the interest.

The size of the loan you will qualify for depends on the type and market value of the securities you pledge, and the purpose of the loan. If you want $15,000 to buy stocks, for example, you must already own shares or convertible bonds worth that amount. That is, with $15,000 as collateral, you can borrow another $15,000 and double your stake in the stock market. But if you want to borrow $15,000 to buy a car, you will need $30,000 worth of these securities. Other forms of securities, such as municipal bonds, Treasury notes and corporate bonds, may also be used for collateral, but brokerage houses differ somewhat on their margin requirements.

Now, say you have an all-purpose asset-management account at a bank or a brokerage house. You can borrow against your deposited assets by cashing checks drawn on the account. The rates vary with the size of the loan, but in mid-1995 they were 8.25% to 8.75%.

Finally, if other lenders will not oblige, you can investigate consumer-finance companies. Such firms make high-rate loans to high-risk customers, and thus are to be avoided if possible.

# Getting Money from Your House

When you borrow against the equity you have built up in your home, your choices include home-equity loans, second mortgages and refinancing. Of the three, probably the least costly are home-equity loans. They are essentially overdraft checking accounts that you can open at a bank or brokerage firm, using your home equity to secure the credit.

They spare you the hassle of securing a conventional second mortgage. An independent appraiser values your house, and then you can usually borrow 70% to 80% of your equity in it. You must borrow at least $1,000 and are likely to pay an interest rate about 1% or 2% above the prime rate, but that is lower than the usual charge for second mortgages. Many lenders may offer a below-market introductory interest rate for the first year (or even three years) to get your business. In mid-1995 the home-equity rates averaged 10.57%. There is no penalty if you pay off your loan early. In addition, the interest up to $100,000 is still fully tax-deductible.

Keep in mind that major brokerage houses and even insurance companies are matching or beating the banks on home-equity loans. One good deal: Prudential Bank & Trust (800-426-4331) offers home-equity loans at the prime rate (8.75% in mid-1995). But you must pay closing costs and a fee.

This type of loan is good for financing a child's education or an addition to the house. But because the funds are so accessible, beware of using a homeowners equity account for risky investments. If you lose all your money, you lose your equity in the house, too!

If you are a retired homeowner, you can get monthly income from your property and still live in it. Look into a so-called reverse mortgage, also referred to by the Federal Housing Authority as a home-equity conversion mortgage. It lets you borrow against the equity in your fully (or nearly) paid-for house and collect the loan proceeds — in the form of monthly payments or a line of credit, or a combination of both. This goes on for as long as you live in the house, or a shorter term if desired. At the end of the term, you have to pay off the loan and the interest, which may mean selling the house.

Elderly parents can tap the equity in their homes by selling their property to their children. The parents then can (1) invest the proceeds from the sale in income-yielding securities and (2) rent the house back from their children. That way, the children get the tax benefits of owning and renting out their property — deductions for property taxes, mortgage interest and depreciation. They must charge their parents a fair market value rent. But they can forgive all or part of this rent by making it a tax-free gift. The limit for annual tax-free gifts is $10,000 from a child to one parent, or $20,000 if both parents are still alive.

Then there's the shared-appreciation type of reverse mortgage. It assures you of income for the rest of your life or until you move. In one variation, you take out a loan against your house and pledge to give the lender (known in this case as the "investor") a specific percentage of any future appreciation on the property. The more you pledge, the higher the monthly payments you collect. When you die, your estate may sell the house in order to pay off the debt. The investor then keeps the agreed-upon share of any appreciation due, plus the interest on the outstanding balance. Anything that is left over goes to your heirs.

# How to Work Off Your Debts

Of all the financial mistakes imaginable, the grimmest is falling too deeply in debt. You do not have to be poor to get bogged down in excessive borrowing. Fortunately, there are ways to figure out how much debt you can comfortably handle.

Think hard about whether you really want to borrow at all. It isn't cheap. As of mid-1995, the short-term rate on personal loans not backed by collateral was about 15.8%. And with inflation at moderate levels, you no longer can count on paying back creditors in significantly cheaper dollars.

Most people, of course, do not have the luxury of avoiding debt altogether. According to the Federal Reserve, between 1980 and 1990, consumer installment debt jumped from 15% of disposable income in 1980 to 17% in 1990.

## Figuring Your Own Upper Limits

Here's a quick, two-part test to help determine how much debt is too much for you:

First, estimate your current annual disposable income — that is, all your income, minus your tax withholdings and your contributions to various personal retirement, savings and investment plans.

Second, map out the year's expenses. Calculate how many of them will require various forms of debt, notably installment loans.

Debt counselors and credit managers warn that no more than 15% of your disposable income should be committed to installment debt, not counting home-mortgage payments. Don't necessarily consider this your own upper limit. You may become nervous at only 10%, particularly if there is only one breadwinner in the family and you have a number of dependents.

Members of Congress are not the only ones having trouble balancing a budget. Many families, too, are struggling to trim their own deficit spending. Just ask yourself:

- Am I approaching the limits of all my credit lines?
- Am I using savings to pay off old bills?
- Am I taking out new loans before I pay off my old loans?
- Am I always late in paying my bills?
- Am I making only minimum payments each month?
- Am I spending more than 15% of my disposable income on monthly installment debts above and beyond my home mortgage?

- Am I constantly forced to dip into my checking overdraft and rarely able to bring it down?
- Do I find it hard to save regularly even a small part of my income?
- Am I borrowing for items I used to buy with cash?
- Are creditors threatening to repossess my car or credit cards, or to take other legal action?
- Do I know exactly how much I owe?

Another obvious trouble sign is if a potential lender — say, a department store or a credit card issuer — denies you credit. In that case, the Equal Opportunity Credit Act requires that the potential lender must state to you the reason for the denial. And the Fair Credit Reporting Act says that if the lender has used a credit reporting bureau to provide your credit history, you must be given that agency's name, address and phone number (see pages 320–21).

These warning signs can serve a constructive purpose. It is precisely when they feel overwhelmed by bills and responsibilities that many people decide to plan for the future as they never have before.

Once you have concluded that you are in trouble, your primary order of business is to determine exactly how much income you receive, and then itemize your monthly expenses. List all your monthly bills in their order of importance. Set priorities for paying them off. Probably the first priority is to pay your home mortgage, and then your monthly utility and installment bills.

If you are still in debt over your head, meet with your creditors and negotiate. Creditors have a great deal of latitude to extend the due date on bills by up to 30 days. They can possibly refinance your debt to arrange a longer term of repayment in smaller amounts each month — even if you are overdue 90 days.

If you have trouble meeting your home-mortgage payments, go to your mortgage lender for help. The last thing a lender wants is to foreclose on your property. He or she would much rather have your cash. So in most cases a loan can be rescheduled and payments reduced if necessary.

You might be tempted to sign up for a consolidation loan to pay off all your debts. That is simply not smart. The lure of a consolidation loan is that a bank or finance company will take over your many debts and you, in turn, will make payments to that one institution. The catch is that the interest rate on such a loan is likely to be high. So you could be replacing a heap of moderate debts with one big one that costs more to carry.

Even while working off your debt, you should plan to save. Setting aside as little as 3% to 5% of your monthly income after taxes will help you start considering saving as an integral part of your budget.

You have certain federal protections if a creditor hires a debt collection agency to press you to pay. The National Foundation for Consumer Credit reports that, under the Fair Debt Collection Practices Act, collection agency employees may not:

- use abusive language to force you to pay
- call at unreasonable hours, that is, before 8 A.M. or after 9 P.M.
- threaten to tell your employer or friends that you have not paid
- try to enter your home under false pretenses with a view to identify or take something of value
- attempt to collect more than you owe
- send you misleading letters that appear to be from a court or government agency

## Using a Credit Counselor

People who have trouble composing a debt-repayment schedule within a workable budget would do well to seek the guidance of a nonprofit counselor. This professional will be sympathetic but firm. A counselor will ask you to provide intimate details about your total monthly income and expenses, a list of your outstanding bills and copies of any correspondence you have had with creditors about debts and loans. He or she will want to know whether you have been dunned by creditors or threatened with legal action, or whether a creditor has sought to have your pay garnisheed.

Next, the counselor will get in touch with your creditors. Counselors have more clout than you might, since creditors often prefer to deal with professionals. Your counselor will intercede on your behalf to reduce and stretch out monthly payments on debts while you organize your finances. The creditors may be in the mood to hold off for a while, because they simply don't want you to default or go bankrupt. They want to be sure to be repaid, and later is better than never. Sometimes a counselor can even knock down the total balance due. Once you have renegotiated the debt terms through your counselor, you make your monthly payments to him or her. Your counselor then manages the debt for you.

Debtors who pay off their obligations with the intervention of a counseling service are on the road to rehabilitation. The path will be rough at first. Many creditors will reject you because of credit-bureau reports of your need for counseling. However, a good word from your credit counselor can help you reopen department-store charge accounts and maybe even finance a new house. Victor Shock, executive director of the Credit Counseling Centers of Oklahoma, in Tulsa, reports, "In our local area we have had great success with mortgage companies by writing letters of recommendation for successful clients."

Before you approach any credit-counseling agency for help, find out whether it is a nonprofit clinic, a for-profit company or simply a bill collector subsidized by your creditors. There are 850 nonprofit consumer credit–counseling organizations across the country. They are almost always better than the for-profit organizations, which charge much more.

Almost half of the nonprofit groups provide free service, and no one is turned away even by those that do charge a fee, currently $8 to $10 a month until the debts are repaid. All groups, however, ask creditors to contribute voluntarily 8% to 15% of the monthly payments the counselors make on their clients' behalf to help defray their cost.

You can also get other kinds of credit help. For aid in creating a budget or a realistic schedule of repayments, call or write to the National Foundation for Consumer Credit (NFCC). To find the nearest of its almost 1,000 offices throughout North America, phone 800-388-2227 — or write to the foundation at 8611 Second Avenue, Suite 100, Silver Spring, Maryland 20910. For example, the foundation can send you one of its pamphlets, *Managing Your Money,* which contains a worksheet that helps you determine both how you spend your money and how you would like to spend it.

The foundation is associated with Consumer Credit Counseling Services (CCCS), a membership organization of local, nonprofit groups supported by banks, credit unions, consumer finance companies and others. CCCS provides credit counseling to anyone who needs it, either free or for a reasonable fee. Its phone is also 800-388-2227.

# Scoring Points with Lenders

To determine whether or not you qualify for a loan, many lenders evaluate you by a mysterious point system. They keep their rating systems secret, so it is hard to find out what information is worth the most points in determining whether you get the credit you seek. Almost certainly, you will be scored on the number and types of existing loans and charge cards you have. It helps a lot if you already have and use other forms of credit. The most desirable types are travel-and-entertainment cards, followed by bank credit cards and department-store charge cards. It's a plus if you have a good record of paying card bills and installment loans on time. But get rid of credit cards that you rarely use. Many lenders, if they see a long list of credit cards issued in your name, will conclude that you have a high potential for indebtedness.

Lenders do not like to see loans from finance companies. A significant percentage of bad credit risks have been in debt to these outfits. If your payment record with such companies is good, though, you shouldn't lose points.

Your income may help you pass the credit test, but lenders know that someone who earns $50,000 a year is not necessarily twice as creditworthy as someone who makes $25,000. If more than 35% to 40% of your gross income goes to paying off current debts, including mortgage and auto loan payments, lenders are not likely to approve your application. In general, you are better off if you own your home rather than rent, and if you already have a checking or savings account.

If at first you don't succeed, get a copy of your credit-bureau report. There may be mistakes. If so, clear them up and apply again. Or go to another lender or credit-card issuer. Each one has different standards.

# Building a Solid Credit Record

*Question:* What will you need in order to lease an apartment, acquire a credit card, rent a car, make hotel reservations or get a loan?

*Answer:* A solid credit history — a record that shows you pay your bills fully and on time.

The records of millions of Americans, almost certainly including you, are held in the huge computers of credit reporting bureaus that sell their services to creditors such as stores and credit-card companies. Most people have built a credit history, but a surprising number haven't — including recent graduates and other young adults, recent widows and immigrants, among others. You can take some steps to establish a credit record, including:

- Open and use a checking account.
- Start a savings account and make regular deposits.
- Join a credit union where you work.
- Take out, use and repay promptly your bills on a department-store credit card. *A tip:* Department-store cards are usually easier to acquire than bank cards, such as Visa or MasterCard, which generally require that you earn a certain minimum salary and have several other credit-card references.

If you want a copy of your credit record, call the credit reporting bureau. Most of these agencies — which gather information on how well and promptly you pay your bills — are part of one of three big companies: Equifax Credit Information Services (800-525-6285), TRW Information Services (800-422-4879) or Trans Union (800-680-7289). TRW will send you a free report even if you haven't been denied credit. Just send your name, addresses over the previous five years, Social Security number and year of birth to P.O. Box 2350, Chatsworth, California 91313.

If you have been denied credit because of a bad-apple item in your file, the company that refused you must tell you the name of the credit bureau that it used in making its decision. You then should write or call that bureau and ask for a complete copy of your report. The bureau is required by federal law to tell you what is in your file. If you request the information within 60 days of your having been denied credit, the bureau will charge you no fee. Otherwise, fees run from a low of $7.50 to as much as $200. CCCS counselors can help you interpret your report.

What if you find information in your report that you think is inaccurate or unfair? Then, (1) write to the creditor who has complained against you and insist that the record be corrected, and (2) write to the credit bureau and request that it get the corrected information from the creditor. You can challenge any information in your file. If the credit bureau cannot confirm the disputed information, it must delete it. If you request it, the bureau also must send a revised copy of your report to *any* credit grantor that received the report in the last six months.

You may also request that the credit bureau send a correction to any employer who has received a credit report on you within the last two years, and to anyone else who has asked for credit information on you in the last six months. It's important that you clear the record because any complaints from creditors or other negative information can stay in your credit report for seven years, or 10 years if you go bankrupt.

Even if the credit bureau finds that its information is valid, you can write an explanation for anything you may have done that is tarnishing your record. The credit bureau should then attach your explanation, or a clear summary of it, to your report. That way, anyone who receives your credit history in the future will also get your side of the story. Try to hold your statement to fewer than 100 words. If you ask, the bureau will send copies to those who requested your report in the past six months or to any employer who requested it in the past two years.

You can also take steps to correct any errors in billings on your charge accounts or credit cards. The Fair Credit Billing Act says that you must dispute the charges within 60 days, in writing. The creditor then must acknowledge your complaint within 30 days, and within 90 days investigate and notify you of action that will be taken. Until the investigation is completed, you cannot be billed or forced to pay any finance charges on the disputed amount. But if the bill ultimately is found to be correct, you then must pay the finance charges.

But what if you have made some very late payments or other credit bloopers in the past? How soon can you start with a clean slate? Most of your mistakes will be removed from your record within seven years after they occurred.

## Holding Down Your Credit Cards

The first step to using credit wisely is to use credit cards wisely. The average American carries a balance of $1,750 per bank card. That's according to Bankcard Holders of America (BHA), a nonprofit organization

## CREDIT-CARD INTEREST COSTS*

On a $1,100 outstanding balance when only the minimum monthly payment is made

| TOP 10 ISSUERS | Minimum (% of outstanding balance) | Annual % rate | Time until payoff | Total interest |
|---|---|---|---|---|
| Citibank | 2.10% | 16.15% | 11.00 yrs. | $1,123 |
| Discover | 2.77 | 15.15 | 10.00 yrs. | 743 |
| MBNA America | 2.00 | 16.15 | 11.80 yrs. | 1,224 |
| First Chicago | 2.08 | 13.15 | 12.75 yrs. | 895 |
| Chase Manhattan | 2.00 | 9.15 | 10.60 yrs. | 502 |
| AT&T Universal | 2.10 | 15.90 | 10.00 yrs. | 931 |
| Household | 2.00 | 15.65 | 16.00 yrs. | 1,440 |
| Chemical | 2.08 | 17.75 | 18.50 yrs. | 1,890 |
| Bank of America | 4.00 | 16.90 | 7.30 yrs. | 522 |
| Bank of New York | 2.77 | 12.15 | 9.00 yrs. | 516 |

SOURCE: BANKCARD HOLDERS OF AMERICA

*1994 figures

dedicated to helping consumers get out of debt and save money on credit. Two pieces of advice: Reduce that balance, and be sure to know exactly what the interest charge is. Federal law requires all credit-card issuers to declare, on all solicitations and applications for cards, the rate they charge, whether it is variable or fixed, and how it is determined.

The BHA makes these additional money-saving recommendations to cardholders:

- Send in your payment as soon as you get your bill. The sooner the bank receives it, the less interest you will pay.
- Pay more than the minimum payment. If you pay only the minimum amount due, it can take you decades to pay off your balance.
- Pay the highest-interest-rate cards first.
- Refuse a card issuer's offer to make no payments for one month. That just digs you deeper into debt.
- Consolidate your cards. The fewer you hold, the easier it is to keep track of them, avoid impulse spending, and reduce your risk if the cards are lost or stolen. Obviously, it also pays to drop a card charging a higher rate in favor of one with a lower rate.
- Beware of "teaser rates," very low initial rates that surge after a number of months. Read the fine print; cash advance fees can be steep to compensate for the low rate. A card from First USA carried a minimum of $5 per cash advance — even if the advance was for only $20.

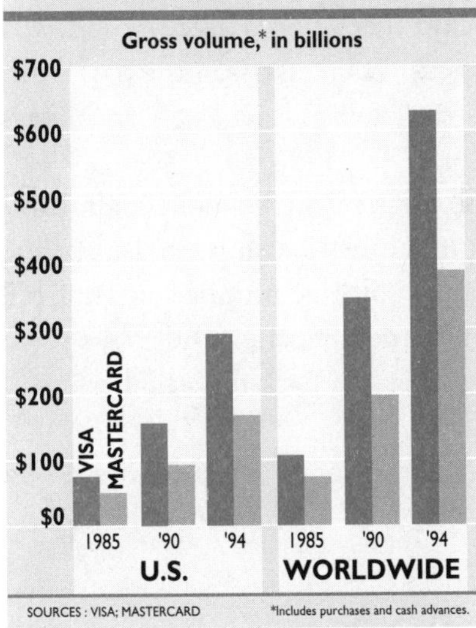


Your best choice is a bank credit card, such as Visa or MasterCard. Both cards are honored by some 9 million establishments worldwide. People really use these cards: In 1994, American consumers charged $291 billion on their 205 million Visa cards, and MasterCard members charged more than $170 billion on their 131 million cards. About one-third of nonmortgage debt carried by Americans is on their plastic.

If you travel extensively or run up a large expense account, you also need a travel-and-entertainment card, such as American Express or Diners Club. Such cards have no preset spending limits. By contrast, the credit line on a bank card can be dented quickly by an airline ticket and a few nights in a hotel. So before you sign up for any card, be sure you will not be cramped by a credit limit that is too low.

Of course, not all credit cards charge you the same interest rate. The annual percentage rate, or APR, ranges from an attractive teaser rate of 5.9% (to entice you to take the card) all the way to a so-called punitive rate of 25%. The latter is the rate banks charge customers they consider risky — late payers, those who carry large balances on a number of cards or those who fail to keep their accounts in "good standing." So it pays to shop around for the most favorable rates.

You might find a lower rate at an out-of-town bank. To locate the best deals, see *Money* magazine's monthly "Your Money Monitor." For more complete details, get the BHA Low-Interest/No-Fee Credit Card List, which names 50 credit-card issuers that offer a low interest rate and/or charge no fee ($4 from Bankcard Holders of America, 524 Branch Drive, Salem, Virginia 24153; 703-389-5445). For a $24 annual membership, you can also receive a bimonthly newsletter, a credit-card registration service, a consumer-dispute hotline and up to 24 publications covering specific consumer issues. People who pay their balances in full each month should find some good deals at the banks on the BHA list.

A low APR can be deceiving. The only way to escape interest charges is to pay your bills promptly or get a card that offers a grace period. Ask for a card with a 25- or 30-day grace period that starts on the date postmarked on your bill. That means you can have as long as 55 or 60 days to pay up interest-free.

People who pay their balances in full might as well choose credit cards from among the many that have no annual membership fee. But before abandoning your present card, phone the toll-free number on your bill and ask your present card issuer for free membership. Quite likely the company will cancel your fee. While you're at it, ask for a higher credit limit. You'll probably get that, too.

Once you go on revolving credit — that is, once you owe interest on balances carried from one month to the next — you generally have to

## SOME ATTRACTIVE CREDIT-CARD DEALS

| | State | Rate | Annual fee | Telephone (800) |
|---|---|---|---|---|
| **STANDARD** | National average: 18.13% | | | |
| **FOR PEOPLE WHO CARRY BALANCES** | | | | |
| Pulaski Bank & Trust | Arkansas | **8.75%** | $35 | 980-2265 |
| Wachovia Bank | Delaware | **9.00** | 88 | 842-3262 |
| Metropolitan National Bank | Arkansas | **9.96** | 25 | 883-2511 |
| Federal Savings Bank | Arkansas | **10.20** | 33 | 374-5600 |
| **FOR PEOPLE WHO PAY IN FULL** | | | | |
| AFBA Industrial Bank | Colorado | **11.90%** | $0 | 776-2265 |
| USAA Fed. Savings Bank | Texas | **12.67** | 0 | 922-9092 |
| Horizon Bank & Trust | Texas | **12.90** | 0 | 571-3462 |
| Metropolitan Savings Bank of Cleveland | Ohio | **13.90** | 0 | 837-6058 |
| **GOLD** | National average: 17.06% | | | |
| **FOR PEOPLE WHO CARRY BALANCES** | | | | |
| Pulaski Bank & Trust | Arkansas | **8.75%** | $50 | 980-2265 |
| Wachovia Bank | Delaware | **9.00** | 98 | 842-3262 |
| Federal Savings Bank | Arkansas | **10.20** | 48 | 374-5600 |
| Simmons First National Bank | Arkansas | **10.25** | 50 | 636-5151 |
| **FOR PEOPLE WHO PAY IN FULL** | | | | |
| AFBA Industrial Bank | Colorado | **11.90%** | $0 | 776-2265 |
| USAA Fed. Savings Bank | Texas | **13.04** | 0 | 922-9092 |
| Amalgamated Bank | Illinois | **13.50** | 0 | 723-0303 |
| Union Planters National Bank | Tennessee | **13.50** | 0 | 628-8946 |

Standard rates are as of July 3, 1995; Gold rates are as of May 31, 1995. All rates are variable and applicable to purchases only.
SOURCE: *BANK RATE MONITOR*

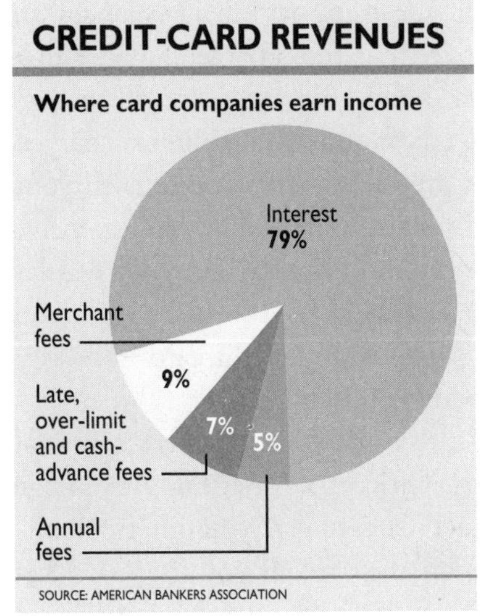


start paying interest on every additional purchase. In other words, once you buy something today, you have to start paying interest on it today. But some bank cards preserve the grace period on new charges. This practice is compulsory in Maine, Massachusetts and Vermont but uncommon elsewhere.

Each month's finance charge depends not only on the APR and grace period but also on the way the card company computes the balance subject to interest. Federal regulations require disclosure of the method, usually in simplified language. The standard methods, assuming that a grace period applies, line up as follows, in descending order of desirability: adjusted balance, average daily balance excluding new purchases, previous balance, average daily balance including new purchases, two-cycle average daily balance including new purchases.

The much ballyhooed access to cash with credit cards is really a type of loan called a cash advance. You may have to begin paying interest on it immediately, whether you hand the card to a bank teller or feed it into an automatic teller machine (ATM) or write out one of those convenience checks that come with the card. A cash advance can be an expensive way to borrow. Check with your card issuer for its rules and fees, and be sure to watch your bills carefully to see what you are being charged. The APR may be higher than on purchases. And many card companies charge transaction fees as high as 5% of the amount borrowed.

Be careful about running up advances and charges that you cannot pay off in full within a few months. Personal bankruptcies, due in part to high credit-card balances, continue to rise: to more than 780,000 in 1994 alone.

Just about every bank offers two varieties of Visa or MasterCard: standard and gold. The gold cards come with higher credit limits and bristle with perks. (But if you want a higher credit limit, it is usually yours for the asking on a standard credit card.) According to Jim Daly of *Credit Card News,* fewer than one-half of all credit cards carry fees. Those that do average about $16 for both standard and gold cards. Extras that go with the gold include insurance against theft or damage to items charged to your card, extended warranties on products that you buy with your card, and car-rental insurance that eliminates the need for an expensive collision-damage waiver. But if you own a home and a car, your regular insurance probably covers lost or stolen possessions, whether or not you paid for them with your credit card. Further, any credit card gives you the right to withhold payment on shoddy goods.

In the battle for customers, credit-card purveyors are offering special rebates, travel bonuses and even cash. Citicorp's American Advantage card and United Airlines' Mileage Plus First card give you one frequent-flier mile for every dollar you charge on the card. If you use GE's Rewards MasterCard, you can get as much as 2% back on annual purchases of up to $10,000. Dean Witter's Discover Card pays cash rewards of 1% a year; if you spend, say, $3,000 in a year, you'll earn $30.

### How to Win at Cards

Simple math tells you: It pays to reduce your card balance, even if you have to dip into your savings account to do it. That's better than making interest payments of 18% or so on your card balances. Remember: Federal law requires all card issuers to declare on all their solicitations and applications just what interest rate they charge, whether it is variable or fixed, and how it is determined.

## Automatic Teller Machines

The ATM card — that handy piece of plastic that you slip into a bank's automatic teller machine to get a quick fix of cash — is spreading out to supermarkets, gas stations and convenience stores. Your card gives you access to your cash whenever and very nearly wherever you happen to be. Through regional and national networks, you can extract money from your checking account at banks that you have never heard of and that certainly have never heard of you. More than 442,000 ATMs are stationed in bank alcoves and outposts in shopping malls and student centers around the world.

But with the conveniences come some costs. You're exposed to losses if a thief figures out how to use your card. Under the federal Electronic Fund Transfer Act, your liability increases in three stages, based on how long you wait before notifying your bank that you have lost your card: $50 during the first two business days after you learn that something is amiss, $500 over the next 60 days, and everything taken after that, including any credit you can draw on through an overdraft account.

Safeguards make it hard for your bank to pin the liability on you. Only someone who knows your PIN (personal identification number) can activate your card, but your bank can't stick you with liability simply because you wrote the number on the back of the card. (As foolish as it seems, many people do just that.) Most important, those stages of liability don't start counting down until you have had a chance to detect any unauthorized ATM withdrawals on your bank statement.

It pays to find out the ATM costs when you shop for a checking account. Many banks build ATM fees into your monthly maintenance fee. Relatively few charge their depositors for using the bank's own ATMs. Those that do may nick you for 50 cents a shot. A larger number charge 50 cents to $1 each for withdrawals via regional networks; many other banks charge $1 to $3 each for withdrawals using a national network.

If you ever have trouble with a bank over your ATM card, seek relief from one of these four federal agencies in Washington, D.C.: If the bank you deal with is a nationally chartered bank, write to the Comptroller of the Currency. If you have a problem with a state-chartered bank, contact the Federal Reserve Board. If your bank is state-chartered but not a Fed member, call or write to the Federal Deposit Insurance Corporation. If your ATM difficulty is with a savings and loan association, write to the new Office of Thrift Supervision. Give any of these agencies four weeks to make decisions and get back to you.

Don't worry too much about being shortchanged by automatic banking tellers. You may be concerned that the impersonal machine will make an all-too-human mistake, that a $400 deposit will somehow show up on your statement as only $40. In a survey by the Federal Reserve Board, 6% of the people who used the electronic banking services claimed they had been victims of a machine error. But 95% of the grievances were settled satisfactorily.

If your automatic teller blows a transaction, simply write the bank a note within 60 days of receiving your statement. By law, the bank must resolve the complaint within 45 days of getting your letter. If it takes longer than just 10 business days, the bank must credit your account for the amount in dispute until any investigation ends. If you still have a grievance, write to the Federal Reserve Board's Division of Consumer and Community Affairs, 20th and C Streets NW, Washington, D.C. 20551.

## The Deal on Debit Cards

ATM cards give you quick access to your money; debit cards are almost a substitute for cash. The debit card, or point-of-sale cash card, is an electronic key to your checking account. Don't confuse it with a credit card.

Some cash cards are issued by banks, others by gasoline companies or supermarket chains for use in their outlets only, like charge cards. Cash cards are increasingly used in department stores, convenience stores, supermarkets, gas stations, fast-food restaurants, and elsewhere. More than 70,000 U.S. retail establishments can now ring up cash-card sales.

Californians are in the vanguard; in 1994 they made an eye-popping 70 million debit-card transactions on the Star System Inc.'s Explore network alone. No wonder: They could use their debit cards not only at all the usual places but also at Disneyland. In Washington, D.C., the Metro Line subway has tested the sale of fare cards through ATMs in its stations. Soon to come are national debit shopping cards comparable in acceptability to major credit cards.

A cash card works like this: At the checkout counter, say, you either hand your card to the clerk like a credit card, or you slide it through a slot in a machine called a card reader and press your secret four-digit personal identification number (PIN) into a keypad on the reader. The clerk's register transmits your tape total, PIN and other data to a distant processing center, whose computer recognizes your bank and relays the signal to it. If your account contains enough money to pay for the groceries, the system approves your purchase. Then the money moves electronically from your account to the store's. The whole process takes about six seconds.

Cash cards are, in fact, more liquid than cash, and that can get scary. If you have shopaholic tendencies, watch out. A cash card gives you instant access to every dollar in your checking account plus every additional dollar of credit in an overdraft checking account. A spendthrift relative entrusted with your card and PIN can drain your account, too.

All cash-card systems are not created equal. Most are limited to participating stores in a specific area, such as one state or a few adjacent states. But two national debit-card networks — MasterCard's Maestro and Visa's Interlink — were established in mid-1992. Together the two companies have over 42 million users, and Visa predicts the number of debit cards it issues will triple by 1998.

Some universal cash cards are acceptable wherever credit cards are honored. Clients of some large brokerage houses get Visa debit cards that function like cash cards, the primary example being the nearly 3 million users of Merrill Lynch's cash-management account and related asset-management accounts.

The major appeal is, of course, convenience. You don't have to carry much cash or worry about stores' accepting your checks. Shopping sprees based on cash-card plastic won't run up credit-card debts at interest rates that have lately been double-digit.

The great disadvantage of cash cards is the loss of "float," the time lapse between the date of a purchase and the departure of the money from your bank account. Shoppers who pay by check enjoy at least a couple days' float. Credit-card users who pay their monthly bills in full can effectively earn the free use of spent money for a grace period of as long as 60 days.

Not all cash cards take away the float. Proprietary cards issued by Mobil Oil and Vons, a California supermarket chain, give two days' grace. Says Virginia Miller, vice president and treasurer of Vons, "Retaining a float helps families whose paycheck for the week has not cleared the bank by Saturday or Sunday, when most people shop. Other debit systems take the money before you get home with the ice cream."

The risk of loss if a thief raids your account is usually minor, though the law itself is not all that reassuring. As with lost or stolen ATM cards, it makes you responsible for charges up to $50 if you notify the bank within two business days after you learn of an unauthorized withdrawal. For the next 60 days, if you still haven't called the bank, your liability rises to $500. Wait any longer and your potential loss is limited only by your bank balance plus any credit line in your account.

In fact, banks seldom try to shift any liability to their customers. To play it safe, however, take the following precautions:

- Choose a PIN that you can easily remember. Cash-card issuers recognize that life is becoming a maze of numbers too long and too numerous to keep track of, so more and more of them let you pick your own number. But don't select one that is on display somewhere in your purse or wallet, like your house or license-plate number.
- Don't write your PIN on your card or keep it with your card.
- Don't reveal your PIN even to friends or relatives. Thieves can have scams for wheedling it out of you, but bankers track most challenged charges to family members.
- Notify your card issuer or bank immediately if your card is lost or stolen or if unexplained charges appear on your statement.

A final note: Mastering the credit-card possibilities calls for clear thinking about where to put your spare cash. When you find yourself with a bit of money to invest, your understandable impulse is probably to tuck it away in an investment for the future. But if you are carrying large balances on credit cards, your best investment by far is to use the money to reduce those debts.

It costs $180 a year to service an outstanding balance of $1,000 on an 18% credit card. Paying off that $1,000 can "earn" you the same 18%. What's more, you take no risk to get that return. To match it with an investment, you would have to take big chances with your money. If you are in the 28% tax bracket, for example, you need to earn 25% before taxes on an investment just to break even with what you would save by paying off the balance on an 18% credit card. You would have to earn 25.7% to match an 18.5% card, and 18.5% is about the rate charged on cards from major institutions from Chase Manhattan to BankAmerica. Compare those returns with the 5.3% yield on a risk-free one-year Treasury bill.

CHAPTER II

# Getting Your Best Buys in Housing

*How to find the right house at the best price, secure the lowest-cost financing, save on taxes — plus the improvements that really pay off.*

▼

As Americans, we expect nothing less than life, liberty — and a house that looks as terrific as Tara and goes up in value every year. Indeed, America's favorite investment is still the family home. It is also by far the biggest investment that most people make.

Though the housing boom-and-bust of the past decade has shaken the faith of many homeowners and wanna-be's, now is a good time to buy a house — if you really need one to live in and have found one you like. In mid-1995 the median price for a new house stood at $133,000. For one that had been previously occupied, the figure was $111,000. In 15 years those numbers had jumped from $55,700 and $48,700, respectively. That's partly because of the general run-up in prices during the 1980s, and the fact that the surge of baby boomers into the housing market lifted demand. But the ride also reflects the fact that people are demanding more house. In the past 25 years, the size of a new house has grown from an average 1,400 square feet to 2,100 square feet.

Are these trends putting home ownership beyond the reach of young adults? No. Contrary to popular wisdom, reports the National Association of Realtors, it is easier to buy a house now than it has been for many years. In mid-1995 the NAR's "affordability" index for first-time buyers showed that anyone with a family income of $30,580 a year after taxes earned enough to buy a starter home costing an average of $76,400. Young renters typically had 80% of that amount because their median income was $24,735. In 1980, by comparison, young renters had only 59.8% of the necessary amount.

What's more, prices of existing homes rose an average of only 4% a year from 1980 to 1992; since then the method of compiling the number has changed slightly, and in 1993 and 1994 prices have advanced an annual average of just 2.9%. With the economy creating new jobs and mortgage rates still not outrageous, home prices in most regions are likely to climb — but only modestly. That's good on two scores. It gives buyers confidence that their life savings won't disappear into a black hole if they invest in real estate. At the same time, price increases that are only moderate help more people qualify for home purchases because costs do not run too far ahead of income.

Prices of existing single-family houses were expected to rise just under 1% in most parts of the country in 1995, and new homes to go up 3.6%, with the strongest markets being in Salt Lake City, Lincoln, Nebraska, and Raleigh/Durham, North Carolina. There was one notable exception. House prices in California were forecast to remain flat in 1995.

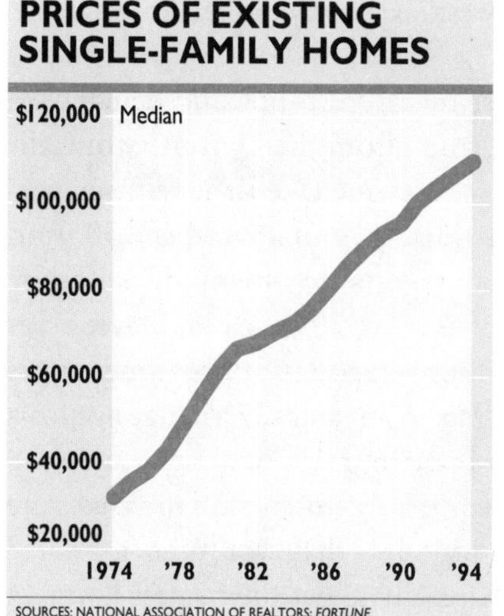


According to the NAR, the median price for an existing single-family home in the second quarter of 1995 ranged from a low of $56,400 in the Waterloo/Cedar Falls area of Iowa, to a peak of $340,000 in Honolulu. Also in the second quarter the nationwide median price for previously occupied homes rose 0.2% above that of one year earlier, to $111,000. Cities where housing costs hovered around the median include Milwaukee, Las Vegas and Baltimore. Some of the most

## EXISTING-HOME PRICES IN 30 CITY AREAS

The top 30 metropolitan areas in the U.S. according to gross metropolitan product

| Metropolitan area | Median price | Metropolitan area | Median price |
|---|---|---|---|
| 1. New York, NY | **$171,300** | 17. Nassau/Suffolk, NY | **$158,300** |
| 2. Chicago, IL | **144,500** | 18. Phoenix/Mesa, AZ | **93,400** |
| 3. Los Angeles/Long Beach, CA | **181,700** | 19. Newark, NJ | **186,000** |
| 4. Boston, MA | **181,600** | 20. Baltimore, MD | **110,600** |
| 5. Philadelphia, PA | **118,700** | 21. Oakland, CA | **245,500** |
| 6. Washington, D.C. | **157,600** | 22. Cleveland/Lorain/Elyria, OH | **100,100** |
| 7. Detroit, MI | **86,200** | 23. San Jose, CA | **244,500** |
| 8. Houston, TX | **78,800** | 24. Pittsburgh, PA | **83,500** |
| 9. Atlanta, GA | **95,300** | 25. New Haven/Bridgeport/ Stamford/Danbury, CT | **137,300** |
| 10. Dallas, TX | **94,400** | | |
| 11. Minneapolis/St. Paul, MN | **102,200** | 26. Kansas City, MO/KS | **88,600** |
| 12. Orange County, CA | **214,900** | 27. Tampa/St. Petersburg/ Clearwater, FL | **77,700** |
| 13. St. Louis, MO | **85,400** | | |
| 14. San Diego, CA | **170,500** | 28. Denver, CO | **121,400** |
| 15. San Francisco, CA | **256,100** | 29. Riverside/San Bernardino, CA | **127,200** |
| 16. Seattle/Bellevue/Everett, WA | **157,500** | 30. Miami, FL | **105,300** |

SOURCE: NATIONAL ASSOCIATION OF REALTORS

reasonable housing — with median prices of around $80,000 or less — could be found throughout the Midwest, as well as in San Antonio and Tampa/St. Petersburg.

The 75 million baby boomers just might keep housing demand — and prices — firm for a long time. A study from the University of California concludes that as Americans age, they increase their homeownership rate and spend steadily more on housing until around age 70. And the Chicago Title and Trust Company reports that many in the prime potential homeowners' generation of 25- to 39-year-olds haven't yet made their move. Chicago Title says the average age of first-time buyers in 1994 was 31.6, a big jump from 28 in 1976, and the average age for a move-up buyer was 41.7, much older than 36 in 1976.

How much of your income can you afford to spend when you are buying a house or an apartment? A little less than you used to. Some years ago it was sensible to stretch financially to get the biggest house in the best neighborhood that you could possibly manage. Inflation was then running away, meaning that your house was likely to spurt in value, and you would be paying off your mortgage debt in ever-depreciating dollars.

Now that inflation is moderate, real estate professionals advise you not to take on more house than you can handle. If you buy well beyond your means, you will not be able to keep the place up, and that will hurt you when you are ready to sell. You'll never get top dollar for a house that's run-down. But since real estate stands to remain a solid investment, the experts do say you may spend a *little* more than you are comfortable with.

When should you trade up to a larger house? Homeowners who bought high in the past have been afraid to move up in today's modest market, worrying that they will have to sell their present home at too painful a discount. But many who have been willing to take the chance have found that they ultimately got a good deal on a better residence.

How you buy can be as important as what you buy. The success of an investment depends largely on getting favorable financing. Put down as little of your own money as possible. Take advantage of the competitive mortgage market to shop hard for the best deal. If you can, get financing from the seller, asking for as long a term as he or she will accept. In some cases, though they're increasingly rare, you might be able to assume the seller's mortgage. You will normally be able to do so if it is a Federal Housing Administration (FHA) loan that was made before December 15, 1989, or a Department of Veterans Affairs–backed loan, or if the mortgage has been in effect for many years.

Househunters' eyes tend to be bigger than their wallets, but that's as it should be. Your job is to find the house you want to live in; it's the banker's job to determine whether you can comfortably carry the financing.

Lenders usually follow guidelines laid down by the Federal National Mortgage Association, known as Fannie Mae. Mortgages, you see, have become commodities in a resale market, where investors trade mortgage securities. Fannie Mae and the other secondary mortgage companies need uniform products to sell. Following these guidelines, here's how lenders judge your ability to pay back a loan:

First, they calculate your housing expense ratio, which is the highest percentage of your gross income that bankers will let you spend on monthly payments. They add up your salaries, dividends and other steady streams of income, such as alimony or child support or disability benefits. That's your gross income.

Then they tabulate the basic costs of ownership. The main items are mortgage interest and principal, real estate taxes and homeowner's insurance. Other possible expenses include mortgage insurance guaranteeing payment to the lender or special tax assessments on the property, such as for use of the sewer system or fire protection. In a condominium or a special housing development, there might also be association dues for maintaining a pool and other amenities.

The lenders then divide your monthly housing expenses by your monthly gross income and multiply the answer by 100 to arrive at your housing expense ratio. If the figure is more than 28%, you probably won't get a conventional mortgage. If it's above 29%, you usually won't qualify for a Federal Housing Administration loan insured by the government.

## The Return of Rentals

Renting apartments is back in style. A new class of renters is arising, and they include affluent older people, single women, childless couples and those who move often with their jobs. Construction of apartments and condos, which was depressed for eight years and fell to a postwar low in 1993, rose 60% to an estimated 260,000 units in 1994. That's still less than half as high as in the mid-1980s, when starts easily topped 600,000. The National Apartment Association reports that the areas where apartments are most in demand are Atlanta, San Antonio, Austin, Tampa/St. Petersburg, Phoenix, Charlotte, Nashville, Albuquerque, Colorado Springs, Tucson, Salt Lake City, Boise, and Portland (Oregon). Markets are also rising in Indianapolis, Chicago and Detroit.

The lenders' second measure, called the total-obligation-to-income ratio, equals the percentage of your gross income that will be needed to pay both your housing expenses and other long-term obligations. To your housing expenses, the loan officer will add your monthly payments on any other nonbusiness mortgages, installment loans, credit-card balances with terms longer than 10 months, and regular payments to an ex-spouse for alimony or child support. You are probably over your head for a conventional loan if your total obligations equal more than 36% of your gross income — or more than 41% for an FHA or VA loan.

Let's assume that you can clear those hurdles. Congratulations! But don't order furniture just yet. You still have to satisfy a lender that you are a worthy risk. Banks and mortgage companies will check out your credit report to make sure you haven't missed payments on other loans. They will make sure your salary and employment history jibe with your answers to loan-application questions.

Oh, and one more thing: the down payment. More often than housing expenses, this obstacle will sour the deal. The lowest regular down payments are 5% to 10% on fixed-rate mortgages and 10% to 20% on adjustable rate and balloon mortgages. Lenders usually press for more. Generally, the higher your income, the lower the down payment that you can get away with. You probably can get a better deal than you think, provided you look around and bargain hard.

What if you're self-employed and can't show the kind of gross income bankers like to see? Don't despair. As the army of the self-employed grows, mortgage brokers in particular are bowing to the new reality and finding other measures of your credit worthiness. Many lenders are willing to accept total obligations of up to half of your income if you show that you can pay your bills on time — or at least, with very few late payments. It helps if you are able to make a down payment of 20% or more.

Folks with shallow pockets and small incomes should investigate Federal Housing Administration or Veterans Affairs (VA) mortgages. The average down payment on all FHA loans is 3%; on a $100,000 mortgage, it is an affordable $4,500. But the FHA puts a ceiling on the loan size. It cannot exceed the median house price in your county. For specific loan size, contact a mortgage company or a local office of the Department of Housing and Urban Development. If you're a vet who qualifies (yes, Gulf War veterans do), no down payment at all is necessary. Anyone who served in the Armed Forces for as few as 181 days in peacetime or 90 days in wartime qualifies.

The Federal National Mortgage Association has a program that allows eligible borrowers to put as little as 3% down. Most lenders make this

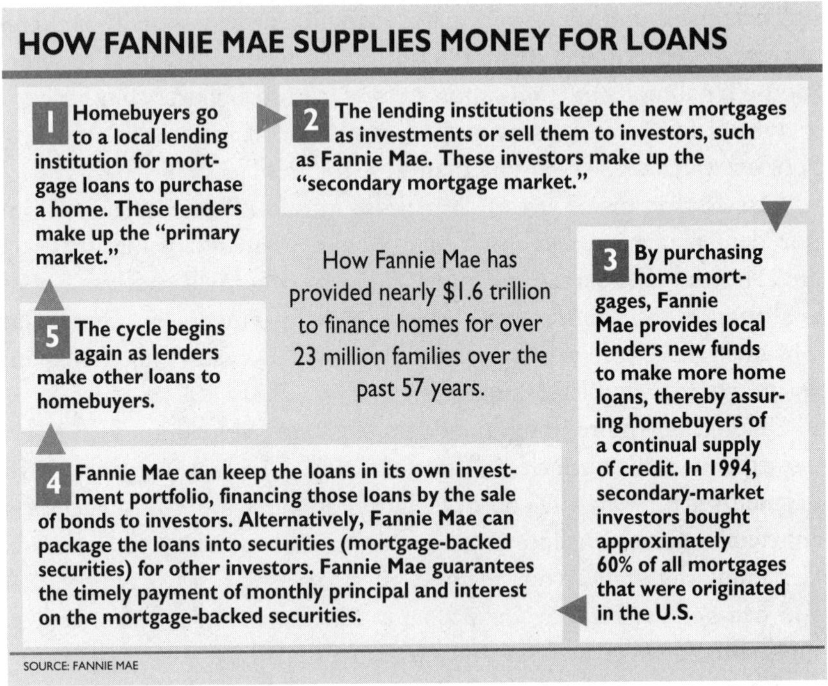

**HOW FANNIE MAE SUPPLIES MONEY FOR LOANS**

**1** Homebuyers go to a local lending institution for mortgage loans to purchase a home. These lenders make up the "primary market."

**2** The lending institutions keep the new mortgages as investments or sell them to investors, such as Fannie Mae. These investors make up the "secondary mortgage market."

**3** By purchasing home mortgages, Fannie Mae provides local lenders new funds to make more home loans, thereby assuring homebuyers of a continual supply of credit. In 1994, secondary-market investors bought approximately 60% of all mortgages that were originated in the U.S.

**4** Fannie Mae can keep the loans in its own investment portfolio, financing those loans by the sale of bonds to investors. Alternatively, Fannie Mae can package the loans into securities (mortgage-backed securities) for other investors. Fannie Mae guarantees the timely payment of monthly principal and interest on the mortgage-backed securities.

**5** The cycle begins again as lenders make other loans to homebuyers.

How Fannie Mae has provided nearly $1.6 trillion to finance homes for over 23 million families over the past 57 years.

SOURCE: FANNIE MAE

Community Home Buyer's "3/2 Option" available to borrowers. It enables a buyer to use a gift or an unsecured loan from a public or nonprofit agency for up to 2% of the required 5% down payment. At least 3% of the down payment must be from your own funds. Contact your local and state housing agencies or Fannie Mae for possible sources of lending. Also check into "Fannie 97," a new Fannie Mae Community Home Buyer's program requiring a 3% down payment for a fixed-rate 25- or 30-year mortgage.

To avoid wasting money on applications for mortgages you can't get, make sure to prequalify yourself for the loan. Get the lender to look over your financials and tell you how much he or she thinks you can afford before you formally apply.

## Picking a House That Will Sell Well

Unless you're sure the house you are about to buy will be your last, select one that not only appeals to you but also stands to be a worthwhile investment. Whether it's a small starter home or a spacious family estate, the same factors affect the resale value:

- Medium-sized houses are better long-term investments than very large or small ones. Those with three bedrooms are easier to sell than those with four or more. Houses in the strongest demand also have at least two full baths.
- Single-family detached houses are better than condominium apartments. Consequently, you'll find a buyer's market for condos or co-ops in popular areas of many cities, including New York and Miami.
- Conventional styles sell more easily — and for higher prices — than unconventional ones do. In the East, "conventional" means split-levels and colonials; in the South and West, contemporaries are more common; in the Heartland, a style known as Midwestern traditional is most appealing. Remember: Today's trendy style may be tomorrow's out-of-fashion oddball.
- Standard interiors attract more buyers and higher prices than unusual configurations do. If you want to sell a pink Cadillac, you will have to find someone who dotes on pink Cadillacs.
- Two rooms add the most to resale value: the kitchen and a second bathroom. The kitchen should have plenty of light and modern appliances. It does not have to be equipped for Julia Child, but it should come with a dishwasher and — if possible — a garbage disposal.
- Even if you live in the Deep South, buy a house with a fireplace. Though wasteful of energy, fireplaces are romantic accessories that usually hold their value in all parts of the country.

The houses in a neighborhood should be of roughly equal value. Stay away from places where there is a wide disparity, because smaller, cheaper dwellings depress the prices of their more elaborate neighbors. If you do find yourself in a neighborhood where house values differ substantially, look for the ugly duckling on a street full of swans: The least expensive house in a neighborhood is a much better buy than the most expensive one. The former will be pulled up by surrounding values even if you do not improve the property; the latter will be held down by them.

Location is paramount. It's hard to beat a house in a neighborhood where the homes and lawns are well cared for. Check the zoning laws. You don't want to see auto body shops or mobile homes springing up among standard single-family homes. One way to pick the right neighborhood is to see how other buyers are voting with their dollars. Are values moving up, or down? What is the variation between asking and selling prices? In choice neighborhoods, the difference is small, often only 3% to 5%.

Another measure is how quickly houses have been selling. For years the thumb rule was that if the average length of time on the market is less than three months, the area is strong and in demand. A corollary was the percentage of houses put up for sale that turned over within 90 days. In an undesirable place, or in an overpriced market, two-thirds of all the homes listed with real estate firms might not change hands within that period or might even be taken off the market without being sold.

## HOUSE-HUNTING TIPS

**NEIGHBORHOOD** Location is essential. For resale value, the worst house in the best neighborhood is far better than the best house in the worst neighborhood. Also, does the school system have a good reputation? How is the transportation? Are other services, like recycling and garbage pickup, well run? What is the general upkeep of nearby homes?

**STYLE AND LANDSCAPE** Is the home appealing? Is it a place you would like to return to every day after a long day at work? It should be a welcoming sight and a place to seek rejuvenation.

**FLOOR PLAN** The layout of the home will affect the way people interact in it. For example, if you enjoy entertaining, an open plan or contemporary home may be best for you. If privacy is what you seek, a more traditional home design is probably what you want.

**APPEALING DETAILS** Custom-made items that will be left behind when the owners move make a home more valuable. For example, built-in draperies or special appliances add great value. Also, architectural elements such as handcrafted wood moldings, tall ceilings and large windows with breathtaking views are in high demand. All these elements should add enjoyment to you and your family while living in it and help in reselling the home.

**IMPROVEMENTS** An updated kitchen or other improvements should be appealing to most buyers. But not everyone is interested in the upkeep of a pool or spa and may not be interested in buying a home with such extras.

**TAXES** Values of homes are significantly affected by city and county taxes. A municipality with lower property taxes usually attracts higher bids for its homes.

**OTHER FACTORS** A home in an area that is growing, with thriving industries and new jobs, is likely to increase in value. The homes in economically depressed areas tend to decrease in value. Unless you have to move immediately, because of, say, a job transfer, it is better to look for a long period of time before you choose a house.

SOURCE: *BUYING, SELLING AND OWNING YOUR HOME MAGAZINE*

But from 1991 to 1994 it took an average of 105 to 110 days before a house was sold, according to the *Better Homes and Gardens* Real Estate Service Housing Cost Survey. To get information about the area's turnover time, as well as the difference between asking price and selling price, call a local board of Realtors, mortgage lenders, a homebuilders' association or real estate brokers.

A smart first step in your search is to look for a community or part of the city that has outstanding schools, whether or not you have school-age children. Parents are willing to pay premium prices to move to an area that offers excellent education. Check to see how much the community budgets for school expenses per child and compare that figure with other school districts in the area. Also find out what percentage of the high-school graduates go on to college; 80% or more is excellent.

Before you buy, be sure to visit a local school and speak with the principal. Simply by asking him or her what distinguishes the school, you can gain some valuable impressions. For example, if the principal boasts, "Our school is almost as good as Smithville's," you might then want to search for a house in the Smithville district.

Sometimes you can also make a sound investment by being an early buyer in a new housing tract. Particularly at times and in places where business is slow, builders are very anxious until they get the first few houses off their hands and see that the development will sell. In such circumstances, smart buyers can capitalize on those fears to knock down the asking price or extract from the seller such extras as better-quality kitchen fixtures.

Of course, being first carries risks. Read the fine print on your home warranty carefully. Many warranties are nearly useless, requiring that the house be unsafe or unlivable before the builder must take remedial action.

Before you buy, find out about the record and reliability of the builder. Investigate other homes constructed by that builder to see how they have held up over time. The builder shouldn't balk when you ask for a comprehensive list of past projects. Better yet, go to the county courthouse, where deeds are registered, find the builder's previous building permits, and call up the people now living in those homes.

▾ ▾ ▾

### Additional Tips for Investing in a House

- If your house has only one bathroom, probably the best improvement you can make is adding a second bathroom. Another profitable remodeling project is redoing the kitchen.
- If you want to build on to your house, do not plan an addition that raises the value of your property more than 20% over the value of other houses in the neighborhood. It will not pay in the end, when you sell your house.
- When it comes time to sell, try to make the sale before you buy and move into another house. Empty houses seldom command their asking prices.
- Before you put your house on the market, get several Realtors to tell you what they think it should go for. Watch out for "quick turn" artists who may pressure you into a lowball offer.
- You stand to earn more profit when you resell a dwelling that you had bought new rather than an old one.

## Getting the Most from a Real Estate Agent

Even before you search for a house or apartment, hunt for a real estate agent. Don't rely on luck and newspaper ads but start with recommendations from friends or other trustworthy contacts in the community. Call the board of Realtors and ask for names of several former Realtors of the Year; agencies earn this designation because they sell a lot of houses and know much about the market. If the board is not listed in the phone book, a local Realtor should be able to direct you to it. Also, go to open houses where the public is invited to look at some of the homes listed for sale with various brokerage firms.

The agent you choose should have access to the local multiple-listing service. This is a computerized network that gives him or her a complete rundown of all the houses listed for sale in the area. The agent should also know the local mortgage market and help you figure out how much house you can carry based on your income and expenses. Once you have found a house you want to buy, he or she will help you negotiate the price and close the sale.

A brokerage firm usually earns a commission of 6% or 7% of the selling price of the house for listing it — that is, putting it on the market — and selling it. If your agent works for another firm, the commission is split 50-50 between the firm that lists and the firm that sells. But the bottom line is that the seller of the house, not the buyer, generally pays the commission.

Almost all agents represent the seller. For this reason, when you have found a house you would like to make a bid on, never tell your agent, "Let's offer the Smiths $200,000 — but we'll go as high as $220,000 if we have to." The agent is obliged by the custom of the trade to share that information with the seller. You should wait until the seller refuses your offer before you volunteer that you are willing to pay more. And remember: It is generally in the broker's interest to downplay whatever faults lie in a house or neighborhood. Some agents may be buyers' friends in disguise. They are so eager to turn property over fast that they will persuade the seller to take less than he or she might get by waiting for a better offer. If you're comfortable with these ethics, you may get a good deal. Of course, watch out for such people when it comes time for you to sell.

Other agents have set themselves up specifically to represent the buyer. Payment is either a flat fee or by the hour. That way the broker will not steer the buyer to more expensive houses in order to get a fatter commission. If the buyer does not find a house he or she likes, the broker usually refunds part or all of the fee.

The broker who works for a buyer will examine houses listed through agencies as well as those advertised directly by owners. He or she will also inspect the house for flaws in construction and check the neighborhood for potential changes in assessments or problems in the schools. Such a broker is likely to strike a much tougher bargain for his or her customer, the buyer, than a conventional broker will. The broker might demand, for example, that the seller guarantee the integrity of the roof or the plumbing for up to one year. When serving the buyer, some real estate agents submit questionnaires to sellers requesting specific details about a house's condition. This tends to flush out the costly little surprises.

If you are selling your house, you will find that the competition among real estate brokers for your business has become fierce, partly because nationwide companies are fighting to expand in the market. Thus, you can make some particularly good deals with them. The large, national organizations claim to offer more tempting services than small, independent agencies can — sometimes including access to listings on the Internet, with pictures.

Independent real estate brokers are fighting back, sometimes offering to work for less than the prevailing commissions. But the kind of deal you get from any agent depends overwhelmingly on how desirable your house is. If you have a sound, attractive structure in a sought-after location, or if the market is very weak, you might be able to offer a broker a commission of 4% or 5% instead of the conventional 6%.

Occasionally you can persuade a broker to give up part of his or her commission just to get a stalled deal moving again. If a buyer and a seller are only a few thousand dollars apart, the broker may agree to cut his or her fee if the seller accepts a lower price. In effect, the broker absorbs some of the seller's loss.

Some brokers have unbundled the traditional package of services and provide, at an hourly rate, only what customers need. Other brokers — the discounters — are charging commissions of about 2%. But these agents use color slides to let the potential buyer screen properties in their offices, and then they expect sellers to show their own houses to prospects.

## Checking Out the House

So you've finally found the house you love. Will it love you back, or break your heart? What hidden problems lurk behind the beautiful wallpaper and the gleaming bathroom tiles?

Unless you're extremely knowledgeable about structures and mechanical systems, hire an inspector to go over the house from top to bottom. The job may cost you about $250 to $300, but it will be worth every penny — both for your peace of mind and, quite possibly, as a tool for negotiating with the seller.

An experienced inspector will go over everything — plumbing, heating and wiring systems; foundations; roofs, windows, floor joists, you name it. He or she will point to small problems as well as big ones.

How can you tell a good inspector from a poser? The business is largely unregulated. Just about anyone can call himself or herself an inspector, regardless of training or qualifications. Credentials may not be what they seem; to join the National Association for Home Inspectors, for example, all someone need do is send in a résumé, a report from one home inspection and a check for $150. Some occasional practitioners are actually building contractors looking for jobs they can take on.

One credential with clout is membership in the American Society of Home Inspectors (ASHI). To be certified, an inspector has to take classes, pass exams, perform 250 verified fee-paid inspections and complete 40 hours of refresher courses every two years. The ASHI will mail or fax you a free list of certified inspectors in your area; call 800-743-2744.

Make sure the person who inspects your home, whether certified or not, has plenty of experience in residential inspections. Ask to see one or more reports from previous inspections. If all you're handed is a checklist, keep searching. A worthwhile report will be a step-by-step narrative rundown, full of details and offering advice on repairs.

## Watching Those Closing Costs

When you buy a home, your real price will be bigger than what you and the seller agree upon. Behind the down payment and the mortgage installments lurk those nettlesome expenses, closing costs. They can be 4% to 8% of the size of the mortgage. On a typical $75,000 mortgage, that means you will pay an additional $3,000 to $6,000.

Among the extras are loan origination fees and points. Origination fees are typically figured as 1% of the mortgage amount, or one point. In addition, your lender is likely to demand one to three points — all up-front interest. Other typical mortgage costs are an application fee ($75 to $300), an appraisal fee ($150 to $300) and a survey ($125 to $300).

And buyers who cannot put down 20% or more of the purchase price in cash are required to buy private mortgage insurance to protect the lender against default. For this, you typically will be charged a one-time fee of one-half to one point plus annual premiums of a quarter-point or more.

Mortgage lenders also want proof that the seller has a clear title to the property you are buying. So you will have to pay for a title search. You also will have to buy insurance to cover the possibility that the search missed something. Figure on the two fees running a total $250 to $650, depending on where you live and the cost of your house.

It is up to you to insure the house against fire, flood, and disasters particular to the region (i.e., California lenders will probably require earthquake insurance). At the closing you must show that you have a policy and that the first year's premium has been paid. That will come to between $350 and $600 for a single-family house. The premium is slightly less for a condo.

Of course, many towns, counties and state governments also muscle in on the closing, demanding their due in sales or transfer taxes. These are usually based on the selling price of the house or the size of the mortgage and can run a couple of points or more.

If you need an attorney to represent you at the closing, figure on spending another $300 to $1,000 — or even more. But a growing number of people, particularly in the South and West, are managing without lawyers, thanks to the continuing standardization of legal and loan documents. Instead, real estate brokers often handle the details, from drafting a contract to ordering a title search and closing the sale. And growing in popularity are escrow agents — intermediaries who do the legal work for both parties. Buyers and sellers share the cost, typically a half a percent of the sale price. The trend began in California and has been spreading eastward. You can find out what your state does — and does not — allow by contacting the state's Consumer Affairs Office, a local chamber of commerce or your state Attorney General's Office.

Just when you think you have paid every conceivable tithe, tariff and tax, a few more bills will crop up. But you will know you have finally reached the end of the line when you pay to have your deed recorded. That little exclamation point usually will cost $40 to $60.

## Raising Money for the Down Payment

Even if you are struggling to come up with a modest down payment, you can still buy a home. Don't automatically assume you have to raise 10% to 20% of the price in cash. If you have served with the Armed Forces, you may be able to get a mortgage insured by the Department of Veterans Affairs for 100% of the cost of the house or apartment — with no down payment. You don't have to be a vet to qualify for a Federal Housing Administration–insured loan that can cover up to 95% of the purchase price. You can apply for VA and FHA loans at banks and savings and loan associations.

If your down payment is less than 20% and your loan is without backing by a government-related agency, you are required to take out private mortgage insurance to protect the lender against the possibility of your defaulting. You need not choose the policy offered to you by the lender. It's worthwhile to shop around among various lenders. To qualify for a low-cost policy, a good repayment record on auto and student loans is essential.

If your employer allows it, you can borrow against your contributions to a corporate profit-sharing program or a 401(k) plan. You will be charged interest at a lower rate than a bank would charge. As a last resort, you may even dip into your own IRA. If you're not yet 59½ years old, you'll have to pay ordinary income tax and a 10% penalty on the amount of your early withdrawal, but these costs may be outweighed by the tax deductions your new house will generate.

Some companies even help out employees to keep them from leaving for other jobs in areas where housing costs less. Colgate-Palmolive, for example, assists all its U.S. workers by paying origination fees on mortgages of up to $200,000 or so. Other corporations work with Fannie Mae's Magnet Program to assist employees who can't make the full amount of a down payment. The employer lends the difference, and Fannie Mae guarantees the mortgage.

If your parents want to chip in, the two of them can give up to a total $40,000 each year to a married child and spouse without having to pay federal gift taxes. Or in return for making the down payment, your parents could become co-owners of the house. That way you could buy a more expensive place than you could otherwise afford. You won't be alone in seeking such help. According to a 1994 Chicago Title and Trust Company survey, only 74.1% of the average first-time buyer's down payment came from his or her own savings and investments.

▾ ▾ ▾

# Finding the Best Mortgage

The excitement of homebuying involves not only the hunt for the right house but also the search for the right mortgage. Lenders are offering many new kinds of loans. Particularly if you are a first-time buyer or are returning to the housing market after many years, you will need to educate yourself.

If you value predictability and need a guarantee that your mortgage payments will not rise, you may well want a fixed-rate mortgage. More than half of all borrowers prefer these, according to the Federal Housing Finance Board. The rate you pay is higher at first than with other kinds of mortgages, but it will remain constant. In June 1995 the interest rates on fixed 30-year mortgages averaged 7.74%, down from 8.54% three years earlier. On a $75,000 loan, for example, the monthly payments worked out to $537, excluding taxes and insurance, down from $579.

While 30-year fixed-rate mortgages still account for most home financing, banks have been pushing 15-year fixed-rate loans. These mortgages often carry interest rates about a half percentage point lower than 30-year mortgages. They allow you to own 100% of your house sooner — and you will pay far less interest over the life of your loan. But

## WHAT'S THE BEST MORTGAGE

Your monthly payment—and the total interest you pay—varies greatly, depending on the type of mortgage you choose.

| Type of loan | Average rate (June '95) | Total points | Total interest on a $100,000 loan | Monthly payment |
|---|---|---|---|---|
| **15-year fixed** | 7.26% | 1.18% | $64,417 | $913 |
| **20-year fixed** | 7.67 | 1.10 | 125,600 | 816 |
| **30-year fixed** | 7.74 | 1.23 | 157,660 | 716 |
| **Five-year balloon** | 7.56 | 1.32 | 36,893 | 703 |
| **Seven-year balloon** | 6.93 | 1.24 | 46,539 | 661 |
| **1/30-year adjustable*** | 5.86 | 1.13 | 34,660 | 591 |
| **3/30-year adjustable**** | 6.99 | 0.90 | 111,773 | 665 |
| **3/1-year adjustable***** | 6.82 | 1.24 | 51,089 | 653 |
| **5/1-year adjustable***** | 7.00 | 1.30 | 64,622 | 665 |

*30-year mortgage with a rate adjustment each year.
**30-year mortgage with a rate adjustment every three years.
***30-year mortgages with a fixed rate for an initial period (three or five years) and a rate adjustment each year for the remainder of the term.
SOURCE: HSH ASSOCIATES

## MORTGAGE COSTS

To compute an approximate monthly payment, multiply the number in the table for your rate and term by the amount of your mortgage without the last three zeros.

| | Length of mortgage (years) | | | |
|---|---|---|---|---|
| Rate | 15 | 20 | 25 | 30 |
| **6.0%** | $8.44 | $7.16 | $6.44 | $6.00 |
| **6.5** | 8.71 | 7.46 | 6.75 | 6.32 |
| **7.0** | 8.99 | 7.75 | 7.07 | 6.66 |
| **7.5** | 9.28 | 8.06 | 7.39 | 7.00 |
| **8.0** | 9.56 | 8.36 | 7.72 | 7.34 |
| **8.5** | 9.85 | 8.68 | 8.05 | 7.69 |
| **9.0** | 10.15 | 9.00 | 8.39 | 8.05 |
| **9.5** | 10.45 | 9.32 | 8.74 | 8.41 |
| **10.0** | 10.75 | 9.65 | 9.09 | 8.78 |
| **10.5** | 11.06 | 9.98 | 9.44 | 9.15 |
| **11.0** | 11.37 | 10.32 | 9.80 | 9.53 |
| **11.5** | 11.69 | 10.66 | 10.16 | 9.91 |
| **12.0** | 12.01 | 11.01 | 10.53 | 10.29 |

SOURCE: MORTGAGE BANKERS ASSOCIATION OF AMERICA

your monthly payments will be higher with the 15-year mortgage because you're paying off the total amount of the loan more quickly. You may be better off going for the 30-year mortgage, and investing — say, in a mutual fund — the amount that you would have spent on those higher payments.

But consider the adjustable-rate mortgage, or ARM, which rises or falls in line with interest rates in general. First-year rates are typically two to three-and-a-half percentage points lower than fixed-rate mortgages. Even though the rates rise to approximate those of fixed mortgages in the second year, the initial savings can make a significant difference — especially if you expect to sell your home within a three-to-five-year period.

ARMs are especially inviting for younger buyers who expect to move on or trade up. It also pays to get an ARM if its lower monthly payments help you to qualify for a loan on the house you truly desire. Just make sure you can really afford the house.

ARM rates are linked to a variety of indexes. The two most popular are the one-year Treasury securities index and the so-called 11th District cost-of-funds rate, based on a composite of interest rates that lenders are paying on deposits and their borrowing costs. The Treasury index moves more quickly, so it's a better bet when rates in general are coming down. The rate on ARMs usually changes annually, though some adjustments are made monthly and some as infrequently as two or more years.

## MORTGAGE RATES

| | April 1989* | Oct. 1993** | June 1995 |
|---|---|---|---|
| **30-year fixed** | **11.22%** | **6.83%** | **7.74%** |
| **15-year fixed** | **10.99** | **6.40** | **7.26** |
| **1/30-year adj.*** ** | **9.44** | **4.15** | **5.86** |

*Recent highs **Recent lows
***30-year mortgage with a rate adjustment each year.
SOURCE: HSH ASSOCIATES

What's the ideal adjustable mortgage?

- First, the loan agreement should include caps that limit the interest-rate changes to no more than two percentage points a year and five to six points over the life of the loan.
- Second, your initial interest rate should be at least two to three percentage points below that of fixed-rate loans.
- Third, when you get your mortgage, you should have to pay no more than two points in loan fees — a point, of course, being equivalent to 1% of your mortgage principal.
- Fourth, your monthly payment should not be capped. If interest rates rise, you could wind up with "negative amortization." The bank then will add the unpaid interest to your principal, inflating the size of your mortgage.

Unfortunately, the perfect mortgage is rare, but you should be able to trade some features for others that are especially important to you. To get a lower interest rate, you can agree to pay additional fees up front. If you're planning to stay in the house more than three to five years, you will probably come out ahead with the lower mortgage rate. But don't let the lender roll the points into your mortgage, because doing so will increase the amount of money borrowed — and over time your interest on the points could cost you more than the points themselves.

If you cannot decide between an adjustable-rate and a fixed-rate loan, the solution may be a convertible mortgage. It starts out with an adjustable rate that is lower than that on a fixed mortgage. But if interest rates drop in the future, you can convert to a fixed-rate mortgage at close to the then-current rate for such loans.

A hypothetical example: Say that you took out a convertible mortgage on which the interest rate started at 6.25%. This was far lower than the 8.5% available on a 30-year fixed-rate loan. After three years your adjustable rate drops to 6.125%, but your lender is offering fixed-rate loans at 7.5%. Worried that interest rates might now start rising, you convert to the 7.5% loan for, typically, $250 — much less than the thousands you would spend on a traditional refinancing. When you convert your ARM, you are essentially getting no-cost refinancing. So the lender will charge a higher-than-market interest rate — about 0.5%

higher. Your mortgage will be based on a formula that is explained in your contract.

When you go shopping for a mortgage, start by seeing what local lenders are offering in your newspaper. Then look for a real estate broker who uses a computerized service, which can make comparison shopping a lot easier and faster. In many cities and suburbs, a broker will enter in a desktop computer the size of the loan you are looking for, the amount of your income and other details of your finances. The computer then displays on its screen descriptions of different mortgages and latest rates that are available from various lenders. It also tells you if you are likely to qualify for a particular loan. In some cases, these services permit you to apply for the mortgage electronically. You never deal with the lender in person, and the papers are simply mailed to you for signing.

The most valuable matchmaking services are clearinghouses for mortgages from many lenders, including those in faraway places where money may be more easily available and interest rates more competitive than in your own area. The nation's largest publisher of consumer-loan information is HSH Associates (1200 Route 23, Butler, New Jersey 07405; 800-UPDATES, or 201-838-3330 in New Jersey). It provides reports on the interest rates charged by various financial institutions for mortgages, home-equity lines of credit, credit cards and auto loans. HSH also reports on what rates different banks and other institutions are paying for certificates of deposit. For $20 you can get a Homebuyers Mortgage Kit that includes the booklet *How to Shop for Your Mortgage* and the latest HSH weekly reports on the terms of loans from dozens of institutions in your state. HSH publishes regional editions for all 50 states and 130 major metropolitan areas. The company also has an electronic version, *PC Mortgage Update,* for $20. By e-mail HSH can be reached on: America Online, HSH ASSOC; the Internet, Info@HSH.com; CompuServe, 70410,3507; and the World Wide Web, http://www.hsh.com. Before you send your check, call and see if HSH covers your area.

Beyond the fixed-rate and the adjustable-rate loans, here are two other mortgages you might consider:

*Shared-equity mortgage.* Would you like to help your grown child buy his or her first house? A shared-equity arrangement allows you to split the costs of buying and maintaining a home and combine two incomes to qualify for the mortgage.

It works like this: Two people purchase a house, but only one lives in it. The other partner is solely an investor. The occupant must pay a fair market rent to his or her partner but keeps the proportion of the rent that represents his or her ownership. Meanwhile, the partner who does not live in the house typically pays a portion of the monthly carrying costs, including the property taxes and first-mortgage installments, and does not collect monthly interest payments. He or she gets to split the deductions for interest and taxes with the co-owner who occupies the house. They eventually divide the value of the property, including any appreciation. Usually after three to 10 years, the owner-occupant must buy out the investor.

Unfortunately, an investor who wants out of a shared-equity arrangement is really stuck. There is no secondary market at all for these investments — not yet, anyhow. But if you want to set up such an agreement, have a real estate lawyer with experience in this field draft a contract. The fee is typically $300, but varies according to your lawyer's hourly charges.

*Shared-appreciation mortgage.* These are generally most popular in times of very high interest rates. Example: Some time ago a young couple in Phoenix spotted a house they wanted to buy. The price was $98,500. They figured that after putting 20% down they could get a $78,800 mortgage at interest rates then at 13.5%. But monthly payments would have come to $950 a month, and that was more than the couple could afford. Their solution was to go to a mortgage company that offered a shared-appreciation mortgage, which lowered their payments by one-third. In return, they promised to give the lender one-third of the profit they make whenever they sell the house. And when they do sell, they still stand to come out ahead because their two-thirds share will probably amount to just as much as the full profit on a cheaper property.

Shared-appreciation mortgages help not only first-time buyers but also elderly buyers who cannot afford to make big payments and who expect to own their houses for the rest of their lives. If you consider such a mortgage, be aware of the risks. Under some agreements, a lender can collect its share of the appreciation after 10 years, even if the homeowner has not sold. If the homeowner does not have the cash to pay, he or she will have to borrow and perhaps take out a new mortgage. This could zap him or her with exploding monthly payments.

The shared mortgage is also a poor choice for a do-it-yourselfer. If you make home improvements yourself, the value that you add to your house is shared with the lender.

## Still More Mortgages

If you can't quite make payments on a conventional mortgage at first but are confident your income will rise within a couple of years, consider the so-called *buydown.* With the typical 2-1 buydown, for example, you pay two percentage points less than the 30-year fixed rate during the first year, and one point less in the second year. You start paying full freight in the third year. The overall cost of the mortgage would be higher than what you would pay for a conventional mortgage, but the reduced starting rate may be worth the extra cost if it gets you a house you could not afford otherwise. Builders often offer buydowns to move their houses in slow markets.

Another way of lowering initial costs is through the *balloon mortgage.* It is structured like a 30-year mortgage, but the first-year interest rate is 0.25% to 0.75% less than that on a typical 30-year fixed-rate loan. This is because you have to pay off the whole mortgage in only three, five or seven years. Often the loan will have a built-in refinancing option, offering you whatever the going rate is at that time. In any case, you must refinance.

On the other hand, if you have cash to spare, you could save much money over the life of your loan with a so-called *biweekly mortgage* that allows you to accelerate your repayments. You ask your bank to deduct your house payments every two weeks from your checking account. Each payment is half of what you would turn over every month in a conventional mortgage. But you make 26 of those payments annually, not 24 — in effect amounting to an extra month's payment every year.

How big are the savings? Take a $100,000 mortgage at 8.5%. Your biweekly payments would be $384, and you wind up paying $769 more a year than if your payments were monthly. But you would be able to retire your mortgage in about 23 years rather than 30. That works out to a savings in your interest payments of $54,000.

For further pointers, the U.S. Consumer Information Center publishes a number of books that can help you through the maze of buying and financing a home. To get its free catalog, write to Consumer Information Catalog, Pueblo, Colorado 81009. Also valuable is the HSH Associates booklet, *How to Shop for Your Mortgage,* mentioned above on page 351. It defines the most popular types of mortgages (without endorsing any one of them) and helps buyers understand the fine print in mortgage contracts. It also contains an easy-to-read page of mortgage payment tables and a prequalification table that lets you calculate the mortgage you can afford. To get a copy, send $9 to HSH.

## Don't Give Up on Refinancing Your Mortgage

Even if you missed the boat back in late 1993, when fixed mortgage rates were down to a 28-year low of 6.83%, it may not be too late to refinance the high-interest mortgage you took out in the early 1980s. Some of those loans carry interest as high as 14%. Saving just one point in the rate on a 30-year, $100,000 mortgage spares you more than $25,000 in total payments. But refinancing involves a lot of hassle and expense. It makes sense only if your new loan brings your monthly payments down enough over the time you plan to stay in your house to offset the immediate out-of-pocket costs.

If there is a prepayment penalty clause in your mortgage, you will have to pay plenty to get out of it — up to 3% of the unpaid balance. That's on top of the usual expenses of refinancing, which are often almost as high as the closing costs on the original mortgage. Costs include the points charged by the lender, typically 1% to 3% of the loan's principal amount. So check carefully to see what these real costs will be, after you figure in your income tax deductions for them. Then compare them with the immediate and long-term savings you can expect by refinanc-

**YOUR SAVINGS BY REFINANCING**

What you save by shifting to a $100,000 mortgage at 8%

| Your current mortgage rate | Current monthly payment | Monthly savings at 8% | Annual savings at 8% |
|---|---|---|---|
| 12.0% | $1,029 | $295 | $3,540 |
| 11.5 | 990 | 256 | 3,072 |
| 11.0 | 952 | 218 | 2,616 |
| 10.5 | 915 | 181 | 2,172 |
| 10.0 | 878 | 144 | 1,728 |
| 9.5 | 841 | 107 | 1,284 |
| 9.0 | 805 | 71 | 852 |

SOURCE: MORTGAGE BANKERS ASSOCIATION OF AMERICA

## Is It Worthwhile for You?

Refinancing can be worthwhile, but it is not for everyone. A general rule is that refinancing becomes worth your while if the current interest rate on your mortgage is at least two percentage points higher than the prevailing market rate.

Refinancing is a good idea for a homeowner who:

- wants to get out of a high-interest-rate loan to take advantage of lower rates (a good idea only if you intend to stay in the house long enough to make the additional fees worthwhile)
- has an adjustable-rate mortgage (ARM) and wants a fixed-rate loan to have the certainty of knowing exactly what the mortgage payment will be for the life of the loan
- wants to convert to an ARM with a lower interest rate or more protective features (such as a better rate and payment caps) than the ARM he or she currently has
- wants to build up equity more quickly by converting to a loan with a shorter term
- wants to draw on equity built up in his or her house to get cash for a major purchase or for his or her children's education

If you decide that refinancing is not worth the costs, ask your lender whether you may be able to obtain all or some of the new terms you want by agreeing to a modification of your existing loan instead of refinancing.
*Source: Mortgage Bankers Association*

ing. You should also be planning to live in your house for at least three more years. Otherwise, the costs most likely will exceed the amount that you would save in monthly payments.

A quick way to see how long it will require for refinancing to pay off is to divide your closing costs by the reduction in your monthly payment. The result will equal the number of months it will take you to break even. For example, if your closing costs are $6,000 and your monthly saving is $150, you will need to keep your home 40 months to break even (6,000 divided by 150 equals 40). If you're struggling to meet your present payments because you've lost your old corporate job and are earning less, many bankers will be surprisingly sympathetic about helping you refinance to lower your payments. Similarly, if your home has declined in value, many lenders will help you by taking advantage of Freddie Mac and Fannie Mae programs that allow borrowers to refinance up to 95% of their homes' value, versus the typical 80% to 90%.

## Buying a Bargain House

Owning repossessed and foreclosed properties is not the business that mortgage institutions want to be in — and that is good news for prospective buyers. These institutions will give you the best deal in town.

Prices vary all over the lot. Many of the foreclosed properties are in the medium range for their area, while others are obviously at the low end. For a real bargain, consider the "handyman's special," the diamond in the rough that can be buffed to brilliance with your own time and energy — and money. Every mortgage institution has some of these to sell. Fannie Mae prides itself on installing new fixtures and carpeting, painting the place and replacing appliances. Freddie Mac also refurbishes. The Federal Housing Administration, the Department of Veterans Affairs and the Federal Deposit Insurance Corporation, on the other hand, all sell a house pretty much as is. These agencies lack the funding to make many improvements.

Check Fannie Mae's list of repossessed houses, *Real Estate Owned (REO) Properties*, which you can get from the Office of Public Information, 3900 Wisconsin Avenue NW, Washington, D.C. 20016. If there are residences available in your state of choice, they will be listed with local Realtors who are members of the multiple listing service.

The Department of Veterans Affairs has 39 regional offices that can give you information on VA-acquired properties. To find the nearest office, call 800-827-1000. You will be given a series of electronic commands to get information about available homes. Then you punch in the zip code of your chosen area and your desired number of bedrooms and baths. If such homes are to be had, you listen to a list of them identified by address, list price and square footage.

This hotline is just one of several innovations that both private and government agencies are using to sell the many single-family homes that are foreclosed each year. Freddie Mac has four regional offices across the U.S. It will send you a list of foreclosed homes in any area but must refer you to a broker if you want to buy. You can call 800-373-3343 for information.

As of early 1995 the U.S. Department of Housing and Urban Development had more than 40,000 homes for sale. You can find out about these homes from a local mortgage company, a local HUD office or newspaper ads announcing HUD auctions. HUD also has a "fixer-up" program, the 203(k), which allows people to consolidate into one mortgage the several loans typically needed to acquire and rehabilitate a house. Contact your HUD office for details.

Hotlines and special programs aside, sale procedures are standard. You can easily spot newspaper ads placed by real estate brokers as well as by agencies holding repossessed properties. Houses are sold through local brokers at fair market prices. Agencies also take sealed bids from any number of hopefuls who submit a price at a predetermined time and place. Highest bids win. If houses languish on the market, agencies may accept lower-than-list prices.

The agencies occasionally hold auctions. But heed a warning from David Kaufman, owner of Kaufman Lasman Associates, a real estate auction firm in Chicago: "Some people come away from auctions with a steal, and others get butchered." You will be competing with professionals, so before rushing out to bid, make sure you know what you're doing. Here's how to survive and even prosper at a real estate auction:

- Avoid the auctions and sheriff sales held by court order. They are aimed strictly at real estate pros. Watch instead for auctions operated by national, regional or local companies on behalf of lenders and developers.
- Prepare for an auction by finding out all you can about the property for sale and the price of comparable houses in the area. Tour the house with a professional inspector. If possible, talk to a real estate broker familiar with the place.
- Get a professional appraisal to help you determine what your maximum bid should be. Remember that a house in a deteriorating neighborhood won't offer much investment potential.

- Hire a lawyer to make sure there are no other claims on the property. You want to buy it free of liens and disputes.
- Arrange financing before the auction. You will have to submit a certified check for $1,500 to $3,000, depending on the auctioneer. If your bid fails, you get the money back. If your bid wins, the check goes toward the down payment. But if you can't qualify for financing, you lose the deposit.

Both the Federal Housing Administration and the Department of Veterans Affairs are prepared to give individual assistance to potential homebuyers at their regional offices throughout the country. Veterans Affairs can provide 100% financing and you needn't be a veteran to qualify. Just reduce the VA's foreclosed houses by one.

## Manufactured Homes

Homebuilders have become more productive and efficient over the years. But for delivering value, hardly any of them can beat the makers of manufactured homes — houses partially or largely built in factories and shipped to your property for assembly. Manufactured houses, including mobile homes, account for 30% to 40% of all new homes in the U.S.

Consider the benefits: lower cost and/or higher quality, quicker occupancy than conventional "stick-built" homes and a wide variety of styles, floor plans and prices. Many manufactured houses are indistinguishable from stick-built homes. Indeed, some are sold as finished homes by local dealers or builders, and the buyers may not even be aware they're getting a manufactured home. Yet they typically cost 5% to 10% less, and sometimes the difference is much greater. For mobile homes, the savings can reach 50%. Banks and other lenders are usually happy to issue mortgages for factory homes once the buildings are complete.

An excellent guide to the possibilities is *Manufactured Houses* by A. M. Watkins, an enthusiastic advocate. His 189-page book explains the subject in clear prose and lists more than 300 manufacturers in the U.S. and Canada. It's available for $14.95 from the Building Institute, 127 South Broadway, Nyack, New York 10960. Ads for manufactured homes also appear in housing and building trade magazines.

Manufactured houses come in four basic types: modular or sectional, panelized, precut, and mobile.

*Modular homes* are the most finished and cost about $50 a square foot. They are typically 95% complete when they leave the factory in two or more sections, depending on the size. At the site, the sections are placed on the foundation and connected — usually by a local contractor with experience assembling modular homes. Modules can be stacked to make two- or three-story houses — or even higher ones. And the finished home can be ready to occupy within a week or two. Prices range from $40,000 for a modest house of roughly a thousand square feet to $300,000 or more for a six-thousand-square-foot home.

*Panelized houses* are less finished but cost as much as homes built to customers' specifications, about $55 a square foot. You pay a premium because they are built more quickly and are ready to occupy sooner, usually in two to three months. Panelized houses consist of completed wall panels, usually eight feet high and up to 40 feet long, designed to be assembled quickly on-site. Some come with "closed panels," which include insulation, wiring and electrical outlets mounted in the interior walls. Windows and doors may also be supplied, sometimes "prehung" in the panels. Some manufacturers will sell part or all of what you need to complete the house, from siding and roofing to screws and nails to bathrooms and kitchens. You can hire a contractor to install the mechanical systems and finish the interior, but the savings with panelized homes are greatest if you can do much of the work yourself.

*Precut houses* are basically kits of parts that cost $30 to $35 a square foot, and are most valuable for serious do-it-yourselfers. Some makers offer only precut lumber for the outer walls, along with insulation, windows and exterior doors. Others sell you practically everything you need — from wiring to plumbing fixtures to hinges and doorknobs.

*Mobile homes,* once sneered at, have changed. While many are still budget models that look like the stereotypical denizens of the old trailer park, a growing number are designed and built like conventional houses: walls finished in wood siding, conventional windows and doors, asphalt shingle roofs — and plenty of room. So-called doublewides and triplewides, shipped in two or three sections, can offer two thousand or more square feet, three or four bedrooms, and ample other living space. Mounted permanently on foundations, they cost about $25 to $35 a square foot and compare with stick-built houses costing twice as much.

For vacation homes, manufactured log, dome or A-frame houses are especially attractive bargains. They come in many styles and levels of sophistication; the fanciest can offer you porches, dormers, lofts, skylights and other amenities. Costs start at $30 to $35 a square foot; they are low because vacation homes often lack insulation or other amenities that would make them comfortable for all four seasons of the year. One big plus: Manufactured homes eliminate the problem of finding good builders and workers in remote areas, often a real challenge, and then overseeing the work from miles away.

The first step in buying a manufactured home is to steep yourself in catalogues. When you see something you like, phone the company to find its local dealer. Check with the Better Business Bureau or your state Consumer Affairs Office to see if any complaints have been filed against the company. Also ask the firm for names of local builders who have assembled its houses. Interview the buyers and visit their homes.

Once you know that you are dealing with a reliable company, you are ready to sit down with its representative to discuss the details of the home you want. Many people work up their own designs. Of course, the more you depart from a standard plan, the more you will have to pay.

# Selling Your House for Top Price

Before you buy a home, it's wise to sell the one you now live in. Otherwise, you risk paying two mortgages and being forced to sell out at fire-sale prices. Don't assume that your present house will sell as fast or for as much money as you think it should, especially if you are in a soft market. Get an appraiser's estimate of its value and ask a real estate agent how rapidly homes in that price range are turning over in your area.

If houses stay on the market for more than two or three months, don't even look for a second home until you have a firm contract of sale on the first. And continue living in the house, if possible, while it is on the market. Untenanted houses give buyers the impression that the owners are desperate to sell.

To put your house into shape for selling, figure on spending several weekends of your time for a minor cosmetic facelift. As the saying goes, "God is in the details." Many seemingly minor defects — little problems you've grown accustomed to and may not even notice anymore — can create the same poor first impression as a rumpled suit or dress. They may break the deal before it even gets under way.

Start with your home's so-called curb appeal, or how it looks from the street. Step back and try to imagine you're seeing the place for the first time. Are plantings trimmed and orderly? Mulching flower beds and bushes with fresh wood chips can greatly enhance the grounds' appearance. Of course, make sure the lawn is neat. Patch cracks and holes in the driveway. Do you need a new mailbox? How about nice brass house numbers? Tubs of pink geraniums flanking the doorway? Such finishing touches often can do more for your house than a major renovation.

You don't need to spring for a full paint job unless the outside walls are blistering and peeling. But touch up the trim. The $200 or so you spend to brighten doors, windows and the like often makes your whole house look freshly painted. Wash the windows, inside and out. When the glare of the sun hits dirty panes, you can see the streaks from the street.

Now step inside and pretend once again to be a sharp-eyed stranger. Thin out your possessions before you show your house. The fewer things you have in a room or closet, the larger it will appear. Repaint rooms that need it, such as those that your kids have graced with unusual colors. Kitchens and bathrooms must always be immaculate. A rusty sink or a ring around the toilet bowl can scare off prospective buyers who might think the plumbing needs repair — or that your commitment to maintenance in general may be shaky.

All homebuyers are conscious of energy costs, so your heating system must work well — and look it. Wipe the boiler and the area around it to remove soot or oil stains. And now's the time to clear all the junk out of the basement, not to mention the attic.

Do anything you can to make the house warm and inviting when prospective buyers arrive. Here's a trick the National Association of Realtors recommends: "Have some fresh bread or a batch of cookies baking in the oven. The aroma will make the buyer feel more 'at home,' and its appeal will carry over to other rooms."

A helpful guide is *100 Surefire Improvements to Sell Your House Faster* by R. Dodge Woodson (John Wiley & Sons, $14.95). It lists projects from small detail work to major improvements, and offers judgments about which ones pay off best.

You may do well selling your house yourself. Some experts recommend preparing a fact sheet that includes a floor plan, utility and insurance costs, and maintenance fees. Such a flyer would answer most buyers' questions while emphasizing the most attractive, or marketable, features of your home. You can also use some new sales devices, such as putting your FOR SALE notice on local cable TV or electronic bulletin boards. When you sell the house yourself, of course, you save the broker's commission. You have little to lose, because brokers will be more than eager to get your business if you're unsuccessful.

Before your house goes on the market, make sure it is correctly priced. It is worth hiring a professional appraiser, but shop around because fees vary. To find several local candidates, write or call the Appraisal Institute (875 North Michigan Avenue, Suite 2400, Chicago, Illinois 60611; 312-335-4100). Or you might solicit opinions from up to three real estate brokers to ensure a competitive price.

While you are awaiting the sale, investigate the area you will be moving to. Drive around and see what neighborhoods best suit you. Survey the prices quoted in real estate ads in the Sunday paper. But don't actually househunt. You could fall in love with a new homestead while you are still wedded financially to your old one.

By selling first, of course, you may have to move out before you have found another house. Try to avoid that possibility in your negotiations with a prospective buyer. For example, you might be able to postpone the closing date to allow yourself time to find a new place.

Such an extended closing period also gives the buyer more time to change his or her mind. So a better solution, if the buyer is amenable, is to close the deal as soon as possible but rent your house back from him or her until you find another one. If the buyer balks at such a provision, resign yourself to renting elsewhere, preferably in or near your future neighborhood. Though a temporary inconvenience, this strategy will acquaint you with the market and make you a smarter buyer.

## Financing Your House Sale

If you are having trouble selling your house, you might consider offering to lend some of the money to a buyer. Sellers typically make loans at rates as much as two percentage points below market rates. But you should not subsidize the buyer, except as a last resort — and then with plenty of professional help. Most people do not have the time or skills to successfully manage so-called owner financing.

Say that you do decide to help provide the financing for the buyer. Your first problem is running a thorough credit check on him or her — a specialized task best left to pros. Then comes enforcement. Though you might be planning to get tough the moment your buyer misses a payment, there is not much you can do. You might figure you could threaten to foreclose — take back your house. Just try it! Foreclosure can drag out for months. All the time, your debtor can enjoy the comforts of your old home — and you cannot exactly expect him or her to treat the house with tender loving care during the whole nasty affair.

Here are precautions you can take if you finance:

- Demand a healthy down payment, at least 10% and preferably more. For an insolvent buyer, it is a lot less painful to walk away from a mortgage contract with nothing to lose but a good credit rating than to lose both his or her credit rating and, say, $10,000. Even the best-referenced buyer can go belly-up. Whatever you can do to make that option as unattractive as possible for him or her will stand to your advantage.
- Enlist help from officers at your bank or savings and loan association. For a fee of 0.5% to 1% of the loan amount, they will service, or collect payments on, the mortgage you give to a buyer. For additional fees, the banker will do a credit check on the prospective buyer and handle a foreclosure — if one becomes necessary.
- Get a lawyer to draft the contract. Real estate agents, who are often involved in arranging owner financing, generally use blank forms that are filled in by the buyer and seller and later checked by the agency's lawyer. If the contract turns out not to be what you want, too bad. For example, most mortgage loans, whether from a bank or from the seller, are not assumable and carry a "due on sale" provision. This means the seller must pay off the mortgage when a residence is sold. If you ever need money before the note comes due, you will have to sell the loan to a mortgage banker for less than its face value.

When selling to a financially marginal buyer, you will get a better price if you arrange the loan at the outset through the Federal National Mortgage Association's Home Seller program. A Fannie Mae–approved bank or savings institution processes your buyer's application. The fee, which is negotiable, is usually paid by the buyer. To get the names of participating lenders in your area, write to the Federal National Mortgage Association, 3900 Wisconsin Avenue NW, Washington, D.C. 20016.

One form of seller financing that some buyers find attractive uses the balloon mortgage. With a balloon, repayment of a large part of the principal is deferred. So monthly payments are low until the loan period ends, when you, the lender, get one big payment.

Balloons can hold a couple of problems. Your money is tied up until the note matures. Even then you may not get paid on time if the buyer doesn't have the money. But an arrangement known by the dismaying name of hypothecation allows you to negotiate a way around that grim obstacle to liquidity. Essentially you use the money owed you as collateral for a new but smaller loan that you get from a bank or savings and loan association. Then you can use the loan money to add to the down payment on your new house. With hypothecation, you might well work out the figures so that the homebuyer's monthly payment to you will be exactly the same as what the bank asks you to pay on your smaller loan. Your buyer could send his or her check directly to your bank and, in one stroke, be paying an installment on both your loan and his or hers. In any case, ask your bank or savings and loan about the possibility of using hypothecation.

In sum, if you are thinking of financing the sale of your own home, here is what you should do:

- Hire a lawyer to write all your contracts — even if you use a real estate broker.
- Cover in writing everything that could possibly happen.
- Get a thorough credit check on the buyer.
- Make sure you get a big enough down payment to keep your buyer from hightailing it.
- Insure your loan with a title insurance company so that you will have an absolute first lien on your former home up to the

amount that you lent to the buyer. The buyer customarily pays for this title insurance on your behalf.

## Limiting the Tax Bite

As with any major financial transaction, the IRS is ready and waiting for you when you sell a home. If you're moving up, you may have no problems. Assuming your new house costs the same as or more than your old one did, you can postpone paying any capital-gains tax on profits from the sale of the old one. You'll pay eventually — the IRS lowers the so-called cost basis of the new home by the amount of the profit, so it will become part of the profit from the eventual sale of that new house. But of course, later is always better when it comes to paying taxes — and substantial capital improvements you make in the new home will reduce the profit.

Be sure you *move into* your new home within two years of the sale date of the old one. Wait a day longer, and the IRS won't let you roll the profit over. And remember, if you've used any portion of your house for business and taken the appropriate deductions, you cannot exclude those rooms from capital-gains taxes. Only the residential part of your home qualifies for exclusion.

There is one exception to the two-year rule. If you had to live overseas in the meantime for business reasons, you'll get a "time-out" equivalent to the time you spent abroad, up to a maximum of two years. One caveat: Generally, converting to a rental property prevents you from rolling over any profit.

If you're older than 55, you get a one-time exclusion from capital gains tax of up to $125,000 of the profit. This is a big help when you are trading down to a smaller home. Be sure the closing takes place after your 55th birthday (it's all right to sign the contract earlier). And the house must have been your principal residence for three of the past five years. Otherwise, no soap. Finally, will this be the biggest gain you're ever going to get from a home sale? If you are sure of a bigger one down the road, hang on to the exclusion until then.

▾ ▾ ▾

# Doing Preventative Maintenance

No matter how new or sound your home may be, the dark forces of entropy lurk everywhere, waiting to eat into its value. Head off problems in the early stages. You will save money by fixing small ones before they get big — and you'll get more for the house when you sell it.

Spring and autumn are good times to take stock with a top-to-bottom physical examination. Not all homes need an exam every six months. For newer houses and those in mild climates, an annual inspection should suffice. But if your house is more than 10 years old or has to weather ice and snow, you are wise to make quarterly checkups. If you're handy, you will be able to do a fair amount of work yourself, especially with the help of a good home maintenance and repair book (several are listed at the end of this section).

In most parts of the country, the worst enemy of your house is water. It does its earliest damage to the roof, and the most vulnerable areas are the flashings — the metal sheeting that covers the joints where chimneys and vent pipes rise through the roof. Cracks and gaps in the flashing sealant should be recoated with tar or latex sealer. Other trouble spots include gutters and downspouts. It's very important to keep leaves and debris from piling up and blocking the drainage; the water will eventually find its way into the eaves and rot them. If you have shingles, make sure that loose or cracked ones are repaired quickly.

Caulk any gaps around windows and doors and the junctures between the foundation and patios and walks. Such steps can save you hundreds, even thousands, of dollars in emergency repairs later on — not to mention significant money in heating costs. And while it is tempting to postpone back-straining brick, concrete and asphalt repair jobs, the consequences of not doing them promptly can be costly. Don't underestimate the damage that can be done by water freezing in masonry cracks.

You can save both time and money by repairing your house in stages rather than all at once. The south side usually needs painting every three to six years, since it takes the worst beating from the sun. The other sides require it only every eight to 10 years.

There's not as much to do indoors, but it is equally important. An oil-fired furnace should be professionally cleaned and serviced once a year.

Charges start at $150. Gas furnaces should be checked every couple of years for soot buildup. If you have a hot-water system, you will probably need to bleed air out of the convectors — particularly the upper ones — at the start of the heating season; air in the system will keep the water from circulating well. Change or clean the filters in hot-air systems and air-conditioners quarterly. Filthy filters can reduce efficiency by 10% to 25%. And don't forget to inspect your smoke detectors and burglar alarms regularly.

Electrical systems don't exactly wear out, but problems can nonetheless develop. If you are frequently blowing fuses or resetting circuit breakers, consult an electrician. You probably have an overloaded circuit. While it's rare, houses have been known to burn down because squirrels or other rodents have gnawed insulation on wires in attics. If critters have been living there, check your wiring.

Minor plumbing problems are easy to deal with. You can usually fix leaking faucets with just a wrench and an inexpensive washer. Your subsequent savings on water can be surprising. Toilets aren't much harder; you can get tank replacement parts for standard types at hardware stores.

## The House Inspection: A Checklist

To head off problems and save money, here are key things to look for:

- Flashing, gutters and downspouts: Seal cracks and gaps, clean out leaves and debris.
- Shingles: Repair loose or cracked ones.
- Door, window and foundation caulking: Fill any gaps.
- Paving: Fill holes and cracks.
- Heating and cooling systems: Clean filters, have the furnace serviced, bleed air from convectors in hot-water systems.
- Plumbing: Fix leaking faucets and toilet tanks — even a small drip can add up to big water bills. If you have a septic tank, make sure it is pumped out regularly.

Fortunately, there is a wealth of books that can help you do many repairs yourself. One way to choose among the wide variety is to focus on a project you know something about. Say you've had experience repairing a faucet: Check that section in several books and buy the one that describes it most clearly. The Time-Life Books series *New Home Repair and Improvement* gets high marks from do-it-yourself advisers. Each volume concentrates on a particular subject — for example, landscaping, basic wiring or kitchens. For $16.99 plus $3.95 shipping and handling, you can buy the specific volume you need. Call 800-621-7026. Other useful books are *This Old House* by Bob Vila and Jane Davison (Little, Brown and Company, $24.95) and *Reader's Digest Home Improvement Manual — Updated Edition* by Reader's Digest Association Inc. ($30).

## Making Home Improvements That Pay Off

Upgrading your home not only will make it more livable but also can yield rewards when the time comes to sell. You may well get back every dollar you spend when you add a bathroom or a bedroom — or more, taking into account tax benefits. But don't go overboard. An extravagant addition can make your home *harder* to sell.

Not every prospective buyer, for example, will love a $15,000 pleasure center with a custom-made whirlpool, hot tub, steam bath and built-in stereo system. It could even be a turn-off. The limits on what a house can sell for are well defined in any neighborhood. If the houses range from $90,000 to $120,000, your top resale price still will not be considerably more than $120,000, no matter how many rooms, baths or skylights you add. You are not likely to recover any costs that raise the value of your property more than 20% over that of similar homes in your neighborhood.

The most profitable interior improvement is to remodel your kitchen — the nerve center in many homes, a combination family room and workplace. It should be sunny and spacious, should have new appliances, plenty of storage and a step-saving layout that positions the stove, sink and refrigerator close together. But try to limit the remodeling expenses on it to 10% of the estimated value of your home. If you put in a deluxe gourmet kitchen and wind up with a buyer who is a canned-soup cook, don't expect to get all your money back.

Adding a second bathroom should return almost its entire cost. A third is popular, too — perhaps a half-bath — but most prospective homebuyers consider more than three unnecessary. Since decor is so much a matter of taste, elaborate remodeling is less likely to pay for itself. But do not skimp on basic quality. An elegant ceramic tile floor creates a far better impression than vinyl.

Fireplaces can be one of your best investments. Yes, they usually waste more heat than they provide, but people tend to feel that the ambience is worth the cost. Central air-conditioning can also help you sell your house even if you live in a colder region, simply because it offers cleaner, pollen-free air.

A deck or patio can recoup 40% to 70% of its cost. So can a conveniently located family room. But plan it carefully, consulting an architect if possible: An addition that disrupts the traffic pattern, or fundamentally clashes with the style of the house, can subtract value. And if you convert the garage to a game room, you eliminate all the buyers who want a garage.

Swimming pools do not add much to the price of a house in cooler regions of the country. Many people worry about the time and trouble it takes to maintain a pool, as well as the potential danger to children. Even in warm areas, recovery of your outlay is uncertain.

Energy efficiency improvements such as insulation and energy-saving windows have paid for themselves ever since the oil price shocks of the 1970s. But trendy innovations — for example, solar heating panels — offer a less certain return. The more personalized a project, the more chancy the payback. Make your improvements yourself only if you have the soul of a craftsman and skills to match. Hiring professionals to do the entire job usually is the soundest investment.

The kicker to major improvements is the tax benefit. When you sell, the expenses are added to the so-called cost basis of your house, which includes the purchase price and is subtracted from your sale price to determine your capital gain. Among the improvements that qualify are rooms, decks, porches, fences, shrubs, trees, storm windows, lighting fixtures, air conditioners — even wall-to-wall carpeting, termite-proofing and waterproofing.

The key word is improvement. The tax people will not let you count normal repairs and upkeep. Keep full records of all your improvements and renovations. That way you can avoid having to guesstimate when the time comes to pay the IRS. You can also add to the cost of your house any legal fees you paid when you bought it. And your legal fees and commissions on the sale of the house will decrease your sale price for tax purposes.

## Financing Improvements

Americans spend just over $100 billion a year on major improvements and additions to their homes — about 70% as much as they spend on new homes. As with new-home purchases, most of the money is borrowed.

Second mortgages, including home-equity loans, are the most popular methods of financing renovations. They account for 48% of all outstanding consumer-credit debt at banks, not counting credit cards. Interest rates are relatively low — and, importantly, tax-deductible up to $100,000. You can sometimes get below-market rates by borrowing from your company profit-sharing plan or against the cash value of your whole life insurance, but the tax-deductibility of second-mortgage interest may make it a better deal. If you cannot tap any of these sources, you can apply for a variety of loans offered by banks and finance companies. Interest rates are lowest at credit unions, higher at banks and highest at consumer loan companies.

The great benefit of the home-equity line is its flexibility. You take out money only as needed, and pay interest only on the amount you've written the checks for. You can use the money for any purpose, not just home renovations. The line can run as high as 70% to 80% of the appraised value of your house, minus the unpaid portion of the mortgage principal, and repayment can be stretched out for 10 years or more. The interest rate is usually adjustable, varying monthly, and pegged at some one-and-a-half to two percentage points above the prime rate (which was 8.75% in mid-1995). An estimated 15 million homeowners have taken out home-equity lines of credit.

Lenders are eager for your business. You can get home-equity lines of credit from banks, brokerage firms, savings and loan associations, credit

## The $1 Million Limit

Congress has put some limitations on mortgage-interest deductions that apply primarily to affluent people and are quite complex. So they take some explaining:

You can fully deduct only the interest you pay on your first $1 million of housing debt, whether you are single or married. (But if you're married and filing separately, you may deduct only the interest on the first $500,000.) This covers debt that you incur when you acquire, construct or substantially improve your principal and/or second residence and that is secured by such property.

But wait — there's a further wrinkle. The million-dollar limit applies only to debt taken out after October 13, 1987. Interest on all debt that you had taken before October 13, 1987, will be deductible even though it exceeds the limit. However, the amount of this previous mortgage debt will reduce the million-dollar limit on all new debt.

Say you had bought a house or apartment with an $800,000 mortgage two years ago, and you want to buy a vacation home this year with a $400,000 mortgage. You will not be able to deduct the interest on your entire debt of $1.2 million, only the interest on your first $1 million of it. But if you already had incurred the $1.2 in debt before October 13, 1987, you may deduct the total interest on it. However, even the very rich can fully deduct the interest incurred on $100,000 of a home-equity loan.

unions and some mortgage-banking firms. Some attractive deals come from national outfits that compete everywhere. For example, Countrywide (800-669-5850), which is the nation's largest mortgage lender, in mid-1995 was charging the prime rate plus 2%. Other leading lenders include First Interstate (800-446-8651) and Harris Trust (312-461-2121). You do have to pay closing costs on most equity lines, but many lenders keep those costs to a minimum.

Traditional second mortgages are a better choice if you're financing a single large project and value the certainty of fixed monthly payments, since you can get fixed-rate loans. Typically you'll be charged one to two points over the first-mortgage rate, along with (sometimes substantial) closing costs. Those offered by the Federal Housing Administration through mortgage banks, commercial banks and S&Ls are usually cheapest. It may cost less to refinance your first mortgage instead, especially if rates have dropped since you took it out. In comparing the costs of second mortgages and home-equity lines, be aware that financing fees for second mortgages are counted toward the annual percentage rate (APR); for the equity line, points are not included. Thus, the advertised APR on an equity line may appear lower, but the loan may actually be more expensive.

## Finding Repairers You Can Trust

A major project is not likely to be a tranquil experience, but neither should it be a calamity. Your satisfaction with the job may depend more than anything else on how skillfully you choose and deal with the carpenters, plumbers, electricians and any other contractors who work on it. Pick these house surgeons as carefully as you would a family doctor.

Nothing beats referrals from friends or neighbors who have had work done on their homes. Failing such contacts, you can get names of financially sound workers from bankers and storekeepers who deal with them. Building-materials wholesalers, such as plumbing-supply houses and lumberyards, can also be a good source of leads. If you pluck a name from the Yellow Pages, make sure your candidate has been in business locally for three years or so and will supply references. Call these people and get an account of the repairer's work, prices, reliability and character. The Better Business Bureau also keeps files on tradespeople who have drawn complaints.

For major remodeling jobs, you will probably need a general contractor to assume command of the entire project. That includes finding designers to draw up your plans, hiring subcontractors for specific jobs, such as plumbing, and arranging for building permits and inspections. Fees vary widely — from roughly 10% to 25% of the entire cost — depending on the complexity of the project.

In addition to the sources above, you may be able to get leads on general contractors from local chapters of such trade groups as the National

Association of Home Builders and the National Association of the Remodeling Industry. The latter offers a free pamphlet, "Select a Professional Remodeling Contractor." Write to the National Association of the Remodeling Industry, 4301 North Fairfax Drive, Suite 310, Arlington, Virginia 22203, or call 800-440-NARI.

Once you have located several candidates for a substantial job, evaluate them carefully. One consideration is rapport. It's a mistake to hire a workman just because he is engaging; yet it's also wrong to dismiss personal chemistry. Pick someone you can communicate with. And visit one of his job sites. If the place is messy and disorganized, it is reasonable to wonder whether the worker takes meticulous care with his work.

When picking a contractor, ask yourself the following questions:

- Was he or she recommended by a trustworthy source?
- Has he or she supplied the names of previous customers whom I can check for references?
- How long has he or she been in business under the same name? More than 10 years is a definite plus.
- Will the contractor give me his or her home address and phone number?
- Has he or she agreed to include start and completion dates in the contract?
- Does a check with the contractor's bank indicate that he or she is financially sound?
- Did he or she offer me a written guarantee?

Finally, if you answer yes to the next two questions, perhaps you should look for another contractor:

- Has the contractor made oral promises that he or she will not put in the contract?
- Did he or she offer you a discount for signing up at once?

If so, those are danger signals you cannot afford to ignore.

For big home improvements, try to get at least three bids. Discard any astronomical ones. But you may want to choose the most highly recommended contractor even if his or her bid is not the lowest. No bid is set in concrete, so negotiate with the person you really want. Contractors expect their profit to be 10% to 25% of a project's total cost. But if they need work, they will accept less.

You will need a tight agreement that cites the details of the job practically to the last nut and bolt. Designate the brand name, model number and color of any appliances and plumbing or electrical fixtures. You should specify materials for cabinetry, countertops and hardware. A standard form, called an owners and contractors construction agreement, is available at many stationery stores. You can also write to the American Homeowners Foundation, 1724 South Quincy Street, Arlington, Virginia 22204. For $5.95 the foundation will send you an eight-page model agreement. And if you want a pipeline to independent expertise on dealing with contractors, become a member of the United Homeowners Association, 1511 K Street NW, Suite 326, Washington, D.C. 20005 (202-408-8842), for $12. The association will answer questions by phone and send a bimonthly newsletter.

Other points to include, and to keep in mind for any job, whether you are renovating your whole house or simply adding kitchen cabinets:

- Specify the start and approximate completion dates.
- Stipulate that all work must be done to the highest standards. The contractor should guarantee to provide replacement materials and necessary additional labor if the work falls short.
- Make sure the contractor takes responsibility for obtaining any required permits.
- Arrange to pay the contractor in stages. Turn over 10% at the start and 30% as each third of the job is finished. Hold off paying the last installment until two weeks after the project has been completed. This way you can make sure there are no surprises.

The last, all-purpose words of advice: Do not skimp on materials or workmanship. As one Houston stonemason remarks, "Cheap workmanship is like cheap wine. The price is right, but you'll regret it later."

CHAPTER 12

# Your Family: Building for the Big Changes in Your Life

MARRIAGE AND COUPLES

## What Every Spouse Should Know

I was tempted to title this section, "The Blushing Bride's Guide to the Last Taboo: Money." I am always amazed at how couples who share so much intimacy in other arenas are so shy and secretive when it comes to talking about their personal finances.

In finance, as in love, it is what spouses do *not* tell each other that hurts. Talking to your mate about what you own and what you owe seems such a simple thing to do. Yet many people just say no. Some husbands rather chauvinistically still assume their wives do not understand finances or are not interested. And some married partners plainly do not trust each other; they would rather share a toothbrush than a bank account. But keeping your mate in ignorance can be dangerous to your wealth.

Surely you should reveal and explain your finances just before you marry, and then regularly go over them in later years. A sensible time to review your assets is when you are writing or rewriting your will — and *both* spouses should have wills. Use the occasion to make or update lists of all the valuable possessions you own separately or in common. Include all real estate, bank and brokerage accounts, cars and boats, precious jewelry, works of art and insurance policies. Keep the separate lists of your assets in the same secure place that you store your wills. Both spouses also should know where other valuable documents are kept, including military discharge papers, birth certificates, marriage license and insurance policies.

You should know the names, addresses, and phone and fax numbers of the financial professionals in your mate's life. They include any stockbroker, accountant, personal banker, attorney, insurance agent and financial planner. You also should learn the details of your spouse's job benefits and work history, such as whether you have survivor's rights to his or her pension. If your mate held a previous job long enough to earn a pension, you could be eligible for additional retirement funds.

Military service often endows survivors with financial rights in the event of a spouse's death. If your husband or wife was in the Armed Forces, you might be eligible for G.I. life insurance, a pension, burial expenses, even a VA mortgage loan. To apply for these benefits, you will need the veteran's discharge papers.

Rent *two* safe-deposit boxes. Put in your own box all the papers you will need if your spouse dies. These should include copies of just about all the documents mentioned above. Banks in many states seal the box of the deceased upon notification of death, and you may have to wait weeks or months for a court to grant permission to open that box. Also leave copies of all necessary documents with your lawyer, and with at least one adult child or some other trusted third party.

## The Perils of Holding Your Assets in Joint Name

At some point in your life you will almost certainly want — or need — to own an asset jointly with your spouse or with your parents, siblings or friends. But before you make that very important decision, you should know a few things about the complex laws of ownership. Sometimes, even for the happiest of married couples, joint ownership is not so smart.

True enough, joint ownership can simplify estate planning and the eventual disposition of your wealth. On your death, your share of jointly held real estate, stocks or other property usually passes automatically to your surviving co-owner. That means it bypasses probate — the often lengthy and expensive process by which a will is proved valid in court.

Yet joint ownership can lead to feuds among co-owners and heirs *and* daunting tax bills. For example, a childless couple may think they can do without wills because they hold all of their property jointly. Not so. If the husband dies, everything passes to his wife without complication. But if the wife then dies later without a will, every cent would go to *her* relatives under state laws known as laws of intestacy. The husband's relatives would be left with no legacy at all.

You can avoid such problems by writing a will that describes how you want the assets disposed. The trouble is, you would not avoid probate this way.

But you can sidestep probate if you set up a revocable living trust. An attorney will draw it up for a fee of several hundred dollars to several thousand dollars. In it, you agree to transfer ownership of your assets, while you are still alive, to a trustee. That person then manages the property on behalf of the people whom you name as beneficiaries. In every state but New York you can name yourself the sole trustee. Then you retain control of the assets in the trust, and, if you also name yourself as a beneficiary, even receive income from them.

You can have the trust written so that, after your death, its assets go automatically to your heirs. Or the assets can remain in the trust, with the income from them going to your heirs. Either way, the assets avoid probate.

Back again to joint ownership: It is dangerous for individuals who own highly appreciated assets — such as a house that has jumped sharply in value — or whose estate is more than $600,000. These people would be vulnerable to heavy estate taxes.

Take a couple who bought a house for $50,000 in 1970 and held it jointly until the husband's death. At that time, let's say the value of the house had escalated to $200,000. Half of the house's value would pass automatically to the wife, leaving her with both her husband's $100,000 share and her own equal share. If she then sells the house for $200,000, the IRS would slap her with a tax on her long-term capital gain of $75,000 on her share.

Here's how the taxman's devastating mathematics works: The house she sold for $200,000 originally cost $50,000, and so the capital gain was $150,000. Because she owned one-half of the house, her half of that gain was $75,000.

But she could have avoided the tax if her husband alone had held title to the house and had passed it to her in his will. The reason: Married couples can leave estates of any size to each other tax-free. Because she would have inherited a house worth $200,000, she would not have had any taxable gain if she sold it at that price.

There is, however, a serious potential problem with this strategy. (Bear with me; very little in the tax code is simple.) The problem: You can seldom be sure whether the husband or wife will die first. If the wife dies first in the above example, the husband would own the whole house and would have to pay taxes on the *entire* capital gain when he sold it.

That is, he would owe taxes on a capital gain of $150,000.

Many spouses also object to putting the house in one partner's name. They fear that their mate might divorce them and keep the house. But contrary to popular belief, you usually cannot keep goods out of your spouse's reach simply by registering them in your own name. Judges simply will not stand for it. And virtually all the states now have equitable-distribution or community-property laws, which divide up property in a divorce regardless of who has title to it.

Despite the tangles that can occur, there are times when joint ownership does make sense. You might elect to own property jointly if you want to shift income to a family member who is in a lower tax bracket. If, say, a mother and her young child own stock together, the child's share of the earnings might be lightly taxed — if at all. Income up to $1,300 a year on savings and investments is taxed at the child's rate, so long as the child is younger than 14; over age 14, *all* savings and investment income is taxed at the child's rate.

Joint ownership also can help you shield assets from creditors. And it can have psychic rewards for a mate who feels happy just holding half of the family's riches. But remember: While joint ownership can give you or your spouse a warm feeling, it can give you or your heirs the chills when it comes time to settle up with the almighty IRS. If you die with assets above $600,000, the excess will be hit by federal estate taxes, beginning at 37% and going as high as 55%, and your heirs will be assaulted with state estate taxes, too. Yet a husband and wife together can shelter $1.2 million from estate taxes by dividing most of their assets between them, owning the assets individually and establishing estate tax credit trusts in each of their wills (for more, see Chapter 23, "Dealing with Wills, Trusts and Estates").

# The Virtues of Prenuptial Agreements

Many modern couples who plan marriage reveal and plan just about everything — except money. It seems indelicate, if not downright greedy, to ask "What's your net worth?" before saying "I do." Nevertheless, more and more engaged people are not only overriding their inhibitions but also writing prenuptial contracts. These specify who owns what property and what should become of it in various contingencies.

You would be wise to prepare carefully and sign legally a prenuptial contract. You spell out in advance just who owns what — and which financial obligations each partner has to the other. Such an agreement is particularly important when the bride as well as the groom has a career, with her own income, assets and obligations. A prenuptial agreement is also a necessity if one partner has children from an earlier marriage and wants to protect their inheritances. Love may be lovelier the second time around, but marriage finances are messier. If one mate-to-be is studying for a profession, a contract can help you pin down how much the other partner's working contributes to his or her future earnings. Finally, an agreement can clarify who owns just what, and just how any pooled assets would be split if the marriage were to dissolve. A doctor or accountant, for example, may stipulate that his or her spouse accept a lump-sum settlement instead of a share in his or her practice or business.

Courts in most states now recognize a contract that tries to head off a battle in the event the marriage breaks up. Such agreements can save hundreds of hours of fact-finding and testimony and thousands of dollars in legal and other fees. A "prenup" can also serve as a basis for subsequent agreements made during the marriage. More important, a prenuptial agreement can resolve ahead of time any mismatched expectations over money and help you set the financial ground rules for a fair, lasting — and loving — marriage.

You can work out the details of your agreement on your own, of course. But each partner should have his or her own lawyer negotiate and review the contract, because judges often suspect that without an attorney to protect the interest of each side, one partner may too easily sway the other. One sign of the effectiveness of prenuptial pacts is that although more and more of them have been challenged in court, not many have been overturned.

# Settling Up Your Finances Before Marriage

Whether or not you sign a prenuptial agreement, you and your mate-to-be should thoroughly discuss the subject of money before your marriage. Take inventory of your separate assets and liabilities. Decide what property you want to keep in your own name and what you want to merge. Most financial advisers suggest that you keep separate as well as joint bank accounts.

Be sure to familiarize yourself with the law. Each state has its own laws governing marital and separate property and stipulating what happens if the two are mingled. *A tip:* If you want to put property in your spouse's name, avoid the federal gift tax by transferring ownership *after* the marriage. The law allows an unlimited marital deduction.

You and your intended should discuss the advantages and disadvantages of various forms of joint ownership. An accountant, lawyer or Certified Financial Planner can explain the nuances. For example, in one form of joint ownership, the title specifies that if one of you dies, all the property goes automatically to the spouse. In another form, however, each of you owns half of the property, and you can leave your share to whomever you wish, such as a child from an earlier marriage. If a married couple takes title to a house as tenants in common, then either partner can leave his or her share of the house to whomever he or she names in his or her will.

Be certain to update your will. If you die without a will, your spouse generally receives only one-third to one-half of your separate property. The rest is distributed among other relatives.

Consolidate or coordinate your medical insurance. If you both have group plans where you work and you are paying part of the premiums, you may be able to save money by dropping one plan and having the other cover you as a family. Or you may be able to keep both policies, naming each other as dependents, and get more of your medical costs covered. And do not forget the obvious: Make sure to change the name of your beneficiary on your IRA, life insurance, pension, profit sharing and annuity.

One of the best approaches for dividing household bills when both spouses hold paying jobs is to have three bank accounts — his, hers and theirs. The common pot might go for food, maintenance of the house or apartment, recreation and joint savings.

## Saving on Wedding Costs: The New, Sensible Sharing

Traditional weddings, with white satin gowns and three-tiered wedding cakes, are in style again. Couples are back to marrying, or remarrying, in old-fashioned ways, even if they have been living together for years. This return to basics, alas, makes a considerable dent in the family's finances. It is expensive to let them eat cake.

The cost for food, drink and dancing — along with flowers, invitations, clothing and church or synagogue fees — comes to a national average of some $16,500. Of course, prices can vary greatly, according to region and extravagance, ranging from $1,000 to six figures. One-third to one-half is spent at the reception. The dinner or buffet, including liquor and champagne, ranges on the low end from $10 a person in small Midwestern towns to an average $100 a head — and often $200 or more — in Los Angeles, Boston or New York. Add 5% to 10% for kosher catering.

Sensible planning can reduce the bill. Some couples getting married on the same day agree to share the cost of flowers at the place of the ceremony. Others save a few hundred dollars by skipping such reception giveaways as printed napkins. Friends can contribute their photographic or musical talents, or even their flower-growing abilities.

### AVERAGE WEDDING COSTS

|  |  |  |  |
|---|---|---|---|
| Invitations, announcements, thank-yous | **$228** | Rehearsal dinner | **$409** |
| Bouquets and other flowers | **463** | Bride's wedding dress | **725** |
| Photography, videotaping | **1,208** | Bride's headpiece/veil | **144** |
| Music | **539** | Bridal attendants' apparel* | **685** |
| Clergy, church, chapel, synagogue fee | **113** | Mother of the bride's apparel | **201** |
| Limousine | **192** | Mother of the groom's apparel | **198** |
| Attendants' gifts | **163** | Groom's formal wear (rented) | **77** |
| Wedding rings (bride and groom) | **2,152** | Men's formal wear (ushers, best man) | **224** |
| Engagement ring | **2,807** | Wedding reception | **5,957** |

**Total $16,485**

*On average, each of five bridal attendants' dresses costs $137.

SOURCE: SURVEY OF *BRIDE'S* READERS

## MOST POPULAR HONEYMOON DESTINATIONS

|  |  |  |
|---|---|---|
| In Continental U.S. | California | 6.0% |
| | Florida | 15.6% |
| | Pennsylvania | 3.4% |
| | North Central | 4.5% |
| | Northeast | 11.1% |
| | Southeast | 22.4% |
| | Mountain West | 12.3% |
| Outside Continental U.S. | Bahamas | 8.3% |
| | Bermuda | 4.8% |
| | Canada | 7.0% |
| | Europe | 7.8% |
| | Hawaii | 19.1% |
| | Jamaica | 7.5% |
| | Mexico | 12.5% |
| | United States V.I. | 5.3% |

Percentages add up to more than 100% because some respondents selected more than one destination.

SOURCE: SURVEY OF *BRIDE'S* READERS

Traditionally, members of the wedding paid for their own dresses and formal wear. But in some cases now, couples and their families sensibly handle these bills instead of giving their attendants costly gifts of jewelry as keepsakes of the wedding. And you can rent bridal gowns and bridesmaids' dresses instead of buying them.

There are many ways to cut costs on wedding receptions, too. Wedding planners, caterers and banquet managers say that newlyweds can curtail expenses by 20% or more without sacrificing quality. It's all in the timing. No matter where your reception is held, you can save money by avoiding the peak seasons, like June, when space and labor are at a premium. The time of day also makes a difference, with afternoon functions generally being less expensive than evening ones.

When planning the menu, remember that smaller items, like reception hors d'oeuvres, count for a lot. A lavish cocktail reception takes some of the pressure off having a showpiece dinner, which is where the

**WHAT AMERICANS SPEND ON HONEYMOONS**

| | All honeymoons | Foreign honeymoons* |
|---|---|---|
| $5,000 or more | 14.8% | 19.7% |
| $4,000–5,000 | 11.1 | 14.2 |
| $3,000–4,000 | 21.7 | 27.2 |
| $2,500–3,000 | 9.4 | 10.9 |
| $2,000–2,500 | 13.8 | 14.0 |
| $1,500–2,000 | 8.2 | 5.9 |
| Less than $1,500 | 21.0 | 8.1 |
| Average amount spent | $3,200 | $3,800 |

*Outside Continental U.S.
SOURCE: SURVEY OF *BRIDE'S* READERS

dollars add up. Wedding caterers suggest you save money by adding a carving board to the reception buffet and eliminating the appetizer at the wedding dinner. The dinner's cost can be reduced even further by making the wedding cake the dessert, not just something to taste during a toast.

Remember, a wedding feast doesn't have to cost as much as a Cadillac, and with more couples paying for part or all of their own weddings these days, cost control is on many people's minds. Your goal should be a wedding dinner that is both elegant and economical. After all, there are more important uses for your money, like as part of a down payment on your first dream home.

And when the bride has tossed her bouquet, where can the happy couple go for the vacation of a lifetime without taking on the national debt? According to *Bridal Guide* magazine's Marriage 2000 survey, 97% of couples go on a honeymoon. Of them, 45% head for tropical islands and 15%, an ocean cruise. A recent survey in *Bride's* magazine found that the average American couple spends $3,200 on a nine-day domestic honeymoon, $3,800 on a foreign trip. Check with your travel agent for cost-saving honeymoon packages.

The father of the bride used to pay the wedding bills, and the groom's father the honeymoon expenses, but that old etiquette is giving way to the new economics. Today, families of the bride and the groom commonly split the costs. Often the expenses are divided four ways — among both sets of parents and the bride and groom. This seems natural to many of today's career-minded brides. After all, their parents funded educations that were intended to prepare their daughters to pay their own way — or at least a good part of it. So parents of the bride can take heart: You may be losing a daughter, but at least you are not obliged to pay the whole bill.

Even pre-wedding festivities are more practical. Gone are the days of a group of women giggling over a sexy negligee at a bridal shower. Now friends often give "couples showers." Guests are encouraged to bring gifts that both bride and groom can use, like gardening tools. Couples who start out willing to share gardening chores can probably count on sharing many years together.

The custom of the bridal registry is "in" again, but with a twist. Many brides circumvent the suburban department store in favor of museum stores, antique shops and upscale catalogs such as Williams-Sonoma's. Even some Home Depot stores have their own bridal registry. The preferred gift of many modern couples is money. At some weddings, ethnic custom dictates that you give cash to the bride or groom at the reception. Or you can mail your check to the couple's home within a week after the ceremony. Although the amount depends on the guest's financial standing and the lavishness of the reception, the average expenditure on a wedding gift is $50. Make that $100 if you and your spouse are giving the gift. And increase it to $100 *per person* if you're invited to a glorious sit-down dinner and, frankly, the crowd is affluent.

For up-to-date, innovative tips on how to scale down wedding costs, read *Bridal Bargains: Secrets to Throwing a Fantastic Wedding on a Realistic Budget* (Windsor Peak Press, $10.95), by Denise and Alan Fields. The authors offer a money-back guarantee on the price of their book if you don't save at least $500 on your wedding. Or call them on their wedding hotline at 800-888-0385.

## Protecting Your Significant Other

Nearly 3 million American couples fit the Census Bureau description of POSSLQ: Persons of the Opposite Sex Sharing Living Quarters. They and other co-habitating unmarried couples have special financial problems, which they can alleviate by taking some sensible steps.

The facts of unmarried life are that the law is muddy about the financial rights of two people living together without benefit of clergy. This is further complicated by variances among the states. Take inheritance, for example. When one member of a married couple dies without a will, state laws typically assure that the bulk of the person's property will pass to the surviving spouse. But when an unmarried person leaves no will, all of his or her earthly goods can be claimed by the next of kin. Even a loathsome great-aunt thousands of miles away stands before a live-in partner in the inheritance line.

The message is clear: If you are living with someone to whom you eventually want to leave some or all of your worldly goods, you had better put your intentions in writing — in an unshakable will that has been drafted by a lawyer, legally signed and properly witnessed. That may sound unromantic, but the stark reality is that placing your financial wishes in writing is the best way to protect a joint venture of the heart. Written contracts can protect your interest if disputes arise with your business partners — or with an ex-spouse or government authorities — over such matters as insurance, other inheritance or debts that you have to pay.

Couples with little money or other assets might get by with the fill-in-the-blanks legal forms found in some books on living together. If your finances are fuller or more complicated, you probably need a lawyer's assistance to draw up a financial agreement. If you chance to do it yourself, your agreement at least should be notarized. Contracts between unmarried couples generally are recognized by the courts as long as they violate no laws and both partners enter into them freely.

Unmarried couples should always own things separately. For example, he buys and owns the car, she buys and owns the computer — though both partners use them. They should acquire as little as possible together and keep receipts or other records of what each buys. Doing that will prevent bitter battles if and when they split up.

For much the same reason, unmarried pairs should not have joint bank accounts or credit cards. In joint charge accounts, each person is 100% responsible for debts incurred by the other. And creditors who may be chasing one of the two partners can freeze and seize all the assets in joint bank accounts.

The tidiest way to split household expenses is down the middle. Many POSSLQs simply put their initials on receipts of bills they pay, toss them into a drawer and square accounts once a month. An exception, of course, is if one partner is enrolled full-time in college or is too ill to work. Then the other, working partner pays the bills. But records should be kept and, ultimately, he or she should be paid back — at least in part.

For example, a young woman in Raleigh, North Carolina, returned to college. Her live-in partner underwrote her expenses with a 7% loan.

She signed an agreement to repay him, whether or not the two continue living together.

Unmarried partners should be sure to do the following:

- Buy medical insurance if either partner isn't covered by a group health plan.
- Name your long-term POSSLQ as a beneficiary of your life insurance policy.
- Sign a so-called medical power-of-attorney permitting your POSSLQ to visit you and to make medical decisions if you're seriously ill.
- And, to repeat because it is most important, write a will leaving to your POSSLQ what you want him or her to have.

Affluent unmarried people face particular problems. You and your unmarried partner may well save money by filing your taxes separately instead of jointly, thus escaping the notorious marriage penalty. But that saving will be minuscule compared with the bigger hit you stand to take on estate taxes. To hold down those taxes, the more affluent partner may choose to give annual cash gifts to the less affluent partner.

Married partners can give unlimited gifts to each other without paying any federal or state gift tax. Similarly, upon death, married partners can pass all their assets to each other, free of estate taxes. But not so unmarried partners. Their gifts are limited to $10,000 annually to each of any number of individuals, plus $600,000 in the course of a lifetime. That means anything that you give to your live-in lover above $10,000 a year, and above $600,000 in the course of your life, is subject to federal and state gift and estate taxes. You can get around at least part of this by buying life insurance and making your live-in lover both the owner and the beneficiary of the policy. For more, see Chapter 13 on life insurance and Chapter 23 on wills and trusts.

# Financial Planning When Expecting a Child

Pregnancy concentrates the mind, notably of those young two-career couples who heretofore have not worried excessively about their financial future. Now they need investments that will help them build up their net worth to support larger living quarters, start a college fund and generally underwrite the high price of parenthood.

If you are expecting your first child, you should — as recommended in Chapter 1 — try to build a cash reserve in a bank money-market deposit account or a money-market mutual fund equal to at least three months' worth of living expenses. To repeat: Only after you have this secure cash cushion should you consider investing — because all investment involves some risk.

A sensible way to invest in a mutual fund is to put in the same amount of money each month, whether the market rises or falls. That is known as dollar-cost averaging. Your money buys fewer shares when the market goes up, and more shares when it goes down. By signing a form provided by the fund, you can have it withdraw the money automatically from your checking account every month.

Before your baby is born, be sure to review your health, life and disability insurance. You may need more coverage than your employer offers. Each working parent should have enough life insurance to replace most of his or her earning power at least until the child has finished school. An insurance agent or, better yet, a Certified Financial Planner who does not himself or herself sell insurance, can help you figure out how much you should have. In addition, you'll need total disability insurance coverage; it should replace about 60% to 70% of your salary.

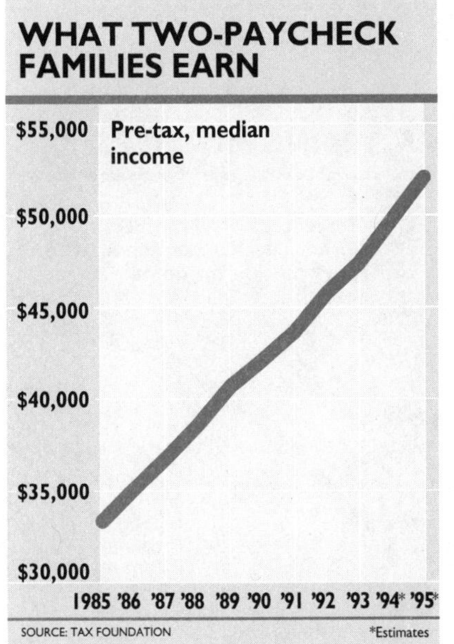


Each parent should have a will. If you don't, have one drawn up by a lawyer. It may cost as much as $700 for each but is well worth the money. Carefully choose a guardian for your child in the unlikely event that both you and your spouse die before your heir apparent reaches age 18. Pick a brother or sister instead of your aging parents.

# Preparing for the Real Cost of Kids

For more than a century, parents have issued the same lament: It has become so expensive to have a baby that only the poor can afford it. True enough, bringing up baby is costlier today than at any other time in history. That is partly because the luxuries of a short time ago are now considered middle-class birthrights: TVs, PCs, VCRs, etc. The U.S. Department of Agriculture estimated that in 1993 the average *annual* cost of raising a child age 15 to 17 was

- $6,260 for a family earning less than $32,000
- $8,500 for a family earning between $32,000 and $54,000
- $11,790 for a family earning over $54,000

The national average cost of raising a youngster age 15 to 17 was $8,290 a year. Naturally, it was far more than that in many big cities.

If Mom stays home until Junior toddles off to kindergarten, her lost income from a job over several years could amount to another $100,000 or more. And that dollar cost may be compounded by atrophying skills and evaporating seniority. So, more mothers are choosing to get right back to work after their child is born.

Knowing when the expenses of childhood rise and fall can help you prepare for them:

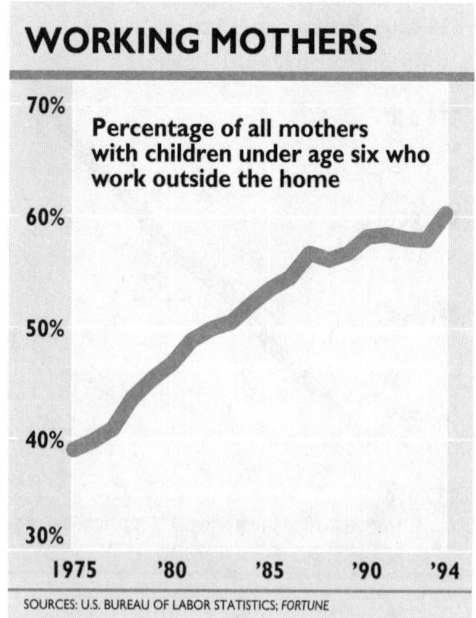


Newborns enter the world at considerable cost. Routine hospital and delivery fees run an average $5,000 in a metropolitan area, and an untroubled cesarean birth adds some $3,000.

But from age one to five or six, the costs of child-rearing are relatively low. This is the time parents should put away and build cash in deep-discount bonds, zero-coupon bonds, U.S. savings bonds, tax-free municipal bonds and other secure investments to pay for the expenses that start moving up as soon as the child goes off to school and skyrocket during the teenage years.

Puberty is pricey, due in part to dating and all its accoutrements. The annual insurance premium on your car can more than double with a 16-year-old son added to the policy as a driver. At age 18, child-rearing costs are exponentially higher than costs incurred in the birth year. Welcome to the groves of academe and the most expensive years in a child's life.

If you have — or plan to have — children, prepare now for those predictable costs ahead. Start by checking what your health insurance covers. A good maternity package in a group policy will pay at least two-thirds of the hospital and physician's fees for the birth of a child. Later on, most policies do not cover the routine examinations of a healthy baby. So, unless you belong to a health maintenance organization, you may have to budget as much as $600 during a baby's first year for those periodic visits to the pediatrician.

## Expecting a Baby?

Here are questions, as reported in the *Wall Street Journal,* to ask your employer about the maternity provisions in your health-care policy before you have a baby. Employers have been cutting back on their coverage, but knowing all the rules can help you get the largest possible reimbursement.

- Are prenatal care, diagnostic tests, pregnancy and neonatal intensive care covered by the plan? If so, what are the co-payments or deductibles?
- What kind of coverage is there for an infant's nursery care?
- Will the policy pay if the child was conceived before the mother or father joined the health-insurance plan?
- Will the insurance cover the costs of having a baby in a birthing center instead of a hospital? What about a midwife?
- When does the plan start covering the child as a dependent?

- Must the mother take certain childbearing education courses to be covered?
- When does the insurer have to be notified that the mother has been admitted into the hospital to have the baby?
- How many days will the insurer allow the mother to stay in the hospital after the baby is born?
- How many extra days' coverage will the insurer pay for if the baby has to stay on in the hospital for additional care after the mother goes home?

## Where to Adopt a Child

If you are childless — and not by choice — you have many new options in adoptions. Today almost anybody can adopt a child, but it may be a rather special one.

Two decades ago public and private adoption agencies had many more healthy American-born babies than they do now. The decline, of course, is due to the wide availability of birth control devices and abortion. Also, changing social attitudes have led to an increase in unmarried mothers who are willing to keep their children.

You can get a directory of agencies that place healthy American-born children by writing to the National Council for Adoption, 1930 17th Street NW, Washington, D.C. 20009-6207. The Council also publishes *The Adoption Fact Book,* a comprehensive 300-page guide that includes a list of adoption resources, a summary of state regulations, and a discussion of the major issues involved in adoption. It is available at the same address for $39.95 plus $4.50 postage.

Would-be parents are becoming increasingly interested in adopting children from other countries and kids whom social workers categorize as hard to place or as having special needs. They include youngsters with physical, mental or emotional disabilities, as well as older children of all races and brothers and sisters whom adoption agencies do not want to split up. Youngsters with special needs account for nearly half the children available for adoption in the U.S. Agencies are finding it easier than ever to place them, often with people who formerly did not qualify as adoptive parents. Single, disabled and low-income people — even couples in their 50s and 60s — are now allowed to adopt.

About two-thirds of all parents adopt through agencies; the rest get children through doctors or lawyers. Public adoption agencies, operated by state and local governments, generally do not charge fees. Private agencies, commonly sponsored by religious and charitable groups, charge an average $9,000, and that often includes attorney's fees. If it doesn't, you will have to pay about $1,000 to a lawyer for preparing adoption papers.

The fees are often reduced or waived for parents who adopt special-needs children. Almost all states also have subsidy programs for parents who take such youngsters. Together with federal reimbursements, the subsidy could amount to $2,000 for use toward adoption costs. You may be able to get additional subsidies to assist with the ongoing special needs of these children.

A small but growing number of corporations are granting maternity leaves and other benefits to employees who adopt. For example, Procter & Gamble and Johnson & Johnson give unpaid child-care leaves plus up to $2,000 and $3,000 respectively for adoption-related expenses. Time Warner gives a week's paid parental leave and up to 51 weeks' unpaid parental leave plus as much as $5,000 in adoption expenses. So, if you are an adoptive parent or are considering becoming one, check to see if your company will provide any benefits.

Your city or state Department of Social Services can give you a list of licensed adoption agencies in your area. For help in finding special-needs children in states beyond your own, write to the National Adoption Center (1500 Walnut Street, Suite 701, Philadelphia, Pennsylvania 19102; 215-735-9988). Or call 800-TO-ADOPT.

If you want to adopt a healthy child quickly, you can seek help from American agencies that specialize in overseas adoptions. The wait is usually no more than 18 months. Most of the children come from Asian countries, especially China, South Korea and Vietnam, as well as from Latin America and Eastern Europe. Babies put up for adoption in Western Europe are even scarcer than those in the U.S., in part because of low birth rates.

Adopting a child from another country costs anywhere from $6,000 to $20,000, and the investment is not without risk. Reports of children in Eastern Europe in need of families have led to some bad experiences, usually caused by incompetence but sometimes by fraud. On occasion, children have been illegally smuggled out of their home countries. Some fee-and-flee foreign lawyers promise to deliver babies but just milk you for money and abscond. If a private adoption goes awry, you will have small chance of recouping any cash you handed over in advance. However, international adoption is better regulated than it used to be; the U.S. Immigration and Naturalization Service works diligently to ensure that children coming into the U.S. have been adopted properly.

In any event, it is best to work only through well-established organizations. You can find many of their names and addresses in *The Report on Inter-Country Adoption,* available for $20 from the International Concerns Committee for Children (911 Cypress Drive, Boulder, Colorado 80303). For a list of lawyers, social-services agencies and orphanages in Central and South America, write to the Latin America Parents Association (8646 15th Avenue, Brooklyn, New York 11228; 718-236-8689). An agency specializing in placing children from all over the world is Holt International Children's Services (P.O. Box 2880, Eugene, Oregon 97402; 503-687-2202).

The U.S. State Department publishes a booklet titled *International Adoption,* which has guidelines for people interested in adopting a foreign child, including visa and immunization requirements. It is available, free, from the Office of Children's Issues, Department of State, Room 4800, Washington, D.C. 20520-4818.

Another way to avoid waiting up to four years to adopt a child is through private placement known as independent adoption — that is, adoption without an agency's help. People who use independent placement find the birth mother on their own and take the baby straight home from the hospital. Many ask for leads from relatives, friends, clergy, teachers, social workers, lawyers and doctors — any person who might help locate a pregnant woman who says she does not intend to keep her child. This way, you can bypass the demands and restrictions that adoption agencies may impose on your age, religion and marital status, and even the adoptive mother's employment; sometimes agencies also demand proof of infertility. The cost of an independent adoption ranges from $3,000 way up to $20,000.

Independent adoption does have drawbacks. It is banned in Connecticut, Delaware, Massachusetts, Michigan and North Dakota. Even where it is allowed, you must find a pregnant woman willing to give up her child and then, typically, pay her medical and legal expenses. There is always the chance that the mother will change her mind as soon as she bears her child — or, worse, try later to reclaim her child in the courts. (This happened to friends of mine. They had paid the mother's considerable expenses all during pregnancy, but when she reneged on the deal soon after birth, they had no recourse and lost all the money.)

To find out more, write or phone the adoption office of your state's Department of Social Services. You also can make contact with local adoption groups through the Adoptive Families of America in Minneapolis (612-535-4829) or, for special-needs adoption, the National Adoption Center in Philadelphia (800-TO-ADOPT) and an organization called RESOLVE (1310 Broadway, Somerville, Massachusetts 02144-1731; 617-623-0744).

## Finding Reliable Child Care

The traditional household — Dad works, Mom stays at home to raise 2.6 children — went out with Ozzie and Harriet, or Desi and Lucy. At least 65% of American mothers hold jobs outside the home; more than 50% of new mothers enter or reenter the work force before their child's first birthday. A University of Maryland study in 1985 found that American parents spent an average of only 17 hours a week with their children — and there's scant reason to believe that the total has risen since then.

Today, parents continue to find themselves away from home more often than not, and many have trouble locating decent child care. Trained, full-time nannies can cost $250 to $600 a week plus benefits. Neighborhood baby-sitters are less expensive, but they are not always as reliable. Increasingly, parents are concluding that the best solution is to put their kids in a child-care center. This can be either a center that is run out of someone's home or a freestanding operation. In 1994, 57% of working moms' preschoolers were enrolled in such facilities.

Many new centers have opened lately, but the number still lags behind demand. Shortages are critical in urban areas that have high concentrations of low-income people; the need is particularly intense for centers that will accept children under the age of two. Child-care centers just cannot find and hire enough capable staff members at fees that are within most parents' reach.

About 65% of the licensed child-care centers in the U.S. are run by churches and other nonprofit organizations. For-profit operators make up the rest. They range from small independent centers to larger chains. Nearly 1,500 employers sponsor child-care centers for their employees or share a center with another employer. About 3% of all major corporations now do so, and the number is growing.

Allegations of abuse or neglect at a few child-care centers are appalling, but they are mostly unproved and almost certainly exaggerated. Many centers offer quality, convenience and affordable prices. Still, providers of group care vary widely in the quality and types of services they offer.

People who operate small group-care programs in their own homes, called family day-care homes, usually are not subject to — or do not bother with — state licenses. Centers quite likely are not licensed if they care for only a few children, are open only a few hours each day, or are run in a church or school. But centers that look after more than 15 kids are almost all licensed. State licenses help ensure that the centers meet minimum standards for health, fire safety and staffing.

Other advantages of large day-care centers over the small home-based programs generally include greater stability and broader curriculums. The operations that allocate a higher percentage of their budget to attract better teachers and reduce staff turnover are often able to provide a higher level of quality in their programs. Staff is the key to quality.

Many big companies offer a free child-care referral service to help employees find a care facility to meet their needs. IBM uses 250 different organizations. The company also has pledged $22 million in recent years to improve the quality of day care in the towns and cities where most of its employees live.

Some smaller companies are paying attention as well. American Bankers Insurance Group, based in Miami, maintains a day-care center for employees' children aged six weeks to five years. After that the child can attend a Dade County public "satellite" school for an additional five years. The school takes care of the child from 7:15 A.M. to 6:15 P.M. and keeps its doors open during school holidays and summer vacations.

The cost of care in a center depends largely on a child's age, the staff-to-child ratio and the experience of the staff. Prices vary throughout the country. Monthly fees for children under age five average about $330, but $600 to $800 is not unusual. Uncle Sam helps to defray day-care expenses with a tax credit for working couples and single parents. Depending on your income, the annual Child and Dependent Care Credit may be worth $480 to $720 for one child and $960 to $1,440 for two or more. (Lower-income families get the larger benefits.)

An alternative fringe benefit, if your employer offers it, is the Flexible Spending Account. Through salary withholdings, an FSA can help reduce your dependent day-care costs by allowing you to use *pretax* dollars to pay for day-care expenses. Here's how FSAs work: Before the beginning of each plan year, you elect how much to deposit into a Dependent Day-Care Account. The maximum annual contribution is $5,000 for married couples filing joint tax returns and single parents filing as a head of household; it's $2,500 if you're married and filing separately. During the year, you pay dependent day-care expenses as they occur and submit claims to the FSA plan administrator for reimbursement up to the amount totaling your initial contribution.

Whether your savings under a dependent day-care plan would be higher than those using the standard child-care tax deduction depends upon your individual circumstances. But studies show that overall savings are greater under a dependent day-care plan. Neither the employer nor the employee pay federal income taxes or Social Security taxes on the money going into an FSA. One caveat: IRS regulations stipulate that FSA contributions not used during a given calendar year be forfeited. So, "use it, don't lose it."

Employers can also set up their own care centers for employees. For example, Time Warner has an on-site emergency day-care center. Employees can use it up to 20 times a year, free of charge, as a back-up to their regular child care. The center accommodates 30 children a day and accepts kids ranging from six months to 12 years old. Johnson & Johnson supports a permanent on-site day-care center at its headquarters in New Brunswick, New Jersey. The company subsidizes part of the cost, but employees using the center still pay $140 to $178 a week, depending on the child's age. Alternatively, the company can pay an employee directly for child-care costs until the kids reach the age of 16. Care for disabled dependents of any age also can be covered. Check with your employer on whether benefits are offered. Since it costs less for a company to pass out child-care subsidies than to build and run a day-care center, many firms may be inclined to make such payments. If you are a working parent, you might ask your human resources department to consider sharing your child-care costs.

Selecting a good center for care is not child's play, but your task will be easier if you ask a few important questions of other parents who use the center and of the professionals who provide the care.

One: How large are the classes? Big groups tend to be too confusing for babies and toddlers, and large centers should break them down into smaller groups. For kids under two years old, the maximum number should be eight per group, with at least two staff members. Toddlers ages two to three should be in groups of 12 or fewer.

Two: What is the ratio of staff to children? There should be at least one adult for every three to four babies or toddlers, according to the National Academy of Early Childhood Programs.

Three: Can you meet with the teachers easily and often? Most centers encourage parents to drop by anytime for a visit. Be wary of those that do not. And you should have at least two formal conferences a year to evaluate your child's progress.

Four: Is there a wide variety of toys designed for your child's age group? Infants like colorful mobiles, mirrors and plastic boxes. With preschoolers, look for musical instruments, games and costumes.

Five: Are teachers conscientious about sanitary conditions? Studies show that kids under age three in day-care centers are more likely to contract gastrointestinal ailments than those who stay at home. Frequent hand-washing is a simple remedy and should be encouraged by the staff.

Six: What arrangements have been made for medical emergencies? A nurse or doctor should be available nearby, ready for a call. Parents should be told promptly when there are outbreaks of illnesses such as chicken pox or measles.

Once you have selected a child-care center, keep monitoring it for changes in its programs or personnel. But your best indicator of quality may be your child's enthusiasm. If your son or daughter hates to leave the center at the end of the day, chances are you made the right choice.

Parents often assume that all branches of a day-care chain meet uniform standards of quality, but this is not always the case. The difference between sound and sloppy centers is determined mainly by the quality of the local director and staff.

Sometimes parents overstress the importance of teaching academic skills in a day-care center. Teaching everyday living skills to children may be more important than drilling them in the alphabet and numbers. But the main point is this: Before placing a child in any center, check it out thoroughly by visiting it and by speaking both with staff members and with parents of other children who attend. For further information on how to find a quality child-care center, write to the Child Care Action Campaign, 330 Seventh Avenue, 17th Floor, New York, New York 10001-5010. The CCAC provides free information, guidebooks and publications addressing U.S. businesses and child care.

To find an in-home caregiver, first ask friends and co-workers for referrals. If nothing turns up, try placement agencies or a classified ad. Placement agencies and nanny training schools are listed in the Yellow Pages under "Child Care Centers" and "Nanny Services." Before employing an agency, check with your local Better Business Bureau to see if any complaints have been filed against the institution.

Once prospective caregivers are recommended, set aside ample time for a detailed interview and to check all references. The Child Care Action Campaign provides a complete list of questions you should ask and recommends that you never hire a caregiver without checking references yourself — even if a placement agency says that it has already done a background check.

## Ten Questions to Ask a Nanny

1. Why do you wish to be a nanny?

   Look for someone whose answers show a love for children. Taking care of kids involves a very big commitment. Don't hire anyone unsure about being a nanny.

2. What is your child-care experience?

   Ask about past jobs, formal nanny training, degrees in child education and classes in child care. If the applicants have worked as nannies before, ask why they left previous positions. Ask about baby-sitting jobs and other child-related work such as serving as camp counselors, play group leaders or tutors. Get the names and numbers of three or four references. Also helpful: Personal recommendations from teachers or clergy.

3. What are your child-rearing philosophies?

   You want someone who can be firm yet gentle and nurturing. Offer specific examples of difficult behavior, such as, "It's time to go to school, but Robin is throwing a tantrum and won't put on her coat. What would you do?" Key: Look for someone with patience.

4. These are the job requirements. Do they sound like something you can handle?

   List the specifics of the job, including responsibilities, hours, days off, salary and benefits (such as health insurance). If the applicant expects only to care for the children and you expect her to cook, too, you'll both end up frustrated.

5. What are your hobbies and interests?

   Look for a nanny with varied interests, such as sports, art, music, travel, etc. Try to find an active nanny for a household of athletic youngsters or a musical nanny for a child who takes piano lessons.

#### WHEN HIRING A LIVE-IN NANNY

6. What qualities are you looking for in a family?

   When hiring live-in help, chemistry is very important. You want someone whose personality meshes with your own. Some live-in nannies expect to be part of the family, while others view the relationship as that of employer/employee. Discuss: Will the live-in nanny travel with you on vacations? Eat with you?

7. What was your upbringing like?

   Was the applicant's childhood stable? Look for someone who can be a wonderful role model for your children. You want someone with similar values and morals.

8. Do you smoke?
   Describe your house rules about smoking. If you are a smoker, make the applicant aware of it.
9. Can you drive?
   Does the applicant have a good driving record? You may want to check with the Motor Vehicle Department. The applicant can authorize the MVD to release this information. Or you can even hire an investigative agency to check the applicant's driving, Social Security and criminal records. Discuss whether the car will be available for the nanny's day off.
10. Do you have any dietary or other restrictions?
    Does the applicant have any allergies or other medical problems? You may want to ask for a doctor's release attesting to good health.

*Source: Bottom Line Personal*

Once you select a front-runner, have her come to your home for a trial weekend. You should pay her for her time, but the money is well spent. If your instincts tell you something is wrong, trust them and continue the search.

The work does not end when you make your decision. Employers of child-care workers are subject to the same labor laws as all employers. You must meet federal minimum wage requirements ($4.25 an hour in 1995), pay Social Security taxes on any employee who earns more than $1,000 a year and pay federal unemployment tax on up to $7,000 of the caregiver's earnings. (One major exception: If a child-care worker is under age 18, and this is not his or her primary job, you pay no taxes regardless of what the worker earns.)

You should also check your homeowner's insurance policy to see if it provides worker's compensation for caregivers. If it doesn't — and most don't — check with your state's Department of Labor or insurance board about buying a worker's compensation policy to cover medical problems or injuries occurring on the job. A policy covering full-time (20 hours a week) child-care providers should cost you about $225 a year.

The IRS has a booklet for household employers and employees. Call 800-424-FORM to request *Publication 503: Child and Dependent Care Credit and Employment Taxes for Household Employees.* For more information on employer-reporting requirements, call the IRS at 800-829-1040. Be sure you know what is expected of you before you hire a caregiver.

Au pairs may be a good alternative. Congress has authorized the U.S. Information Agency to issue special one-year visas to women ages 18 to 25 from 17 European countries. Au pairs live with American families and work up to 45 hours a week taking care of the children. Your cost is usually $9,000 to $10,000 a year, or some $175 a week — far less than you would pay for a live-in nanny who would typically have some type of professional child-care training. The sum covers training, transportation, health insurance and up to $300 in tuition at a local college, which is part of the deal. An au pair also gets two weeks' paid vacation, which most of the au pairs use to tour the U.S.

The major disadvantage is having to entrust your kids to a youthful foreigner whom you have never met or interviewed. But au pair candidates must have at least one year of child-care experience, a secondary-school education and fluency in English. Screening and interviewing are done by offshoots of student-exchange organizations with uniform requirements: Au Pair Care (800-288-7786), AuPair/Homestay U.S.A. (202-408-5380), Au Pair in America (800-727-2437), EF Au Pair (800-333-6056) and Euraupair (800-333-3804). Each group can issue visas to 2,840 au pairs a year. Using an au pair from one of these five sponsors simplifies your tax life because you are not required to withhold any tax from the weekly stipend.

The one-year limit on an au pair's stay puts off those parents who hope for a long-term relationship between child and caregiver. But 68% of participating families reapply for a new au pair. If you judge an au pair under the USIA program to be incompetent or incompatible with your family, a program coordinator will try to arrange a swap with another family who also finds its au pair unsuitable. Failing that, a new candidate may be flown in. But about 85% of the original matchups succeed.

▾ ▾ ▾

# Setting a Sensible Allowance for Your Child

With ice-cream cones costing about $2, children are being pinched by high prices, just like Mom and Dad. So they are getting jobs at younger ages, doing their own comparison shopping for toys and clothes and turning to a price-fighting tactic as time-honored as the tooth fairy. Kids are clamoring for increases in their allowances. What principles should parents follow when giving them? Experts in child-rearing suggest that children should start getting allowances early, along with some basic lessons in cash management. Even preschoolers can figure out that a quarter is worth more than a dime.

The amount of the allowance should grow along with the child and his or her spending needs. A good rule is one dollar per week for every year of the child's age. That is, a nine-year-old would get nine dollars a week. Bonnie Drew, author of *Moneyskills: 101 Activities to Teach Your Child About Money,* says that allowances should be large enough to enable your child to make budget and spending decisions. Dr. James McNeal, a

## WHAT YOUR KIDS SHOULD KNOW ABOUT MONEY

| | |
|---|---|
| **•AGE 3** | How to identify coins and bills by name.<br>How to trade coins for something when shopping. |
| **•AGE 4** | How many cents each coin is worth. |
| **•AGE 5** | How to manage a small allowance.<br>How money is obtained (usually through work). |
| **•AGE 6** | How to identify larger-denomination bills and coins.<br>How to make simple change. |
| **•AGE 7** | How to read price tags, look for sale items and make sure they get correct change. |
| **•AGE 8** | How to estimate the total cost of purchases.<br>How to save toward a short-term goal (maximum one month).<br>That they can earn money at odd jobs.<br>How to make savings-account deposits. |
| **•AGE 9** | How to create a simple weekly spending plan.<br>How to comparison shop.<br>How to find ways to earn extra for special goals. |
| **•AGE 10** | How to save a small amount weekly for a large expense.<br>How to read and understand sale ads.<br>How to use a phone book to call stores for information. |
| **•AGE 11** | How to save for longer periods in the bank.<br>How the principle of compound interest works. |
| **•AGE 12** | How to formulate and operate on a two-week spending plan.<br>The value of wise investing. |

SOURCE: *MONEYSKILLS: 101 ACTIVITIES TO TEACH YOUR CHILD ABOUT MONEY*, BY BONNIE DREW, CAREER PRESS, $9.95

children's marketing specialist at Texas A&M, says kids can begin to handle money at the age of three and a half; by age four or five, they are full-fledged "penny-candy purchasers who exhibit mastery of the purchase concept." McNeal also believes that we as a society are growing more concerned with our children, creating a "filiarchy" in which parents are spending less money on themselves and considerably greater amounts on their children. More and more, children are emerging as central decision makers for household expenditures.

Youngsters' spending money should be enough to cover regular expenses and still leave something to save or spend as they choose. If they blow it all, parents only hurt them by giving more, except in very special cases. A child must be taught to manage well and live within his or her income.

Child psychologists also warn parents to beware of inadvertently causing children to confuse money with less tangible family gifts, such as love and attention. Sometimes divorced parents pay their kids hefty allowances to compensate for their absence — and that does the youngster no good at all.

But children can profit from a special clothing allowance as soon as they are old enough to spend large sums wisely, usually by age 12 or 13. How much to give? One guideline is what the government figures a middle-income family spends to clothe a child — about $69 a month for a 14-year-old, $71 for a 17-year-old in 1994 .

The buy now–save later psychology of many adults seems to have permeated children's minds. By many measures, teenagers are saving less than they ever did. So, to encourage thrift, many parents open bank accounts for their kids. Wise parents also believe that just as kids must be taught to save, they must learn to give to charity. As a small child, David Rockefeller, retired chairman of Chase Manhattan Bank, was required by his father to give 10% of his $1 a month allowance to charity. He later became an outstanding philanthropist.

## Teaching Your Child to Invest

Do you have a child who is curious about the stock market? With encouragement, your budding Warren Buffett can learn the ABCs of investing and perhaps earn a little pocket money.

Most kids who are keen on the stock market get their inspiration from investment-minded parents. To be soundly schooled in the market, it is best that your children invest real money — yours or theirs. Investing is not child's play. And it is hard to capture a kid's imagination with hypothetical stock picks.

Investing can be fun when kids buy into companies they know, such as fast-food chains or computer makers. You also can tap your youngsters' enthusiasm by suggesting that they follow and select stocks of highly visible firms in your hometown. Of course, investing real money means real money may be lost.

With some exceptions, children are usually better off investing in individual stocks rather than a mutual fund. Funds offer diversification and professional management, but they are not necessarily well suited to teaching your youngsters about the market. With stock, children are introduced to the idea of owning a piece of a known company that they can follow. This concept will become increasingly important to them as they grow older. You, however, will have to buy, sell and register the stock in your name as the child's custodian. Under state laws, minors legally can own securities — but not trade them by themselves.

Kits and publications are increasingly available for the child who shows a leaning toward lucre. The Consumers' Union publishes *Zillions,* a bimonthly magazine aimed at 8- to 14-year-olds and patterned after *Consumer Reports.* A subscription costs $16, and you can order by calling 800-234-2078. Fidelity Investments, the mutual-fund company, will send a free kit called *Kids and Money,* directed to fourth-to-sixth-graders (800-544-8888). The Federal Reserve Bank of New York offers several colorful and informative comic books about money, banks and credit. You can get them free by writing to the Public Information Department, 33 Liberty Street, New York, New York 10045; or call 212-720-6134.

Since 1994, Steinroe Mutual Funds has offered the Young Investor Fund. It's a no-load fund, and 65% of its assets are in companies that children might relate to, such as Coca-Cola and McDonald's, or with companies that deal with products such as toys or children's software. The minimum investment is $500 and the fund requires monthly investments of at least $50. Young investors get a beginner's kit and regular newsletters.

# Choosing a Legal Guardian

Chances are your minor children will never need a guardian, but you should make provisions for their future in case anything happens to you and your spouse. Most people put off the uncomfortable chore of selecting someone to look after their children if they become orphans. Yet if you should die and there is no one ready to assume responsibility for your minor children, the surrogate's court or the probate court will appoint a guardian. Often it is a relative. The judge will not be able to grant your wishes unless you have expressed them in print.

The way to avoid this potential misfortune is to name a guardian in your will. There are two kinds of guardianships. A guardian of the person handles the children's day-to-day upbringing. A guardian of the property manages whatever money or property you have left for the kids. Generally, a guardian of the property must submit to the court an annual accounting of how he or she is managing the assets and often must request permission to make various expenditures on behalf of the kids.

Though this system protects the children's interests, the guardian gets tangled in red tape. The guardian must post a bond to protect the estate in case he or she absconds with the money. A bond on a $250,000 estate would run about $1,300 a year, and the estate pays the bills, somewhat diminishing what you leave for your children.

To avoid these costs and complications, lawyers often recommend that you nominate a guardian of the person and property but pass any assets along to your kids in a trust. The trust document, which should be drawn up by a lawyer, should spell out how you want the money spent — on schooling, clothes, music lessons and so forth. A trustee then can write checks up to limits set by the trust without having to ask the court for approval. Some lawyers recommend that the guardian not be the same person as the trustee; if two individuals are chosen, each can oversee the other. But others recommend that the nominated guardian also be the trustee, for convenience of administration.

The hard part is picking the right person to be the guardian. Choose someone who is about your age and, preferably, related to you. If you are not close to your relatives, select a person who would bring up your children in the manner you would. Make sure you ask the people you have in mind whether they would be willing to take on the responsibility of guardianship. Discuss with the guardians the financial arrangements you have made for the children and how you want them brought up.

A guardian named in the will is under no legal obligation to accept the responsibility and can refuse it, in which case the court will have to find another person, who may not be someone you would choose. For that reason, attorneys urge that you also name at least one backup guardian in your will. Where appropriate, children, too, have the right to know who their guardian is going to be. So consult at least your older children before you make a decision. Every few years, or whenever personal or financial circumstances change, review the guardianship provisions in your will. The brother you have named may have been divorced or your best friend may now run a head shop in Malibu. If you think you should name a new guardian, tell the current one and draft a new will.

If someone asks you to be a guardian, think hard about whether you should accept. Find out what the parents expect of you and whether the children are to live with you. Ask how the parents want the children educated and if there are any restrictive conditions, such as a statement in the will that the children cannot be moved out of the country. Inquire about money. You should be told what funds are available for the kids' day-to-day upkeep and to carry out any special wishes, such as sending Junior to Harvard.

Ask your lawyer or the lawyer who drew up the will to explain your obligations and rights. And, if you have children of your own, find out how they would feel about having other children in the household.

## Preparing for College

Ideally, you should start saving for college as soon as your child is born. It's probably wise to put as much as you can into stocks or stock mutual funds. Yes, stocks can and do go down from time to time, but if you have your money invested for long periods, history says you'll come out ahead.

From infancy to, say, age eight, it makes sense to invest 65% to 90% of your college fund in stocks. Then, for safety's sake, between the ages of nine and 13, shift to about half stocks and half bonds. And from age

14 onward, move gradually to U.S. Treasury notes or government money-market funds; they are totally safe, and with college fast approaching, now is not the time to take any chances with your money.

Although it usually pays to invest in your child's name instead of your own name, be aware that that may undermine his or her chances to get financial aid. The aid formula requires a child to contribute as much as 35% of his or her savings, but parents are expected to contribute no more than 5.6% of theirs.

To reduce college expenses, your child may consider going to a school that offers a bachelor's degree in only three years. More and more of them do. In this way, Albertus Magnus College of New Haven, Connecticut, cut the cost of a degree by $13,000. Middlebury College in Middlebury, Vermont, says its three-year program will save students between $10,000 and $12,000. To make up for the fewer years, schools are extending the time the students spend studying, either by adding 10 minutes or so to the length of each class period, increasing the length of the semesters or adding mandatory summer sessions. The payoff may be not only one year's less college bills to pay but also one year's sooner earnings from a job after graduation. (For more, see Chapter 15, "Financing Your Education.")

## YOUR PARENTS

# Discussing Finances with Your Aging Parents

If your parents are near or beyond retirement age, you should broach certain sensitive subjects with them now to help ensure their well-being. Raising matters of money and mortality requires delicacy. But it is crucial that you have an understanding of your parents' financial affairs in case you are called on to manage them.

Start by asking your parents to make a list of their assets and liabilities. They should note whether these assets are held in joint tenancy, tenancy in common or in one parent's name. Then a lawyer who is expert on estate and tax matters should evaluate whether their forms of ownership are the most advantageous ones for estate purposes. If your parents are reluctant to discuss their finances, suggest that they draw up the list in private and keep it in a sealed envelope or a locked box at home. They should let you know where it is. Of course, urge them to consult a lawyer to make sure that they have taken steps to preserve their estate from excessive taxes.

Next, you should determine whether your parents' income is sufficient to meet their retirement needs. For example, do they have low-interest-bearing bank savings accounts and World War II vintage savings bonds that they could cash in and use to buy bank CDs paying more? Their house also could be a source of income even while they live in it. Ways to unlock this equity include so-called reverse mortgages, sale leasebacks, charity life agreements and home-equity credit lines.

If your parents are age 65 or older, they qualify for Medicare. But they also need supplementary health insurance that pays the deductibles and the percentage of doctor and hospital bills not reimbursed by Medicare. Discourage your parents from piling on one policy after another. They cannot be reimbursed more than once for the same bill.

Most nursing-home costs are not covered by Medicare or private health insurance. Your parents can, of course, buy special insurance to cover some or all of nursing-home costs. And they may be eligible for government programs designed to supplement income and cover the medical costs of the needy, such as Medicaid. Check whether your parents are eligible, and if they are not, find out how they can become eligible. The rules vary from state to state, the most important factor being how low your parents' own assets must go in order for them to qualify for Medicaid. In some states they have to spend almost every last penny that they possess. This is particularly tragic when only one spouse requires nursing-home care but the other spouse has to exhaust practically all of his or her remaining assets as well. Fortunately, a number of states are becoming more liberal, allowing the elderly to hold on to more than before. To repeat, check up on the rules in the state where your parents live. (For more, see Chapter 14, "Cutting Your Health-Care Costs.")

Do both your aging parents know how to handle financial matters? Often in marriages one mate manages the money. If that spouse dies first, the survivor may be at a loss to assume the task. While both parents are alive, you might suggest that the partner who is unaccustomed to balancing the checkbook take over the bill-paying for one month a year. And both your parents should know where important papers are kept.

Senility, illness or accident could leave one or both of your parents unable to manage. If no provisions have been made, a court will appoint a guardian, committee or conservator — even if one partner is still competent. So *each* of your parents should sign a durable power-of-attorney agreement. This is an inexpensive way to ensure that someone whom your folks trust will manage their affairs when they cannot. Your parents should give the power of attorney to each other — and also name a successor, either you or one of your brothers or sisters, in case they both become unable to make important life-and-death decisions.

Ask your parents how they feel about life-prolonging hospital procedures. They might not want extraordinary measures to keep them alive. An advance directive, such as a living will or a health-care proxy, may give you control over their health-care decisions. In a living will your parents may declare just which heroic life-extending procedures they do — or do not — want, and under what circumstances. A health-care proxy names someone to make decisions that they cannot. Almost all states provide legal standing to living wills, health-care proxies, durable powers of attorney for health care or other decision-making documents for this purpose.

If your parents' wills are over five years old, or if your folks have moved to another state since their wills were written, these documents should be reviewed. A lawyer can update the wills to take into account changes in estate tax law such as the unlimited marital deduction.

Finally, you should know where your parents keep all their important papers. The best place is in their attorney's office. They and the executor of their estates should have copies as well. Your parents should keep their copy of these papers in triplicate — with one copy in a safe-deposit box, one in a fireproof box at their home and another at one of their children's homes.

## Knowing the Ins and Outs of Powers of Attorney

When aging parents — or anyone else, for that matter — fall ill and cannot handle their own financial affairs, their families can run into frustrating barriers to acting on their behalf. In cases of prolonged disability, you must ask the courts to appoint a guardian, sometimes called a conservator, to handle the stricken person's finances. This is a time-consuming and expensive process, which might result in the appointment of a stranger. Still worse, while the legal process unfolds, your hands are tied. The prices of the stricken person's stocks may be falling, or a great offer may come in on a home he or she had up for sale. But you can do nothing.

The way out of these and other impasses is for everyone who owns valuable assets to give a durable power of attorney to someone trustworthy and wise. A document prepared by a lawyer and properly signed and witnessed will do the job. The fee normally shouldn't be more than $200. You can even create your own durable power of attorney, though that is not recommended. Stationery stores carry standard forms, but many financial institutions may refuse to comply with boilerplate forms. Each state has its own laws and court rulings about how to execute a durable power of attorney. So it's best to employ a lawyer.

In addition, ask your banker and stockbroker to let you execute their own company's durable-power-of-attorney form. Financial institutions can be balky about acknowledging outside attorneys' documents even though they are perfectly legal.

What if your parents resist letting anyone, even their own child, mess with their investments while they are in their right mind? Then there may be another way to protect them. They might be willing to give you something called a springing power of attorney. This document specifies the conditions in which you can act on behalf of your mother or father. It might say, for example, "This power of attorney shall become effective only upon the disability or incapacity of the principal." Springing powers of attorney are legal in most states.

Either a durable or a springing power of attorney should list specific powers, says Sanford J. Schlesinger, a national authority on elder law. For example, the person being appointed should have right of access to safe-deposit boxes, power to sign tax returns and settle tax disputes, power to make decisions about how a pension should be collected, power to collect money due from Medicaid, Supplemental Social Security and other government entitlements, and possibly even power to make gifts.

▾ ▾ ▾

# When a Parent Needs Your Money

As people live longer, more and more grown children will be called upon to give financial help to their aging parents. But how much support should you provide, and how can you do it without making grave sacrifices yourself?

A wrenching dilemma arises when the financial needs of the older generation conflict with those of the younger generation. Nobody has developed a formula for resolving it. Even the clergy provide varying responses.

Rabbi Stanley Schachter, former vice-chancellor of the Jewish Theological Seminary of America, says, "Children have an obligation to maintain their parents at a level of their highest dignity, ideally in the manner to which they are accustomed."

John Rhea, a Presbyterian minister who is an expert on the subject, has another view: "The top priority for an adult child is not to make the parents happy but to make them comfortable, to make sure their basic needs are met."

And Monsignor Charles Fahey, a former chairman of the Federal Council on Aging, says, "There is a strong responsibility to care for and love your parents, but that does not necessarily equate with economic support. Your primary responsibility is to your own children."

These differing outlooks mean that each individual has to decide for himself or herself. Still, you can get guidance from a trained social worker or other professional. A hospital, nursing home or senior-citizen center can refer you to such a counselor.

Most people want to take care of their parents, and they do an admirable job of it. In approximately 80% of cases, any help the elderly require comes from family members. And the National Council on the Aging reports that up to 11.8% of the U.S. workforce is involved in providing care for elders — a figure expected to jump dramatically as the number of aged people surges in the years ahead.

A large new network of sources has sprung up to provide care and support for the aged. To find out what is available locally, consult your city or state Department of Aging, listed in most phone books. Also try Family Service America, a nonprofit group representing 280 accredited family-service agencies. It will direct you to its local agency. Write to Information Center, Family Service America at 11700 West Lake Park Drive, Milwaukee, Wisconsin 53224, or call FSA at 800-221-2681.

## How and Where to Get Good Care for Aging Relatives

Just about everyone has heard an aged parent or grandparent plead, "Whatever you do, don't send me to a nursing home." Take heart. Only about 17% of people will be in a nursing home for more than five years. You also have several new alternatives.

Getting your elder involved in outside activities is one way to prolong his or her interest in staying well in the first place. Family Friends, a program sponsored by the National Council on the Aging in 26 sites around the U.S., has elderly volunteers visiting regularly with chronically ill and special-needs children (for information, call 202-479-6675). The University of Pittsburgh's Generations Together organizes phone links between senior citizens and so-called latchkey kids — children who return to empty homes after school. Such programs are available in most major metropolitan areas through your state's local office for the aging, your community's family-services bureau and religious organizations. You might call a neighborhood senior citizens' center; its employees can guide you to programs for older people.

The U.S. Administration on Aging toll-free ElderCare Locator Information Line directs elders or their families to local service agencies. Dial 800-677-1116, Monday through Friday from 9 A.M. to 8 P.M. Eastern Standard Time.

When your elder is impaired — that is, in need of some supervision — the least painful venue for all concerned is usually the geriatric day-care center. Nearly 3,000 adult day-care centers in the country now give respite to the caregiver and provide health maintenance and monitoring for the elder. At minimum, adult day-care centers offer elders a place for interaction, exercise and a hot lunch. Activities include games, craft and cooking classes, musical shows and field trips. These centers are located primarily in nursing homes, but you'll also find them in churches, community centers and hospitals.

The Stride-Rite Corporation has built an intergenerational day-care complex, accommodating aging relatives as well as children of its employees at its headquarters in Cambridge, Massachusetts. The child-care operation is well used by employees. The elder-care part is used less by employees than by people from the community at large. But employees take good advantage of the elder-care coordinator, who dispenses advice to them. All this has sparked interest from state agencies, private hospitals and other corporations, and the complex has become a model for others of its kind. Stride-Rite gets some 12 to 15 calls a week from other companies that are looking into the idea.

An intergenerational center also was opened in 1991 at Lancaster Laboratories in Lancaster, Pennsylvania. The elder-care part is filled to capacity with 25 handicapped or frail adults who cannot be left alone to take care of themselves. Most are not relatives of Lancaster Laboratories' employees. Costs for adult day care by geriatric social service professionals in community-based group programs vary all the way from a few dollars (for social activities and a daily meal) to $150 a day (for more serious nursing care, like physical therapy). Your best source for further information is the National Institute on Adult Day Care at the National Council on the Aging, 409 3rd Street SW, Suite 200, Washington, D.C. 20024; 202-479-1200.

Services available to the elderly in their own homes are expanding rapidly, and so is the number of government, charitable and for-profit agencies that provide such care. One example, a state-sponsored program in Florida, Community Care for the Elderly, has been successful in helping more than 38,000 older people, providing them with extensive at-home services. These elders can have meals delivered to their homes, get assistance for personal care and homemaking and in some districts get transportation to needed medical services. Your local Department of Aging will know of other similarly innovative services in your area.

When medical support is needed, look into home medical care. Limited services by a registered nurse are 100% reimbursable by Medicare if they are related to a hospital stay, and this care may extend for an unlimited time as long as the necessary qualifying conditions are met. Medicare will also pay for the services of a home health aide in conjunction with skilled nursing care. Sometimes, even if an older person doesn't require skilled nursing, private health-insurance policies will pay for personal care and home health services.

To determine whether the agency providing home care is a good one, you can review the checklist in *How to Choose a Home Care Agency*, a free publication from the National Association for Home Care, 519 C Street

NE, Washington, D.C. 20002. Be sure to ask whether or not the agency is certified by Medicare; if it is, that means it has complied with federal guidelines.

If home care is not an option, check into apartment buildings designed specifically for the elderly. So-called residential-care facilities provide room and board, limited health care and social and recreational programs. Then there are continuing-care retirement communities. They sometimes look like college campuses and offer up to three living choices: apartments for people who are well enough and desire to live alone; intermediate-care facilities for those who need some medical attention; and often another facility that offers around-the-clock skilled care. Continuing care can be ideal for the elderly person who is independent but realizes that the day of infirmity inevitably may come. For more information on continuing-care retirement communities, contact the American Association of Homes and Services for the Aging; 202-783-2242.

Still, nursing homes may be the only choice for some families with elderly relatives. In general, those homes have improved significantly in recent years. The best tend to be nonprofit institutions sponsored by religious, union or fraternal organizations.

You can get names of better nursing homes in your area by asking your doctor or hospital social worker. Also, inquire at a senior citizens' center, your state affiliate of the American Health Care Association, or the American Association of Homes for the Aging, 901 E Street NW, Suite 500, Washington, D.C. 20004.

You should visit any homes you are considering at least twice — once on an official tour and once as a surprise, if possible. Supervisors of a well-run home will welcome you and your questions. Make sure the residents seem content, clean and neat. Taste the food. To get brochures on choosing a nursing home and finding financial aid, send stamped, self-addressed envelopes to the American Health Care Association, 1201 L Street NW, Washington, D.C. 20005.

Inescapably, nursing homes are expensive: from $1,500 a month to $6,000 or even more, depending on the locality and the kind of accommodations. The national average is $31,000 a year, or $86 a day. Medicare, which is commonly thought to cover the costs of care, in fact pays for less than 5% of nursing-home costs nationwide. Among the many stipulations: The patient must have been in a hospital for at least three days, the patient must enter the skilled-care facility within 30 days of his or her discharge from the hospital and the facility must be approved by Medicare.

If all conditions are met, Medicare pays in full for the first 20 days; from the 21st to the 100th day, the patient shares the cost by paying a nationally set daily rate of $89.50. The average length of stay paid for by Medicare is only 26 days. To find out if your elder is covered, call your nearest Social Security office. If your elder is interested in acquiring Medicare medical insurance, which may help pay for covered services received in a nursing home from a doctor, the Social Security office can assist you with that as well. But remember that you can sign up for the insurance only in the first three months of the calendar year.

Long-term-care insurance, which accounts for less than 1% of nursing-home payments, is available in most states from the American Association of Retired Persons (601 E Street NW, Washington, D.C. 20049; 202-434-2277), from some employers and from increasing numbers of insurance companies. The Health Insurance Association of America reports that if you are 50 years old, a policy offering $80 per day in nursing-home benefits for up to four years with a 20-day deductible period costs about $435 a year. The same policy costs $983 annually if you are age 65, and about $3,998 if you are 79. Premium costs have been declining slightly over the years.

Make sure any long-term-care policy you consider has no hidden obstacles to collecting claims. Reject any plan that makes even a day or two of hospitalization a prerequisite for the payment of benefits. Look for a policy that covers three levels of nursing care — skilled, intermediate and custodial — and that pays an amount equal to at least half the nursing-home benefit for any home care your elder may need. The policy should explicitly cover Alzheimer's disease, Parkinson's disease and other nervous disorders that are organic in origin. It should pay for care needed because of pre-existing diseases. The daily benefit rate should climb from year to year to protect against rising nursing-home costs.

Medicaid, the program for patients who have no money, is now the major financier of long-term care, covering about 52% of nursing-home bills nationally. Eligibility depends on need, and "need" is defined differently by Medicaid programs in different states. Some states not only require the impoverishment of the patient but also place a limit on the assets of the patient's spouse.

However, federal law allows spouses who remain at home to retain a "maintenance needs allowance" of up to $1,870 a month. The new law establishes new rules for the transfer of assets to children or other relatives. In doing so, the spouses disqualify themselves for Medicaid, but only for a limited time. Under the new federal guideline, they can become eligible for Medicaid in 36 months or less after applying for it and after transferring assets to others.

Children of applicants who anticipate a long nursing-home stay should consider suggesting that their parents do this: Give to their potential heirs all of their assets except the amount of money needed either to pay for or to insure the next 36 months of care. A family entering this process should seek the advice of a lawyer knowledgeable in this field. In addition, all should be aware that federal law prohibits nursing homes from requiring large cash registration deposits from those who qualify for Medicaid.

DIVORCE

# The New Economics of Divorce

Marriages may be made in heaven, but more and more divorces are being negotiated in accountants' offices. Because of a revolution in property settlements, splitting up a marriage is becoming much like the dissolution of a business partnership. Alimony is out, a concept called "equitable distribution" is in, and court decrees are so unpredictable — and so expensive to obtain — that couples should go to extreme lengths to avoid trial.

Instead of fighting bitterly over who did what to whom, smart couples now are more likely to concentrate on tallying all the dollars and cents that were acquired during their life together so that they can be split equitably. State legislatures and courts across the country are acknowledging that both parties put effort into a marriage, so both are entitled to their fair share of the assets if they divorce. Both the spouse who pays the bills and the partner who works as a homemaker or who earns less are credited with their contributions.

Most states have adopted new concepts of what marital property is and how it should be split. The prevailing theory is that any property accumulated during a marriage should be divided not only fairly but also finally so that each partner can move on to the next stage of life, unencumbered by leftover financial ties. This is based on the two modern realities that many marriages do not last and that women are increasingly able to support themselves.

A dozen years ago, women could not count on receiving any assets that had not been held in their own names. Recently, though, more and more women have been getting at least half of the marital assets, even in the 41 states without community-property laws on the books.

Now most states hold that all assets earned during a marriage, no matter by whom or in whose name they have been held, go into a common pot to be divided in whatever way a judge decides is fair. The only exceptions are anything that a spouse owned before marriage, received as compensation for personal injuries or received as an inheritance or gift during the marriage. Such property continues to belong to him or her.

At the same time, women are getting less alimony. Just 16% of divorced wives receive these payments, and short-term alimony is becoming more common than long-term. In sum, courts are more reluctant to burden a husband with an ex-wife's maintenance until she remarries — if ever — and with an obligation to completely support the children until they are grown. It is expected that most women will work for pay and support themselves. So rehabilitative maintenance usually is awarded just long enough for a woman to re-enter the work force or train for a better job. And support of children is considered the responsibility of *both* parents. Prodded by federal law, states now have percentage-of-income guidelines for child support.

What are really on the rise are lump-sum, one-shot settlements based on an analysis of the couple's financial assets. Figuring out the size of those assets, and just which partner is entitled to what, can mean lengthy litigation and high accounting and legal fees. Property judgments by a court are unpredictable at best, and sometimes downright unfair. If the couple cannot decide for themselves who gets what, the judge will. But these decisions are only as equitable and intelligent as the judge himself or herself.

Divorce is becoming so prevalent that more and more couples make an inventory of their assets every several years, just in case. They evaluate what they own, from cars and carpets to stocks and bonds. Then each partner outlines his or her individual contributions to this joint balance sheet, including the value of the wife's services if she is at home caring for children. Such written tabulations can save hours of high-priced legal time and help ensure a fairer division of property if a couple ever separates. In general, the one who keeps the best records comes out ahead in the divorce. It may seem cynical if your marriage is in full flower, but you'd be prudent to keep careful financial records, including mutual-fund statements, income tax returns, canceled checks and transactions of any business you might own.

Because of the radical changes in the economics of divorce, anyone thinking about dissolving a marriage is well advised to do some serious financial planning first. Divorce lawyers now orchestrate elaborate financial settlements, and they often call in help from property appraisers, accountants, tax specialists and the like. The cost of divorce varies according to the length and complexity of the case, the value of the assets at stake and the scale of lawyers' fees in different localities. It can easily run to $10,000 for a middle-class couple with children, a house and other assets — and that is when they settle out of court. If they insist on going to trial, the fee could double or triple.

## The Virtues of Divorce Mediation

Divorce does not belong in the courts. Being there puts the couple into an adversarial position and tends to drive them farther and farther apart. You can reduce the cost and pain by using a professional mediator to help determine the settlement. Mediation is not for every couple. Sometimes differences are too sharp and hurtful for both people to sit down and reason together.

The first chore of a mediator is to search for common ground. If the three parties — husband, wife and mediator — agree that the mediation can work, the couple then faces a tough homework assignment: to bring budgets, balance sheets, tax returns, pension information and other financial reports to their next meeting. It may take anywhere from two to a dozen or more sessions for a couple to reach financial agreement. It may involve payments for child support and alimony, division of pension and retirement funds or simply a division of the spoils of a lifetime — including the dog and the cat.

One reason for lopsided splits of marital property may be that despite a generation of women's liberation, wives still typically come to the divorce table ill-informed and therefore ill-equipped to negotiate. In many cases, the woman has not taken an active role in handling finances other than the household budget.

Under the guidance of a competent mediator, divorce becomes an educational process for both spouses. In sharp contrast, a divorce hammered out between lawyers for each party tends to stop the flow of information. Still worse, says Robert Coulson, former president of the American Arbitration Association, lawyers often widen the gap between couples. In his or her proper role as an advocate for one party in a dispute, a lawyer may instruct a wife, for example, to pull all the money out of a joint bank account, or advise a husband to close his wife's charge accounts.

A meeting of minds offers opportunities to keep enormous sums out of the tax collector's reach. Take the sale of a house. Let's say she's 55 years old and he's 57. The house they have owned and lived in for 30 years originally cost $30,000. The house is now debt-free and worth $500,000. Neither spouse wants to live in it any longer. In the throes of an adversarial separation, a couple will often sell their house and split the proceeds. As joint owners over age 55, they can together claim a once-in-a-lifetime $125,000 exemption from taxable capital gains. That way, each might net about $180,000 from the sale.

Under a mediator's patient tutelage, however, the couple might agree, while still married, to change title of the house from joint ownership to tenants-in-common, giving each a separate one-half interest in the property. Then, by waiting until after the divorce to sell his or her share, each ex-spouse would become eligible for a separate $125,000 capital-gains exemption. Instead of netting $180,000, they would each take away $200,000 or more.

Some divorce mediators are attorneys; others have backgrounds as social workers, teachers, clergy, financial planners, psychologists or therapists. Where their financial competence is limited, they may call in actuaries, accountants and attorneys to complete the job; in some cases they may even refer overwrought clients to psychotherapists.

How much does divorce mediation cost? Anywhere from $80 to $170 an hour is the typical fee for drawing up a separation agreement, which will probably go through several revisions. Responsible mediators advise their clients to review the settlement with their own attorneys.

If the divorce mediator is also a lawyer and drafts the formal settlement, there will be additional fees: perhaps $1,500 for the agreement and $1,000 for filing it in court. In most cases, the entire cost of a mediated divorce is below $5,000. Although that is far less than the usual charge for an adversarial divorce, few practitioners recommend mediation strictly as an economy move. Rather, they say, mediation is a less traumatic and more effective way of reaching a fair deal.

How to locate a trained divorce mediator? The Academy of Family Mediators (1500 South Highway 100, Suite 355, Golden Valley, Minnesota 55416) requires practitioner members to meet certain standards, and can provide names of those in your area. Or try the American Arbitration Association, listed in the Yellow Pages under "Mediation Services." It has offices in 35 cities and, for a $300 fee, will recommend a mediator who meets its professional standards. For a free pamphlet titled "Family Mediation Rules," write to its Publications Department at 140 West 51st Street, New York, New York 10020-1203.

Undoubtedly, the best divorce settlements come when both partners are able to put aside personal squabbles and concentrate on enlightened self-interest. They accept that neither will come out ahead but that both will be able to make a clean break and to start anew. Just remember: A peaceful divorce settlement is almost always better than a trial, because it is much cheaper and is less stressful to family life.

## The Tax Consequences of Divorce

If you are estranged from your spouse, you may take comfort in the federal laws affecting the tax consequences of broken marriages.

It is much simpler than it was a dozen years ago for a divorcing couple to divide ownership of their property, such as houses and stocks. In the past, if a man transferred a house to his ex-wife upon their divorce, he would owe capital-gains taxes on any estimated appreciation in the property's value. Under the new rules, though, the man owes nothing. In fact, neither the man nor his ex-wife owes any taxes until the house is sold — perhaps many years from now. But when the ex-wife eventually sells the home, she will be liable for taxes on any rise in its value since its original purchase by the husband, although there are two ways she can avoid or defer paying Uncle Sam.

First, if she is older than age 55, she can take advantage of the once-in-a-lifetime exclusion of up to $125,000 in capital gains on the sale of a primary residence. Or, she can buy another home of equal or greater cost within two years of the sale, allowing her to save her exclusion for the future. Unfortunately, these special provisions do not apply to other property that one spouse transfers to another in a split-up, such as stocks. The ex-wife must still pay capital-gains taxes on these assets when she sells them.

An example: Say a man owns a house that he bought for $100,000 but now is worth $150,000. Say, too, that he gets a divorce and puts the house in his ex-wife's name. He owes no tax on the gain. On the other hand, if and when his ex-wife sells the house, she stands to end up owing taxes on all its appreciation since her ex-husband first bought it.

The basic rule on the tax treatment of alimony shapes many divorce settlements. If you receive alimony, the IRS considers it just like any other income, and you have to pay taxes on it. Similarly, if you pay alimony to an ex-spouse, the IRS considers it an expense, and you can deduct it from your taxable income.

The federal law says that alimony in most cases is what goes clearly to the ex-spouse alone. Here is how the current rules work:

Say you pay $1,500 a month to your ex-spouse, and she uses $500 of it for the children. You can deduct only $1,000 a month from your taxable income, but you cannot deduct the $500 that is spent for the children. This money is considered child support, and you have to pay taxes on it. There are some instances, however, when money that benefits both the ex-spouse and children can be considered alimony. One tax break for a nonworking spouse who receives alimony lets him or her shelter as much as $2,000 of it annually in an Individual Retirement Account.

It is also possible to claim a share of your former spouse's pension. You can start collecting as soon as your former mate reaches early-retirement age, normally 55 years old. Or you can demand your share in a lump sum if the company pension allows it. You can postpone taxes on the lump sum by rolling it over into an IRA.

Another point: Deadbeat divorced parents who miss child-support payments are in big trouble. Strict child-support rules in every state provide for withholding of state tax refunds and the placement of liens on the assets (such as real estate and bank accounts) of parents who don't pay. The money is diverted instead to help provide for the child. Delinquent parents may be required to post a bond and their poor payment history could be reported to credit agencies. It's about time: The Census Bureau found in 1989 that only 44% of children of divorced parents receive any money from their fathers.

CHAPTER 13

# Insuring Yourself Sensibly

## Buying Life Insurance Wisely

> There are too many complicated schemes or plans of insuring and . . . too many and too elaborate forms of contract or policy. Each new company announces some new feature in its business which is to enure greatly to the advantage of the insured, and thus, with some seventy different companies, each urging their superiority over all others, he who seeks insurance, if he stops to hear all the arguments, and deliberately determine which is really the best company, is likely to die before he reaches a conclusion.
>
> *Eleventh annual report of the Superintendent of the Insurance Department of the State of New York, April 1, 1870*

More than 600 companies and 200,000 agents sell life insurance today, but not everything has changed in 126 years. If you listen to one sales pitch after another, you're almost certain to feel confused. That's the wrong way to shop for life insurance.

The right way is to spend a few hours learning how to make smart decisions, so that you can get more for your money. Buying life insurance is a skill, and you can become good at it. You need to understand the wise uses of life insurance, the main types of policies you're likely to encounter, and ways to get better value. By learning the basics, you — rather than a salesperson — will be in control.

Salespeople can come up with endless reasons for you to buy life policies, but there are only three sensible uses:

- to replace lost income caused by a breadwinner's premature death
- to provide liquidity for your estate, protecting your heirs against having to sell off assets like the family business in order to pay estate taxes, or to provide money to equalize the shares of an estate
- to serve as an investment, allowing you to build up money to fund college, retirement or other objectives, or to increase the value of your estate

Most insurance advice comes from agents and brokers who receive commissions — often very fat ones — for selling policies to you. If you don't buy, their kids don't eat.

Commissions on whole life insurance policies typically run 50% to 90% of the first-year premium, and 3% to 5% every year thereafter — as long as you pay the premium. Agents have a strong incentive to push cash value policies, because they cost — and pay — so much more than term policies. A $250,000 term policy with a $300 premium might pay the agent only $150 for several hours' work, versus at least $1,500 from a $3,000 premium on a $250,000 whole life policy.

It's easy to see why sales pitches often emphasize "permanent" (cash value) over "temporary" (term) insurance. It's also easy to see why affluent families are attractive prospects for agents. If an agent can sell a $1 million second-to-die policy with a $20,000 premium, he or she can earn $10,000 in the first year and $1,000 a year thereafter.

Commission-based sales dominate the market because most people won't buy insurance without sales pressure. As the old line goes: Life insurance is sold, not bought. When an agent gets a call from a customer saying he might just want to buy some more insurance, the agent suspects that the prospect has just received a very bad report on a stress test.

High front-end commissions are needed because most sales efforts fail and because it takes time to explain the policy and go through the application process. The obvious disadvantage of the system is that you can't be sure the agent's advice is not distorted by the need to sell product. Some agents overcome this inherent conflict, others don't.

▾ ▾ ▾

## Some Misuses of Life Insurance

- *Insurance on children.* The pitch here is that you'll be giving your child a head start in life by getting permanent coverage in place while he or she is still young. The main purpose of life insurance is to protect against the financial consequences of death. Unless your child is the main breadwinner of your family, put those premium dollars into no-load mutual funds for college.
- *Pension maximization.* If you're eligible for a pension through your employer, you'll probably have to choose either a joint-and-survivor income that continues until you and your spouse both die or a higher income that stops when you die. Elect the higher single-life option, agents say, and use part of the extra money to buy life insurance to provide an income for your spouse. This may work to your advantage, or it may not, depending on the pension figures, your ages and health, interest rates and other benefits linked to your pension, such as cost-of-living adjustments and health insurance. Be aware that agents who use unrealistic numbers can make life insurance look good in every case. Choosing a single-life pension is an irrevocable decision, so before proceeding you should get an unbiased evaluation from a financial planner, insurance consultant or employee benefits specialist.
- *Private pension plan.* This is just a fancy name for cash value life insurance. The idea is to invest money in a life insurance policy and then take out tax-free loans later to provide an income in retirement. On paper, this scheme may give you more after-tax money than annuities or taxable investments, but it depends on favorable tax treatment that may change in the future. The agent's numbers may also be based on unrealistic assumptions about the future performance of the policy. If you want a less risky "private pension plan," invest your money in no-load mutual funds.

Agents also differ in their dedication to giving you service after the sale. Front-loaded commissions reward agents more for finding new customers than for keeping existing customers happy, so even though you're entitled to "lifetime service," you may have trouble getting your phone calls returned.

It's best to interview several agents by phone and then pick the one whom you like best. It may seem wise to invite several agents to make proposals, but often you'll wind up with mountains of paper, confusingly conflicting assertions and no quick way to get the truth.

You can increase your chances of getting a knowledgeable agent who places your interests first if you ask a few questions:

- How long have you been in business? (Most new agents don't last even five years before moving on to another occupation.)
- Are you a Chartered Life Underwriter, and if so, do you participate in the PACE (Professional Achievement in Continuing Education) program? (Participation represents a dedication to becoming and staying knowledgeable, though it's no guarantee.)
- Which companies get most of your business and why? (Though an agent can represent hundreds of companies, he or she usually has a few favorites.)
- Are you willing to disclose your compensation for selling me the policy? (Such willingness may help you judge whether the agent sees himself or herself as a professional adviser or a salesperson.)
- What services do you provide after the sale? (These may include an annual review of policy performance relative to your original expectations and to similar policies in the marketplace, a copy of rating agencies' reports on the insurance company's financial strength, and any suggestions on making more effective use of your policy as your needs change — for example, by investing more money in the policy to save for college tuition or retirement.)

Get referrals from friends, accountants or attorneys, but remember that agents often have cross-referral relationships with other professionals. So it's wise to verify the agent's qualifications yourself.

You can also consult one of the fee-for-service insurance advisers, though they are few in number and not easy to find. They act much like fee-only financial planners, but they come in two types. *Fee-based* insurance advisers earn most of their income from fees, though they may also represent and receive commissions from insurance companies for selling policies. *Fee-only* advisers get no compensation from agents or companies for policy sales; they work strictly on a fee basis. Expect to pay $100 to $200 an hour for their analysis. For a referral to fee-for-service advisers, call the Fee Insurance Alliance (800-874-5662) or the Life Insurance Advisers Association (800-521-4578).

To help you determine any potential conflicts of interest, ask the adviser to disclose the sources, nature and amount of his or her overall compensation.

A low-cost way to get a second opinion before you accept an adviser's recommendation is to consult one of the computer on-line services, such as America Online, Prodigy or CompuServe. They have forums devoted to insurance topics, where you can get opinions from other buyers and even agents.

## How Much Insurance Do You Need?

Insurance agents offer simple formulas to answer this complex question, but they cram many different kinds of people, with different requirements, into the same pigeonhole. How much coverage you require hinges on what you want it to do for you. Don't make the mistake of expecting it to do too much. Insurance should be designed to maintain, not raise, your immediate family's standard of living.

To figure out how much life insurance you should have, estimate your family's annual living expenses. Then determine where that money will come from, if you should die. Include your Social Security benefits, savings, assets that can be sold and your spouse's income. The gap that's left between what costs you expect and what income you can count on is what you need to cover with life insurance. So, if you are a middle-income person with dependents, you are likely to need life insurance coverage in six figures.

To approximate your current need, multiply the annual after-tax

**LIFE INSURANCE NEEDS FOR:**

| | Today's dollars | Number of years | Total |
|---|---|---|---|
| **CAPITAL NEEDED TO ACCOMPLISH YOUR GOALS** | | | |
| Living expenses for survivors<br>While children are at home<br>After children leave home | | | |
| Education expenses | | | |
| Mortgage payoff | | | |
| Miscellaneous needs | | | |
| Final expenses | | | |
| Inheritance for children | | | |
| Other: | | | |
| **Total capital needed** | | | |
| **CAPITAL AVAILABLE TO ACCOMPLISH YOUR GOALS** | | | |
| Current investments<br>Retirement plans (IRAs, 401(k)s, etc.)<br>Other investments | | | |
| Pension | | | |
| Social Security<br>While children are at home<br>After children leave home | | | |
| Spouse's earned income | | | |
| Other: | | | |
| Less: Settlement costs and estate taxes | | | ( ) |
| **Total capital available** | | | |
| **SHORTFALL/(EXCESS)** | | | |
| Less: Life insurance in force | | | ( ) |
| **ADDITIONAL LIFE INSURANCE NEEDED** | | | |

SOURCE: GLENN S. DAILY

## The Biggest Mistakes That People Make

- *Failing to keep other goals in mind.* Every dollar spent on insurance expenses is a dollar that's not available for other goals. No responsible person wants to leave dependents in penury, but premature death is only one of life's risks. You don't necessarily have to buy as much life insurance as a computer program says you "need."
- *Buying cash value life insurance rather than term.* Term is probably more appropriate for most people who want life insurance while their children are growing up. Instead of listening to sales pitches for high-commission cash value products, make maximum use of tax-deductible retirement plans and buy low-cost mutual funds.
- *Not shopping around for term insurance.* Prices vary enormously, and it takes only a few phone calls (see pages 441–42) to find competitive policies.
- *Buying full-commission cash value policies.* You can get quality low-load policies from a few companies without paying commissions, and you can also reduce commissions on some agent-sold products by "blending"; that is, substituting low-commission term insurance and paid-up additions for high-commission base coverage. Either way, you'll get better value for your money.
- *Ignoring cash values.* High cash values are your safety net against unforeseen events, such as poor policy performance, concerns about the company's financial condition, or a shorter-than-expected need for insurance. Most people drop their policies within 10 years of purchase, with large losses. Low-load policies (see the list on page 445) usually have very high first-year cash values, and you can increase the cash values of some agent-sold policies by blending.
- *Replacing an existing cash value policy without an adequate evaluation.* After you've paid the start-up costs for a policy, it's usually not advisable to start all over again with a new policy. Before getting rid of what you have, get unbiased advice. The

Consumer Federation of America's Life Insurance Rate of Return Service (202-387-6121) is one good source.

- *Failing to take full advantage of existing cash value policies.* Your existing policy may be a good place to save more money for other goals, or you may be able to reduce the coverage as you get older and keep the policy going with a lower outlay. If you bought a high-commission policy with low cash values, you can exchange the policy for a deferred annuity and use the excess cost basis to shelter future investment gains from income tax. For example, if the premiums total $50,000 and the cash value is only $30,000, you can roll the $30,000 into a deferred annuity, let it grow to $50,000 and cash out the annuity without owing any tax on the $20,000 gain.
- *Setting up the policy improperly.* You may incur unnecessary estate, gift and income taxes if you're careless in choosing the owner and beneficiary of the policy or in making changes later. For large policies, you may want to consider using an irrevocable life insurance trust. You should avoid situations where the insured, the owner and the beneficiary are all different; at death, this creates a taxable gift from the owner to the beneficiary. An experienced attorney, accountant, agent or other adviser can help you stay clear of these pitfalls.

*Source: Glenn S. Daily*

expenses by the number of years you will have to pay for those expenses. Do a similar calculation for the sources of income that would be available at your death, in all cases using after-tax estimates. The difference between money needed and money available is your life insurance need.

It is not unusual for the amount to be shockingly high, especially if you want to maintain your spouse's standard of living for decades. Suppose you have two young children and a 35-year-old spouse, and you want to provide $30,000 after taxes for living expenses for 60 years, plus $20,000 each year of college for each child, plus $150,000 to pay off the mortgage, plus $50,000 for miscellaneous expenses. All that takes

$2,160,000 of capital, and even more if you don't want to touch principal. Total Social Security payments might be worth an equivalent lump sum of $600,000, and perhaps you have another $200,000 in spendable assets such as certificates of deposit or listed stocks. That still leaves $1,360,000 to be provided by life insurance.

You may decide to make your goals more modest or to buy less insurance than you "need." Perhaps you'll conclude that your spouse won't live to be 95, can get by on $25,000 a year, or can be counted on to earn at least $20,000 a year after taxes. Remember that the chances are high you won't die before reaching retirement, and every dollar you spend on reducing the risk of premature death is a dollar that can't be saved to reduce the more likely risk of outliving your money.

If you're buying life insurance to help pay estate taxes at some future date or to equalize the shares of assets passing to your children, you'll need to get a projection of those taxes and asset values from your lawyer, accountant, financial planner or insurance agent. Again, you may decide not to buy all the insurance that you "need," after taking other goals into account.

An important point: Your beneficiaries will not have to pay income taxes on the benefits they receive from your life insurance. But your estate will have to pay estate taxes on the benefits, unless the policy is owned by a third party, such as a carefully drafted irrevocable trust for your heirs. (For more on irrevocable trusts, see Chapter 23, "Dealing with Wills, Trusts and Estates.")

## Choosing Among the Types of Life Coverage

Insurance companies have a talent for thinking up new products to sell, but their most popular policies continue to be term, whole life and universal life. Meanwhile, variable universal life is becoming more widespread. Which is best for you?

In pondering this question, bear in mind that you need life insurance early in your career, when your children are young and your assets are low. But if you plan properly as you grow older, your insurance needs may decline or even disappear.

Let's examine in more detail the different kinds of policies.

There are two basic types of life insurance: term and cash value. Term

## SELECTING FROM THE DIFFERENT KINDS OF POLICIES

These are typical annual premiums for a newly issued $250,000 policy. Term insurance is, of course, much less expensive than whole life. If you get annual renewable term, the company guarantees to renew your policy year after year. But it will not guarantee you the rate, which may rise more than you expect. You can, however, lock in a fixed rate for a 10-year or 20-year term, if you are willing to pay more from the very beginning.

| | Issue age | Annual renewable term | 10-year term | 20-year term | Universal life | Whole life |
|---|---|---|---|---|---|---|
| **MALE** | 30 | $210 | $240 | $340 | $1,000 | $2,000 |
| | 40 | 250 | 350 | 535 | 1,500 | 3,250 |
| | 50 | 385 | 700 | 1,170 | 2,600 | 5,500 |
| | 60 | 830 | 1,560 | 2,600 | 4,900 | 9,600 |
| **FEMALE** | 30 | $185 | $210 | $300 | $800 | $1,700 |
| | 40 | 225 | 285 | 420 | 1,300 | 2,750 |
| | 50 | 315 | 510 | 790 | 2,200 | 4,500 |
| | 60 | 565 | 950 | 1,590 | 3,900 | 7,600 |

SOURCE: GLENN S. DAILY

insurance is pure protection and builds up no cash value that you can draw out in the future. Cash value life insurance requires a higher initial outlay but it builds savings inside the policy for your future use. For example, you can withdraw the money to supplement your retirement income or to help pay your children's college tuition.

For most people term insurance is the appropriate choice because it requires a lower initial outlay, and carries no long-term commitment. Also, the policies are easier to understand and compare than is the case with cash value policies. The two most common varieties are:

*Annual renewable term.* The premiums you pay typically increase each year, and you can renew the policy each year until you reach a maximum age. Example: For a $500,000 policy from Northwestern Mutual, a healthy, nonsmoking 40-year-old man would pay $580 in the first year. The premium would steadily rise to $835 at age 45, $1,235 at age 50, $1,935 at age 55. The man could renew the policy up to age 69, when the premium would be $11,350. If he smokes, his premium each year would be twice as high.

*Level-premium term.* Premiums remain flat for five to 20 years, after which the policy can be renewed at a higher premium for another multi-year period. To qualify for favorable renewal rates at the end of that period, you usually must provide evidence of insurability. Otherwise, the policy reverts to expensive annual renewable term.

Example: First Colony would charge a healthy 40-year-old man $655 a year for a $500,000 10-year level-premium policy. If he's still healthy at age 50, he could renew for another 10 years at $1,340; otherwise, his premiums would rise from $1,170 at age 50 to $3,740 at age 55. If he could afford the steadily steeper premiums, he could renew up to age 99, when the premium would be a neat $365,120.

In contrast to term insurance, cash value life insurance combines protection with savings. After paying the agent's sales commission and other expenses, the insurance company puts the balance of your premium into an internal fund, where it is invested and earns interest. The growth in this fund allows the company to keep your premium level for life.

Example: For a $500,000 policy, a 40-year-old man who doesn't smoke might pay about $7,400 a year. That premium wouldn't change. But the cash value might build up to $39,000 by the fifth year and $92,000 by the 10th year. At that point, he could probably stop paying more premiums, and the policy would continue for the rest of his life. When he died, his beneficiaries would receive $500,000.

If he decides to drop the policy after 20 years, he might get back a cash surrender value of about $156,000. So, in this example, he would have a gain of $82,000 over the $74,000 he paid in, and he would have insurance protection throughout the 20-year period.

Many are the kinds of cash value policies. All work basically the same way but are distinguished by four characteristics:

- *Fixed premium or flexible premium.* With a fixed premium policy you must pay a specified amount each year to keep the policy in force, and there is a rigid relationship between the cash value and the death benefit. You cannot change one without changing the other. A flexible premium policy lets you vary your premium payments by increasing or decreasing them, or stopping them for a while.
- *Fixed interest or variable.* With a fixed interest policy, the insurer declares an interest rate each year based on the yield of its overall portfolio of investments, primarily bonds and mortgages. In contrast, a variable policy's return is determined by the performance of the investment funds you select to support the policy.

- *Unbundled or bundled.* In an "unbundled" insurance policy, the insurance company discloses all the insurance and administration charges and investment earnings. "Bundled" policies do not disclose the charges and credits separately, only the total cash value and dividends.
- *One insured or multiple insureds.* Single-life policies insure one person. Multiple-life policies are written on more than one life, such as a husband and wife.

Specific cash value policies are:

- *Traditional whole life.* This is the oldest type and still has the largest market share, about 48% as measured by total life insurance coverage (term insurance has 14%). Premiums are fixed and based on conservative assumptions that interest rates will be quite low and mortality rates will be quite high. Each year the company pays a dividend to its policyholders that reflects the difference between actual and assumed experience.

  You may use dividends to, among other choices, reduce the premium or buy more whole life insurance — called *paid-up additions* — at bargain rates. Many companies allow you to add term insurance and paid-up additions to a whole life policy to design your own customized insurance plans. This is called blending, and it increases the flexibility of whole life by letting you choose a lower premium. The trade-off is that you won't be able to use dividends to make the death benefit grow, because dividends are used to pay the term costs. For example, by replacing 25% of the whole life coverage with term insurance, you could reduce the premium by about 25%.

  You may also be able to request a *partial surrender*; that is, you can surrender a portion of the policy, with a pro-rata reduction in your premium and the amount of coverage.

  Example: At age 55, you buy a $300,000 USAA policy with a $7,656 annual premium. In the first year the company earns more than the assumed interest rate of 4.5% and pays out less than the assumed death claims of $6.36 per $1,000 of coverage on all its policies. So, at the end of the year it pays you a dividend of $1,725. You could use that to reduce the second-year premium from $7,656 to $5,931 or to buy $4,706 of additional paid-up insurance. ("Paid-up" means that you don't have to pay any premiums on that insurance for the rest of your life.)

- *Universal life* (also called *adjustable life* or *flexible-premium universal life*). This flexible policy lets you change the premium and the death benefit every year, within limits. There is no fixed premium, but the policy will lapse if there isn't enough money in your account to pay the various charges for insurance and administration. All monthly credits for interest and all deductions for insurance and administration are shown in an annual statement. If you drop the policy during the first 10 to 20 years, most companies hit you with a declining surrender charge based on the amount of premiums paid. These charges disappear after you've held the policy for about 20 years.

  One common myth is that universal life lacks a guaranteed premium that will keep the policy in force for life. You can get the same guarantees that whole life provides if you pay a whole life premium each year. If you pay a lower premium, you take some risk that you'll have to pay a higher premium later, but you can avoid surprises by asking the company to give you a new projection of policy values every few years.

  Example: A 38-year-old woman buys a $200,000 universal life policy from the Ameritas insurance company. If she pays $1,000 each year, the policy probably will stay in force for life, unless the company's interest earnings fall or its death claims rise. If that happens, she can increase the premium to put the policy back on track. If she pays $2,184 each year, the policy is guaranteed to stay in force for life. If she pays $5,000 for one year only, the policy will probably stay in force for at least 20 years.

- *Interest-sensitive whole life* (also called *current assumption whole life* or *fixed-premium universal life*). The monthly interest credits and insurance deductions are shown in an annual statement, as with flexible-premium universal life, but there is a fixed premium, as with traditional whole life. If the internal funds build faster than assumed, you can use the excess to reduce the premium.

- *Variable life.* This kind of policy hitches an old-fashioned whole life policy to the unpredictable investment markets. Part of your premium goes into managed investment pools that *you* — not the company — select. Depending upon the company, you can put your money into stock funds, bond funds or a money-market fund. Or you can put some in each. Although there are some restrictions, you can switch among funds in search of the highest total returns. Unlike whole life, the cash value of your policy — and its death benefit — can sink as well as soar.
- *Variable universal life.* This combines some of the advantages of universal life and variable life. Ordinary universal life offers you so-called flexible-premium features, which allow you to vary from year to year the amount of your premium going into insurance coverage and the amount going into investments. But variable life additionally lets you switch among your investment options. With variable universal life, you can alter your premium allocations *and* change your investment choices, so you have maximum control over where your investment money goes. About 30 companies sell variable universal life, including Prudential, Equitable, IDS and John Hancock. As with all life insurance that combines insurance with investment, any earnings are tax-deferred until you cash in the policy. If your beneficiary receives the earnings, they are exempt from federal income taxes.

  Is variable universal life sensible for you? The answer might be yes if you plan on keeping the policy for 15 years or longer. Otherwise, high fees and commissions — especially at the front end — will eat into your early cash buildup.
- *Second-to-die* (also called *survivorship* or *last survivor*). These policies insure two lives — usually a husband and wife — and pay off only at the second death. Consequently, their premiums are lower than for a policy covering a single life. For example, the premium for a $1 million whole life policy on a 60-year-old man might be about $38,000, whereas the premium for a $1 million second-to-die policy on a 60-year-old man and woman could be about $25,000. Second-to-die policies are used mostly by affluent people to pay estate taxes. Most

companies offer a policy split option that lets you switch to two single-life policies in the event of divorce or a change in estate tax laws, though you may need evidence of insurability. Second-to-die versions of each single-life type of policy are available; for example, you can get second-to-die whole life, universal life or variable universal life.

- *First-to-die.* These policies insure two or more lives and pay off at the first death. The annual premium is 20% to 30% less than the combined premiums of two single-life policies. This can be an economical way to satisfy the protection needs of a dual-income family or retired couple, where money is needed at the first death but not the second. Most first-to-die policies are universal life.
- *Riders.* These are supplemental provisions that expand the benefits of a policy. Some carry an additional charge. A *beneficiary purchase option* attached to a single-life policy creates a second-to-die benefit; a *first-to-die* or *single-life term rider* attached to a second-to-die policy provides a benefit at the first death.

  *Accelerated death benefit riders* have gained in number and popularity in recent years. They allow seriously or terminally ill policyholders to collect part of the death benefit before dying.

## Choosing Between Term and Cash Value Policies

In general, short-term needs require term insurance and long-term needs — those lasting beyond age 60 or so — require cash value insurance. Needs that fall in between can be satisfied with either type.

One factor in the choice may be your tolerance for complexity. Cash value insurance is more complicated than term, and its performance — that is, the growth in death benefits and cash values in relation to what might be expected, given the current interest rates in the marketplace — is harder to monitor. Critics often fault the insurance industry for its lack of disclosure. It may be difficult for policyholders to get even basic information, such as the interest rate used in calculating their dividends, or the internal charges that they'll be paying for insurance protection. After you invest your money in a policy, you may get only a cryptic annual statement of your current death benefit and cash value — and an invoice for more money.

Even top-quality companies fall short on disclosure. For example, almost no company tells you how your policy's performance compares with the alternative of buying term insurance and investing on your own. Disclosure of this information — which has been advocated for years by the Consumer Federation of America Insurance Group — could help policyholders avoid the dual mistakes of dropping attractive policies and keeping unattractive ones.

You should buy a cash value policy only (1) after you have taken full advantage of investing your money in tax-sheltered retirement plans such as 401(k)s and IRAs and (2) if you're sure you'll keep the policy in force for at least 15 years. The reasons: The tax-sheltered plans are better investments than cash value policies, and because of the high selling expenses of most such policies, you lose part of your investment if you drop out early.

One strategy is to buy term insurance and invest your savings. The table below, which like most of the tables in this chapter was prepared by

## CASH-VALUE LIFE INSURANCE vs. TERM

This table shows how much you'd have to earn (or lose) each year to match the cash value of a Northwestern Mutual whole life policy if you bought Northwestern Mutual's term insurance and invested the difference in premiums elsewhere. For example, you would have to lose 23.4% each year for three years to have only $12,516 of cash value after paying total premiums of $22,338 (i.e., $7,446 x 3). Or, you would have to earn 3% for each of 10 years to have $80,609 of cash value after 10 years. The projected cash values are based on an 8.5% dividend interest rate.

| Year | Premium | Death benefit | Cash value | Average annual return |
|---|---|---|---|---|
| **1** | **$7,446** | **$400,000** | **$189** | **–97.3%** |
| **2** | " | **400,781** | **6,025** | **–44.4** |
| **3** | " | **403,155** | **12,516** | **–23.4** |
| **4** | " | **407,046** | **19,701** | **–13.2** |
| **5** | " | **412,429** | **27,630** | **–7.4** |
| **6** | " | **419,225** | **36,366** | **–3.7** |
| **7** | " | **427,419** | **45,961** | **–1.1** |
| **8** | " | **436,956** | **56,487** | **0.7** |
| **9** | " | **447,813** | **68,011** | **2.0** |
| **10** | " | **459,956** | **80,609** | **3.0** |
| **15** | " | **537,539** | **161,003** | **5.7** |
| **20** | " | **636,725** | **276,008** | **6.7** |

SOURCE: GLENN S. DAILY

fee-only insurance adviser Glenn Daily of New York City (212-249-9882), shows how much you would have to earn to make this strategy work. In the example shown, says Daily,

> It would take eight years before the cash value in the policy begins to equal what you would have if you bought cheap term insurance and invested at 0% interest. Up to that point, you would have more money if you bought term insurance and simply kept your savings under a mattress. The reason: All of the "savings" in the policy during the first year and 5% to 10% of them for several years afterward go to pay the agent's commissions and the company's other expenses for marketing, underwriting and administration.
>
> The problem with cash value policies is that you have to hold them a long time before they build up enough assets — that is, cash value — to begin to equal what you could get with other conservative investments. But many people just don't hold their policies for a long time. Less than half of cash value policies are held for at least 10 years, and less than one-quarter are held for 20 years. People lose far more money each year from ill-advised purchases of cash value policies than from the well-publicized insolvencies that attract media attention.

On the other hand, if you actually hold a cash value policy for a long time, it's likely that you'll do better than with term insurance. Cash value life insurance enjoys two significant advantages that make it a competitive long-term investment.

First, earnings grow tax-deferred within the policy and escape income tax entirely if you die. Your beneficiaries do not have to pay federal, state or local income tax on life insurance death benefits. (But they will have to pay estate taxes unless there is a third-party owner, such as an irrevocable trust, just as with any other asset.)

Second, if you cash in the policy, your cost basis is the sum of the premiums, without any reduction for the value of the insurance protection you've received. Say that you pay $1,500 a year into a universal life policy, then cash it in after 20 years and collect a cash value of $43,000. Your taxable gain is only $13,000, even though some of your money was used to pay insurance costs. In effect, these costs become tax-deductible, because they are not added back to your cash value when the taxable gain is computed.

Say you pay $1,500 in the first year, get $100 in interest and pay $100 in insurance costs within the policy. If you could cash in the policy and receive $1,500, the IRS says you don't have any gain, even though you earned $100 interest. In effect, the insurance costs were deducted from the interest earnings, so instead of having to pay income tax on $100 — which you would if you bought nondeductible term insurance and invested in a taxable CD — you don't owe any tax.

Cash value insurance produces the greatest benefit when it is held until death, because the accumulated investment earnings are free of income taxes. In most cases, the favorable tax treatment overcomes the high expenses, so your beneficiaries will receive more money on average than if you had invested the premiums in alternatives of similar risk, such as short-term municipal bonds or short-term bond funds.

## Selecting a Term Policy

When shopping for a term policy, you'll find that no company's policy is superior to others in all respects, so you'll have to make trade-offs. The important factors to consider are, in no particular order:

*Cost.* To measure costs, look at the present value of premiums over your intended holding period, plus or minus a few years. Or, if you don't compute present value, you won't go too far wrong just adding up the premiums.

*Guarantee period.* If premiums are not guaranteed, you need to consider the risk that the company will raise its rates in the future, or that you'll have to pay high premiums if you're no longer in good health.

Guarantee periods range from one to 20 years. State regulations have a big impact on guarantees; rules requiring that a company maintain a certain level of assets to back its term insurance liabilities affect the cost of providing long-term guarantees.

The National Association of Insurance Commissioners has proposed a regulation, awaiting adoption by individual states, that would increase the money that companies have to set aside to meet their obligations from term sales. If they are adopted in 1996, companies probably will

## RISKS OF TERM POLICIES

**RISK: If you don't keep the policy as long as you expected, you'll probably pay more than necessary for the coverage. Example: 10-year level term is cheaper than annual renewable term over 10 years, but it's more expensive in the beginning.**

WHAT TO DO:
- Give some thought to future needs as well as current needs.
- Compare policy costs for different periods to see the trade-offs.

**RISK: If you keep the policy longer than you expected, you'll probably pay more than necessary for the coverage. Example: Five-year level term is cheaper than 10-year level term over five years, but it's more expensive over 10 years.**

WHAT TO DO:
- Give some thought to future needs as well as current needs.
- Compare policy costs for different periods to see the trade-offs.

**RISK: If you buy a level-premium policy and are not in good health at the end of the level-premium period (usually five to 20 years), the premiums will increase steeply.**

WHAT TO DO:
- Choose annual renewable term.
- Convert to a cash-value policy.
- If you don't qualify, it probably means you're not in the best of health, so be pleased you have life insurance, even if it's not cheap.

**RISK: If the policy isn't renewable and you have trouble passing a medical exam, you might lose your coverage.**

WHAT TO DO:
- Choose a policy that is renewable to at least age 69.
- Convert to a cash-value policy.

**RISK: Nonguaranteed premiums may rise.**

WHAT TO DO:
- Choose a policy with a long guarantee period.
- Go with a company that has not raised its term rates in the past.

**RISK: If the company's cash-value policy isn't attractive and you want or need to convert, you'll pay more than necessary for permanent coverage.**

WHAT TO DO:
- Buy a low-load term policy that is convertible to a low-load cash-value policy (see the list on page 445).

**RISK: The company may get into financial trouble.**

WHAT TO DO:
- Choose a company with high financial-strength ratings.
- Don't worry excessively about it.

SOURCE: GLENN S. DAILY

raise the price of these policies or stop offering them altogether. Existing policies would not be affected. Meanwhile, if you need term for more than five years and want to lock in a guaranteed rate, you should buy a policy now, before the rate goes up — possibly by 25% or more.

*Renewability.* Most term policies are renewable to at least age 69, but there are exceptions. Renewability simply means that you have the right to keep the policy in force, but it doesn't guarantee that you'll be happy with the price, which rises with the years. Anyhow, try to get a policy that's renewable for as long as possible, unless a nonrenewable policy is available at a lower cost and you're sure your insurance need won't extend beyond the short renewability period.

*Convertibility.* This gives you the right to convert to one or more of the company's cash value policies without evidence of insurability. Find out how long you have the option to convert, and how attractive the company's cash value policies appear to be. If you buy a level-premium term policy and aren't able to demonstrate good health after an initial term period ends, it may make sense to convert because the cash value policy will be issued at standard rates, whereas the term insurance rates will reflect the company's expectation that the remaining policyholders are in poor health.

*Insurer's financial strength.* This is not as important for term as for cash value insurance. If history is a guide, you can expect death claims to be paid promptly and in full even when regulators take over a company. That happened in such cases of failure as Executive Life, Mutual Benefit and Confederation Life. The main risks of shaky financial condition are that nonguaranteed premiums may rise and that the conversion option will be much less valuable. A lesser risk is that the low guaranteed premium might not be honored.

A list of the major rating agencies and their phone numbers appears on page 443. Because ratings are revised continuously, check the current rating of any company that you are considering. Ask also whether the company is on a watch list for a possible change in its ratings.

There are hundreds of different kinds of term policies in the marketplace, but you can narrow the choices quickly with a few phone calls:

- Northwestern Mutual Life (call a local agent) offers competitive annual renewable term policies, convertible to high-quality, agent-sold cash value policies.
- USAA (800-531-8000) offers several types of term policies, convertible to no-commission cash value policies; it sells by phone and mail, and through salaried representatives.
- Wholesale Insurance Network (800-808-5810) offers several low-load policies from a handful of insurers. The policies usually are convertible to low-load cash value policies.
- Quotesmith (800-556-9393) provides free quotes of term insurance from its database of 160 companies and can sell

policies or refer you to agents who subscribe to its on-line quote service.

- Compulife (800-567-8376) gives you referrals of agents who are licensed to use its term-comparison software.

To sum up, the chart on page 440 shows the main risks of term insurance and how to deal with them.

## Choosing a Cash Value Policy

For most people, the important features to consider are (in no particular order): expected future performance, high early cash values, flexibility and the insurer's financial strength. Again, no insurance product is superior to all others in all respects, so you have to make trade-offs.

On large purchases, it's sensible to buy more than one policy for diversification. No matter how careful you are in choosing a policy, you can't eliminate the possibility of being disappointed. Spreading your purchase among several policies is as prudent for life insurance as it is for other investments, such as common stocks and mutual funds.

In judging future performance, many life insurance buyers confuse premiums with price. With cash value policies, you have to consider not only the premiums but also the cash values and the death benefits over the *entire period* that you might hold the policy. A policy with a higher premium for the same initial coverage could easily turn out to be a better buy if it produces higher benefits later or if it is based on more realistic assumptions about the insurance company's investment yields, death claims, and lapse rates (that is, the number of people who drop their policies each year).

The benefits you get for what you pay ultimately will be determined by the insurer's selling expenses, investment and underwriting expertise, administrative efficiency, lapse rates, reserve method, reinsurance costs, profit objective and treatment of existing policyholders. Unfortunately, no outsider can make a comprehensive examination of all these factors because the company keeps some of the necessary information to itself. So life insurance buyers typically rely on projections and illustrations of possible future benefits, supplied by the sales agent; histories of company performance prepared by the A. M. Best ratings company; and the

### PHONE NUMBERS OF RATING AGENCIES

| | |
|---|---|
| A. M. Best | 900-555-2378 |
| Duff & Phelps | 312-368-3100 |
| Moody's | 212-553-5377 |
| Standard & Poor's | 212-208-1527 |
| Weiss Ratings | 800-289-9222 |

ratings and reports of all major ratings agencies. (See list of ratings agencies at left.)

Sales illustrations are projections of future premiums, cash values and death benefits prepared by the company or its agents. Illustrations are useful for understanding how a policy works, because they show the effect of choosing different dividend options or premium amounts. With universal life, for example, an illustration can show what happens if you pay the maximum premium each year rather than just enough to keep the policy going. With traditional whole life, an illustration can show what happens if you use dividends to buy paid-up additions rather than to reduce the premium.

Illustrations are good for explaining concepts, but you should be very cautious about relying on the projected numbers — because it's easy for companies to produce projections that have little chance of coming true. For example, a company can assume that it will continue to earn the same rate of return for the next 50 years on the bonds in its investment portfolio, even though it knows that its new bonds are yielding less than its maturing ones.

A Society of Actuaries task force concluded in a 1992 report that illustrations should *not* be used to compare the expected performance of different policies, because the reasonableness of the underlying assumptions varies from one company to another. State insurance regulators are developing guidelines for illustrations, and many of the rosiest projections used today would probably be banned. So, be skeptical when one company claims it can provide the identical benefits that another company does, for a much lower premium, without explaining in detail how it can accomplish that feat. (Low-load policies can offer lower premiums because they save on commissions.)

Performance certainly does vary among companies, but sales illustrations are not a reliable indicator of these differences. If history is a guide, only about half the policies with illustrated values in the top 25% among their peers will actually deliver top-25% performance, as measured by interest-adjusted cost indexes for traditional whole life or cash values for universal life.

On the other hand, illustrations do tend to be reliable at predicting poor performers. If a policy has below-average illustrated values, it's not likely to deliver superior performance. For example, in A. M. Best's survey of 10-year universal life performance, only three out of 27 policies that had below-average illustrated cash-surrender values in 1984 actually performed in the top 25% in the 10-year period through 1993.

You can increase the chances that your policy will perform well by reducing the high selling expenses — agents' commissions and expenses for office rent, sales conferences, training and other benefits — that typically consume 15% to 25% of all premiums paid. Savings in distribution costs occur immediately and are therefore easy to verify. You can get a good idea of what you are paying by comparing the first-year premium with the first-year cash value on an illustration. Many policies sold by agents have *no* first-year cash value, because all of your money is used for commissions and other expenses. In contrast, no-commission policies usually have a very high cash value; the first-year cash value may even exceed the premium.

If you look for policies with (1) first-year cash values equal to at least 50% of the first-year premium and (2) long-term illustrated values that are the same or better than those of similar policies, you'll have a fine chance of getting top value for your money.

Here are two ways you can reduce the selling expenses of cash value policies:

*Consider low-load policies.* A few companies sell policies directly to consumers by mail and over the phone, or through fee-for-service insurance consultants and financial planners. For these policies, *first-year* distribution costs are usually less than 25% of the premium, versus more than 100% for most policies sold by agents.

The difference, of course, is the front-end-loaded commissions paid to agents. The lower costs show up in high cash values in the early years of the policy and, all other things being equal, lower premiums or higher long-term values. High cash values offer more protection than high financial-strength ratings, because they provide a safety net against unforeseen events that may move you to cash in the policy. You can dump the policy without a large loss if its performance is disappointing, as measured by the growth in death benefits and cash values in relation to a new policy that you could buy, or by the rate of return in relation to term insurance. A high cash value also gives you the ability to bail out if

## LOW-LOAD LIFE INSURANCE POLICIES

| Company | Policy name and description | Where to get them |
|---|---|---|
| **American Life of New York** | 5-Year Term, Variable Universal Life | Directly from company (800-872-5963) |
| **Ameritas** | Low-Load Universal Life, Low-Load Last Survivor Universal Life, Low-Load 5-Year Term, Low-Load Variable Universal Life | Directly from company (800-552-3553) or from fee-based advisers (800-255-9678) |
| **Federal Home Life** | Universal First-to-Die (first-to-die universal life) | Fee-based advisers affiliated with Fee For Service (800-874-5662) |
| **First Transamerica** | TransUltimate (universal life) | Fee-based advisers affiliated with Fee For Service (800-874-5662) |
| **John Alden** | Pioneer Universal Life, Pioneer Survivorship Life (universal life), Pioneer 10-, 15-, 20-Year Term | Fee-based advisers affiliated with Fee For Service (800-874-5662) |
| **Life of the Southwest** | FBTLife (5-, 10-, 15-year level premium term) | Fee-based advisers affiliated with distributors (800-228-4579) |
| **Lincoln Benefit** | Achiever VI (universal life), Entrepreneur II (term) | From company or from fee-based advisers (800-525-9287) |
| **Security Benefit** | Security Ultimate (universal life), Security Elite Benefit (variable universal life) | Fee-based advisers affiliated with Fee For Service (800-874-5662) |
| **Southland** | Legacy Immediate Equity (universal life), Survivorship IE | Fee-based advisers affiliated with distributors (800-872-7542, x 6518) |
| **USAA** | Universal Life, Whole Life, Annual Renewable Term, Seven-Year Term, 10-, 15-, 20-year level premium term | Directly from company (800-531-8000) |

Note: Many of these policies are available through the Wholesale Insurance Network (800-808-5810). They may not be available in all states. This list does not include savings bank life insurance or low-load policies that are available only to corporations, wealthy individuals or association members.

SOURCE: GLENN S. DAILY

the company's financial condition becomes questionable, as measured by a sudden drop in its financial-strength ratings. Even if you do nothing and the company is later taken over by state regulators, you'll be in a better position with a high cash value, because you can draw upon it to keep the policy going without having to throw good money after bad. The list above shows the main low-load policies.

*Look into blended policies.* You can reduce commissions on agent-sold policies by substituting a "blend" of term insurance and paid-up additions for high-commission whole life. The paid-up additions generally pay a commission of only 3% to 4% to the agent, whereas the commission on the whole life component is usually more than 50%. With a blend, a portion of the agent's commission, in effect, is retained within the policy to enhance future cash values and death benefits.

Agents often argue that blending is risky, but that's true only if you pay a lower total premium. If you add enough paid-up additions to the term and base components—so that the total premium is similar to the premium you would pay without blending — you'll actually reduce risk. The reason is that more money will be available within the policy to pay future premiums if necessary. Because blending reduces commissions, you may have to look around for an agent who will follow your request without trying to talk you out of it.

Blending is more common with traditional whole life than with universal or variable universal life. Whole life policies offered by Guardian, Massachusetts Mutual and Northwestern Mutual are a good place to start. Ask the agent to prepare two sets of illustrations, one for 100% whole life and another for the minimum whole life percentage (generally 10% to 40%), using the same initial death benefit and the same total premium in each case.

The table below compares a low-load policy with an agent-sold policy, with and without blending. The annual premium for all the policies is $7,500. Because of lower selling expenses, the low-load policy has higher cash values and death benefits for at least 10 years. This is true even though, here, the 7% credited rate of interest of the low-load universal life policy is 1.5% less than the 8.5% dividend interest rate of the whole life policy. It's reasonable to expect the 8.5% whole life rate to de-

## GETTING BETTER VALUE WITH LOW-LOAD AND BLENDED POLICIES

A lower commission for the agent translates into higher cash values and death benefits for you. You can reduce the agent's commission by buying a low-load (i.e., no-commission) policy or by blending low-commission term insurance and paid-up additions with high-commission whole life.

| | FULL-COMMISSION POLICY | | BLENDED POLICY (25% whole life, 75% term) | | LOW-LOAD POLICY | |
|---|---|---|---|---|---|---|
| Policy year | Death benefit | Cash value | Death benefit | Cash value | Death benefit | Cash value |
| 1 | $465,000 | $0 | $465,000 | $4,900 | $467,000 | $7,500 |
| 5 | 467,000 | 28,400 | 465,000 | 37,000 | 500,000 | 39,900 |
| 10 | 484,000 | 76,700 | 465,000 | 93,300 | 554,000 | 94,500 |
| 20 | 611,000 | 245,900 | 574,000 | 296,800 | 741,000 | 281,300 |

Issued to a male nonsmoker, age 40, $7,500 annual premium
Full-commission and blended policies: Whole life with 8.5% dividend interest rate
Low-load policy: Universal life with 7% credited interest rate

SOURCE: GLENN S. DAILY

cline over time as the company's portfolio yield is affected by lower interest rates, so the illustrated values in this comparison *understate* the advantage of the low-load policy. Agent-sold policies can catch up with low-load policies over the long run only if they have sufficient advantages in other pricing areas to offset the drag of high selling expenses.

The blended policy is about 25% whole life and 75% term and paid-up additions. The first-year cash value is $4,950 higher than with the 100% whole life version ($4,950 versus $0). The death benefit of the blended policy is lower for at least 20 years, but it will be greater well before you are likely to die. The table below shows the main risks of cash value life insurance and how to deal with them.

## RISKS OF CASH-VALUE POLICIES

RISK: **The policy might not perform as well as expected; that is, premiums may be higher than expected, or death benefits and cash values may be lower than expected.**

WHAT TO DO:
- Buy policies with high immediate cash values, so that you can switch to another policy with minimal loss if you're in good health.
- Reduce selling expenses with low-load policies or blended agent-sold policies, to give yourself an immediate performance advantage.
- Request sales illustrations using an interest rate 1% below the current rate, to reduce the risk of disappointment.

RISK: **The insurance company might get into financial trouble.**

WHAT TO DO:
- Choose carriers with high financial-strength ratings.
- Choose variable or variable universal life, so that you'll be able to get all of your money even if the company becomes insolvent.
- Diversify among companies.
- Buy policies with high immediate cash values, so that you can switch with minimal loss if you're in good health, or take out a maximum policy loan while waiting to see what happens.
- Choose a flexible-premium policy, so that you can stop paying premiums for a while.

RISK: **Your plans might change; for example, you might not need insurance for as long as you expected.**

WHAT TO DO:
- Buy policies with high immediate cash values, so that you can drop the policy with minimal loss.
- Choose a policy, such as universal or variable universal life, that lets you change the premium or amount of coverage.

RISK: **New types of policies might become available.**

WHAT TO DO:
- Buy policies with high immediate cash values, so that you can switch to a new policy with minimal loss if you're in good health.

RISK: **Service after the purchase might be unsatisfactory.**

WHAT TO DO:
- Deal with experienced agents or directly with the company's home office.
- Ask the company to appoint a new agent of record for your policy.
- Send a complaint to your state insurance department.

SOURCE: GLENN S. DAILY

# How Life Insurance Agents' Predictions Can Let You Down

In the 1980s, when everybody came to expect high interest rates on investments, insurers stepped up the marketing of "interest-sensitive" policies. They ground out glowing illustrations showing that you would not need to pay premiums after a few years, even as the policies' cash-surrender value and death benefits rose majestically. Those illustrations, known in the trade as ledger statements, have a capacity to mislead you badly if they are based on overly optimistic assumptions about various insurance costs and, most of all, the rate of return on the insurer's investments of policyholders' money.

In so-called vanishing-premium policies, you theoretically can pay large premiums for a few years and, by plowing all dividends back into additional insurance, generate enough internal tax-deferred earnings to pay for the policy for the rest of your life. But the dividends that agents show you to demonstrate how the premium can vanish are *not guaranteed.* Far from it. They are refunds paid out of surplus, the size of which depends mainly on the company's operating expenses and return on investments.

In the heat of competition, notably beginning in the mid-1980s, aggressive companies puffed up their policy illustrations. They did so by assuming that the high interest rates they were then earning on real estate loans and junk bonds would be available practically forever. Then came the economic slump of 1989–92. Commercial real estate values tumbled. Developers defaulted on their mortgages. And the low-rated bonds of financially shaky companies sank in value. Even insurers that had invested cautiously in government and high-quality corporate bonds had to reduce their dividends.

The predictable result is that some policyholders are now being told they'll have to pay more premiums than they expected when they bought the policies, and a number of them are filing lawsuits against the companies and their agents. Responsible insurers may keep their sales illustrations within reasonable bounds. But that does not stop their agents from grinding out ever-prettier numbers with their impressive new software. So cast a skeptic's eye on agents' numerology. Ask the agent to give you a copy of the company's responses to the Illustration Questionnaire prepared by the American Society of Chartered Life Underwriters and Chartered Financial Consultants. (This is a series of questions answered by the company about the assumptions underlying its projected policy values.) Stay with insurers that get high grades for claims-paying ability from two or more independent rating services. Ratings are not ironclad, but they are all you have to go on.

## Checking Your Insurer's Safety

You buy life insurance in case something happens to you. But what if something happens to your insurance company?

That's no idle question. In 1991 state regulators had to take over six major insurance organizations: the Executive Life Insurance companies of California and New York, First Capital Life of California, Fidelity Banker's Life of Virginia, Monarch Life and Mutual Benefit Life. All except Mutual Benefit and Monarch collapsed into insolvency because they were overloaded with junk bonds worth a fraction of their face value. In Monarch's case, the parent company went bankrupt, producing one of the biggest failures in the history of the life insurance industry. And it was followed by the failure of First Capital Life and its affiliates, in which American Express Corporation had a large ownership position. State regulators suspended payment of cash surrender values, but not death and annuity benefits, while state life insurance guarantee funds and the life insurance industry tried to patch together a plan to keep the promises made to the failed companies' policyholders. In 1994 seven life insurance companies failed or were taken over.

Before you buy any policy, check with your state insurance department to make sure the company has a license to operate in your state. This was a lesson learned the hard way for dozens of Koreans who were operating grocery stores in South Central Los Angeles during the 1992 riots. According to Sean Mooney of the Insurance Information Institute, these grocers fell victim to an insurance swindle that had them mailing monthly payments to a post office box in Chicago. Taxi drivers were hired in Chicago to forward the checks to the Cayman Islands. And when the grocers looked to their insurance companies for help after the riots, there was none.

If you are worried that your insurance company may collapse, your only readily available checkpoints are five independent ratings services that judge the ability of insurers to pay their claims. Yet until a little more than a year before it went under, Executive Life got top ratings from A. M. Best Company and Standard & Poor's.

Depending on their financial strength, every year insurance companies are assigned one of 15 letter ratings by A. M. Best. These range from A++ to F for firms in liquidation. A. M. Best bases its ratings on many factors affecting the insurer's financial stability, including policy-renewal rates and the performance of the firm's investments. An A++ or A+ is supposed to give strong reassurance that a life-insurance company will not fail. Of the 1,753 companies Best reported on in 1995, 215 were placed in its top rating categories — 50 received an unqualified A++ and 165 received A+. Fully 580 did not qualify for a letter rating because they did not meet the minimum size requirement or they lacked sufficient operating experience.

While Best is well known, several investment advisers to corporate-benefits departments find the ratings of Standard & Poor's, Moody's Investors Services and Duff & Phelps to be more thorough. Standard & Poor's top rating of AAA went to 47 companies out of more than 1,066 life and health companies on its evaluation list of April 30, 1995. As of mid-1995 Moody's had 10 U.S. life insurance companies out of 122 rated Aaa. Duff & Phelps gave its top rating of AAA to 49 out of 180 companies as of March 31, 1995.

You can get Best ratings by calling or writing to the insurers you are considering, or their agents. Or you can look up the ratings in *Best's Insurance Reports* at public libraries. For another free opinion, phone S&P at 212-208-1527, Moody's at 212-553-5377 or Duff & Phelps at 312-629-3833. And for a fee that depends on the extent of the request, you can get an opinion from Weiss Ratings, Inc. (800-289-9222).

## Discounts for Healthy Habits

Being conscientious about your health and fitness can trim not only your figure but also your insurance bill. Nonsmokers get 5% to 25% price breaks from almost all companies on their life, health and disability premiums. Some companies also give the discounts to policyholders who smoke only cigars or chew tobacco.

To qualify, you may have to pass a medical exam certifying that your weight, blood pressure and cholesterol levels are normal. You will also have to declare on a questionnaire that you exercise regularly. Allstate Insurance's term life policies, for instance, are roughly 15% cheaper for physically fit nonsmokers who say they exercise three to five times a week, use seat belts while driving and avoid excessive salt. But you must not have a high-risk occupation or hobby, such as auto racing.

If you suffer from hypertension, you can cut your premiums by as much as half by taking steps to correct your condition. Compared with those who have normal blood pressure, hypertensive people pay an average of 50% more for term insurance and up to 25% more for health policies. Both costs drop if the policyholder's blood pressure comes down. A 30-year-old man with moderately high blood pressure will pay $290 annually for a $100,000 renewable term life policy with Allstate. If he reduces his blood pressure to normal levels for a year or two while

## WHAT YOU PAY WHEN YOU'RE NOT A TOP RISK

People who have the best health histories and pass all the tests are classified as "standard" risks and pay the lowest rates. Individuals who don't quite make that grade are rated by certain "tables" and pay more. Here are examples of a $250,000 term policy and a $250,000 whole life policy offered by the United States Life Insurance Company for a 45-year-old man. The higher the table, the higher the number of claims the insurance company assumes it will receive each year from that group and the higher the premium charged. The company's anticipated claims above the norm are listed below under "Percent above standard premium."

| | TERM INSURANCE | | WHOLE LIFE INSURANCE | |
|---|---|---|---|---|
| CLASS | Annual premium | Percent above standard premium | Annual premium | Percent above standard premium |
| **Standard** (healthy individuals) | $395 | — | $3,143 | — |
| **Table 1** (e.g., mildly overweight people) | 490 | 25% | 3,755 | 20% |
| **Table 2** (e.g., diabetics) | 583 | 50 | 4,353 | 39 |
| **Table 4** (e.g., individuals with uncontrolled hypertension) | 770 | 100 | 5,547 | 77 |
| **Table 8** (e.g., people with liver problems) | 1,145 | 200 | 7,938 | 154 |
| **Table 12** (e.g., people with uncontrolled diabetes and abnormal EKG) | 1,520 | 300 | 10,328 | 231 |

SOURCE: MARVIN N. STRAUSS CLU, THE STRAUSS AGENCY

## Guidelines for Some Groups of People

- *People with health problems.* Over 90% of life insurance applicants pass the medical exam with flying colors and are considered so-called standard risks, but if you have a significant health problem, you'll probably have to spend more time finding a policy. People with the same condition may be treated more favorably by one company than another, because of more reliable mortality data, more liberal requirements or special arrangements with a reinsurer (that is, an insurance company that assumes some of the risk from the primary carrier). You can start by looking for low-load or high-quality agent-sold products, but you may need to extend your search. For difficult situations, an agent who specializes in impaired risks may be helpful in placing the coverage. Many agents have a relationship with impaired-risk specialists for hard-to-place cases, so it's probably easier to find them indirectly. Of course, if your employer or some organization you belong to offers a group policy that doesn't require a physical, carefully consider buying it.
- *Young people without dependents.* You probably don't need life insurance. Agents will tell you that it's costly to wait, because the premium rises every year and, even worse, you might become uninsurable. That's true, but it's far from the whole story. The vast majority of people do not become uninsurable from one year to the next. Also, if you save and invest the money you'd otherwise spend on unnecessary insurance, you'll probably have more than enough to cover the higher premiums later. If you insist on buying insurance now, stick with convertible term and put your savings into tax-deductible retirement plans or no-load mutual funds.
- *Married couples with one income.* You probably need insurance on the breadwinner's life, especially if you have children. Cheap term is likely to be more appropriate than cash value policies. However, if you already have a cash value policy, it probably is wise to keep it, and it might even make sense to put more money into it for education and retirement goals.

- *Dual-income couples.* You may or may not need insurance, depending on whether each of you can get by on your own income. If you can and you have children, it might make sense to buy a low-load second-to-die policy to provide for your children's support in the highly unlikely event that you both die. If neither income is enough by itself, you can buy two term policies. A first-to-die cash value policy might seem appropriate, but the selection is limited, and there is no performance history.
- *People in or near retirement.* If you want life insurance to provide a bigger estate for your heirs or to pay estate taxes, you'll need cash value policies. Consider buying more than one for diversification. If you already own life insurance, this is a good time to look at what you've got. You may be able to reduce the coverage or switch to an annuity, or you might find that your existing policies fit in well with your estate plan just as they are.

*Source: Glenn S. Daily*

maintaining a healthy lifestyle, his premiums sink to about $154. Insurers are willing to offer lower rates because people who reduce their high blood pressure with medication and diet have a near-normal mortality rate.

Such incentives are beginning to show up in health insurance policies, too. Employers are beginning to reward their employees who have healthy habits by giving rebates, or paying for a greater percentage of their health bills.

## Help for the Hard-to-Insure

If you have a serious health problem or hold a dangerous job, you probably will find that some insurance companies are willing to take chances and sell you life, disability and health policies. They cost you more — in extreme cases several times as much — or give you less coverage than a regular policy.

Ask an agent to refer you to an insurance broker who specializes in high risks. Brokers usually deal only through agents, and each is familiar with a number of insurance companies.

Even for a hard-to-insure person, term life insurance — straight protection without any cash value — is less expensive than whole life. Another option is to buy a so-called graded-death-benefit policy. With it, the death benefit gradually increases over a period of years until it equals the face value of the policy. The disadvantage is that if you should die shortly after the policy is issued, your survivors will receive less than the policy's face value.

If you are a high-risk person, you may not be able to get disability insurance at all. Though there are common standards that insurance companies follow, one person's medical problem may be viewed differently by various companies — with different conclusions. If you do qualify for a disability policy, expect to pay 20% to 100% more than the usual rate. You may be able to cut the premium by agreeing to accept lower monthly benefits, by waiting longer for benefits to begin and by collecting them for a shorter period of time. You may also reduce your premium by taking out a policy with a limited exclusion rider that disallows benefits if the disability is caused by a condition that existed before the policy's purchase. This type of plan, which covers other disabilities, costs only as much as the coverage sold to people who are not high-risk.

## Managing Your Existing Policies

If you put your policies in a drawer and forget about them, you may miss out on opportunities to spend your insurance dollars more wisely. For example, you might not need as much coverage now as you did when you bought the insurance, or you may be paying more than necessary for what you do need. For each type of policy, here are some things to re-examine periodically:

- *Term insurance.* Are the premiums still competitive with current policies? If you own a level-premium policy, you should compare prices when the initial period ends, usually after five to 20 years. You should also compare prices whenever an insurer raises the premiums above what you had expected to pay when you bought the policy.

- *Traditional whole life.* Are you taking advantage of the right to use dividends to buy paid-up additions? Are you paying for any riders that you no longer need? Do you have policy loans that you could pay off with money that is earning less than the loan costs? If you no longer need as much coverage, will the insurer let you reduce the face amount and premium in a partial surrender? Is the policy still performing well in relation to a new cash value policy or term insurance? This can be difficult to determine; one solution is to get an in-force illustration and then request a rate-of-return analysis from the Consumer Federation of America, 1424 16th Street NW, Suite 600, Washington, D.C. 20036 (202-387-6121). (An in-force illustration is a year-by-year projection of death benefits and cash values, similar to a sales illustration for new policies.)
- *Universal life.* Is the planned premium still sufficient to keep the policy going? Your annual statement may tell you when the policy will expire under various assumptions about future premiums and interest rates. Is the policy still performing well? Look at the annual statement each year to see what the insurance and expense charges and the interest rate are. If the interest rate seems low in relation to seven-year Treasury note yields or if the cost-of-insurance rate is higher than what the agent told you it would be when you bought the policy, you should request an in-force illustration from the agent or the company's policyholder-service department. If your insurance need has decreased, consider reducing the face amount of the policy, but watch out for partial surrender charges. It may also make sense to put more money into the policy for other savings goals, such as education funding — if the interest rate and expense charges are attractive. You can get this money out later by taking withdrawals or loans.
- *Variable universal life.* Ask the same questions as with universal life, with a few additions. Are the investment funds performing well? An annual report will discuss fund performance, and you

can get additional information from Morningstar publications (800-876-5005). Is your allocation of premiums and account value among the various stock and bond funds still appropriate? You may want to rebalance your allocation or make adjustments to reflect changing needs. For example, if an international stock fund has performed exceptionally well, consider shifting some of the gains to other funds within the policy, to restore your desired allocation. If you own stock funds with large gains outside the policy and want to reduce your exposure to the stock market, consider shifting from stocks to bonds within the policy, rather than incurring income tax by liquidating your other investments.

Before dropping any cash value policy, consider a tax-free exchange (called a 1035 exchange, referring to the tax code section) to another life insurance policy or a deferred annuity. This lets you postpone income tax on gains within the policy. If the premiums you've paid exceed the surrender value (so you have no taxable gain), a tax-free exchange lets you use this excess cost basis to shelter future gains. This is a valuable benefit that shouldn't be carelessly discarded.

# Knowing What to Expect from Social Security

A vast system of social insurance helps see one in six Americans through the expanding years of old age or the hardships of illness or death. You don't have to be poor or pass a means test to receive Social Security benefits. You just have to have worked in a covered occupation long enough — as briefly as 18 months in rare cases. Almost all occupations are covered.

When an American breadwinner dies, his or her dependent children up to college age are usually entitled to monthly income checks. Similarly, benefits usually flow to a surviving spouse until the youngest child is 16 years old. Widows and widowers can again get benefits at age 60, this time for life. Parents under age 29 earn the right to survivors' benefits for their families after paying Social Security taxes for a mere 18 months, provided they have been married for at least that period of time. Older people need more so-called work credits — up to 10 years' worth for those born before 1930.

As generous as they may seem, survivors' benefits surely do not eliminate the need for life insurance. For a 35-year-old parent with a relatively high annual income of $50,000 who died in 1995, survivors' benefits ranged up to $2,264 a month. The survivors' benefits for the average family were much lower, $1,288 a month for a widow and two children. But like all other Social Security payments, survivors' benefits rise each January to match the increase in the cost of living during the 12 months through the previous September.

Children are eligible for survivors' income until their 18th birthday, with an extension to age 19 if they're still attending high school full-time. A child who becomes disabled before age 22 continues getting income for as long as the disability persists. So does a parent who takes care of the child.

But a working parent or a child who holds a job may lose some or all of his or her benefits by earning more than a limited wage. Here's how the system works:

For every two dollars earned above $8,160 in 1995 by a person under age 65, Social Security took back one dollar in benefits. So if your 1995 benefit was $12,000, earning $32,160 would have wiped out every penny of it. Starting at age 65, the penalty eases; in 1995 the earnings threshold was $11,280. If you're between 65 and 70 years old, each three dollars of higher earnings costs one dollar of Social Security. There's no penalty after age 70.

Social Security also pays income to disabled wage earners and their families. To qualify, you must be a lot worse off than you would have to be to collect on a disability insurance policy. You must be so severely disabled, physically or mentally, that you won't be able to do any kind of work for at least a year. Or else your doctor must attest that your illness is expected to end in death. If you lose your sight, though, you can work for limited pay and still collect disability income. General disability coverage usually starts in the sixth month of disability and ends at age 65 if you live that long. Quite often, applications are rejected at first. They can be appealed, with some hope of reconsideration.

After 24 months of disability, beneficiaries become eligible for

Medicare, Social Security's hospital and medical insurance plan designed primarily for retirees.

If you are under age 24, you earn Social Security disability coverage after working for 18 of the previous 36 months. The work time expands with age, reaching five years (20 calendar quarters) for people ages 31 through 42. The longest anyone has to work to qualify is 10 years.

Income extends to your spouse and one child, or to two children, under the same conditions as survivors' payments. The maximum benefit for a single disabled 25-year-old in 1995 was $1,409 a month; the benefit increased to $2,113 if the recipient had a spouse and children. The national average family benefit for 1995 was $1,178.

## Avoiding Mistakes with Your Health Policy

How much should you be paying for health insurance, and what kind should you buy?

Unless you can join a group plan through your company or professional association, you will have to buy an individual policy. Each is custom-made according to age, health status, region and the deductible, so the costs may vary greatly. At Blue Cross/Blue Shield, for instance, a 35-year-old single man might pay around $2,600 a year, depending largely on his health and the type of coverage, while a family of four might pay close to $5,800. Again, this would vary considerably by region (and other factors), costing much less in California (where there is strong competition from HMOs) and much more in New York. Policies that provide a set dollar amount for each day in the hospital may be good supplemental coverage, but are not intended to replace your basic health-insurance plan.

The indispensable coverage for most people is a comprehensive major medical policy covering hospitalization, outpatient services and doctors' bills or membership in an HMO. Major medical policies are available from Blue Cross/Blue Shield and commercial insurance companies. The policies make you pay a maximum of 20% of most expenses in addition to a certain deductible, but no more than $1,000 in any one year. And the best plans place no ceiling on benefits. (For more, see Chapter 14, "Cutting Your Health-Care Costs.")

# Long-Term-Care Insurance

A long stay in a nursing home can wipe out a lifetime of savings. Medicare pays for 20 days in a skilled nursing facility and part of the cost for the next 80 days, but only after a stay in a hospital, and pays nothing for long-term custodial care. Even care in your own home can reduce you to a pauper's level, though not quite as rapidly. Studies indicate that more than 40% of all Americans who turn 65 years old in the mid-1990s will eventually enter a nursing home, and many others will require paid help to continue living at home. The numbers are bound to increase as the baby boomers grow older. Well over one-fifth of all Americans will be older than 65 in the year 2030.

More than 100 companies and 26 Blue Cross plans offer a variety of long-term-care policies. Some pay as much as $200 a day toward a range of benefits, including skilled nursing care at home and in nursing homes. They also cover custodial care if you don't need medical attention but do require some help with dressing, eating and walking. The best policies include home care as well as day care in a nursing center. Some 968 employers offer long-term-care insurance, and over 400,000 policies have been sold, according to the Health Insurance Association of America.

Health-insurance costs vary tremendously, depending on your age, when you buy the policy and the benefits you elect. Though long-term care is rarely needed for people in their 50s and 60s, the price is far lower during those years than it is if you wait until you are age 70 or older. For example, the average cost for a policy paying $80 a day for nursing-home care and $40 a day for home health care with a maximum coverage period of four years is about $440 a year at age 50. At age 65, the cost of such a policy is about $898, and at age 79, it goes up to about $3,727. And with 5% compounded inflation protection, which ensures that you won't lose benefits as long-term-care costs surge, prices rise to $630 a year at age 50, $1,452 at age 65 and $5,076 at age 79.

Ask your insurance agent these key questions before you buy:

- Does the policy cover the whole spectrum of nursing care? "Skilled care" generally includes such services as giving injections that can be performed only by (or under the direct supervision of) nurses, physical therapists or other medically trained experts. "Intermediate care" must also be under the supervision of skilled medical personnel, but registered nurses are not required to be on 24-hour duty. "Custodial care" does not require highly trained or licensed people. Most long-term nursing-home patients need custodial care, as do patients in their own homes. "Day care" is for people who live at home but need supervision, or company, while they are up and around.

Look for a policy that provides all these kinds of care if you should ever need them, that will cover you even if you need only intermediate or custodial care, and that allows you to enter a nursing home without a prior hospital stay.

- How generous is the daily benefit? It can range all the way from $25 (for at-home care) to $200 (for nursing-home care). The nationwide average for care in a nursing home is $30,000 to $40,000 a year. Home care including physical therapy, help with medication and preparation of food costs at least half that much.
- How long does a person have to be in a home before benefits begin? Some policies cover you from the moment you enter a nursing home. Others require that you be confined for a certain number of days, usually 20 to 100, before payments start. You might want to remember that the longer the waiting period, the lower your insurance premiums will be. Avoid any policy that makes prior hospitalization or a stay in a skilled nursing home a prerequisite for coverage.
- How long do benefits last? Plans typically cover you for your lifetime in nursing homes.
- Does the policy include protection against inflation?
- Are any illnesses, injuries or pre-existing conditions excluded from coverage? Don't buy a policy that excludes nursing-home stays due to mental or nervous disorders such as Parkinson's or Alzheimer's disease. And be sure the policy is guaranteed renewable.

# Selecting the Best Disability Policy

The biggest gap in many people's insurance protection is the absence of a disability policy. Even if you are young and healthy, the odds are uncomfortably short that someday you may need such coverage. Almost half of all people now age 35 will be incapacitated for three months or longer before they're 65 years old. So, for protection in case you are laid up, it makes sense to buy a disability insurance policy. It can cost from a few hundred dollars to $1,500 or more a year.

In tailoring your policy, aim to replace 60% to 70% of your current pretax earnings. That should be enough to maintain most of your spending power, because disability benefits are tax-free if you have paid for your own insurance. Don't rely on Social Security to replace your lost wages in case of serious illness or accident. As explained above, to get disability benefits from that source, you must be so severely disabled, physically or mentally, that you won't be able to do any kind of work for at least a year or you must be suffering from a fatal illness. Even then you will have to wait at least five months from the onset of the disability for payments to begin. The average benefit in 1995 was $1,076 a month for a family.

You are probably best off with coverage that provides lifetime benefits, but you can save hundreds of dollars a year in premiums by settling for coverage that will pay you benefits to age 65. Reducing the duration of benefits further may leave you unprotected against a catastrophic disability. A better way to reduce premiums is to increase the number of months you must be disabled before the policy starts paying. Take a man age 35 who wants a $1,000 benefit per month. If benefit payments begin one month after he is disabled, his policy at Minnesota Mutual would cost him about $746 a year. But if he increases the waiting period to three months, the price falls to $412. A four-month or six-month waiting period would further reduce these premiums.

Recognize the difference in quality between a Concorde supersonic jet and a one-prop puddle jumper, and then realize that the differences in protection among disability policies is even greater. That difference most often explains the disparity in policy premiums. Look for a policy with the fewest exclusions. Generally the fewer the exclusions, the higher the quality of the policy. You don't want a policy that allows the insurance company to point out an exclusion that denies your benefit payments after you're disabled. Zero exclusions would be the ultimate choice.

Disability-income policies offer more riders than an old John Wayne western. A few are important and worthwhile. To protect yourself against inflation during a long-term claim, you can choose a rider that will increase monthly benefits automatically to a specified annual maximum. If you go all-out, a rider can push up your premium by 25% or more. Limit your cost-of-living boosts to a yearly percentage (4%, 6% or 8%), depending on what you expect inflation will be in the future. Inflation since 1967 has averaged 5.55%. To get real inflation protection, be certain to select a cost-of-living benefit that increases on a compound, not simple, basis.

One of the latest riders, available from The Guardian and a few other companies, lets you order a large addition to your benefits during periods of extended disability. Called a future increase rider, it can catch your income up to the merit raises you got before you were sidelined, as well as keep pace with inflation. But you may have to wait many months for the increase to take effect. Activation occurs after the next anniversary date of your policy, plus a waiting period equal to the one for regular benefits. The Guardian's future increase rider adds 10% a year to your original premium.

Still another rider to consider ensures your eligibility for long-term-care insurance. For the price of its basic policy bought before age 45, CNA, a leading writer of long-term-care insurance, lets you convert your disability coverage into a high-quality long-term-care policy anytime from age 55 to 72. UNUM Life Insurance Company guarantees your right to add long-term-care insurance to your disability policy, often at a discount from the ordinary premium for people your age. This opportunity is restricted to four 90-day periods when you're 56, 59, 62 and 65 years old.

Two things you don't want an insurer to do are to raise your premiums and cancel your coverage. Any disability contract worth considering should be at least guaranteed renewable. The best type of policy is noncancelable; it both guarantees renewal and freezes the premium at its original level for as long as you keep the insurance. Above all, buy a policy that covers all types of disabilities and that also protects you if you are only partially disabled. Some weasel-worded contracts give the company an "out" by considering you to be disabled only if you are confined to home.

The most important decision is to choose the right insurance company. If you become disabled, you will be destined to have a relationship that may last for years. A few companies write most of the high-quality individual disability policies. The leaders include Connecticut Mutual, Minnesota Mutual, Mutual of New York, Northwestern Mutual, Paul Revere, Provident Life and Accident, and UNUM.

## Auto Policies

The cost of auto insurance has doubled in the last 10 years. The standard policy in a liability state contains six basic types of coverage: bodily-injury liability, property-damage liability, uninsured motorist, medical payments, collision and comprehensive. In the 14 no-fault states, personal injury protection is also available. This insurance provides medical and wage-loss benefits to a person injured in a vehicle accident, no matter who is to blame.

Don't skimp on bodily-injury liability and property-damage liability coverage. If you or anybody driving your car with your permission is in an accident in which someone is killed or injured, this coverage pays for an attorney to defend you against lawsuits by victims of the accident. It also pays other court costs and any judgments against you. Property-damage liability covers property that you do not own. The average driver should carry a policy that would pay up to $100,000 for a single injury, and up to $300,000 for all injuries in any one accident. It should also cover up to $50,000 in property damage. If you have substantial assets or a high salary that could be seized to pay off a court judgment that exceeds your auto coverage, raise your bodily-injury liability limits to $500,000 or more. If you need further coverage, consider an umbrella policy. A $1 million umbrella costs about $150 to $200 a year in many states, and protects you in case you are sued, by offering additional protection that exceeds the dollar limits on your auto and homeowner's policies.

In some states you are required to buy uninsured-motorist coverage. It pays you for injuries, pain and suffering caused by a hit-and-run driver or someone who cannot pay a judgment. If you have adequate health and disability insurance where you work, you may not need medical-payments coverage. It may largely duplicate protection already supplied by your regular medical policy.

Many are the ways to save on your policy. According to the Insurance Information Institute, you should take as large a deductible as you can afford on collision and comprehensive, which covers fire, theft and vandalism. The deductible is the amount you agree to pay before the insurance kicks in. For instance, increasing the deductible to $500 from the common $200 may reduce your collision premium about 15% to 30%. A $1,000 deductible can save you as much as 40%. If your car is paid for or more than five years old, or if its value is under $1,500, consider dropping collision and comprehensive coverage.

Shop around for companies that offer the deepest discounts. The insurer may give you a discount if you have a good driving record. Driver training could cut as much as 15% off your premium. And people age 50 and older can often get discounts of 10% to 20%.

Canvass companies for price quotes. To get a benchmark price, call State Farm. It's the nation's largest auto insurer and, in many areas, one of the least expensive. You will also want to learn about a company's reputation for service. Check with your state's insurance department. The larger states, including Illinois, New York and California, publish annual lists of companies with the highest and lowest percentage of consumer complaints.

As you survey the companies, find out what you can about which of them are most forgiving if you have an accident. For example, if you are at fault for an accident that results in a payment of more than $400, the Nationwide Insurance Company will usually raise your rates 30% for the next three years, while State Farm may disqualify you for a discount — or if you already have one, may withhold it for three to six years. Companies will also reward you for accident-free years. Nationwide does not raise your rates in the situation mentioned above if you have been a policyholder for at least five years and have not had an accident in the past three.

There are often significant differences in collision and comprehensive premiums for various car makes and models. Cars that are easily damaged in accidents, are popular for joyriders or are a valuable source of spare parts are more expensive to insure in every state. Collision and comprehensive insurance is cheaper on cars that are harder to damage and easier to repair.

Many states have drafted insurance companies into the war against auto theft. If you live in one of those states and you have installed special alarms or other antitheft devices, you can arrange for your premiums to be reduced; you might get 10% to 25% off the comprehensive premium. There are many other steps that drivers everywhere can take to improve their insurance against auto theft.

You will probably have to bear some of the expense of renting a car while waiting for the insurance settlement. Most policies pay about $15 a day toward a rental car. Renting is likely to cost you two or three times that much per day, and you may not get a settlement within a month. Thus, it is wise to buy a little-known rider, which at State Farm typically costs $15 to $40 a year, depending on your age and location, and extends your period and amount of coverage. The rider also pays up to $400 for meals, lodging and transportation while you are waiting for your own car and covers a substantial share of your policy's deductible if you have an accident driving the rental car.

Your insurance coverage for the theft of accessories or possessions you have in the car may not be as extensive as you expect. Some insurance companies that classify removable radios as a portable accessory do not cover their theft. If you have resorted to toting your expensive stereo or radio around when you are out of the car, consider buying a disguise for it instead. For about $20, a plain plastic front gives your equipment the look of an ordinary factory-installed radio. You should also check with your insurance agent for car phone coverage. If a phone is a portable, it should be scheduled for coverage under a homeowner's policy. If a car phone is permanently installed, it should be added by endorsement to the auto policy.

Neither your auto policy nor any extra coverage applies to other things that a thief might steal from your car, such as a $1,000 set of golf clubs or a $400 designer blazer. But you are probably covered anyway. Most homeowner's policies apply to anything taken by someone who breaks into your car. There is a hitch, though: You have to prove that the doors were locked at the time of the theft.

Whatever kind of insurance you are buying, you can save money and worry by remembering this: Never risk more than you can afford to lose. But don't pay to insure what you can afford to risk.

# Homeowner's Policies

Every owner of a house or apartment needs insurance to protect his or her residence and its contents against calamity, but how much coverage is enough? The amount you should have depends on the replacement cost of your house. That is, what you would have to spend to rebuild your castle as it now stands.

Insurance companies offer policies that cover your home and its contents for 100% of their replacement cost. Premiums are higher, of course, than for a standard homeowner's policy. You also can add a package deal to a standard policy that guarantees replacement costs for home and contents. Extra coverage for the contents, for example, tacks only an extra dollar or two per $1,000 onto your annual premiums. But not all houses are eligible for total coverage. Most insurers won't guarantee the replacement cost of damage to older homes that have handiwork that would be expensive if not impossible to replace, and the construction of some older homes might not meet current fire codes.

Insurers recommend that you insure your home for 100% of its replacement cost. However, total losses are relatively rare and you may be adequately covered for partial damage with 85% of the replacement cost. Be sure that your policy indexes the replacement cost to inflation. And if you make a substantial improvement to your house, raise your coverage to reflect its new value.

Although standard homeowner's policies cover your personal possessions, they set limits on what you can claim. Usually they reimburse you only for what you paid for the item — minus depreciation — and not for what it would cost to replace it today. That's why policies that cover replacement costs of contents have become so popular. Your yearly premium may go up about 10%, but the extra protection is worth it.

If you have a home-based business, a standard homeowner's policy provides coverage for about $2,000 of office equipment, including personal computers and typewriters. Such a policy can generally be expanded to cover $15,000 of property. The policy does not cover liability costs related to the operation of the business. For example, if someone delivering business-related goods falls in your driveway and decides to sue, your homeowner's insurance would not cover you. A separate business insurance policy would be needed.

You can hold down your insurance costs by taking advantage of special deals offered by most companies. There are premium discounts of up to 20% on new homes, 2% to 5% for installing dead-bolt locks and smoke detectors and 15% to 20% if you put in an elaborate fire and burglar alarm. Allstate reasons that retirees age 55 and older are often at home and gives them a 10% discount on homeowner's policies.

Increase your deductible to $500 from the standard $250, and you will save on your annual premium. How much depends on the company you select, the state you live in and the amount of insurance you buy. But never scrimp on overall coverage just to keep costs down.

No homeowner's policy covers all perils. The most popular, called HO-3, provides top-of-the-line coverage. It will reimburse you not only for fire and windstorm, but also if your water pipes freeze and burst, though not for floods or earthquakes. For that you need to seek extra coverage at higher cost.

If you live in an apartment, a co-op or condominium, you also need insurance to protect you from fire, burglary and even liability. True, landlords, co-op corporations and condo associations have insurance. But their policies cover only the building itself and mishaps that occur in common areas. So you need your own policy.

It should cover excess living expenses (for example, if your apartment is damaged by fire, the insurance company will pay for your stay in a hotel) and full replacement costs for articles that are stolen or destroyed. Apartment insurance, which 41% of renters carry, generally costs anywhere from $90 to $300, with a standard deductible of $250. Homeowner's and tenant's policies set low limits on the payments for personal articles, such as jewelry, furs, silverware and collectibles. But you can buy endorsements that protect your valuables at an additional cost — $10 to $30 a year for $1,000 of value on jewelry, or about $12.50 a year for $2,500 coverage on silverware, depending on where you live.

Consider buying a personal articles policy. Under it, the value of your personal articles is agreed upon in advance, and the coverage includes loss or mysterious disappearance, which is not covered under most homeowner's policies.

Your homeowner's policy does include some liability coverage. That pays your legal expenses to defend yourself in case you are sued for injuries to people on or off your property, and pays the damages if you lose or settle the claim.

But what if you get sued for ramming into a highly paid executive on a ski slope and crippling him for life? The possibility is remote, yet if you were hit by such a lawsuit, the $100,000 or so that most homeowner's or renter's policies pay on such claims wouldn't go far. Ask your agent about higher liability limits in an umbrella policy. This supplements the protection you already have against injury claims in your homeowner's and automobile policies. As noted earlier, you usually can buy a $1 million policy for $150 to $200 a year, and a $2 million policy for an additional 50%.

The best contracts cover almost every kind of liability claim except those related to business activities. They should protect you if you are sued for libel, slander or invasion of privacy, malicious prosecution, wrongful eviction, defamation of character or discrimination. Some policies insure against bodily injury or property damage resulting from your use of reasonable force to protect persons or property. Your policy should extend to everyone in your household who is related to you by blood, marriage or adoption, including children away at school.

## Making a Household Inventory

Close your eyes and try to list all your living-room furnishings or the contents of your jewelry box. If you have trouble coming up with a complete tally, imagine how hard it would be when you are upset, after a fire or burglary. Making a written inventory of your household goods can be one of the best money-saving steps you can take. A list not only guarantees that any insurance claim you submit after a burglary or a fire will be complete, but it also assures you of a smooth claims process. Your insurance company probably can give you an inventory form to fill out.

The Insurance Information Institute recommends a video inventory as a time-saving measure. A quick shot inside the closet doors, accompanied by your recorded verbal descriptions, will save you from having to write up the entire contents. Some independent claim services and camera stores will provide — for a fee — a total video inventory of your home, or you may prefer for privacy's sake to do it yourself.

Insurers are not likely to question claims based on such inventories, especially if you submit them along with photos, receipts or appraiser's statements for valuable items. You should leave a copy of your inventory of household goods with your insurance agent or in your safe-deposit box.

What should go into your inventory? Write down the date you bought each item of value, plus its price. If an appraiser has estimated the value of any of them, record the figure and the date. Make sure the appraisal is precise and explicit. Highly generalized descriptions will not back up a claim. In a written inventory, describe each object as graphically as possible. Be sure to include its age, brand name, size, model number and other relevant details. For tableware, note the manufacturer, pattern and number of place settings.

For some types of property, though, you may wish to lump together a number of articles and attach a single estimate of value. This is a wise tactic with clothing. Unless you have closets full of designer evening gowns, there is no sense driving yourself crazy counting and describing everything in your wardrobe. Even a couple of priceless Hawaiian shirts should not be too hard to describe if an insurance company asks you to. For more, see Chapter 21, "Getting the Best in Services," in the section titled "Keeping Records to Reduce Your Loss."

CHAPTER 14

# Cutting Your Health-Care Costs

Though President Clinton's plan to re-engineer our health-care system was DOA, it stirred the country's desire for change. The feeling is strong that the system has to be altered fundamentally, but in ways that would be far less extensive, expensive and intrusive than Clinton's total health reform. The search is on for means to hold down the climbing costs of care.

Already market forces and a flood of state reform laws are revamping the nation's health-care system and reducing medical inflation. The cost of care continues to rise, but the rate of medical inflation has slowed steadily since it peaked in 1990 at 9%. The increase in 1994 was 4.8%. There is a surplus of hospitals and of medical specialists, so more of these providers are willing to discount their services. Meanwhile, more employers are offering financial incentives to their workers to switch to health maintenance organizations for their medical-insurance coverage. Because HMOs operate on flat prepaid fees from members, they work hard to reduce expenses.

But medical costs are still steep enough that you should take every sensible step to contain the price of your own family care. The average fee for a visit to the doctor has increased almost fivefold in the last two decades, from $11 to more than $50, and the average cost of a day in the hospital has soared from $74 to roughly $1,000 (in some cases, even more). Though health-insurance policies subsidized by your employer may cover most of your bills, you may well face some sizable uninsured costs if a family member becomes ill or injured. But you *can* negotiate with your doctor, save on drugs and use other safe strategies to trim the bills that your policy does not pay:

- Ask your doctor to lower his or her price — if you consider it out of line or think that your steady patronage entitles you to a discount. Physicians' fees are surprisingly negotiable.
- Save on drugs. Health insurance may pay up to 80% of your pharmaceuticals bill, but your 20% payment will be of a smaller amount if you buy generic drugs. Almost all are virtually identical to brand-name pharmaceuticals. Ask your doctor to write out the generic name or to note on his or her prescription that the pharmacist may substitute a generic equivalent of a brand-name drug.
- Buy from a chain drugstore or mail-order firm. Because they buy in bulk, you'll probably get a better price than from an independent druggist. No central source lists mail-order firms; but the American Association of Retired Persons runs a pharmacy service that is open to non–AARP members. By calling 800-456-2277, you can order free catalogues that list more than 1,500 generic and brand-name products. Two reliable mail-order companies are Express Pharmacy Service and Action Pharmacies. Express (800-926-8850) offers only prescription drugs. Action (800-452-1976) sells both prescription and over-the-counter drugs. For names of other mail-order companies, ask your doctor or call your health plan's administration office.
- Do comparison shopping for a dentist, an important step because only one out of every two Americans with employer group health coverage has dental insurance. In New York, for example, you can pay anywhere from $20 to $75 for a routine cleaning.

  You can go to a clinic at any of the 55 U.S. dental schools for simple procedures. Clinics charge fees that are roughly half of what you would pay a regular dentist. Students are in the final two years of their four-year dental school education, and you will be relieved to know that they are closely supervised. The trouble is, they may keep you in the chair up to three times as long as experienced dentists.

  A less trying way to reduce costs may be to seek out a dental clinic run by a hospital. These clinics are staffed by new graduates. They are faster than students and command higher fees.

Still, they charge as much as one-third less than private practitioners. Or consider a prepaid dental plan, which can lower costs for you and your family.

- Reduce your costs of eyeglasses and contact lenses. A basic step is to recognize the distinctions among ophthalmologists (medical doctors who diagnose and treat all eye disorders), optometrists (those licensed to give eye exams, determine if you have vision problems and prescribe glasses and contact lenses but who are not medical doctors) and opticians (technicians who make and fit prescription lenses but have no medical training — only about half the states require formal licensing for opticians).

  Ophthalmologists charge $30 to $90 for a routine exam and up to $250 for a pair of soft lenses. They provide the contact lenses that they prescribe, but usually you must take an ophthalmologist's prescription for ordinary eyeglasses to an optician.

  If you don't have complex vision problems, you may not need an exam by an ophthalmologist. True, everybody should have his or her eyes checked by one of them to spot eye diseases or disorders; the American Academy of Ophthalmology recommends that people 20 to 39 years old should see an ophthalmologist every three to five years; those ages 40 to 65, every two to four years; and people older than 65, every one to two years. Anyone who works for long periods staring at a computer should have an *annual* exam by an ophthalmologist, simply because we do not know what the long-term effects of such activity may be.

  For a *routine* eye exam, an optometrist may suffice, but be careful: An article in the October 1993 *Review of Optometry,* titled "Cheap Exams, Expensive Glasses," reports that some optometrists continue to mark up the price of glasses in order to charge a lower eye-exam fee, which attracts new customers. The trade magazine *20/20* in its 1994 Group Buying Survey found little difference between optometrists' and opticians' prices. The cheapest option for buying glasses is probably large optical chain stores, where you can get your eyes tested, choose from a large selection of frames and have prescriptions made into glasses in an in-store laboratory. But an article in the August 1993 *Consumer Reports* found that people who bought at these large stores were less satisfied with their service than those who went to individual practitioners. The chains that received the highest ratings by *Consumer Reports* were Price Club Optical, For Eyes, Frame-n-Lens and Visionworks.

By far the most important step to control your medical costs — and your treatment — is to find the health-insurance policy that meets your needs at a reasonable price. It should be a comprehensive policy, covering all possible maladies, plus hospital care and, ideally, dental care. Don't waste your money on the so-called dread-disease policies, which insure you (at high cost) against specific illnesses such as cancer. That's like insuring only part of your car. You and your family need *total* coverage.

Unless you are already covered by a plan where you work, look for a policy that picks up at least 80% of your doctors' bills, and 80% of your stay in a semi-private hospital room. Some policies will even pay 100% for a "reasonable" period of time in a hospital. You can get such coverage with an *individual major medical policy.* To find out which insurance companies in your state offer such policies, call your state's Department of Insurance. Blue Cross/Blue Shield and Mutual of Omaha offer individual policies in most states.

Because this insurance is so expensive, anyone considering leaving a job that provides insurance should be aware of the law known as COBRA (for Consolidated Omnibus Reconciliation Act). It enables you to continue group coverage for 18 months, though at fairly high rates (see below). Another option is to find out if your policy can be converted from a group to an individual rate. This would be less expensive and offer fuller benefits than if you just went out and bought an individual policy.

The drawback of Blue Cross/Blue Shield is the cost. Its fees, among the highest in the nation, vary widely from place to place but commonly run close to $2,600 a year for an individual and $5,800 for a family of two adults and any number of children under age 19. On top of the fees, the yearly deductibles can be high: from $100 to $5,000, depending on your premiums.

Most health plans limit the total benefits you can collect in a lifetime. To be safe, you should have a limit of at least $1 million for each family

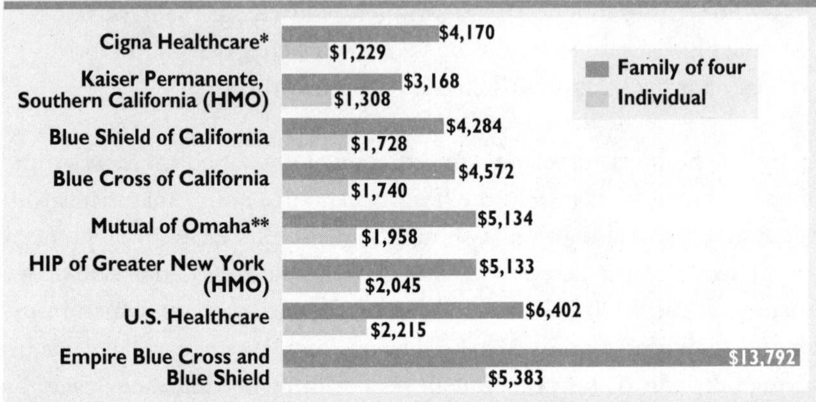


member. Two-thirds of all plans provide that much. If you are ill at ease with your plan's maximum, you can supplement it at a reasonable price. Mutual of Omaha is one company that offers many supplemental policies.

About the only thing you cannot buy additional insurance for is your deductible for such outpatient expenses as visits to the doctor, prescription drugs, lab tests and private nurses in your own home. The deductible is the bare minimum you absolutely have to pay. It varies anywhere from $50 to $5,000 a year, though the average is $200 for a single person and $450 for a family.

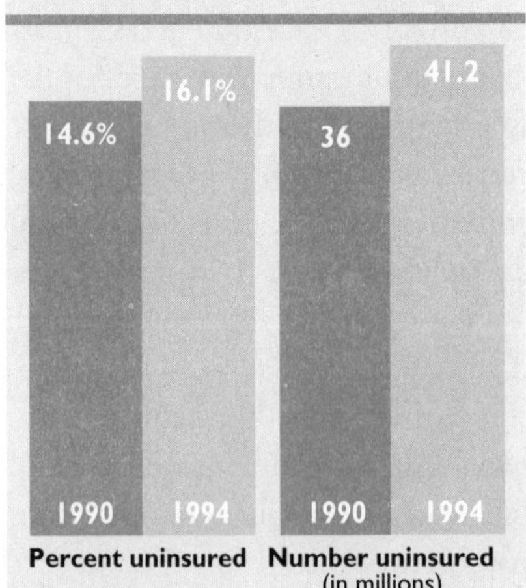


Give your health insurance its routine physical, and you will discover that some expenses are just not covered. Two-income couples with different employers have two policies to scrutinize; the strengths of one may make up for the weaknesses of the other. But remember: Family benefits are on the decline. A survey by the Northwestern National Life Insurance Company shows that while seven out of 10 *employees* believe their employers should provide health benefits for their families, nine out of 10 *employers* say they plan to reduce or eliminate coverage.

Indemnity or fee-for-service plans are also declining. A Bureau of Labor Statistics report on employer-sponsored health-care benefits found that in businesses with 100 or more employees, participation in traditional fee-for-service plans dropped from two-thirds of all employees in 1991 to one-half in 1993.

A policy's value is determined by the annual deductible, the out-of-pocket limit, and the co-insurance rates (that is, how much of the premium the employee has to pay). Foster Higgins, a benefits consulting firm, cites some figures for workers in large companies of 500 employees or more who bought the traditional indemnity plan in 1994: the average co-insurance payment was 20% of the premium, the average monthly contribution by the employee was $33 for an individual and $110 for a family, the median annual deductible was $200 for an individual and $500 for a family, and the median annual out-of-pocket maximum was $1,200 for an individual and $2,250 for a family. While the co-insurance rates and monthly contributions for HMO participants are similar, the difference is that in managed care plans, you pay an average of only $8 for each visit to the doctor.

Though it is illegal in most states to cancel group policies, individuals are still not protected. A company may cop out on you at the end of your policy's term — usually one year — if you get sick a lot and require treatment many times, or simply belong to a group that does. To prevent cancellation, buy a guaranteed-renewable policy. It specifies that the company can neither cancel your coverage so long as you pay the premiums, nor raise your rates merely because you have filed several expensive claims. But rates can go up as medical costs rise.

If you work beyond age 65, you may choose between continuing your employer's health plan or adopting Medicare. Employers are required to offer workers 65 or older the same health-insurance benefits under the same conditions as younger workers. But if you want Medicare, it's your responsibility to apply for it at your local Social Security office no later than three months after you turn 65. If you do not apply and then become ill, you may have to pay your own medical bills.

If you are retiring before age 65, make sure you are still covered under your group plan. Otherwise, you will have to buy a policy on your own. And if you are laid off or fired, ask your employer to continue your coverage for at least 30 to 90 days. If you do not get that protection, shop around for an interim policy to insure you until you land a job.

If you work for a company with more than 20 employees and are laid off or fired, you and your dependents have the right by federal law to be covered by the company's group plan for 18 months. You will have to pay for the full cost of coverage yourself, but at no more than 2% over the full group premiums. Still, this will be much more than you paid when you were an employee because your employer is no longer sharing the cost of premiums.

COBRA also gives a child turning 19 — or 23 if he or she is a student — the right to enjoy his or her parent's group coverage for 36 months, again by paying for premiums that are 2% more than the group premiums. The same period of coverage holds true for your spouse and minor children if you die or get divorced. Again, they would have to pay the full cost of the group premiums.

Finally, if you should become one of the 41 million or so people under age 65 who according to the Employee Benefits Research Institute do not have health insurance, you might turn to your local public, voluntary or private hospital. You can never be refused emergency care, unless the hospital does not have an emergency room. For nonemergency care, hospitals can refer you to a public state or city-run outpatient clinic, where you can enroll on a sliding fee schedule; the fees depend on your income and ability to pay. The trouble is, these clinics are very busy, and you might have to wait a long time to see a doctor. For inpatient nonemergency care, you can get public aid from the state in the form of MANG (Medical Aid No Grant) to cover some expenses, though there is considerable paperwork involved in applying. You may also check your state Department of Social Services to see if you qualify for Medicaid, the government-funded health insurance for low-income people.

▾ ▾ ▾

# The Pros and Cons of HMOs

Health maintenance organizations are often called the best prescription for achieving high-quality, economical group care. They are not like traditional group plans, in which you pick your own doctors and send the bills to your insurance company for reimbursement. An employer using HMOs usually gives several choices to his or her employees. They generally can choose between a "pure HMO" and an "open HMO."

- The "pure" variety requires members to use doctors and hospitals that belong to that HMO's network; after you pay an initial annual fee, the costs of these services are small.
- The fast-growing "open" HMOs or point-of-service (POS) plans allow members the choice of using doctors and hospitals in the HMO network or going to a provider outside the network. If you do go outside, you must pay a percentage of the costs incurred — the co-insurance rate — and a deductible.

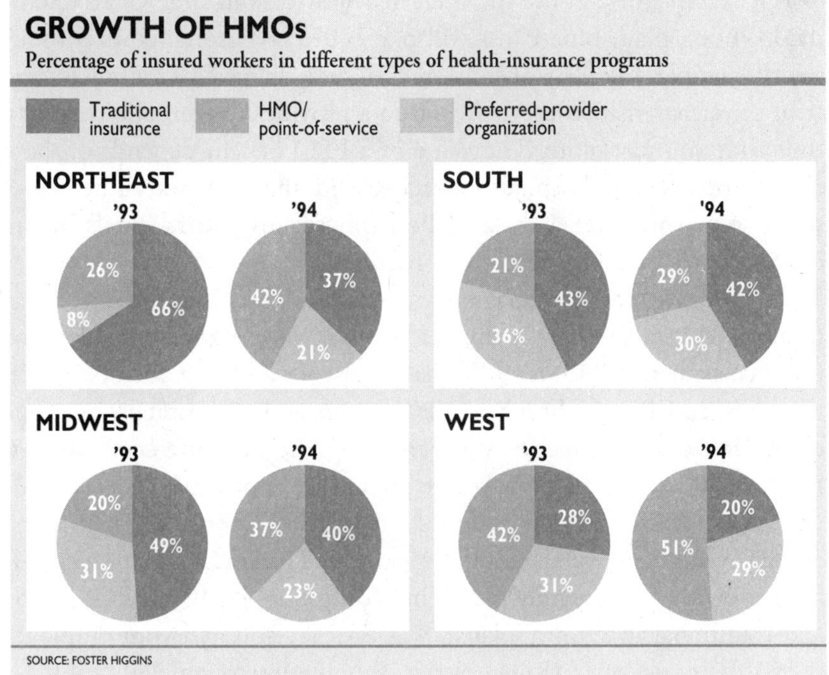

The average deductible for single coverage in POS plans is $296 if you use out-of-network providers. But if you are like most people enrolled in POS plans and choose to use the network's doctors and hospitals, you will have to pay only a small co-payment — $5 or $10 — each time you receive care. (The co-payment comes on top of the premium cost, which you share with your employer.) Co-payments are designed to make people think twice before going to the doctor.

Another type of managed care plan is the preferred provider organization, or PPO. It is offered by many large insurance companies, Blue Cross associations and hospital chains. A PPO works like a traditional fee-for-service health plan, but you get the option of paying lower deductibles and co-insurance by using the plan's own providers. If you do so, your deductible will be about $135 and your employer will reimburse you for about 80% to 100% percent of your medical costs. If you choose your own doctor and hospital, your deductible will be an average $250 and your employer will cover about 70% to 80% of your costs.

For example, if you use the preferred providers in Blue Cross's Standard Option plan, Blue Cross will pay 100% of hospital costs without any deductible, pay 95% of surgical costs and charge $10 for any outpatient physician visit. You can switch to a provider of your choice at any time, but you pay more. The value of a PPO benefit depends on how many doctors and hospitals participate in the network. Blue Cross stands out, with over a third of both physicians and hospitals in the country participating as preferred providers.

Still another kind of managed care plan is the exclusive provider organization. An EPO offers a smaller network of preferred providers for lower costs than a PPO. If a PPO has a network of 2,000 doctors and 20 hospitals, an EPO might have 1,000 doctors and 12 hospitals, but your co-insurance and deductibles are cheaper. The big difference with an EPO is that it does not allow you to go outside to other providers. EPOs tend to be less strictly regulated by states than PPOs or HMOs.

The average cost for all employer-sponsored health care plans in 1994, both individual and family plans (including pure HMOs, PPOs, POSs and traditional indemnity plans), was $3,741. You and your employer share this annual cost, with employers shouldering roughly 80% of it.

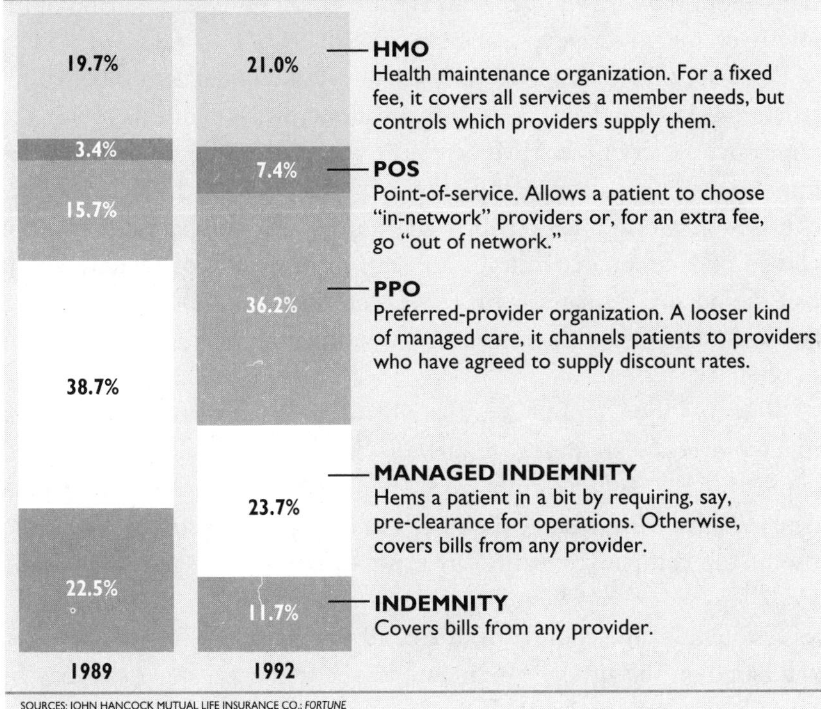


If you are self-employed, unemployed or retired and not a member of a group plan, you pay the full fee yourself. An HMO's doctors handle almost all your medical needs for no extra charge. HMOs usually cover a higher percentage of surgical and hospital costs than do traditional group policies, and you do not have to pay any deductibles. As a result, you may save 20% to 40% a year.

Health maintenance organizations bet that they can keep you well, and so they stress preventive medicine, starting with well-baby care and comprehensive exams. HMOs do whatever they can on an outpatient basis. And they often reward their doctors with year-end bonuses and profit sharing if they succeed in holding their costs below a set amount; and the best way to do that is to keep members out of the hospital. One result: Costs of operating HMOs are rising no more than 3% annually.

This is generally a good deal, but not always. Managed care organizations may not offer the best care for complex, costly illnesses; some have turned down bone marrow transplants for cancer patients on the grounds that those are experimental treatments. If you have any questions about the care you get at an HMO, you should get a second opinion — even if you have to pay for it yourself.

Be aware that your HMO physicians will be under a number of restrictions. At some HMOs, members cannot always count on seeing the same doctor every time. HMOs require you to use not only their doctors but also the hospitals, labs and other facilities with which the HMO has contracted. Most "pure" HMOs will not pay for any part of the bill if you go outside the network for a doctor or hospital. Fortunately, about half the doctors affiliated with HMOs are specialists. But it is the total freedom to go out of the network at any time that makes the POS plans so popular.

More and more employers offer a broad menu of managed care plans to employees. Xerox is a model. Its highly successful program has enrolled 55,000 U.S. employees, plus retirees and eligible dependents. Called HealthLink, the plan was developed to combat the rapid rise in the company's health-care costs — up 51% between 1987 and 1990.

Throughout the country, Xerox contracts with 204 different HMOs, and based on the zip code of an employee's residence, he or she may be offered from two to 12 HMOs. Xerox pays a certain amount for each employee a year — $5,438 for full family coverage — and the remainder of the HMO fee is deducted from the employee's pay. The most efficient, lowest-cost HMO that Xerox offers, known as the benchmark plan, costs $4,997. So if an employee chooses the benchmark plan, he or she actually gets a refund of $441. Other HMO prices are $5,597, $5,847 and $5,999. The more the employee pays, the more complete the coverage that his or her family gets.

If an employee chooses not to go with an HMO but with the Xerox Medical Plan — a conventional fee-for-service plan that lets the employee choose any doctor — he or she will get an 80% reimbursement (after the deductible) for approved charges. The employee also will pay $2,214 a year on top of the Xerox allowance of $5,438, making this the most expensive option.

HealthLink's HMOs include Kaiser, Blue Cross/Blue Shield of Rochester, New York, UltraLink, PruCare, The HMO Group and U.S. Healthcare. In a 1993 survey 83% of Xerox's employees said they were satisfied with their plan, and 88% said they would definitely or probably recommend it to family and friends. This is fairly typical; in surveys of other HMO groups, members generally profess to be quite satisfied.

## Xerox's Requirements of HMOs

Here is what Xerox's well-run health-care program demands of participating HMOs. When choosing your own HMO, these are good guidelines to follow. Each HMO must:

- be accredited by the National Committee for Quality Assurance
- have internal, ongoing quality assurance programs
- report on a wide range of performance measures using a national standardized data report system, including the provision of appropriate preventive and early diagnosis screening care (e.g., pap smear tests, immunizations, mammograms, well-baby care)
- participate in special studies of quality of care and efforts to improve outcomes and effectiveness of care (e.g., reduce cesarean rates)
- be easily accessible for all types of care (emergency, urgent, illness or routine)
- have well-published methods for appealing decisions that the patient does not understand or agree with
- be committed to regularly surveying member satisfaction and continuously evaluating and improving the quality of care and service
- have a relatively low number of member complaints and grievances and handle those responsibly

By and large, HMOs do provide sound care at reasonable cost — as their 55 million members can attest. (The number is estimated by InterStudy, a health-care policy research organization, to rise to 66 million in 1997, and that will give HMOs even more leverage to pare the prices

## THE TEN LARGEST HMOs

| HMO | Members (millions) | Principal area served |
|---|---|---|
| **Kaiser Permanente** | **6.7** | California and 15 other states |
| **United HealthCare** | **3.7** | Minnesota, Florida and Illinois are biggest among 20 states |
| **U.S. Healthcare** | **2.2** | Strong in Northeast |
| **Humana** | **2.1** | Illinois, Florida and 12 other states |
| **FHP International** | **1.7** | California and 10 other western and midwestern states |
| **Health Systems** | **1.6** | California, Colorado |
| **PacifiCare** | **1.5** | Southern California |
| **HIP** | **1.2** | New York |
| **Foundation Health** | **1.0** | California and eight other states |
| **WellPoint** | **0.7** | California |

SOURCE: *WALL STREET JOURNAL*

they pay for hospital stays, prescription drugs — and doctors.) A 1992 study by the U.S. Health Care Financing Administration, a division of the Department of Health and Human Services, concluded that treatment at HMOs was as good as conventional health care.

Still, HMOs vary widely in quality, just as independent physicians do. So before signing up, ask friends or co-workers who belong how they rate a plan. You should phone the administration office of any HMO you are considering joining to ask if it is affiliated with a well-regarded local hospital and if most of its physicians are certified by specialty boards. Get this information on paper and signed by a responsible authority.

Beware of HMOs' boasts that they are the best as ranked in a regional survey. To check out an HMO, call the National Committee for Quality Assurance (NCQA) in Washington, D.C., at 202-955-3500. It is a private group financed by foundations, government grants and fees charged to each health plan that applies for accreditation. The NCQA does the most thorough investigation of any organization. It measures not only customer satisfaction but also the quality of an HMO by examining such matters as the participating doctors' credentials and what preventive medicine procedures — such as immunizations — are commonly followed. It has reviewed nearly half of the country's HMOs. The NCQA publishes the Accreditation Status List, which shows each plan's current accreditation status — full, provisional, one-year, denial or

## HOW ONE TOP HMO RATES ITS QUALITY

Kaiser Permanente's Northern California regional HMO judges its performance versus state and national averages.

| | | **Kaiser Permanente** (Northern California) | **Benchmark** (state or national average) |
|---|---|---|---|
| **WHERE IT SAYS IT DOES BETTER...** | % of children who get meningitis shots | 93.2% | 45.1% |
| | Meningitis cases per 100,000 people | 0.1 | 0.9 |
| | % of births by cesarean section | 16.1% | 22.5% |
| | Infant deaths within 28 days of birth per 1,000 births | 8.7 | 9.5 |
| | Heart disease deaths per 100,000 people | 157 | 219 |
| **THE SAME AS STATE AVERAGE...** | Colorectal cancer deaths per 100,000 people | 16.1 | 16.6 |
| **...WORSE** | Gall bladder removals per 100,000 people | 167.5 | 158.3 |

SOURCE: *FORTUNE*

under review. The NCQA also offers consumers guidelines and other information on how to choose an HMO.

Another source is Washington Consumers' Checkbook. Every year it publishes a nationwide poll on how federal employees rate the many HMOs and fee-for-service plans offered to them. The report focuses on customer satisfaction and includes patients' opinions of many features of each plan, from how easy or hard it is to get a doctor's appointment to the extent and quality of follow-through care. The results are in the *Checkbooks' Guide to 1995 Health Insurance Plans for Federal Employees.* It also compares costs of various plans. To get the report, send $10.45 to Checkbook Insurance Guide, 733 15th Street NW, Suite 820, Washington, D.C. 20005, or call 202-347-7283. Washington Consumers' Checkbook also has a new member-satisfaction ratings guide that gives plan-to-plan comparisons for 250 HMOs (which comprise about two-thirds of HMO members) titled the *Consumer's Guide to Health Plans.* The book is useful for consumer concerns — it shows, for example, that roughly 89% of HMO members gave their plans favorable ratings overall. But it does not provide the more telling outcome-related data for acute medical concerns. You can order the guide by writing to or calling the address or number on page 483.

It is a favorable sign if an HMO belongs to the Group Health Association of America, a trade organization that sets medical and financial standards for its 350 member plans. Also, ask directors of the HMO whether it is federally qualified — meaning it provides a specific range of services. About one-half of the 545 HMOs in the country are federally qualified, and 76% of the people who are enrolled in HMOs are in them.

Because some of the newer, smaller HMOs are operating in the red, you will also want to conduct a financial checkup. Phone the state office that regulates HMOs — usually the Department of Insurance, except in California where it's the Department of Corporations — for an opinion on the one you are considering. The state offices can tell you if there have been complaints against a health plan. But for any further information, you must go in person and view the files. The HMO is probably sound if it has been in business for five years or if it is sponsored by a big insurance company or some other substantial institution.

A. M. Best, the insurance rating firm, publishes reports on the financial health of 13 HMOs. For a copy of *Best Insurance Report* or *Best Managed Care Report,* call 900-555-BEST. The call costs $2.95 and each report is $4.95.

**EMPLOYEES' RANKINGS OF HEALTH PLANS**

A survey of 24,300 employees of Xerox, GTE and Digital Equipment showed they preferred fee-for-service plans, but when costs and other factors were considered, group-practice HMOs that run their own health centers scored highest. Independent Practice Association (IPA) doctors see other patients. Point-of-service plans let you go outside your HMO.

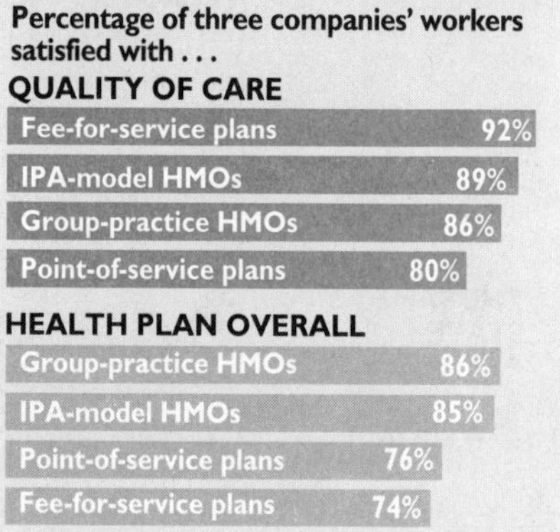

**Percentage of three companies' workers satisfied with . . .**

**QUALITY OF CARE**

|  |  |
|---|---|
| Fee-for-service plans | 92% |
| IPA-model HMOs | 89% |
| Group-practice HMOs | 86% |
| Point-of-service plans | 80% |

**HEALTH PLAN OVERALL**

|  |  |
|---|---|
| Group-practice HMOs | 86% |
| IPA-model HMOs | 85% |
| Point-of-service plans | 76% |
| Fee-for-service plans | 74% |

SOURCE: *FORTUNE*

# Finding a Good Doctor

One of your most important investments, surely, is your investment in health care. So it is smart to spend at least as much time selecting a good doctor as it is, say, picking a new car or a house. Not all doctors are created equal. You can measure them against certain yardsticks of quality, but you must be willing to do some research.

Start your search by asking neighbors, friends and fellow workers for recommendations. If you are moving to a new town or neighborhood, get a few names of prospective physicians from the doctors you have been seeing in your old community. Request referrals from your company's medical department; that is the simplest way to learn the names of professionals who have earned reputations among patients for reliability. Also ask local medical and dental societies for names of practitioners who take new patients.

You can consult the *Directory of Medical Specialists,* available in large public libraries. It lists the names, educational backgrounds and specialties of all U.S. doctors. You can phone the internal-medicine or family-practice department of the nearest university-owned or university-affiliated teaching hospital and get the names of doctors who are on the staff. Finally, you might ask your pharmacist to suggest doctors who he or she feels are well qualified. Pharmacists know which ones are up to date on the latest drugs.

Once you have found two or three candidates, call their offices and speak with the doctor if you can. Ask what he or she charges for some selected procedures such as a basic physical exam. If the physician will not say, move on to the next. You can even drop by for a get-acquainted interview. Doctors often do not charge for a few minutes' talk with a potential patient.

Find out whether the doctor practices alone or as part of a group or in an HMO. There is little evidence to suggest that your care will be any better or worse in one type of practice or another. As time goes on, more and more people will enroll in some form of managed health-care plan.

Studies indicate that the prestige of the doctor's medical school or its location — in the U.S. or abroad — may not, by itself, foretell the quality of care that he or she delivers. Two other criteria are far more important.

First, where did the doctor complete his or her residency? The best training programs generally are at university-affiliated hospitals.

Second, has the doctor passed a certification exam given by the professional organization that oversees his or her specialty? Certification is no guarantee of excellence, but it is the best yardstick you have. Again, you can check the doctor's credentials in the *Directory of Medical Specialists.* You can also check if your state medical society publishes a directory. For example, the Medical Society of New York State's directory lists the name, location, position and credentials of 46,000 physicians. It also provides general information on the state's hospitals. You can buy the directory for $100 in New York by calling 800-523-4404, or check your local library.

When you judge a doctor, also consider the hospitals he or she uses. You can't check in to a hospital, except in an emergency, unless your doctor can admit you there. To do that, he or she must have been screened by its credentials committees and granted admitting privileges. Good doctors use good hospitals, so selecting the right physician can solve two potential problems. Conversely, if you favor a specific hospital, you should select your doctor from among those with admitting privileges at that hospital.

When planning a trip, check what coverage your health-care plan provides away from home. Many insurance companies require special documents from any doctor or hospital you visit out of your city. Your HMO may have a reciprocity agreement with an HMO in the area you'll be traveling in. If not, you may need those special documents to get reimbursed.

For names of practitioners in an unfamiliar place, try the county medical or dental society. The Travelers Aid Society, found in most large cities, will also give you the name and address of the nearest hospital. Be sure to take along an ample supply of any medication you may need. Carry it with you — not in a suitcase that might be lost or separated from you during a long plane journey. If you run out, you probably will need to see a local doctor for a new prescription.

When you are overseas, a U.S. embassy or consulate can provide names of English-speaking doctors, though the U.S. government does not guarantee their expertise. Doctors' and hospital bills overseas usually must be paid in cash, but your health-insurance program may reimburse you — after you return home. Blue Cross/Blue Shield will reimburse you for medical emergencies outside the country. The Oxford Health Plan covers catastrophic medical expenses while traveling in the U.S. and overseas. It is a good idea to double-check the extent of your medical coverage *before* you travel. Every contract is as different as the company and the buyer. Your benefits may be reduced once you are outside your medical service area, even in the U.S. If your plan is not adequate for overseas travel, you can buy supplemental insurance. See Chapter 20 for more details on these plans.

## Checking Up on Your Doctor

In the past, medical professionals were blindly trusted and all too seldom second-guessed. No longer. Lately, with employers scaling back health insurance and employees getting new choices in coverage, Americans are demanding information. HMO "report cards" — with data on individual hospitals' death rates for heart surgery and other information — are starting to reveal who has the most effective treatment.

Wyoming's Jackson Hole Group — an association that convenes several meetings each year of executives of major companies, government officials, doctors and researchers — is working to circulate more data on medical outcomes. Its president, Dr. Paul Ellwood, is a leading proponent of quality accountability in health care. He thinks it is the only way you can determine which HMO keeps its members the healthiest. The group is developing a comparative study of quality information, projected to be available sometime in 1996, to help consumers choose among the growing number of health plans. Many communities from Seattle to Hanover, New Hampshire, circulate report cards, citing mortality rates and health-care outcomes of hospitals. These reports reveal the results of surveys of customers' satisfaction with health-care providers and track which hospitals are keeping more people alive. The reports are forcing the medical profession to account for its performance and thus deliver a better service.

The report cards have led hospitals with high marks to share information about their surgical procedures with hospitals that have low marks. Result: Hospitals increasingly are using uniform surgical procedures, and that uniformity is improving outcomes. Hospitals where certain operations are performed regularly are better at them than where they are seldom done. Patients are about *six times* as likely to die of risky pancreatic cancer surgery at small hospitals that rarely perform the procedure than at hospitals that perform it more routinely, according to a Johns Hopkins University study released in 1995. The outcomes depend greatly upon the experience a surgeon gets by performing the procedure many times over.

## Uncovering the Performance Records

With very few exceptions there is little comparative outcome-based information on hospitals nationwide. One way to discover which hospital in your area has the best record in overall quality and performance is to look at the reports published by the Joint Commission on Accreditation of Healthcare Organizations. The Joint Commission accredits more than 11,000 organizations, including 80% of the nation's hospitals, and measures their level of performance in a range of categories. You can find out if a hospital near you is accredited by calling 708-916-5800. If it is, you can order the report for $30, or the institution itself may have the report available.

Your state health department can tell you whether a hospital has any outstanding quality-of-care problems, and it may be able to give you outcome data for certain procedures. In New York, for example, the state health department has statistics on cardiac surgery and neo-natal mortality for each hospital. Beware of judging a hospital's overall quality based on isolated procedures, like neo-natal mortality, which may not account for certain risk factors like patient profile and hospital location. Washington Consumers' Checkbook publishes two articles to help you choose a high-quality hospital in the San Francisco Bay and Washington, D.C., areas. They provide information on emergency and inpatient care, including death-rate data for selected procedures, and opinions of nurses, physicians and consumers. You can order them by writing or calling the address or number cited on page 483.

Also ask your surgeon and your hospital; it's your right to know. Put hard, specific questions to them: "How often do you do this operation? What are the risks and results? How do they compare with other hospitals and doctors? I want numbers. Tell me."

You may ask a member of your employer's human resources

department to call the National Business Coalition Forum on Health at 202-775-9300 in Washington, D.C. A private group that serves business, it tracks hospital quality standards in some areas of the country.

# How to Pick a Hospital

Your choice of a hospital is closely tied to your selection of a physician because only a doctor with staff privileges can admit you to a hospital. It is therefore wise to consider these two factors together. Ask about the basic gauge of a hospital: whether it is approved by the nonprofit Joint Commission on Accreditation of Healthcare Organizations. You can be sure that an accredited hospital has met national health and safety standards of excellence in 24 categories.

For most medical problems, accredited community hospitals without teaching programs may be satisfactory. Their staffs are competent, their costs are 15% to 25% lower than at university hospitals and they have the reputation of being more hassle-free. For fairly routine treatment, it usually does not matter whether the hospital is privately owned and nonprofit or privately owned and for-profit.

But for certain types of complex surgery or serious illnesses, it just does not pay to be anywhere but in a university-affiliated hospital or a specialty center such as a children's hospital or an institute devoted to the treatment of a particular disease. Teaching and specialty hospitals tend to have doctors who are the most up to date. Those institutions generally see hundreds of patients a month. In medicine as in most disciplines, practice makes nearly perfect.

Especially in surgery, volume is key. If the surgeons at a hospital do not each perform 40 to 50 operations a year, they are probably not maintaining their skills. For heart surgeons, the number is higher. According to the American Heart Association, the recommended minimum number of open-heart surgeries at a hospital is 200 to 300 annually; the minimum per surgeon is 100 to 150.

How do you find out about a surgeon's or a hospital's volume? Just ask. If your doctor does not want to tell you or is vague, that's a clear warning signal. Try to gather information from local consumer groups, from your state's medical society, from life insurance companies and from your state hospital association. Another source is *The Consumers' Guide to Hospitals,* which reports on the number of Medicare cases each hospital has handled for various types of diagnoses and also cites hospital-by-hospital death rates. The handbook tells how often a hospital does a treatment and the procedures used. It is published by Washington Consumers' Checkbook, a nonprofit program of the Center for the Study of Services, and costs $12. The phone number in Washington, D.C., is 800-475-7283.

When surgery seems called for, a second opinion is essential. It can save your insurer money and you an operation. Many of the nonprofit insurers in the Blue Cross network have recognized the importance of second opinions. In some states, insurers are requiring and paying for them. If you need a second opinion, you can call the federal government's second-opinion hotline at 800-638-6833. You can also make more informed decisions if you learn about your condition and its treatment by doing research in your local or hospital library.

If you get a major hospital bill that is bigger than expected, check it carefully. When you (or a relative) are released from a hospital stay, insist on an itemized statement of charges. Ask for an explanation if you find items or services that you suspect weren't delivered. If you're still not satisfied, notify your insurance company, whose demands for an explanation will carry more clout. Some insurers and employers offer financial incentives to people who uncover excess charges on their medical bills.

## Avoiding the High Cost of Hospitals

Long, expensive and sometimes unnecessary hospital stays are a major cause of medical inflation. But hospitals have found new ways to avoid the high price of inpatient care.

In more than half of all surgical operations, patients now can return home the same day. Surgical lasers have reduced hazardous bleeding, and lighter anesthetics eliminate the hours of grogginess and nausea. As a result, many routine procedures such as hernia repair and cataract removal are being done safely, efficiently — and economically — outside of hospitals.

These same-day operations can be performed at hospital-affiliated clinics, in doctors' offices and at independent surgical centers. About 2,000 freestanding ambulatory surgery centers have sprung up, and their success is largely due to their freedom from the tyranny of hospital schedules, as well as the savings they offer the patient. The doctors' fees are usually the same wherever an operation is performed, but other costs are 40% to 60% less than in a hospital because the overhead is lower and there are no room charges.

Some emergency-room treatments and many recuperative services also don't need the vast — and vastly expensive — resources of a fully equipped hospital. So entrepreneurs and hospitals have set up about 5,000 independent immediate care centers across the country. They're staffed mainly by physicians specializing in emergency medicine or family practice. True, an immediate care center is no place to go with a serious illness or injury. But for minor burns, sprains, cuts and colds, it can deliver faster, more convenient and often less expensive care.

Private business is also offering home-care services that are priced lower than the same care in a hospital. Some 12,000 agencies now provide home care, and about half of them are Medicare-approved. They send out nurses, homemakers and even companions to people who are confined at home but don't need hospitalization. So if you are ever headed toward a hospital, you might pause a moment to consider your growing range of alternatives.

## Keeping Healthy by Keeping Informed

High tech has come to the home health field, and now you can get software programs that help keep you informed. For example, Medical HouseCall answers your questions about diseases, drug interactions, poisons, medical tests and first aid. The software also has a medical encyclopedia, nutrition information and a program to maintain your family medical records.

You enter symptoms of an illness and answer questions that the software puts to you. The software generates a list of possible causes; it also gives you information about your doctor's diagnoses, prescribed treatments and medication, and tests he or she may want you to undergo. This may help you ask better questions of your doctor. But don't try to second-guess your doctor; he or she can see many things that you cannot.

The software was developed by Applied Medical Informatics (2681 Parleys Way, Suite 204, Salt Lake City, Utah 84109; 800-584-3060 or 801-464-6200). It costs $55 to $60, or up to $70 for a CD-ROM version, and is available for Macintosh and Windows-based computers.

You can call the U.S. Public Health Service's Agency for Health Care Policy and Research and ask for medical documents and publications. By mail or fax, it can send you a wide variety of clinical practice guidelines on topics from early HIV infection to the prevention of pressure-induced ulcers. You can request a list of all information available to familiarize yourself with it. The agency is in Rockville, Maryland; its phone number to order publications is 800-358-9295. If you have a handset on your fax you can call the agency's InstantFax at 301-594-2800. Guess what? The information is free.

More and more libraries in urban areas are offering a complete health library on CD-ROM. Called the Health Reference Center, it was developed in 1990 by Information Access Company (362 Lakeside Drive, Foster City, California 94404; 800-227-8431). It has considerable information from consumer-oriented magazines and professional journals, medical education pamphlets and health reference books. The abstracts are written in language that laypeople can understand, and medical terms are well defined. If you are a computerphobe, not to worry. The CD-ROM program is easy to use and designed so that you will not need librarian assistance to conduct a complete search that may be personal in nature. Many employers and HMOs, including the largest, Kaiser Permanente, make the Health Reference Center available to their employees or members. You may want to check with your health-care provider, employer or library to see if they have it.

## Prepaid Dental Plans

If dentists' bills are taking a big bite out of your family budget, you may be able to chop these costs by joining one of the prepaid dental plans. Typically, they have been limited to members of employee groups, but now individuals can buy into a few such plans. At Northeast Dental Plan of America (800-828-2222), annual fees run $85 for individuals,

$155 for a couple and $195 for a family with any number of dependents; also, for people age 62 and over, fees are $75 for an individual and $135 for a couple. There are no deductibles, no restrictions for pre-existing conditions, no waiting period for treatment, no charges for checkups and no age limits.

While there are charges for procedures, they are generally 25% to 50% below usual fees. For example, at Northeast Dental, the flat rates are $27 for a silver amalgam filling, $10 for a basic cleaning, $10 for a full set of X-rays — and $405 for a porcelain-on-metal cap, which normally costs $600 to $900. All prepaid plans place some restrictions on your choice of a dentist. Some require you to select one at a dental center that has a contract with the plan. But Northeast Dental lists more than 3,000 dentists and dental specialists whom you can use. You can also call 800-828-2222 to get free information on the plan, a complete fee schedule, a list of participating dentists and an application kit.

If your employer offers you the choice of joining a prepaid plan, first ask your benefits counselor how many of the plan's dentists practice close to where you live or work. Inquire whether your whole family has to go to the same dentist. This could be a nuisance if you prefer to use one near your office and your family needs one close to home.

Ask the directors of the plan whether complicated dental work, such as a root canal or oral surgery, is handled by a specialist. Any dentist is licensed to perform such procedures. Make sure you will be referred to a specialist if you need periodontal, endodontic or orthodontic care.

Find out how the plan handles emergencies. The better plans guarantee 24-hour availability for care, even when your chosen dentist is not reachable. This means that you will not be forced to pay for treatment by a dentist who is not part of the plan. Also ask about grievance procedures to settle possible disputes between you and your practitioner. The plan should offer arbitration by a patient-relations administrator or, ideally, pay for a second opinion from an independent dentist.

You can get prepaid dental plans — and HMOs that include dental care as part of the package — in most parts of the country. To find one in your area, check the Yellow Pages under "Dental Service Plans," or call the American Dental Association at 312-440-2746 and ask for its brochure that lists HMOs and PPOs with prepaid dental plans.

# Finding a Psychotherapist

Picking a therapist can itself be a source of anxiety: Psychotherapy is expensive and practitioners range from geniuses to charlatans. More than 600,000 therapists practice in the U.S., offering over 250 types of treatment. Anyone can hang out a shingle as a psychotherapist and, with a little knowledge and a lot of brass, can succeed. So as you search, remember that credentials are critical. Accredited mental-health professionals fall into seven classes: psychiatrists, psychoanalysts, clinical psychologists, psychiatric social workers, psychiatric nurses, marriage and family therapists, and pastoral counselors.

Psychiatrists and most psychoanalysts have M.D. degrees, meaning they can prescribe drugs and hospitalization; these may be needed to treat severe illness. Clinical psychologists have Ph.D.'s in psychology; psychiatric social workers, marriage and family therapists, and pastoral counselors must have at least a master's degree; and psychiatric nurses are registered nurses who have at least a master's degree in mental-health nursing.

The best way to find a therapist is to ask your family doctor. You can also consult state offices of professional societies, which give out names of members over the phone. Other good sources are mental-health associations, university medical centers, hospital clinics or self-help groups such as Alcoholics Anonymous or International THEOS, an organization for widowed people.

To check a therapist's credentials, contact the state chapter of the appropriate organization — for example, the American Psychiatric Association (if you call 202-682-6220, the association will give you the number to phone for referrals in your area) or the American Psychological Association (call 202-336-5500 to get the phone number of your state association for a referral service, or call the state chapter directly). The American Psychiatric Nurses Association (202-857-1133) has a national referral service that provides a list of advanced practice psychiatric nurses by state. State boards for nursing verify whether a nurse is licensed and sometimes reveal whether any complaints have been filed against him or her — all state boards for nursing verify this information. Other state boards provide different kinds of information. For example, the New York State Education Department of Professional Licensing

Services (518-474-3817) verifies credentials for all licensed mental-health workers (including certified social workers, psychologists, psychiatrists and nurse therapists).

The National Mental Health Association (703-684-7722) has a referral service for mental-health centers across the U.S. The services offered vary from center to center, but they include individual, family and group therapy. Payment is on a sliding scale, determined by income.

When you first meet a therapist, remember that you are a customer as well as a patient. Ask about credentials and fees. Some therapists will reduce charges if you are unable to pay the full rate. Feel free to get a second consultation or to change therapists.

Fees depend largely on the type of therapist you choose. Psychiatrists charge the most; in private practice, their sessions of 45 to 50 minutes cost \$60 to \$150 or even more. Psychologists with Ph.D.'s charge \$60 to \$100 a session, while social workers bill \$40 to \$60. You can save considerably by going into group therapy: A number of people share their problems and try to solve them under the direction of a therapist. Medical-insurance coverage for psychotherapy can vary greatly, so before beginning treatment, check with your insurer about what is reimbursed.

## New Options in Births

A number of pregnant women prefer not to give birth in a hospital delivery room, and they now have several cost-saving options. Certainly a hospital delivery room is the safest place to have a baby and the *only* wise choice for women who are considered to have risky pregnancies. Some women dislike the routine hospital procedure and want more control over their birthing experience. So they are choosing alternatives to the steel-and-tile delivery room.

One option is the hospital birthing room. Unlike the standard delivery room, it is usually furnished with beds, plants, stereos and other comforts of home. Members of the family — including children — can often stay in the room with Mom. Labor, delivery and recovery all take place in the same congenial setting, where a nurse-midwife or preferably an obstetrician is in attendance. The average charge for a routine delivery in a hospital birthing room involving a one-day stay in 1993 was

$5,436. This compared with an average charge of $6,034 for the usual two-day hospital stay.

There are also 135 birthing centers away from hospitals that are licensed by 32 states, and the number is growing fairly fast. The centers are usually staffed by certified nurse-midwives, and all have consulting physicians on 24-hour call. They also have arrangements with nearby hospitals so that a woman who suddenly develops complications can be transferred quickly to a delivery room. Freestanding birth centers charge 30% to 50% less than hospitals. The average cost in 1993 was $3,268 for the usual one-day stay. Most major health insurers reimburse birth centers 100% of their charges; the average postpartum stay in a birthing center is seven hours, but can range anywhere between two and 24 hours. But it cannot be stressed enough: The *safest* place to have a baby is the hospital.

## Infertility Solutions

Nearly one out of 12 married couples of childbearing age who try to conceive a child fail to do so. The fight against infertility can be exasperating and expensive, but new methods can increase your chances of success — at reasonable cost.

With modern therapies, these couples now have more than a 50% chance of parenthood once a diagnosis is made. And it is possible to identify the cause in 80% to 90% of the cases. The testing and treatment can cost $15,000 to $30,000 — and sometimes more. Insurers cover only part of this. Couples usually have to pay at least 20% to 30% of the bill themselves.

If you are trying to overcome infertility, above all get expert medical help. Your family doctor or gynecologist may be able to clear up minor difficulties. But if your doctor's treatments have had no effect after several months, see a fertility specialist. For names of specialists and fertility clinics, write to the American Society for Reproductive Medicine, 1209 Montgomery Highway, Birmingham, Alabama 35216-2809.

Closely question any specialist you are considering. Ask about the tests and treatments he or she administers, how long he or she has specialized in infertility, how successful he or she has been in helping couples conceive. Check your health-insurance coverage. Some companies do not consider infertility to be an illness. But even they will pick up part of the bill for tests and treatment of conditions that may interfere with reproduction. Your compensation may depend on the wording a doctor uses when filling out insurance claim forms. One infertility specialist advises, "Insurance generally covers the cost, as long as you do not state that the work is being done for infertility per se, but instead use such terms as ovulation disorder, tubular obstruction or pelvic adhesion."

## When Should You Have Elective Surgery?

Every year, many thousands of Americans face a difficult choice: whether or not to have elective surgery. It can be costly, let alone painful. Aside from the usual fears, you have to consider many other factors, including lost income, uninsured medical expenses and extra outlays for convalescence. If you have any lingering doubts about undergoing a procedure, ask a number of tough questions. Many of them should be directed to an internist or a family practitioner rather than a surgeon, because surgeons are oriented toward surgery. Learn the following:

- Can your condition be controlled by medication, diet or a medical device in lieu of surgery? If so, are you likely to stay on the prescribed regimen?
- What are the chances that the disorder will suddenly get worse, resulting in emergency hospitalization?
- Will leaving your condition untreated limit your lifestyle, work or recreation?

If you decide on surgery, find out the chances of its success. You will also want a confirming second opinion before you proceed. Almost all health insurers will pay not only for a second opinion, but even for a third if the first two conflict. When seeking another opinion, go to a doctor you have found independently, not a colleague recommended by your surgeon.

To locate another specialist on your own, phone the referral service of a major hospital, preferably one that has a medical school connected with it. Or call your county medical association. Pick a doctor who has *diplomate* status. That means he or she both has experience and has passed extensive exams in his or her specialty. The second doctor may insist you repeat the same tests you have already had, but if there is even a remote possibility that you do not need surgery, it is probably worth it.

## The Costs of Cosmetic Surgery

Cosmetic surgery to fight sags, bags, drags and wrinkles is performed on more than 1.2 million patients a year. What are the costs — and the real value — of those operations?

Depending on the procedure and the doctor, fees diverge widely. They average from $1,300 for common dermabrasion to more than $15,000 for extensive body contouring. But plastic surgery performed right in the doctor's office eliminates steep hospital expenses for many patients. A single overnight stay in a hospital for a face-lift might easily cost $3,500 to $8,000 for operating-room fees and a private room; in a surgical outpatient facility, the same patient might pay only $500 to $1,500 in fees for the room and various equipment — in addition to the doctor's bill, of course. Operations are now routinely done in doctors' offices. An office nose job, for example, can take as little as two hours. Then the patient spends a couple of hours resting in a recovery room and goes home with a long list of dos and don'ts and a phone number where the doctor can be reached, if necessary. In some states, such as California, there is another alternative: hotel-like recovery centers staffed by nurses to ease postoperative care.

Beware, though, of heavily advertised cosmetic-surgery clinics. In a few of these body shops, surgeons perform as many as 12 operations a day. This high-volume approach sometimes results in short-order workmanship. Make sure your surgeon's facility is a member of the American Society for Aesthetic Plastic Surgeons (800-635-0635) or a member of the American Academy of Cosmetic Surgery (312-527-6713). Also, verify that the in-office surgical facility is accredited with the American Association of Ambulatory Plastic Surgery Facilities (708-949-6058) or the Accreditation Association for Ambulatory Health Care (708-676-9610).

The American Academy of Cosmetic Surgery (401 North Michigan Avenue, Chicago, Illinois 60611-4267; 312-527-6713) reports the number of plastic surgeries conducted on men increased 11% from

1990 to 1994; nose reshaping jumped 30%. Surprisingly, over the same period, the number of men undergoing face-lifts fell 35%. The top five procedures for men are, in order, hair transplants, nose surgery, eyelid surgery, liposuction and chemical peeling.

How much do doctors charge? So-called tummy tucks are $2,170 to $6,000. Because of safety concerns, silicone gel breast implants can no longer be used routinely, but saline implants may still be used, and the average cost is $3,500. A face-lift averages around $4,000 but can run anywhere from $2,870 to $8,000. A total makeover — with face-lift plus work to smooth the neck and lift eyebags, chemical peeling and so on — can easily run $10,000 to $20,000. The price depends on such variables as the areas to be worked on, the qualifications of the surgeon and his or her geographic location; prices are steepest in big cities on both coasts. In one technique, the surgeon not only tightens the skin but also resculptures the jaw line and neck by removing excess fat. Then he or she cuts and resews a neck muscle to form a kind of sling to support the neck and chin. Pain should be minimal, and discoloration should be gone in 10 days or so.

The news about nose jobs is that they are no longer the assembly-line reshapings of a decade or so ago. For $3,000 to $9,000, you should get a nose that is natural and fits your face. In one technique, the operation is done mostly from the inside out, so there is no visible scarring.

Hair transplantation is another growth business. In the past you commonly would have had to endure up to four or possibly five painstaking — and often painful — sessions with a plastic surgeon or dermatologist. Sometimes the plugs of hair did not thrive, or they sat in such neat rows that they often look as if they have been sowed by John Deere. But new techniques have improved hair transplants. Done properly by an experienced surgeon or dermatologist, the result is a rather natural hairline, with single hair grafts used in front of the line. The bill can reach hair-raising proportions: from $5,000 for a minimal procedure to $25,000 to $35,000 for more extensive balding, which may require perhaps four scalp reductions and eight to 10 hair-graft transplant procedures. A dermatologist doing hair transplants and skin peelings should be certified by the American Board of Dermatology (Henry Ford Hospital, One Ford Place, Detroit, Michigan 48202-3450; 318-874-1088).

Whatever the cost, a plastic surgeon usually will not raise his or her scalpel until you have paid at least half of the fee. If insurance will pay some, then 50% up-front is typical; otherwise, you must pay the entire fee before the surgery. The doctors say that since the surgery is elective, high postponement and cancellation rates mess up their busy schedules. More likely, doctors fear that some patients would refuse to pay after seeing the results. If you are less than pleased, your only recourse is to sue.

Medical insurance probably will not pay for the operation unless the work is considered health-related or rehabilitative, such as breast reconstruction. Similarly, plastic surgery rarely qualifies for a medical deduction on your income tax. But no matter how much you have to pay, do not expect the moon. While cosmetic surgery can help you turn back the clock, you cannot stop it forever. As one surgeon warns, "We can't make people into movie stars or mend broken marriages — the only way to get rid of every line and wrinkle is to embalm you."

If you pick a plastic surgeon, do it as though your life depended on it. In rare cases of complications, it might. An alarming number of practitioners are charlatans. Nothing prevents an M.D. from calling himself or herself a plastic surgeon and making extravagant advertising claims. The head of a plastic surgeons' watchdog committee in San Francisco says misleading ads have resulted in many catastrophes and several known deaths in California.

One way to measure a surgeon's skill is to check his or her certification. If specializing in reconstructive procedures and aesthetic procedures, he or she should be certified by the American Board of Plastic Surgery (1635 Market Street, Suite 400, Philadelphia, Pennsylvania 19103; 215-587-9322); if a surgeon does all kinds of cosmetic surgery, he or she should be certified by the American Board of Cosmetic Surgery (18525 Torrence Avenue, Lansing, Illinois 60438; 708-474-7200); if focusing on procedures from the neck up, he or she should be certified by the American Board of Facial, Plastic and Reconstructive Surgery (1 Prince Street, Alexandria, Virginia 22314; 703-549-3223).

For a list of surgeons certified by the American Board of Plastic Surgery, write or call the American Society of Plastic and Reconstructive Surgeons (444 East Algonquin Road, Arlington Heights, Illinois 60005; 800-635-0635). If you tell the society what operation you are considering, it will provide the names of 10 board-certified doctors in your area who perform the procedure and can send you information on its own financing program.

Your surgeon should be affiliated with a reputable hospital or a medical school, even if he or she performs most of his or her operations in the office. Without the right qualifications, a hospital would not accept the surgeon. Also, doctors on hospital staffs are subject to review by their peers.

A plastic surgeon should be willing to spend plenty of time answering your questions. Some charge nothing for the first consultation, particularly if you decide to go ahead with surgery. Others ask for $50 to $100 or even more as a consultation fee. If you do not think a particular surgeon is right for you, it is better to write off the consultation fee and find someone who merits more confidence. The stakes in plastic surgery are always high. Your best protection is to put yourself in the hands of a responsible surgeon.

About 10% of all U.S. plastic surgeons use imaging computers, which help the patient and doctor to determine what surgery might achieve. The computer takes a video camera shot and projects it onto a screen. With a mouse-like device, the doctor can transform the image as the patient explains what he or she wants. Some doctors oppose this system because they feel that it can mislead the patient — the image is the work of a computer, not a doctor. Instead, they rely on photographs of their actual work to help guide their patients.

## How Medicare Works

Medicare, which is Social Security's hospital- and medical-insurance plan, is mainly for people age 65 and older. It also covers anyone of any age receiving disability benefits, after he or she has been out of action for 24 months. Inflation has slowed dramatically in private health care, but not in Medicare and Medicaid. The two government programs account for 31% of the nation's health-care costs. Their spending grew 13% in 1994, to $162 billion; it was expected to leap another 10% in 1995, as beneficiaries increase and services expand. Congress is determined to cut this growth to the 5% to 7% range (or even below that), lest the system go bankrupt early in the 21st century. Almost certainly some of the benefits will be reduced.

But at this writing in late 1995, everyone eligible for Social Security retirement benefits was getting Medicare coverage at age 65 — whether retired or still working. In all, Medicare serves 37 million Americans. Some of them desperately need all that Medicare can provide; 10% of the beneficiaries account for 70% of the spending; 78% of Medicare beneficiaries earn less than $25,000 a year.

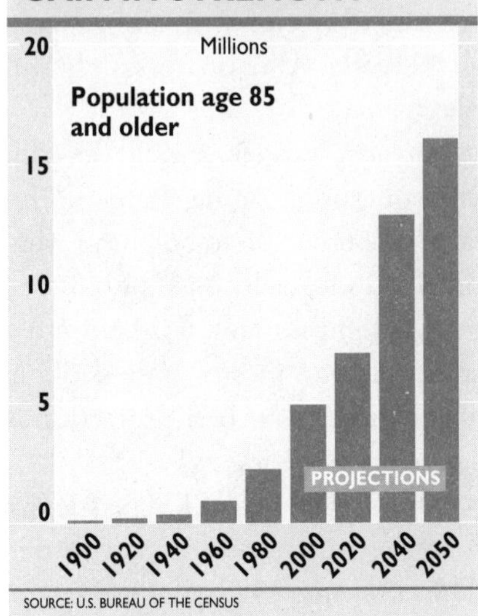


Medicare has two basic elements:

*Part A* is hospital insurance, and it covers almost every Medicare recipient. Most people don't have to pay any premiums for it. But Part A has deductibles and "co-insurance" — amounts that you must pay for yourself or through coverage with another insurance plan that may pay for what Medicare doesn't.

*Part B* is medical insurance, and it is optional but essential. It charges premiums: $46.10 a month in 1995. Social Security deducts the premium from monthly retirement checks. Part B also has deductibles and co-insurance that you must pay yourself or through coverage by another insurance plan.

Here, in brief, are Medicare's benefits (subject to change by Congress):

Under Part A, in 1995 you paid a total of only $716 for the first 60 days of hospital costs in a semi-private room. But for the next 30 days, you paid $179 a day. In the rare cases where you are hospitalized longer, you have 60 days of coverage that can be used over the rest of your life; for those, you pay $358 a day. After 150 days, you pay *all* hospital costs.

If you go from a hospital to recuperate at a nursing home that provides skilled care, Medicare covers all costs for the first 20 days, and everything over $89.50 a day for the next 80 days. After that, benefits stop. The accent here is on "skilled," meaning the home must offer care that can be performed only by licensed nurses, such as physical, occupational and speech therapy. Only a minority of nursing homes are skilled. Medicare doesn't pay for nursing homes or home care devoted primarily to maintaining an older person or providing long-term care.

Other Part A benefits include home *medical* care. If you meet the Medicare conditions, home health-care coverage includes skilled nursing care for up to 35 hours a week, or for eight hours a day, for a finite and predictable period of time. Benefits also include home health services like physical or speech therapy. If you meet the conditions and your physician determines that you need home health care, he or she sets up a home health plan for you with a home health agency that participates in Medicare. Medicare will not pay for 24-hour-a-day nursing care at home, drugs, home-delivered meals or blood transfusions. You have to pay 20% of the approved amount for durable medical equipment, such as oxygen gear and wheelchairs. All hospice care is paid for the terminally ill.

Under Part B, you are partly reimbursed for doctors' fees up to amounts approved by Medicare. You pay the first $100 per year and 20% of the rest of those approved rates; you also pay the difference between the approved fee and the higher amount that some physicians charge. Doctors accepted the amounts paid by Medicare in all but 4% of cases in 1994, down from 9% of cases in 1993. Medicare does not pay for prescription drugs.

Certainly, Medicare will not be enough to see you through when you retire. Parts A and B together reimburse an average of no more than 60% of medical expenses, and the total may well go down as Congress chops away at Medicare spending. But they do cover most catastrophic costs.

Given the gap, and the lack of any Medicare coverage outside the U.S., it's usually wise to supplement Part B with a "Medigap" policy. Most large corporations provide it for retirees after Medicare phases in, and many employers continue their regular group plan coverage until then for early retirees, often at company expense. In all, 89% of Medicare beneficiaries have supplemental coverage: 37% through Medigap, 33% through employer-sponsored plans, 12% through Medicaid and the rest through other sources. Federal law states that you have six months after retirement to buy any Medigap policy without having to undergo a medical exam or answer questions about your health.

You can escape most of the expense of a Medigap policy — usually $720 to $1,200 a person per year — by joining an HMO. It will cover just about all doctors' bills and prescription drugs. Only one in 11 Medicare beneficiaries belongs to an HMO, but more seniors are likely to join as Congress tightens Medicare. Increasingly, HMOs are signing deals under which Medicare pays a fixed per-capita fee to HMOs for covering just about all the medical needs of seniors.

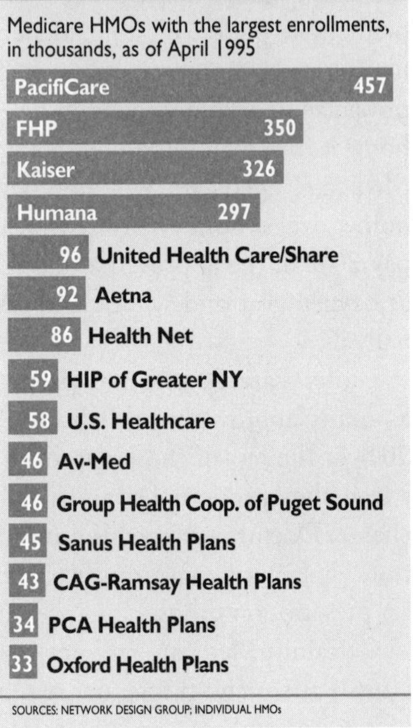


One good HMO example: Oxford Health Plan, which operates in four states (Connecticut, New Jersey, New York and Pennsylvania) from its base in Norwalk, Connecticut, is well-suited for retirees. It offers unlimited hospitalization, a $500 annual benefit for pharmaceuticals and a $10 charge per doctor's visit — with no deductibles and no extra premiums beyond the basic HMO charge. Oxford and similar HMO plans can offer this to Medicare patients because they can cut costs that Medicare cannot, because of its bureaucracy and red tape. For instance, Medicare requires patients to spend three costly days in a hospital before becoming eligible for much less expensive home care. Like all HMOs, Oxford emphasizes preventive care — such as annual checkups, fitness and asthma programs; and in 1996 Oxford, in conjunction with the New York City Department for the Aging, will launch a falls prevention program for the elderly — and works to reduce the number of hospital visits. HMOs have cut the number of hospital stays for their Medicare patients by 17%.

The elderly who join Oxford must use doctors from this HMO's list and specialists whom those doctors recommend. Also, Oxford's doctors, as in any other HMO, choose the treatments they deem appropriate; in short, you can't have everything you may want. But the pluses usually outweigh the minuses.

New Medigap regulations prescribe 10 standardized policies, designated by the letters A through J in most states. Seniors can choose the bare-bones Plan A — one that picks up the patient's 20% share of allowable doctors' fees and 100% of the eligible hospital expenses for an extra 365 days of inpatient care during the policyholder's lifetime. Plan B covers this plus the $716 inpatient hospital deductible. All other plans provide these benefits and more, and beneficiaries can tailor a policy to their needs and ability to pay.

The premium for Prudential/AARP Medigap basic Plan A is roughly $375 a year; for the most extensive Plan J, it is $1,420. Prices in California, Nevada and especially Florida are higher. Prices vary by location (cities are more expensive), insurance company and sometimes the age of the buyer.

Plans H, I and J include some reimbursement for prescription drugs. You can choose a plan that pays for either $1,250 or $3,000 worth of pharmaceuticals per year, but only after you pay a $250 deductible plus 50% of bills above that. So a patient's annual pharmacy bill would have to reach either $2,750 or $6,250 to capture the full insurance benefit.

New rules should also protect you against overinsuring yourself. In the past many Medigap policyholders were sold redundant additional policies. But except for long-term nursing-home coverage, which is not included in any supplemental plan, one good Medigap policy should cover all you need. It is now illegal for insurance agents to sell you more than one Medigap policy.

If your pocketbook permits, buy a plan with at least these features:

- *Full coverage of doctors' bills.* By far the largest gap in Medicare is that it pays 80% of doctors' fees, after a $100 yearly deductible.
- *Full coverage of hospital bills after Medicare runs out.* There is a sizable deductible for each hospital stay. It was $716 in 1995 and goes up every year. To reiterate, Medicare pays the rest for the first 60 days of a hospitalization, and all but $179 a day for the next 30 days. In rare cases of even longer stays, you can draw on a lifetime reserve of 60 hospital days, at $358 a day. Add it all up, and your out-of-pocket bill could reach $27,566 a year. Medigap insurance should reimburse you for all of that. Under the most basic policy, Plan A, all but the $716 hospital deductible is reimbursed. Plans B through J do cover the deductible.

- *Early coverage of existing illnesses.* The best policies immediately insure the patient for pre-existing illnesses. Others put benefits on hold for one to six months.
- *Guaranteed-renewable coverage.* Group Medicare policies covering retired members of professional societies, religious groups and other associations are seldom guaranteed-renewable. The insurer can drop the whole group after reasonable notice. Some commercial policies are "conditionally" renewable; if a company decides to pull out of a particular state because it is losing money there, it can cancel all its policies in that state. Make sure your policy is guaranteed-renewable.
- *Nursing-home coverage.* The first 20 days of post-hospital care in a skilled nursing home are Medicare's complete responsibility. The next 80 days cost the patient up to $89.50 each day. A Medigap plan should cover that. But don't expect any Medigap plan to pay for care in a custodial nursing home, where people with chronic illnesses spend the rest of their lives. That calls for a special long-term-care policy.
- *Illnesses while you're out of the country.* Even some otherwise comprehensive policies don't cover them.

To help you evaluate the new Medigap policies, United Seniors Health Cooperative has updated its booklet *Managing Your Health Care Finances* ($10, United Seniors Health Cooperative, 1331 H Street NW, Suite 500, Washington, D.C. 20005). And consult the 1995 *Medicare Handbook,* free at Social Security offices throughout the U.S. There is also a Medicare Hotline (800-638-6833) through which you can get Health Care Financing Administration publications and information about Medigap insurance and Medicare. And the National Insurance Consumer Helpline (800-942-4242) answers questions about health, life and property casualty insurance.

## Alternatives to Nursing Homes

Technology, improvements in home care and the spread of continuing-care retirement communities are offering alternatives to nursing homes for the mentally competent elderly. Medicare's nursing-home coverage is

## WILL YOU NEED A NURSING HOME?

| LENGTH OF STAY | CHANCES FOR MEN | CHANCES FOR WOMEN |
|---|---|---|
| Enter sometime in your life | 33% | 52% |
| Three months or more | 22% | 41% |
| One year or more | 14% | 31% |
| More than five years | 4% | 13% |

SOURCES: UNITED SENIORS HEALTH COOPERATIVE; *FORTUNE*

limited to short recuperations from major illness or injury. Costs of longer-term nursing homes average $80 to $90 a day, or some $31,000 a year. But these costs can reach up to $60,000 a year. Almost 70% of people in nursing homes rely on Medicaid; many of them are middle class but were driven to impoverishment because of the costs of long-term care. *The Directory of Nursing Homes,* an annual publication by HCIA Inc. (a health-care information company based in Baltimore), has detailed information about the prices, programs and services of 16,500 homes, listed by state and city. The directory costs $249; to order call 800-568-3282, or check your local library.

There is a common misconception that Medicare will cover long-term care. It does not. The fact that so many people in nursing homes rely on Medicaid shows that large numbers fail to insure themselves for the long term. With the expected cuts in Medicare and Medicaid, and the rise in the number of people age 70 and older, LTC (for long-term care) insurance is even more needed. About 3.5 million people have bought such policies from 118 insurers, and the number is growing about 25% a year.

When choosing an LTC policy, be aware that 45% of nursing-home stays are less than three months, just over 33% are for more than a year, and with most plans coverage for pre-existing conditions doesn't kick in until six months after the policy is issued; however, most plans do cover Alzheimer's disease, are guaranteed-renewable and have a 30-day free-look period. Long-term-care insurance covers nursing homes, home care and assisted living in communities that offer help with daily activities (feeding,

## CLIMBING COSTS OF NURSING HOMES

Average yearly rates for nursing-home care based on a rate of $29,930 in 1990

| INFLATION RATE | 1990 | 2000 | 2010 |
|---|---|---|---|
| 5% | $29,930 | $48,910 | $79,570 |
| 6% | 29,930 | 53,655 | 95,995 |
| 7% | 29,930 | 58,765 | 115,705 |
| 8% | 29,930 | 64,605 | 139,430 |

SOURCES: UNITED SENIORS HEALTH COOPERATIVE; *FORTUNE*

dressing, bathing, light medical care, etc.) for people too frail to do everything themselves but too healthy to be in nursing homes.

It is best to buy LTC insurance from the well-known organizations: American Express, Blue Cross/Blue Shield, Bankers Life, CNA and the American Association of Retired Persons. Buyers generally have to be ages 50 to 84. Most policies pay a fixed amount for each day you receive care. They also offer an inflation adjustment so that the benefit rises each year at a specified rate — say 5% compounded — but this adds 30% to 65% to your premium. The premium depends on your age, level of benefits and the deductible period, anywhere from zero to 100 days.

## The Cost of Nursing-Home Insurance

Here are average annual premiums for four years of coverage with a 20-day deductible:

For $80-a-day nursing-home coverage and $40-a-day home health care:

- If you're age 50, the base plan costs $337, and $630 with 5% compounded inflation adjustment.
- If you're 65 years old, it costs $898 and $1,452.
- If you're age 79, it costs $3,727 and $5,076.

For $100-a-day nursing-home coverage and $50-a-day home health care:

- At 50, it costs $405 and $770.
- At 65, it costs $1,086 and $1,896.
- At 79, it costs $4,372 and $6,033.

There are other alternatives. Medicine is keeping the elderly healthier longer. They are becoming disabled much later in life. Many of them stay relatively healthy, and able to live at home, until their 90s.

Technology assists them. Video magnifiers (allowing a vision-impaired person to read enlarged print from a TV screen) and devices that lift you into a bath or enable you to send out an emergency message if you get into trouble — all these, and more, help keep many of the elderly functioning at home.

They are not cheap; the video magnifier is about $3,000. But prices are low in contrast to nursing-home bills, and the independence and self-esteem the elderly get can be priceless.

Continuing-care retirement communities, or CCRCs, are growing in popularity. The appeal for many residents is that they have become a form of long-term-care policy. In a typical CCRC you move into an apartment and as care needs increase, you can get assisted living or move into a nearby nursing home. In 1994 the average entrance fee for a one-bedroom apartment was $59,000 to $86,000, with monthly costs of $1,000 to $1,400. The entrance fee for a two-bedroom apartment ranged from $88,000 to $121,000, with monthly costs of $1,250 to $1,600. (In many cases, if you leave the community, you or your heirs get some refund.) You can get assisted-living services, for a fee, in about 75% of the communities.

The American Association of Homes and Services for the Aging publishes *The Consumer's Directory of Continuing Care Retirement Communities.* It lists over 550 CCRCs, with information on their costs, size, setting, location and services. It comes out annually, costs $24.95 and can be ordered by calling 800-508-9442. From the same source, for $6.95, you can also get *The Continuing Care Retirement Community: A Guidebook for Consumers.* And the American Health Care Association (1201 L Street NW, Washington, D.C. 20005) publishes consumer brochures on selecting different types of care.

Other sources include the AARP at 202-434-2277; the National Rehabilitation Information Center (NARIC), 8455 Colesville Road, Suite 935, Silver Spring, Maryland 20910 (800-346-2742) and ABLEDATA at the same address (800-227-0216). The NARIC is a library and information center on disability and rehabilitation. ABLEDATA has information on new technologies and rehabilitation equipment. If you have a product in mind, like the video magnifier, you can call ABLEDATA for more information. The Eldercare Locator (800-677-1116) identifies local aging agency offices that provide information on services for the elderly, especially long-term-care insurance.

# Treatments for a Drinking or Drug Problem

Mary Tyler Moore, Johnny Cash and Betty Ford have something in common with millions of other Americans. All have battled drinking or drug problems, or both — and won.

Does someone you know have an addiction? According to the National Clearinghouse for Alcohol and Drug Information, telltale signs include: a person drinking immediately when faced with a problem, drinking changing a person's basic personality, the person attempting to handle all stress and social functions with alcohol, and missing work regularly.

Often it is as tough for a family member to admit that a loved one has a problem as it is for the addict. The sooner you confront the problem, the better. Some people shy away from treatment because they think they will have to take a leave of absence from work. With cutbacks in the workplace, many are worried that their jobs could mysteriously disappear while they are away. The fears are often unfounded. Many effective treatments are conducted at hours that would not keep one away from work. Some of these treatments are even free.

The number of treatment centers is huge and growing because the number of addicts is growing. In all, 50,000 Alcoholics Anonymous (AA) groups and 11,316 rehabilitation clinics, hospitals, halfway houses and outpatient programs offer help. The prognosis for those who seek help and complete treatment is good. The rate of recovery — defined as complete abstinence for one year — averages 60% and is much higher for those who regularly attend an after-care or peer-support program.

The costs range from nothing in the case of AA to $650 a day or even higher for private clinics. More and more people are getting the help they need at an affordable price because treatment is increasingly covered by health insurance.

Of the almost 25 million workers in companies with 100 employees or more surveyed by the Bureau of Labor Statistics in 1993, 98% had group health-insurance coverage for inpatient alcohol and drug detoxification. Roughly 80% were covered for both inpatient and outpatient rehabilitation following the acute stages of substance abuse treatment. For those enrolled in HMO plans, 62% were covered for inpatient rehabilitation and 77% for outpatient care. Medicare also covers up to 80% for approved inpatient detoxification programs and 50% for outpatient psychiatric care.

Specialists argue persuasively that confrontation with one's peers is an effective way to break down an addict's denial of his or her disease. This can be done in group therapy.

For addicts who recognize their problem and want help, the first step is detoxification, the elimination of alcohol and drugs from the blood. In the most serious cases, detoxification in a hospital usually lasts five to eight days and costs $300 to $700 a day. But it is covered by insurance even when policies don't pay for other aspects of treatment.

Once a patient has banished chemicals from his or her bloodstream, the roots of the addiction can be addressed. According to the National Clearinghouse for Alcohol and Drug Information, there are three kinds of treatment programs: outpatient, transitional and residential.

About 87% of alcoholics or drug addicts who receive treatment get it from clinics and rehabilitation centers but don't stay there overnight. Outpatient programs are well suited for people with an addiction not severe enough to put them in the hospital or a home to recover. They allow the person to continue to work or attend school. The programs are designed to work with the person's schedule so that his or her employer and co-workers will never know. The costs run from $10 all the way up to $100 a visit, depending on the type of counseling provided and, in some cases, what the patient can afford. They are generally much less expensive than in-house treatments.

The most prominent of the self-help groups, of course, is Alcoholics Anonymous. Health-care professionals praise AA — and it is absolutely free. Similar associations that have borrowed AA's tenets are Narcotics Anonymous and Pills Anonymous. What does AA offer? Trust and anonymity, continuous help and support from those recovered or trying to recover, and education about the effects of the disease and its progression. All can help lead to recovery.

Transitional programs are the halfway houses. They provide a drug-free place to live while working or attending school. Counselors live with the patients and, by offering their own recovery experiences, help patients adapt to living drug-free again. Patients also gain support from the other tenants.

Residential programs are for people who have to be watched around-the-clock in order to break their addiction. Given the supervision, these programs are the most expensive. Clinics charge an average $400 a day for typical 21- or 28-day stays. Generally, insurance reimbursement for inpatient care is limited to about one month per year. Although celebrities have gravitated to some clinics, everyone is treated as an equal.

There are several types of residential programs: intensive hospital, residential hospital care, residential care and therapeutic communities.

An intensive, in-house program for patients with serious psychological or medical problems can cost as much as $35,000 a month, though most in-house programs are $5,000 to $7,500 per month. A typical stay is 28 days. Programs for teens generally last two to four months. Intensive hospital programs are designed primarily for addicts who are severally dependent and have serious withdrawal symptoms requiring detoxification.

Residential hospital care programs provide 24-hour treatment and rehabilitation but are not as restrictive or as intensive as hospital programs. They are designed for people who earlier had tried to break the addiction and failed. Patients are given the supervision they need in an environment that is drug-free to help them overcome their dependence. They emphasize therapy, education and counseling. The cost varies with the length of the stay. The average is one month.

Residential care programs in homes, not hospitals, are for people who are not in danger of experiencing severe withdrawal symptoms. Counseling and therapy are used as treatments, but there is 24-hour surveillance.

Therapeutic communities are either privately run or government-sponsored homes. These communities, reports the National Institute on Drug Abuse, are particularly good with addicted adolescents who are considered troublesome to help. Typically, they are kept busy 16 hours a day in a very structured program designed to keep the adolescents stimulated, not bored. Boredom is suspected to contribute to youthful addictions.

Both the halfway houses and therapeutic communities offer extended inpatient care for people who would be likely to slip back into their old ways after a standard 30-day inpatient program. Room and board can cost $775 to $2,500 a month or even more in rare cases.

Several groups address the needs of the family members of addicts: Adult Children of Alcoholics (310-534-1815), the National Association for Children of Alcoholics (301-468-0985) and Alanon/Alateen (800-356-9996).

When you are ready to examine specific programs, ask your doctor for recommendations. You also can get information from the National Council on Alcoholism and Drug Dependence. To locate one of its 200 chapters, call its 24-hour hotline at 800-NCA-CALL. Also, the National Clearinghouse for Alcohol and Drug Information (800-729-6686) will send you free copies of reference materials on addiction. You can also call the Center for Substance Abuse Treatment hotline at 800-662-HELP. Local churches generally know of support groups. Your phone book lists all self-help groups in your area. State, county and city health and education organizations generally offer programs for addicts. Hospitals give education seminars as well as treatment. You would be wise to look for therapies that are conventional and well tested. For example, you're best off avoiding any doctor who tells you that alcoholism or drug addiction can be treated with prescriptions alone.

When you meet with the administrator of a program, be wary if he or she suggests admittance before taking a complete case history. Also beware of any evasiveness about costs or of a willingness to shave a few days off a program to match your insurance coverage. Think of the interview as your chance to assess a program's quality. Ask if the clinic meets the approval of the Joint Commission on Accreditation of Health Care Organizations, as well as state licensing agencies. Don't be afraid to inquire what type of patients tend to use the program. Many of the best programs use group therapy. But if the other people in the program have radically different backgrounds from your own, you may find it difficult to identify with their problems. Also ask the administrator for recovery rates and inquire whether these are monitored by an outside agency, such as the Comprehensive Assessment and Treatment Outcome Research (CATOR) in St. Paul. A fair measure of success is one year of abstinence, but two years is better.

## For Further Help

These addresses and phone numbers may be useful:

Adult Children of Alcoholics
P.O. Box 3216
Torrance, California 90510
310-534-1815

Alanon/Alateen
World Service Office
P.O. Box 862
Midtown Station
New York, New York 10018
800-356-9996 (general information)
800-344-2666 (meeting referral)

Alcoholics Anonymous
World Service Office
P.O. Box 459
Grand Central Station
New York, New York 10163
212-870-3400 (general information)
212-647-1680 (New York meeting referral)

National Association for Children of Alcoholics
11426 Rockville Pike
Suite 100
Rockville, Maryland 20852
301-468-0985

National Clearinghouse for Alcohol and Drug Information
P.O. Box 2345
Rockville, Maryland 20847
301-468-2600
800-729-6686

National Council on Alcoholism and Drug Dependence
12 West 21st Street
New York, New York 10010
212-206-6770
800-NCA-CALL

National Drug Information and Treatment Referral Hotline
800-662-HELP
800-66-AYUDA (español)

National Families in Action
2296 Henderson Mill Road
Suite 204
Atlanta, Georgia 30345
404-934-6364

American Society of Plastic and Reconstructive Surgeons
444 East Algonquin Road
Arlington Heights, Illinois 60005
800-635-0635

Applied Medical Informatics
2681 Parleys Way
Suite 204
Salt Lake City, Utah 84109
801-464-6200
800-584-3060

National Committee for Quality Assurance
202-628-5788

Washington Consumers' Checkbook
733 15th Street NW
Suite 820
Washington, D.C. 20005
202-347-7283

National Rehabilitation Information Center (NARIC)
8455 Colesville Road
Suite 935
Silver Spring, Maryland 20910
800-346-2742

ABLEDATA
8455 Colesville Road
Suite 935
Silver Spring, Maryland 20910
800-227-0216

American Dental Association
312-440-2746

Here are the phone numbers of counseling programs in each state that give free information and assistance on Medicare, Medicaid, Medigap, long-term care and other health-insurance benefits:

Alabama 800-243-5463
Alaska 800-478-6065
Arizona 800-432-4040
Arkansas 800-852-5494
California 800-927-4357
Colorado 303-894-7499 ext. 356
Connecticut 800-443-9946
Delaware 800-443-9946
District of Columbia 202-676-3900
Florida 904-922-2073
Georgia 800-669-8387
Hawaii 808-586-0100
Idaho 800-247-4422
Illinois 800-548-9034
Indiana 800-452-4800
Iowa 515-281-5705
Kansas 800-432-3535
Kentucky 800-372-2973
Louisiana 800-259-5301
Maine 800-750-5353
Maryland 800-243-3425
Massachusetts 800-882-2003
Michigan 517-373-8230
Minnesota 800-882-6262
Mississippi 800-948-3090
Missouri 800-390-3330
Montana 800-332-2272
Nebraska 402-471-4506
Nevada 800-307-4444
New Hampshire 603-271-4642
New Jersey 800-792-8820
New Mexico 800-432-2080
New York 800-333-4114
North Carolina 800-443-9354
North Dakota 800-247-0560
Ohio 800-686-1578
Oklahoma 405-521-6628
Oregon 800-722-4134
Pennsylvania 717-783-8975
Puerto Rico 809-721-5710
Rhode Island 800-322-2880

South Carolina 800-868-9095
South Dakota 605-773-3656
Tennessee 800-525-2816
Texas 800-252-3439
Utah 801-538-3910
Vermont 800-642-5119
Virginia 800-552-3402
Virgin Islands 809-774-2991
Washington 800-397-4422
West Virginia 304-558-3317
Wisconsin 800-242-1060
Wyoming 800-438-5768

CHAPTER 15

# Financing Your Education

## Getting the Most Financial Aid for College

Parents of teenagers heading toward college are being struck with an American affliction: tuition shock. But there is some therapeutic news. Even though federal aid has not kept pace with climbing college costs, you can still get much help from government and private sources.

For the academic year 1994–95, tuition, fees, and room and board averaged $18,261 at private colleges and $8,398 at public institutions. The fact that those figures are averages means the charges at many universities were higher. With the 1993–94 school year, Yale became the first university to cross the six-figure threshold. At a number of elite colleges, tuition, room and board, and fees now cost over $25,000 a year — more than $100,000 for four years.

So, what strategy should you pursue to ensure that your children get the education you — and they — want for them?

First, of course, start saving for college as soon as possible after your child is born.

Second, look for quality bargains in higher education. Many colleges manage to keep their academic standards up and their total costs down. Every year, *Money* and *U.S. News & World Report* publish detailed lists of these colleges.

Third, press your hunt for financial aid. Sometimes it is available even for families with annual incomes of $100,000 or above. In tough competition to recruit high achievers, quite a few schools have recently changed their policies on scholarships, giving them to desirable students regardless of their need. Many a high-school student is in the running for an academic scholarship if he or she has at least a B average, ranks in the upper third of the class and has Scholastic Aptitude Test (SAT) or American College Testing (ACT) scores above the national norm — now a total 849 for the SAT and a composite 20.6 for the ACT. For more prestigious universities, you will need higher scores, but don't put off applying because you think you can't afford it. Sometimes the costliest schools give the largest scholarships. The competition among colleges to attract minority students who score well on the SATs or ACTs is notably intense. Many of those students can get substantial scholarships.

The National Association of Student Financial Aid Administrators has a handbook, *TIPS (Timely Information for Parents and Students),* designed to help parents of high-school students through the aid process; the book contains detailed calendar checklists that tell you what steps you have to take and when you have to take them. Send $9 to the NASFAA, Department T-2, 1920 L Street NW, Suite 200, Washington, D.C. 20036-5020.

Almost half of all undergraduates received some public or private assistance in the 1994–95 academic year, as aid reached a record of nearly $39.7 billion. The federal government provided more than $26 billion; it funded federal grants and scholarships that students don't have to pay back, as well as student loans and work-study programs. Colleges supplemented these programs with more than $7.3 billion of their own aid. It is often from the colleges themselves that middle- and upper-middle-income families get their help.

To learn whether you qualify, you go through an incredibly complex and demanding process called need analysis. Financial need is defined as the difference between the cost of undergraduate education and what your family can contribute. This process should start shortly after January 1 of your child's senior year in high school. It is in your interest to submit the forms as soon as the needed information is available. To do so, you must have your tax information long before the April 15 deadline.

When applying for financial aid, you have to complete the Free Application for Federal Student Aid (FAFSA). It asks for detailed information concerning your family's finances: family size, taxable and nontaxable income of parents and students, cash and investments and the debts against them, and other information.

## WHERE THE SCHOLARSHIPS ARE

Elite schools award aid on a need basis. But most colleges shower money on talented students even if they are affluent. Here's a sampler from *Fortune*.

| | *Tuition and fees 1995–96* | *Room and board 1995–96* | *% receiving grants* Average grant* | *% receiving merit awards* Average grant* | *Comments* |
|---|---|---|---|---|---|
| **IVY & OTHER ELITE SCHOOLS** | | | | | |
| AMHERST | $20,710 | $5,560 | 45%<br>$13,250 | None | Even parents making more than $135,000 have qualified for financial aid at this elite liberal arts school. |
| HARVARD | $20,865 | $6,710 | 45%<br>$12,200 | None | Cleaning bathrooms is one way that students earn cash to pay bills. Scrubbers can earn $8.90 an hour. |
| PRINCETON | $20,960 | $6,116 | 41%<br>$13,000 | None | "Be all that you can be" with the help of an ROTC scholarship at this highly selective Ivy. |
| STANFORD | $19,695 | $7,054 | 44%[1]<br>$11,100 | 4%[2]<br>$21,000 | Water polo could help you splash down happily at this school, which offers various water-sports scholarships. |
| SWARTHMORE | $20,186 | $6,880 | 48%<br>$15,440 | under 1%<br>full tuition | Half the students average a walloping $15,440 in grants, thanks to a $500 million-plus endowment. |
| **OTHER PRIVATE SCHOOLS** | | | | | |
| BARD | $20,677 | $6,382 | 63%<br>$14,500 | 5%<br>$19,800 | Strapped for cash? Top-10 public high-schoolers can go here for the same price as their state university. |
| BOSTON UNIVERSITY | $19,420 | $7,100 | 54%<br>$12,100 | 10%<br>$12,000 | An accomplished bassoonist should toot his own horn when applying to BU, which likes to fill its orchestra. |
| CASE WESTERN RESERVE | $16,300 | $4,940 | 57%<br>$7,842 | 58%<br>$7,624 | Get your creative juices flowing to compete for three awards of $8,000 each in dance, theater and art. |
| DUKE | $19,500 | $6,320 | 35%<br>$11,565 | 3%<br>N.A. | Calculating types who finish in the top 10 in the North Carolina math competition can collect full tuition. |

| | | | | | |
|---|---|---|---|---|---|
| **GEORGE WASHINGTON** | $19,032 | $6,590 | 40%<br>$10,368 | 27%<br>$8,196 | Cheerleading awards are among the multitude of diverse scholarships to root for at this D.C. school. |
| **LAFAYETTE** | $19,621 | $6,000 | 66%<br>$12,066 | None | Starting in 1996, Marquis scholarships will grant at least $10,000, along with funds to study abroad for a semester. |
| **LAKE ERIE** | $12,320 | $4,906 | 66%<br>$2,138 | 33%<br>$2,888 | It pays to be a twin here. The small Ohio college has a buy-one, get-one-free tuition policy for all four years. |
| **LEHIGH** | $19,650 | $5,440 | 50%<br>$11,900 | 3%<br>$6,000 | Battling Penn State for students, this school offers $7,000 merit awards to the top 100 applicants. |
| **MARQUETTE** | $13,010 | $5,100 | 63%<br>$6,051 | 43%<br>$3,696 | Interested in cleaning choppers? Bite into a $5,000 scholarship offered by the Dental Hygiene program. |
| **NORTHWESTERN** | $17,184 | $5,781 | 53%<br>$9,542 | 4%[2]<br>part to full | If you're academically strong, financially needy and love golf, take a swing at a scholarship for caddies. |
| **NOTRE DAME** | $17,830 | $4,650 | 27%<br>$7,150 | 4%<br>$14,100 | Women can set themselves up for a free ride here playing volleyball for the Fighting Irish. |
| **U. OF ROCHESTER** | $19,175 | $6,730 | 71%<br>$13,750 | 6%<br>$1,950 | Science whizzes can see their dreams come true with a Bausch & Lomb scholarship worth at least $5,000. |
| | | | **STATE SCHOOLS** | | |
| **U. OF CALIFORNIA** (Berkeley) | $4,354[S]<br>$12,053[N] | $6,466 | 47%<br>$4,860 | 9%<br>$1,033 | An incredible deal for Californians. Their tuition is a paltry $4,354 per year, vs. $12,053 for nonresidents. |
| **U. OF MICHIGAN** (Ann Arbor) | $5,268[S]<br>$15,900[N] | $4,659 | 40%<br>$5,000 | 28%<br>$2,500 | Are you a Churchill, or a Jack Welch? This place awards full scholarships to those with leadership qualitites. |
| **U. OF NORTH CAROLINA** (Chapel Hill) | $1,575[S]<br>$9,100[N] | $4,350 | 27%<br>$3,301 | 1%<br>$5,395 | Visit exotic locales and even study abroad for free, courtesy of the Frances L. Phillips travel award. |

*1994–95. [S]State resident tuition costs. [N]State nonresident tuition costs. [1]Includes loans and work-study.
[2]Only merit athletic scholarships awarded.

SOURCE: *FORTUNE*

The data are analyzed by a central processing system, which arrives at a figure known as the Expected Family Contribution, the amount colleges can reasonably expect you to pay annually out of your own pocket. The product of this analysis is called the Student Aid Report (SAR). Most private colleges with substantial endowments also require applicants to complete the Financial Aid Form (FAF), to determine whether the student is eligible for one of the college's own programs. In addition, you will probably be asked to complete an institutional financial aid form and send it along with a copy of your 1040 income tax form for the most recent year. But don't despair, a lot of the information overlaps.

If college costs are higher than the SAR number, the school's financial aid officers will try to figure out ways to make up the difference by creating a package combining a college grant, federal loans and, possibly, a work-study program.

To determine the level of federal-loan funding a student is entitled to, the aid administrators must use the Federal Methodology Formula developed by Congress, which takes into account a family's income and some of its assets. If you seek additional aid from the school, you may be asked to complete yet another form, which uses the federal methodology and counts equity in the family house.

Each financial aid administrator has the authority, under law, to make judgments in individual cases and can differentiate within the college's financial aid formula. Administrators can use their own discretion to adjust a family's contribution in special cases of unemployment, excessive medical expenses or multiple tuition requirements (i.e., for other siblings). The system does take into account unusual circumstances. Roger Koester, Financial Aid Director for the Colorado School of Mines in Golden, says, "A family can have an income in the one-hundred-thousand-dollar range and have five kids — three of them in college — and still show some eligibility. On the other hand, a family with one child in college, no unusual circumstances, and a sixty- to seventy-five-thousand-dollar income will generally not be eligible for aid at most colleges."

Being a single parent may qualify as an unusual circumstance. Some single parents with relatively high incomes have qualified for financial aid. The point is that you should not be discouraged from applying; you have to be persistent and you may be pleasantly surprised.

Whatever the circumstances, they must be documented in some way to qualify for special treatment. The FAF has a section where you can explain your special circumstances. In most of these cases, the financial aid administrator will base family contributions on future expected income rather than on current earnings.

You can usually increase the aid your child gets if you know how to massage your finances. There's nothing wrong with doing so. An advantageous application for college aid, like an honest tax return, violates no law or ethical principle.

*Rule number one:* Be careful about putting savings or investments for college expenses in your children's names. Yes, as mentioned elsewhere in this book, your child is in a lower tax bracket than you are, so you can save taxes by investing in your child's name instead of your own. But consider this: Under the federally legislated aid formula, the required family contribution to the child's education must include only 2.6% to 5.6% of the parents' assets per year. That means the bulk of most families' wealth is never counted against them. But students are expected to spend up to 35% of *their* assets each year. Conduct a family accounting, and estimate what you stand to save on taxes by investing in your child's name, compared with what you would lose in college aid.

*Rule number two:* Adjust and reposition your assets to minimize your wealth as measured by the aid system. In surveying your net worth, the system recognizes some forms of wealth as assets but not others. Bank accounts, stocks, bonds and mutual funds count against you, but the cash you accumulate in most retirement funds, insurance and annuities does not. Some financial planners therefore advise clients to move part of their investments into universal life or deferred annuities a few years before a child is ready for college.

Alas, that situation may change in the future. The FAF and institutional forms now ask how much you've contributed to your 401(k) plan in the most recent year. You might be able to borrow from those funds for college.

To get an idea of how much aid you may be eligible for, write for the guide *Don't Miss Out* (Octameron Press, P.O. Box 2748, Alexandria, Virginia 22301; $7). This thorough guide to financial aid is updated annually, and it provides an eligibility worksheet in its appendix.

When it comes to borrowing, the cheapest money around is available through federally subsidized *5% Federal Perkins Loans.* A student can borrow as much as $3,000 annually directly from the school, up to a total of $15,000 over his or her entire undergraduate career. Students enrolled at schools with low default rates can borrow still more money. (Contact your school to see if it qualifies.) Repayment begins nine months after the completion of studies and extends for up to 10 years.

The old *Guaranteed Student Loans* are now called *Federal Stafford Loans.* They are part of the Federal Family Education Loans (FFEL) program and are offered through lenders such as banks and credit unions. Students can qualify for a maximum of $2,625 for the first year, $3,500 for the second and an annual maximum of $5,500 for each remaining year, or a total of $23,000 for an undergraduate education. Interest rates are set at 3.1% above the three-month Treasury bill rate, with a cap at 8.25% for 1995. Repayment begins six months after graduation.

Students who are deemed ineligible for full or partial Federal Stafford Loans may make up the difference with *Unsubsidized Stafford Loans.* These have the same rates and limitations as the Federal Stafford Loans, but the student, not the government, pays the interest while he or she is enrolled, starting with the day the loan is disbursed until it is repaid in full. The student then pays back the principal amount after graduation. (Congressional Republicans want to stop subsidizing interest for Stafford Loans, but as of mid-1995 the subsidies were intact.)

A federal offering mercifully free of a family needs test is the *Federal Parent Loans for Undergraduate Students,* known as the FPLUS loan. Its fluctuating interest rate equals the one-year Treasury bill rate plus 3.1%, with a cap of 8.98% for 1995. The maximum that may be borrowed in an FPLUS loan is the difference between the school's cost and the other financial aid the student is expected to receive. There is no annual or cumulative maximum for borrowing. You get the loans through participating banks or other commercial lenders. But repayment — again, up to 10 years — begins within 60 days after you take out an FPLUS loan. The longer repayment period, however, means smaller monthly payments than for most bank loans.

Recently the federal government started phasing in the Direct Loan program with the intention of streamlining the financial aid process and saving money. This program now involves the student, the college and the U.S. Department of Education. The need for the middleman (the bank) is eliminated. To apply for the loan, all the student has to do is fill out the FAFSA, the Free Application for Federal Student Aid. The school determines the amount to be borrowed, forwards that information to the Department of Education for approval and receives the funds electronically. The borrower repays the loan directly to the government, and a variety of repayment options are at his or her disposal. In the first year of the program (1994–95), 104 institutions participated. In the second year (1995–96), about 1,400 institutions participated.

When you file the Financial Aid Form (FAF), you are initially applying for the Pell Grant, which is the basis of all other financial aid packages. The Pell Grant is geared to low-income families. But colleges expect you to apply for the Pell Grant, and only when you're turned down will they consider you for other forms of aid.

Many *states* offer subsidized student loans to residents. Among the most generous are Alaska, Illinois, Minnesota, New York and Pennsylvania. To apply, see your college loan officer or go directly to your state education agency. Loan programs are often limited to in-state colleges, but students from Illinois and Pennsylvania can take a state loan along with them, wherever they enroll.

Another source of help may be close to home — in the form of scholarships financed by local communities, clubs and other private organizations. Every year thousands of students win more than $200 million worth of scholarships sponsored by many noncollegiate organizations. Just a few examples: The Knights of Columbus gives 50 four-year scholarships, each worth $1,500 a year for tuition at a Catholic university, to children of members. Even a nonmember's child is eligible for scholarships from the Elks National Foundation (an average $1,200 a year). Some 400 companies, unions and trade organizations sponsor National Merit Scholarships, usually worth $500 to $2,000 or more a year and covering all four years of college. And if you are a veteran, ask at your local American Legion post about awards available to your children.

If your child is willing to spend a minimum of four years after college in military service, consider the Navy/Marines, Army or Air Force Reserve Officer Training Corps (ROTC). All three programs can pay full tuition, fees, books and $100 a month tax-free. Each year 3,000 to 5,000 high-school seniors are granted full four-year scholarships, but shorter-term awards are available to students who qualify after starting college.

Because the pool of high-school seniors is smaller than it was a few years ago, the schools themselves must work harder to attract students. Consequently, many colleges are developing attractive financing

## FINDING FINANCIAL AID

**Federal Student Aid Information Center: 800-433-3243**
**Student Loan Marketing Association (Sallie Mae): 800-831-5626**
**American College Testing (ACT) Federal Student Aid: 319-337-1200**
**Nellie Mae: 617-849-1325 or 800-634-9308**
**ProPlan: 718-803-0900 ($69, 100% money-back guarantee)**
**Peterson's College Quest: 800-858-9952 (sells software for family: $49, and for businesses: $295)**
**CollegeCredit™: 800-831-5626 (for free information and applications for family education loans)**
**CSS/College Money Planner™: 609-771-7839 (to order a personalized planning tool for financing a child's education: $14.95)**
**College Cost Explorer FUND FINDER®: 212-713-8165 ($495 for single computer license; $745 for multicomputer/network license)**

SOURCE: THE COLLEGE BOARD

programs. They are offering more and more academic scholarships — from a few hundred dollars to full tuition — for students with top grades. Among the most generous and prestigious are the University of North Carolina's 54 Morehead scholarships and the University of Virginia's 21 Jefferson scholarships, both of which cover the entire cost of attending the respective schools.

You can find out about scholarships of all kinds from high-school guidance counselors, college admissions officers and books such as Oreon Keeslar's *Financial Aids for Higher Education,* published by William C. Brown ($72.50; 800-338-5578). Who knows? You might find a scholarship that few people compete for. At Harvard, for example, the William S. Murphy Fund divides nearly $17,000 each year among needy collegians with the surname Murphy.

Here are some other forms of help:

- A number of colleges have adopted guaranteed-tuition programs: Families can prepay all four years of tuition at the freshman rate. Participating schools include Case Western Reserve University in Cleveland, Washington University in St. Louis and the University of Southern California. The University of Pennsylvania will even lend parents the money — at favorable rates — to prepay tuition.
- For families whose incomes are too high to qualify for existing loan programs, there are also new student-loan plans. North-

western's Parent/Student Loan enables families with incomes over $40,000 to borrow up to the full tuition cost of $15,804 a year at 6.75%.

- Many colleges now let you pay off a year's tuition bill month by month. Some sponsors of these installment plan programs: Knight Insurance Agency (800-225-6783), Tuition Management Services (800-722-4867) and Academic Management Service (800-635-0120).

Another means of stretching college dollars is to have your child substitute a job for a loan. Colleges are concerned about student debt and are thus expanding work-study programs. This is an excellent way for a student to help finance his or her own education while simultaneously gaining expertise in a chosen field. Students alternate terms on campus with terms working at a real job. Last year, more than 200,000 young adults enrolled. Some 900 colleges offer co-op programs, and students have their pick of over 300 majors. Among the leaders are Northeastern University in Boston, Drexel in Philadelphia and the University of Cincinnati. For example, at Northeastern tuition is about $13,686 a year, and students can choose from a wide range of majors and paid jobs with more than 2,000 government agencies and private firms.

In a typical cooperative education program, a student takes a responsible job with a company that has agreed to participate. Students often work as trainees, earning an average $8,000 for a year's work, though some earn up to $15,000. Part of these earnings, minus taxes, are usually figured into the student's financial aid package back at school; and the grants and loans he or she would otherwise need may not be necessary.

Wages reflect those of the marketplace. Therefore, engineering students tend to earn significantly more than their counterparts enrolled in the liberal arts. Co-op jobs are scarcer for humanities students than for technical students or those with specific job skills, such as nursing majors. Most co-op students are in business administration, computer science, other hard sciences and engineering. While the majority of students work for private business, the biggest single employer is the federal government. It put some 14,000 students to work in the 1993–94 school year. And the government usually keeps about 45% of its students on the payroll after graduation.

The students commonly find that time spent on the job is a boon to their careers. They usually receive no academic credit for their work, but they learn skills firsthand. Many positions become full-time after graduation and pay a much higher salary than a less-experienced applicant could expect.

To learn more, write to the National Commission for Cooperative Education, 360 Huntington Avenue, Boston, Massachusetts 02115. Also, an excellent pamphlet is "Earn & Learn: Cooperative Education Opportunities Offered by the Federal Government." It is published by Octameron for $4 and you can get it by calling 703-836-5480.

Finally, see whether it might be feasible for your child to accelerate his or her studies and graduate in three years instead of four. To do so, he or she will need to take advance-placement exams in high school. If your youngster scores highly, usually a 4 or a 5, he or she can skip some beginning college courses at most colleges — and save a good deal of money along the way. Remember: Any child who graduates in three years can save a whole year's costs, and these days that can range from about $6,000 to $25,000.

## Saving for College

If college costs grow at the rate of 3% or 4% a year, a bachelor's degree in 10 years' time could cost $150,000 at a good university. Clearly, you will need a pile of savings and investments to finance it.

A convenient parking spot for savings is the custodial account that comes under the UGMA (Uniform Gifts to Minors Act) or the UTMA (Uniform Transfers to Minors Act). The tax code specifies that if your child is younger than age 14, the first $650 annual investment income in his or her name is tax-free; the next $650 is taxed at his or her rate (usually 15%); and any dividends, interest and capital gains above $1,300 are taxed at your rate. Once your child turns 14, *all* the income is taxed at his or her rate. As mentioned above, you have to balance your tax savings against the possibility that you may get less financial aid if your child has assets of his or her own to tap for college costs.

The best strategy with custodial accounts is to concentrate initially on high-growth, low-income investments such as long-term growth mutual funds. Once the child is within five years of entering college, the emphasis should switch to low-risk, income-generating investments such as

**AVERAGE ANNUAL INCREASE IN COLLEGE TUITION AND FEES**

From 1987-88 to 1994-95, at four-year colleges

| Year | Public | Private |
|---|---|---|
| 1988–89 | 5% | 9% |
| 1989–90 | 7 | 9 |
| 1990–91 | 7 | 8 |
| 1991–92 | 12 | 7 |
| 1992–93 | 10 | 7 |
| 1993–94 | 8 | 6 |
| 1994–95 | 6 | 6 |
| Annual cost | | |
| 1994–95 | $2,686 | $11,709 |

SOURCE: THE COLLEGE BOARD

certificates of deposit, money-market mutual funds or short-term bonds.

Fidelity Investments, the biggest mutual-fund group, has a college-savings plan that uses a number of its funds. They are Cash Reserves, a money-market fund; Blue Chip, a stock fund; Growth and Income, a dividend-oriented stock fund; and Asset Manager, a mixture of stocks, bonds and money-market securities. Investors can mix and match these funds in a custodial account in any proportion they wish. For a minimum initial investment of $1,000, Fidelity waives the 2% sales charge on its Growth and Income Fund.

A different approach, based on the historic behavior of stock prices, lets you put somewhat more of your college money into the stock market. Over the past 70 years, rising stock prices and reinvested dividends have produced an average annual compound return on Standard & Poor's 500 stock index of just over 10%. Despite sharp declines in some years, losses over any five-year period have been rare. Going by past performance, a parent probably can preserve the value of college money in stocks by selling shares *gradually* after the student's 13th or 14th birthday and putting the proceeds in CDs or a money-market fund.

An investment program designed to do exactly that is available from Twentieth Century Investors, a no-load mutual-fund company in Kansas City, Missouri. Through its College Investment Program, parents or grandparents can have fixed amounts of $25 or more a month transferred from their checking account to Twentieth Century Select Investors, a growth stock fund. Starting when the college-bound child is 12, 13, or 14 years old (your call), the company will transfer fixed monthly amounts from the stock fund to Twentieth Century's Cash Reserve money-market fund (800-COLLEGE).

Bonds have become popular with parents, because over the years bonds produce interest that can be reinvested, while the bonds themselves can be timed to mature when the child is ready to go to college. And you *do* want to invest only in bonds that will mature and pay off at full face value at precisely the time when you need them. Don't buy a very-long-term bond that you'll have to cash in to pay tuition bills before it matures; if you do, you'll find that bonds can be as volatile, vulnerable and unpredictable as stocks. Their face values go down when interest rates go up.

U.S. Savings Bonds pay *tax-free* interest to anyone using them for college education, as long as the parents' joint incomes are $68,250 or less, or $45,500 or less for single parents. The interest exclusion phases out beyond that amount and disappears altogether at $96,200 for couples and at $59,150 for single parents.

A number of states have passed legislation creating College Savings Bonds, also known as "baccalaureate bonds," which are municipal bonds, free from both federal and state taxes. You can buy them from brokerages and from some banks for prices that generally range from $900 to $5,000. Some states offer a financial incentive if the child attends a school within the state. In Illinois, for example, parents who pay around $1,000 for a bond now will collect $5,000 in 20 years. If that money pays for costs at a public or a private college in Illinois, the family collects a $420 bonus at maturity.

Baccalaureate bonds belong to the larger family of zero-coupon bonds, which get their name because you receive no income until the bond matures. You buy a zero at a substantial discount and collect its face value when it matures. Though you receive no income until then, you have to pay taxes on the accrued interest — except on municipal or state zeros, both of which are tax-free. Tax-free zeros are fast becoming one of the most attractive long-term investments for college education. The risk with zeros is that their value fluctuates more than that of conventional bonds, as interest rates rise and fall.

## Financial Aid Consultants

Financial aid forms are so difficult to fill out that many parents are getting advice from academe's equivalent of tax advisers: college financial aid consultants. They charge from $70 to $800, depending upon how much individual attention you get. Consultants guide you through the aid application process and make sure no options and opportunities are overlooked. You may also want to write to the national firm Octameron Associates (P.O. Box 2748, Alexandria, Virginia 22301; 703-836-5480), which publishes 15 to 20 books on student financial aid.

A consultant typically begins by reviewing your finances. Then, using his or her knowledge of what the schools offer, he or she can figure out what kind of aid — and how much — you stand to get from the colleges you are considering. He or she will also point you to money available from sources other than the schools — for example, state loan programs or private scholarships. Of course, the consultant will help you fill out the aid forms; you have to repeat that arduous task every year. To find a consultant in your area, ask a financial aid officer at a local college or a high-school guidance counselor. Check the references of each consultant and try to speak with several past clients. Stay away from anybody who makes big promises about how much financial aid he or she can squeeze out for you or anyone who urges you to misrepresent yourself on the forms. The applications you file are checked for accuracy. And financial aid consultants are required to sign the aid application forms they prepare in much the same way tax accountants must sign the returns they file on a client's behalf.

There is no accreditation or licensing process to screen consultants, so be careful when selecting one and when considering the advice he or she provides. Opinion varies on their usefulness. If you do your homework, you can gather — free of charge — much of the information that they offer. The point is, get references and question the consultant closely — about his or her background and what he or she can do for you — before you engage him or her.

# Choosing the Right College

Not just football and basketball stars, but fully 60% of the students who enter college as freshmen do not graduate from that school. Most leave early because they realize they chose the wrong college. It is easy to make that mistake — but it is also easy to avoid it. Your decisions about what college to attend determine where you spend several important years, and many thousands of dollars.

The surest way to select is to visit several schools; meet with faculty members, students and administrators; and make your own evaluations of some key points. When comparison shopping, see that your needs as a student are going to be met. For example:

- Do the students share your talents and interests? To gauge the caliber of the competition you will face, compare your high-school grade point average with the average for the current year's freshmen. College admissions officers will give you the data. If your scores are higher than the average for the entering class, you may find yourself underchallenged.
- Consider the school's program in your planned major. If you intend to concentrate in science, for example, ask when the laboratories were last re-equipped. Find out where students who take your major go after graduation. It is a good sign if many get into prestigious graduate schools or win scholarships.
- Take note of class sizes. At small colleges, the ratio of students to faculty is a sound indicator of how much personal attention you will get. A ratio of 10 students per teacher is excellent. Ask an admissions officer to estimate the class sizes for courses in your major.
- Find out about any special academic programs. You might be interested in completing your bachelor's degree in three years instead of four; a growing number of schools will let you do so. Or you may well want to spend your junior year abroad, say, studying art in Italy. Ask which foreign universities you may attend.
- Determine what the total expenses are for the colleges you are weighing and decide whether you and your family can afford them. Consider whether the added cost of a private college justifies itself or whether a well-rated state school can deliver academic excellence. You will not spend money just on tuition and room and board. You will also make at least one round-trip — and probably more — between your home and campus each year. And you will have to pay for books, entertainment and almost certainly a personal computer.
- If you will require financial aid, ask college officials how your needs will be met. See whether the college offers most of its as-

sistance in the form of grants or loans or job opportunities. A school that can afford to give out most of its aid as grants is more financially attractive than one that cannot.

- Ask yourself if graduating from a certain college will enhance your career. You can expect a precise answer if you have a specific goal. An aspiring engineer, for example, can find out the percentage of recent graduates in his or her field who received job offers — and how much those offers were for.
- Try to get a feel for how loyal the college's alumni are. Ask college officials for evidence of alumni networks. This can help you get a job after you graduate.
- Find out about the school's financial condition. A college that must survive mostly on tuition because of its tiny endowment may well have crowded classes, run-down dormitories and outdated labs. To compare colleges fairly, divide endowment by the number of undergraduates, and determine which has the largest endowment per student.

# Getting a Degree in Business

What is the most popular undergraduate course on college campuses? It's business. One out of four students is aiming for a degree in business, and many hope it will be a ticket to job security and advancement after graduation. It can be — if you choose the right school.

Carefully check out the quality of the school before enrolling, because strong demand for business teachers has produced a serious shortage. Look closely at *who* will be teaching you. At the best schools, at least 70% of the teachers hold Ph.D.'s. Also, look at *what* they will be teaching you. Highly specialized areas are often quickly outdated by technology. The American Assembly of Collegiate Schools of Business, the association that accredits business programs, has approved only 268 of the 1,200 or so colleges that offer undergraduate business degrees.

The University of Virginia's McIntire School of Commerce is one of the most elite undergraduate business schools. Over the past five years 85% to 90% of the graduates landed jobs within three months of graduation. Though recruiting has tapered off at some universities, the best schools attract legions of corporate job recruiters. For example, at

Indiana University, more than 500 corporations send recruiters to meet promising students. And representatives from nearly 600 companies visit the University of Texas.

If you are interested in accounting, check out the University of Texas and the University of Illinois. Their accounting departments are among the best. For marketing and information systems, consider the University of Minnesota. If you want to study liberal arts as well, the University of North Carolina is one school that offers courses in logic, writing and public speaking. The Wharton School at the University of Pennsylvania offers the only Ivy League undergraduate business major. It's known for its expertise in accounting, applied economics and finance.

Other schools with strong, selective undergraduate business programs include the University of California at Berkeley, Carnegie-Mellon, MIT and the University of Wisconsin–Madison.

## Does an MBA Still Pay?

To earn one of those cherished master's degrees in business administration costs $11,000 to $36,000 a year in tuition and expenses for a full-time student, in addition to salary lost by studying rather than working for two years. But does it still pay to get an MBA?

Studies by the American Assembly of Collegiate Schools of Business and the U.S. Department of Education show that the number of MBAs granted each year has more than tripled since 1970, to 89,064 in 1994. Almost 237,000 students, including part-timers, are enrolled in one of the more than 700 graduate business and management programs. Consequently, an MBA no longer guarantees you an advantage in the race to top management positions. Tempting jobs open to MBAs from even the most prestigious business schools are somewhat harder to land than they were in the late 1970s and 1980s. On-campus recruitment has decreased and job offers have been fewer. The ratio of starting salary to tuition has also fallen. Starting salaries are still high, but many no longer seem as startling as in the past. The College Placement Council reports that in 1995 an MBA with little work experience and a nontechnical undergraduate degree was offered a job paying an average of $39,035.

Still, attending a first-rate university pays big dividends. The top graduate business schools include those at Stanford, Harvard, Michigan, Chicago, Pennsylvania, Northwestern, MIT, Columbia, Berkeley, New York University, Dartmouth, Virginia and Carnegie-Mellon. (Full disclosure department: I am a member of the Board of Overseers at New York University's Stern School of Business, so I may have my own biases.) The payoff of attending one of those schools can be impressive, particularly for people who study the most demanded specialties: finance, marketing and international business. It is also helpful to have earned a degree in science or technology before going to graduate business school. The MBAs with undergraduate majors in engineering or hard sciences usually get jobs more easily than those without such backgrounds.

Another smart move is to work for a few years before going to graduate business school. The most successful combination for a new MBA is to have a technical or scientific undergraduate degree and work experience. In 1995 such graduates with two to four years' work experience typically started at an average salary of $65,268 — almost $25,000 higher than MBAs who majored in liberal arts as undergrads and had never held full-time jobs.

## Opportunities Without Elite College Degrees

We live in what might be called a Bachelor of Arts economy. Graduates of four-year colleges have a significant and growing financial edge over other workers. The latest Census Bureau statistics show that in 1993 the median income for men age 25 and older with four years of college was $41,591 — 55% higher than the income of men with one to three years of college at $26,777, and 80% more than the amount earned by those with only a high-school diploma at $23,127. Every bit of evidence since then shows that the gap is widening.

Even so, many job openings call for skills that are more likely acquired in a technical school or on the job than on some ivied campus. Technical school graduates are landing some jobs with a higher starting pay than newly minted bachelors of arts can command. Aircraft technicians fresh from a 2½-year program can earn $32,000 a year or more, which is on par with the starting salaries for most engineers with bachelor's degrees. Tuition runs to $19,000 at the College of Aeronautics at New York's La Guardia Airport, one of about 140 institutions in the nation that offer such a program. A computer programmer who completes a six-month course can earn $22,000 a year while an English major is still home rewriting a résumé.

Technical training is expensive but, because it is condensed, costs far less than a $70,000 university degree. At one technical school, for example, an 18-month program that trains electronics technicians costs $10,000. Many two-year community colleges and private junior colleges offer vocational training at considerably lower cost than do private technical schools. Tuition averages about $1,022 a year for such job-oriented studies as data processing, police science, real estate sales and auto mechanics.

What is most valuable in vocational education at either a community college or a technical school is hands-on training. When choosing a program, first visit the school and ask many questions. Inquire about the school's resources as well as about the time devoted to learning by doing. Check which companies hire the most graduates. Then query those companies' personnel managers on how they rate the school's courses. A bachelor of science graduate of a 36-month course at the De Vry Institute of Technology can get a job starting at about $22,500 a year. That's a fair return on an investment of $23,490 in tuition and registration fees.

The ideal, of course, is to get paid while learning a skill. High-tech companies that need a competent workforce often educate people in specialized skills. The list includes AT&T, IBM, Xerox and Control Data. Competition for on-the-job apprenticeships has always been stiff, but businesses' need for trainees is growing. Some companies are helping to train students for the workplace before they leave high school. For example, Sears, lacking well-qualified repair people, established a curriculum in 1992 in a suburban Chicago vocational high school that gives students the training they need to go to work as beginner technicians right after graduation. Sears hires a high percentage of the graduates.

The Labor Department's Bureau of Apprenticeship and Training supervises nearly 43,000 apprenticeship programs. Along with the standard apprenticeships for plumbers, pipefitters and carpenters, there are programs in hundreds of other occupations, including biomedical equipment technician, meteorologist and chef. For more information, contact your local Office of Apprenticeship and Training at the Department of Labor or the state apprenticeship agency, both of which are usually listed in the new Blue Pages of the phone book. Even without training, high-school graduates can find worthwhile jobs in marketing, retailing and a few other fields. And in some government-regulated sales fields — particularly real estate, securities and insurance — a beginning file clerk can impress a boss by studying hard and passing a licensing exam.

## Cutting Costs at Community Colleges

You can get an effective and economical start toward earning a college degree by attending a two-year community college. Nearly 6.2 million students attend such schools. Public community colleges cost an average of just over $1,000 a year; that is about one-fifth to one-half of what tuition and fees alone average at your four-year state university. And you can economize on room and board by living at home and commuting.

Check the catalogue to make sure that your college has a transfer program to a four-year school. The college should be able to meet liberal-arts requirements for transfer and offer courses in English, math, history and science that look like the core curriculums at a state university.

You can judge academic merits by consulting *Peterson's Guide to Two-Year Colleges* to see how many students go on to four-year programs. Anything over a 60% transfer rate is encouraging. Another sign of quality is the on-campus presence of a chapter of Phi Theta Kappa, the honor society often considered the two-year counterpart of Phi Beta Kappa.

You also can earn a four-year bachelor's degree entirely by mail or over the phone. Most correspondence programs require some classroom attendance, but the Center for Distance Learning at Empire State College does not. The college is part of the State University of New York, and its correspondence program is accredited by the Middle States Association of Colleges and Schools. Through the Center you can get a degree in business, human services or interdisciplinary studies. Each credit will cost you $90 as a matriculated student, and you need 128 credits to graduate. If you have had previous college experience or other training, you can usually count most of it toward your degree. For more information, write to the Center for Distance Learning, Empire State College, 2 Union Avenue, Saratoga Springs, New York 12866.

## College Credit for Life Experience

You can earn college credits for any learning you have acquired on your own — simply by taking a test. Quite a few accredited colleges administer such exams in what are generally called "external degree programs." Two of the biggest and best known are at the University of the State of New York (Regents College, 7 Columbia Circle, Albany, New York 12203-5159) and Thomas Edison State College (101 West State Street, Trenton, New Jersey 08608-1176). Neither school has a residency requirement; both take students from all over the world.

To earn academic credit for work experience, you can take standardized tests. Or the college will tailor an exam to your special circumstances. To enroll in a Regents College degree program of the University of the State of New York, you pay $480 the first year, plus a record-keeping fee of $240 each year thereafter. For more information you can also contact the College Level Examination Program (CLEP) of the College Board (45 Columbus Avenue, New York, New York 10023; 212-713-8064).

## Budgeting for Students

One extracurricular activity that every college student should master is personal money management. But a student's day-to-day spending is typically as ad lib and unbuttoned as a fraternity beer blast. That does not mean you cannot keep your undergraduate from overspending.

During a school year, the average college student will lay out about $2,000 for books, other supplies, transportation and personal expenses

## HOW MUCH STUDENTS SPEND—AND WHAT FOR

Estimated average student expenditures in non-fixed budget components, 1994–95*

| SECTOR | ALL STUDENTS | RESIDENT STUDENTS | | COMMUTER STUDENTS | | |
|---|---|---|---|---|---|---|
| | Books and supplies | Trans-portation | Other expenses | Board only | Trans-portation | Other expenses |
| **Two-year public** | **$566** | ** | ** | **$1,716** | **$934** | **$1,095** |
| **Two-year private** | **552** | **$569** | **$975** | **1,850** | **908** | **1,192** |
| **Four-year public** | **578** | **592** | **1,308** | **1,684** | **892** | **1,314** |
| **Four-year private** | **585** | **523** | **991** | **1,809** | **884** | **1,123** |

*Data in this table were weighted by enrollment to reflect the variable expenses of the average undergraduate student at a particular type of college.

**Sample too small to provide meaningful information.

SOURCE: THE COLLEGE BOARD

at a state university. There is plenty of room for economizing, and the first place to look is at food and phones. Two surveys have illustrated the point. At Penn State, boarding students forked out an average $415 a year for all those 2 A.M. pizzas and their accompaniments. And at the University of Connecticut, students spent more than $50 a month each on long-distance phone calls.

While many students seem to think that it costs less to live off campus than in a dorm, they may be wrong. In college towns with a lot of demand for off-campus housing, accommodations within walking distance of campus tend to be expensive. Of course, off-campus students can save money by sharing housing and doing their own cooking. If landlords demand a one-year lease, students should hold out for subleasing privileges.

Most parents have to send money at one time or other. But doling out funds regularly by the week or month may tend to foster an unhealthy dependence. Instead, try giving your undergraduate a lump sum each semester and make it clear that the money will have to last. If you give your child spending money, be certain to sit down and discuss your mutual expectations. To avoid unnecessary strife, you need to know the student's assumptions about spending. And the student, in turn, should know when a check is coming, its amount and any rules about its use.

Ideally, college students should take full charge of a semester's spending. If the first semester seems too soon, put it off until the next term. But the parents' lives will not get any easier until the student runs his or her own finances.

## Coaching Courses for the SATs

If you are a high-school junior planning to take the all-important Scholastic Aptitude Test or the redesigned American College Testing assessment, it makes sense to invest your time and money in a coaching school — particularly if a high score is crucial to your getting into your top college choice.

Test results show that coaching can improve your SAT and ACT scores. True enough, designers of the tests measure the kind of reasoning ability developed over a long period of time. But leaders of the Stanley H. Kaplan Educational Center, the oldest and largest coaching school, claim that its students raise their SAT scores by an average of 92 points. Among those who stand to benefit most from coaching are first-time test-takers. Familiarity with instructions, types of questions and time pressures help to improve your performance. Coaching also aids those who tend to choke. They can learn how to pace themselves, make informed guesses and take shortcuts.

The best courses last for a month or more. But stay away from the so-called cram houses that offer three sessions or fewer, no matter how many hours they run. Before you sign up for any courses, sit in on a session and find out if students are satisfied with the instruction.

The Kaplan Center has 150 branches with 600 satellite locations where classes are offered nationwide. Call 800-KAP-TEST to find the one nearest you, or write to the Kaplan Center, 810 Seventh Avenue, New York, New York 10019. For SAT coaching, the branches offer 40 hours of class in 10 lectures plus two workshops over eight to 10 weeks for $595. Scholarships are available for needy students. Seven sessions of coaching for the ACT test cost $345. Another reputable school with 60 branches is The Princeton Review. For an office near you, call 800-2-REVIEW.

If you do not feel the need for formal coaching, you might try examining the many workbooks available. One is *How to Prepare for College Board Achievement Tests* (each subject sold separately), published by Barron's at $9.95; another is called *Real SATs,* published by the College Board at $14.

## Classes for Elders

Many colleges are opening their classrooms to knowledge-hungry people age 60 and older. You can choose from thousands of week-long, noncredit courses through a nonprofit organization called Elderhostel. An average of $300 pays for one to three courses taught by regular faculty members at U.S. colleges. That fee includes tuition, room and board, and extracurricular activities such as films and parties. You can also sign up at universities in European and other countries, including Israel and Mexico. Two- and four-week foreign seminars on every continent except Antarctica range from about $1,600 to $5,000, including airfare.

Elderhostel enrolls more than 250,000 students a year at 1,800 institutions. For information, write to Elderhostel, 75 Federal Street, Third Floor, Boston, Massachusetts 02110-1941, or call 617-426-7788.

# Courses in Public Speaking

In a survey, 2,500 Americans were asked, "What are you most afraid of?" The most frequent reply was not death, illness or poverty, but speaking before a group. Yet people in all types of jobs are asked routinely to speak at staff meetings, sales presentations and trade conventions. Their success or failure at the podium often influences their careers.

More and more men and women are signing up for courses that promise to help make them better public speakers. Fees range from $50 (or even less at a community college or YMCA) all the way up to $3,600 for a commercial course. If you can demonstrate that the course will help you perform better on the job, your employer may be willing to pay for the instruction.

The grandfather of public-speaking courses is the Dale Carnegie course. It consists of 12 weekly evening sessions for about $800 to $1,100, depending on region, and is offered at more than 1,100 locations across the country.

You also can practice and learn through the nonprofit Toastmasters International, whose members attend a series of meetings to sharpen their speaking skills. You pay $25 to $50 a year at one of more than 5,000 affiliated clubs, plus a one-time $12 fee to join. At meetings, there is no formal instruction. Instead, 20 or so members typically take turns giving five- to seven-minute speeches. Their peers then critique their performance.

Once you have picked a course, ask for the names of graduates in your field or profession. Call them and press for candid comments on the nature of the course, the quality of the instruction and the relevance of the program to your specific needs.

You may even become sufficiently proficient to earn a second income as a professional lecturer. True enough, very few people can collect big money, but you can make public speaking pay. Try approaching schools, libraries, PTAs and other civic and business organizations and institutions to offer your services. If you're good, your name will spread among local groups. At first, you may want to speak for free, and then as your reputation spreads you might start charging. When you can command perhaps several hundred dollars a speech, the smaller booking agencies may be willing to take you on.

## Learning a Foreign Language

Getting an assignment abroad for several years is an increasingly important step on the road to advancement in the modern multinational corporation. And in our global economy, it certainly helps to master one or more foreign languages.

The least expensive way to start is to take a self-taught course on audiocassettes. The Audio-Forum Company (96 Broad Street, Guilford, Connecticut 06437; 800-243-1234) markets sets of cassettes in 91 languages. There are 230 courses, each in one of three categories: tourist, refresher or comprehensive. The tourist tapes teach the words and sentences you will need for such basics as checking in to and out of hotels and getting around on public transportation.

For more comprehensive courses, consider the cassettes sold by the Foreign Service Institute, the branch of the State Department that trains diplomats and other federal employees in languages. Instruction in one of more than 50 languages costs $32 to $300 for a series of tapes lasting from five to 48 hours. You can buy them through the National Audiovisual Center (Order Section, 8700 Edgeworth Drive, Capitol Heights, Maryland 20743; 800-788-6282).

You can enroll part-time in top-quality language classes offered by many colleges and continuing education schools. The language division of Continuing Education at the University of Houston, for instance, charges $280 to $385 for a 32-hour accelerated-learning course in languages as varied as Arabic, French and Chinese. Also check out classes at cultural institutes sponsored by foreign governments and located in many major U.S. cities. For example, the Goethe Institute is a German cultural center with branches in many places. Its Chicago branch offers German language courses that meet once or twice a week for 10 weeks. The cost is $160 for the once-a-week course and $300 for the twice-a-week course. Similar courses are offered in many large cities.

If you want the convenience that cassettes afford and the personalized attention you can get in a class, hire a tutor. That will cost $15 to $40 an hour, but an instructor from a commercial school will be much more expensive. The most affordable instructors are foreign-exchange students or foreign-language majors at local colleges. Ask instructors there to recommend tutors. You can also find teachers through the cultural institutes.

For a very intensive language-learning experience, go to classes offered by such chains as Berlitz and Inlingua. But be warned: Commercial courses are costly. Expect to spend about $4,800 for a 12-day total immersion course in any language at Berlitz. For that price, you will get day-long private lessons from a team of instructors.

To make your vacation a learning experience, enroll in a study-abroad program run by both U.S.-based and foreign schools. You can study as briefly as several days or as long as four weeks — or more. Many of these language classes for travelers are reasonably priced.

Want to learn Russian? Moscow State University and Leningrad State

University permit foreign students to take language classes and to stay in the university dormitories. Clark Malcolm's Custom Tours (800-688-3301) specializes in setting up group study courses in the former Soviet Union and Eastern Europe. They typically include five hours of language instruction daily, as well as meals, activities and a shared hotel room for about $60 a day.

CHAPTER 16

# Enriching Your Career

## Where the Opportunities Are

The U.S. is in transition from an industrial society to an information society. In this new world, the individual and the computer will have to work together as a team. People who want to get ahead will need not just one skill but more likely several skills. Humanists had better be able to communicate with technicians. Engineers should know how to read a balance sheet. With global trade expanding, you would be wise to know one or more foreign languages.

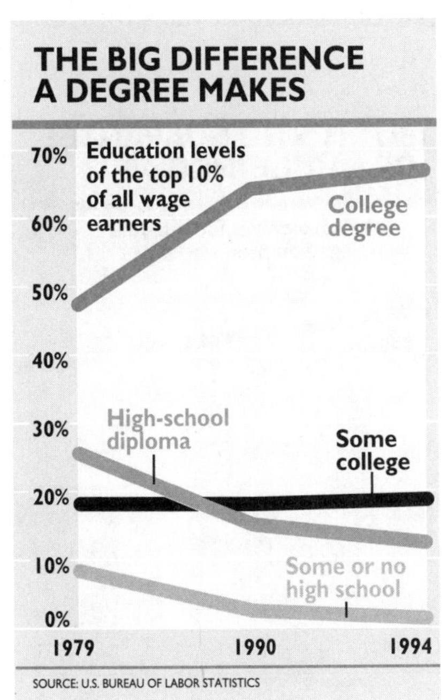


The workplace is shifting from an emphasis on the narrow specialist, who is in danger of becoming obsolete, to the multiskilled generalist who can adapt. A college degree helps but, increasingly, it is not enough. The most desirable workers will be those who constantly upgrade their skills and keep on top of the latest technology. And forget about the nine-to-five workday. With home computers and faxes, you may be expected to work whenever — and wherever — the job requires it. With all this in mind, you have to start actively managing your career.

Ask a career counselor for the hottest career prospects, and you may well hear that the future lies in two areas: high tech and health care. Indeed, shortages of people with skills in those areas has created great demand for such professionals as technical writers, systems analysts, computer engineers and scientists, and biomedical workers. The Bureau of Labor Statistics estimates that from 1992 to 2005, the number of jobs will rise 138% for home health aides, 88% for physical therapists and 71% for medical assistants. But unless you feel an urgent desire to care for the ailing or work with computers, you would be making a mistake to follow the herd into either of those fields. The wisest counsel in looking for a job is to pursue your own interests and ambitions. A surprising number of determined men and women are finding good jobs in fields that the career prophets had written off.

When recruiting young adults for management-track jobs, companies look for so-called hard skills like accounting, finance and marketing. But some other qualities have become much more important than they used to be. In a *Fortune* poll of top executives, the ability to work in teams was cited as the most important new skill for business school graduates. Companies also want people who can think beyond their own discipline, be it accounting or marketing, to solve complex problems. Even if it's not your specialty, you have to know enough about technology to understand how your company makes its products or delivers its services.

Corporations are looking for people who can think globally. Besides mastering foreign languages, that kind of thinking includes understanding the different ways work gets done in other parts of the world. An assignment overseas used to be seen as a career graveyard; now it is increasingly a passport to advancement.

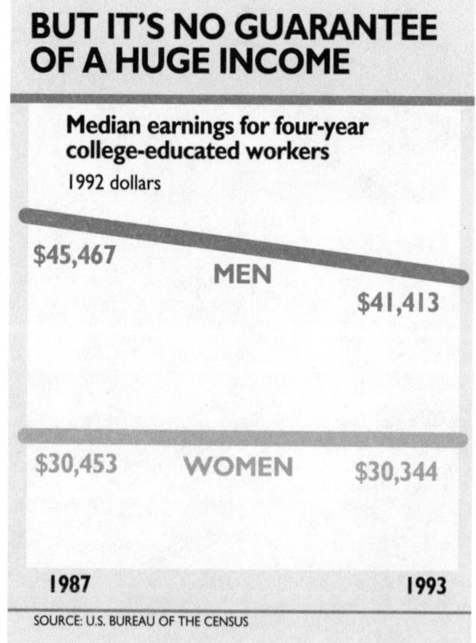

## WHERE THE JOB GROWTH WILL BE

Projected percentage change in employment by broad occupational group, 1992–2005

|  |  |
|---|---|
| Production | 0% |
| Agriculture, forestry, fishing | 3% |
| Laborers, handlers, equipment cleaners and helpers | 17% |
| Administrative support, including clerical | 14% |
| Mechanics, installers and repairers | 16% |
| Construction trades and extractive occupations | 22% |
| Transportation and material-moving machine and vehicle operators | 22% |
| Marketing and sales | 21% |
| Executive, administrative and managerial | 26% |
| Technicians | 32% |
| Services | 33% |
| Professional specialty occupations | 37% |
| ALL OCCUPATIONS | 22% |

SOURCE: U.S. BUREAU OF LABOR STATISTICS

Believe it or not, the world can use another writer — in fact, many of them. They will be needed to analyze events and make sense of the computer data flood. Newsletters, TV cable services and trade journals all will require people who can convert raw data into readable English.

More than ever before, women are realizing career opportunities in every industry. Many women are now using their skills to start their own businesses. Since 1990 the number of sole proprietorships owned by women has been growing almost twice as fast as those owned by men. Dun and Bradstreet estimated in 1995 that there were 7.7 million firms owned by women. They employed some 15.5 million people, 35% more than the Fortune 500 companies, and generated $1.4 trillion in sales.

Demand is rising for personal services. As the population ages, one of the fastest-expanding careers will be geriatric nursing. But the real surprise may well be teaching. Millions of computer buyers will need instruction, and so will millions of semi-literate workers. Hundreds of corporations already run remedial English and math classes. Jobs for preschool and kindergarten teachers are expected to increase by 54% over the next decade, and the number of teaching jobs in special education should rise 74%. Even college and university faculties are expected to grow 26% by the year 2005.

Small companies provide the biggest job growth. The old Fortune 500 largest industrial companies have shed more than 5 million jobs since the late 1970s, and in 1994 employed only 11.4 million people. Companies employing 500 or fewer have added more than 13 million jobs since 1980.

While it is commonly believed that half or more of all new companies don't last more than five years, that survival rate may be improving (see page 598). Venture capitalists are more flush with cash than ever. Funds committed to venture firms by big institutional investors increased from $1.4 billion in 1991 to $4.2 billion in 1994, and some banks, chastened by fiascos in real estate and overseas investments in recent years, are exploring ways to expand in the small-business market.

Prospects for economic growth appear to be brightest in the Mountain states, the Southwest and the Midwest. High-tech and other companies continue to move into Texas, Arizona and New Mexico to take advantage of a willing workforce, low taxes and a welcome climate. In the Southeast, job growth has decelerated outside the major metropolitan areas, but such cities as Atlanta and Charlotte are surging.

Growth is moderate in the Middle Atlantic states, and weakest in the expensive Northeast. In Southern California the long-anemic economy has started to come back, lifted by the entertainment industry as well as tourism and exports. Northern California is stronger.

One of the most promising places to build your career could be the Midwest. While there remains a threat that the auto industry may weaken, the industrial heartland has trimmed its costs, built its efficiency and now is one of the most productive and competitive manufacturing bases in the world. In the Northwest, high-tech investment — notably for computer semiconductor plants — is expanding vigorously in Washington, Oregon and Idaho. It is also rising fast in Utah and Colorado, among other states of the West. Indeed, it is the Mountain states that probably will experience the most vigorous growth. Always a magnet for people who crave wide-open spaces, this region also offers to employers a dedicated, well-educated workforce, relatively low costs and all those marvelous wide-open spaces.

Private businesses in the U.S. added nearly 3 million workers in 1994. Unfortunately, many new jobs won't provide long-term security or great benefits. At many corporations, paternalism has passed into history. Temporary jobs are now a permanent part of the corporate landscape. Temps are being hired for every kind of work, from soldering and wiring jobs to accounting and computer programming. These days more employees need to learn to leverage short-term jobs into permanent positions; Manpower, Incorporated reports that more than 40% of its temps were offered permanent jobs in 1995, up from 25% in 1992. Instead of taking out want-ads, companies are turning to temps — trying them out for short periods to see if they would make good full-time workers.

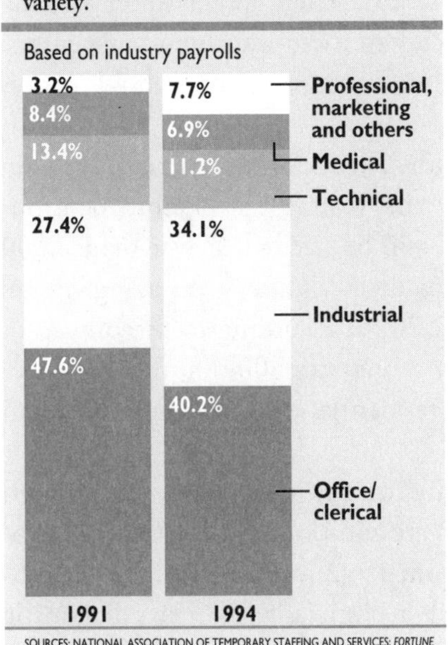


Auditors and accountants, financial analysts, human-resources managers and other business specialists are also in demand. Jobs for accountants and auditors will grow by as much as 39% over the next 10 years. According to surveys by recruiter Robert Half International, newcomers to accounting in 1995 typically earned starting salaries of $24,000 to $30,000, depending on the size of the firm. Experienced senior accountants can earn $33,000 to $44,000 — or more with CPA accreditation and a graduate degree. The range for corporate accounting managers can be $43,000 to $63,000 — or higher in very large cities. Other business specialties require a combination of technical and management training. A benefits administrator in human resources averages about $40,000, but a well-rounded human-resources director of a major company can command a salary of more than $120,000, and vice presidents can earn more than $230,000 at a huge corporation like AT&T.

Financial-services jobs are expanding because of the new attitude people have toward money: They want to take control of it, and make the most of what they have. More Americans are willing to invest the effort and expense to plan their savings and investments, so brokerage houses and insurance companies are strengthening their financial-planning departments. Banks, real estate companies and other financial concerns will be hiring more analysts, portfolio managers, marketing specialists and, above all, salespeople. Some financial jobs will require MBAs — master's in business administration degrees — but would-be stockbrokers who have sales experience in any area will be eligible for training programs at the brokerage firms.

From 1992 to 2005, according to the Bureau of Labor Statistics, as many as 2,671,000 new sales and marketing jobs will open up — an increase of 21%. Meanwhile, the increase in two-career couples will provide more work for the relocation, personnel and headhunting firms that will have to solve the problems of moving an executive who also has a working spouse (known as "the trailing spouse").

Child care is another obvious growth area. There are 9 million working mothers with young children, and many of them want day-care centers. Small businesses that help with time-consuming household chores should also do well.

With the 65-and-older group rapidly expanding — some 37 million Americans will be among them by the year 2005 — more pension-planning and retirement consultants will be needed. Fewer than 2,000 doctors now are expert in geriatric medicine. Clearly, an aging nation will demand many more. By the year 2005, according to the Bureau of Labor Statistics, there will be jobs for more than 500,000 therapists, researchers, nurses and workers in residential-care communities and group-living centers for older people.

The American concern with staying healthy, particularly when faced with an aging population, will also create additional jobs. Of the 10 projected fastest-growing occupations from 1992 to 2005, four are health-related. Medical centers will need technicians to run diagnostic equipment; office managers, marketing executives and accountants to handle the books; and nurses to treat patients. The two best places to set up your health-care business will be New England and Florida. By the year 2010, 14% of New England's population and 21% of Florida's will be over age 65.

Nurses of all kinds will do well. Salaries vary by region, of course, but on average nursing school graduates now start at around $30,000 on hospital staffs. The industry average is $36,618. Head nurses earn, on average, about $45,000. Pay is highest on the East and West Coasts: In New England the average annual salary is $37,785; on the West Coast, it is $41,315. A master's degree improves earnings because it offers new options — for example, in management or research. Nurse anesthetists, for example, have an average salary of $76,000. More than 750,000 new nursing jobs may open up by the year 2005, raising the total to 2.6 million.

Of course, computers will create jobs — but not only where you expect them. More openings will come in banks, utilities and other businesses that use the mighty microchip than in those that make it. Companies will be looking for programmers and systems engineers. Anyone who can develop software will not have to hunt long for work.

As *Fortune* has noted, technicians of all kinds — including clinical laboratory technicians, emergency medical technicians, engineering technicians, computer programmers and science technicians — are part of a large and fast-growing worker elite that is transforming the American labor force. The technician is becoming the core employee of the digital Information Age. One of every four new jobs goes to a technical worker, with estimates that the broad category of technical workers will represent one-fifth of total employment within a decade.

Two large forces are giving technicians new responsibility. First, increasingly powerful, versatile and user-friendly technologies are eliminating the need for workers to perform many time-consuming routine tasks, thus freeing them to tackle more challenging activities that require judgment and skill. Second, as more companies come to depend on such technologies to eliminate quality defects, speed up production and product development, and improve customer service, technicians more than ever are the workers relied upon. They are the caretakers of the computer and telecommunications networks that keep businesses running, and they are important in the design of presentations used by any sales force to entice customers. Some organizations are starting to make the mastery of a technical specialty a prerequisite for career growth.

Here are some other promising careers for the late 1990s:

- *Water-resource experts.* Water shortages could become severe in many places. We will require more hydrologists, environmental engineers and others to preserve our most important of all resources.
- *Environmental accountants.* From a disaster like an oil spill to local disputes about garbage disposal, environmental issues have become everyone's concern. Businesses and agencies at all levels of government will need accountants versed in ecology, environmental regulations, damage assessment and insurance.
- *Personnel, training and labor-relations specialists.* With the new emphasis on enhancing industrial and office productivity, these experts will be called on to work out corporate agreements between management and labor. Employee-training experts will also be in high demand, as many workers seek or require retraining. This profession is expected to grow 36% over the next decade.
- *Development economists.* People with college degrees in international economics and business will help to market American products abroad.
- *Nurturing-service workers.* These professionals provide specialized personal services — for example, home health-care workers, licensed massage therapists, exercise physiologists.
- *Entrepreneurs.* The U.S. needs plenty of these risk takers to start new businesses. For anybody who has a marketable idea — from the highly technical world of electronics and computers to the everyday realm of retailing — entrepreneurship can offer one of the best careers of the era.

And finally, what about selling your skills and experience abroad? As U.S. companies seek position and profits in the European Community market, jobs are opening for Americans. Harold Messmer's *Staffing Europe* (Acropolis Books, $24.95) surveys job opportunities for enterprising Americans.

# Getting a Fast-Track Overseas Assignment

An assignment abroad, once thought to be a career dead end, has become a ticket to speedy advance. And an increasingly necessary one. Already the headhunters are putting a premium on people who have worked overseas. Says Dick Ferry of Korn/Ferry International, "A foreign posting some time in your career is now almost required for senior-level jobs. And that doesn't mean just working in London for a couple of years."

Many business leaders believe that when you're immersed in a foreign-language culture, you learn to be sensitive to other points of view. You gain mental flexibility. You learn to function in multiple environments. You discover that there are different ways of solving problems. Ludo Van Der Heyden, dean of the Insead graduate business school in Fontainebleau, France, says that American businesspeople abroad experience what it is like to be a member of a *minority*. In short, you get a crash course in what it takes to be a cross-cultural leader in today's global business. When abroad, you are also loaded with a lot of frontline responsibility in a hurry, handling all kinds of situations and often dealing with all types of people (factory managers, labor chieftains, government ministers).

Of course, the foreign exposure is most necessary in industries that have the most international of markets: aircraft, telecommunications, computers, chemicals, pharmaceuticals, energy and auto assembly. (Small wonder that the CEOs of Detroit's Big Three all lived abroad for many years and headed their companies' international operations.) But more and more companies in other fields are catching on to the value of overseas experience. The number of expatriate executives jumped 30% in 1994.

How do you land these plum assignments? Sure, it helps to have some fluency in languages. The most important ones, in order of preference, are Spanish, German, French, Japanese, Chinese, Italian and Korean. Farsighted managers are also learning the languages of Russia and India. But the best thing you can do is to tell your boss clearly and often — and his or her boss, too — that you want a foreign assignment. More and more companies — United Technologies, Honeywell, S. C.

Johnson — map out three- to five-year career programs for young executives, often including foreign service.

Make certain that your spouse and children are aware of the rough spots and eager to go. The toughest problems for managers abroad focus on the family: Many kids rebel at being tossed into a foreign environment; most spouses cannot get work permits for themselves. (Only one in eight of the U.S. executives abroad is a woman.)

There are professional risks, too. While you're away, the jumpy politics of your company may shift, and your busy mentors may lose contact. So you have to take the time to stay plugged in. Neil Marchuk, 38, jokes about having two jobs: his day job as vice president of S. C. Johnson in China — and his night job communicating over the phone with friends at headquarters in Racine, Wisconsin. Keeping linked up should not be too hard if you make the effort. After all, the company has made a huge investment in you by sending you overseas — $300,000 a year in salary, benefits and expenses is not unusual.

That's one reason why people younger than 45 usually draw the overseas assignments; companies can count on many more years of service from them. Still, quite a few older managers are picked, often as a nice climax to their productive careers. It's almost never too late to benefit, and short tours abroad can help, too. Bill George, 52, CEO of Medtronic Inc., the world's dominant maker of pacemakers and other medical gear, is sending himself from his Minneapolis headquarters to Asia or Europe for a month or two. "I want to get really in depth with customers, and find out how things are done." To find extra reality, he says, "I'll be renting a small flat. I'm not going to stay at the Hotel Imperial."

## Where the Big Pay Is

Some companies have a tradition of paying well, notably those exploring the frontiers of science and the new technologies. But within any industry, salaries commonly are 15% to 20% higher than average at the most openhanded firms, according to Reggio and Associates, a compensation consulting firm in Chicago. The principal factor is size: obviously, the bigger a company's sales, the greater its pay is likely to be. Low-profit companies can be expected to pay low or give meager raises, or both.

Old companies or those in established fields such as steel and autos tend to offer a larger share of total pay in the form of fringe benefits than those in new businesses do. But the new ones give more stock bonuses and options.

Investment banking, stock brokerage, management consulting and executive recruiting offer outsized rewards for partners, directors and top producers, but not so much for the many service workers who back them up. In a number of other fields, mostly those considered glamorous, starting salaries are small. But they climb sharply in the upper-middle to upper ranks. Television and advertising are examples.

Starting pay at law firms ranges all the way from the low 20s to the 80s. Although a handful of big-city firms offer stratospheric salaries, that remuneration has less to do with an individual's immediate performance than his or her future promise. *A warning:* Even during recessions, it is unwise to take a job paying less than you think you deserve. In bureaucratic corporations with ossified pay systems, employees who start out cheap may never catch up.

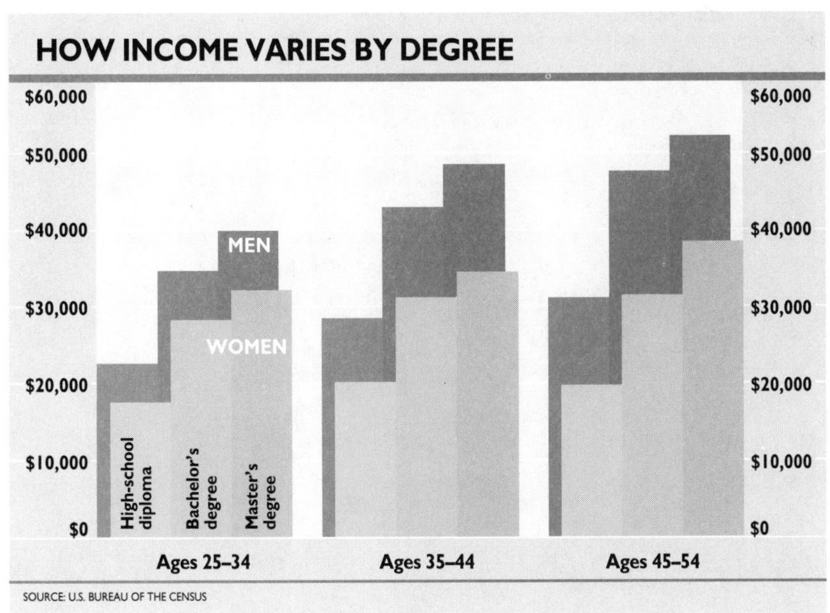

# Second Careers for Women

For many wives and mothers, work resumes at 40. But any woman who wants to re-enter the job market will find that she needs some smart strategies to do it.

The most serious difficulty is a lack of confidence and focus: Too many re-entry women tend to undervalue their previous experience. If you are one of them, you should know that many of the skills needed to manage a household or organize a charity bazaar can be transferred to business. Are ill-defined ambitions a problem? The solution may be career-planning workshops offered by countless nonprofit agencies, individual counselors and almost every university and community college. Courses vary from two days to 10 weeks and cost about $150 to $500. There are also single career-counseling sessions and/or workshops for less than $30 up to about $100.

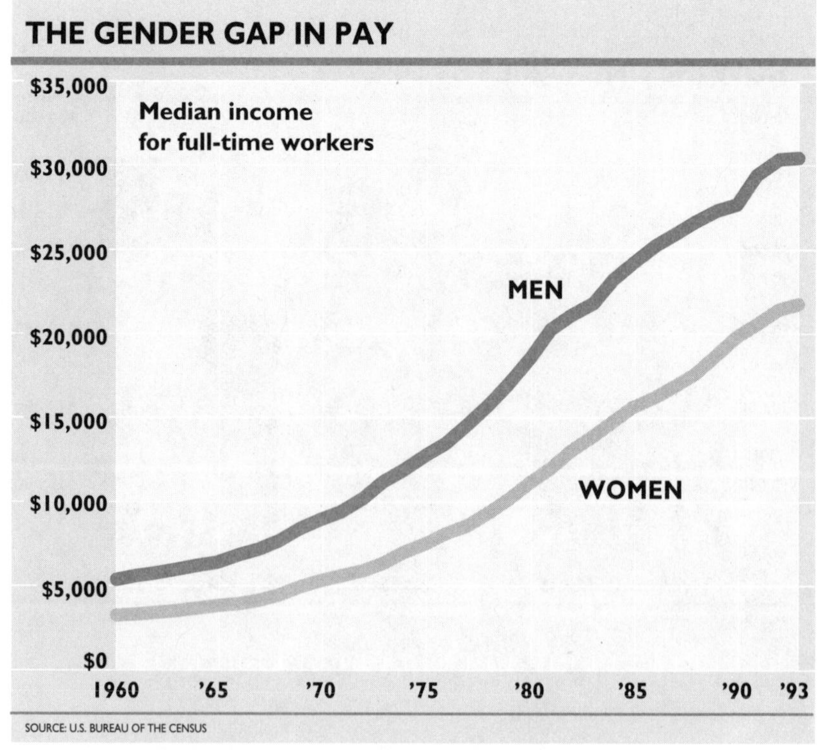

After determining your career objective, you may discover that you need to refurbish your skills before you try them out again. That's fine, but beware of the temptation to go to college year after year, stacking degree upon degree, never braving the rougher waters of the marketplace. You may think that you have to be able to do a job before you can take it. Don't "overcredentialize" yourself and hold back from the day of reckoning.

As a first step back into the market, draft a résumé. You will want to present yourself on paper in a way that is meant to fit your specific goal. Unless your educational credentials are recent or sterling, you will probably want to downplay them and play up your volunteer and other experience. Employers are often unimpressed with degrees or other credentials older than your children.

Omit the personal details. By law an employer cannot ask your age, marital status or whether you have children. This information is best left out of a résumé. When many employers see "children" written in a résumé, they think of sick days. Your instinct may be to run off 200 copies of your résumé and wallpaper the town. Instead, you should treat this master copy as a draft and customize your résumé to the specific opening you are trying to fill.

To get a job interview, begin by phoning friends and telling them that you are leaving the homestead for the wage-paying world. Use that grapevine of contacts you have developed — everyone from old school friends to members of clubs you have joined.

Even if you have had many years of significant but unpaid experience, your first re-entry job is likely to be on the lower rungs of the labor force. You should not be either insulted or excessively concerned if it is less glamorous, less responsible and lower paying than

## TIMES HAVE CHANGED

Proportion of jobs in various occupations filled by women

| Occupation | 1970 | 1990 |
|---|---|---|
| **Accountant** | **31%** | **54%** |
| **Architect** | **4** | **15** |
| **Bartender** | **26** | **52** |
| **Chemist** | **16** | **29** |
| **Dentist** | **5** | **13** |
| **Doctor** | **11** | **21** |
| **Economist** | **15** | **44** |
| **Farmer** | **7** | **15** |
| **Industrial engineer** | **3** | **27** |
| **Lawyer/judge** | **6** | **26** |
| **Librarian** | **85** | **83** |
| **Nurse** | **94** | **91** |
| **Physicist** | **6** | **12** |
| **Police detective** | **5** | **13** |
| **Psychologist** | **46** | **58** |
| **Public official** | **25** | **59** |
| **Secretary** | **98** | **98** |
| **Teacher** | **74** | **74** |

SOURCE: PROGRAM FOR APPLIED RESEARCH, QUEENS COLLEGE, NYC

you expected. What is critical is that the job positions you for growth within the company or your chosen field.

One starting spot that rewards initiative is often overlooked — or looked down upon — by women. That position is sales. Insurance, brokerage and real estate firms will pay you at least a modest salary to learn the business, and commissions can plump up the pay envelope once you master the skills. Most important, sales jobs provide avenues for advancement.

# Part-Time Jobs for Professionals

A new class of high earners is working less and enjoying more. The number of part-timers is fast expanding, and so is the list of employers welcoming them — and willing to pay them well. Nearly 30 million Americans work part-time — over 20% of the labor force. A surprising number — about 4 million — are professionals, from surgeons to sales managers. Some work part-time voluntarily, others are motivated by economic forces. Whatever the reason, about one out of five professionals forgoes full-time employment.

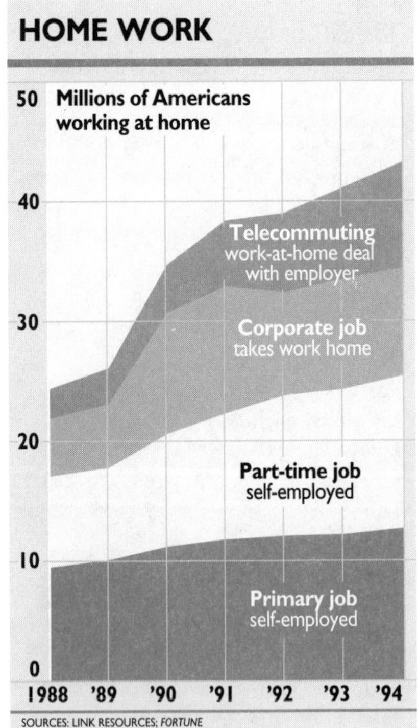


Part-time opportunities are best for people with highly specialized skills, including medicine, law, accounting, engineering and, especially, data processing. Many find part-time positions in federal agencies and state governments.

Part-time professionals can profit from the trend toward flexible working arrangements. Since managers offer part-time work as a way to hold on to valued employees, your chances of reducing your hours on an existing job may be better than your chances of finding a new, part-time position. One way to convince your boss to cut your hours is to keep a record for two or three months of exactly what tasks you do and how much time you need to do them. That will help you estimate how much you could get done if you worked fewer hours, and give you some idea of what responsibilities could be shifted to others. You should also be able to show how you would keep up with responsibilities that normally require full-time hours, such as travel and staff meetings. Always stress the quality of your work above the money the company would save on your salary.

One company at the forefront in promoting part-time employment is NationsBank, a large national bank headquartered in Charlotte, North Carolina. Its SelectTime program not only has proved to be popular with staffers but also has drawn in professionals who need to divide their time between the workplace and home. You have to work for the bank for one year before you are eligible to participate. NationsBank (formerly, NCNB) gives full benefits to employees in this program. But other companies typically provide part-timers with pro-rated benefits, and many companies do not give them any benefits at all.

Employment agencies that handle part-time professionals and managers are springing up in large cities. The Pickwick Group in Wellesley, Massachusetts, places a broad range of specialists in Boston and other New England communities. In San Francisco, $M^2$ Management Maximizers acts in a similar capacity for the Bay Area.

You may wish to deal directly with a company rather than use an agency. In that case, send to any prospective employer a résumé with a brief cover letter stating your qualifications and what services you can provide — part-time. If you get an interview, be prepared to explain how you would handle specific problems that a job might present for a part-timer. Offer to work a scaled-down schedule on a trial basis for a few months. Also, volunteer to go full-time when emergencies arise.

For more information on how and where to get part-time jobs, write or call the Association of Part-Time Professionals (Crescent Plaza, 7700 Leesburg Pike, Suite 216, Falls Church, Virginia 22043; 703-734-7975).

## Making Moonlighting Pay

More and more people hold down not one job but two — or more. If you are one of these moonlighters, there are some rules you should follow to make the most of your extra efforts — and to stay out of trouble with your primary employer, with the taxman and with your own family.

Over 7 million Americans work at second jobs, putting in an average of 13 hours a week. They moonlight to earn more money, of course, but also because they may feel stuck on a plateau in their primary job, because they want to lay the groundwork for a new career or just because they yearn to explore some skill or hobby and have fun. They do a vast variety of things: A Long Island pediatrician conducts wine-appreciation courses on weekends and Wednesday evenings; a Kansas City, Kansas, family therapist is a weekend auctioneer; a New York civil engineer moonlights as a cabinetmaker and resurfacer of paddle-tennis courts.

If you want to take on additional work, here are some rules to follow:

- Tell your boss at your primary job that you are moonlighting, but assure him or her that your other work won't interfere with your regular responsibilities.
- Be sure to charge enough for your moonlighting. Bill any clients one-third to one-half more than your regular daytime wage. After all, you are working overtime, and you do have some expenses and taxes to pay on your income.
- Schedule your time so that you have some regular hours for relaxation and to spend with your family. If you find that you are having more than the usual tension on your regular job or that you are becoming tired or irritable, cut down on the moonlighting.

No one wants you to succeed in your part-time career more than the Internal Revenue Service. Naturally, your moonlighting earnings are subject to income tax at ordinary tax rates. If you are a self-employed moonlighter, you will also have to pay Social Security and Medicare taxes of 15.3% on your free-lance income. This 15.3% consists of two taxes: the Social Security portion — which is 12.4%, up to a maximum of $60,000 — and a Medicare component, which is 2.9% on all income earned. But any Social Security and Medicare taxes you paid on wages from your regular job would count toward these maximums. In other words, you wouldn't have to pay twice. And if your net self-employment income after deductions is less than $400, then no self-employment tax is due.

But the self-employed can get special tax breaks as well. As noted in Chapter 9, "Saving Money on Your Taxes," if you run an enterprise and show a profit in three years out of five, you are presumed to be running a business and can deduct from your entire taxable income any losses your enterprise generates. You must, however, keep detailed, accurate records of the income and expenses of your moonlighting activities.

Some of the benefits you will get if you qualify:

First, you can deduct the cost of all supplies used in your venture, plus the business mileage on your car, parking fees and tolls. The standard deduction is 30 cents per mile.

Second, if you have an office or workspace at home that you use *only* for business, you can deduct the portion of your rent, heat and utility costs that goes into maintaining the office. But you cannot deduct more than your net income from the business.

Third, you can deduct from your sideline income a certain amount of your business equipment purchases. The maximum deductible varies, depending on how you and your spouse file your taxes and other factors. You can deduct up to $17,500 as long as your business equipment purchases are less than $200,000 for the year. If you spend more than the deductible amount, you can choose another option: you can decide instead to depreciate your total expenditure over the life of the equipment. But you cannot both deduct and depreciate. (Again, for further details, see Chapter 9.)

# Computer Jobs

The belief is common that computers are wiping out countless jobs. In fact, lower-paying jobs — as computer operators who simply type in information — are shrinking as the machines become more powerful, versatile and easier to run. But some high-level jobs created by the computer are going begging; not enough people have the necessary skills. According to the Bureau of Labor Statistics, demand for people with the right training in many areas of the computer industry is expected to increase as much as 112% by the year 2005. We shall need more than 1.5 million specialists in computer fields.

Good jobs should be available for several kinds of workers: for systems analysts, who devise ways for computers to handle information; for programmers, who tell the machines what to do; for technicians, who maintain and repair the complex equipment. There is also some need for teachers who can instruct others to use the machines. After some retraining, schoolteachers are finding jobs teaching corporate computer classes. As the late John Kemeny said when he was president of Dartmouth College, "It is as unforgivable to let a student graduate without knowing how to use a computer as it was in the past to let him graduate without knowing how to use a library."

**FASTEST-GROWING OCCUPATIONS REQUIRING A COLLEGE DEGREE, 1992-2005**

| Occupation | Projected rise |
|---|---|
| Computer engineers and scientists | 112% |
| Systems analysts | 110% |
| Physical therapists | 88% |
| Special-education teachers | 74% |
| Operations research analysts | 61% |
| Preschool and kindergarten teachers | 54% |
| Psychologists | 48% |

SOURCE: U.S. BUREAU OF LABOR STATISTICS

People throughout the workforce can improve their job status if they learn to use computers. Word processing skills are now becoming almost universally necessary for secretaries, and the fastest-moving business managers will be those who are the most creative in employing computers to streamline operations, thereby saving time, effort and money. You can plug in to the world of computers by taking low-cost night courses at community colleges. Beginners can learn about various parts of the world of computers through books, especially ones with "for Dummies" in the titles, and videotapes that are available at bookstores, computer stores and the public library. One thorough and easy-to-read text is *Overcoming Computer Illiteracy: A Friendly Introduction to Computers* by Susan Curran and Ray Curnow (Penguin Publishing, $12.95).

Career opportunities continue to open up for analysts who design computer systems — for example, to expedite billing or keep track of inventory moving around the warehouse and devise ways to pull together a company's financial records. Analysts are the troubleshooters of the electronic age, employed by most large companies, as well as schools, hospitals, government agencies and a rapidly growing number of firms that develop and sell software to other companies. From 1992 to 2005 the Bureau of Labor Statistics estimates that jobs for computer systems analysts will increase nearly 110%, to nearly 1 million jobs. Systems analysts' starting salaries average more than $35,000. For top people with experience, the national average is $50,000. Jobs for computer engineers and scientists are expected to increase by 112%, to 447,000.

Rapid technological changes will also create a sizable new elite of high-tech employees — from production workers who operate computer-aided manufacturing systems to that indispensable outside consultant who brings specialized expertise to the company's staff. For example, consultants can develop a new Lotus Notes application or a home page to establish the company's presence on the Internet's World Wide Web.

Suppose you would like to become a computer analyst. To qualify, you usually need a few years' experience in the industry where you want to work; it helps considerably if you understand the company's business and you have had exposure to its financial dealings. Companies are looking for people with a bachelor's or even a master's degree in business or computer sciences from a school with a well-regarded curriculum.

Additionally, companies need database administrators who know Oracle, Sybase or another leading database management software system. Also in great demand are people to manage local area networks and to staff the "help desk" to answer computer users' phoned-in questions and assist them with problems. Programmers, who develop applications for the computer, more than ever need to be proficient with a popular application development tool such as Visual Basic and PowerBuilder.

One way to gain experience in a particular area or to learn a needed skill with a software product is to work in an internship program. Many nonprofit organizations have such programs. You will not be paid, but you will gain valuable experience to put on your résumé.

What opportunities does a career in computers offer for advancement? If you establish a record of delivering trouble-free projects on time and demonstrate communication skills and leadership qualities, you can be promoted to project leader and or to other management positions within the company's information systems department. You can aspire ultimately to become Chief Information Officer, or CIO, the highest-ranking officer in a company's information systems organization. The CIO has overall responsibility for all the corporation's computer projects and its strategy for acquiring new technology and computing equipment.

Some CIOs have complained in the past about a glass ceiling that keeps them from being considered for the top spot in the corporation, but this is less true today than it was a few years ago.

Free-lance consulting offers another opportunity. An independent computer consultant can earn from $25 to $150 an hour on technical and project-management assignments, depending on his or her skills and experience with various software products and what the contracting company is willing to pay.

## Engineers

Prospects for engineers remain bright, enhanced by the computer revolution and the need to upgrade the country's aging infrastructure. The Labor Department estimates that the U.S. will need about 300,000 more engineers in the year 2005 than it had in 1992, raising the total to 1,660,000. Even civil engineers, who traditionally suffer during construction slumps, are expected to prosper. The government anticipates that about 41,000 more civil engineers will be needed by 2005, increasing the total to 214,000.

Demand is rising for women and African-Americans and other minorities in engineering. In fact, women sometimes start out at higher pay than men do. In the early 1970s only 3% of all engineering students were women; today they make up about 20% of undergraduate engineering classes. And young black and Hispanic men are beginning engineering studies in numbers closer to their representation in the population at large: they made up about 15% of the entering undergraduate students in the fall of 1994.

Highly regarded engineering schools include Cal Tech, Purdue, Georgia Tech, Illinois, Michigan, MIT, Stanford, Penn State and Texas A&M. Of course, quality teaching is available in many lesser-known schools.

For students straight out of college, engineering jobs pay the highest of the major professions — about $40,000 for entry-level chemical engineers in 1995. Generally, the oil, chemical and drug companies and major research and development labs pay the most, and government agencies and colleges the least. In many companies, engineering is a route to the top.

The higher the climb, the less engineering is practiced. Some engineers who prefer the drawing board to administrative chores choose not to advance to management. So a number of companies promote pure technicians to some sort of consulting or distinguished-fellow status. These jobs carry salaries of $70,000 to $80,000 and sometimes more — roughly equivalent to upper middle management. With the rapid pace of technological change, engineers constantly have to re-educate themselves. They say that their usable knowledge has a half-life of eight years. That is, half of what an engineer knows when he or she starts out is obsolete in that time.

## Financial-Services Jobs

The question I hear most often is a plaintive "Where can I find a good financial planner?" And for "financial planner" you could just as easily substitute "stockbroker," "insurance salesperson" or "tax adviser." Americans increasingly recognize that they have to take control of their finances, that they have to save and invest wisely and systematically to prepare for their retirement. This means increasing demand for the services of financial professionals.

People who sell — stocks, bonds, mutual funds, insurance, annuities — begin with some of the most modest salaries but also have the potential for the highest incomes because they collect commissions. The money does not come easily. Starting out as a securities salesperson requires pursuing new accounts aggressively, often making cold calls all day long and hearing people — from close friends to total strangers — say "no." Small wonder that the chief requirement for brokerage and insurance salespeople is personality.

People who do the hiring are not too impressed by flashy applicants. They are looking for the ability to persuade, negotiate and collaborate. That's true even in banking; most bank jobs still involve some kind of selling. Lending officers in particular are expected to drum up new business.

Financial planners can do particularly well. These professionals analyze clients' entire financial situation and then recommend how to allocate assets, make investments and save money. To become a fully trained financial planner, you have to pass six to 10 college-level courses. Two schools offering these courses are the College for Financial Planning (4695 South Monaco Street, Denver, Colorado 80237-3403) and the American College (270 South Bryn Mawr Avenue, Bryn Mawr, Pennsylvania 19010).

Planners often start out as salespeople at brokerage or insurance companies, working on commission. Then they may set out on their own to become planners and charge fees for their advice. Sometimes they also sell mutual funds, insurance and tax shelters and collect commissions.

Insurance is a tough career — you have to suffer a lot of rejection — but it can be highly rewarding for people at the top. You have to be a super salesperson because, as has often been said, "Life insurance is not bought; it's sold." And whenever an insurance salesperson gets an unsolicited call from a prospective client asking to buy some insurance, the agent presumes that the client must have just received a failing grade on a stress test.

But life-insurance sales have grown strongly over the last decade and agents' commissions are up, thanks to the renewed popularity of cash value policies. Full-time agents average about $38,000 in earnings. Typical top pay averages about $55,000. But it's not unusual to find agents who target wealthy buyers earning six-figure or even seven-figure incomes. Consider: An agent who sells a $1 million whole life policy could collect an immediate commission close to $40,000 and lesser commissions in subsequent years.

Insurance companies commonly hire people in their late 20s and early 30s who have had little or no experience selling. Salaries start at $23,000 on average and gradually decrease as the agents' commissions increase. Many insurance companies do not have their own sales corps but instead rely on independent agents. The independents offer customers a broad line of policies and annuities from any number of companies. A fast-growing part of the business now is selling policies to small businesses and big corporations or, through them, to large groups of employees.

## Health Administrators

Health-care administration is a flourishing profession that enables you to do well by doing good. Managing a hospital or nursing home is much like managing any enterprise — except that the decisions can determine whether someone lives or dies.

What an administrator does depends largely on the size of the institution he or she works for. A veteran leader of a 1,100-bed New York hospital spends his days and about a third of his evenings in meetings — on how to raise funds, contain costs and recruit specialists and whether to invest in the latest equipment. His annual salary is around $275,000. The administrator of a 70-bed hospital and nursing home in a small town in Idaho has plenty of meetings, too, but typically they are with surgeons about improving the light in the operating room or with dietitians about how to contain the costs of meals. She also squeezes in visits to patients. Her salary is $65,000 — but like her big-city counterpart, she also comes away with a sense of accomplishment.

As running medical institutions has become more complex, the administrative ranks have swelled to include not only the director, but also middle managers skilled in accounting and market research. Some 500,000 people were working in the health-care administration field in 1995.

Many will be outside the medical institution — for example, in government agencies, where administrators may analyze regional needs for health care. Some experts are also hired by insurance companies, where they may design new types of coverage. Quite a few of the best opportunities are in the fast-expanding health maintenance organizations, which sell prepaid medical plans offering the services of a staff of salaried physicians.

One obvious problem: The number and kinds of jobs depend largely on the future shape of health-care reform, and that is most uncertain. On the one hand, promises to extend coverage to millions of uninsured Americans could lead to more jobs; but on the other, efforts to curtail health-care costs will likely squeeze administrative jobs. Perhaps the best way for administrators to ensure their futures is to acquire many special skills.

Jobs in health administration can be both exciting and frustrating. At any moment, a hospital administrator is apt to get a call: A child needs a blood transfusion but her parents forbid it on religious grounds. On the spot, the administrator must decide whether to get a court order or go ahead with treatment.

These jobs call for stamina and patience. Administrators must wrestle with aggrieved patients and their relatives, feisty community groups, unions, demanding doctors and trustees. Administrators share chronic problems: too little money, too few nurses, constant turnover among low-paid aides, and strict, ever-changing government regulations. But the emotional rewards can be rich.

To land a job in the field, you usually need to have a bachelor of science degree or, for high-level positions, a master's of business administration or a master's of health administration degree. Some thirty schools offer undergraduate degrees in health-services administration that are accredited by the Association of University Programs in Health Administration. Among the outstanding graduate programs, all two-year courses, are those at the universities of Michigan, Minnesota, Washington, Pennsylvania and California at Berkeley.

A Hay Management Consultants' survey shows that an assistant administrator with a graduate degree can earn from $50,000 to $80,000, except in nursing homes, where the range is $30,000 to $40,000. With 10 years' experience, a nursing-home director can command a salary of $40,000 to $75,000. A hospital administrator with 10 years' experience earns from $100,000 to $180,000 — less in small towns, more in big cities. The head of a hospital chain earns $250,000 or more. Salaries in health administration depend largely on the size of the institution.

People who want hospital careers can improve their prospects by joining chains such as Columbia HCA or Humana. And nursing-home administrators are in such short supply that a number of states allow them to head more than one nursing home each.

## Management Consultants

These corporate doctors are enjoying some of the best of times. Bright young business school graduates rush into the field, eager to help companies plot high strategy to cope with changes among the customers, competitors and workforces. It's a romantic profession. Top performers can expect heavy demands, endless and long-distance travel, high compensation and, frequently, early burnout. But many who leave consulting firms after five or 10 years parachute into top management jobs elsewhere or start their own, generally successful businesses. The field is most attractive for enterprising generalists or for graduates with a solid

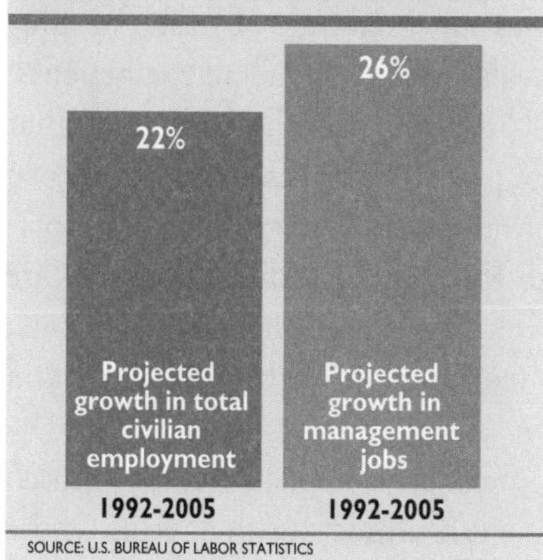


background in a specialty such as accounting.

To land a job with a top outfit, you usually need an MBA from a first-rate school. A few years' work experience will also get you in the door. People seeking a second career in management consulting can bring it off only if they offer solid grounding in a specialty. A product manager at a major consumer-goods company, for example, could turn into a consumer-marketing consultant. A star writer on computers could become a computer consultant.

It is not uncommon for high-ranking graduates of the best business schools to start in consulting firms at $65,000 or more — sometimes much more. Partners and directors of top firms earn over $300,000. Since their services are so expensive, successful consultants must be able to get to the root of a problem and produce solutions quickly. A consultant must be articulate, assertive and versatile enough to sell his or her solution to the assistant plant managers and the company president, without offending either.

One drawback is all that travel. Top consultants easily spend 60% of their time on the road. Another complaint is that consulting gives you influence but no real power to enforce decisions. But for bright young comers, consulting provides tremendous learning experiences — and a ticket to a commanding corporate job.

## Military Officers

Long the nation's employer of last resort, the military is becoming downright upscale. To get a few good men and women, the Army, Air Force, Navy and Marines have offered increased pay, abundant fringe benefits and generous pensions. From 1980 to 1995, military compensation rose more than 75%. Some people, notably college graduates, can find remarkable opportunities as officers. A second lieutenant can collect more than $25,000 a year, and a full colonel with 26 years of service easily commands $70,000. These earnings are made up of base pay plus tax-free allowances for housing and meals. Added on are all the benefits: 30-day vacations, free family medical care and a retirement plan that provides pensions equal to 75% of base pay after 30 years. There are also discounts at commissaries even after retirement, Veterans Affairs mortgages and postgraduate education with full pay. In addition, women are usually granted six weeks of paid maternity leave. The Navy, for one, employs more than 55,000 women, working on both combatant and noncombatant ships.

Though Uncle Sam may want you, these days he may not have much room. Military commissions that were yours almost for the asking in the early 1980s are now harder to come by: In the post–Cold War years the services see no pressing need for large numbers of junior officers, and they are even offering middle-level older officers cash incentives to retire. But recruiting hasn't ceased; it just goes on at a slower pace.

There are three main routes to earning an officer's commission. First are the most prestigious sources: the Military Academy at West Point, the Air Force Academy at Colorado Springs and the Naval Academy at Annapolis. West Point pays cadets an allowance of $6,500 per year in addition to room, board, tuition and medical care. After they are commissioned, graduates must spend at least six years on active duty.

Here is how to apply: In the fall of your junior year in high school, write to the academy of your choice for an application kit. Each academy will have many requirements for admission. West Point's include a qualifying medical exam, physical aptitude test, and an ACT or SAT test; you have to be between 17 and 21 years old. Follow the instructions in the kit, then write to the U.S. Congressman for your district and to both of your U.S. Senators, asking them to nominate you. The legislators' staffs look for students with grades in the top fifth of their classes, good health, participation in athletics, leadership potential and gung-ho personalities. Each academy chooses enough candidates to fill the legislator's quota of five students in each of the academies at any given time.

Second, the broadest channel to a commission is college ROTC. It produces about 7,000 officers a year. To become one of them, you take two to four years of military-science courses, drill periodically and show up for summer training. Some 60,000 students were enrolled in ROTC in 1995. Many have scholarships, with the government picking up the bill for full tuition, books, and subsistence allowances ($150 per month), for as many as four years of college. After they graduate, scholarship recipients must serve at least four of their eight-year obligatory commissioned service on active duty.

Third, the officer candidate and training schools of the Army, Air Force, Navy and Marines are still the fast track to a commission for those who were not in ROTC. These schools enroll enlisted people who have shown qualities of leadership, as well as a limited number of civilians. All candidates must be college graduates. To apply, contact one of the 7,500 recruiting stations that the services maintain across the country. Once you become an officer, you will be obliged to serve at least three years on active duty.

# Paralegals

For a solid career in the law without spending the time and money to get a law degree, become a paralegal. The Bureau of Labor Statistics estimates that from 1992 to 2005, paralegal jobs will grow 86%, to as many as 180,000 in the year 2005. The average starting salary is about $24,000, but after 10 years in the field working for a good law firm in or near a major city, you may expect $50,000.

Paralegals research cases and draft documents for lawyers. There is no standard licensing exam. Some law firms train their own paralegals, but many others prefer to hire graduates of certificate or degree programs. These are usually one or two semesters long, and they are offered by colleges and vocational schools. For a list of such programs, write to the National Association of Legal Assistants, Inc. (1516 South Boston Avenue, Suite 200, Tulsa, Oklahoma 74119–4013). Or send $7.50 to the American Bar Association's Standing Committee on Legal Assistants (750 North Lakeshore Drive, Chicago, Illinois 60611) for a general information packet on paralegal training, the schools that offer it and the jobs it can lead to.

# Secretaries

Partly because many women are turning their backs on traditional career roles, pleas for secretaries are increasing in the want-ads. Not long ago, the Bank of America declared that on any given day it was advertising openings for 30 secretaries. Of those who responded, many were overqualified college graduates who could not find jobs in their chosen fields, so they were unhappy from the start. Quite a few of the rest were inadequately trained high-school graduates. The shortage of competent secretaries remains severe, and it is likely to grow worse. The Labor Department estimates that nearly 385,000 new secretarial jobs could open up by the year 2005. Employers will probably court secretaries by boosting pay and by making it easier for them to advance to better jobs.

More than 3 million secretaries are now employed, many of them back-to-work wives who got their training 20 years ago and are willing to stay in secretarial positions. Their skills, employers report, tend to be superb, and their work ethic excellent.

The average salary is about $25,000. Pay tends to be lowest in the South and highest in the West and in large cities. The range for experienced secretaries in New York City, for example, is from $25,000 to $50,000, though some executive secretaries earn nearly $70,000. Shorthand still can mean a salary premium for secretaries in law firms. And an applicant with a bachelor of arts degree can command up to $5,000 more than one with a high-school diploma.

Job aspirants willing to invest about $8,000 may take a nine-month course at Katharine Gibbs, the country's best-known secretarial school. The curriculum includes the usual skills plus electronic word processing and accounting. There is also a course in poise — called "professional development" — which requires students to observe themselves on videotape as they perform their duties. A dress code prevails, too: no jeans, culottes, sneakers or clogs.

The payoff for top skills in many companies is that a secretary's career path follows his or her boss's. When the boss gets a promotion, he or she takes the secretary along, a practice sometimes called "fate-sharing." Some complain that this reduces secretaries to appendages of their bosses. They urge management to post job openings scrupulously and to encourage secretaries to apply for higher-ranking jobs. Indeed, many secretaries do move into management. With demand for able secretaries at an all-time high, opportunities to advance should become greater than ever.

Secretaries who stay in their jobs say they enjoy them for two reasons. They get to know a lot about what is going on in a company without having to take the heavy responsibility for it, and they enjoy helping a boss be more productive. They make it easier for him or her to succeed, and when he or she does, they share the satisfaction — and some of the financial rewards.

## Teachers

Many teachers are finding lucrative jobs outside the schools and colleges. They are switching from the schoolroom to the corporate-run training room.

During the late 1990s millions of computer buyers will need instruction. So will millions of office and factory workers. Already hundreds of corporations provide classes in English and math, spending billions of dollars each year to train employees. The person most likely to do the hiring of teachers is the director of training and development.

If you are a teacher, an essential strategy for making the switch is to develop — and use — acquaintances in business. Serve on school committees that have ties to local industry, or participate in community organizations where you are likely to meet people in business. Once you are in the corporate door, you can pick up other industrial-training specialties. And from there you may be able to move to a job in management. You may also want to read *Your Career in Human Resources* (write to the American Society for Training and Development, 1640 King Street, Box 1443, Alexandria, Virginia 22313, or phone 703-683-8100).

Men and women are also going back to school by the millions to study an enormous range of subjects. The boom in adult education has brought a roaring demand for part-time teachers of subjects as diverse as programming a computer and finding a mate. If you have a skill, you may be able to earn some extra money by teaching it. The teachers whom most adults prefer are not ivory-tower academics but those who have direct experience to share. As a part-time teacher of an adult education course, you can expect to earn perhaps $18 to $20 an hour. But if your course is extremely popular, you can make as much as $400 an hour. Most expenses connected with teaching — such as professional dues, subscriptions, travel to and from professional meetings — are tax-deductible. There are non-monetary rewards, too, such as learning more about your field and gaining potential clients and business contacts.

The most popular adult education subjects are starting a small business; making money in stocks and bonds; and how to buy, use and program computers. Demand is also brisk for courses in physical fitness; assertiveness training; practical topics, such as plumbing and bicycle repair; and affairs of the heart, from divorce to middle-age dating.

Beyond corporations, the best places to get part-time jobs in adult education are at community colleges, municipal recreation agencies or the fast-spreading, noncredit independent learning centers. If you teach through a learning center, you may function as an independent contractor, generally taking 30% to 50% of the fees. Tuition can start as low as $30 per student per course but often ranges much higher. For its cut of your fees, the center will promote your course in its catalogues, handle student registration and give both you and your curriculum a sense of legitimacy.

# Successful Techniques for Job Hunting

Job hunting is a skill, and it is fairly easy to learn. Once you master a few techniques, you will substantially improve your chances of getting a job — whether you are entering the employment market for the first time or looking for a new position.

Take a case of how *not* to do it:

He seemed to have everything a job hunter could want: intelligence, charm and one of corporate America's prized credentials — a Harvard MBA. To distinguish himself, however, he wore a baseball cap as well as his three-piece suit to job interviews. Despite dozens of interviews, he got no offers.

The problem, of course, was the cap. Instead of marking him as a go-getting individualist, the hat told recruiters that he lacked maturity and was overly concerned with image. He had tried but misapplied the first rule of job hunting: Stand out from the pack. The way to do that is to do your own research into the company and its business, ask probing questions and project certainty about yourself and your career goals without appearing smug.

The first hurdle is to get an interview with prospective employers. Perhaps friends, business acquaintances or alumni of your high school or college can recommend you to employers whom they — or their friends — know personally. If all else fails, you might get an interview by writing directly to the employer. Send a forceful letter outlining your achievements and likely contributions to the company. But don't use such ruses as implying that you are something other than a job applicant.

Résumés are important, but they are not worth the incredibly long hours many job seekers invest in them. You probably can better spend your time in researching the company and thinking about how you specifically can be useful to it. The ideal résumé is no longer than one page. It should concentrate not on descriptions of your previous jobs but on your accomplishments: "I increased sales 50% in six months." Do not exaggerate. An applicant who stretches the truth, even about something innocuous, will be branded as dishonest.

Though many recruiting professionals prefer the homemade résumé you write yourself, you may want help. If you have a PC, look into software packages such as WinWay Resume 2.0 ($39.99) and Job Search Pro, the latter produced by Softkey Software of Cambridge, Massachusetts. This $40 package includes a résumé and cover letter as well as extra features such as follow-up letters and the wherewithal to create a database of company names and addresses. A similar program, Perfect Resume, is available for $39.99 from Davidson & Associates Inc. of Torrance, California. You can also get a résumés-only program called Resume Writer for only $11.99 from Expert Software of Coral Gables, Florida. If you're a college graduate, find out whether your school's placement office sends alumni résumés to prospective employers, either on its own or through services such as Skillsearch of Nashville, which dispatches computerized résumés to corporate employers.

Once you've landed an interview, start considering yourself as a product for sale — cold-blooded as that may seem. First, you have to decide what the product is going to be — what skills and qualities you have to offer. The next step is to package your product well and to devise a strategy for selling it. Like any salesperson, you might practice your pitch on friends. But be prepared for the interviewer to throw some tough stock questions. One favorite is, "Tell me a little about yourself." A poor response begins, "Well, I was born on . . . " You would do much better to say something like: "Lately I've discovered that I can combine my abilities to . . . " and then go on to state specifically what you can do.

What you wear to the interview matters less than you may think. Of course, a serious applicant for a job at a traditional firm should not wear a scarlet jacket and white bucks or a diaphanous dress with a plunging neckline, not to mention a baseball cap. When in doubt, the best advice is to dress conservatively.

Since interviewers are impressed by applicants who ask sharp questions, it is wise to study the firm and its industry. You can read the company's annual report, ask a stockbroker for any written analyses of the firm and learn more about it in business reference books at a library.

Your sales presentation begins the moment you show up for the interview. Some personnel managers base their judgment partly on the office receptionist's reaction. If the applicant is rude to the receptionist, he or she will not get the job, no matter how smart he or she looks in the interview. It shows that he or she is a two-class person, smiling up and spitting down.

Corporate recruiters recommend some techniques to help you stand out during an interview:

- Carry a folder marked with the company name — and take notes. That shows you are well organized.
- Convey enthusiasm. Try to turn your weaknesses into advantages. If an interviewer suggests that you lack qualifications, you can say that you are a fast learner who welcomes challenges — and then give an example.
- Prepare what vaudevillians used to call a "get-off line" — a parting comment that moves the recruiter closer to an offer. You might ask, for example, whether he or she sees any obstacles to hiring you.

There are other crucial questions. You might ask what happened to the last person who had the position you may be taking. If he or she was promoted, you will get some idea of where the job is likely to lead. If, instead, the person was fired, you may learn early on about a major stumbling block that could trip you up, too.

If negotiations get warm and you are invited back for a second or third interview, ask to talk with someone at the company who is doing much the same job that you are being hired for. This person probably will be one of your soundest sources. Ask him or her whether your prospective boss is really as charming as he or she seems. Or ask about the least appealing aspect of working for the firm.

A good way to learn about a company's style is to do some research into the job and educational backgrounds of the top managers. Look them up in Dun & Bradstreet's *Reference Book of Corporate Managements* or in *Standard & Poor's Register of Corporations, Directors and Executives,* available at major libraries. For example, if all top managers are Ivy League graduates, that may tell you something about your chances for promotion. If you are a woman, you may want to learn how many women have advanced into upper management.

Find out as much as you can about the company's financial health. Is the firm growing? And where is this growth coming from? Your chances of advancement, of course, are greater if the company is expanding. Ask a stockbroker for research reports on the company. On the basis of its business outlook and strategy, consider where the company might be in five years.

Ask your prospective new boss or the person hiring you how and by whom your performance will be measured. You and your employer should agree on specific goals for you to accomplish — and a reasonable timetable for achieving them. You will also want to know how the company will help you meet the goals you have agreed on. Your boss should stand ready to grant you powers commensurate with your responsibility.

Ask what the salary range is for similar jobs in the organization. While you should aim to come in at the top of the range, this may still be too low. Many candidates will not consider changing jobs without a nice raise over their current pay. What other compensation does the company offer? This might include bonuses and benefits such as health plans and pension and profit-sharing programs. Your potential employer probably will be most impressed if you try to tie your compensation to your performance in as many ways as possible. Once you have worked out an agreeable compensation package, it is often a sound idea to have your prospective employer set down the details of the offer in a written memorandum.

But formal employment contracts, which spread widely in the 1980s, are now uncommon. They are generally limited to senior vice presidents, chiefs of major divisions and still higher officers. In some cases it's enough for you to simply ask for a letter confirming the broad outlines of your employment terms. However, if you are dealing with complicated subjects such as stock options, you may want a more formal agreement. Pay particular attention to passages detailing the circumstances under which you may be fired. Avoid ill-defined words, such as "incompetence," which are subject to broad interpretation.

Be alert for provisions that could restrict your activities if you leave the company. Some employers may ask that you agree not to work for a competing firm. Make sure that what constitutes "competition" is defined as narrowly as possible. And after you have struck a bargain, submit the proposed contract to your lawyer — before you sign it.

## What to Do When the Headhunter Calls

One of America's big-trophy headhunters received a call from his grown daughter, who works overseas for a major multinational. "Hey Dad," says she, "you'll never guess: Your top competitor phoned and wants to recruit me for a hot job."

"Well," asked the doting Dad, "what did you say?"

"I told him," she related, "that I don't want to move, so good-bye."

To which, father admonished: *Wronnnng answer!*

"Call back that rival recruiter," he urged. "Say that you are indeed pleased with your current job, but tomorrow might be another day, so why don't we talk?"

For any ambitious person, that real-life story carries three lessons:

First, never say never to a recruiter. Business is changing so fast that the job you love today may be quite different tomorrow.

Second, it sure pays to get known by a headhunter — and get your résumé into his or her databank. This way the searcher, and his or her clients, will get to know you.

Third, and most important: You have to actively manage your career. You can't count on your employer to do it for you.

Almost all the recruiters whom I know make that last point — forcefully. Hob Brown, chief of Russell Reynolds, put it this way: "Everybody has to think of himself as sort of a mobile business." Or listen to Dale

Winston, of Battalia Winston International: "The biggest change in business in the last five years is that you have to take over the management of your own career. You have to ask yourself, 'What am I going to be doing in this company next year? Am I just going to repeat what I did last year?' If so, it's time to jump. People who think they can be cradle-to-grave executives with the same company are making a dramatic mistake. There ain't no such thing anymore."

Re-engineering and the last recession taught us that almost no job is forever. As a result, when a headhunter phones, smart people no longer play hard to get. But what should *you* do and say?

The basic rule is the simplest: Answer the headhunters' calls. If you have a secretary, advise him or her not to brush them off. (Some overly protective — or apprehensive — assistants do just that.) If you are really happy and secure where you are, tell the recruiter so and offer to suggest other candidates. You might say, "I almost certainly won't leave my job, but if I can help you, I'm pleased to do it." That keeps your lines open, and the recruiter will appreciate your candor. At the very least, the headhunter will ask whom else you could recommend for the job. He or she will probably call you back on other searches in the future — one of which may just produce the job you want when you want it. Remember, you're already on his or her preferred list. Most headhunters narrow down their list of candidates before making these calls. By the time you hear about a top job, a recruiter has likely cut his or her candidates to 15 or 20.

If you are among the increasing number of executives willing to consider an immediate job change, keep your résumé updated and handy. One U.S. manager based in London faxed his résumé to the headhunter over his PC in the midst of that first, unexpected phone call. That told the recruiter both that his quarry was well prepared for anything — and that he knew how to exploit the new technology. If during that first interview you can find out the name of the company with a job to fill, you can score an even bigger point if you pull up information about the company from your desktop database and refer to it in your conversation. Searchers want to know how computer-literate you are. So they'll ask questions like, "How do you write your letters and memos?" One troglodyte killed his chances forever by replying, "I call my gal in to dictate."

Headhunters commonly ask what you do for fun.

Poor answer: "I like to watch basketball on TV."

Fair answer: "I like to take my kids to basketball games."

Great answer: "I play basketball three times a week."

Everybody out there is searching for a junior Lou Gerstner: A change agent who has shown success in several varying environments (Gerstner's résumé includes McKinsey, American Express, RJR Nabisco and, most recently, IBM) can come into an alien culture and shake it up, and can quickly raise profits and the stock price. Just like IBM, companies are looking outside more than ever for leaders who can accomplish a lot in a very short time with fewer resources. Hob Brown points out that some major corporations have even given up recruiting on campus; it's too expensive and takes too long to show results. They prefer to hire a 33-year-old who has learned lessons elsewhere.

But age counts for less than you think. Says headhunter Jack Cleary of Chicago's Andrews & Cleary, "I don't care how old you are, or how young you are — it's what you've done with the years you have. If you're thirty-three and a staff accountant for Arthur Andersen, you're probably over the hill. If you're fifty-five and a group executive at GE, you're exceptionally fast-track."

So how do you get on the recruiter's most-wanted list? How can you pull yourself above the crowd? The answer is, you have to get in a position where you *run something,* where you can show demonstrable *results.* If you can't make the next step up, you have to agitate for your company to move you around to new jobs — the trendy term is "broad-banding" — but don't get stuck too long. At General Electric, becoming a member of the traveling audit team is an elite job. Cleary says three years on that team is too little, five years is too much, four years is about right. Increasingly, companies are assigning their best young talents to their most troubled operations, with a view to turning things around. That's manna for star-quality strivers.

It's important to become known in your field — known by a circle of influential competitors, suppliers, stock analysts, management consultants and former employees of your company — so that people can recommend you when they are called by a recruiter. Gary Knisely of the recruiting firm of Johnson Smith & Knisely Accord recommends that you build a list of about 25 people in your field — folks at your level or higher — and call them every three to six months, just to say hello or perhaps discuss some industry issues.

It pays to become active in professional groups, to get into their directories and attend industry meetings. Searching for a general counsel for a large health-care company, Cleary started by studying the list of attendees at a seminar of the Health Law Management Association.

Sorry, but becoming active in charities and community affairs doesn't count for much in this era of the bottom line. Says Pen James of Pendleton James Associates, "No client has ever told me, 'I want a good community person' — never."

Oh, yes, what ever happened to the headhunter's daughter with whom we began this passage? She did call back the recruiter; they did speak, and she was startled to discover that his client was a premier company offering a platinum job. She hasn't jumped as of this writing — but now the recruiter will keep on calling her, again and again.

## The Smart Way to Change Jobs

People are switching jobs so frequently that U.S. business is beginning to look like a French bedroom farce. The new morality says you have to be loyal to your career more than to your company, and the new math adds that if you're typical, you'll have about 10 employers during your working life. In this jumpy atmosphere, it's wise to think about how you should behave if you're ever romanced by another employer and decide to make The Big Switch.

First, as with any love affair, figure out what you're giving up. It's probably more than you think. If you're like most people, you just don't know the real value of your pension and other retirement plans and exactly what you would be leaving behind.

Before telling anyone where you work of your plan to leave, ask your human resources department to give you a routine estimate of what all your benefits are worth *and* the total value of any stock options, restricted shares and other deferred compensation that you can't yet cash in. Then spend some money to hire an outside expert — a financial planner or accountant — to give you a studied, impartial estimate of all that plus your pension. He or she should have software capable of figuring out the value of options you may hold. You might think you already know the value because you know the company's stock price, but that's not the whole story. The value of options is also a function of their longevity, so you'll need help figuring it all out.

Don't expect your employer to speed up the vesting of those options now as a warm and fuzzy farewell gift. After all, the reason those options were stretched out was to handcuff you in place. Besides, under complex new tax rules, companies have to charge against their earnings any profits you make from exercising options.

Only when you know what you're leaving behind can you intelligently negotiate the terms of your trade. Your new employer is much more important than your old one in these talks, and not only because you should be looking forward instead of back. You don't have a lot of negotiating room with the company you're leaving. Maybe you can ask to take along your computer (many managers get passionately attached to their computers), but that's about all. It's the new employer who can make you whole.

If an employer really wants you, he or she really wants to make you whole — and add something to the pot. What's a good package? Answer: A raise of 15% to 20% in salary and bonus, *plus* a sign-on bonus or some extra benefits to make up for all the "bennies" you left behind.

To calculate what they should add up to, you need to ask many large and small questions. For example:

- How long is the waiting period for joining the new company's 401(k) plan? One year is common. That will cost you, because you'll be giving up one full year of company-matching contributions.
- When does my new health-insurance plan start covering me? Sometimes you have to wait 60 days after joining the company. Federal law allows you to carry your old employer's medical policy for up to 18 months, but at very high rates.
- Does my new health plan cover "pre-existing conditions?" Most do, but not all. Note: Under federal law, no employer can ask you to take a physical exam, unless the job demands a certain level of health — say, as an airline pilot.
- How long can I wait before exercising all my existing stock options? Sixty days is common; to pick up those options, you may ask your new employer for an immediate cash grant or low-interest loan.

- How soon can I start exercising the options granted to me by my new employer? Many companies now make you wait, and let you cash in only 25% of them a year. If your old company was on a faster schedule — it let you cash in 25% of your options every six months — ask your new employer for more options to make up the difference.

Indeed, if you fall short in any areas of benefits or bonus, ask for something extra to make up the difference — a bigger relocation allowance or real estate loan, a richer life insurance policy, a company car or a longer vacation. If you've been recruited by a headhunter, you'll have more leverage.

You'll probably work out the deal with the person hiring you. Try to make the talks seem not like a tough negotiation, but a fact-based discussion of fairness. You want to say, "This is what 'making whole' means to me." Only if you're jumping to a very high-level job — $250,000 and above — should you withdraw from the talks and bring in a lawyer to deal for you. At the senior-vice-president level and above, top lawyers often do this work for negligible fees; it's a loss leader to develop a relationship with you. Bluntly, they hope to attract business from you and the company once you join it.

Don't ask for an employment contract, unless you're joining up as a senior VP, major division head or higher. Three-year to five-year pacts were popular during the 1980s, but they are rarely given now. Says the human resources chief of a Fortune 200 company, "Employers have learned that contracts benefit only the employee. The employee can sue for breach of contract, but you never see a company suing the employee to continue working for it. And you don't need a contract to prevent an employee from jumping to a competitor and taking trade secrets with him." The law prevents employees from doing that, anyhow.

But you should seek a general letter of agreement outlining your pay, benefits, job title and responsibilities. It should include a short-term, fail-safe clause to cover you if the mating doesn't work out. Companies commonly give you six months' pay, or will make you whole, if you — or your new boss — decide that your move was a mistake. You should also seek a change-of-control agreement, guaranteeing that you will get everything you agreed upon should hostile forces conquer the company and bounce you.

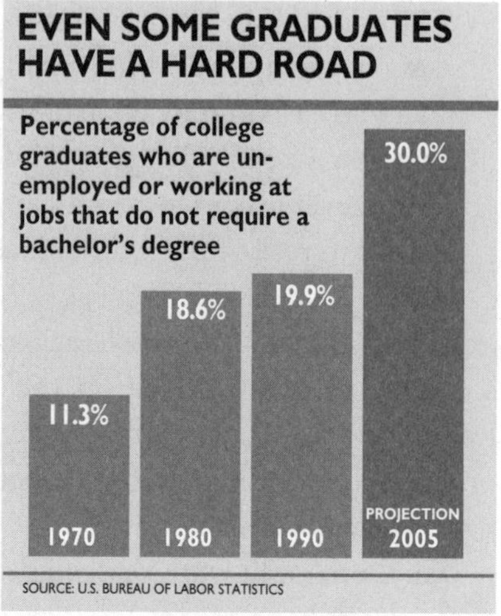

**EVEN SOME GRADUATES HAVE A HARD ROAD**

Percentage of college graduates who are unemployed or working at jobs that do not require a bachelor's degree

| 1970 | 1980 | 1990 | Projection 2005 |
|---|---|---|---|
| 11.3% | 18.6% | 19.9% | 30.0% |

SOURCE: U.S. BUREAU OF LABOR STATISTICS

Only after you have buttoned up every detail should you tell your present employer that you're decamping. Says New Jersey attorney Steven Gross, who has negotiated deals for many a switching executive, "A lot of this has nothing to do with economics but a lot to do with style and manner. Try to explain to your former boss that it has been a grand career, but there's an opportunity you just can't pass up."

Should you be open to a counteroffer? "I think not," Gross advises. "You can change your decision, but you can't remove the cloud of suspicion that you were somehow disloyal because you were prepared to leave." Of course, time heals. One reason for acting with class, calm and courtesy is that in most industries, it's a small community and a long career. With all the mergers and job-hopping now, it's just possible that in five or 10 years you'll be back in bed again with your old employer — just like in those French farces.

## How to Move Off a Plateau

Because of the crowd of baby boomers, stiff competition in the job market and the downsizing of corporations, many people's careers are stalling at lower levels and at earlier ages than before. It takes more talent and drive to get ahead today than it has for many years. But by learning new skills and seeking added responsibilities, you can move up and off a career plateau. Several tactics:

- Fortify yourself with knowledge. Take courses at a community college or specialized school to learn a new skill such as computer literacy or public speaking. Investigate executive MBA programs in which you attend classes on weekends. Quite possibly your company will subsidize your tuition.

- Get involved in community or business projects. You can broaden your experience and heighten your visibility by holding office in a professional group, writing an article in a trade journal or organizing a conference. If given the chance to make a speech, seize it.
- Look for new responsibilities to add to your job description. The delicate objective is to shine before superiors without alienating your immediate boss or co-workers. You don't want them to consider you an opportunist or a troublemaker. What you need is an idea that will make your superior's department look good and therefore win his or her blessing. Propose the plan to your immediate boss. With his or her approval, you can present it more formally to the company's higher-ups. If they let you try it and it works well, you're in a position to bargain for a new title or a raise or more authority. By showing eagerness to grow in your present job, you'll avoid being classified as deadwood.
- Tell the folks on top exactly what you think you can do to contribute further to the enterprise. Don't let them take you for granted. Also, arrange for feedback from peers and people who report to you. Perhaps you're not communicating, delegating or producing as effectively as you might think.

Sometimes the wise way to move a career off dead center is by trading your job for another at the same level. Many people turn down transfers to other cities because they don't want to uproot a working spouse. If you are single, it could pay for you to offer to move to some distant branch office where opportunities may be richer.

It's harder than it once was for up-and-coming managers to find out where they stand, because the rules of climbing the corporate ladder have changed drastically since the days of the so-called "organization man" of yesteryear. Restructurings have flattened many a traditional corporate hierarchy. So many managers are sitting in their jobs longer, regardless of their skills. And lateral moves within a corporation are becoming routine, even desirable. You may be wise to talk to your boss about transferring to a different type of work in which you would gain new skills. For example, an engineer who switches to a personnel job can acquire the managerial experience necessary for a higher-level technical assignment.

Another option is to continue doing the same job but in a department with room for advancement or with a specific need for your abilities. Even if such a horizontal shift doesn't lead to a promotion, the new challenges can get you out of a deadening routine.

To move sideways successfully, you need a history of credible job performance, a sound plan and influential supporters. The first step is to find the right department and job in your organization. Do not just listen for grapevine gossip. Check the employment office to find out who is hiring. Ask department heads to tell you their long-range plans. Scan trade magazines and securities analysts' reports to learn which parts of your industry are ripe for expansion.

Get help from insiders. Make lunch dates with people at your level or above. Ask about advancement opportunities and what it takes to land the job you're after. Only if every route off the plateau ends in a cul-de-sac should you look for a new employer.

If you think your boss takes you for granted or doesn't value you highly enough, one way to get his or her attention is to look for another job. As an executive recruiter at the Paul Ray Berndtson firm says, "This is the way to ask management, 'Just how valuable am I, and what are your plans for me?'" Roughly three-quarters of the 1,400 executives who responded to that firm's survey had put out feelers in 1993. Of those, 12% accepted new jobs. Many others advanced within their own companies.

# Negotiating a Transfer

The Employee Relocation Council reports that about half a million employees will be transferred by their companies this year. If you are a transferee, take care to negotiate with your employer to get the best deal on moving expenses.

Most large companies have standard moving policies that supposedly leave little room for negotiation. But no matter how rigid the company position seems, employers sometimes make adjustments. If you know what to ask for, you can get more — and save yourself some unpleasant financial surprises.

The standard package begins with the company paying all the costs of transporting your household goods. If you own a house or condo, the company typically will arrange for the purchase of it at a price set by two or more local appraisers. If you sell the house yourself, your employer should pay any real estate brokerage fees.

The company should cover any prepayment penalty on your old mortgage and pay for one or two househunting trips to the new location. Also ask for temporary living expenses for up to six weeks and up to three points for mortgage origination fees. And the company may provide interest-free or low-rate loans for down payments on your new house.

Ask for a raise at least large enough to offset any higher cost of living in the city where you are bound. Also ask for a $1,000 to $5,000 allowance to cover the costs of carpets, draperies and any other items you have to leave behind. These allowances are taxed as ordinary income by the federal, state and local governments. So most companies give you still another allowance to offset that extra liability.

You should get help in finding a job for a working spouse. Try to have the company hire a relocation firm to assist with résumés and job counseling. And ask for compensation for child-care costs while your spouse is job hunting.

# The Perils of Job-Hopping

For those people who wonder whether the surest way to the top is to hop from job to job within a given field, or to stay with one company, here's a good word for fidelity. Job-hopping is becoming much more frequent and acceptable. But those at the top know it can pay to stay with one employer. Eugene Jennings, a Michigan State University professor emeritus, tracked the careers of corporate presidents since 1953. He found that more than half of them remained loyal to one company.

True enough, job-hopping can help you gain valuable training and experience. The best reason to switch jobs, however, is to overcome obstacles, such as a hostile boss or a demotion. Yes, job-hopping is the normal way to move up the ladder in some volatile lines of work, such as advertising, television, fashion design, marketing, publishing and retailing. In recent years the demand for hoppers has risen especially in high technology and information processing.

But elsewhere, restless job switchers are sometimes suspected of being merely opportunistic, perhaps unable to get along with co-workers or to complete a job. The rewards of job-hopping can be fleeting. Professor Jennings found that though managers increased their salaries by 35% on average when they changed companies, those of equal ability who stayed on did even better. Some job-hoppers may sacrifice substantial benefits, such as pension increases.

Jennings calls job-hopping a "high-risk maneuver" that "fails as often as it works." New jobs sometimes do not turn out to be as alluring as first perceived, or new bosses as dynamic. Even if the hopper succeeds at fulfilling a specific new assignment, he or she risks being stereotyped as fit only for that role. Job-hoppers sometimes deceive themselves into thinking they have improved their position. In one survey 85% of those who changed their jobs thought that their moves had helped them, but their new bosses reported that only 46% had actually advanced. Unless you are unhappy or dead-ended in your current job, you should jump to another job only when you get a clear new opportunity or a meaningful raise in pay or an important advance in rank or responsibilities — or all three.

## How to Change Your Career

The reasons for veering off established career paths to explore whole new fields are often quite different today from what they were a few years ago. Career counselors say that midlife job changers no longer complain as much about too little advancement or too little pay. Their reason for switching now is as likely to be a desire for personal satisfaction as for money.

More and more managers are walking away from careers with big companies to venture out on their own. It's not hard to see why. Corporate cutbacks of the 1990s left fewer opportunities for ambitious executives at many companies. And some managers just get fed up with the stress of bigger workloads after yet another round of downsizing. Other competent, creative managers finally decide that working for a large company is just too confining.

Teachers, social workers and doctors often say they reach a burnout point of physical or mental exhaustion; they tend to seek out less-demanding professions. One teacher of emotionally troubled children contends she felt guilty when she first took a job as a tour consultant for a motel chain. Now she wonders why she did not make the change several years ago.

Above all, the successful career changers are adaptable. Many managers who have left one job to start their own businesses say that at first they really missed the secure sense of identity that a corporate job offers, to say nothing of that regular paycheck. People who move on to start their own businesses also find that they suddenly need to nurture skills that are not always encouraged at a big company — like creativity, risk-taking and flexibility. Not to mention doing countless administrative chores themselves.

You can lessen your chances of making a big mistake in career switching if you turn to the right sources of information and counseling. For a good start, read a book titled *Career Burnout: Causes and Cures* (Free Press, $12.95). *Career Burnout* provides a thoughtful description of this increasingly common problem and ways to deal with it. The most popular book that coaches people in career switching is Richard Bolles's *What Color Is Your Parachute?* (Ten Speed Press, $14.95). This perennial paperback best-seller emphasizes self-evaluation and defined goals.

For information about specific jobs, start in the reference section of the public library. Look for the Department of Labor's *Occupational Outlook Handbook* or the *Encyclopedia of Careers and Vocational Guidance.* Both tell you how to break into a field, and explain the kind of work done in a variety of occupations. Then head again for a bookstore. The *American Almanac of Jobs & Salaries* (Avon, $16) lists pay scales in various fields.

If the change you are contemplating requires you to earn a college degree, shop for a school that will give you academic credit for your achievements in life. A handbook, *Earn College Credit for What You Know,* includes a list by state of colleges and universities that award credit for nontraditional academic work. You can order it for $21.50 plus $5.00 for shipping and handling from the Council for Adult and Experiential Learning (243 South Wabash Avenue, Suite 800, Chicago, Illinois 60604; 312-922-5909).

Since you cannot learn everything from books, speak with people in your desired fields. Professional and trade associations and college alumni groups will give you names. Use your free hours to work part-time in your new job before you plunge in. Even a pot-scrubber learns about such frustrations of running a restaurant as no-show reservations, late deliveries and long hours. If you do better with a team than a tome, take one of the courses or workshops in career change offered by community colleges, universities, YMCAs and YWCAs. The cost of courses varies greatly depending upon their length and nature. Private career counselors charge $300 to $1,000 for several sessions. University services charge less, sometimes on a sliding scale. Some public libraries offer free courses in self-assessment and job evaluation.

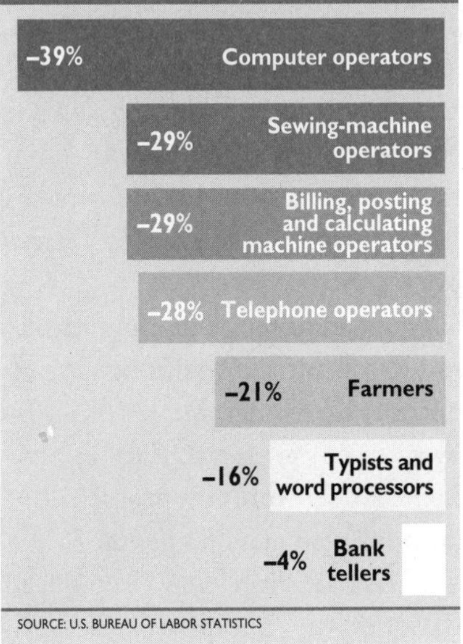


Most of us have undiscovered talents — artistic skills or money-making aptitudes — that we might not be aware of. If you want to make a career change and need help discovering a slumbering skill, you can have your abilities professionally tested. One of the oldest and best-known testers is the Johnson O'Connor Research Foundation. It charges $480 for seven to nine hours of testing and evaluation of your aptitudes for logical analysis, artistic or musical talents, and even executive ability. The foundation has 11 testing centers around the country. For a list of them, write to Johnson O'Connor Research Foundation (11 East 62nd Street, New York, New York 10021) or call 212-838-0550.

## What to Do If You Get Fired or Laid Off

In cost-cutting drives, jobs are usually the first casualty. The phrase "reduction in force," hardly softened by its acronym RIF and used apologetically by corporations peeling back, spells unemployment for hundreds of thousands of workers, from the mail room to the boardroom. A 1993 survey showed that when companies restructured, the most common activity was downsizing. Fully 74% of the corporations polled by the Wyatt Company reported cutbacks and one out of four reduced its workforce by more than 20%. It should be no surprise that the number of temps and part-time workers has risen so dramatically. Managerial downsizing cut deepest in companies with more than 5,000 employees. Fully 90% of these outfits have reduced the white-collar payroll in the past five years. Two out of five of the top human resources executives polled say that the number of managers is likely to shrink further in the next five years.

Those being wrung out can do little about saving their jobs, but sometimes quite a bit about negotiating the terms of their departure. Companies usually start with early-retirement packages. They may offer valued long-time employees a year's worth of severance pay or several years' extra credit toward pension benefits. Or they may ease you out with a consulting assignment at half your final salary.

Early-retirement packages can put you in a bind unless you are only a few years shy of normal retirement age. The hard truth is that you are likely to accrue as much as two-thirds of your total pension in your last 10 years on the job. But turning down a retirement offer has its own risks. The company may be telegraphing the news that your department may soon be eliminated, and your job with it.

Early-retirement offers and outright layoffs are part of a long-term corporate restructuring trend. Right Associates, a consulting firm that specializes in "outplacement" — the current honeyed term for helping the fired cope and relocate — surveyed companies about their severance policies. About 40% said they paid a week's salary for each year of employment; but 5% gave a full month's pay per year of service. In addition, some 40% continued their laid-off employees' group health and life insurance, usually for the same number of weeks or months.

Whatever the set policy, try to bargain for better terms, especially if you are older than 40. Some companies have a practice of not offering you outright all that they are prepared to give. They are willing to kick in more, figuring that it's a good thing if you leave with the feeling that you have "won" something. Severance packages usually come with a paper to sign, releasing the company from any further liability for your firing; your company doesn't want any pesky discrimination suits. A 1990 amendment to the Age Discrimination in Employment Act gives people age 40 and older a set time to ponder the deal, seek to negotiate better terms and consult a lawyer. That period is 21 days if you are being laid off individually and 45 days if your job is part of a mass reduction in force. Further, after signing a release form, you have seven days to revoke it.

Robert B. Fitzpatrick, a lawyer in Washington, D.C., specializing in employee rights, has a battle plan calculated to leave a company vulnerable to litigation when it fires someone. The strategy begins at the first hint of a layoff. Employees who are warned of deficiencies during annual evaluations should take their supervisors literally by keeping a record of their own efforts to improve performance. "Bosses are lazy and they are busy," Fitzpatrick says. "So they don't give much time to evaluations and record-keeping. Prepare a work improvement plan if you're told to shape up. In it, outline the goals you expect to attain. Then attain them."

If you're fired anyway, you can go quietly or try to get yourself a fancier deal. Labor-law attorneys like Fitzpatrick advise many laid-off workers to threaten suit as a way of trying to wrangle better severance benefits. Possible improvements might include extra weeks of severance pay or its reclassification as compensation for the hardship of being fired after age 40. Severance money under that label may be tax-free and can leave you immediately eligible for unemployment insurance.

Sweeteners to group health-insurance coverage are also well worth some hard negotiating. It's true that federal law gives laid-off employees the right to continue their group health-insurance coverage for 18 months. But the premium may be more than you can afford when you're out of work.

More important than squeezing your former employer for the last ounce is making preparations to get on with your career. Starting over may require redefining what you do. Dee Soder's Endymion Company counsels senior executives, and she says that defining exactly what one does in a managerial job is difficult. So managers may want to begin a job search by taking a tough, truthful inventory of their own strengths, weaknesses and aspirations. It's helpful to get outside perspectives. Soder notes that the higher one is on the slippery pole of corporate America, the tougher it is to step out of the echo chamber and hear some real criticism.

The chances of becoming re-employed improve significantly if you proceed in a businesslike way. Keep your emotions in check and your wits sharp. Remember, there is considerable truth in those counselors' platitudes that you should devote at least six hours a day to the search, write 15 to 20 letters each week and consider job hunting to be a job in itself. I would add that any day without a serious interview, or scheduling an interview, is a wasted day.

A natural impulse is to call friends in other companies in the hope of immediately finding a new job. But that's simply trying to prove to your ex-boss and yourself that he or she had poor judgment in letting you go. The right time to begin calling around for leads is after you have a résumé and know where you would like to work. When you update your résumé, list your objectives only in broad terms so as not to limit the kinds of openings interviewers might consider for you.

Getting interviews is easier if you can use your friends for entrée. But if you have to start cold, write an enticing letter to the person who is in a position to hire. In four crisp paragraphs, outline why you are writing, who you are (in terms of your previous titles and responsibilities), what you can do for the corporation you are writing to, and why you deserve a hearing. Follow up in a week or so with a phone call, but try not to sound too eager for the interview. If a potential employer senses that you are desperate, you've had it.

What do you say when an interviewer asks whether you were fired from your last job? Don't hide it, lie about it or even dance around it. Being fired just does not carry the same stigma that it did 10 years ago. With so many mergers and corporate consolidations, it can mean simply that you were in the wrong place at the wrong time.

Personnel managers are impressed by people who talk openly and honestly about themselves. You can battle nervousness by rehearsing the job interview with a friend, preferably someone who personally has done some hiring. And though you want to cast yourself in a radiant light, managers really do appreciate a balanced self-appraisal. They like to hear a job applicant volunteer not just what he or she is good at, but where he or she is weak, too. No one ever fits an employer's requirements perfectly.

It is equally important to have done your homework about the company and its field. Someone who has analyzed the firm's record and can speculate about its future impresses personnel executives much more than a job seeker who comes in asking, "What do you have open?" But don't be afraid to come right out and ask for a promising job. Like a salesperson who is reticent about closing a sale, a job hunter who is squeamish can wreck his or her own carefully constructed campaign.

Even if an interview goes splendidly, you will probably have to wait for a job to open. Without being overly pushy, the dedicated hunter finds reasons to keep in touch with potential employers. It is always wise to mail a thank-you note. You might even send along some new clippings or other information that may intrigue your interviewer.

While you are in the process of securing and conducting interviews, you should examine every option, including moving to another city. The biggest mistake some people make in their lives is to act as if they were born with a tag on their big toe that reads, "I'm a middle manager" or "I'm an auto worker" or whatever. But do not lurch into rash career decisions. Do not switch careers out of anger at what has just happened to you. And do not go back to school simply to get away from the competitiveness of the job market.

You might browse a book that career counselors recommend: *The Termination Handbook* by Robert Coulson (Free Press, $16.95). Another useful book is *The Perfect Resume* by Tom Jackson (Doubleday, $12).

## Time Management

In many ways, nothing is more devastating to a career than making it apparent that you are unable to manage your time properly. Others may see that as translating into an inability to manage your company's business. In these days of around-the-clock global communication, work is never finished. But somehow smart executives manage to stay on top of their jobs. How do they do it? A large part of the answer is that they have a talent for picking their priorities and concentrating on the essential questions of their jobs.

Managers could greatly improve their productivity and reduce their stress by taking the time to restructure their datebooks. Smart people leave room on their daily calendars for the unexpected. If you have an agenda cram-packed with meetings, it doesn't necessarily mean that your career is going well: It may mean you aren't thinking straight. The worst thing that can happen with an overcrowded appointment book is that you could — and, of course, you will — start running late. As a result, you will find yourself unable to keep up with your plan.

Technology can help you manage your time. Many executives say that their most useful tool is a car phone. Yet plenty of high executives will agree with Laurel Cutler, former vice chairman of the FCB/Leber Katz ad agency, who says her ultimate time-saving technique is learning to just say no.

First, unjam your schedule by taking on less. Have the nerve to say no to those requests to head the Chip-and-Dip Committee for the company picnic or write a memo on the misuse of company stationery. Then there are the tasks that you can delegate to others. That is just what a Los Angeles career couple did when they went to the extreme measure of hiring a 22-year-old person to do their shopping, pick up their cleaning and perform other household chores. The couple called him their "wife."

Getting it all done usually requires following the standard practice of making a list. Writing the list just before you leave work at the end of the day helps get you off to a fast start the next day. You might even keep a second list detailing all the foreseeable tasks you want to accomplish. Each day you pick 10 items from that list and put them on your daily sheet.

You might be wise to construct a personal time log. Write down everything you do for two weeks. That way, you can get a sense of the amount of time you typically need to perform certain jobs. Try to drop or delegate those tasks that take huge amounts of time but produce small rewards. Concentrate on the chores that produce large benefits for the time you put in.

Do you keep putting off little tasks because they are boring and have nothing to do with your real goals in life? If so, make an appointment with yourself once a week when your energy is running low to get through all the niggling but necessary paperwork that has to be dealt with.

Are you the victim of unwelcome interruptions such as drop-in visitors who plunk down in a chair and keep you from accomplishing anything? Maybe you are encouraging them — for instance, by making eye contact as a co-worker passes your desk. Some time-management specialists recommend turning your desk around so that you sit sideways to the door. That should keep you from making the first fateful eye contact without alienating co-workers.

Is your desk a mess? Just throw out the clutter, the memos, clippings, reports and monthly summaries you keep. Chances are you will never look at most of what you save. If you could readily replace a document, then why not chuck it? As for the material you do decide to keep, try sorting it into four piles: first, items that require your action; second, papers that must be referred to other people; third, all reading material; and fourth, items that have to be kept in your files because it is part of your job to keep them.

Unfortunately, each mail delivery brings with it more paper, including a request that you do something at a future date. To organize all those new piles, take an accordion-shaped file folder and number the compartments from one to 31, for each day in the month. File the papers in them. Then, first thing each morning, run through the file for that date and act on all those notes that say what you must do that day.

If you are really in a mess, you may have to seek professional help. It is available from specialists called time managers, who stand ready to sort out your schedule and your clutter. Some may be listed in your Yellow Pages under "Management Consultants." Fees for time-management consultants vary widely. One example: The Work System course by Workability (914-764-0250) in the New York metropolitan area costs $335 and includes a four-hour seminar plus a binder of daily planning sheets.

CHAPTER 17

# Gaining from Small Business and Entrepreneurship

## The Art of Getting Rich

Big companies may continue to shed workers, but that doesn't mean that economic opportunity has evaporated. On the contrary, the fast pace of technological and social change opens fresh frontiers — and America's new economic hero is the entrepreneur. If you are one of those enterprising men or women, endowed with unending drive and a talent for the intelligent management of risk, you can still get rich in America by starting your own business.

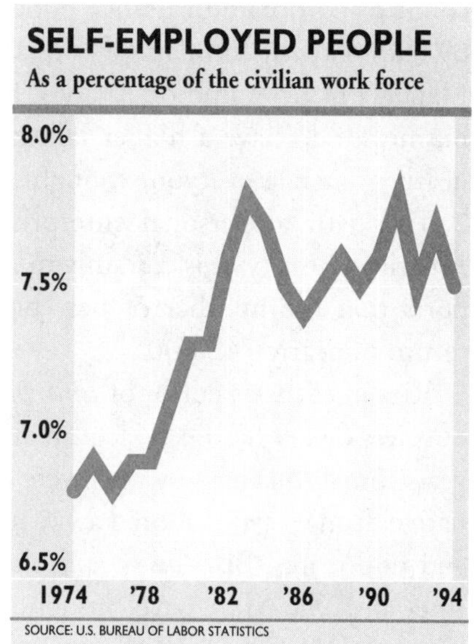


The professional occupations

of doctor, lawyer, investment banker and hired manager have provided a route to affluence for many postwar Americans, but entrepreneurship has always been the most reliable path to the biggest pots of wealth. More millionaires come out of small businesses than out of big corporations. Just ask Microsoft's Bill Gates. Or Dell Computer's Michael Dell. Or Sam Walton's heirs, who inherited billions. They started with next to nothing.

An entrepreneur's ultimate prosperity depends on the nature of his or her product and service, personal drive, luck, and the scope of his or her vision. If successful, he or she can create a lifestyle in scale with his or her dreams. Gates is now the richest man in America. Though not quite as fabulously wealthy, the founders of smaller successful companies can still live at a standard that the rest of us would envy. Owners of printing companies, video-rental franchises, home-security services and metals-recovery companies enjoy country club memberships, his-and-her BMWs, pleasure boats and luxury cruises through the Baltic, the Black Sea and Southeast Asia.

The risks in starting an enterprise are legendary: Between 50% and 80% of all new businesses have been said to fail within the first five years. But a new study suggests that the fabled failure rate of start-ups may have been exaggerated. The Dun & Bradstreet Corporation tracked every company that established a new trade credit, company bank account or corporate insurance policy between 1985 and 1994. In 1994, 69.7% of these companies were still in business. Says Doug Handler, Manager of Econometric Analysis for Dun & Bradstreet, "While smaller businesses do have a higher failure rate than larger companies, it's not nearly as high as everyone thought."

The path to personal enterprise may now be clearer than ever in American history. It is certainly more popular. Dun & Bradstreet also reports that the number of new business incorporations in 1994 hit a record of nearly 742,000.

Rieva Lesonsky, editor of *Entrepreneur* magazine, notes that the small-business owner has been "legitimatized" — and glamorized — in recent years. Small-business owners were once looked down upon as unimaginative drudges who labored away in burger-flipping operations or mom-and-pop stores. But the spectacular successes of the likes of Microsoft, Intel and Wal-Mart have brought entrepreneurship new attention and high regard. Today's small-business owner can also call on sources of

**GROWTH IN SMALL BUSINESSES**

| | One-year decline in business failures | Increase in new incorporations* |
|---|---|---|
| **LARGE CITIES** | | |
| Atlanta, GA | 15.9% | 9.7% |
| Minneapolis/St. Paul, MN | 44.1 | 8.5 |
| Kansas City, MO | 8.3 | 15.2 |
| Phoenix, AZ | 11.1 | 22.1 |
| Seattle/Everett, WA | 13.0 | 11.7 |
| St. Louis, MO | 35.4 | 15.2 |
| **MID-SIZED CITIES** | | |
| Springfield, MO | 23.3 | 15.2 |
| Eugene/Springfield, OR | 34.0 | 11.4 |
| Tulsa, OK | 19.2 | 8.7 |
| Salem, OR | 50.0 | 11.4 |
| Portland, OR | 24.1 | 11.4 |
| St. Cloud, MN | 9.9 | 8.5 |
| **SMALL CITIES** | | |
| Medford, OR | 35.8 | 11.4 |
| Clarksville, TN/Hopkinsville, KY | 29.5 | 8.4 |
| Eau Claire, WI | 29.8 | 8.1 |
| Columbia, MO | 48.6 | 15.2 |
| Biloxi/Gulfport, MS | 77.8 | 16.8 |

*Information available only at the state level.

SOURCE: *ENTREPRENEUR*

support that didn't exist a generation ago. The personal computer, the electronic database and the proliferation of books, magazines and weekend college courses about small-business management support the entrepreneur as never before. A number of schools, including Babson College in Boston, offer MBAs with an emphasis on entrepreneurship.

## What It Takes to Succeed

What you need to start your own business are an idea, a feel for the market (and a true willingness to serve), a business plan and capital. Add to that devotion, an iron gut and an ability to be flexible; family and friends who support your entrepreneurial mania; and a team of experts and colleagues who know what you do well — and are prepared to tell you what you don't do well. Perfect timing and excellent luck are not required but will come in handy if available.

Historically, the entrepreneur has taken five main roads to fortune in America: investing in the stock market, investing in real estate, drilling for oil, publishing and retailing. But Ian Morrison, who heads the Institute for the Future in Menlo Park, California, believes that entrepreneurial opportunities in the 21st century will come from three key trends that are well under way: the "explosion" of new technology, the aging of the baby-boom generation (now ages 31 to 50) and the globalization of business. This does not mean that you must invent an amazing new product or master some obscure technology. Many of the most successful entrepreneurs simply make something better, serve a customer whom others have neglected or spy a need that others have missed.

Profitable ideas can be monumental or mundane. Operating systems for mainframe computers were around long before Bill Gates. But Microsoft prospered because it seized the opportunity to put basic operating systems into the personal computer, which represented a new wave of technology. Judy George, chairman and CEO of Domain, a chain of 22 home-furnishing stores, saw that the hard-working baby boomer was growing up. George reasoned that this new consumer would be spending more time at home, wanting more than utility or uniform style. "I saw the home more as a sanctuary, a fashion statement." It didn't hurt that George was willing to "break all the rules, mixing classic design with comfortable home furnishings." Her company, born in 1985, rang up revenues of $40 million for fiscal year 1995.

Some start-ups are capitalizing on one of the 1990s' most enduring (and painful) trends. Large and medium-sized companies are downsizing, often because it's too expensive to keep experts in computer operations or training on staff. But they still have work that needs to be done. So they have "farmed out" the work to small firms and individuals who specialize in serving particular kinds of companies or needs.

Such niche service businesses have proliferated in accounting, public relations, photocopying, training, and credit reporting and collection services, in part because their start-up costs are low. Some need little more than a computer, a room and a bank loan (and, of course, an experienced hand). With $5,000 to $10,000, you can buy the computer equipment you need, for example, to do bookkeeping for other small-business firms.

## GOOD PLACES TO START A BUSINESS

Based on an educated labor pool, reasonable wages and real-estate costs, and growth in personal income, these 20 cities in four regions were chosen by *Entrepreneur* magazine as top places for new business.

| Top 20 cities by region | 1992 population | Estimated 1997 population | % with college degrees | Average clerical salary | Growth in income 1980-93 | Average office real-estate cost per sq. ft. |
|---|---|---|---|---|---|---|
| **WEST** | | | | | | |
| Albuquerque, NM | 496,251 | 548,000 | 26.7% | $17,195 | 44.34% | $14.25 |
| Phoenix, AZ | 2,224,211 | 2,416,000 | 22.1 | 17,519 | 66.53 | 16.14 |
| Tucson, AZ | 688,139 | 769,000 | 23.3 | 18,547 | 49.91 | 17.50 |
| San Diego, CA | 2,616,354 | 2,772,000 | 25.3 | 19,799 | 56.00 | 17.70 |
| Salt Lake City, UT | 1,115,354 | 1,233,000 | 22.9 | 16,488 | 34.35 | 15.00 |
| **SOUTH** | | | | | | |
| Ft. Worth, TX | 1,407,445 | 1,404,000 | 22.6 | 16,357 | 52.79 | 13.50 |
| Columbia, SC | 466,673 | 497,000 | 25.3 | 16,784 | 50.22 | 13.75 |
| Austin, TX | 832,909 | 911,000 | 32.2 | 17,678 | 77.37 | 15.00 |
| Raleigh-Durham, NC | 772,978 | 841,000 | 34.8 | 17,813 | 77.38 | 17.25 |
| Dallas, TX | 2,679,134 | 2,710,000 | 27.6 | 17,280 | 47.30 | 14.00 |
| **MIDWEST** | | | | | | |
| Wichita, KS | 495,450 | 481,000 | 21.5 | 16,097 | 22.19 | 14.50 |
| Omaha, NE | 632,509 | 671,000 | 22.8 | 17,023 | 29.39 | 17.57 |
| Indianapolis, IN | 1,283,984 | 1,397,000 | 21.1 | 16,898 | 27.93 | 17.50 |
| Kansas City, MO | 1,599,338 | 1,693,000 | 23.4 | 17,727 | 30.19 | 18.38 |
| Minneapolis, MN | 2,546,689 | 2,746,000 | 27.1 | 18,434 | 38.81 | 21.55 |
| **NORTHEAST** | | | | | | |
| New Haven, CT | 533,235 | 823,000 | 27.4 | 19,717 | 41.64 | 14.00 |
| Worcester, MA | 441,683 | 751,000 | 23.4 | 18,705 | 35.29 | 15.00 |
| Hartford, CT | 773,934 | 1,131,000 | 28.1 | 19,956 | 42.91 | 17.75 |
| Middlesex, NJ | 1,046,058 | 1,055,000 | 30.2 | 20,866 | 63.32 | 17.25 |
| Boston, MA | 2,857,064 | 3,865,000 | 33.1 | 21,013 | 38.27 | 19.75 |

SOURCE: *ENTREPRENEUR*

While change creates opportunity for any entrepreneur sensitive enough to tune in to what's up (and what's out), some of the most ingenious creators have built businesses around ideas that are utterly simple. Alexander Mautner made a place for his Metro-Clean Express by removing not just garbage but also graffiti for clients in the New York City area. Gary Kvistad created Woodstock Percussion, a $14 million-a-year company in West Hurley, New York, by engineering and marketing a more melodic wind chime. The list goes on and on—and the next winning idea is probably close at hand.

## STATE CORPORATE INCOME TAX RATES

| State | Rate | State | Rate |
|---|---|---|---|
| Alabama | 5% | Nebraska | 5.58-7.81% |
| Alaska | 1-9.4 | Nevada | None |
| Arizona | 9 | New Hampshire | 8 |
| Arkansas | 1-6.5 | New Jersey | 9 |
| California | 9.3 | New Mexico | 4.8-7.6 |
| Colorado | 5 | New York | 9 |
| Connecticut | 11.5 | North Carolina | 7.75 |
| Delaware | 8.7 | North Dakota | 3-10.5 |
| Florida | 5.5 | Ohio | 5.1-8.9 |
| Georgia | 6 | Oklahoma | 6 |
| Hawaii | 4.4-6.4 | Oregon | 6.6 |
| Idaho | 8 | Pennsylvania | 10.99 |
| Illinois | 4.8 | Rhode Island | 9 |
| Indiana | 3.4 | South Carolina | 5 |
| Iowa | 6-12 | South Dakota | None |
| Kansas | 4 | Tennessee | 6 |
| Kentucky | 4-8.25 | Texas | None |
| Louisiana | 4-8 | Utah | 5 |
| Maine | 3.5-8.93 | Vermont | 5.5-8.25 |
| Maryland | 7 | Virginia | 6 |
| Massachusetts | 9.5 | Washington | None |
| Michigan | 0–2.3 | Washington, DC | 9.975 |
| Minnesota | 9.8 | West Virginia | 9.0 |
| Mississippi | 3-5 | Wisconsin | 7.9 |
| Missouri | 6.25 | Wyoming | None |
| Montana | 6.75–7.25 | | |

SOURCE: TAX FOUNDATION

# Critical Elements: Planning and Capital

The most critical period in the life cycle of a start-up is the first two or three years. That's when a new enterprise is most likely to fail. The businesses that make it through this tunnel are those that have been most carefully planned and provided for.

You will need to draft a detailed business plan, including cash-flow projections. But that step is premature if you haven't first "road tested" your idea. Ask successful business people you know and trust what they think of your idea. Just as important, ask your potential customer. When Judy George started her Domain furniture company, she had years of experience as president of Scandinavian Design, a retail home furnishing firm with 86 stores nationally. Yet even she did some basic research, interviewing customers who came out of existing competitors' stores to find out what they were looking for — and to make sure it was what she planned to sell.

Your sound business idea is the foundation for a useful business plan, a road map for your company's future. It should be about 60 to 80 pages long and include weekly or monthly projections for the first two years. Itemize what it will cost to develop, manufacture, sell and market your product or service. Take the competition into account. Estimate your company's sales and share of market over the next three years on a quarter-by-quarter basis. Do the figuring yourself to become familiar with production, distribution and marketing. A realistic cash-flow projection may be even more critical to your company's success. You need sufficient cash flow to make sure your business will have the financing and income it requires to survive.

A growing number of sources provide help to you in formulating your first business plans. One such source is the Small Business Administration (409 Third Street SW, Washington, D.C. 20416; 800-827-5722 or 202-205-7701). An SBA-affiliated volunteer group, Service Corps of Retired Executives (SCORE), operates about 400 chapters throughout the U.S. to advise new owners and fledgling businesses. The SBA also sponsors some 60 Small Business Development Centers, which in turn direct close to 900 smaller groups.

The SBA also has two computer bulletin boards — SBA OnLine and SBA Home Page — that offer information about starting and running a small business, SBA services and publications, and its loan procurement assistance and business development programs. The address for both OnLine and Home Page is: http://www.sbaonline.sba.gov., or call via modem 800-697-4636. To download software files, send or receive e-mail with other small-business owners, or get greater access to other federal agency bulletin boards, such as the IRS, that offer advice to small-business owners, call 1-900-463-4636 (cost: 14¢ per minute).

To test that your assumptions are sound and you have provided for the unexpected, have your business plan reviewed by more sophisticated, objective counsel. Your banker, lawyer and accountant may provide valuable feedback, but they do not have the benefit of experience in the market you have targeted. People who serve the customers you are aiming for do. If you want to open a benefits consulting firm for small- to medium-sized businesses, for example, ask an employment recruiter who knows the companies in your market how quickly potential clients pay their bills.

Consultants to start-up enterprises can also be useful at this stage, particularly if your experience with business or finance is limited. Ask an accountant, lawyer or banker — or a friend who has successfully launched his or her own business — to refer you to a reliable professional. Expect to pay $1,000 to $1,500 for a relatively brief encounter with a consultant, and more if you hire an accounting firm. Even if you have considerable experience, the investment may be worth it.

These professionals may also be able to show you how to use potential customers and suppliers as sources of financing, and how to cut costs by leasing, rather than buying, equipment. They can give you information that will help you decide what legal form your business should take — corporation, sole proprietorship, S corporation, personal corporation, or limited partnership — and advise you on the tax implications of each.

Local colleges and universities may be a source for general guidance. There are 483 SBA-supported Small Business Institutes at colleges and universities across the U.S. Faculty members oversee advanced undergraduate and graduate students, who for one full term work with a designated small business on market studies, promotional strategies, accounting systems and operations plans. The service is free for qualified businesses.

You may consider seeking aid from a company that provides "business incubation" services. About 550 business incubators in the U.S. and Canada provide beginning entrepreneurs with inexpensive space, support and services — from copying equipment and secretarial assistance to business consulting and accounting as well as networking opportunities. Some incubators have their own "angel" network of investors and seed-financing programs. For information about incubators in your state, write or phone the National Business Incubation Association, 20 East Circle Drive, Suite 190, Athens, Ohio 45701; 614-593-4331. The International Venture Capital Institute also publishes a directory of incubators that can be ordered for $19.95 from IVCI at P.O. Box 1333, Stamford, Connecticut 06904; 203-323-3143. As with any professional you hire, do ask the managers of business incubators to give you references from other entrepreneurs they have helped.

# How to Raise the Money You Will Need

Insufficient financing is the number-one killer of new businesses. Undercapitalization pits the entrepreneur against the clock — and against competitors who are better financed — in a losing race. Entrepreneurs can and do tap a broad range of sources for capital: their own assets, family, friends, former business associates, finance companies, banks and venture capital firms. Plan to spend at least three months acquainting yourself with the sources of financing before you try to raise any significant amount. And be prepared to ante up whatever you've got.

Entrepreneurs put up what is called "first money" in order to get enough of their own dream on paper to convince investors it's viable. The determined entrepreneur uses all his or her sources of credit, including putting a second mortgage on his or her house and even "maxing out" his or her credit cards. (The SBA reports that a large majority of the women who have started low-overhead service companies in recent years financed them with "loans" from their credit cards.) If the basic business idea and planning are sound, the creator will impress other potential investors with his or her commitment. Just as important, by maximizing his or her own stake in the business, the new owner will retain tighter control of the enterprise.

When you solicit friends and relatives — and later, friends of those friends and relatives — ask them to lend the money rather than obliging you to sell them stock in your company. That way, you won't have to put up with Uncle Bill telling you how to run "his" business. To get names of potential investors you don't know, ask accountants, bankers, lawyers, brokers and other business owners. They often are aware of who has money to invest or lend.

Local business groups like the chamber of commerce can provide more leads. So can simple ingenuity. Bill Rosenzweig found backers for his New Age tea company, The Republic of Tea, in Mel and Patricia Ziegler, the entrepreneurs who started the Banana Republic leisure-clothing company. Rosenzweig ran into Mel on a plane, and they just started talking business. Moral: Seize every opportunity.

Once you have exhausted your individual financing sources, it is time to approach the institutions. You may be rather pleasantly surprised: Money to finance promising new businesses is fairly plentiful. Though some banks in the Northeast have been nervous about small-business lending, after years of drought banks are making loans to small businesses again. Professional venture capitalists are loaded with cash — so much that they sometimes complain they cannot find enough small companies worthy of investment. And investment banking firms, universities and insurance companies are betting on small business through their own venture capital units. Judy George started her Massachusetts-based Domain furniture company with $3 million from Harvard Private Capital Group, Chemical Ventures (a unit of Chemical Bank), The Travelers Insurance Company, Bain & Company management consultants and Robertson Stephens and Company.

The best sources for loans of $100,000 or smaller are the banks, commercial finance companies, the SBA, and business-development agencies and companies. You can find these sources through the SBA answer desk (800-827-5722), your state economic development office, your local chamber of commerce, and trade associations.

The SBA's guaranteed-loan program made 36,480 loans to small businesses totaling $8.2 billion in 1994 (up from $6.7 billion the year before). About a quarter of such loans go to start-ups. The SBA can back as much as 90% of loans of up to $500,000 (the average is $170,000)

## BIG LENDERS TO SMALL BUSINESSES

| Bank holding company | | Small-business loans (% of total) | Domestic small-business loans (billions) | Domestic business loans (billions) |
|---|---|---|---|---|
| **First of America Bank Corp.** | Kalamazoo, MI | 57.3% | $2.34 | $4.08 |
| **Norwest Corp.** | Minneapolis | 51.1 | 4.23 | 8.27 |
| **KeyCorp** | Cleveland | 42.6 | 5.80 | 13.60 |
| **Banc One Corp.** | Columbus, OH | 39.0 | 6.15 | 15.77 |
| **Boatmen's Bancshares** | St. Louis | 36.2 | 2.25 | 6.21 |
| **Fleet Financial Group** | Providence, RI | 31.8 | 3.81 | 11.98 |
| **First Union Corp.** | Charlotte, NC | 31.3 | 5.09 | 16.26 |
| **First Bank System** | Minneapolis | 31.2 | 2.22 | 7.11 |
| **SunTrust Banks** | Atlanta | 30.3 | 3.33 | 10.99 |
| **National City Corp.** | Cleveland | 29.3 | 2.71 | 9.22 |

Note: Small-business loans consist of commercial and industrial loans of $1 million or less made to firms with U.S. addresses as well as mortgage loans of $1 million or less backed by nonfarm, nonresidential properties. Total business loans remove the $1 million limitation.

SOURCES: EDWARD P. FOLDESSY FROM COMPUTER TAPES OBTAINED FROM THE FEDERAL BANKING AUTHORITIES; *WALL STREET JOURNAL*

from both bank and regulated nonbank lenders such as The Money Store. Proposals now under consideration may raise the SBA's ceiling on loan size to $1 million. The prices for SBA loans are also under review, but the agency caps rates at 2¼ to 2¾ points over prime, plus a fee equal to 2% of the loan amount.

The SBA has made recent changes that give new companies a boost. In 1994 it introduced a "low documentation" program for loans of $100,000 or less. The banks that give SBA-backed loans had been turning away small-business owners because the SBA's loan application was too cumbersome. So the SBA reduced the form to one page. Result: 56% of the SBA's loans in the first five months of 1995 were for $100,000 or less, compared with 30% in 1993.

The SBA also makes direct loans to certain kinds of small businesses, such as those run by the disabled (though there has been some talk in Congress of curtailing these loans). Further, if you need funds for research and development, you may get help from the SBA-monitored Small Business Innovation Research program (202-205-6450). The program coordinates and oversees R&D funding agreements with small businesses and 11 participating agencies, such as NASA and the Environmental Protection Agency. Through SBIR guidance, the participating agencies spent about $645 million on R&D in fiscal year 1993.

Small-business investment companies, or SBICs, are private venture firms that borrow some of their money under an SBA guarantee. Apple, Intel and Federal Express all got through their early years with the help of SBIC-guaranteed venture financing. (In the case of FedEx, the SBIC financing arrived like the cavalry, just as the company was about to close its doors.) In addition to the 270 all-purpose SBICs, there are 90 SBICs that invest exclusively in concerns at least 51% owned by those whom the agency considers to be "socially or economically disadvantaged" people, such as minorities and the poor.

In about three-quarters of the states, quasi-public business-development corporations, or BDCs, make loans to small companies to create local jobs. For details, ask your state's economic development agency where you can find a BDC. You can also turn to the little-known local development corporations, composed of local government officials and private citizens who borrow funds from the SBA and from banks and re-lend the money to entrepreneurs in need of long-term financing.

Target which banks to approach by finding out first which ones are the "friendliest" to small business. *Entrepreneur* magazine publishes a list of such banks (for example, in its June 1995 issue). Your local or regional newspaper may do so as well, and your area chamber of commerce may provide leads. See also page 606. Don't overlook the company that manages your mutual funds. Some, including Merrill Lynch, have venture capital units that make direct investments in start-ups.

Don't expect that your bank or financial-services company will give you a loan just because you have money on deposit or invested with them. But if they are not interested in the financial needs of small businesses, move your money. As Kathryn D. Barrios, managing director of Americas Consulting Group, advises, "Give your patronage to someone who will help you build your business."

For loans of $500,000 and above, reach out to venture capital firms. Don't seek help from a venture capitalist if you are not willing to give up a piece of your own company. Venture capitalists do not make loans; they buy private stock in your company, hoping to sell it at a profit when your business has grown.

Because of the unusual success of some recent new businesses, notably in high tech and services, financiers are willing to take greater risks than just a few years ago — if they figure that they may also reap greater rewards. And the best venture capitalists will serve your company with advice about developing management depth, investing in information systems and more. Keep in mind, however, that you are selling an ownership stake in your business to someone who will have substantial influence over its future. Wesley Hayne's virtual reality software company, Virtual Express Ltd., folded, he says, because his backers pulled the plug. They were disappointed in the speed with which the market for his product was developing.

You may look for a local venture capital association; about 150 such clubs operate in the U.S. and abroad. They hold monthly luncheon meetings at which entrepreneurs and investors discuss ideas and funding for new products or businesses. Members include venture capitalists, bankers, attorneys and corporate executives. For a directory of the clubs, send $9.95 to the International Venture Capital Institute, P.O. Box 1333, Stamford, Connecticut 06904.

In searching for financial help, be wary of firms that advertise that they are professional finders of money. Many of them charge high fees simply for sending out mass mailings to investors. But one reliable source of names of potential angels is the National Venture Capital Association. To get its membership directory, write or call the association at 1655 North Fort Myer Drive, Suite 700, Arlington, Virginia 22209, 703-351-5269.

The national bible for shopping the venture capital firms is *Pratt's Guide to Venture Capital Sources,* published by Venture Economics Division of Securities Data Publishing, Inc., 40 West 57th Street, New York, New York 10019. The guide contains a listing and profiles of over 950 venture capital firms in the U.S. and abroad, including their recent investments, geographic preferences, industry and product preferences, and types of financing available, along with names of their principals and phone numbers to call. Look for it in a good public library and save yourself the price of $249. Venture Economics can provide "most active investor" listings in specific technology and industry fields through its Newark-based information services group (201-622-3100). *Guerrilla Financing* by Bruce Blechman and Jay Conrad Levinson (Houghton Mifflin, $11.95) is also a source for finding a wide variety of financial backers.

Speak with tax attorneys, accountants and brokers who have experience getting a group of high-bracket investors to invest in a business in return for tax write-offs and potential profits. You may even have to make a private offering of stock. The disadvantage is that it reduces your stake in your own company. The less you are compelled to surrender, the more you can offer later to attract skilled managers and additional capital to your company.

## Tax Breaks for Investors

Fortunate investors in small businesses can get a capital-gains tax break. If they buy stock issued after August 1993 in some small companies and hold it for at least five years, their capital-gains taxes will be cut in half. The tax regulation regarding this kind of small-business investment is complex, so you'll want to consult a CPA or tax attorney to see if your company qualifies.

# Growing Your Business: Do You Have What It Takes?

While poor planning, lack of capital or plain bad management will do a company in, so can a founder who doesn't have the true entrepreneurial temperament. Studies of entrepreneurs show that those who succeed share certain traits. They have an appetite for calculated risk and the flexibility to learn from their mistakes. They tolerate failure well. Many of them stumbled along the way, then quickly picked themselves up, analyzed their errors and applied what they learned. They are devotees of the dream, giving themselves totally to the business they tend.

The successful entrepreneur doesn't just have an idea, or an urge to get out from under a boss. He or she wants to go beyond the dream — delving into detail, imagining the future and making it plausible through a business plan. Entrepreneurs who make it are persistent and patient, often beginning with little money but considerable determination. In their heart of hearts, they are unstoppable. Michael Ray, a professor of innovation, creativity and marketing at the Stanford University Graduate Business School, says that many entrepreneurs liken starting a company to going through the process of birth: dark, frightening and ultimately thrilling, as something new is brought to life.

You may wish to start a business all by yourself, but studies show that teams enjoy better odds for success than individuals. The right blend of management skills makes a difference, and more partners bring to the table more contacts, more experience and more money than you alone can.

But where do you find the right people to be your partners? Building an enterprise simply on blood ties, friendship or a shared enthusiasm for golf can be dangerous. True, your relatives and chums may have funds to invest. But starting a company is strain enough without the added trauma of firing someone dear who does not work out. Or, worse yet, having to keep him or her on board.

We all tend to surround ourselves with people like ourselves. It's comfortable. But it's a mistake in managing a business. Seek those with complementary talents. An engineer who pairs up with a manufacturing or marketing person is better prepared for the challenges of entrepreneurship than a trio of engineers, even if their business is the next generation of computers. You will be more confident, and be able to move more quickly, if you have worked with your new partners before. To balance potential rewards with the hard work required early on, all partners should invest some capital in the business, or at least forsake some salary during the start-up phase.

Even if you have the perfect partners and more than enough cash, your new business still can be done in by poor record-keeping. Well before you open, you will need to have sound financial information keeping you up to date on operating expenses, inventory costs, accounts receivable, debt obligations and income. Accurate financial records are an indispensable warning system. With all that, if your small business can then survive two or three years of growing pains, the odds for continued success will be in your favor.

For more information, look at a number of first-class books written for and by entrepreneurs. Two of the most useful primers are Jane Applegate's *Succeeding in Small Business* (Penguin, $12.95) and *The Republic of Tea* by Bill Rosenzweig (Doubleday, $22.50), which gives an up-close and personal chronicle of the nail-biting and second-guessing Rosenzweig went through as he created his Republic of Tea company. *Built to Last* by Jim Collins (Harper-Collins, $25) tells how to create a company that will endure.

## Learning to Be an Entrepreneur

In the days when small business was an enterprise limited to the candy store or the car dealership, entrepreneurs learned everything they knew from the famous academy of hard knocks. But to survive and compete in today's economy, small-business owners — like the proprietors of big ones — can benefit from management skills acquired through formal training. More than 600 U.S. colleges and universities offer courses in starting a small business. Some, including Babson College, Baylor University, the University of Southern California and the University of Pennsylvania, have introduced undergraduate majors in entrepreneurship. If you have neither the time nor temperament to work toward a degree — or if you'd like to develop your idea in the safety of a supervised laboratory — you can choose from a variety of commercial and SBA-sponsored courses.

A worthwhile course will cover such fundamentals as evaluating an idea, raising capital and dealing with suppliers and customers. Students are often asked to prepare a detailed business plan for their firm's first five years. You can size up a course's content not just by studying the catalogue but also by talking with faculty and former students; get their names and phone numbers from the sponsors of the course.

The SBA also offers workshops at more than 100 district and branch offices, where accountants, bankers, marketing consultants and government officials offer pointers to small-business people. The nonprofit Center for Entrepreneurial Management holds seminars on entrepreneurship at many private clubs. For courses in your area, write to the Center at 180 Varick Street, Penthouse, New York, New York 10014.

# How to Get the Right Franchise

In the era that began with Ray Kroc colonizing America with a company called McDonald's, you could have invested in a fast-food franchise and cooked up a fortune. It is not too late to acquire a worthwhile franchise. If you pick wisely, the odds of surviving and succeeding as a small-business man or woman multiply impressively.

While fast-food franchises still dominate the field, the 1990s have seen the rapid rise of the office-service franchise. You can sell business services such as typing, copying, telexing and mail pickup. Mail Boxes Etc. USA, based in San Diego, has given with-it franchisees a chance to get in on its growing success. Other promising franchise opportunities include printing, specialized employment agencies and business brokers. These brokers bring together people who want to sell their small businesses and people who want to buy them. By doing

**BIGGEST FRANCHISES**

| Rank | Franchise chain | Number of outlets |
|---|---|---|
| 1 | McDonald's | 12,643 |
| 2 | 7-Eleven | 12,469 |
| 3 | H&R Block | 9,228 |
| 4 | KFC Corp. | 8,187 |
| 5 | Radio Shack | 7,000 |
| 6 | Subway | 6,862 |
| 7 | Burger King | 6,490 |
| 8 | Century 21 Real Estate | 6,150 |
| 9 | Pizza Hut | 5,745 |
| 10 | Dairy Queen | 5,347 |
| 11 | Domino's | 5,145 |
| 12 | Jazzercise | 4,782 |
| 13 | Little Caesars | 4,117 |
| 14 | ServiceMaster | 4,076 |
| 15 | Snap-On Tools | 4,000 |

SOURCES: INTERNATIONAL FRANCHISE ASSOCIATION; *ENTREPRENEUR*

just that, one Atlanta grandmother earned some $240,000 in commissions in only her second year of operation. Another group of franchises performs household services for people who are too busy to do them. These chores reach from housecleaning to performing home maintenance when the owners are away.

Franchises for stores that sell educational products and services are growing 10% a year and now are a substantial business. There are franchised learning centers for children and adults, day-care centers and diet centers that "re-educate" you about your eating habits.

You can also find opportunities in franchising's traditional backbone — retail stores. Franchisers account for just over one-third of retail sales in the U.S., or about $800 billion a year. The potential is strong for stores that sell home computers, TV equipment and inexpensive furnishings. Restaurants that serve ethnic food are doing well, too.

Professional franchise brokers can help you locate the business you want; for names, call the International Business Brokers & Consultants Limited (617-696-5800). There are indeed professional franchise consultants, but be careful in choosing one. The International Franchise Association, a trade association of franchisers and franchisees, says some people with little experience have set themselves up as consultants and promise much more than they can deliver. Before hiring a consultant, ask for the names of past clients and call them. When you get serious about buying, deal with a lawyer who is familiar with drafting franchise contracts and with Federal Trade Commission rules. For a recommendation, try a local franchise operator or the bar association.

For a description of 5,000 franchise companies in the U.S. and overseas and information on how franchising works, get *The Franchise Opportunities Guide,* produced by International Franchise Association Publications (800-543-1038). The price is $15, plus $6 for shipping and handling. Another comprehensive list of the offerings is in *The 1996 Franchise Annual Handbook and Directory.* You can get it for $39.95, including postage, from Info Press (728 Center Street, P.O. Box 550, Lewiston, New York 14092).

Before you sign a contract to buy a franchise, the parent company must give you a disclosure statement. From it you can get the names and phone numbers of several franchisees. Phone them to find out how well they are doing.

When you buy, you pay the franchising company an initial fee and later a continuing royalty that averages 4% to 5% of gross sales but can reach 10% or higher, particularly for service businesses. In return, you can use the company's trademark and franchising services for a set period, usually five years, with renewal options up to 25 years. The basic franchising service is to give operating instructions, often covering everything from sales tactics to the color of the office carpeting. Capable companies also help you pick a business location and buy equipment and inventory (some of which you may be required to buy from the franchisor). Their representatives sit in with you when you hire your first employees. The best ones hold your hand through crises.

Instead of running franchises themselves, many investors hire managers to operate them. But franchisors usually feel that the owner's attention is crucial and therefore will not sell units to absentee owners. That is understandable: Few salaried managers will put in the 60 to 80 hours of work each week that it often takes to make a business succeed.

When you start investigating franchises to purchase, do your homework and cast your net wide. Talk to other franchisees in other areas of the country (they will be less likely to view you as a potential competitor than one in your vicinity) and speak with franchisees in competing companies. Get the "buzz" on relationships between the franchisor and its franchisees. Read *Entrepreneur* magazine, which ranks franchises in terms of their "desirability" as an investment (see *Entrepreneur*'s January 1995 Franchise 500 list). Go to the library and look for articles in the business press about the financial health of your company. When America's Favorite Chicken Company, owners of Popeye's and Church's fried chicken and biscuits fast-food restaurants, declared bankruptcy a few years ago, franchisees who had planned to sell were temporarily stuck.

More research tips: Ask to talk to senior executives of the franchisor and find out about their growth plans and strategies. Check to see if there's been a recent change in senior management at the franchisor that could signal a new strategy for the future. Look at the ratio between company-owned stores and stores owned by franchisees. The more stores owned and operated by the franchising company, the more likely it will be to support franchisees and act out of a long-term interest for the franchise's quality and reputation.

Suits between franchisees and the franchisor are common. Franchise owners of Carvel Ice Cream Bakery Stores have been rebellious because the Carvel company has begun selling its products in supermarkets, cutting into franchisees' sales. In 1994, 42 filed suit against Carvel, controlled by a Bahraini investment company, in New York state court.

Try to distinguish between franchise trends and fads. Take-out food restaurants have grown explosively as two-income families looked for meals to serve on nights when Mom got home late, or when it was Dad's turn to cook. Given this trend, and Americans' interest in healthier eating, franchises that sell full meals featuring chicken that is roasted or broiled rather than fried may have a future. But in the 1980s some investors got burned when they bought franchises in catfish cafés and chili restaurants designed to look like bordellos.

## Making a Family Firm Survive and Succeed

Many of the almost 20 million small companies in the U.S. are family-dominated, but keeping such a business alive — and the family happy — takes work. The survival rates are dreadful. Only a third make it to the second generation, and only a tenth to the third generation. That's partly because of heavy estate taxes (see Chapter 23 on wills, trusts and estates) and partly because the founder often has tremendous difficulty giving up control of the business to his or her heirs.

Parents often do not parcel out enough authority to their children because they fear their own authority will be diminished. Conflicts between generations typically boil over when founding fathers are in their 60s and their children are in their 30s. At that point, the children have learned the business, and as professionals wish to apply what they've learned — perhaps by introducing new products and services or otherwise expanding the business. But parents want to protect their retirement security by keeping the business on a course they feel most comfortable with. The drama that then unfolds often is a cross between *King Lear* and *Long Day's Journey into Night.*

Sibling rivalry is a major problem. So is indulging a beloved relative. Profits fall and nonfamily employees are driven away when nepotism keeps family members in key jobs despite poor performance.

Here are some tips on how to manage a successful succession in a family business:

- Heirs to the business first should get jobs outside the family firm. After they've proved themselves in these neutral surroundings, they can confidently return.
- When the time comes to pick a successor, the founder and his or her heirs should put family loyalty out of their minds. The big question is, Who can run the business best? It may not be the eldest son, but a daughter or an in-law or even a hired manager.
- If two or more heirs wind up sharing control, they should agree in advance on some orderly way to settle disputes that may arise between them. They might agree to hire an independent arbitrator.
- Above all, the aging chief should gradually but steadily hand over control. The patriarch of a family firm can do everything else right, but if he doesn't designate an heir — and then show his support for that heir, and let go of the reins — he has failed the business.

## Business in Your Home

Tens of millions of Americans now work in their homes. If they make it past the 13th month — the critical test, say home-business consultants — most find rewards in both income and lifestyle. The fastest-growing of these enterprises are computer data and word processing, direct sales for commissions, and general business services, including accounting, bookkeeping and typing.

If you want to start a home business, first make sure local zoning regulations allow it. Some communities outlaw home businesses, as do some apartment leases and condo bylaws. But an increasing number of communities are changing the rules to accommodate the needs of workers who have been laid off, and others will grant an appeal for a permit or variance. Also make sure that you are operating within federal and state laws. Some laws, originally designed to prevent sweatshops, regulate what goods can be produced commercially at home.

Hire a lawyer who has worked with other home businesses. He or she can shepherd you through the layers of regulations that apply to home business. According to Donna Chaiet, a Manhattan attorney who works with entrepreneurs, issues that affect a start-up are considerably different from those of an ongoing medium-to-large company.

For example, you have to decide what legal form your business should take. Most small businesses start as sole proprietorships, which require little expense or government approval to set up. One big advantage of a proprietorship is that both you and your business are taxed as individuals. Thus, if you have a full-time job and a part-time business that loses money, you may be able to write off your losses against other income. Be careful, though: Tax law stipulates that you must "materially participate" in a business in order to offset income from your full-time job.

Since you are employed by yourself, you will be responsible for making quarterly tax payments to the federal government and the state, as well as to Social Security. Just as if you had started a company with employees, keep a record of actual and projected income and expenses so that you can estimate your income for the year and your likely tax bracket. Consider your pension options, too: a SEP-IRA for self-employed people offers different advantages than a traditional IRA. In making these choices, an accountant who has experience with others working at home can be indispensable.

A major disadvantage of a proprietorship is that in case of a lawsuit, your personal liability is unlimited. That is just one reason why you should be sure to get adequate insurance. A regular homeowner's or renter's policy probably is not enough. You will need extra personal liability coverage.

Forming an S corporation protects your personal assets against liability. But you then need to file federal and state corporate tax forms because the corporation is a separate entity. Therefore, you'll be responsible for making sure that S corporation tax returns are filed to the federal and state government every year that your business is in existence.

The biggest potential tax advantage of your home enterprise is that you may be entitled to deduct not only for regular business expenses but also for a host of household expenses that you can prove are directly related to your work. Such deductions are limited to the annual net income from the business. If you work full-time from your home and deduct mortgage or rental expenses as business costs, IRS and Social Security regulations also require that the work you do must be performed at home — not in the offices of your clients.

Putting your husband or wife on the payroll of your home business can be a tax saver, but you will need to follow some IRS rules. By employing a spouse who has not previously been working for pay, couples can increase their combined maximum annual contributions to their tax-saving Individual Retirement Accounts from $2,250 to $4,000. Your business can also deduct your spouse's salary, as well as any amounts it pays in for his or her pension or profit-sharing plans, worker's compensation, life insurance or health policies. Employing your husband or wife will not trigger a tax audit. But the IRS will not permit the extra deductions if it believes you hired your wife or husband solely for tax reasons.

If you are audited, be prepared to prove that your spouse was hired for a legitimate business purpose. The more evidence you have that he or she is considered just another employee, the better. So write a job contract. It should cover your spouse's duties, pay, benefits and the expected length of employment. Keeping a time sheet of his or her work hours and a description of the work will also be useful.

Be certain to pay your spouse a reasonable salary. As evidence, clip newspaper ads for similar jobs. Or call a local employment agency and ask for the going wage. Try to get a letter from the agency documenting the quoted salary range, or at least keep legible notes on the conversation. One useful guide for helping you create your home office is Paul and Sarah Edwards' *Working from Home* (Jeremy P. Tarcher, $15.95).

## How to Profit from Your Leisure

Walk through an outdoor shopping mall on Saturday or Sunday, and you may well find table after table of crafts for sale by local residents — some of whom have grown quite skilled. To enhance their incomes, more and more Americans are finding ways to make money from the things they do for fun, turning spare-time hobbies into ready cash. People play the saxophone, perform magic, hybridize plants, make jewelry — all for money.

As always, the range of possibilities is limited only by your imagination, experience and interests. Mature former athletes stay in the action, for example, by becoming referees. A basketball referee can start out officiating at high schools for $25 to $70 a game. After a while he or she can graduate to college basketball for $100 to $470 a varsity game.

Working just 50 nights a year, a college referee can earn more than $23,000.

Some hobbies hardly ever become money-makers. Forget about gardening; commercial growers offer such wide variety and low prices that you simply cannot compete. But the market for crafts seems insatiable. There are more than 30,000 crafts fairs a year, and most of them are markets for amateurs. A growing number of boutiques and even department stores also provide outlets, though their standards for handmade items are high. To learn about crafts shows, you may subscribe to *Sunshine Artist* magazine (2600 Temple Drive, Winter Park, Florida 32789; $29.95 for 12 issues). Each month it reviews many shows and gives tips on displaying and pricing your work.

A primary rule for any hobbyist is that only quality sells. So whether you want to weave a rug or blow a trumpet for money, you have to do it well. Even the amateur has to be professional, businesslike and original. Countless talented people fail because they never grasp the importance of such business basics as sensible record-keeping or promotion.

Hobbies are treated under a special section of the tax code. Any expenses you incur can be deducted, but only from the income you derive from the hobby. Suppose you spend $1,000 to buy yak teeth. Later you find you have overestimated the market for yak-teeth bracelets and you can sell only one of them for $8.75. Result: You can deduct from your hobby income just $8.75 of the $1,000 you spent.

This loss limit is waived when your hobby becomes a business. Then you can take deductions larger than your hobby income — that is, you can create a shelter for other income. If you manage to make a profit in three out of five years, the IRS automatically assumes your hobby is a business. Even if you cannot pass the three-years-out-of-five test, you may still be able to convince the IRS that you are seriously trying to make a profit. You can help create a solid case by keeping accurate and up-to-date records, showing you work hard at your avocation and make a consistent effort to sell your work. If you are convincing, the tax authorities may let you claim losses for a decade or more, even though you cannot muster one profitable year.

In a cash business — most craft and part-time paid activities are strictly cash — the temptation to ignore the taxman is strong. Since there is no record of the transactions, the IRS probably will never hear of them. But your anonymity will not last long if your work is original and you are determined to succeed. Then you will become profitable, maybe even rich and famous, and even the taxman will come and find you. (For more on taxes, see Chapter 9.)

## How to Get Your Invention to Market

As much as Americans like to make things, they like to make things better. While the entrepreneur dreams of creating a company, the inventor dreams of making his or her product a reality. The lonely inventor faces tremendous obstacles and risks — and rousing rewards if he or she plays it right.

More than 113,000 patents were granted in 1994, but only 5% of all patented inventions ever make it to the marketplace, and scarcely 1% of them earn money for their originators. Still, individuals have brought forth plenty of recent products, from a new wheel for in-line skating (i.e., rollerblading) to a protein-based antifreeze with medical, cosmetic and food-related applications.

Not all bright ideas can be legally protected. But start by trying to get a copyright, a trademark or a patent. For example, computer games, other software and what lawyers call "artistic or literary property" should be copyrighted. It costs $20 to register a copyright for your lifetime plus 50 years.

Apply for a trademark as soon as you plan to sell your product in more than one state. A trademark will set you back $245, but it will keep other people from using your product's name, logo or emblem.

A patent protects your distinctive product design or process from imitators who may try to copy it and sell it. But it will not protect you against someone who develops a process or product different from yours — for example, his catalytic converter works with charcoal instead of filter paper.

Does your invention have a unique graphic or pictorial design? A design patent will protect the product's appearance against design pirates. If your creation is a useful new device, compound or mixture, or process, you will need a utility patent.

For a fee of $300 to $800, a patent attorney or agent will conduct a search to see if your idea is already covered by one of the more than 5 million existing patents. If it is not, you then apply for a patent by writing to the Commissioner of Patents and Trademarks, Washington, D.C. 20231. After paying roughly another $2,000 to $5,000 in attorney fees for the preparation of the patent application and its prosecution, and waiting an average 18 months, two out of three inventors get a patent. A utility or plant patent protects your invention for 20 years and is not renewable. A design patent will protect your original design for 14 years. You may also need to apply for patents in other countries, at a cost of about $1,000 in attorney fees per country (plus local patent-office charges) — or else you could find your idea being exploited abroad.

In very special cases, you may have to build a prototype of your invention; that can cost from $5,000 to $20,000. Before making such an investment, have your invention evaluated for its market potential. If the invention is energy-related, you can have it evaluated free of charge by the National Institute of Standards & Technology in Gaithersburg, Maryland. A few universities also provide evaluation services. Baylor, Texas, charges $150 and the University of Wisconsin–Whitewater, $225. They are part of the SBA program sponsoring institutes at nearly 483 colleges and universities that aid entrepreneurial inventors with such tasks as market research and feasibility analysis.

Once you have your invention patented and evaluated and perhaps have built a prototype, the hard part begins: getting it produced and bringing it to market. You can accomplish that in many ways.

Arthur D. Little Enterprises, Inc., of Cambridge, Massachusetts, gives marketing, technical and legal support to selected inventions, generally in the consumer market. The firm typically pumps some $50,000 into research, development and market studies for each product, though the amounts can range from $15,000 to more than $500,000. Then the company uses its considerable connections to bring the invention to market and shares equally in the proceeds.

But beware of firms that want their money up-front and in alarmingly large amounts. A number of so-called development companies promise to mount a marketing campaign that will turn the seed of a hopeless idea into a money tree. Such unscrupulous outfits prey on inventors' gullibility, vanity and pocketbooks. They extract $1,000 to $3,000 in exchange for little more than sending a form letter to prospective backers culled from the Yellow Pages.

Don't count on selling your invention to big corporations. They are seldom receptive to products that are N.I.H. — "Not Invented Here."

But small businesses are much more willing to buy a stake in outside innovations because it is cheaper than doing their own research. So roughly half of all new products and services are bought by small businesses.

## Publishing Your Own Newsletter

Thanks to the decline in prices of computers and printers, and the growing availability of software that lets you do the job at home, many entrepreneurs who have a way with words and an eye for the way things look on the page now publish their own newsletters. According to Howard Hudson of Hudson Newsletter Clearinghouse, there are more than 100,000 newsletters in the country. Publishers range from husband-and-wife teams to corporate giants. Start-up costs generally are less than $10,000.

Some of the largest and most profitable newsletters deliver information about health care, the beverage industry, off-price shopping opportunities and the investments made by money managers of large mutual funds. But people have created successful newsletters on such highly specialized subjects as recipes and shopping tips about chocolate, prescriptions for restoring old houses, advice on child development and where to find special and unspoiled vacation destinations. Some of the latest newsletters offer tips to computer users and health-conscious consumers.

The field is crowded, and the failure rate is high, so you will need to have an original idea that will appeal to a large number of customers — as well as the expertise to give them information that is superior to what's already available. You can find out if a competitor has beat you to the punch by consulting directories such as the *Oxbridge Directory of Newsletters* (Oxbridge Communications, 150 Fifth Avenue, New York, New York 10011; 212-741-0231, $415) or *Hudson's Subscription Newsletter Directory* (Hudson Newsletter Clearinghouse, P.O. Box 311, Rhinebeck, New York 12572; 800-572-3451, $159). They are available at many libraries.

Think about how frequently your readers will want to receive a newsletter about the subject you have picked, how much it will cost you to produce (do you require new software, or computer training?) and how much profit you will need to make. Then set a subscription price.

Prices span from $5 to as much as $4,500 a year. Some newsletters serve limited audiences who are willing to pay more for high-quality, useful information; others have broader appeal but less critical information and sell for a lower price.

Test the market's interest in your idea before you start publishing. Use direct mail to reach potential subscribers: It allows you to zero in on only those people you want to reach. You can rent mailing lists through list brokers. To find names of brokers, consult the *Direct Marketing List Source* guide (Standard Rate and Data Service, 1700 Higgins Road, Des Plaines, Illinois 60018; 800-851-SRDS, $345 subscription for six issues). It is available in many libraries. Costs per thousand names range from $45 to more than $100. A test mailing should cost a few thousand dollars at most. Ideally, it should yield a response of 1% to 3% and should bring in enough subscriptions to cover your direct-mail expenses.

## How to Get Your Book Published

Book publishers receive more than 100,000 unsolicited manuscripts annually — and send nearly all of them back with all the speed and compassion of Andre Agassi returning a cream-puff serve. It is by no means impossible to get your first work of fiction or nonfiction published. To do so, you will need talent and tenacity. And you will have to persuade a publisher or an agent merely to read your manuscript.

It is perfectly legitimate for an unknown author who gets a nibble from a publisher to recruit an agent before proceeding further. The proper approach to an agent or to a publisher is to write a letter explaining the kind of book you have in mind. Enclose a chapter or at least a sample of your writing. Outline briefly what you have already published, if anything. Above all, include a self-addressed, stamped envelope if you want your chapter returned.

In fact, most book publishers will not deal with unknown authors except through an agent. You can find lists of well-known agents in two books at your public library. They are *Writers' Market* and *Literary Market Place.* Using an agent offers another advantage: If a publisher bites, the agent probably will get you a better deal than you can negotiate on your own. If you are not a well-known writer, don't expect anything more than an advance of $5,000, plus royalties if your book sells well.

For their services, agents customarily charge 10% to 15% of whatever the writer receives.

Some agents also charge a fee just for reading manuscripts. Before you agree to pay anything, find out what services you will be getting for your money. If an agent insists on a written contract, hire a lawyer to approve it before you sign.

The easiest way to break into print is by writing what is known as popular fiction — that is, mystery stories, spy thrillers and adventure tales. Romances alone account for more than 40% of all fiction published between hard and soft covers. Advances on romances are relatively low. Harlequin Books, which started the boom in romantic fiction, pays an average advance of about $2,500 with royalties of 6% of the book's retail price charged against the advance. Other publishers may pay higher rates, and an experienced writer who catches on and learns the formula may earn $15,000 or more a book.

In nonfiction, a fresh and sharply focused idea is more important than writing style. But the novice author had better be an expert in his or her subject. Readers want specific information on specific topics. Books on cooking and dieting do well, as does anything connected with ways to make money. And sex is definitely here to stay.

If you cannot find a publisher who is captivated by your manuscript, don't despair. For a fee of $3,000 to $15,000, a so-called vanity publisher will design, print, bind and promote your book. Vanity books, however, are seldom taken seriously by other publishers or critics. Or, you can do what Virginia Woolf, Walt Whitman and Mark Twain did, and publish your own book.

Two monthly magazines offering an abundance of tips and information for aspiring authors are *Writer's Digest* and *The Writer. Literary Market Place* also lists the names of publishers. Check to see which houses are putting out books in your field. *Children's Writer's and Illustrator's Market* is a good guide to one of the hottest areas in publishing today, children's books. Be patient, and don't expect an instant embrace from the first publisher you send your submission to. Many best-sellers were rejected by scores of well-known publishers before finally being accepted.

CHAPTER 18

# Computers for Fun and Profit

Quite suddenly, the world of home computing has been transformed from a relatively small group of solitary users to a huge, global community of people sharing information over a sprawling electronic highway. This is not the same Infobahn that Bill Clinton envisioned in the early 1990s, but instead a loose confederation of networks that make up the Internet and such on-line services as America Online, CompuServe and Prodigy. Through these "nets" people the world over dip into great storehouses of information, ask questions of experts and speak with one another.

The popularity of the networks, and of interactive multimedia software (you communicate with it, and it talks or sings to you) has rocketed the demand for home computers. In 1994, for the first time, Americans spent more on home computers than on TV sets, and the home computer market grew twice as fast as the business computer market.

It's getting harder to find excuses not to buy a PC. Too difficult to learn? The new programs are easy enough for a six-year-old to master. Too expensive? You can get the whole works — computer, color monitor, modem to send faxes and plug into the information highway, CD-ROM drives for playing games or tapping into encyclopedias and much more — for under $2,000. You also can get a stripped-down version for close to $1,000, and a superfast, capacious, bells-and-whistles setup for $5,000. You figure you won't have enough use for a computer? If you have stocks to manage (and select), taxes to calculate, children to educate or letters and memos to write, you will soon wonder how you could have survived so long without a computer. And because it is becoming such an indispensable tool for creating graphics, your PC may enable your small business not only to communicate with customers but also to impress them with classy presentations.

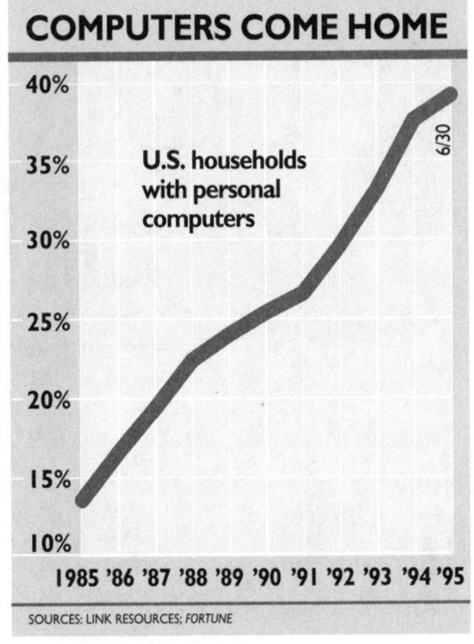


## SELECTING THE RIGHT HARDWARE

When you shop for a computer, the first question a retailer will ask you is which of the two often-irreconcilable families you wish to buy into: Apple or IBM and its compatibles. Apple, favored by schools, has 11% of the global market (down from 15% in 1993). IBM and a host of "clones" that use the same operating system are favored by business and command 89% of the market. If you buy IBM compatibles, you can pick and choose: You can purchase a computer from one company, a printer from another, a modem from still another.

On the other hand, one reason that Apple users tend to love their Macintoshes is that everything comes from the same company. A CD-ROM from Apple plugs into your Mac and goes right to work; Apple printers mate with your Mac system without a hitch.

But the once-sharp split between IBM and Mac is blurring as an increasing number of software conversion packages help people on both planets use the same data files, documents and multimedia programs.

A few years ago, Apple was the costlier competitor. But it has cut prices, so today Macs cost the same or, at most, a few hundred dollars more than the PC rivals. The Apple desktop Performa sells for $1,450 to $2,500, depending on the amount of memory. (The more memory you have, the bigger, more complicated programs your computer will run. Games, for example, need a lot of memory.) The newer Power Mac comes with much more memory, software and fancy features; it was originally intended for the business market but has proven also to be popular for home use. The price spans from $1,400 to $4,500 for a high-end Model 9500 that is more than adequate for a very sophisticated user in the corporate world. If you want a portable, there's Apple's 7.3-pound PowerBook. The least expensive PowerBook 520, which sells for $1,300, has a black-and-white screen and very little memory. For $4,500, you get a top-of-the-line PowerBook 540C with a color screen and loads of memory.

Beginning in late 1995, all Apple products were scheduled to be built around the new PowerPC chip. Developed jointly by Apple and IBM, it is their answer to Intel's famous Pentium chip, which is used in PCs. Although programs written for older Macs will run slightly faster on the PowerPC, you will get the full benefit of the PowerPC's superior performance with software specifically written for it.

Apple has long held an edge in ease of use. That's because it has always had the advantage of a GUI (pronounced "gooey"), or Graphical User Interface. In plain lingo, that refers to the clever little images on screen — the pull-down-and-click-on-the-picture "icons" that users found easy to handle. Or at least easier than the text-based operating system known as MS-DOS (Microsoft Disk Operating System), or DOS for short, on which IBM-compatible machines run. DOS requires you to use strings of commands, some of which can be complicated and a bit intimidating.

Back in 1985 Microsoft gave a big marketing push to its Windows system, which looked and acted much like the Mac GUI. Still, Apple had an edge in ease of use. Microsoft aimed to gain dominance by bringing out in August 1995 its much-heralded new operating system, Windows 95. Some of the new features of Windows 95: It will allow you to run several programs simultaneously without having to wait while the computer is tied up with any one of them, and it will let you easily connect with the Internet.

The old aphorism — software dictates hardware — may convince you to choose IBM PCs, since there is still more software for them than for Macs. But the most popular programs are being issued for both platforms.

It's unwise to hold out for fear of obsolescence. Six months after you make your choice, the technology will turn itself inside out, and yesterday's fastest and best will look as fresh as old pancakes. Accept this fact, and aim for a system that will meet your basic needs for at least several years. (I have used my portable computer for three years, and it has substantially speeded and smoothed my work on this book.) You don't have to have the very latest to be far advanced. It's possible to run a modern spreadsheet on a 10-year-old computer, and some people still do. A $2,000 PC of 1995 has about as much computing power as a $2 million mainframe of 1980, so it should not become obsolete very soon.

Not only does technology change but so do the major players. Packard Bell, the biggest seller of home computers in 1994, was largely unknown two years earlier. By the second quarter of 1995, Packard Bell had relinquished the top spot to Compaq. The five leaders were Compaq, Apple, Packard Bell, IBM and Dell. Hewlett-Packard, number one in sales of printers, has moved into the retail market for PCs and has become a formidable competitor.

Technological change centers on your computer's microprocessor. This is the silicon chip with fabulously complex semiconductor circuitry that rules how fast your software programs will work and whether or not you will be able to run several programs at once, use parts of one program in another, or hook yourself up into a local area network of computers (a LAN is good for two or more users who want to share files or communicate with each other via electronic mail). The faster your microprocessor, the more versatile your computer will be. The corollary is that the older the microprocessor, the cheaper the computer will be. Pentium, Intel's fifth-generation silicon chip, was introduced in 1994. In early 1995 the average price of a PC with a 60-megahertz Pentium chip dropped nearly 40%.

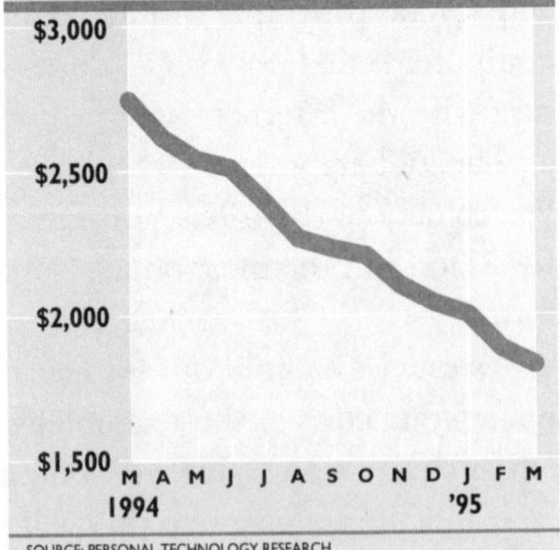


A major consideration is how much memory you will need. Memory, or RAM (random-access memory), is the amount of room you have on your computer to run software programs. RAM is like a tabletop — the bigger it is, the more things you can put on it. RAM comes in clumps of two megabytes; a megabyte is the equivalent of one million characters. The more RAM you have, the more things you can do at the same time, such as receiving a fax while simultaneously writing a letter or filling out your tax form.

If you don't have enough RAM, some programs won't run at all. With eight megabytes of RAM you will be able to run Windows and use all the current versions of the software mentioned in this chapter; it will keep you going for a few years before you need an upgrade. But if you have big plans for exotic, addictive or educational computer games, or you intend to buy Windows 95, you should most likely get 16 megabytes now. Buying a new PC with 16 megabytes instead of eight will cost you about $350 more. Today, a separate memory upgrade for your existing PC costs about the same.

Also very important is the capacity of your computer's hard disk. The hard disk is like a filing cabinet where your programs and data are stored. You should get a hard disk with at least 500 megabytes.

Most computers include the monitor as part of the price, but be sure this screen has the size and features you want. For running Windows, don't get anything smaller than a 14-inch screen. (Monitors, like television screens, are measured diagonally.) A 15-inch screen adds $100 and hardly makes a difference over 14 inches. But a 17-inch version really does make a difference and may well be worth an extra $250 to $350, especially if you're creating fancy graphics or using games. If you're creating illustrated four-color brochures or newsletters with photographs and artwork, you may want to go for a 20- or 21-inch screen, which can display a two-page spread. But these "oversized" monitors are sold separately from computers and cost $2,200 to $3,500.

Bear with me for some valuable specifics:

For a sharp image and extensive detail on your screen, choose a noninterlaced SVGA model with a dot pitch of .28 or less. A VGA monitor with a .39 dot pitch is less expensive, but you may get jagged letters, your spreadsheets may be able to display only a few columns, and the image won't be supersharp. For good graphics capability, tell the dealer that you want an SVGA monitor with at least one megabyte of memory dedicated to displaying 8-bit color (256 colors) at 1,280-by-1,024 resolution (good for Windows). A screen refresh rate of at least 70 hertz will ensure flicker-free images; and the flatter the screen, the less distortion there will be.

You want to consider health and environmental issues. The findings are not all in on the dangers, if any, of subjecting yourself to hours and hours of low-level radiation from your nearby monitor, but it can't hurt to be careful. Swedish researchers have established a low-radiation standard called MPR-2, and many monitors on the market meet this standard.

As for environmental issues, most new computers conform to the U.S. government's Energy Star standards. So-called "green" machines are made using recyclable plastic and have more efficient cooling systems that save power. When you haven't used the machine for a while, the monitor powers down automatically. This prolongs the life of your screen and reduces your electricity bill.

CD-ROM — which stores vast amounts of text, music and action video on compact discs — is an option that is fast becoming standard equipment. (CD-ROM stands for Compact Disc Read Only Memory — "read only" because you can read or listen to, but not alter, the content.) You can add a CD-ROM drive to your existing system — for a cost of about $400 — or buy a new machine with a built-in CD-ROM.

The CD-ROM programs are hard to resist. For example, DeLorme's Street Atlas USA (at discount, $79) gets more than *1 million* color maps onto a single compact disc; with a few keystrokes, you can call up on-screen any part of just about every city, town or rural area in the U.S. DeLorme's Global Explorer ($79) does much the same thing for the world. True, watching a CD-ROM encyclopedia play the national anthem of every country in the world may lead us to ask, "So who needs it?" On the other hand, it's one thing to try to describe "scat singing" to your children — and quite another to turn on Ella Fitzgerald and see and hear her demonstrate it. Kids love electronic encyclopedias. Two of the best-sellers are the Grolier Encyclopedia ($66) and Microsoft's Encarta ($59). For example, in Encarta's illustrated timeline of 15 million years of world history, you can select "Rebirth of Trade in Europe" from the 1100 A.D. to 1200 A.D. period and get a summary of the subject. A few more keystrokes will retrieve a description of Marco Polo's travels, illustrated by a map with moving arrows that trace his expeditions across Asia, and also get you past and present facts and historical highlights of Venice, Mongolia and the Gobi desert.

A CD-ROM will also save you trouble when you install large software packages. A lot of programs take up so many floppy disks that companies have started distributing their software on CDs. It's much easier and quicker to put a single CD into a drive than to feed floppy disks one by one into your computer.

For multimedia — which gives you the ability to interact with software filled with pictures and sound — you'll need a double-speed or faster CD-ROM drive. Newer quad-speed drives (which add about $150 to your bill) display motion with less jerkiness. You'll also need a 16-bit sound card and self-powered, magnetically shielded speakers. Computer "cards" contain specialized functions, such as sound, video or CD-ROM capability, that can be added to a computer. Cards have different shapes and sizes. For desktops and smaller computers, they look very much like credit cards. A desktop card is a four-inch-by-seven-inch piece of rigid plastic with little blobs of solder and cylindrical and rectangular objects attached to it; it looks somewhat like a miniature industrial park with buildings and parked cars. It's smart to buy a machine that has multimedia components built in, so you know they all work well together.

Installing separate multimedia components in a working computer can be a mind-boggling experience even for a technical professional, according to business technology writer Emily Andren. It can take many frustrating days, and uncounted rounds of adjustments, to coax these new elements to work congenially with the operating system and other existing devices in the PC. To minimize these problems, buy a multimedia upgrade kit of all the components, which costs about $400.

A modem is the key option that allows your computer to talk to other computers — for example, when you use the Internet and other on-line services or dial into your office to get into your company's database. With a fax modem, you can also send and receive faxes from your computer. Many computers come with built-in internal fax modems, but you can also buy external modems and attach them. An internal modem takes up less space, and all you have to do is plug a phone line into your computer. The speed at which the modem sends and receives information should be no slower than 14.4 kilobits per second (kbps) for data and 9,600 bits per second (bps) for fax transmissions.

When sending data, a 14.4 kbps modem will transmit the equivalent of 1,000 words of text, or about four and a half double-spaced pages, in four seconds, while a 9,600 bps modem will take six seconds to send it. With the very slow 2,400 bps modems, it will take 25 seconds. The higher the transfer rate, the less time you'll spend staring at your monitor waiting for graphics to materialize, such as the striking pictures on the Internet's World Wide Web. Fax transmission is much slower than data transmission. You can fax about two pages a minute at 9,600 bps. With 4,800 bps and 2,400 bps modems, faxing takes even more time and means longer calls on your phone bill.

Pentiums are faster than the older Intel 486 machines, but like the PowerPCs in the newest Apples, they need software written specifically for them to make the most of the added speed. Windows 95 will take full advantage of the Pentium chip's speed and will also run on 486 machines. Spending an extra $300 for a Pentium machine instead of a 486 is a form of insurance against obsolescence.

When you go shopping, what can you expect? You can get Pentium-based computer systems for $1,200 to $2,400 (street prices) that have lots of RAM and hard disk space, a color monitor, a CD-ROM drive and a built-in modem, and include some of the most popular software packages (which would add up to $1,000 if bought separately).

The least expensive of these packages is the $1,195 Packard Bell Legend 300CD, which on its hard drive has only 420 megabytes, less than the recommended 500 megabytes. A Hewlett-Packard Multimedia computer costs $1,900 to $2,000, depending on the monitor you select, and has a 540-megabyte hard drive. For $1,799 a Compaq Presario CDS 792 includes a 735-megabyte hard drive and quad-speed CD-ROM. An Apple Macintosh Performa 6115CD with a 60-megahertz PowerPC 601, a 700-megabyte hard drive and dual-speed CD-ROM is $1,899, which is at the high end of the price range of the IBM look-alikes.

Computers with Intel's older 486 chips, introduced in 1990, are much less expensive and still a viable alternative. They will run Windows and all types of software described in this chapter. But make sure that any system you buy can be upgraded to a Pentium.

When buying a 486 machine, it's worth getting a 66-megahertz DX2 processor — which makes the computer run faster — even if you can purchase a slower model for as much as $250 less. With a DX2 processor, you won't have to wait as long while a program is getting started (brought into RAM from the hard disk) or while a huge spreadsheet crunches through hundreds of calculations. You have a wide choice among 486-generation computers with a 500-megabyte hard drive and the same memory capacity as the Pentium examples above. For $1,599 (discount), you can get a Gateway 4DX2-66 Family PC, a Micron PCI

Magnum or an IBM Aptiva 535. The Aptiva comes with IBM Online Housecall, a software program that lets a support person at IBM's help desk see exactly what you see on your computer when you call with a problem.

All of the machines mentioned here are highly rated. For a desktop, you can't go wrong buying from Compaq or Dell. Compaq, the largest seller of PCs in the world, has been a strong force in the market for over 10 years. Dell has built a solid reputation selling high-quality PCs by mail order at very competitive low prices and provides very good support.

## Desktop or Portable?

In making this decision, ask yourself just how movable you want your computer to be. For anyone who travels a lot, let me tell you, a portable is indispensable. If you do decide that you need to work on a plane or commuter train, or that your kids will want to carry their machine to and from class, then what should you choose?

You will pay at least twice as much for a portable as for the equivalent desktop; and the smaller the portable, the more it costs. Designers at Digital Equipment have actually managed to cram a 340-megabyte hard disk, eight megabytes of RAM and a 9.5-inch color monitor into the slim four-pound HiNote Ultra (about $3,080). Portables are getting more expensive, but they also are becoming lighter and more powerful, with better screens and keyboards. They also have more features such as multimedia — including a built-in CD-ROM drive — and come with preloaded software. The ones with built-in CD-ROM drives are fairly new and can cost up to three times as much as comparable desktops.

When buying a portable, you basically have two choices in terms of size and weight: Notebooks weigh around seven pounds; subnotebooks usually weigh four to five pounds.

Then there are electronic organizers, which are miniatures that can fit into a breast pocket or purse and weigh a pound or less. They are the electronic equivalent of time-management books like DayTimers. A strong candidate is Sharp Electronics' $499 Zaurus ZR-5000, which is 6.7-by-4-by-1-inch (about the size of a paperback book), weighs 13.6 ounces, and serves as calendar, scheduler, to-do list, telephone directory and world clock for telling the time in 212 cities. You can use a stylus to write notes to yourself or select what you want to do, such as check your calendar or look up a phone number, from the four-by-three-inch pressure-sensitive screen. But unlike the earlier Sharp Wizard, the Zaurus cannot decipher handwriting. It has a tiny keyboard that you use to enter information like names and addresses.

The Zaurus has a modem that will hook up to a regular or cellular phone to communicate with another Zaurus or a computer with special software enabling it to exchange data with a Zaurus. With this connection, you can send or receive electronic mail, gain access to on-line services like CompuServe, and get information to update your expense report. For an extra $100, you get a fax modem card, which enables your Zaurus to send and receive faxes.

Pen-based machines, which let you write with a stylus instead of typing on a keyboard, have not achieved the success anticipated a few years ago. That's especially true of Apple's hand-sized Newton and other machines that promised to develop the ability to read your writing. The pattern-recognition technology that enables the machine to read handwriting works only in a limited way. The computer does learn to read each of your longhand letters — no matter how difficult they are to grasp — if you are consistent. The machine will expect the next such letter to look just the same, or close. But in most instances, you have to learn to write longhand without connecting any of the letters. Most computers can't completely handle real cursive handwriting — yet. So-called neural networks, which enable computers to learn over time, will improve. Someday, students may well be able to scribble notes during lectures and print them out later as editable type.

Subnotebooks are portables weighing under seven pounds and small enough to fit into a briefcase. Until recently they were largely a flop in the marketplace. To make subnotebooks lighter, manufacturers took the easiest and cheapest route: little screens and calculator-sized keyboards — exactly what customers didn't want.

Now manufacturers are getting smarter. IBM's diminutive ThinkPad 701C weighs only 4.3 pounds and has gotten good reviews for its pop-out two-part keyboard, called the Butterfly, that slides out of the 9.7-by-8-by-1.7-inch case and locks together to form an 11.5-inch-wide typing platform. Other features reviewers like are the 10.4-inch color screen (larger than some full-size, heavier notebooks), 14.4 kbps fax modem (most of the competition offers slower modems) and stereo sound system. Prices start at $3,100.

The highest-rated portables in the notebook category weigh as little as possible over seven pounds. Many of them now come with a built-in CD-ROM drive, as well as eight megabytes of RAM and a 500-megabyte hard drive, and with Windows installed.

What you want to look for in a notebook computer are things like battery staying power (at least three hours), a small and light AC adapter/recharger for recharging batteries, and the ability to add more memory and hard disk capacity later. Adding memory costs about $65 per megabyte, so loading on eight megabytes comes to $520. To increase your hard disk capacity, you will have to add a second hard disk, about the size of a cigarette pack, to your computer. A three-megabyte disk runs about $300. When you choose a notebook, try out the keyboard to be sure it feels comfortable and that the keys are large enough for real word processing.

If you're going to spend hours working in the Windows environment, invest the extra money in a color screen or you'll get very tired of looking at gray-scale icons. It's even more important not to make keyboard and monitor compromises if you're buying a notebook as your only computer and plan to use it a lot. If you're spending all your computing time between two places, it might actually be cheaper to buy two desktops and get a software program like Traveling Software's LapLink IV, which sells for $100. If you're in one place and have older versions of your data and documents on your computer, LapLink will dial long-distance, via your computer's modem, into your other computer; retrieve the latest versions; and store them on the computer you're using.

A highly rated choice is the IBM's multimedia ThinkPad 755CD, which weighs 7.3 pounds, has a well-engineered front-loading CD-ROM drive and starts at $5,295. The ThinkPad 755CX without a built-in CD-ROM drive has all the same features as the ThinkPad 755CD, even sound, costs $900 less and weighs 6.1 pounds. However, you will not be able to upgrade it to have a built-in CD-ROM drive — you will have to buy an external drive ($329), which does not have full-motion video capability and is an extra piece of equipment to carry around.

Toshiba's Satellite T2150 CDT, which has a built-in CD-ROM drive and a more compact keyboard than the ThinkPad, is considerably less expensive at $3,595. It also has an external floppy disk drive that is not included in its stated weight of 6.8 pounds.

If a CD-ROM drive isn't essential, you can get a 6.4-pound Dell Latitude XPI Pentium notebook with a 10.5-inch color screen for $2,999. You can add a card that plays sound ($199) and an external CD-ROM drive ($349) to this model. And the company will ship it to you at no-nonsense speed; place the order by noon Central Time, and you'll usually have your new system the next day.

An excellent choice for notebooks is any model in IBM's broad ThinkPad product line, with their high-quality screens. Another is any of Dell's Latitude XP series, which have a long battery life — six to eight hours — and that's important for true road warriors.

# Printers

One of the most dramatic changes for the home user is the drop in prices of ink-jet and laser printers. No longer do you have to put up with the shrill whine and fuzzy print quality of dot-matrix printers, or the difficulty of getting them to print at the top of the page of continuous, pinhole-feed paper. You can now buy a black-and-white ink-jet printer for what a lower-quality dot-matrix printer cost in 1993. Color ink-jet printers, which used to cost thousands of dollars, are as low as $250, but they are slow — it takes from two to six minutes to print a color page.

You're always safe in buying from Hewlett-Packard, whose ink-jet and laser printers have become the industry standard. If you do buy another brand, make sure it's "HP-compatible," meaning that your computer and software will work with it as easily as they do with a Hewlett-Packard printer.

Ink-jet printers are as small as Canon Computer Systems' BJC-70, which can be put in a briefcase. It weighs only three pounds, prints four black-and-white pages a minute and costs $339. Canon's BJC-600e prints one color page, or up to four black-ink-only pages, in a minute and sells for $449. The Hewlett-Packard DeskJet 660C, available as the Desk-Writer 660C for the Mac, sells for $365 and prints beautiful color pages at the rate of two to three minutes per page. The $250 Lexmark Exec-

Jet IIc was the first ink-jet color printer to break the $300 price barrier.

The trouble is, ink-jet printers just don't produce black-and-white pages that look as good as those from laser printers, especially from one of the PostScript models, even if the number of dots per inch is the same. Most ink-jet pages smear when the ink is wet, and cartridges cost around $30, more than those for laser printers for the same amount of printing (about 1,000 pages per cartridge). Most of the lowest-price color ink-jets produce black on color pages by mixing black from the color palette, resulting in a muddy gray-green that is sometimes called "process black." This saves the cost of adding another color ink to the color cartridge. Some printers, like the Lexmark ExecJet IIc, produce a very high-quality process black that looks like the real thing. More expensive ink-jets, such as the Canon BJC-600e and the Hewlett-Packard DeskJet 600C and DeskWriter 600C, use real black ink in both their color and black-and-white cartridges.

Laser printers produce a smear-proof page with a cleaner, sharper image than can be obtained from an ink-jet printer with the same dots-per-inch resolution. More expensive than ink-jets, they can print from four to 10 pages a minute and can handle just about any type of job, no matter how sophisticated. Laser printers for PC compatibles have dropped several hundred dollars in the past couple of years. The Hewlett-Packard LaserJet 4L, introduced in 1994 at $849, is still very popular and now sells for $445. It is small (14.5-by-14-by-6.5 inches) and efficient, prints four to six pages a minute and is a good choice for home use. The Epson ActionLaser 1000, a six-page-per-minute printer, has declined from $799 to $499 in the last couple of years. For higher speed, the Hewlett-Packard LaserJet 4 Plus prints 12 pages a minute at 600-by-600 dots per inch and costs $1,279.

*A warning:* Not all printers will work with all computers. So check to make sure.

Two or three years ago, the cheapest ink-jet for Macs sold for $479 and printed only one page a minute; today Apple's black-and-white StyleWriter 1200 costs $270 and is three times as fast. The color StyleWriter 2400 ($400) prints one color page in two or three minutes, and three black-and-white pages in one minute. Most other ink-jets for Macs operate at similar speeds. Hewlett-Packard's DeskWriter 660 is a good black-ink printer for $299, with a color version for $399 that prints "process black." For users requiring photographic quality, the

Epson's Stylus Color printer ($529) has 720-by-720-dots-per-inch resolution and can print on glossy and other special paper.

Laser printer prices for Apple have also been plunging. In 1993 they were about $1,500 to $2,500. Today, for $1,289 you can get an Apple LaserWriter Select 360 that prints 10 pages a minute. The Hewlett-Packard 5MP with 600-by-600-dots-per-inch output sells for $1,000, and the lower-resolution 300-by-300-dots-per-inch Texas Instruments microLaser PS23 is $599. These are all discount prices.

## Fax Machines and Copiers for Your Home Office

If you have a home office, you'll almost certainly need a computer, a copier and a fax machine. To get tax deductions for this machinery, your office has to meet certain stiff requirements, which are spelled out in Chapter 9, "Saving Money on Your Taxes." For further details, call the IRS (800-829-3676) and ask for forms and publication 586, "Business Use of Your Home."

To minimize the space all this equipment will take up, look for multipurpose devices as well as machines that have a small "footprint." You may be able to avoid buying a fax machine and copier by using a fax program and a fax modem on your computer. One of the best programs is Delrina's WinFax PRO for Windows (discounted for $79), which makes sending your faxes through a fax modem as easy as printing a document; in fact, WinFax PRO lets you fax anything on your computer that you can print. You can also receive faxes, make notes on them (not handwritten, however) and send them back to the same person or someone else.

A new breed of multipurpose machines combines printer, fax machine and copier in one unit. Lexmark's Medley, which retails for as little as $849, is 15 inches wide, 15.4 inches deep and 12 inches high, and weighs only 17 pounds; it is the first of these devices to offer color printing. Like the $250 Lexmark ExecJet IIc ink-jet color printer mentioned earlier, the Medley prints three black-and-white pages a minute and one color page in three to six minutes on plain paper, and has a 14.4 kbps fax modem that transmits a page in six seconds. Plain paper and high-quality 300-dots-per-inch scanning and printing make it a viable choice as a copier. You can also scan images directly into your computer to include them in a document you are creating, or you can send them to someone else. You can even scan your letterhead and signature, incorporating them in letters you fax from the computer.

If the Medley or a similar machine can't handle your demand for high-volume printing or copying, you might buy a separate fax or copier. Here are the prices and features of these two major home office components:

For a good fax machine, figure on paying $500 to $1,200, though you can get stripped-down models for $300. Transmission speed has been pared to between 10 and 18 seconds a page, but thermal paper, with its unpleasant waxy surface, is still unavoidable on machines going for less than $500. Plain-paper fax machines can double as copiers, but thermal-paper faxes really can't. Thermal-paper copies often come out unpresentably crinkled or fade over time, and you might even have to sacrifice a page from a book or magazine by tearing it out in order to copy it. Most plain-paper fax machines cost $700 and up, and they outsell the thermals. Canon, Sharp and Toshiba all make reliable fax machines, and you could consider the leasing option, too. You might be able to get a much better fax machine for your money.

Personal copiers, the briefcase-sized copy machines that sell for $400 to $1,600, have one great advantage over their office-grade big brothers: They are more or less maintenance-free. All the parts that cause trouble in the big machines, such as the toner container and the photosensitive drum, now come as sealed units that are simply tossed out and replaced when used up. Even the cheapest copiers made by Canon, Brother and Sharp, among others, should give years of solid service.

A new class of retailer has appeared to serve the needs of the home office, selling machinery that has been downsized and even color-coordinated to fit the home environment. Stores such as Staples and Office Depot specialize in this gear. Mass retailers like Kmart and Sears sell fax machines and computers a few aisles away from toasters and irons. Though you'll find little personalized assistance, warranties are honored; and more often than not if there is a problem, the item will simply be exchanged for a new one. A word of caution: Home office machinery is evolving at a rapid pace, and this year's wonder machine could become next year's forgotten fad.

Generally, but not always, mass-marketed machinery will be less up-to-date. It's best to begin with a visit to a store specializing in office equipment, where you can see the latest developments in a particular machine. Then make your purchase based on price and service. You may find that the blue-light special at Kmart is just what you want, or you may prefer to buy from a specialist.

Don't be wowed by — or pay more for — features you'll never use. One big-office feature you probably don't need is polling, the ability to scan several other fax machines to see if there is a transmission waiting for you. But if you ever need to have your fax machine send the same message to a group of other machines — salespeople often want to send out a promotional fax to a group of customers — you might be interested in the feature known as broadcasting. If you have a small and dependable customer group, you may find yourself faxing to the same places all the time; if your machine can automatically dial a dozen or so numbers from its memory chip, it might be worth the extra $50 or $100 that the broadcasting feature will cost you.

Good news: Home office software is getting better and better. A nice package from Starfish Software is Sidekick ($50), which combines a calendar, an address book that looks like a card file, and a notebook — all under one software roof. You can even get electronic timers and reminders that will tell you when it's time to pick up the kids. Sidekick will create labels from your address book and dial phone numbers, provided you have a modem.

## Where to Go for Help

For many people, not being "computer literate" is the biggest barrier to buying a home computer. In this do-it-yourself environment, manufacturers expect you to unpack the components and plug them together, using instruction manuals for guides. Computers are indeed becoming easier to set up, but they're not completely foolproof. They have very few moving parts and rarely break down; software errors are more frequent, though still relatively uncommon. The vast majority of problems new users have result from the fact that things so often don't work in an intuitively obvious way, or the way the instruction manuals seem to indicate. The question of who you're going to call when you need help is a very important factor in deciding where — and what — to buy.

Virtually all computer and software companies and most stores have telephone support staffs to answer questions and address your problems.

The service you get varies from one source to another, depending on how expert the support staff members are, how long you have to wait on the phone line to get through to them and what — if anything — they charge.

Most of the leading manufacturers offer toll-free 24-hour technical support for hardware, but sometimes you can be put on hold for 20 minutes or told that the lines are too busy to accept your call. Chain stores usually offer support over toll-free numbers, but, unlike most manufacturers, often will give you less free help after you have made a major purchase. Before buying any PC, check out the company's or store's tech support lines by calling them yourself. Many local boutique-like stores with strong reputations offer prices competitive with high-volume chains and also provide good support for technical questions and troubleshooting. Most of these stores will set up your computer for you. If you buy a computer with all the features you need, you can lean on the seller to make it work; if you add them later, you may be on your own.

Many people prefer to ask for help from someone else who is using the same product. Maynard Nicholl, a consultant in the Gaithersburg, Maryland, area, who for the past 10 years has set up computers for home users and small businesses, says that unless you're an expert, you would be better off with the most popular product even if it isn't the best one, because you would then have a larger user population who can help. The Internet and other on-line services have bulletin boards and discussion groups where you can get hints and tips on avoiding snags and can ask questions about your problems.

## Mail-Order and Used

Dell and Gateway 2000 have become major brands by selling over the phone. Other brands that sell directly and through dealers have entered the mail-order business. More and more PCs are bought this way, even though it would seem to be far riskier than shopping hands-on in a neighborhood store.

But experience has shown that you are likely to get high-grade hardware, technical support and repair service with mail-order computers — if you stick to tried-and-true brands like Dell (800-426-5150), Digital

(800-344-4825), Gateway (800-523-2000), IBM (800-426-2968) and Zeos (800-423-5891).

If you want a computer right now and can't wait for prices to be reduced further when the next generation of machines comes out, consider buying a used model. You can get a used 486 IBM clone with eight megabytes of memory, a 420-megabyte hard disk, an SVGA color monitor, fax and data modem, and CD-ROM for $1,060 — which is $440 less than the price of a new one. You can find a used Macintosh Performa with a color monitor but half as much RAM and disk space for $650. Cost when new: $2,000. Much older machines are much cheaper, but they have less than 25% of the amount of RAM and disk space. A used IBM PS/2 Model 70 that sold for $3,000 in 1991 now goes for only $200.

If you can't find a used-computer dealer in your area, Computer Renaissance in Minneapolis (612-520-8563) may help you locate one. Two companies that match buyers and sellers for a wide variety of desktops, laptops and notebooks are NACOMEX USA in New York (212-614-0700) and the United Computer Exchange in Atlanta (404-612-1205). To check out the credibility of used dealers, call the Computer Leasing and Remarketing Association in Washington, D.C. (202-333-0102).

## SOFTWARE
## WHAT — AND WHERE — TO BUY

A computer without software is like a camera without film. Software translates your commands into a digital language that the computer can understand and create something from. The software industry is a movable feast: It is expanding incredibly fast, keeps changing by the moment and offers a vast variety — from the wacky to the wonderful. Software designers, taking advantage of the increasing power and speed of hardware, are writing programs of increasing complexity that can do amazing things. These programs need a lot more memory and hard disk space than older, simpler programs, and thus require a more powerful computer than you would have needed a few years ago.

Most new computers come loaded with software that's ready to go when you turn on the switch. The package usually includes popular versions of a word processor, a spreadsheet and a money manager. Multimedia systems include CD-ROM drives as well as several popular games, a dictionary, an atlas and a four-color encyclopedia that talks (for example, you can hear Robert Frost recite his poetry). Some computers that have a built-in fax and data modem also give you introductory subscriptions to the most popular on-line services — America Online, CompuServe or Prodigy.

If your computer purchase doesn't include software, and your needs are likely to remain basic for a while, try one of the so-called integrated software packages. They have something for everyone: word processing, spreadsheet capability and graphics. The price of all this is often under $100. The most popular integrated programs are Microsoft Works ($85) — which also includes Microsoft Money for financial analysis — and ClarisWorks ($129). Both have Mac and PC versions.

To entice first-time buyers who may be computer-averse, Microsoft in early 1995 brought out a new software program named Bob, which has a different "social interface," as Microsoft calls it, from Windows. Instead of the standard Windows icons, Bob shows you a Disney-like representation of a room with a calendar, Rolodex and checkbook — each representing things that you can do with the computer. Comic strip–style characters then appear with speech balloons over their heads, giving you options for what to do next. Bob lists for $99, but can be bought at CompUSA and some other places for $75.

Bargains abound at computer superstores — sometimes 60% to 80% off list price. Many, including CompUSA, offer training classes for a fee. Other franchises where you may or may not get good help include MicroAge, J&R Computer World, Software City and Software Etc stores. Sears, Office Depot and Staples sell software, too, but if you want specialization (though not always the lowest price), try Egghead Discount Software (170 stores across the country). One mail-order establishment with separate divisions for IBM PCs and Macs that has reasonable prices and excellent technical support is PC Connection and Mac Connection (800-800-0021). An alternative pair, also giving good support, consists of Micro Warehouse (800-367-7080) and Mac Warehouse (800-255-6227).

▾ ▾ ▾

# Sharing the Wealth

It is quite possible that right now we are in the midst of a significant turning point in the information age. The pivotal event is simply that, in large part, the information highway has arrived — and it is called the Internet. The Internet: the vast, burgeoning web of corporate, research and educational computer networks that span the globe, networks where people and companies can communicate with each other, where you can get information from all over the world. More than 30 million people in over 160 countries now have access to the Internet, and the total is growing fast.

If you're on the fast-growing part of the Internet called the World Wide Web, not only can you send text to all the other users but you can also provide them with four-color photos, video clips and graphics — at very little cost. A lot of products and services are displayed on the Web. You can browse through product information and pictures, put in an order to send flowers to someone in another city, read magazine and newspaper articles, and even look for a job.

On other parts of the 'Net, you can send electronic mail or messages to anyone on the Internet, participate in on-line discussion groups with users around the world on just about any topic you can think of, and swap software programs (called "shareware") with other people.

If you're in education or the government or doing research, your employer has free access to the Internet from its computer. Everyone else pays. Home users can get an account to dial into the Internet-connected computer of one of the rapidly growing number of local and regional Internet service providers, such as Pipeline in New York, NearNet in Boston and CERFnet in San Diego. Service providers give you a connection to the Internet through their computers.

Internet service providers charge an hourly rate of $2.50 and up for Internet use, or a monthly fee of as little as $15 for an unlimited number of hours. They will also give you software that enables your computer to use the World Wide Web, electronic mail and other parts of the 'Net. Your computer will have to make a phone call to the service provider and stay on the line as long as you're using the Internet; so, to save long-distance charges, get a local provider, or a national or regional one with a local or toll-free phone number.

America Online, CompuServe and Prodigy, the leading on-line services, in mid-1995 had a total of 7 million subscribers — and counting. All three have electronic mail, discussion groups, bulletin boards and shareware, and charge the same rates for connect time: $9.95 for the first five hours and $2.95 an hour therafter. The information ranges from financial news and weather reports to almost any interest or hobby. You can even get particulars for planning a vacation and then make your own airline reservations. This material is catalogued and centralized, much better organized and easier to find than similar sources on the Internet. Subscribers also have access to the Web and can exchange electronic mail with anyone on the Internet. The three services have clipping services that find articles on topics you specify and send those articles to you electronically, for varying fees.

As part of Windows 95, Microsoft is introducing its own on-line service, the Microsoft Network, and its goal is to blow right by the other on-line services. If you have Windows 95, just click on a button and you'll be on the Microsoft Network. Click on another button, and you'll be on the Internet.

Computer bulletin boards, numerous and growing, are a sign of how widespread the grass-roots digital community is. If you want to participate in a local and even global bulletin board — to get free software or send messages to other bulletin board members and participate in on-line discussions of various topics — call the Association of Shareware Professionals in Muskegon, Michigan (616-788-5131); it lists 472 member bulletin boards. Or you might look at *BoardWatch,* a monthly bulletin-board magazine available at some newsstands and software stores; it publishes lists of bulletin boards and reviews software programs, many of which are given away free (303-973-6038). Some bulletin boards are hooking up with the Internet.

A few other well-known bulletin boards — which sometimes have new shareware programs even before CompuServe and GEnie (which is General Electric's on-line service) — are Channel 1 in Massachusetts (617-354-3230), Aquila in Chicago (708-820-8805) and EXEC-PC in Wisconsin (414-789-4210).

▼ ▼ ▼

# Virus Protection

There is fun software, and there is useful software. Virus-prevention software definitely belongs in the latter category and should be part of your computer's arsenal.

A virus is a destructive program created by some prankster to electronically cripple your system, wiping out or scrambling the software on it. Increasingly common, viruses can make their way into your system whenever you exchange files with other computers via modem or disk. Fortunately, you can both get antivirus software and take preventive measures. Two basic rules:

First, always, always back up your important files by making copies of them on floppy disks. But be forewarned that even your back-up files could be infected, as some viruses work like time-release capsules, waiting until you call up a file that activates the viruses or allows them to spread. A good program that automates the process of periodically backing up large numbers of files is Peter Norton's BackUp (from Symantec, for IBM compatibles only), which discounts for $84; for the Mac there's Retrospect from Dantz Development at $140. FASTBACK PLUS ($125) from Symantec has DOS and Mac versions, and some utility programs (see below) have back-up programs built in.

It's wise to back up the entire contents of your hard disk from time to time. Backing up a 500-megabyte hard disk would take piles of floppies; a better alternative is to use a tape back-up unit. A popular one is from Colorado Memory Systems, costs about $200 and comes with its own back-up software.

Second, never boot up (that is, start your computer) using a floppy disk that is not your own, since floppies are the likeliest source of trouble. If you boot up with an infected floppy, the virus loads into memory and never leaves your system. Every time you then turn on the PC, the virus loads into memory and infects other floppies. One consolation: viruses — so far, at least — do not damage hardware, the machine itself, but only the programs and data that are stored on it.

If your computer is struck by a virus, your best recourse is to use one of the antivirus programs — but they aren't foolproof. You might lose everything on your hard drive — the equivalent of going into your local library and dumping every card out of the card file. The books may stay on the shelves, but you can't get to them.

And you will always be at risk, since most antivirus software searches only for known viruses, and new viruses appear all the time. Even brand-new, shrink-wrapped software has been known to come infected directly from the manufacturer, though this is extremely rare.

Viruses can spread like wildfire through communications networks, such as the Internet. You may worry about programs that you obtain from an on-line service. America Online, CompuServe and Prodigy check all their programs for viruses, but the Internet and on-line bulletin boards can be risky. If you load software into your computer from reputable sources (rather than exchanging floppies with friends), you are likely to be safe.

But do get an antivirus program. You'll be very glad you did if you run into trouble.

Should a black box appear on your screen (the sign of the Jerusalem virus, of which there are more than 40 known variants); should you see the message "Your computer is now stoned" (this is the Stoned virus, which vies with Michelangelo — the infamous virus that infects computer files on the artist's birthday every March 6 — as the most prevalent of all); or should your screen characters appear to drop down to the bottom of the display (a sign of the Cascade virus), save your file and turn off your PC. Boot up from a clean floppy with the write-protect switch on (to prevent the computer from altering the floppy's contents) and thank your stars you've got an antivirus program.

Two of the best ones for the IBM PC are McAfee Associates' VirusScan 2.1 ($50) and the antivirus program that comes with Symantec's PC Tools ($129). For the Mac, there is Symantec's SAM ($64); Mac Tools 4.0 ($89) also includes antivirus software. Before buying software, check that the manufacturer offers a subscription for updates. If you need more help (whether or not you have antivirus protection), someone at the National Computer Security Association (717-258-1816) can walk you through a few basic self-help steps (for free).

All on-line services offer antivirus help of one kind or another. If you subscribe to CompuServe, there is an antivirus forum that advises on how to beat the bugs (just type GO VIRUSFORUM). Perhaps best of all, from Symantec comes Untouchable ($95 at discount), a program for

Macs and IBM compatibles that is not dependent on constant upgrading; it looks for certain kinds of changes that indicate the presence of a virus. This may prove to be the most effective way to get them before they get your hard drive.

## Using a Computer to Manage Your Money

Managing money is largely a matter of managing numbers, and that's what computers do best. The impressive computational powers of the microchip enable even the greenest practitioner to perform dizzying feats of pure mathematics and practical calculations previously reserved for professional money managers.

Managing money additionally involves common sense, prudence and self-discipline — and in these departments the personal computer is brain-dead. Also, to crunch your personal financial numbers in a PC, you have to feed in all your cash-flow data into the machine first. This process, called data entry, can be tedious; and in order to get an accurate picture of your finances, you must do it regularly (many people make daily entries, though once a week — and sometimes once a month — is usually enough). So with these two caveats noted, everyone who wants to streamline his or her personal finances ought to take a serious look at how computer software programs can help.

All sorts of financial software are available: programs for personal finance management, for investments, for tax planning and filing. Newer versions of some of them include hints and tips at appropriate points from subject-matter experts whom you can see and hear on CD-ROM. An astonishing wealth of information is quite literally at your fingertips, so your computer can serve as an important asset to your financial well-being.

The best financial programs offer the advantages of personal financial planners and books without the disadvantages: the programs are economical, unbiased, convenient, complete, comprehensive and easily tailored to your specific needs. They arm you with information you need to make intelligent decisions. Personal finance software helps you keep track and take control of all your money coming in and going out and performs all sorts of related activities. These can be as far-reaching as helping create a strategy to save for the future and work down your debts, and as immediate as paying your bills and balancing your checkbook. By tracking and categorizing where your spending goes, the programs will help reconcile your electronic checkbook with your personal budget.

These programs will flash you built-in reminders when rent or mortgage and utilities payments are due, show the net worth of all your combined accounts and calculate your tax liability. When you shop for personal finance software, ask whether it will transfer data directly to either your favorite tax-preparation program or to a spreadsheet.

Several excellent personal finance management programs are available for the Mac and Windows environments. Prices fluctuate widely. Those cited below reflect the best information available in late 1995. Intuit's best-selling, easy-to-use Quicken (anywhere from $34.95 down to $16.95) has over 8 million users. (Full disclosure: I appear as an on-screen "expert" in the Quicken Deluxe CD-ROM version.) The very popular Managing Your Money ($35.45 list) from MECA Software has a well-written manual and on-screen tutorial wit.

Two good personal finance management programs for Windows only are Microsoft's Money ($24.95 list, $15.95 street) and Simply Money from Computer Associates ($69.95 list, $32.50 street). Home offices and sole proprietorships can use the accounting, payroll and petty-cash functions in Simply Money. Other options for small businesses are Intuit's QuickPay ($50) payroll program and QuickBooks 3.0 ($99), a simple accounting and inventory management program.

You can use personal finance management programs to keep track of investments and, if you have a modem, retrieve current stock quotes of individual securities on-line. Quicken updates stock prices from IDD Information Services' Tradeline Electronic Stock Guide; Managing Your Money gets this information from the Dow Jones News/Retrieval service; Simply Money retrieves them via CompuServe; and Money uses the Reuters Money Network.

All four programs mentioned above provide you with a way to get personalized paper checks that feed through your printer. Just be forewarned that you'll have to buy special, somewhat expensive checks. If you want them anyway, try to get them from a business-forms dealer instead of from the software company — you'll save money.

Citicorp and other banks for years have offered home banking software that gives you bill-paying capability and up-to-date checking-account information. To pay bills, you can specify a payee, the amount and date of a one-time or recurring (weekly, monthly or other time interval) payment. At the appropriate time, the bank debits your account and transmits the funds electronically or mails a check to the payee. Now some banks are offering this software in a form that enables you to do home banking directly with your personal finance program. You can also transfer information on your checking-account activity — the checks you wrote, your deposits, your balance — from the bank's files into your PC, eliminating the burden of entering the data yourself. Microsoft has tailored versions of Money to work with banking software from Chase Manhattan, First National Bank of Chicago, Michigan National Bank and U.S. Bancorp and is creating versions for several other banks. As of September 1995, Intuit and Microsoft had lined up more than 20 banks to integrate their home banking programs with Quicken. Citicorp's Direct Access works with Managing Your Money. Monthly fees for personal computer banking services vary by state and for individual users range from free to $11; for small businesses, fees are four to five times as high.

If your bank does not have software that works with the money-management program of your choice, Quicken, Managing Your Money, Simply Money and Money offer another way to automate paying your bills. Instead of your payment specifications going to a bank, the information is transmitted to CheckFree, a company that pays bills for you from your existing bank account. CheckFree clears checks through a link with the Federal Reserve and charges you around 40 cents per payment.

If you have the latest version of Lotus 1-2-3 or Microsoft Excel, you might wonder whether you couldn't just use a spreadsheet to manage your money. Although spreadsheet programs can be made to do almost any combination of calculations, they were never intended to be household managers; they are best for analysis and "what-if" scenarios. The leading spreadsheets are versatile, though, in their ability to exchange data with other programs such as WordPerfect and Harvard Graphics. And they pride themselves on offering presentation-quality features: Borland International's Quattro Pro comes complete with visual and sound effects and even offers an electronic slide-show feature that can produce 35mm color slides.

For do-it-yourself analysis, Morningstar's U.S. Equities OnFloppy

(DOS only) has data on over 6,000 stocks and has software you can use to select and evaluate these shares. For example, you can select all stocks in the retail grocery industry with a more than 2% dividend and a price/earnings ratio 15 or less. One-time purchase of U.S. Equities On-Floppy is $55; you can also get periodic updates for a year — quarterly ($145), monthly ($295) or weekly ($995). Value Line Publishing lets you study and compare financial statements of 1,600 companies in its DOS or Mac Value/Screen III database. Value Line will mail you four quarterly updates for $325, or 12 monthly updates for $465. You can also receive the database electronically for 12 months ($495) or 52 weeks ($1995). For analyzing trends in the stock market and tracking the market in aggregate, Market Analyzer PLUS (from Dow Jones at $499 for IBM compatibles, $349 for Mac) is capable of converting a smorgasbord of statistics into an easy-to-read chart. Dow Jones' Spreadsheet Link ($149 for IBM compatibles only) enables you to download Dow Jones News/Retrieval service data into whatever spreadsheet you're using.

If you have a modem and don't need the advice of a broker, you can execute your own securities trades with discount brokerage firms — Quick & Reilly, E*Trade Securities, PC Financial Network — through the leading on-line networks. You can reach several other firms and deal with them directly on the Internet's World Wide Web. With discount brokers' proprietary software, including Charles Schwab's StreetSmart 1.0 ($39) for Windows and Macintosh and Fidelity's DOS-based Online Xpress ($49.95), you can execute buy-and-sell orders directly. Some of the software also gives you access to quotes, analyst reports, and current and historical data on securities and mutual funds. For example, Schwab's newer StreetSmart 2.0 (Windows only) provides information on 900 mutual funds as well as news and financial information from Standard & Poor's and Morningstar via Reality Online's Reuters Money Network. Schwab and Fidelity offer a 10% commission discount for online trades.

What if you just want to do retirement planning? If you have questions about whether you're putting enough into tax-deferred savings, whether you are adjusting properly for inflation, or how long your resources will last, you may want to look at a couple of helpful programs. Vanguard's Windows-based Retirement Planner, a bargain at $15 plus $3.00 for shipping and handling, shows you charts and snapshots of how you might invest, depending on whether you specify a conservative or aggressive profile. Plan Ahead for Your Financial Future ($39.95, plus $1.95 for handling and shipping) from Dow Jones includes articles from the *Wall Street Journal* on determining how much money you will need for education and Social Security, in addition to retirement.

Wouldn't it be nice to determine from your spending and saving patterns and your existing insurance coverage how much and what type of insurance you really need, without having to listen to a sales pitch from an agent? Price Waterhouse, the Big Six accounting firm, lets you do just that with its Survivor Income Planning System ($45). In addition to providing for your survivors, with this program you can plan to have enough money for your children's college tuition and your own retirement. If you start making realistic projections now, it can make a major difference to you and your family later.

## Computerizing Your Taxes

Because computers are great organizers and calculators, they can save you time and money on your taxes. With tax software, you can devise strategies, do all the necessary calculations for your tax returns and then print out your completed federal and state forms or file them electronically.

Two highly rated packages for ease of use and solid advice for preparing returns are Intuit's TurboTax for Windows and MacInTax for the Macintosh (both $29.95) and Block Financial Corporation's Kiplinger TaxCut ($29.95) Other best-sellers are Computer Associates' Simply Tax ($34.95) and Parsons Technology's Personal Tax Edge ($19). Personal Tax Edge offers fewer frills but takes you through the forms-preparation process efficiently and gives good value for the money. All have Windows and Mac versions, except for Simply Tax, which runs in Windows only. Because federal tax laws and forms are constantly changing, you'll have to buy a new version every year. Not all these packages, however, have versions for every state. State versions, when available, cost around $25.

Several programs use a simple question-and-answer format to help you fill out your tax forms. These programs walk you through a line-by-line process of answering questions displayed on one half of the screen, while your answers appear on the other half in replicas of that year's tax forms. The fun begins when you punch a key and all the computations — percentages, depreciations and deductions — are figured in an instant. Many programs then run an audit check, which reviews your forms and flags any answers or omissions that are likely to trigger an investigation. TaxCut even noticed, in auditing a sample return, that the cost of the tax software itself hadn't been listed among the itemized deductions. The TurboTax program, meanwhile, caught a mortgage-interest deduction that the IRS would consider too high relative to the filer's income.

The CD-ROM versions, TurboTax Deluxe and MacInTax Deluxe (Intuit, $44.95), Kiplinger TaxCut Multimedia (for Windows only, Block Financial Corporation, $29.95) and Personal Tax Edge Deluxe for both Windows and Mac platforms (Parsons Technology, $29) include full-motion video and audio interviews giving explanations of each IRS form, as well as suggestions for additional tax-saving deductions and how to resolve discrepancies in your answers to questions. Kiplinger TaxCut users can also get the phone number of the nearest H&R Block office to call for free advice.

All of these tax programs can save you the trouble of entering financial data by retrieving the appropriate information from the most popular money-management software.

Unfortunately, the 1995 versions of TurboTax and MacInTax had bugs that caused errors in 1% of 1.4 million users' returns, forcing them to submit amended returns. But Intuit moved quickly to repair the damage, replacing the flawed software and in some cases offering to pay any interest or penalties, so by the time you read this, there should be little cause for concern.

You may be able to deduct at least part of the costs of the computer and software, as long as you use them for help with your taxes, investments or overall money management. They would be considered miscellaneous deductions. You can deduct only the amount by which your total miscellaneous unreimbursed deductions exceed 2% of your adjusted gross income.

## The Delights of Word Processing

Remember the not-so-good old days, when a few mistakes on the typewriter meant you had to start the letter all over again? We are light-years away from that now. The simple function of defining a block of text and moving it has radically changed the way we put words onto paper, and with improved mouse, trackball and stylus technologies, and widespread voice activation right around the bend, the writer's (and editor's) life is only going to get better. Putting an envelope into an old-fashioned typewriter and typing a name and address requires fewer steps than doing the equivalent on a computer, but electronic cutting and pasting surely beats the scissors-and-tape method. It's neat to turn out letter-perfect copy, every time.

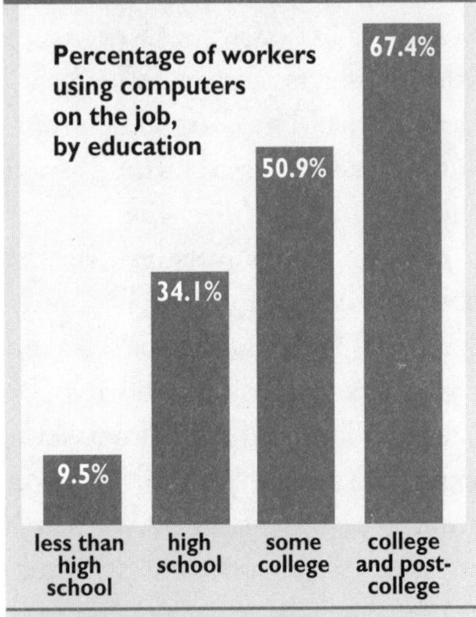


If you are an executive, a student or a person who devotes more than four hours a week to writing or editing, you need a word processor. Bypass the $200 to $300 "smart" electronic typewriters entirely — they have some storage and retrieval capabilities but are very limited — and go for a computer. Experience shows that, when it comes to word processing, trying to save expense by opting for a typewriter is an invitation to frustration. Even if you're just looking for a good machine your teenager can take to college, consider the low-cost 486 personal computers, where for well under $1,000 you can give that student some serious power and versatility. However, a computer at this price will have little or no multimedia capability.

You have a wide range of choices for word processing software. Three top sellers, WordPerfect 6.1, Microsoft Word 6.0 and Ami Pro 3.1 are so powerful that they can just about brush your teeth for you. These programs certainly make the PC smarter than the smartest electronic typewriter, give it infinitely greater memory (the working memory of a "smart" typewriter can keep only 2 to 5 pages at a time in memory), are exponentially faster and can be upgraded.

The pre-Windows and Windows versions of these programs may differ in small but significant ways; if you're upgrading, it's best to test them yourself. If you're swapping electronic documents with other people, it's easier than ever to convert the files into the format of other word processors, such as from Microsoft Word to Ami Pro or WordPerfect, and vice versa, provided they are all running Windows. In fact, it's easier to share documents created on different word processors than to switch between new and old versions of the same one. For example, if you're using Word 6.0, you can work with a document that was produced on the older Word 1.0 or 2.0, but if you're still using Word 1.0 or 2.0, you won't be able to do a thing with a document created on Word 6.0.

Language translators have improved to the point where the translation can usually be understood, though it probably will not be grammatically correct and might give the reader a chuckle or two. Some of these are available for the desktop. The Language Assistant series by Globalink translates English documents to and from French, Spanish, German or Italian ($59 for each language version). For any translator now on the market to produce an intelligible translation, the original document must be written in flawless English.

# Desktop Publishing

High-quality desktop publishing, until recently limited to the Mac world, has started to spread into the IBM-compatible universe. Now that QuarkXPress has a Windows version that performs well, thanks to the speed of the Pentium chip, some very serious graphics designers have a wider choice of Windows-based layout packages. QuarkXPress, which sells for $589, has the tools to create a page layout containing text, drawings and photos.

QuarkXPress may have a serious competitor in Corel, long famous for CorelDRAW, a graphics package for creating images and drawings from scratch. Since Corel acquired Ventura Publisher from Xerox and did a major overhaul, this premier PC-based page layout composition package works seamlessly with CorelDRAW. You can now get Ventura 5 as a freestanding composition tool ($445 on diskettes, $375 on CD-ROM) or integrated with CorelDRAW ($649 on diskettes, $499 on CD-ROM).

Reviewers have given high marks to Adobe's PageMaker 5.0 ($549), praising its user-friendliness and excellent customer support. Although not quite so complex as QuarkXPress and Corel's Ventura, PageMaker should still be able to handle most desktop publishing projects with ease.

You may not need four-color magazine quality. You'll spend less on software and a lot less on hardware if you want to design and produce merely good-looking documents illustrated with a few drawings and photographs — newsletters, fliers, business forms, invitations — that look as if they may have been produced at the neighborhood printing store.

To achieve that, you'll need a computer with all the characteristics recommended earlier in this chapter: the 66-megahertz 486DX2 machine with eight megabytes of RAM and a 520-megabyte hard disk, or preferably a one-gigabyte disk (a gigabyte is 1,000 megabytes, equal to one billion characters). A Pentium machine is even better. More RAM is always a smart idea. You will also need at least a 17-inch or 21-inch SVGA; the bigger the monitor, the easier it is to see what you're doing. A laser printer with 600 dots per inch will give you quality output. The least expensive of these printers is $1,000.

The leading word processing programs have many features that help with layout and design. The Windows version of WordPerfect 6.1 can incorporate graphics from other sources and create tables and an index. Other worthwhile programs include Adobe Home Publisher ($49 on diskette, $69 for the deluxe CD-ROM version) and Microsoft Publisher (about $90).

Many type fonts are now available on CD-ROM. From Bitstream, you can get 500 fonts for only $29; most word processors have about 30 fonts. As an alternative to creating your own artwork or using expensive scanners (a scanner is an optical sensing device that converts an image — a photograph, a drawing, a logo or a magazine illustration — into digital form for manipulation by your software) to bring color or black-and-white illustrations into your documents, check out CD-ROMs with a wide variety of professionally drawn visual images, called clip art. Corel's Gallery ($35) has 10,000 images, 6,000 of them in color. If you need to produce a spectacular four-color promotional brochure, or if you want automatic letter spacing, text rotation (the ability to rotate text on its axis), vertical justification or automatic indexing (good for longer documents), you'll need bigger-ticket hardware and software.

For highly detailed drawing, the mouse is a klutzy instrument, and the other pointing devices that come with most computers are even worse, if not impossible. It is much easier and faster to draw with a cordless stylus on a horizontal tablet connected to your computer. The results look as though you were writing right on the screen of your monitor. A Wacom UD-1212-RM, which includes a 12-by-12-inch graphics tablet with a cordless pressure-sensitive pen, plus Painter 3 software to make it work, sells for $749.

Not least, you'll need a scanner and scanning software. Hand-held scanners are available for anywhere from $150 to $500, but they are limited in what they can do. Most can capture only a four-inch-wide band at a time, so you have to make multiple passes and electronically "sew" the pieces together, which is a time-burner. For small images, though, they may be your best choice. For a real estate agent wanting to scan snapshots of houses for sale, or for someone just scanning Junior's graduation picture into the family's electronic scrapbook or calendar, it's acceptable.

For more sophisticated results, look at flatbed color scanners, such as the 600-dots-per-inch Epson Action Scanning System ($799), or the 1600-dots-per-inch Hewlett-Packard ScanJet IIc (list, $1,599; street price, $1,395), or even Agfa's Arcus II, which has tested very well and discounts for about $3,500. Some scanners come bundled with Adobe PhotoShop software for editing scanned photographs, such as changing colors and contrast or correcting flaws.

You'll need all this expensive hardware just to produce a few sharp copies of your document. Because volume color printing in your home office is prohibitively expensive and slow, and the equipment takes up a lot of space, chances are you'll want to farm out this step to a print shop. With a modem, you can transmit your electronic document directly from your computer to shops that are equipped to receive it, or you can take it on a disk or cartridge to the print shop.

If you find all of this intimidating, check out how the small commercial output services are easily doing modern desktop publishing. Kinko's Copies has over 700 stores in the U.S. Alphagraphics, another big chain, prides itself in keeping up with the latest in advanced technology. Often these stores can provide help and technical support.

Some computer retailers have found it profitable to rent out desktop publishing equipment — a sound way for you to learn the ropes and better define which hardware and software will best satisfy your needs. Desktop publishing rental storefronts are popping up everywhere. They are quite common around universities, as merchants hurry to provide students with a means to produce eye-catching reports and posters at a reasonable rate.

One last word: Desktop publishing is not easy to pick up, and you should at a minimum go through the tutorials provided with the software you acquire. Training classes are definitely advisable. You may find organizations providing training in the Yellow Pages under "Desktop Publishing." Local MacUser Groups also conduct desktop publishing classes. To find the MacUser Group nearest you call Apple (800-538-9696).

# Picking Educational Software

Electronic-age children find computers irresistible and need no convincing about the urgent necessity for computer literacy. Today, close to 70% of college- and postgraduate-educated people use computers on the job. This number should increase greatly when today's kids graduate from college. Anyway, kids and keyboards go together. There's something for everyone here, from shape-recognition games for preschoolers to brain-teasers for older children. After a few years of using educational software, many kids over the age of 10 are so computer-wise that they prefer the same graphics, word processing and spreadsheet programs that grown-ups employ.

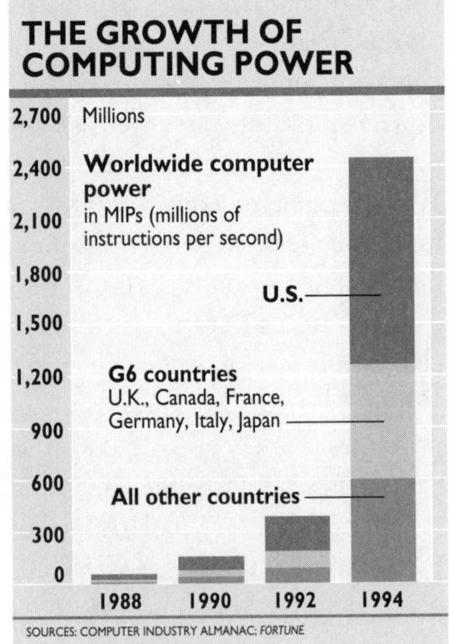


The only problem is that with over 15,000 educational programs to choose from — most priced between $25 and $60 at discount chains such as B. Dalton's, Software Etc and Egghead Software, or from large mail-order houses such as Educational Resources in Elgin, Illinois (800-624-2926) — how can you determine which ones are best? Since the programs are shrinkwrapped in plastic, you can't test them in the store. Some video outlets have begun to offer rentals; the only other way to assess what you're buying is by word of mouth or reading product reviews.

Educational software for grade-school children used to be little more than electronic flash cards: A question popped on the screen, students answered it and the computer said whether they were right or wrong. Critics claim that a "drill and kill" approach promotes passivity and stifles the imagination because students tend to memorize the answers. Even so, interactive learning and instant feedback can make a game out of the multiplication tables or the state capitals that have to be memorized anyway.

New "edutainment" software is a lot more fun. It encourages exploration and creativity as a reward in itself, with tools for kids to paint, draw, create their own animated characters, write poetry and report news. This software is a notorious user of computer power and megabytes of hard drive space, mostly because of its sophisticated animation and color graphics, and it will continue to become more power-hungry and an even bigger hog of your hard drive. The learning value of these programs may not come cheap, but it is unsurpassed.

In the next few years, educational software will actually learn while your kids are using it. Programs will be able to detect how quickly or slowly your children are grasping the material, and adjust the pace or teaching approach to match their learning speed. Doing this will require a faster computer and even more complicated programs.

"Ssh! Don't tell them they're learning!" So say designers at the Learning Company, producer of such educational software as the Reader Rabbit and the Math Rabbit series. These animated games cover ages two to nine, beginning with Reader Rabbit Ready for Letters and Math Rabbit Deluxe. In Reader Rabbit 3, for ages six to nine, kids learn the who, where, when, why and how of news stories and improve their sentence structure by playing the role of a reporter.

Broderbund is the company that created the award-winning paint program Kid Pix and its add-on Kid Pix Companion. With the newer Kid Pix Studio, children can paint, as well as create their own plots and characters and produce talking, animated stories. The Amazing Writing Machine is a writing tool that helps kids create their own prose and poetry. If their creativity needs a little help, they can ask for suggestions on words, phrases and humorous topics to stimulate ideas. All of them exist for the Mac, complete with QuickTime technology (or quick video takes). The word processing program Print Shop Deluxe, good for printing greeting cards, posters and even business cards for kids and adults alike, also comes from Broderbund.

Then there is Broderbund's Carmen Sandiego family of programs, including Where in Space Is Carmen Sandiego?, Where in the World . . . ? and Where in the U.S.A. . . . ?, which teach kids about geography, trade, history and cultures of various locales as they follow clues to track down an elusive band of thieves. Where in the World Is Carmen Sandiego? Junior for ages five to eight uses clues that are read aloud, accompanied by colorful photographs, illustrations and animation. The chase uncovers some fascinating facts, one being that if Brazil hadn't been discovered, there wouldn't be any chocolate in the world.

Edmark's Imagination Express series helps kids of all ages create QuickTime movies with their own scripts, music, background scenes, props and movable animated characters; the children have a wealth of items to choose from and embellish. Each package in the series has a different theme — two are rain forests and castles.

From Maxis comes the Sim series, popular with older children, that has them work to a goal or a solution, making trade-offs, such as creating a workable ant colony or building an entire city. SimCity 2000, for ages 10 and older, invites players to address zoning issues, lay down roads and power lines, and solve traffic problems; SimEarth Color, for ages 12 and up, involves geology, evolution and spacefaring; SimAnt, for ages eight and older, gives students the experience of managing an ant colony; and the latest, SimLife, has a genetic-engineering simulation program for ages 10 and up.

Davidson, producer of the world's best-selling electronic math product, Math Blaster Plus, offers more good software: Kid Works, for ages four to 10; and What's My Angle?, an ambitious geometry program in the form of a miniature golf game, for ages 14 and up. A Davidson program, Star Trek: The Next Generation Interactive Technical Manual, puts you in charge of inspecting the Starship *Endeavor,* examining every cranny of the same sets used in the TV series. With a new version, you'll be able to take it on an expedition.

Some of the most engaging offerings come from smaller companies. A piece of inspired whimsy from Sierra On-Line is The Incredible Machine, a sort of Rube Goldberg emulation in which your kids are invited to build a better mousetrap — but they'd better stick to the rules! — using belts, pulleys, treadmill mice and bike-riding monkeys. And the sequel, The Even More Incredible Machine, makes learning about the effects of gravity, air pressure and mechanics an entertaining experience. Easy in the beginning, the program becomes more challenging as users get into it in more depth. An unlooked-for treat from Mecc is The Oregon Trail, a simulation program in which students make the famous trip and are called on to decide how many bullets and blankets they'll need to take. The Amazon Trail, for ages 10 and up, leads kids on a journey on the great river in search of a life-saving medicine for an Inca king and his dying people. The program's designer made the journey himself and uses his photos in the program.

From Mindplay comes a cooking program called Bake and Taste that elementary school math teachers have been known to use to teach fractions. Kids choose real recipes, and they have to complete a meal by the time guests arrive. They can make mistakes (if they do, guests may taste the dish and stick out their tongues), and there is a whimsical sponge for wiping up spills. A program called GeoClock (available as shareware on many bulletin boards) helps kids understand time zones. From Kinder-Magic comes an exploration of symmetry in tiles and tessellations called Mosaic Magic Enhanced.

Don't overlook the possibilities of on-line services, especially the family-oriented America Online and Prodigy, where your kids can find pen pals, get homework help and look things up in an electronic encyclopedia. On Prodigy, they can watch NOVA programs geared for children and play a "Smart Kids Quiz." On CompuServe, they can learn how the stock market works and follow individual company stocks. Adults — and some children, too — play CompuServe's simulated E*Trade to compete with others to see who gains the most wealth in a month.

To help high-school students with their SAT and ACT tests, there are dozens of programs with drills and sample tests. The highly rated One on One with the SAT, from the College Board, the national association that sponsors the SAT, sells for $50. You can get Davidson's Your Personal Trainer SAT for $38; Cliff Notes produces Studyware for the SAT, also $38. Aiding students in the search for schools to attend, Lovejoy's College Counselor has extensive information about colleges and universities, including what financial help is available. But before buying anything, see if what you need is available free on the Internet or in school libraries.

You might also want to get some CD-ROM edutainment for yourself. There is CD-ROM software for buying a car, planning a trip, creating a photo album (provided you can scan in photographs), or just about anything you can think of. 3D Architect, from Books That Work, can help you build a deck or porch; design and furnish a room; or plan lighting, wiring, plumbing, windows and fireplaces, among other projects. The same company's 3D Landscape guides you through the design and planting of your yard, from a database of plants, shrubs and trees, and lets you view it in three-dimensional color. And the price of $50 is considerably less than a landscape designer's fee.

CHAPTER 19

# Getting the Most from Your Car

## When to Buy a New Automobile

Time to replace Old Faithful? Tens of millions of Americans have said yes since 1993, when the average age of cars on U.S. roads peaked at a record 8.3 years. But when you consider that the typical family today has to spend four to six months of its annual income to buy a new vehicle, you may conclude that you will do better by squeezing some more miles out of the one you have. The best way to reduce your automobile costs is to drive your present vehicle — assuming it is safe and reliable — until just before it sputters to a permanent halt. Recognizing that moment takes skill, but here's a tip: Look for a sharp rise in repair costs.

Drivers who heed the maintenance instructions in their owners' manuals usually can roll up 100,000 miles before facing transmission overhauls or other costly repairs. If you have been taking your car to a reliable mechanic for regular maintenance checkups, quiz him or her about what is likely to go wrong next.

Don't panic over a single big repair bill. Repair costs rise steadily through a car's first 10 years. The costs of running a car (gas, oil, repairs and maintenance) go up along with the miles registered on the odometer, but nowhere near as swiftly as the fixed costs (depreciation, financing and insurance) are going down.

The savings from keeping your car for at least eight years showed up in a 1994 study by Runzheimer International of Rochester, Wisconsin, transportation consultants to corporations. Runzheimer's analysts posed two choices for the owner of a four-door, six-cylinder 1991 sedan: Drive it for another four years or trade it in on a 1995 model and drive that car for the next four years. The four-year-old car originally cost about $14,000 and gets 21 miles to the gallon. The new car costs about $17,000 and also gets 21 miles to the gallon. The older car is debt-free. You would need to finance the new car with a four-year loan, paying 8.5% annual interest. The finding: By sticking with the 1991 model, the owner stood to save more than $9,000 by 1998.

Writing in the *New York Times,* Hubert B. Herring compared the total costs of buying a new car for $20,000 with those of buying an equivalent used car for $11,000 — and holding each for three years before reselling it. His conclusion: It cost a total $5,300 more to own and drive the new car for three years.

To get the most out of your car, maintain it faithfully, using a knowledgeable mechanic. See that brakes, tires and steering stay in top condition. In high-pollution areas, keep your auto garaged as much as possible. Consider renting a car for longer trips, if you are worried about pushing your old auto to its limits. Review your repair records regularly. Americans average 39 cents a mile to own and operate the family car. If your costs suddenly shoot up, it's probably time to trade in.

In that case, now could be a good time to take advantage of both a benevolent market — prices of new 1995 U.S. cars went up just 2% over 1994 models — and technological improvements, especially in American cars. Credit, too, may be easier to get, particularly if you qualify for a General Motors or Ford credit card. The GM card, for example, charges no annual fee, offers interest rates of 10.4% above the prime rate and provides up to a $500 rebate toward the purchase of a new GM car. Ford offers a similar deal.

But banks are usually a cheaper source of financing than dealers. For buyers with good credit, the difference is about half a percentage point. Sometimes, however, getting the lowest interest rate isn't the most important consideration. When it isn't, you can do better at a car dealer.

The reason is simple: Banks are in the business of lending money; car dealers are in the business of selling cars. The dealer offers loans backed by a finance company that is either owned by the car manufacturer itself, or has an agreement with it. A car dealer can offer you quick loan approval, sometimes in minutes. If your credit record is less than perfect, dealers will bend over backward to get you approved. After all, they want to make a sale. And if you are late with a payment or need an extension, car dealers are more likely to give it to you. They don't want that car coming back to them.

The price that a dealer quotes to you for a new car represents the first offer in a round of haggling. To negotiate with confidence, you need to know the dealer's cost or invoice price. It may be $500 to as much as $4,500 less than the sticker price.

Information on new-car prices is widely available in automobile and consumer-affairs publications. One valuable source of objective information is *The Car Book* from The Center for Auto Safety (2001 S Street NW, Washington, D.C. 20009; $15.50). A specialized source is *Consumer Reports'* Auto Price Service, which supplies a computer printout for each model you request, comparing invoice and sticker prices and listing the cost of all factory-installed options. One printout on a single make/model/style costs $12; two printouts are $22. Call Auto Price Service at 800-933-5555 or write to P.O. Box 549027, Chicago, Illinois 60654-9027. If you are in a rush, Auto Price Service will fax back your data within four hours at no added cost.

When you've done your research, total up the dealer's cost for your car, including all optional features. Then make your first offer, at $125 to $200 more than the invoice price. The dealer will bid that up, of course. But try to hold out for a price $200 to $500 over invoice for an American-made car — and no more than $500 over invoice for a foreign one. Be sure you know what the rebate is and look out for extras that add to the invoice price.

For $20 plus $3 postage, a car-pricing and referral service called the Global Shopping Network will send you a computer printout listing dealer cost and suggested retail price on all standard equipment and factory options. Then, if you wish, a personal counselor will be appointed to guide you, at no extra cost, through the car-buying process. If you prefer not to negotiate your own deal, Global Shopping Network's buying service will haggle on your behalf, for an additional fee of $99 and up.

The dealers listed by Global Shopping Network typically charge $50 to $150 over invoice for domestic cars and as low as $300 over invoice for imports. To use this buying service, call 800-221-4001. During East Coast business hours a live operator can usually answer your questions and refer you to a dealer in two to five minutes. Also, the Center for the Study of Services' Car Bargains Service (202-347-9612 or 800-475-7283) will get five competitive bids from dealers near you for a fee of $150.

## Tips for Buying the Best Car

- Take a few moments to assess your current vehicle. Determine what you like about it and what you don't. This will give you a good starting point to choose your next car.
- Make a wish list for your next vehicle. Do you want more passenger space? A bigger trunk? More prestige? Lower monthly payments? Write down key items of importance to you. This will aid salespeople at dealerships in understanding what you want when the time comes to visit the showroom.
- Examine your finances. Most cars are bought with a certain percentage of the price as a down payment and the rest paid monthly over two to five years. Determine how much cash you can afford to spend as a down payment or how much your current car will bring if you trade it in and use the proceeds as your down payment. Then figure what you can afford as a monthly payment. Finally determine how long you plan to keep the vehicle. The term of your repayment should never exceed the length of time you plan to own the car.
- Using your list of key criteria, settle on the type of auto that you'd like to acquire. This is a key step, because it's easy to be dazzled and confused by the more than 250 models on the market. When you pick a vehicle type, say, sport utility or luxury sedan, you can compare apples to apples rather than grapefruits to tangerines.
- To help you in this winnowing process, pick up one or more of the buying guides published by magazines such as *Car and Driver, Road & Track, Automobile, Motor Trend* and *Popular Mechanics.* These guides do little more than give you a thumbnail sketch on each car, but they do list the specifications and the Manufacturer's Suggested Retail Price. They will help you narrow your shopping list to the vehicles within your budget. The magazines also do in-depth tests of most new models, worth looking at once you've shrunk the field. Often these reports aren't very critical, so if one gives you the impression the reviews are only lukewarm about the car, that means the judges

probably actively dislike it. The exception is *Consumer Reports,* which is consistently ruthless. The magazine's annual car issue is especially useful. It lists the history of each make's reliability based on reader surveys and provides helpful information about negotiating with dealers.

- Consult the J. D. Power and Associates Initial Quality and Customer Satisfaction Index Studies. The highlights of these studies are in *The Power Report,* available from the marketing consulting firm by calling 800-274-5372. While virtually all carmakers have made giant quality strides over the last 15 years, the relative quality of various makes and models still varies widely.
- Once your list is down to three or four models, go to the showrooms, not to buy, but simply to look. Make a pact with yourself that you're not going to purchase, and then examine the models you're interested in. Sit behind the wheel and in the backseat. Check out the trunk space. Take a test drive. What you need to decide is which vehicle you want to drive for the next several years of your life. As with marriage, be careful what you fall in love with, but don't be afraid to fall in love. You're likely to have your new vehicle for several years. Why not spend that time with something you really like?
- Once you've picked the make, model and equipment you want, you still have to come to terms with a dealer. This is a less onerous task than in years past, because the dealers as a group have made great strides in providing higher levels of service and customer satisfaction. If you feel you aren't being treated as you'd like, walk out. You'll find that same make and model at another dealer, most often nearby. You have the power to say yes or no. Feel free to use it.
- As to price, you'll find that most stories of "giant discounts" and "steals" are just that — stories. It isn't hard to determine the "dealer invoice" price these days, a close approximation of what the dealer paid the factory for the vehicle. Obviously, the dealer has to get more than that simply to stay in business. If you shop around at two or three dealerships asking about the cash

price for a particular model equipped a particular way, you'll find the prices various dealers quote you will be very similar. For most models most of the time, a middle ground between the sticker price and the dealer invoice is fair for both you and the dealer.

*Source:* Jack R. Nerad, former editor of *Motor Trend* magazine, is the co-host of the Mutual Radio Network program, "America On the Road."

# Buying a Used Car

With the average cost of a new car pushing past $18,000, a clean, late-model used car can look like an attractive alternative. But you lose thousands of dollars to depreciation the moment you drive off the dealer's lot; the car's value can decline by half over the first three years. Today's cars are built to last longer with less maintenance than those of, say, a decade ago. So why not let someone else pay that penalty?

Your safest source for a used auto is a new-car dealer. Prices tend to be higher than those of independent used-car outfits or private sellers. But because dealers need to protect their reputations, they have much to lose if they sell you a lemon. They usually offer a warranty (30 days is typical). If you're fortunate, you will find a car that the dealer has maintained, with service records.

If you buy from a used-car specialist, private seller or other non-dealer source, you take more chances. Unless you're mechanically sophisticated, bring your potential purchase to a professional mechanic for a thorough checkup. Fees typically run $35 to $60. In some parts of the country, you can find companies that specialize in such examinations, and some American Automobile Association branches offer a similar service.

You can probably negotiate prices with a dealer. Compare the asking price with those of similar cars in newspaper ads and local specialty want-ad publications. And check with *Consumer Reports'* Used Car Price

Service. For under $20 on average, you can get current prices for a wide variety of vehicles, based on age, mileage, options and condition, plus information about reliability drawn from *Consumer Reports'* frequency-of-repair records (900-446-0500). Some auto clubs offer used-car valuation services.

A relatively stress-free way to get a used car is to buy one from a major car-rental company. Avis, Hertz and National operate used-car lots made up of 10- to 18-month veterans of their fleets. Prices are not negotiable but are well below retail for used cars. You can get a complete maintenance record for each former rental.

Auto dealers frequently offer attractive deals on cars that have been lent to salespeople for their personal use or for showing to potential buyers. After three to six months and usually between 3,000 and 7,000 miles, these demonstration cars are sold at discounts of 15% to 20%. Most demos are covered by what remains of manufacturer's warranties, and many dealers will extend those warranties for a small charge.

The cars also qualify for the special financing packages that are available on brand-new cars. Before you buy, compare the price of a demo with the price that the dealer may be offering on a leftover car from the previous model year that has not been driven at all. The leftover car will sell for less. But the higher resale value of the previously driven but still newer demo probably will provide you with a better deal in the long run.

# The Advantages of Leasing

Detroit and the nation's auto-financing companies are luring more of us to a leasing way of life. In recent years Ford, Chrysler and General Motors as well as the major import brands have devised programs that cut the cost of leasing. Now that the interest you pay on car loans is no longer tax-deductible, leasing your new car can make sense.

For those who have it, paying cash is still the cheapest way to buy a car. For everyone else, financing still beats leasing. But if you lack the money for a down payment or don't want to tie up your cash or plan to keep the car for four years or less, leasing may be for you. The four-year rule applies because new cars depreciate so fast that if you buy one and sell it any sooner than that, it could fetch far less than the unpaid balance of your loan.

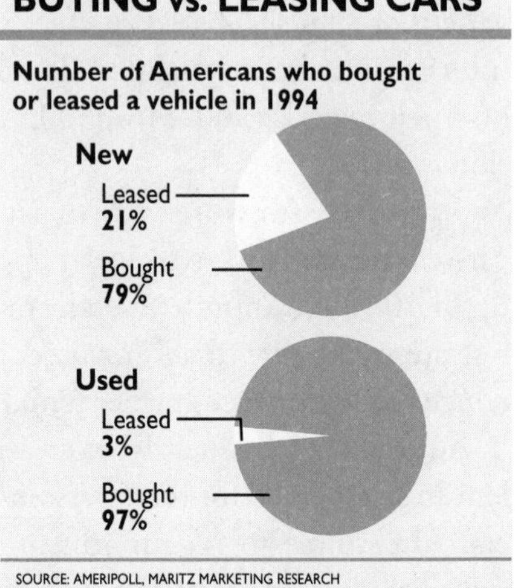


Under General Motors' SmartLease program, you can drive away a new $16,029 Pontiac Grand Am for a $275 security deposit and $270 a month (excluding sales and use tax) for three years (assuming no other down payment or capitalized cost reductions). That's considerably less than the $462-a-month payment on a loan with a $500 rebate and an 11% interest rate. In this case, however, the advantage fades when, after three years, you would own the financed car but would have to spend another $7,053 to buy the leased one.

If you decide to lease, shop the new-car dealers first and then check rates at local banks and independent auto-leasing firms. Some of the information you'll need is straightforward and easy to get, such as the mileage limit, the monthly payment and the cost of insurance. Other crucial details may require some digging. Key questions to ask:

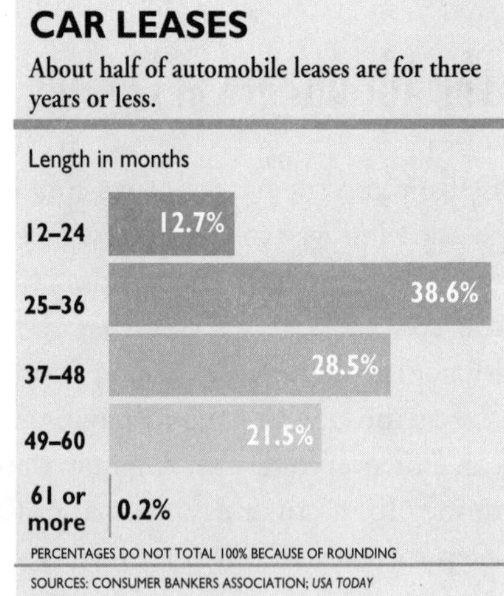


- What is the car's capitalized cost, and what is its residual value? The former is industry jargon for the selling price — the car's value at the start of the lease. You should bargain it down as far as possible, just as you would in buying a new car. Residual value is what the car is worth at the end of the lease. The bigger the difference between the two, the more money you pay through depreciation.

- What is the "money factor"? That's the interest rate, and only the dealer knows — it's not in the fine print of the contract. It is usually expressed as a fraction — say, .0038. You'll have to multiply it by 24 to convert it to an annual interest rate. If the dealer won't tell you, find one who will.
- Does the lease contract provide for "gap" protection? If you have an accident, gap protection pays off your contract when your insurance carrier doesn't provide a large enough settlement to cover the amount you owe on your lease.
- How much do you pay up-front? A deposit equal to one or two monthly payments is unavoidable and eventually refundable. But watch out for something called a "capitalized cost reduction" payment. It can amount to 10% to 20% of the car's value, due in advance.
- What will it cost to get out of the lease early? To keep monthly payments down, some firms rope you into a longer lease than you need and then charge a hefty fee if you attempt to escape.
- How much are the "disposition" fees? These cover the company's cost of selling the car once you are through with it. Any more than $250 is too much. Some companies (GMAC is one) do not charge a fee.
- What constitutes "excessive wear and tear"? Leasing companies must state the kinds of damage charges they may impose on you after the lease ends. Make sure the description is specific.

If you might want to buy the car when the lease runs out, look closely at the terms of a "closed-end" lease. Don't settle for a vague price based on fair market value. Insist on a contract stating an exact, fixed purchase option price. Then, depending on used-car prices at the end of the contract, you can either buy at a bargain figure or walk away from the deal.

The best deals tend to be leases subsidized by an automaker trying to build sales volume. They're easy to spot, because they are heavily promoted. Manufacturers typically subsidize by calculating a high residual value or by setting a below-market interest rate.

If you have a computer, consider getting a program called Expert Lease, by Chart Software (800-418-8450). It gives advice on negotiating a lease and information to help make the lease/buy decision. The cost is $59. For $99.95, Chart will send you an advanced version with more features such as *The Automotive Lease Guide,* which lists residual values. You can buy the *Lease Guide* in hard copy for $12.50 or find it in some libraries.

## Buy or Lease? Tips for Making the Buy-or-Lease Decision

There is no simple answer to the lease/buy question. Making the right decision is a matter of your personal desires, values and current financial status.

*The key advantages of leasing are:*

- You need only a minimal amount of cash to initiate a lease (as opposed to conventional financing, where you often need a down payment of at least 10% of the purchase price).
- You can structure the lease term to match your trading cycle. If you normally buy a new car every two years, you might be better off with a two-year lease.
- You can dispose of the leased car with no hassles at the end of the lease term — no need to sell the old car privately, no dickering at the dealership over trade-in allowance.
- You can buy the leased car at the end of the lease term by making a payment negotiated at the beginning of the lease.
- For the same monthly payment, you can lease a much more expensive vehicle than you can buy.
- On the other hand, there is one key advantage to purchasing your next vehicle — as you make payments, you build equity in a real asset. For many people, this one advantage far outweighs all the advantages of leasing.
- Look at it this way. Would you rather lease or buy your home? Sure, by owning the home you have to put up with all the troubles that are involved — maintenance, upkeep, repairs — but you're also building something for yourself and your family. It's a tangible asset that has psychic rewards as well.

*Given this basic premise, there are still a few instances when it's better to lease than buy. Among them are:*

- You simply can't afford to buy your dream vehicle but you're confident you can make the lease payments through the end of the lease term. (Always plan on staying with a lease through the end of its term because it is very difficult and expensive to terminate a lease before its completion.)
- You feel the quality and dependability of the vehicle is a bit questionable, but you'd still love to have it. Leasing allows you to try it out for a couple of years. If you love it at the end of the term, you can buy it; if you hate it, you just drop it off and say good-bye.
- You want to have a bright, shiny new vehicle every two or three years.
- The manufacturer is making a lease offer that's so financially compelling that you can't afford to pass it up. Many manufacturers now put models on sale not by lowering the price but by offering special lease deals.
- You can't stand the complications and the bargaining involved in selling your old car and buying a new one.

*Need-to-know tips on getting the best lease deal:*

- Negotiate the cash purchase price of the vehicle down from the Manufacturer's Suggested Retail Price (MSRP) and then make the lease deal.
- Demand to see the interest rate you're paying on the lease; don't rely on the monthly payment to determine if you're making a good financial deal. Remember: If you're leasing, you're only purchasing the use of the car over a small portion of its useful life and you're gaining no equity. To reflect this, the monthly payment should be much, much lower than if you were to buy.
- Never lease for a term longer than the manufacturer's warranty on the vehicle. Otherwise, you might be stuck dipping into your pocket to fix a car you don't own.

- Be realistic with yourself about the number of miles you drive in a year. Most leases have annual mileage caps of 12,000 or 15,000 miles, and you pay dearly at the end of the lease if you exceed them.
- Watch out for manufacturer-sponsored special lease deals. Television and newspaper ads touting a specific monthly payment are an obvious giveaway that the manufacturer is putting the car on sale. But remember the deal is no good if it's on a model you don't want.

*Source:* Jack R. Nerad

# How to Find a Mechanic

To enjoy years of trouble-free driving, finding the right auto technician can be almost as important as finding the right car. Beyond getting recommendations from friends, the best way to discover a competent mechanic is through the growing network of reputable repair shops that are identified and appraised by the American Automobile Association (AAA). This is done through AAA's Approved Auto Repair program.

It is the first nationwide effort to identify and evaluate reliable repair shops. The program covers every kind of shop, from franchised dealers to independent neighborhood garages. It includes 4,229 garages in 31 states and the District of Columbia. The AAA inspectors apply such rigorous standards that more garages fail than pass their first inspection. The repair bays, equipment and mechanics' qualifications are checked. Then the AAA queries customers whose names an inspector picks from the shop's files.

You do not have to join the association to take advantage of the program. Simply look for a garage with AAA's red, white and blue sign and the inscription "Approved Auto Repair." Or phone the local affiliated auto club for names of approved shops in the area.

One of AAA's measures of a worthy shop is whether or not its technicians are certified by the National Institute for Automotive Service Excellence, or ASE. The institute supports itself entirely from examination and registration fees. To earn a certificate of competence, a mechanic or technician must have passed at least one of ASE's eight auto-specialty tests and have two years of hands-on experience.

Shops lacking AAA approval may still do first-rate work. Those that display the ASE sign have at least one mechanic certified in one of the institute's specialties. Or go a step further and have the mechanic show you if he or she has an ASE certificate that says he or she is qualified to repair the system that you need to have fixed.

New-car owners are inclined to have repairs done by the dealer because that's where their warranty is honored. The dealer usually has good facilities and makes a special effort to please a customer who has bought one car and may buy another. But dealers tend to be expensive. For specific services, such as buying and installing a muffler, you may get the best price at an independent repair shop. According to the September 1994 *Consumer Reports,* its readers were most satisfied with independents. For brakes and mufflers, their prices were better than either chains or dealers; for transmissions, chains were the most expensive and least satisfactory.

But don't let bargain prices lure you away from an able general mechanic — if you have been lucky enough to find one. When you take a sick car to him or her, describe the symptoms in detail or even write them down. Request a written estimate and ask him or her to call if something unexpected or expensive turns up. Also ask the mechanic to give you any old parts that are replaced. But don't offer your own diagnosis. That is the mechanic's job.

## Devices That Deter Theft

Professional car thieves are so swift and experienced that police, insurance underwriters and even manufacturers of antitheft devices feel that it's hard to thwart them. But although alarms and other preventions are not foolproof, the right ones can save you anguish and expense. Even if nobody ever tries to steal your car, you will get a 5% to 15% discount on your auto insurance.

If you own an expensive auto, and particularly if you live in a big city, your best protection against theft is never to leave your car on the street. Professional thieves are a match for almost any antitheft equipment. But you should seriously consider buying alarms and locks to discourage joyriders and casual miscreants.

Antitheft devices are now so varied and sophisticated that you can outfit your car to do just about everything but roll over and play dead when it is attacked. You can buy these gadgets at stores that sell automotive accessories.

Start with an alarm that will scare away the nonprofessional thief. Good alarm systems, such as those made by Harrison Electronic Systems Corporation in Wilkes-Barre, Pennsylvania (800-422-5050), cost anywhere from $125 to $350 installed. The most expensive type sets off a siren at a variety of intrusions — for example, if someone bangs a window or jolts the car. Two other antitheft systems are the Crimestopper Stiletto ($350) and the Vehicle Security Electronics Quantum Pro ($500 plus installation).

If you figure an alarm may not be enough to scare off the professionals, invest in a device that prevents them from starting the car. You can get the Safestop Starter Interrupt, which costs about $100 including installation, from Harrison Electronic Systems. It disables the starter each time the ignition is turned off. The car cannot be started until a hidden pressure switch is touched.

If what thieves want is your wheels and tires, you can complicate their task by installing locking lugs. A set of four plus the special wrench needed to unlock them costs $12 to $45. The most ambitious type of protection is a vehicle-tracking system such as LoJack. Police cars equipped with special receivers can track down your car and the thief. Many police departments use this product to follow their own fleet. Costs average about $600. (For more, see Chapter 21 on getting the best in services and personal security.)

## Choosing Among the Auto Clubs

Worried about being stranded in a disabled car on a snowy night, millions of motorists have sought reassurance by joining an auto club or one of the assistance programs offered by insurers, banks, oil companies and retail chains. If you or other drivers in your family have any doubts about coping with breakdowns on your own, the question is not whether you should join a club but which one.

## Renting a Car

Never cheap, renting a car has become more expensive in the mid-1990s. Several rental-car companies raised their daily prices by $5 a day and they have added mileage charges of 20 cents a mile. The companies say they need the increases to make up for several years of thin profits.

As *Fortune*'s auto expert, Alex Taylor III, notes, the cars aren't quite as shiny either. Because Detroit has cut back on its sales to rental-car fleets, the companies are keeping cars in service for six months or so, instead of three to four months as in the past. Extra charges are still a nuisance, particularly the notorious collision-damage waiver, which can cost $10 a day or more. You probably don't need it if you are covered by your own auto insurance policy or hold one of several major credit cards that pay for damages in an accident. Fill up the tank with gas before returning the car and you'll also save paying the rental company's refueling charge.

If you rent a car, bear in mind that nationally advertised companies like Hertz, Avis, Budget and National give good service but are expensive. Try to get a corporate discount if the company you work for has an account with one of them. If you aren't in a hurry, look for a rental-car company that is located in a shopping center or office location, away from high-rent airport sites. Enterprise has grown into one of the biggest rental-car companies in the country by offering cars that are somewhat older in less-than-prime locations. It claims its rates are as much as 30% lower than its better-known rivals.

Annual fees range roughly from $50 to $70. Besides roadside assistance, you can expect a menu of such other benefits as bail bond service, trip planning, accident insurance, car-rental reimbursements, and discount coupons for services and accessories. But your choice should be dictated primarily by the quality of an auto club's road help.

A number of national clubs offer so-called dispatch service: Members need only to call the club's number and wait for help to arrive. These clubs include the American Automobile Association (800-222-4357), Amoco Motor Club (800-782-7887), Allstate Motor Club (800-776-9292), and Autovantage (800-999-4227), available from many banks through their MasterCard or Visa cards. If your club does not offer dispatch service, you will have to find help on your own. Some other clubs provide a directory of affiliated service stations or a toll-free number to call for the name of an approved station near where you've broken down. In most of these cases, the club pays for the emergency service, but it is usually limited to towing and minor roadside repairs such as tire changing and battery recharging. Still other clubs merely reimburse you for service you arrange on your own, which can be no boon to the panic-prone.

**AUTO RENTAL COMPANIES**

Top companies by revenue

| Company | 1994 Revenue (thousands) | Telephone (800) |
|---|---|---|
| **Hertz** | **$4,800,000** | 654-3131 |
| **Avis** | **3,000,000** | 831-2847 |
| **Budget** | **2,300,000** | 527-0700 |
| **Enterprise** | **1,975,000** | 325-8007 |
| **Alamo** | **1,275,000** | 327-9633 |
| **National** | **1,000,000** | 328-4567 |
| **Dollar** | **650,000** | 800-4000 |
| **Thrifty** | **452,200** | 367-2277 |
| **Carey** | **222,000** | 336-4646 |
| **Value** | **150,000** | 825-8538 |

SOURCE: *BUSINESS TRAVEL NEWS*

Whether the club pays directly or reimburses you later, the payments are often unrealistically low. There is always either a dollar limit or a mileage limit for towing. The limit for road services generally ranges from $50 to $100, and you pay anything over that.

Be sure to read the fine print of any club's membership contract. Some demand an initiation fee and charge extra for a spouse; others do not. Some clubs cover emergency service on any car you're driving; others limit coverage to cars you own or lease long-term. *A tip:* If you rarely travel far from home, you may find that regional auto clubs offer road service equal to or better than that provided by many of the nationals.

# Neo-Classic Cars

Buying and owning collector cars remains a popular hobby for people who want to drive a piece of history. Sporty cars from the 1950s, 1960s and early 1970s are particularly sought after by baby-boom era men and women who want to acquire a car they yearned for in their youth, when they couldn't afford it. Remember, though, that you should purchase a vintage automobile only if you want something to drive on Sunday afternoon or to tinker with in your garage. Don't regard it as an investment. Like fine art and real estate, prices of collector cars crashed at the end of the 1980s after a big run-up. They are stable now but are growing only slowly, if at all.

If you do buy an older car, stick to two-door or convertible models. They were made in much smaller quantities than standard sedans. They are also considered sportier and thus more desirable, which makes them easier to sell. Stick to cars made before 1974, when emission regulations started to slow the output of high-horsepower models. And shop around. John Iafolla, editor of the monthly *Collector Car and Truck Prices,* says prices tend to be highest in the Northeast and on the West Coast, where demand is greatest.

Iafolla maintains a database of 90,000 car transactions and updates it constantly. Today's prices look cheap compared with the boom years. For example, the 1963 Corvette Sting Ray, a design milestone with its split rear window, cost $4,527 new and rose as high as $40,000. Now you can buy one in good condition for $19,800, or pay up to $33,800 for a spotless one. An original 1964 Ford Mustang convertible, which sold for $2,368 three decades ago, once commanded $20,000. More recent prices ranged between $8,025 and $15,700. And the 1957 Ford Thunderbird convertible now goes for $11,900 to $22,750, versus $47,000 at the peak at the end of the 1980s.

If your tastes run to the more off-beat, there are lots of bargains. A racy 1957 Studebaker Golden Hawk runs between $7,325 and $12,950. An Edsel station wagon in mint condition will cost you no more than $6,000. And a Volkswagen Beetle from the 1970s should set you back at most $4,700.

CHAPTER 20

# Making Your Travel Dollars Go Farther

## How to Find a Reliable Travel Agent

As one who is a frequent-flier million-miler, and has bunked down everywhere from fleabag youth hostels to five-star grand hotels, let me tell you that a smart, sensible travel agent is worth his or her weight in gold cards. This Sherpa can guide you through the thicket of fares and tour packages to get you the lowest prices and the smoothest trips. But where do you find such a knowing professional?

Ray Greenly, a vice president at the American Society of Travel Agents (ASTA), says you need to match your own vacation interests and expectations with the capabilities of the agency. As he puts it, "You can't kick the tires on a trip to Hawaii." You have to rely on the agent to find the trip that fulfills your desires. A key question: Is your agent's taste compatible with yours? What are his or her favorite hotels and sights in places that you have visited and are well acquainted with?

Just about anyone can set himself or herself up in the business. Window decals that boast affiliations with national travel agent associations guarantee that the agency meets some standards, but not necessarily very high ones. Agents who have completed a two-year course given by the Institute of Certified Travel Agents and have five years of travel industry experience can use CTC (Certified Travel Counselor) after their names. This label at least suggests above-average commitment and knowledge. An ASTA designation means that the agency has been in business for three years and has agreed to uphold a code of ethics. The ASTA can tell you how long one of its agencies has been in business, as well as whether or not the society has received any complaints against a particular agency. Recently, the society launched ASTAnet, a website on the Internet that features a global directory of ASTA members, each of whom has a "page" through which Internet users will be able to conduct their travel business.

The best assurance of a competent agent is word of mouth. If you are trying an agent on someone else's recommendation, then tell the agent who sent you. Agents work harder if they have to please old customers as well as new.

Solid professionals are interested in the outcomes of trips. They usually take the initiative to call customers on their return. If you have complaints that are well founded, travel agents can help you get at least some of your money back.

Before settling on an agent, interview two or three on the phone. Ask where each has traveled in the past year. Conscientious agents can share firsthand experience of the places and services they recommend. They probably take two or three weeklong trips and several weekend excursions a year to keep their information up to date. An agent who is unfamiliar with a destination should be willing to refer you to a colleague or another customer who has recently been there. You can tell an agent knows a place fairly well if he or she speaks authoritatively without continually consulting guidebooks and maps.

Don't hesitate to prod the agent to find the lowest fare. You will know the agent is really digging if he or she suggests times or dates that would result in cheaper tickets. On the other hand, be sure to investigate carefully any extremely low-priced package tours. Sometimes they cut so many corners that the hotels and meals aren't anything you would care to remember.

Until 1995 you could expect the agent's services to be free. But a new cap on commissions paid by airlines for domestic flights set off an industrywide debate on pricing policies, and a number of agencies began charging travelers for some services. American Express travel agencies, for example, now charge you a $10 fee when you buy a ticket costing less than $300. Some Carlson affiliates have a similar charge for ticket-only bookings. When you're shopping for an agent, always inquire about possible service charges.

Agents are still getting their standard commissions on international air and rail travel, cruises and hotels abroad. Thus, it's only natural that travel agents prefer writing expensive foreign tours to planning a trip in the family car to the nearest beach. Some may push hotels that offer better commissions for the agent than they do rooms for the traveler. They may even guide you to package tours that are easier to arrange than customized itineraries. Be prepared to call a number of travel agents before you finalize your plans.

Travel agencies range from hometown mom-and-pop operations to the giant chains such as US Travel or American Express, though more and more smaller agencies are hooking up with larger networks. Customers who want personal service often do better with small agencies that have local reputations to protect. But large chains and agencies frequently offer a wider selection of services and staffs that know about more areas of the world. Volume also breeds influence. Agencies that send planeloads of travelers to a destination can get scarce hotel rooms more easily in peak seasons and have greater access to deeply discounted fares. Yet, while larger agents who deal in volume business may get you a nifty deal on standard package trips, you may experience better service with a boutique agency in planning a more complex, less conventional trip.

For a brochure on how to choose a travel agent, send a self-addressed stamped envelope to the American Society of Travel Agents, Fulfillment Department, 1101 King Street, Alexandria, Virginia 22314.

Travelers with particular needs should seek out specialized agents. Some are expert in adventure or cruising trips, still others in the needs of singles or disabled travelers. To find such specialists, consult travel guidebooks and magazines geared toward those interests. National tourist offices also can be invaluable guides to agencies familiar with their countries. There may be a trend toward travel superstores, such as Travel Fest, in Austin, Texas, a store the size of a basketball court, where you can book a ticket to Java, get a map of Chicago, buy a new suitcase — and accommodate just about any travel need.

A number of travel agents specialize in family vacations. They include: Families Welcome (4711 Hope Valley Road, Durham, North Carolina 27707; 800-326-0724 or 919-489-2555) and Rascals in Paradise (650 Fifth Street, Suite 505, San Francisco, California 94107; 800-872-7225 or 800-443-0799).

# How to Get the Best, Cheapest Plane Rides

When you buy an airline ticket, you enter a bazaar of wild negotiating and sometimes wonderful opportunities for bargains. Ticket prices vary sharply, depending upon how far in advance you make your reservation, what day and which time of year you take your flight and from whom you order. The person sitting next to you on the plane may have paid much more — or much less — than you did. This apparent confusion is governed by a process the airlines call yield management. It takes many factors into consideration and determines how many different fares will be offered on a particular flight and how many seats will be sold in each of those fare categories. But those figures change — often daily — as the airline tracks sales on a particular flight. If demand for it is low, the airline will increase the number of inexpensive tickets available and may reduce their price.

You get the very lowest fares by ordering and paying for your ticket months in advance, but you can still get progressively smaller discounts 14 days and seven days before your departure. After that, you'll usually pay full fare. Tom Parsons, publisher of *Best Fares,* a discount travel magazine, says that when you plan an air trip, you should consult a map and consider flying in and out of nearby cities to take advantage of specials. It costs less to fly into Washington's Dulles than into National, and it might be so much cheaper to fly into Baltimore that you could take a limousine from there to Washington and still save money. A few carriers reduce their prices for night flights, usually beginning between 7 P.M. and 9 P.M. Weekend travel may cost approximately $10 extra each way, but a flight beginning on a weekday and including a Saturday-night stay is almost always one of the least expensive.

Sometimes travel agents get better deals than you alone can, so it pays to use them. But just as one airline can give you lower prices on the same run than another line can, one travel agent can bring a nicer bargain than another. And there will be times when you can actually land the sweetest travel deals yourself, direct from the source. Obvious moral: It pays to shop around, among the air carriers, travel agents and discounters.

Discounters, known in the field as consolidators, offer coach tickets — and sometimes business and first-class — at 20% to 50% below full list price. As one airline executive has said, empty space on an airplane is "like overripe fruit in the supermarket — if you don't move it, it becomes worthless." When airlines cannot fill seats, they sell the tickets to consolidators at a considerable discount. Cut-rate consolidators have been legal since airline deregulation in 1978. There are over 100 across the country. Three reliable ones that have been in business for most of that time are Council Charter (800-800-8222), Travac (800-872-8800) and UniTravel (800-325-2222). You can buy consolidator tickets through your travel agent as well. *A warning:* Consolidator tickets are nonrefundable and may have other restrictions. Also, in many cases you cannot get preassigned seating or frequent-flier mileage.

In June 1992 all the major U.S. carriers descended into war with suicide fares, averaging about $200 for any round-trip flight in the 48 contiguous states. The conflict, precipitated by American Airlines' attempt to simplify fare structures, lasted through the summer and ended when American abandoned its campaign. The period stands out as one of the industry's biggest money losers. Though those days of wholesale cuts are over for the present, the deep discounting concept is entrenched. In 1995 USAir had a deep-discount $38 round-trip from Baltimore to Cleveland. Continental sold an Indianapolis to Paris round-trip for $380.

Discounts aren't the only airfare deals. For example, in 1995 travelers flying to Mexico City on Aeromexico from certain U.S. cities got a free round-trip ticket to a Mexican beach destination of their choice. Southwest Airlines pioneered the friends-fly-free concept, which allows a passenger paying a regular fare to take a companion at no charge or at a very low price. Several other airlines have picked up the idea. Northwest teamed with a New England bank to offer qualifying bank customers up to 65% off published fares; all the customers had to do was buy a $1,000, one-year CD or open a $500 IRA. Most such specials are laden with restrictions, but the prices are the lowest available. You can track these and other bargains in the monthly *Best Fares* ($58 a year, P.O. Box 170129, Arlington, Texas 76003).

Since deregulation, plenty of new, entrepreneurial airlines have rolled onto the tarmac. Most of the early ones met the fate of People's Express. But newer lines seem to be following Southwest's tenacious example and shouldering their way into the market. The operations are lean, and the airlines cover many routes that had been thinned or abandoned by larger carriers. Frontier, for example, regularly flies from Denver to Billings and Bozeman, Montana. Midway, once out of Chicago, is operating out of Raleigh-Durham, where it fills a void created when American cut that area's regional service.

Reduced pricing and less-restrictive fares (no Saturday-night stay, no advance purchase and no round-trip purchase to get the lowest fare) appeal to travelers. If full meal service and plenty of legroom are important to you, ask your travel agent or the airline reservation clerk what you'll get before you reserve a seat. You can book flights on smaller lines yourself or have your travel agent do it. If you choose the latter, mention that you are interested in the smaller airlines or the agent might not pursue their flights. ValuJet, one of the better new lines, is not on the agent's computerized reservation system. It is headquartered in Atlanta and flies mainly throughout the Southeast, though service is expanding into the Midwest and Northeast.

There are other strategies to get the lowest fare. If you can't stay a Saturday night — a common requirement for the cheapest fare — you may buy two round-trip tickets that each include a Saturday stay: one ticket from your home to your destination and the other from your destination back to your home. The two round-trip tickets are often less than the one fare without a Saturday-night stay. Most travel agencies will book these tickets, though airlines technically don't allow the practice. If they discover it, they may try to charge you the full, regular fare. You may save money by splitting your ticket. To fly from Baltimore to Chicago, for example, you can buy one round-trip ticket from Baltimore to Cleveland and one from Cleveland to Chicago.

Once you have found the best price for a flight, buy your ticket right away. You then will avoid any fare increases before your departure date. Fares can and do go up overnight, sometimes steeply. But should the price of your flight decrease between the time you buy and the time you fly, most airlines will either give you a credit toward future travel or actually refund you the difference, though you probably will have to pay a $50 fee to have the ticket reissued. It is up to you, however, to check the prices at the time of your departure.

The majority of travel agencies can track the very lowest fares through the Apollo or Sabre reservation computer systems. For instance, Traveltron, operated by a travel agency in Monrovia, California, guarantees to locate the least expensive fares on flights between U.S. cities and continues to search for a lower fare even after you've bought your ticket. Just one example: Fliers recently paid as much as $760 for round-trip coach tickets between New York City and Los Angeles. Traveltron directed callers to a rate of $308. *A warning:* Lower-priced tickets typically have heavier restrictions on them, so the penalty for changing the ticket could wipe out your savings. To use Traveltron, call 818-358-8818. You must pay a one-time membership fee of $49.95.

The key rule: You can get the most for your money if you plan in advance. Wise travelers always try to reserve their seats well before the flight. Though you can usually buy your air ticket as many as 300 to 350 days before your flight (depending on the airline), you may not be able to reserve a seat that far ahead of time. When you book your ticket, find out when you can reserve your seat. You can also save time, and help guarantee yourself against being bumped, by asking for your boarding pass ahead of time.

You will have a smoother flight if you avoid the rear of the plane. Tailwinds cause the most turbulence there. On rear-engine planes like the 727 or DC-9, you will escape engine noise and vibration by sitting as far forward as you can. Doing so, you also avoid the crowds when you leave the plane. Being one of the first out the door can speed you on your way — provided you have only hand baggage and do not have to wait for checked luggage.

On any plane, you will get the most legroom by taking the seat next to an emergency exit, since there must be enough space to permit easy exiting from the plane. Some airlines, however, won't assign these seats until two hours before departure. So if you want one, get to the airport early and make your bid at the ticket counter. Other carriers will allow these seats to be booked in advance. Regardless of such variations, airlines consistently require that persons occupying these seats be age 15 or older, English-speaking and both willing and able to vacate in an emergency. In the coach section, another desirable seat is in the first row, behind a bulkhead. You usually have extra legroom and a good view out a window that is unobstructed by the wing. On Boeing's new 777, some coach seats are 1½ inches wider and have two inches more legroom than normal. But other seats, particularly in the center aisles, are the standard 17 inches wide, with 31 inches of legroom. So seat selection is important; ask to reserve one of the roomier seats.

Avoid, if you can, flying at the busiest times: early mornings and late

## BEST TIMES TO FLY

### DEPARTURE: BEST HOURS TO TAKE OFF

| Airport | Best hour(s) | % of flights on time | Worst hour(s) | % of flights on time |
|---|---|---|---|---|
| Atlanta | 6–7 a.m. | 94.0% | 10–11 p.m. | 48.3% |
| Boston | 9–10 p.m. | 96.2 | 10–11 p.m. | 60.0 |
| Chicago | 11 p.m.–6 a.m. | 100.0 | 7–8 p.m. | 59.2 |
| Cincinnati | 8–9 a.m. | 95.7 | 6–7 p.m. | 56.3 |
| Dallas | 7–8 a.m. | 95.1 | 11 p.m.–6 a.m. | 68.3 |
| Denver | 11 p.m.–6 a.m. | 96.7 | 3–4 p.m. | 61.1 |
| Houston | 10–11 p.m. | 100.0 | 8–9 p.m. | 62.8 |
| Los Angeles | 6–7 a.m. | 94.8 | 8–9 p.m. | 63.2 |
| Miami | 8–9 a.m. | 96.1 | 9–10 p.m. | 60.9 |
| Minneapolis | 10–11 a.m. | 93.5 | 6–7 p.m. | 64.0 |
| New York: La Guardia | 6–7 a.m. | 95.3 | 7–8 p.m. | 70.5 |
| New York: Kennedy | 8–9 a.m. | 95.3 | 9–10 p.m. | 65.0 |
| Philadelphia | 6–7 a.m. | 97.0 | 6–7 p.m. | 60.3 |
| Phoenix | 6–7 a.m. | 96.0 | 9–10 p.m. | 65.5 |
| Pittsburgh | 6–7 a.m. | 93.2 | 6–7 p.m. | 66.0 |
| St. Louis | 6–7 a.m. | 93.4 | 10–11 p.m. | 62.3 |
| San Diego | 6–7 a.m. | 97.0 | 9–10 p.m. | 71.6 |
| San Francisco | 6–7 a.m. | 94.1 | 8–9 p.m. | 65.0 |
| Seattle | 6–7 a.m. | 94.9 | 9–10 p.m. | 59.0 |
| Tampa | 6–7 a.m. | 96.2 | 6–7 p.m. | 67.0 |
| Washington, D.C. (Dulles) | 6–7 a.m. | 94.6 | 7–8 p.m. | 69.7 |

### ARRIVAL: BEST HOURS TO LAND

| Airport | Best hour(s) | % of flights on time | Worst hour(s) | % of flights on time |
|---|---|---|---|---|
| Atlanta | 7–8 a.m. | 90.3% | 6–7 a.m. | 51.0% |
| Boston | 8–9 a.m. | 93.6 | 7–8 p.m. | 51.4 |
| Chicago | 9–10 a.m. | 94.1 | 6–7 p.m. | 61.1 |
| Cincinnati | 8–9 a.m. | 93.6 | 10–11 p.m. | 62.5 |
| Dallas | 7–8 a.m. | 95.5 | 10–11 p.m. | 75.4 |
| Denver | 8–9 a.m. | 89.2 | 10–11 p.m. | 62.9 |
| Houston | 7–8 a.m. | 89.4 | 7–8 p.m. | 57.2 |
| Los Angeles | 7–8 a.m. | 94.9 | 12–1 p.m. | 52.2 |
| Miami | 8–9 a.m. | 91.5 | 2–3 p.m. | 51.6 |
| Minneapolis | 7–8 a.m. | 93.9 | 8–9 p.m. | 65.5 |
| New York: La Guardia | 9–10 a.m. | 92.9 | 9–10 p.m. | 57.6 |
| New York: Kennedy | 9–10 a.m. | 100.0 | 7–8 a.m. | 53.5 |
| Philadelphia | 9–10 a.m. & 1–2 p.m. | 88.6 | 6–7 a.m. | 52.2 |
| Phoenix | 6–7 a.m. | 98.1 | 11p.m.–6 a.m. | 64.4 |
| Pittsburgh | 11a.m–noon & 2–3 p.m. | 91.8 | 8–9 p.m. | 59.7 |
| St. Louis | 1–2 p.m. | 86.3 | 5–6 p.m. | 63.6 |
| San Diego | 7–8 a.m. | 96.3 | 9–10 p.m. | 57.2 |
| San Francisco | 7–8 a.m. | 94.9 | 9–10 p.m. | 59.9 |
| Seattle | 8–9 a.m. | 89.3 | 3–4 p.m. | 62.2 |
| Tampa | 8–9 a.m. | 90.0 | 6–7 p.m. | 47.5 |
| Washington, D.C. (Dulles) | 8–9 a.m. | 90.0 | 9–10 p.m. | 58.8 |

SOURCE: U.S. DEPARTMENT OF TRANSPORTATION

afternoons on weekdays. For reasons travel experts have not fathomed, the most crowded day of the week usually is Thursday. The least crowded days tend to be Tuesday and Saturday. Take direct flights whenever possible, and if you must change planes, try to avoid delay-prone airports, such as those in Chicago, Atlanta and Dallas. When you make your reservation, ask whether the flight you want is often delayed.

There is no foolproof way to avoid being bumped off an oversold plane. A wise plan is to call the airline the night before and ask how full the plane is. If it is only 60% full, don't worry. If it is full, and you absolutely have to make that flight, arrive at the airport at least an hour early.

## HEAVIEST TRAFFICKED AIRPORTS

Airports ranked by number of passengers, 1994

| | Airport | Passengers |
|---|---|---|
| 1 | **Chicago (O'Hare)** | **29,970,000** |
| 2 | **Atlanta** | **25,670,000** |
| 3 | **Dallas/Fort Worth** | **25,435,000** |
| 4 | **Los Angeles** | **19,885,000** |
| 5 | **Denver** | **14,789,000** |
| 6 | **San Francisco** | **14,452,000** |
| 7 | **Phoenix** | **12,452,000** |
| 8 | **Detroit** | **12,256,000** |
| 9 | **Las Vegas** | **11,998,000** |
| 10 | **Newark** | **11,864,000** |
| 11 | **St. Louis** | **11,603,000** |
| 12 | **Minneapolis/St. Paul** | **10,892,000** |
| 13 | **Miami** | **10,832,000** |
| 14 | **Boston** | **10,668,000** |
| 15 | **Seattle** | **9,962,000** |
| 16 | **New York (La Guardia)** | **9,806,000** |
| 17 | **Houston** | **9,681,000** |
| 18 | **Orlando** | **9,167,000** |
| 19 | **Pittsburgh** | **8,997,000** |
| 20 | **New York (Kennedy)** | **8,908,000** |

SOURCE: U.S. DEPARTMENT OF TRANSPORTATION

Of the 477 million passengers who flew domestically in 1994, 780,250 were bumped. But if your plane is overbooked, you may be able to turn the situation to your advantage. Before bumping anyone, the airline must ask for volunteers willing to give up their seats. The carrot may be cash or a later flight at no charge — basically anything you and the airline can agree on. More than half of all those who get bumped choose to do so. If only a little money is offered, you may be able to bargain for more. Generally, the airline's ticket-counter people up the ante if there are not enough immediate volunteers. A free ride can be well worth a few hours' wait.

When you are involuntarily bumped, the airline must get you on another flight that is scheduled to arrive within an hour of your original arrival time or it must pay you a sum equal to your one-way fare up to a maximum of $200 and still fly you to your destination. If the airline cannot get you on a flight due to arrive within two hours of your original arrival time on a domestic flight or four hours on an international one, the penalty doubles to a maximum of $400. In cases when you are forced to make an overnight layover at a city not on your itinerary, the airline should pick up your hotel bill, though it is not legally obligated to do so.

Every line has its own "contract of carriage," spelling out its responsibility to you. You can get a copy simply by asking for it at the ticket counter or by writing to the airline. The contract is also printed on the back of most tickets.

Don't check baggage that you don't have to. When you make your reservations, ask how much you are allowed to carry on and pack accordingly. One advantage of buying a first-class ticket is that you can carry aboard an almost unlimited amount.

One more tip: You can order a special meal by calling the airline at least a day in advance. Your travel agent can also order the meal for you. Quite a few lines offer a remarkable array, from Muslim to non-dairy, but many veteran fliers say that you get the best meal, and the freshest food, by ordering a vegetarian or kosher plate.

Finally, the ultimate bargain: Imagine getting a round-trip flight to Amsterdam for 50% or more off the regular fare. For such deals, you just have to travel for one of several companies that use freelance couriers.

Here's how: Some of the smaller overnight package express companies don't have their own fleet of planes. So they hire freelancers to take commercial flights, and use all or part of a freelancer's baggage allowance to send their packages. (That limits your own baggage space.) The courier company usually pays at least half of the ticket price — and often more if the trip is last-minute. Couriers depart from only five U.S. cities — Chicago, Los Angeles, Miami, New York and San Francisco.

You can apply directly to one or more of the many courier companies around the country. One consistently successful company is Now Voyager (212-431-1616). For a $50 yearly fee, you can land such rare bargains as $150 round-trip restricted-stay tickets between New York and Mexico City. Or get in touch with the International Association of Air Travel Couriers (8 South J Street, P.O. Box 1349, Lake Worth, Florida, 33460). For $45 a year you can become a member; that entitles you to receive its newsletter, which lists courier opportunities and consolidator fares, and to have access to its on-line travel database. Twice a day the association posts a last-minute list by fax. For an overview of courier travel, see *Air Courier Bargains: How to Travel World-Wide for Next to Nothing,* by Kelly Monaghan (Intrepid Travel Guides, $14.95).

# Free Trips for Frequent Fliers

If you travel fairly often, it pays to become a steady customer of one or more airlines and enroll in their frequent-flier bonus programs. You can earn free trips, upgrades and hotel accommodations. In fact, it is smart both to concentrate your flying on one or two carriers so that you can accumulate miles quickly and to join every frequent-flier club you can; you don't know just when you may be taking several trips on a particular line and may qualify for some of its giveaways. Your spouse should join, too.

The awards commonly start after you have piled up 10,000 miles, which entitles you to get an upgrade to first class or business class for the price of a full-fare coach ticket. The free rides usually begin at 25,000 miles — it was only 20,000 miles until early 1995 — and the rewards grow progressively richer. At the highest levels, most airlines will take you to foreign countries, either on their own planes or via linkups with European carriers, as well as Air New Zealand, Qantas of Australia and some Asian lines.

To passengers who have logged 150,000 miles on a single account, United Airlines gives two business-class round-trip tickets to Asia or the South Pacific, plus a 50% discount for up to seven nights in a Westin Hotel, and a one-week car rental in the U.S. For 50,000 miles Delta will give you and a companion two coach tickets to anywhere in the U.S. (except Hawaii); for 80,000 miles, one business-class ticket to anywhere it flies in Europe, and for 90,000 miles, one business-class ticket to Asia. Northwest World Perks has varying mileage requirements, depending on the time you want to travel — peak, standard or off-peak. For example, in the off-peak season (September 1 to November 15), you need 35,000 miles for a European destination, 45,000 for an Asian destination. You may lose your miles if you don't use them. Northwest miles earned in 1996, for example, will expire December 31, 1999.

Frequent-flier award systems have become just about as complicated as the federal income tax; each airline has its own wrinkles and special perks. You can get help from the Frequent Flyer Club. With two levels of membership, for $99 or $124 a year, the club provides a member help line and computes your usage and mileage record on a monthly basis; the club will flag you two months ahead of your mileage expiration. Call

800-333-5937 for the Frequent Flyer Club or visit its Website on-line (http://www.insideflyer.com).

Randy Petersen, president of the club, offers these tips:

- Concentrate your miles in a program that makes it easy to get the kind of reward that you want. Programs vary in the number of miles they require for first-class upgrades and overseas travel. Some allow you to transfer your miles to another person; some allow you to get merchandise for your miles.
- Increase your miles by using program partners, such as other airlines, credit cards, hotels and car rental companies. For example, on a flight from Chicago to Denver, you can earn an extra 2,000 miles (round-trip) from a combination of 1,000 bonus miles for your hotel and 1,000 bonus miles for your rental car.
- Take advantage of affinity credit cards, which pay one dollar for every dollar you spend. Look for other specials. At various times, AT&T, MCI and Sprint have teamed up with airlines to allow customers to earn frequent-flier miles based on long-distance calling. In other promotions, United doubled from 500 to 1,000 the mileage points for a Radisson stay charged to American Express; and Delta dropped its mileage requirements for a ticket to Asia or Europe from 70,000 to 40,000.
- Plan your award use. Free seats on each flight are limited, and popular international destinations are often booked up three months or more in advance. Allow one month to get the awards sent from the airline's service center.
- Read your monthly frequent-flier mailings carefully. Besides giving your mileage statement, they will tell you all the new ways you can earn miles, and they may contain bonuses, such as passes to airline clubs and coupons for discounted — or even free — flights.

## Travel Clubs and Other Discounts

Discount coupon books offer a superior value for most travelers. The best deal is Entertainment Publications' *Entertainment National*™ *Hotel*

*& Dining Directory,* which will get you 50% off at over 3,500 hotels and 20% off at over 2,500 restaurants throughout the U.S. and other parts of the world. Even travel agents use these coupons as the price often beats the rate available to them. The book costs $37.95 and you can get it from Entertainment Travel Editions, 40 Oakview Drive, Trumbull, Connecticut 06611; 800-445-4137.

In addition, discount books are available for 77 U.S. cities, six Canadian cities and a variety of foreign cities. The Paris edition ($48), for example, lists 130 restaurants where you can get 25% off the bill, drinks included. With the current exchange rate, you could pay for the book with just one or two meals. If you've bought one book during the year, you can get the second at a discount.

Other discount books are *ITC-50,* which includes over 3,500 hotels and 1,200 restaurants ($36; 6001 North Clark Street, Chicago, Illinois 60660; 800-342-0558), and *Encore* ($49.95; 4501 Forbes Boulevard, Lanham, Maryland 20706; 800-638-0930). Singapore has a free discount book, *Singapore Plus,* that offers reductions at 155 shops, restaurants and attractions. You can get it in the U.S. before you go by calling the Singapore tourism office in Los Angeles, 213-852-1901, or in New York, 212-302-4861.

Many coupon books — used as premiums and incentives by businesses such as Cellular One and Post cereals — are custom-created by Entertainment Publications or another discounter. They cost little or nothing. These deals are usually well advertised in newspapers and magazines and on product packaging.

Travel clubs cover a wide range. The American Automobile Association (AAA), the best-known club, is actually an association of 121 clubs, with basic membership fees of $40 to $60 a year. Emergency road service, travel services — including Triptik — maps and hotel discounts are part of the deal. Depending on the club you join, you can get dozens of other benefits, including discounted movie tickets and no-fee traveler's checks. Emergency roadside service is the main attraction of all the motor clubs and oil company clubs, such as Amoco Motor Club and the Cross Country Motor Club (for more, see Chapter 19). For only $8, you can join the American Association of Retired Persons (AARP) and, along with its panoply of other benefits, get roadside service through Amoco Motor Club and discounts at hotels nationwide. Membership is open to anybody age 50 or older. One of the most expensive travel clubs is Players Club, at $144 a year. Geared to gamblers, it gives you discounts on hotels, cruises, shows and dinners at gaming resorts.

Don't join a club if you are simply looking for hotel deals. You will be better off with one of Entertainment Publications' books or a hotel discounter such as the Room Exchange (see page 697). Look to a club for a broad range of services and discounts, such as you get with AAA and AARP. Or join if the club focuses on your particular interests, such as Hideways International, which offers vacation rentals of villas and homes (see page 702).

# How to Choose a Cruise

Since the Love Boat sailed off into the sunset, cruise lines have shed their too-exclusive image and positioned themselves as a viable alternative to landlocked vacations. With the lines trying to be more competitive, tourists have benefited from larger staterooms, a wider range of activities and more predictable pricing. Cruise lines now use a system similar to the airline industry's yield management, giving the biggest discounts to passengers who place their orders well in advance. You can also find deals if you can sail the first week of January and during the fall.

The 1990s have also been a decade of expansion. At the end of 1994, there were 133 ships operating in the North American market; 27 new ships are scheduled to be launched by the end of 1998.

For travelers, particularly dual-income families who have little time to plan a trip, a cruise is a sound vacation idea. You get a clear-cut itinerary, you pack and unpack once, you know what your accommodations will be like and what your trip will cost. Almost everything — except tips, drinks and some shore excursions — is built into the price. First-time cruisers tend to underestimate how much they will spend tipping. Depending upon the ship, you may find yourself paying $10 per day per traveler.

Your challenge is to choose the cruise that matches your tastes and interests. The differences are far broader than the glossy cruise-line brochures suggest. You can sail for three days or three months; you can have 100 fellow travelers or 2,600. Lines differ and even ships within a line may vary. Carnival, as its name implies, bubbles round-the-clock with activities and entertainment — like a Las Vegas–style resort at sea.

Windstar's Wind Song feels more like a private club — low-key and upscale. The Delta Queen is unique in providing a view of America by her riverways.

A knowledgeable agent is a must. Ask your agent how many cruises he or she has taken and how many ships he or she has looked over. The designation of MCC — Master Cruise Counselor — means that an agent has taken at least five cruises, inspected more than 10 ships, done case studies and hours of classroom work. Four knowledgeable and reliable agencies that specialize in cruises are: Brennco Travel, Kansas City, Missouri, 800-765-8226; San Marin Travel, Novato, California, 415-892-7777; and The Cruise Line, Inc., Miami, Florida, 800-777-0707; and JWB Travel, South Pasadena, Florida, 800-727-3993.

Let the agent help you narrow your selection to a couple of lines and ships, then do research on your own. One of the many fact-packed guidebooks is *Fielding's Worldwide Cruises* by Antoinette DeLand, updated annually (Fielding Worldwide, $17.95). Another in-depth source is *Cruise Reports,* a bimonthly newsletter that publishes ratings of five or six ships, based on evaluations of at least 15 travel agents. A year's subscription is $24; single issues — you can request the reviews of the ships you are considering — are $4; 212-867-7470. Ask your travel agent for "Cruising: Answers to Your Questions," a particularly useful brochure published by the Cruise Lines International Association, 500 Fifth Avenue, Suite 1407, New York, New York 10110. It is valuable for its charts, which detail which lines go where and what activities they offer.

A must before setting sail: Check the U.S. Public Health Service's sanitation score for the ship you're considering by writing Chief, Vessel Sanitation Program, National Center for Environmental Health, 1015 North America Way, Room 107, Miami, Florida 33132. A score of 86 or higher indicates acceptable sanitation.

## Getting Good Value on Package Tours

Almost every would-be tourist has heard horror stories about package tours. Don't let them scare you away. You can get top value provided you know how to examine your package in advance. Here are questions to ask:

- Does the package include an inexpensive and convenient charter flight? Regular coach fares are down so much on some routes that you could wind up saving only about $25 on round-trip charters from New York City to London. When the savings are substantial, make sure that you don't have to stop en route in two or three other U.S. cities before heading for Rome — via London and Brussels.
- What do "first-class" accommodations really mean? The best European hotels are rated "deluxe." All that first-class gets you is a clean bedroom with a private bathroom. You can determine if you are going first-class or fleabag by looking up the amenities of your hotel in *The Official Hotel and Resort Guide,* available at travel agencies and libraries. The guide also lists the price you would pay for the room if you booked on your own. If the daily cost of the hotel on your package tour is less than the hotel's usual room rate, you know you are getting a deal.
- How many people will be on your tour? Having 59 fellow travelers is a totally different experience from having nine.
- Will you actually get to tour the sights listed in the brochure? The lineup may be dazzling, but it's apt to lose its luster if you do all your viewing through a bus window.
- Will the meals consist of foie gras and roast pigeon, or tomato juice and roast chicken? Tour operators won't tell you what you will eat at meals included in the package, but they can give you hints. If you find you are to dine in hotel restaurants, remember that they seldom are great gastronomical palaces.
- What happens if you have to cancel? Read the brochure's fine print carefully. Rules vary widely from company to company, but generally, the closer you get to the departure date, the more you'll lose. If you cancel at least 60 days in advance, you'll probably get back most of your money minus a small processing fee — $25 to $100. After that, the scale slides from losing about 20% of your land package to, if you cancel just days before departure, losing the total amount. Airfare refunds generally depend upon the carrier's regulations.

For security, check out your tour operator with the Better Business Bureau, pay by charge card and consider buying trip-interruption insurance. Don't buy the insurance from the tour operator. You can buy it from your travel agent in a package that includes other coverage such as accidental death and medical insurance. And make sure that the tour company belongs to an organization such as the U.S. Tour Operators Association (212-750-7371), which has a $1 million consumer-protection plan. If a USTOA member goes bankrupt, you can file a claim for deposits or payments you've lost. To get a claims form, call 212-421-1285.

## Special Deals in Hotels

Gone are the golden days of the late 1980s — when the number of hotel rooms was up and travel was in a slump — but you still can find special bargains. The key is to plan travel around these specials, use discounters (the hotel equivalent of airline consolidators) and to stay in hotels that offer more than lodging.

Smart travelers simply do not pay the rack rate (the standard published rate in hotels). They use a variety of means to lop 5% and 50%, or sometimes even more, off the bill — often by combining deals. For example, the rack rate for double occupancy at the Grand Hyatt Capitol Hill in Washington D.C., is $259. A promotion in 1995 dropped the rate to $98, and travelers could use a 50%-off USAir frequent-flier coupon to bring the price down to $49.

Furthermore, those lavish "honeymoon" packages at hotels and resorts are not only for newlyweds. Many times they are offered to anniversary celebrants as well — and it is a rare hotelier who will demand that you celebrate your anniversary on its true, verifiable date. Next time you book a room for two, simply ask for the hotel's anniversary or honeymoon rate. For instance, the Beverly Hilton in Beverly Hills offers a "Romance Package" — one night's stay in a deluxe room for $175, including chocolate-covered strawberries and champagne upon arrival and breakfast the next morning. The average rack rate for the room alone is $220.

Even luxury resorts offer deals. At El Conquistador in Puerto Rico, a family package for two adults and two children for three nights is $1,080. It includes two hours of tennis lessons per person for the parents, two days in the resort's camp for the kids, airport transfers and all taxes. Priced separately, the cost would be $1,567.

At other hotels, special weekend packages usually include a double room for two nights with extras that can range from ballet tickets to dinner by candlelight in your room. You pay one price, usually much less than everything would cost à la carte. In some cases, the savings can amount to 50%. Midweek packages are also money savers. Stouffer's Stanford Court in San Francisco was recently offering two nights for $339. The "Cable Car Package" included champagne, breakfast and two three-day cable-car passes.

As noted earlier, Entertainment Publications' discount book gives you up to 50% off at hotels and for some restaurant meals. So does the Privilege Card (404-262-0222). You also can get reduced rates through hotel discounters, who operate much like airline consolidators. Two to add to your Rolodex are the Room Exchange (800-846-7000; in New York 212-760-1000), which books rooms worldwide at 35% to 60% off rack rate; and Hotel Reservations Network (800-964-6835), which provides discounts of up to 65% in various cities worldwide.

There are a growing number of hotels specializing in suites — many at prices below traditional hotels. Some suites come with kitchens, so you can save still more by doing your own cooking. For instance, the Windsor Court in New Orleans gives you a bedroom, a sitting room with either a balcony or a bay window, a full kitchen and up to three telephones for $375 to $475 a night. At the Embassy Suites hotel in Los Angeles, you pay $109 to $159 a night, depending on the day of the week and the occupancy rate, for a bedroom and sitting room, kitchen facilities plus breakfast, cocktails in the evening and transportation to and from the airport. For further discounts off the rack rate, you can also call the hotel directly, as opposed to calling a central 800 number, if it is part of a chain.

For a listing of the more than 1,200 all-suite hotels in the U.S., as well as some 200 office suite enterprises offering space and office services on a daily basis, see Pamela Lanier's *All-Suite Hotel Guide* (Ten Speed Press, P.O. Box 7123, Berkeley, California 94707; $14.95 plus $3.50 postage and handling). It is important to ask ahead of time what the suite includes. One hotel's definition of a suite could be a room with a hot plate.

Whenever you stay in a hotel, ask if it gives travel bonuses for repeat customers. For an annual fee of $10 you can become a member of Holiday Inn's Priority Club (800-272-9273) and can stay with your family for the single-person corporate rate any day of the week and get room upgrades when possible. It doesn't cost anything to join Stouffer Hotel's Club Express; you can earn free weekends, U.S. savings bonds and American Express gift checks. Hilton Honors is also free; members earn hotel points that can be used toward vacations, including cruises, and merchandise. You earn both hotel and airline miles for each stay, and the program allows members to trade hotel points for airline miles, and vice versa.

## Bed-and-Breakfast Accommodations

Tired of champagne prices and no-fizz accommodations at hotels, travelers in the millions have turned to bed-and-breakfast guest houses. Fast growing, those accommodations now number an estimated 20,000 across the U.S. They have the comforts of home, often at down-home prices.

B&Bs range from private homes that open one to three spare bedrooms for guests at $45 to $75 a night, to B&B inns, which are commercial establishments as varied as restored mansions and modern inns, where rates begin at $75 and can go up above $250. Hosts offer the kind of hospitality that is rare at hotels, eagerly sharing with you insiders' insights on restaurant finds and shopping bargains along with a common room for mingling with other guests. But at private homes, you may miss some amenities available at even moderately priced hotels. You probably won't have a TV or phone in your room. You may have to share a bathroom. Staying at a B&B inn is closer to a hotel experience and may even include fine dining.

Within this broad spectrum, you may find a gem on your own, but you are better assured of a grand time if you rely on a guidebook or one of the reservation agencies that handles B&Bs. Only about half of the B&Bs are in compliance with all the applicable local and state laws and only about 10% regularly open their doors for inspection to organizations such as the American Automobile Association and the American Bed and Breakfast Association.

You can find a listing of nearly 500 B&Bs in a book, *Inspected, Rated and Approved Bed & Breakfasts and Country Inns,* published by the American Bed & Breakfast Association. Available through bookstores or by calling 800-769-2468, the book is updated annually and costs $17.95 plus $3.50 for shipping. It includes a listing of reservation agencies. They often send free brochures describing members' houses and an application asking for your itinerary, how long you plan to stay and whether you insist on comforts such as air conditioning. Sometimes you can choose your B&B; other times you are assigned to one. The booking agencies may take a week or two to confirm reservations, so plan your trip in advance. Remember: The more the agency knows about what you are looking for and why you are traveling, the better job it can do in matching you with a B&B.

You can find other B&B listings in tour books published by the American Automobile Association and Mobil, as well as *The Innkeepers' Register,* published by the Independent Innkeepers' Association. The book is given as a gift to guests staying at the inns listed, or you can call 800-344-5244 to order it for $12.95, including shipping. The National Network of Bed & Breakfast Agencies (Box 4616, Springfield, Massachusetts 01101) will send you a list of agencies that meet its strict standards. Two agencies specializing in city B&Bs are Urban Ventures, which represents about 700 hosted and unhosted apartments and townhouses in New York City (306 West 38th Street, New York, New York 10018; 212-594-5650), and B&B International, which focuses on San Francisco, the wine country and Monterey and represents 350 properties (800-872-4500).

# Dude Ranches and Farm Vacations

For a moderately priced family vacation, consider a week at one of America's 300 dude ranches. Each can offer a private cabin, three hearty meals a day and a companionable horse for the price of just a room in a big-city hotel. A week at a ranch typically costs $550 to $1,900 per adult — less for children. The ranches are mostly in the open spaces of the West, but the East and South have a sprinkling of smaller spreads.

Many of the ranches still raise cattle for profit and let visiting dudes help round up the herd, brand a steer or lend a hand with chores. But the emphasis is on horseback riding. Ranches offer easy, medium and fast rides, and sometimes real cattle drives. Other activities can include fishing, hiking and swimming. The newest breed of ranches couples conventional resort fare such as tennis with an Old West setting. But the more frills a ranch offers, the more expensive it is likely to be.

To find a dude ranch, write or phone the tourist office in the state or states you would like to visit. For a list of 110 dude ranches in the western U.S. and Canada, send $5 to the Dude Ranchers' Association at P.O. Box 471, Laporte, Colorado 80535. Or call the association at 970-223-8440.

Figuring your budget is simple because the rates are inclusive, though there may be charges for off-property trips, such as rafting excursions. You need add in only your transportation and clothing costs. It can cost less than $150 to outfit you from head to toe for a dude ranch. The biggest and most important investment is cowboy boots. You can buy them for $60 or less if you catch a sale at a western gear store. However, many ranches have boxes of old boots in a variety of sizes that can be lent to their "dudes." You'll also need a couple of pairs of broken-in jeans, flannel shirts and a warm jacket for cool morning or evening rides. Other essentials are a snug straw cowboy hat (about $20) to shield your eyes from the sun and dust, and sunscreen.

On farm vacations, your time is filled with fishing, hayrides and exploring the workings of a farm. These stays are particularly well suited to families. But unlike the dude ranchers, the farm hosts have no central organization that you can call upon for information. Some are listed with B&B reservation agencies; many can be found by contacting state tourism bureaus. Two states with farm-stay programs and brochures that describe the farms and explain how to arrange a stay are Pennsylvania (717-232-8880) and Vermont (802-828-2416).

A warning about farms and dude ranches: Don't expect luxurious rooms and gourmet meals. At all but the most expensive ranches, both rooms and meals are simple.

## Rent-a-Villa Vacations

For a terrific vacation at a bargain price, you can rent apartments or houses in a tropical seaside resort. They offer more privacy — at less cost — than a hotel. For a cold-weather escape into the sunshine, rental apartments can be especially reasonable for a large family or several couples traveling together.

The best places go fast, so it is wise to book two or three months ahead. Hawaii and Mexico have the widest choice of medium-priced houses or condos. For example, on the Hawaiian island of Maui, six people can stay in a three-bedroom, three-bath beach-side condo for $50 a person per day. A luxury hotel nearby easily can cost three times as much.

The Caribbean has much to offer, too. Rents can be fairly low, particularly on Jamaica's north shore. For a three-bedroom house during the winter or spring, prices can be as low as $595 a week — more standard would be $1,200 to $2,000. (Of course, you get more if you pay more.) On Barbados, St. Bart's and St. Martin, for anywhere from $2,500 up to $10,000 per week, you will get a three-bedroom house with a swimming pool and in most cases a full staff — at the very least, daily maid service. The amenities you can expect relative to the price you pay will vary slightly from island to island, as will the government occupancy taxes that you will be charged. Such specifics are important to verify with your travel/rental agent in order to accurately evaluate what is truly good value. During off-peak season, rents are cut nearly in half.

You can find a villa to rent through ads in three magazines, *Travel & Leisure, Town & Country* and *Travel/Holiday.* Or look in such city magazines as *San Diego* or *New York.* But the risks of renting someone's private home sight unseen are obvious.

So the best way to ensure you don't wind up spending a week in a tropical Gulag is to find a villa through a reliable rental agency. Among them are WIMCO (West Indies Management Co., P.O. Box 1461, Newport, Rhode Island 02840; 800-932-3222) for homes in the Caribbean and the South of France; At Home Abroad (405 East 56th Street, Suite 6-H, New York, New York 10022; 212-421-9165), which concentrates on Europe, Mexico and the Caribbean; Creative Leisure International (951 Transport Way, Petaluma, California 94954; 800-426-6367), which specializes in properties in Hawaii, Mexico and the Virgin Islands; and At Home in France (965 Elizabeth Street, San Francisco, California 94114; 415-920-9628).

Agents' fees can be as much as 20%, but usually the cost is built into the rental price. The charge may well be worth it. A responsible agent won't handle a rental unless the owners have hired someone locally to maintain the place and take care of unexpected problems with plumbing, electricity or anything else that goes bump in the night.

Hideaways International (767 Islington Street, Portsmouth, New Hampshire 03801; 800-843-4433 or 603-430-4433 in New Hampshire) is a vacation/travel club that specializes in rental properties in U.S., Caribbean, Mexican and Hawaiian resort areas but also rents apartments and villas all over Europe. You become a member by paying $99 annually, which also gets you two directories and four newsletters a year, with a total of some 2,000 listings; $39 will buy you a four-month trial membership, with a 60-day money-back guarantee. A copy of the 136-page *Hideaways Guide,* guaranteed to make you start packing, is $15. Hideaways also runs ads for weekly vacation-home rentals, as well as yacht charters, and will list your own vacation home for a fee. For example, you'd pay $75 for a 25-word listing in the newsletter and $295 for a new, quarter-page black-and-white listing in the directory.

## Saving by Swapping Homes

Many people would rather swap their children than their homes, but you can cut your holiday costs in half if you are willing to let another family use your house while you use theirs. Thousands of Americans trade homes every year, often with foreign families. For a few weeks, they enjoy comfortable accommodations, often with a car at their disposal. And all that comes without worrying about hotel reservations, restaurant bills and rental cars.

When making exchanges, Americans tend to prefer Europe in the summer. Your chances of cinching a swap are better if you live on Martha's Vineyard rather than in Des Moines. Start searching for a desirable swap at least three months before your scheduled trip. Summer vacation directories become available in January or February.

To find out what is available, join a vacation exchange organization. Get its directories and start writing to the owners whose listings you like. Better yet, start phoning them. You will find descriptions of houses up for exchange in places as diverse as Tasmania and Turkey.

Property owners pore over the directories for a house in the right spot and then negotiate trades with each other. Most clubs give advice on contracts, insurance and other details but otherwise aren't involved in swaps. All allow members to advertise their homes for rent as well as exchange.

The largest of them, Vacation Exchange Club, lists about 15,000 homes in one big directory and four supplements published during the year. For information, contact the club at P.O. Box 650, Key West, Florida 33041; 800-638-3841. About one-third of its listings are in the U.S., Canada, the Caribbean and Mexico; close to two-thirds are in Europe, with a smattering in other countries, including Australia, New Zealand and South Africa. It costs $70 to get all five publications and to list your house in one of them; for $18 more you get a listing with a photo.

A couple of tips: When you find a likely family to swap with, ask for references from people who have exchanged homes with that family in the past. And to avoid any unpleasant surprises, be sure to request a photograph of the interior of the house.

## Time-Shares

A family of four can easily spend more than $2,000 to rent two hotel rooms on the beach for a week during spring break. In the face of this, time-shares offer a seemingly attractive alternative. You pay a one-time fee for the right to go to the same place year after year for a week or two. But if you do not choose carefully, your bargain can become a burden.

More than 1.5 million Americans have been swept up in the vacation time-share boomlet. It began in the mid-1970s, when many builders of resort condominiums adopted the European idea of dividing expensive real estate among many buyers. Developers learned that they could double their profit by selling approximately 50 weekly shares in every apartment. The time-share concept quickly spread to hotels and motels as well as to yachts and campgrounds. Meanwhile, exchange services sprang up that enabled buyers to swap their time-shares in one resort for vacation weeks at another resort. In recent years, Disney, Hilton and Marriott have all built time-share resorts.

Prices of time-share vacation units vary from $5,000 for one week every year in a one-room efficiency unit in New England to nearly $25,000 for a week every year in a luxurious three-bedroom condo at Lake Tahoe. The average cost in the U.S. is $9,500 a week. However, if you buy from an individual owner rather than a resort developer, you may find an ideal condominium for a third or less off the regular price.

During its early, rampant-growth years, the time-share business was known for its fierce competition for customers and high-pressure sales tactics. Today, growth in the U.S. has slowed, and every state except Wyoming has a law governing time-share sales. All those laws include a rescission period, allowing the buyer to change his mind with impunity. Florida, the state with the most time-shares, has the toughest law.

Outside the U.S., the picture is different. Growth is still strong, high-pressure sales tactics are common in some places such as Spain and the Canary Islands, and the industry is not as tightly regulated. Before considering a foreign property, find out what laws protect you and govern the resort. Also, make sure that you're buying a time-share, not just a vacation club membership entitling you only to use of certain properties for a number of years. Club membership can be a gyp if the club doesn't own or hasn't made adequate arrangements to use the properties it is offering to its members. Promises of weeks in Hawaii might entice you to buy a 30-year membership, when the club has secured space in Hawaii for only five years.

Never, ever, buy a time-share on the spot, and be wary of aggressive sales tactics. Take home copies of the proposed contract, the schedule of maintenance fees and the disclosure statement, and study them carefully. Also, ask the salesperson for customer references. It is best to buy from firms already running other resorts. The time-share owners at these locations can tell you how well the developer is meeting his or her obligations. Check the firm's reputation further with the state attorney general's office or, in some states, the special agency that regulates time-share offerings.

Look in the sales contract and other documents for a statement of your rights in the event the resort runs into financial trouble. If you are buying a so-called right-to-use time-share, make sure the contract includes a nondisturbance clause. It obligates the developer's lender to recognize your occupancy rights in case of foreclosure. Ask the lender whether the same clause is in the mortgage or construction loan. If it is not, the clause — and your claim — are worthless.

In the disclosure statement and schedule of maintenance fees, see whether the developer is setting aside a part of the maintenance money for major repairs. If not, you could be socked for heavy special assessments in later years. And have a real estate attorney who is familiar with time-shares review any documents before you sign them. Your own lawyer should be able to refer you to such a specialist. His or her fee for an hour or two of time will be a good investment for you.

If you buy a vacation time-share but later become bored with visiting the same old place, you have two options. The first is to exchange the time you own at your resort for time at another resort. Most resorts have agreements with one of two services that can arrange this trade. They are Resort Condominiums International (3502 Woodview Trace, Indianapolis, Indiana 46268; 800-358-3333) and Interval International (6262 Sunset Drive, Penthouse 1, South Miami, Florida 33143; 800-622-1861). More than a million people exchanged time-shares in 1994. You'll get the best trade if you own a time-share in a popular place at a desirable time of year. There is a charge for swapping, roughly $93 for a transaction within the U.S., Canada and the Caribbean.

The other option when you want to unload your time-share is to sell. But selling the wrong season and the wrong resort may be next to impossible. Time-shares should never be purchased with the hope of selling out at a profit. You're buying future vacation time, not real estate. But it's smart to think about the possibility of having to sell even before you buy.

More and more resort developers are handling resales, and using one of them will be your best option. If your resort developer or manager doesn't offer a resale service, ask for a recommendation. Before you work with any resale brokerage office, ask for referrals and check with the local Better Business Bureau. Never pay an up-front fee of any kind, and don't work with a brokerage that demands such a fee. A reputable brokerage will work on a commission that typically ranges from 12% to 35%. But don't count on selling at anywhere near your purchase price.

So if you are thinking of buying a vacation time-share unit, be sure to satisfy this all-important test: Find a place you will love to be in that same time year after year. Here are some further guidelines to picking the right time-share for you:

- If you buy a time-share unit *in fee simple,* which means you own it outright, brokers recommend you pay no more than 10 times the going rate for a comparable week in a hotel or rental apartment.

- If you buy the *right to use,* which in effect is a lease of 10 to 40 years, then divide the price by the number of years you get to use the property. If the amount is less than the cost of an equivalent rental unit, then the price is right.
- Buy one- or two-bedroom units during the peak season at a popular area. This enhances your chance of swapping, renting or selling.
- Buy in a place that cannot be overbuilt because of geography, local building codes or moratoriums on further time-shares.
- Buy your time-share from an experienced developer. You will be less likely to wind up with poor maintenance, bad management or unforeseen liabilities. Also, big developers are more likely to help you rent or resell your time-share.
- Buy from a resort that has a solid homeowners' association in place. When resorts sell all the available weeks, management is turned over to the owners, who must set up a structure for running the resort. As more U.S. properties mature, the strength of the homeowners' association becomes as crucial as the reputation of the builder.
- Buy in a place that is easy to reach. If it is not, that inconvenience may discourage potential swappers or buyers.
- Buy a time-share because you want a place to take a vacation. If you make the right choice — but only if you make the right choice — you may have the double pleasure of *regular* access to a nice vacation spot.

For a free consumer's guide with information on buying a time-share, write to the American Resort and Residential Development Association, 1220 L Street NW, Suite 510, Washington, D.C. 20005.

## Holding Down Costs of Foreign Travel

The decline in the value of the once mighty dollar may be a tonic for the nation's anemic trade balance, but it sure is tough on American tourists. Foreign travel is devilishly more expensive than a decade ago. Bargains do exist in Portugal, Turkey, Spain and Eastern Europe (though hotel prices are rising rapidly), but Western Europe, for the most part, is not comfortably affordable. In Asia, which is the rising destination, some countries, including Indonesia and Malaysia, offer good values. Japan, though, is one of the costliest countries in the world for Americans. By contrast, Mexico is one of the best values. *A tip:* The most affordable way to see Scandinavia and parts of Northern Europe is by cruise ship, where you avoid the high hotel costs.

To prevent any unexpected blows to your pocketbook, prepare a sensible budget in advance. Before you go, read (or at least skim) one or two up-to-date guidebooks. They will help you arrive at a reasonable estimate of what your trip will cost. At least half a dozen travel newsletters also offer reliable cost information tailored to specific clients, such as retired travelers or singles. You can find out where to subscribe to them from travel agents, ads in travel magazines and your own special-interest groups.

After you have done your homework, sit down and make a daily budget. Add up the estimated costs of hotels, food, tips, taxis and incidentals. Then tack on at least 25% more for the unexpected.

Don't plan to spend the same amount each day. Try the "budget-splurge" method of travel. Cut back on certain days by eating delicatessen take-outs in the park for dinner. Then you can afford a really terrific restaurant the next day.

Prepay as much of your trip as you can before you leave. That avoids budget-busting surprises. And when you plan a trip as far ahead as possible, you can get the lowest airfares and lock in the best deals at the hotels you want. Look for airfare specials months in advance of your travel date and buy your ticket at least 21 days out. For summer travel to popular destinations, book your hotel room three months in advance. Last-minute choices may limit you to high-price rooms, inconvenient locations or dismal lodgings.

Package tours are surely the cheapest way to travel. But some stripped-down tours have more hidden costs than France has churches. Hotel and restaurant managers may ask you to pay extra for items you thought had been taken care of well in advance. You will have a hard time trying to collect when you get back home. Spare yourself grief by inquiring exactly what you are paying for before you leave. (For more, see "Getting Good Value on Package Tours," pages 694–96)

Arrive in a country with about $150 in local currency, which you can acquire at the best exchange rate through Ruesch International, 800-

292-4685. If you want to pay the overnight charge, you can get it in two days; otherwise allow 10. Ruesch will also buy back your unused foreign money for $2 per transaction. Beth Haas, president of the Mid-America Chapter of ASTA, advises her clients who are traveling on tours to have at least $100 in currency for every country they are visiting. By doing so, they avoid wasting time standing in line to exchange money. Plan to pay for your expenses abroad with a combination of traveler's checks, credit cards and cash withdrawn from ATMs. American Express traveler's checks can be cashed for free at American Express overseas travel offices. But banks generally offer the best exchange rates for traveler's checks and cash. Large department stores and some small shops won't pinch you too hard on the exchange rate, but hotels will soak you.

Before departing, call your credit-card company to find out when it begins charging interest on your purchases and whether or not it assesses any conversion or transaction fees or charges made in a foreign currency. Generally, it pays to use credit cards because the transaction is converted into U.S. dollars using a wholesale exchange rate, which is more favorable than even the bank rates. ATMs also give you good value because they, too, use the wholesale exchange rate. Before you go, make sure your PIN will work in foreign countries, find out about limits on cash withdrawals and get a guide to ATM locations abroad. In 1995 Visa introduced another option for payments in the U.S., Britain and Mexico: a money card, the electronic equivalent of a traveler's check.

If you enjoy train travel, one of the world's last real bargains is the Eurailpass. It allows you to travel first class as much as you want in 17 European countries for $498 for 15 days. Children under 12 years old go half-price; under four years old they ride free. If you are 26 years old or younger, Eurail offers a similar second-class package called Youthpass for $398. There is a separate pass for Eastern European countries. Call Rail Europe at 800-438-7245 or 800-848-7245 and buy the pass before you leave. Some trains, such as the high-speed ones, require reservations, which you can make in advance in the U.S. for $10.

Many countries offer their own national passes, some of which (but not all) cost less than the geographically unrestricted Eurailpass. Britain is not covered by the Eurailpass but has its own version, BritRail, which allows an adult 15 days of first-class travel by railroads all over England, Scotland and Wales for $515; standard class is $355. Children ages five through 15 travel for half-fare. Call BritRail at 212-575-2667 for information and reservations.

European trains are usually fast, clean, comfortable — quite superior to most of their American counterparts. Some are also good for stretching out and sleeping in — which is a clever way of saving a bundle on a hotel room every now and then.

For travel in Europe and many other countries around the world, you can also buy airline passes, similar to the Eurailpass. Before you pounce on one of these, such as the Visit Spain Airpass, have your travel agent compare the cost of the pass to individual tickets for your intended route; they might be cheaper.

Just about everywhere, you can save money by avoiding the costly capital cities and trekking off to the provincial centers and the countryside. For example, rural Britain is not only charming but also far less expensive than swinging London. But wherever you decide to go, you might follow the advice of the most savvy and seasoned travelers: Take half of what you plan to pack and twice as much as you have budgeted.

## Traveling Abroad with Children

You do not have to wait until your children have graduated from college to take them on a vacation to Europe. You can go now and take the children with you without breaking the bank at Monte Carlo. The money-saving trick is to stay away from places like the bank at Monte Carlo. Travel with children has become so common that many travel agents specialize in finding the best deals for the family as a whole.

Peter Carry, executive editor of *Sports Illustrated,* who has spent many summers in Europe with his wife and their children, advises that the first rule of international travel with the under-five-foot-tall set is: Don't travel. Rent a house and stay put except for family day trips and the occasional parental overnight. Hauling youngsters from one hotel to another and in and out of restaurants calls for the resources of the Aga Khan and the forbearance of Mother Teresa.

The key part of planning a family trip is finding the rental house. A rental agency will conduct the search for you. Avoid cities and well-known resorts. In a small town or village, your rent is likely to be relatively low, the chances that you will have friendly neighbors is relatively high, and you can absorb local culture that isn't gussied up for tourists.

Beyond rental agencies, comb the classified ads in the Friday edition of the *International Herald Tribune,* available at major newsstands in large cities. The national tourist office of the country you want to visit, its consulate in your area or its embassy in Washington can also point you in the right direction.

Your largest single expense probably will be plane fares. There are ways to hold them — and other costs — down. Check consolidators. Ask about special discounts for children. Sometimes the country where you will be staying is not the one you should fly to. For example, if you are traveling to the south of France, you may be wise to check to see if there is a specially inexpensive New York–London fare, and then pay extra to fly from London to Marseilles. Or you might want to fly to Barcelona because it is often cheaper to rent a car in Spain than in France. A word of caution: You could wipe out your rental car savings if you, your family and luggage won't fit into the rental car and you must make alternate plans.

Regulations on how much luggage you can carry on a transatlantic flight can vary widely from airline to airline, depending upon your destination. Most carriers have a system that limits each passenger to two bags of certain dimensions with a combined maximum weight of 140 pounds, plus carry-on. Ask your travel agent or reservation clerk how much luggage you will be allowed.

Disposable plastic and paper household products are much costlier in Europe than at home. So stuff all your leftover luggage capacity with them if you are renting a home for several weeks. If you are traveling with infants, remember that an army duffel bag can hold more than 200 disposable diapers.

Consider springing for another plane ticket — and bring a baby-sitter along with you. That's right. If you usually have a mother's helper at home or often use baby-sitters, you probably can buy a seat to Europe for the same amount as these services cost. And because there seems to be an endless supply of bright, responsible American teenagers who will baby-sit in exchange for a chance to go to Europe, you need not pay more than expenses. A mother's helper means freedom for mother — and father — to get away, if only for an hour at the local café for coffee and a *digestif.*

If you're visiting London, you can drop off your children at Pippa Pop-Ins (44-171-385-2458), a sleepover hotel for children whose parents want to go out for an adult evening. Though not as widely available abroad as in the U.S., some resorts have programs for child care and activities, and some hotels, such as Hyatt, will "childproof" a room for you, plugging up exposed light sockets, covering the furniture to be "bumpproof," and in a number of cases, providing furniture built to scale for your child's comfort. So when planning your travel, always ask about special accommodations for children.

For grandparents interested in travel with the grandkids, several tour operators offer group trips devoted to such pairings. The companies plan escorted tours to places such as Washington, D.C., Hawaii, and Africa, among many other destinations, for about two dozen grandparents and grandchildren at a time, ensuring that there will be plenty of age-appropriate companions for everyone. Two reliable companies are Grandtravel in Chevy Chase, Maryland (800-247-7651), and Rascals in Paradise in San Francisco (800-U-RASCAL). The latter specializes in family vacations in general.

## Special Values for Seniors

At last I've discovered something good about growing old: You get travel bargains galore. The 50-plus crowd represents about a quarter of the population but controls half of all discretionary income. Travel purveyors are eager to send seniors packing, and they woo them with discounts.

The key to vacationing for less, says Charles Barnard, travel editor of *Modern Maturity,* is to ask for the discount. A 25-year-old hotel clerk may not be able to judge your age and may not wish to risk offending you by suggesting that you're old enough for a senior discount. The proof of seniority that carries the most clout is an AARP card, which anyone age 50 or older can get for $8 by contacting AARP, 202-434-2277. Your driver's license may not qualify you for a discount, no matter how old you are. Occasionally, you must join a separate travel club to get the best discount. For example, Ramada has a $15 lifetime membership in its Best Years Club that gives you a discount of 25%, plus points toward awards; AARP membership alone garners a 15% discount.

Almost all airlines have discounts of 10% for passengers age 62 or older, and usually a companion. You can often find a promotion that offers an even better deal. (If you do get a better deal, ask if you can take your 10% senior discount off *that* price.) Seniors also can buy bulk tickets at considerable discounts. For example, Delta issues senior travel books of four coupons for $596 and eight coupons for $1,032. Each coupon is valid for a one-way coach trip in the continental U.S. Two coupons are needed to go to Hawaii or Alaska. Flying days are unlimited, and the coupons are valid for one year after you buy them. Across the board, hotels, cruise lines, rental-car companies and restaurants offer older travelers discounts that may go as high as 50%.

*A warning:* Prices for tours, cruises and hotel rooms are usually based on double occupancy. If you're traveling alone, you may pay a single supplement — and your fare will range between 110% and 200% of what you would pay if you had a companion. On tours and cruises, you can often qualify for the double occupancy price by agreeing to accept a roommate. A woman is more likely to get a roommate because there are more single women traveling than there are men. A man may get the double-occupancy price without the roommate.

Three respected travel companies that are geared to the older market are Saga, 800-343-0273; Grand Circle, 800-221-2610; and Elderhostel, 617-426-8056. Saga, a British company, has been doing business in the U.S. since 1981. Grand Circle is noted for its extended-stay program, which, for example, offered a 16-day London-Paris tour including airfare from Boston for $1,695, with a London extension available for $295 a week. Elderhostel, which in 1995 lowered its age eligibility to 55, is a nonprofit organization that offers educational travel to universities the world over. Though there are no exams and no grades, participants go to classes and stay in dormitories or similar facilities, while exploring topics as varied as the Civil War, Agatha Christie or Balinese art.

More? You can get a $10 lifetime pass to national parks once you hit 62; at age 70 you'll ski for free at Vermont's Sugarbush; and in San Francisco the $1 fare for public transit is slashed to 35 cents for seniors. Senior discounts change almost as often as hotel rates. *Consumer Reports' Travel Letter* will help keep you up-to-date. A handy reference book is *Unbelievably Good Deals & Great Adventures That You Absolutely Can't Get Unless You're Over 50,* by Joan Rattner Heilman (Contemporary Books, Inc., $8.95).

# How to Survive Customs Inspections

You are just back from a grand trip overseas, and the only obstacle between you and your waiting family is a cold-eyed U.S. customs agent. How can you best survive the inspection of your overstuffed baggage?

Even before they leave home, smart travelers communicate with an office of the U.S. Customs Service and get its leaflets. One is *Know Before You Go.* Among other things, it lists the articles you cannot legally bring home, including fresh flowers, pre-Columbian art and monkeys. The second, *International Mail Imports,* explains regulations about shipping home goods you've bought. You can get these publications and other information by writing to U.S. Customs Service, P.O. Box 7407, Washington, D.C. 20044, or calling 202-927-6724. Be sure to include the name of the leaflet — Customs publishes many others.

A few items are duty-free no matter where they are bought. Among them are original paintings, antiques, and cut and unset diamonds.

In addition to them, each returning traveler, even an infant in diapers, is allowed $400 in duty-free merchandise or $1,200 if you are coming home from the Virgin Islands, Guam or Samoa. A family can pool their allowances. For example, a family of four — Mom, Dad and two children — get a total allowance of $1,600.

Pack your new purchases together and keep receipts handy to tabulate your total and to show inspectors. They are not easily fooled. Customs inspectors have price lists for popular goods such as French perfumes and Scottish woolens. They can spot amateurishly stitched American labels on clothes — a sure sign that somebody bought the garment abroad.

Inspectors are tougher at some gateways than others. The easiest entry into the country is often from Canada, since there is less concern about contraband traffic from the north. The strictest entry points are from the Orient, the Caribbean and South America because that is where drugs originate. So it is small wonder that Honolulu and Miami have a well-earned reputation as the roughest U.S. customs checkpoints. Though 90% of air travelers go through customs in less than 10 minutes — and some in no time at all — a customs inspection in rare cases could delay you as much as a couple of hours. That's all the more reason to leave plenty of time between international and domestic connections.

When you go through customs, you invite suspicion — and a search — if you act nervous or belligerent or carry something bizarre, such as a fur coat in summer. If an examiner finds an item you have not declared, he or she can charge you a fine equal to its U.S. value price. On top of that, the agent can confiscate the item and charge you with a criminal offense.

So the best advice, of course, is to do your homework, keep your bills straight, tell the truth — and if you have overbought your $400 per-person limit, be prepared to pay your duty, which, after all, is only 10% of the amount over limit, up to $1,000. Above that, you pay the rate of duty that applies to each specific item.

## What to Do If Your Baggage Is Lost

The best-laid travel plans can be spoiled if your baggage goes astray on an airline trip. One way to prevent this problem is to carry all your luggage with you on board, as do experienced air travelers pulling their rolling carry-ons. Airlines limit what you can carry with you, so if you must check a suitcase, don't pack anything in it you might need within 24 hours, including pharmaceuticals — or the only copy of your millionaire uncle's will. Above all, don't pack jewelry, expensive cameras or other valuables in your checked luggage. (I've known several people who have lost such items to thieves somewhere in the baggage chain.) For ways to minimize baggage loss, write to the Aviation Consumer Protection Division, Department of Transportation, C-75, Washington, D.C. 20590, and request its free brochure, "Plane Talk."

The reassuring news is that only about 0.5% of all bags are lost, even temporarily, and almost all eventually are found, usually within a few hours. If you cannot locate your bag, your first step is to report the loss to the airline's baggage service representative *immediately;* the bag may still be on the plane you came in on. (That happened to me recently in Madrid — and was I happy that I had insisted that airline personnel search the plane's baggage compartments yet again!)

If a search turns up nothing, you will be given a lost baggage form to fill out. Do not leave the airport without completing and handing in the form — and keep a copy for your records. Get the name and, if possible, the company identification number of the person who collects the form.

(You may need it if the baggage does not turn up and airline officials contend they cannot find your form.) Ask to have your luggage delivered to you if and when it is found.

If you will be bagless overnight, most airlines will give you either a toilet kit or the money to buy one. The airlines are stingier about replacing clothes. Many a weeklong vacation has been hampered, if not ruined, because an airline did not pay for clothes until the vacation was almost over. Even then the carrier might pay only half the cost.

When luggage is lost, the airline is liable for damages, usually up to $1,250 per person on domestic flights and $9.07 a pound on international flights. If your luggage and its contents are worth more than the airline's liability limit, you can buy baggage insurance from your travel agent. Carriers typically charge $2 to $5 for each $100 worth of coverage, up to $5,000. Even so, some airlines may refuse to insure jewelry, cash and breakable items, including antiques and electronic equipment. Keep in mind that most homeowner's or tenant's insurance covers losses above an airline's liability limits (though not for jewelry, unless you have a special policy rider).

Once your bag has been missing for four or five days, you should file a claim form. Extensive dickering over the worth of goods is fairly common. In the end, the airlines usually will reimburse you for your wayward belongings' fair market value, not the replacement cost. The airline will insist on your documenting everything — for expensive items you may need to show receipts of your purchase — and the line won't pay beyond the $1,250 limit. So you stand to collect *less* than the original cost of your property.

Count on waiting six weeks for the payment. If you feel the settlement is unfair, take the matter to small-claims court — before cashing the airline's check. Also, you can complain to the Aviation Consumer Protection Division at the address above.

The major causes of missing bags are mix-ups when they are moved from one place to another, failure to remove old airport tags and theft — usually by someone hanging around the baggage carousel. To avoid loss, always pull old airport tags off a bag before checking it; that prevents confusion about where it is heading. Learn the tag code letters for airports to which you often fly so that you can be sure your bag is properly ticketed. Make sure your name, address and phone number are marked on the outside *and* inside (sometimes tags get ripped off) of any checked luggage. If you do not have baggage tags, the airline will give you stick-on labels. In brief, bright, clear identification is your best guarantee that your bags will get to their destination when you do. And avoid checking expensive luggage; it's an invitation to thieves.

Here are my own rules for avoiding painful loss:

- Carry on as much as you can; check as little as you must. Often, you can carry on more if you go business or first class, or if you hold one of the airline's frequent-flier cards.
- Don't pack jewelry, cameras or other small, easy-to-steal-and-conceal valuables.
- Lock all bags.
- Place identity tags on both the outside and the inside of all checked bags.
- Avoid super-expensive bags or tags that attract a thief's eye. Once I lost a bag between JFK and London's Heathrow that bore a big, bright green tag with the name of the magazine I then worked for: *Money.*

## Protecting Yourself Against Medical Emergencies and Losses

Travel-insurance companies offer a variety of policies that cover trip cancellation due to medical emergencies, as well as offering medical-expense reimbursement and emergency evacuation. Check in advance to see exactly what your own health-insurance policy will cover should you need medical attention while abroad. Often your policy will reimburse you only for what a procedure would typically cost in the U.S., and you will have to make up the difference if it costs more in another country. (A North Atlantic evacuation can cost up to $20,000.)

Two well-known purveyors are Travel Guard International (800-782-5151) and The Travelers Insurance (800-243-3174). Travel Guard offers simple medical insurance for $39 for a trip of one to five days. For approximately 6% of the total cost of your trip, you can buy an all-inclusive policy that includes trip cancellation or interruption, baggage loss, default or bankruptcy insurance (which protects you against loss of the payments you have made if your tour operator goes out of business) and medical assistance (including hospitalization and evacuation) in case of sudden illness or accident. To get reimbursement, it is safest to pay bills abroad with major credit cards, although you should not assume their acceptance. Make sure you obtain the required proof of expenditures; a simple receipt may not be sufficient. Ask the insurance company about its specific requirements.

Vacationers are easy marks for pickpockets and thieves, but you can take steps to make any loss you might suffer less harmful to your holiday. Before you leave home, prepare several lists of all important ID, credit-card and phone numbers. Photocopy key documents, such as your passport and plane tickets. Take all these with you. If you are traveling abroad, also take along extra passport photos and a certified copy of your birth certificate. And leave a second set of copies with someone back home whom you can easily reach.

If your passport is stolen, go immediately to the police and then to a U.S. embassy or consulate. An officer there will ask you to present a police report of the theft and, if possible, to show proof of citizenship — for example, your birth certificate. A photocopy of your passport, or a written record of your passport number, place and date of issuance plus any personal information — exactly as it is written on the document — will also help. You should be able to get a new passport within a day or so. The fee is $65.

If a thief swipes your cash, you can usually have money electronically transferred from your own bank to a nearby bank. If a bank transfer isn't possible and you're in a city with a U.S. embassy or consulate, you can rely on Uncle Sam. Get a friend or colleague to wire money via Western Union to the State Department in Washington, D.C. It will authorize the overseas embassy to give you the cash, less a $15 fee. Most transfers can be completed within 24 hours.

When traveler's checks or credit cards are stolen, report the theft to the issuing companies. If you have your receipt with the traveler's checks' serial numbers, you may be able to get some of your money as fast as you can make it to the company's nearest refund location. Often it is a local bank, travel service, hotel or rental-car agency. Without the serial numbers, your refund could take hours or even days, while the company tries to verify your original purchase.

Credit cards are tougher to replace. Only American Express promises to issue a new card through its local office within 24 hours. Visa and MasterCard often can provide the same service; the time it takes sometimes depends on which bank issued your card.

Losing a plane ticket can be costly. In the U.S., you fill out a Lost Ticket Application (there's typically a $60 to $75 processing fee), then wait several months for a refund to come through. Alas, there may be no refund at all if the stolen ticket is used. And some airlines, including Southwest, treat tickets as cash and don't offer refunds. On the other hand, if you lose your ticket halfway through your travel, you may have to pay only a slight ticket-change fee, or in some cases no fee at all, instead of having to buy a new ticket altogether. Find out before you travel what penalties pertain to your ticket. An international passenger may stand a better chance of receiving a new ticket at little or no added cost because all passengers have to show their passports before boarding.

A new trend, ticketless travel, may ease this problem. With the ticketless system, you charge your tickets and get a reservation number, which you use at the airport to get your boarding pass. If you lose the number, the airline can find your reservation by your name alone. By late 1995 many U.S. airlines were trying the ticketless idea on some of their routes, and United Airlines had it available systemwide.

To find out about special problems in destinations abroad, such as widespread theft or terrorism, contact the State Department at 202-647-5225 or you can access State on many on-line computer services through the OAG Electronic Edition (OAG stands for Official Airline Guide). For the specific pathway for your service, you may call OAG at 800-323-4000.

CHAPTER 21

# Getting the Best in Services

## Long-Distance Phone Service

It's been more than a decade since a federal court decree ended AT&T's monopoly of the nation's telephone service, but old Ma Bell still retains about 60% of Americans' long-distance business. Of its two chief rivals, MCI claims about 20% and Sprint 10%.

What does this competition mean to you? If you live in Chicago and have family in San Diego or abroad, if you travel a lot, or if you own a small business, you can tailor a telephone service plan that will save you serious money.

Basic rates don't differ much among the major providers. They all charge about 80 cents (exclusive of taxes) for a three-minute call from Chicago to San Diego, and about 41 cents for such a call at night. It's their many special long-distance plans that could offer you particular advantages.

With MCI's Friends and Family, for instance, you can get a 25% discount on all calls you make as long as you spend a minimum of $10 a month. If you call other MCI customers in your calling circle, you save 50%. Sprint counters with Sprint Sense. With this plan, state-to-state evening and weekend rates are just 10 cents a minute and peak rates are 22 cents.

Not to be topped, AT&T introduced its True Savings plan for long-distance calls: You get a 25% discount if you spend $10 to $49.99 a month, 30% if you spend $50 or more.

Don't overlook what local long-distance companies — yes, there are such businesses — have to offer. One example is Least Cost Rating, an option offered by Cincinnati Bell Long Distance that serves Ohio, Indiana, Kentucky, western Pennsylvania and the Lower Peninsula of Michigan. Each long-distance call is charged at the lowest rate offered by AT&T, MCI, Sprint, ALLNET and LCI International — a real boon for Cincinnati Bell's clientele of residential and small-business customers.

You're somewhat daunted by the prospect of choosing among all these options? TRAC — Telecommunications Research and Action Center — will send you a chart, updated twice a year, showing the long-distance rates of major carriers and comparing special features such as volume discounts. Send a self-addressed, stamped envelope and $3 for a chart of residential phone service rates, plans and service features of seven carriers and 28 calling plans, or $5 for a chart covering small-business options, to TRAC, P.O. Box 12038, Washington, D.C. 20005 (202-462-2520).

What kind of service can the big companies provide when you're traveling? You're probably familiar with AT&T's Calling Card: You can charge a call to your home phone from almost anywhere in the world just by dialing a local number and giving the operator your Calling Card number (usually based on random digits or a number that you preselect). And AT&T's USA-Direct can help you in 125 countries and territories. You can call a local number and reach a U.S. operator — and get quite a saving on calls to America if you're staying in one of the all too many hotels that add huge surcharges for foreign calls.

Possibly the ultimate for connections at home or abroad is MCI's Friends and Family Personal Number. For $3.95 a month, an MCI customer gives his or her own 800 number to family and friends, who then can call him or her from anywhere in the U.S.; all calls are billed to the 800 customer at 27 cents a minute during business hours or 19 cents a minute off-peak.

AT&T is also offering a 500 personal number that it describes as the "last number you will ever need." By dialing your own 500 number you can program up to three phones to ring in sequence and set call forwarding in approximately 200 countries. In addition you can accept charges from callers whom you provide with your PIN. The service is available only in the lower 48 states and Hawaii. The cost ranges from $1 to $7 a month. (For an additional $5.95 you can add voice mail and call screening.)

The long-distance phone companies certainly aren't neglecting their fellow businesspeople, including those with payrolls a fraction the size of AT&T's. MCI offers "Proof Positive," in which customers always get MCI's lowest rates. Every quarter they receive a statement of what they have saved compared with AT&T's rates, plus recommendations on how to save still more by using various new MCI programs.

To counter MCI, AT&T has its Partners in Business program, offering points to frequent callers, which they can exchange for services such as travel. With the AT&T Small Business Advantage Plus program customers can combine all their business calling — 800, residential, domestic and international direct dialing — into one billing plan. If they bill over $25 a month, they get a 10% discount. The basic fee of $5 a month is waived with $5 in usage. AT&T has other similar programs as well, including its Customnet, which combines all calls that a business makes — local, long-distance and international — into one bill for a volume discount. The program also gives a 10% discount on calls to the U.S. area code dialed most and on international calls to the two countries called most often.

Finally, Sprint's The Most for Business plan guarantees its small-business customers prices at least 20% lower than AT&T's direct-dial rates.

There's hardly a field covered in this guide to personal finance — with perhaps the exception of airline fares — where the competition is fiercer or the options for customers more numerous, and more likely to change literally from week to week. Not to speak of the extra goodies: You might find a frequent-caller program that offers you discounts on car rentals or has a tie-in with one of your credit cards. But keep your head. Whether you're shopping for phone service for your home or for your business, first determine what you need and then look for a company that will give you exactly that. Chances are these days you'll soon find what you're looking for.

## Package Delivery Services

Sending a package overnight to almost any city in the country, and many outside the country, is a cinch these days. Several delivery services do the job — but which does it best?

Among the overnight package couriers, probably the most esteemed is Federal Express. It has been in the business since 1973 and gained fame offering next-day delivery domestically before 10:30 A.M. FedEx recently lost by a hair to United Parcel Service as the company with the widest reach. Big Brown, the longtime ground deliverer, boasts overnight air service to every address in the United States, including Puerto Rico. Federal Express claims it serves areas containing 99% of the population. There are two other major companies: Airborne Express and Emery Worldwide.

The U.S. Postal Service is also in the race. It will take up to 70 pounds overnight between major markets. Like the commercial services, the postal people will make a special trip to pick up your package. But if your letter carrier works out of an Express Mail post office, you can leave a package in your mailbox stamped and ready for pickup.

Prices vary greatly for the overnight delivery of, say, a two-pound package from New York to Los Angeles. The U.S. Postal Service charges $15. United Parcel Service charges $16.75 for same-day pickup and next-day delivery. Federal Express charges $24.25 if the company picks up the package from you, or $21.75 if you drop it off yourself. Emery Worldwide, specializing in business-to-business deliveries and heavy packages, charges $25, including pickup and delivery, while Airborne Express charges $14.50. But if you are willing to have the same package delivered within *two* days of pickup, Airborne Express offers the best value: $9.

All of these services offer delivery of lighter-weight letter packages for lower fees than their two-pound rates, though these vary by company as well. And many also provide delivery service overseas. For delivery of an eight-ounce document package holding up to 30 sheets of paper, prices for next-day delivery are: Federal Express, $15.50 if they pick it up, $13 if you drop if off; UPS $9.50 if you drop it off and $14.25 if they pick it up; Emery Worldwide, $25 — $17.50 extra if they pick it up and another $17.50 if they are delivering to a residence; and Airborne Express, $14 including pickup and delivery. Express Mail charges $10.75 for overnight delivery between major markets. Smaller markets take two days. Of those companies, only Federal Express also provides next-day service from New York to London, at no additional cost.

Whatever service you choose, if you are sending a package to some out-of-the-way place, you may have to pay an additional fee. Post offices and delivery-service agents can tell you whether a town is on their regular rate list. Even so, it is wise to phone the person on the receiving end and find out whether one courier seems more reliable than others in his or her area.

## SERVICE WORKERS FOR YOUR HOME

# Plumbers

Every householder needs a list of good servicemen, and the best way to avoid panic is to have them lined up before you need them. For example, don't wait for your pipes to burst before you start looking for a reliable, affordable plumber.

When checking a plumber's reputation, ask how quickly he responds to emergencies, if he can be reached at night and on weekends and, of course, how much he charges. But how do you find the name of a plumber to check out? If asking your neighbors does not turn up a satisfactory specialist, try the local affiliate of the National Association of Plumbing-Heating-Cooling Contractors (180 South Washington Street, Falls Church, Virginia 22046). It has offices in 47 states, and sometimes it is listed in the phone book as the Plumbing-Heating-Cooling Contractors Association. Most members are licensed and covered by liability insurance and workers' compensation. Their records probably will be fairly clear of complaints. The association's local affiliates often work with city agencies to resolve disputes that arise over a plumber's work or charges. You pay less if you use an unlicensed, unaffiliated plumber, but if something goes wrong, you are more likely to be stuck.

So-called master plumbers are the most seasoned and best trained and can handle the toughest assignments. They have at least five to 10 years' experience and must pass a state exam. When you have a major job, the master plumber gets the appropriate building department permit. He also hires the apprentices and journeymen who do simpler repairs and installations, and he is responsible if anything goes wrong.

You also may locate reputable plumbers by calling the United Association of Journeymen and Apprentices of the Plumbing and Pipe Fitting Industry of the U.S. and Canada. In plain English, that is the plumbers' union, and it is probably listed in your telephone book under "Plumbers and Pipe Fitters Local Union." The voice on the phone line will not recommend a specific plumber but will give you names of contractors who do use union plumbers.

Still another source is the building or plumbing inspection department at city hall. Inspectors see the work of every plumber in town, so they know good craftsmanship firsthand. If they do not want to recommend a plumber, at least they will give you an opinion about any whose names you have.

What can you expect to pay a reliable plumber? You have probably heard the old story of the brain surgeon who calls in a plumber to fix a leaky faucet. The plumber tinkers around for a few minutes and then announces, "That'll be $50."

"Heavens!" exclaims the customer. "I'm a brain surgeon, and I don't get $50 for a few minutes' work."

"Neither did I," says the plumber, "when I was a brain surgeon."

Plumbers have a well-earned reputation for high prices. Expect to pay between $21 and $55 an hour — and more than that at night and on weekends. That range can be deceptive; often it applies to plumbers' travel time as well as the time they spend on the job. And rather than raise their already steep hourly rates to cover increases in the cost of insurance and their other expenses, many plumbers choose the artifice of a so-called cartage charge of $2 to $3 tacked onto the bill for each visit. Not surprisingly, the prices are highest on the East and West Coasts and lowest in the South and Midwest, notably in rural areas.

You will not be able to negotiate the price on an emergency repair job. But if you have work that can be planned in advance, you should get bids from several contractors. Plumbing is highly competitive, and you would be surprised how much the bids differ.

Some people try to save money by buying parts for their plumber. That makes no sense. You will have to buy at retail, and plumbers buy at wholesale. You will not save any money, but you will run the risk of buying the wrong parts.

Do not assume all plumbing repairs require a plumber. There are many jobs you can tackle yourself. Anyone mechanically inclined can patch small leaks, warm frozen pipes, unclog drains, repair faucet drips and replace ceramic tiles. But beware of getting in over your head. A workman who did was cleaning the filters in a Cincinnati winery one December when he accidentally knocked open a water valve connected with the vats of wine. The rising pressure of fermenting wine caused a backflow into the municipal water system. The resulting Christmas present for the people of Cincinnati: sparkling Burgundy on tap, somewhat diluted.

## Home Entertainment Repairers

Getting your television set, VCR or stereo repaired need not be as suspenseful or traumatic as an episode from *As the World Turns.* Well-trained repairers abound, and here are some tips for finding a reasonably priced one.

Although TV sets are generally sturdy, they probably will malfunction at least once during their average 10-year life span. If your set's problem is covered by a warranty, it must be repaired by one of the manufacturer's authorized service dealers. Their addresses usually come with the TV. A relatively small percentage of TVs need repairs during standard manufacturer warranty periods, which are generally 90 days for labor, one year for parts and two years for the picture tube.

The question remains: What to do when the warranty runs out? More and more dealers are offering their customers the option of buying service contracts, or performance guarantees, which extend significantly beyond the life of the manufacturer's warranty. For example, American TV of Madison, Wisconsin (414-521-1002) sells to its walk-in and mail-order customers extended warranties underwritten by American Bankers Insurance. Service can be obtained from any service center in the U.S. For a five-year carry-in service contract covering all parts and labor, prices are: $69.95 for a 27-inch television, $59.95 for a VCR, $69.95 for a mid-priced ($500–$800) stereo. Chuck Bergen of American TV strongly encourages his customers to buy extended service contracts on their home entertainment purchases, especially stereos and VCRs, which have many delicate moving parts that may break down before their time. He says that the cost of the service contract will, in most cases, equal the cost of one service call.

Of course, if nothing goes wrong with the appliance during the period of the service contract, you're out the extra money. In this era of rapid technological advancement, consumers often prefer to replace a faulty or outdated appliance rather than invest one-third to one-half of the cost in an extended service contract. After all, large-screen TVs will continue to deliver bigger and better video images.

If you feel that you must buy a service contract, the best time is a year or two after your purchase — once the warranty has run out and you have some idea of potential repair problems. Check newspaper ads for discounts that manufacturers sometimes offer. Be wary of contracts that are not sold by manufacturers or well-regulated dealers. As one executive in the service contract trade warns, it is a fly-by-night business.

Even if your warranty has expired, it is wise to use an authorized dealer for repairs because he or she will stock parts for your set and will have experience in fixing appliances like yours. You can find authorized dealers in the Yellow Pages under "Television and Radio — Service and Repair." If you cannot locate an authorized service dealer, make sure the repairer you choose has a place of business, not just a truck and a phone number. Some elusive operators pick up your equipment and are never heard from again.

Membership in groups such as the International Society of Certified Electronics Technicians and its affiliate, the National Electronics Sales and Service Dealers Association, provides some evidence that the repairer is competent, as well as interested in maintaining a reputation for reliability. If possible, take your TV, stereo or VCR to the repair shop to save on the house-call service charge. Ask for a written estimate of costs in advance.

When a repairer finishes work, he or she should give you an itemized bill that guarantees the work for at least 30 days. He or she should also return to you all parts that have been replaced, except the picture tube.

Above all, do not try to repair your TV yourself. For one thing, opening the back of your set can be dangerous because color picture tubes release electrical voltage for hours after the set has been unplugged.

# Domestics

With the proliferation of two-income couples, more and more people find that they can afford — and in many cases absolutely need — household help. But how can you find and screen good applicants for domestic jobs?

First of all, recognize that you will have to pay a lot. Full-time domestics in big cities earn $500 to $800 a week. New York City's Pavillion Agency has placed several nannies who earn more than $1,200 a week. Day workers are paid $80 to $120 for an eight-hour day, depending on their experience.

One reason for the relatively high wage is the shortage of domestics. Their numbers decreased by almost 50% in the decade of the 1970s alone.

The best sources for candidates are newspaper ads, friends who have household help and employment agencies that specialize in domestic workers. The agencies will charge you a fee ranging from $2,100 to $3,500, or a sum equal to four and one-third weeks' pay for the person you hire, and their workers tend to command top dollar. You can also ask at churches, colleges and senior citizens' centers for names of people looking for part-time or full-time employment.

If you advertise for help, try the small ethnic newspapers such as Chicago's *Polish Daily News* or New York City's *Irish Echo,* as well as the large metropolitan dailies. If you live in a big urban area and are looking for a live-in baby-sitter, consider advertising in small-town newspapers. Many young women and, in growing numbers, men are eager to spend a year or so in an exciting city but want to live in a secure household.

Whether you locate applicants yourself or get them through an agency, take the time to interview them thoroughly. Rely on your common sense and intuition, but also be sure to check references meticulously. That's the only way you can guard against hiring a thief. Call three former employers and ask pointed questions such as: Did you like her personality? Did she often skip work? How was she with children? And, most important, do you have any reason to doubt this person's honesty?

Once you hire a person on a regular basis, you will have to pay her or his Social Security and other taxes. The procedures you must follow, and the forms you must fill out, are maddeningly complex. But you had better do so, as any number of frustrated would-be appointees to high government office can warn you. The paperwork is so complicated, however, that you would be wise to turn it over to your accountant to execute.

# Caterers

Entertaining can be draining, but if you are thinking of having a party, you can save time and trouble by having a catered affair. But how do you keep the price within bounds?

It pays to bear in mind that small parties cost more per person than large ones with the same menu. A catered meal at home for fewer than 25 people approaches and occasionally surpasses restaurant prices. In New York City, a trendy dinner at home for 12 could run up to $1,000, plus an additional $300 for three people to help serve; liquor and wine would be extra. So if your group is smaller than a couple of dozen, a restaurant might be cheaper.

Still, it is possible to treat yourself to the luxury of a catered affair without paying luxury prices. Shun large caterers and those that emphasize exotic foods. They can charge $85 a person for food alone, although a recent rise in do-it-yourself entertaining caused many to drop or agree to negotiate their prices. Depending on the menu and the number of guests, the national average is $30 a head for dinner. You would do well to seek out small caterers or those new to the business. They often give far better service at lower prices. And look for catering firms that will prepare dishes you can heat and serve yourself.

Beware of caterers who operate out of their homes; in many cases they will be in violation of health codes. And don't rent china, silver or linen. You could pay about $10 to $20 a setting. You are better off borrowing, or even buying, your own.

Another way to pare costs is to get by with less help, particularly those bartenders and waiters who collect $80 to $120 for an evening's work. Instead of the caterer's workers, waitresses or bartenders, enlist some college students or neighborhood teenagers who serve for half as much.

Don't let caterers provide drinks or setups. The markups on them are intoxicating, so buy your own — unless, of course, your caterer can purchase liquor at a discount through a wholesaler, in which case you may be able to save a few dollars. And if you want music or live entertainment, you can save a lot when you hire talented students from a local college or music conservatory to do the playing.

Cocktail parties, of course, are cheaper than fancy dinners. You also can lower food costs by scheduling your cocktail party for a time when people tend to be less ravenous. Guests may only nibble at the hors d'oeuvres at an open house scheduled on a weekend from 3 P.M. to 5 P.M., but a reception from 6 P.M. to 8 P.M. substitutes for dinner for many party-goers. Caterers estimate that most guests will average two drinks at a two-hour party.

Wedding receptions introduce special expenses. Mary Dearborn of New York City's Restaurant Associates says that for 100 guests, a wedding cake might add $300 to $1,200. Champagne for a toast could mean at least 20 bottles — at a total cost of $150 to $600 or even more, depending on the quality of the champagne. Again, if possible, try to pay wholesale rather than retail prices.

The Yellow Pages list columns of caterers. Still, the best way to find one is to ask people who have used caterers in the past. If you work for a company, check with the person there who arranges corporate entertainment. Sometimes officers of churches, synagogues and fraternal organizations, as well as restored-home associations, also know the reputations of local firms that cater parties in their halls.

Once you have gathered a few recommendations, call and get a price estimate from each firm. Before you telephone, figure out what you can spend, and then try to get the best value for your dollar.

Ask any caterer you are considering if you may observe — at a discreet distance — a party he or she has arranged. Most caterers will agree and also let you sample the food. Once you have chosen a firm, be prepared to sign a contract that protects both sides from surprises. For instance, taxes and tips are rarely included in the quoted food price. And the cancellation policy should be clearly stated. Once you have signed the contract, count on paying a deposit of up to 50%, with the balance due immediately before or after the party.

Book at least a month in advance for a cocktail party, and at least several months for a large wedding. You would be wise to call even earlier for a date in May, June, November or December — they are the peak seasons.

If you must cancel, call the caterer immediately. Weddings are generally nonrefundable — that's another inducement for the bride and groom to show up for the ceremony. But with enough notice, many caterers will return part or all of your deposit for a cocktail or dinner party in the hope that you will reschedule and call them again.

# Appraisers

Are you buying insurance to cover your jewelry or silverware? Are you buying or selling or refinancing your house? You will probably need a knowledgeable and reliable professional appraiser to certify its value.

If you're looking for, say, a real estate appraiser, ask your banker, lawyer or insurance agent for recommendations. Get the names of several candidates and then call each one. Ask each about his or her background and fees. Find out if he or she belongs to one of several appraisal associations. They include the Appraisal Institute, the American Society of Appraisers and the National Association of Independent Fee Appraisers. Members tend to be trustworthy and experienced because each of these organizations subscribes to the Uniform Standards of Professional Appraisal Practice defined by the Appraisal Foundation. That is important because few states license real estate appraisers.

A real estate appraisal fee will vary, depending on the size and condition of your house and on how long it takes to compare your property with others in the neighborhood. The cost also differs by region. The average cost of a residential property appraisal in the New York metropolitan area is $550. In other areas you might pay $350 or even less.

For personal property appraisers, once again seek advice from your banker, lawyer or insurance agent; museum curators also can suggest names. The two major associations are the American Society of Appraisers (800-272-8258) and the Appraisers Association of America (212-889-5404). Both can refer you to gem or jewelry appraisers in your area that are members of their organizations.

Appraisers use two measures to establish the value of your possessions. One is the *replacement cost,* which is what you would have to pay to replace the item. Usually you insure the property for the replacement cost. Then there is *fair market value* — it's the price a willing buyer would pay to a willing seller.

The fair market value is used for settling an estate, dividing property for a divorce or donating a work of art for a tax deduction. It is usually only half the replacement cost. That is because a dealer's markup is often 100%. An appraiser might tell you to insure a Chippendale highboy for $10,000 because it would cost that much to replace one. But if you wanted to sell the highboy, a dealer might pay you only $5,000.

An appraisal must be precise and explicit to back up an insurance or tax-loss claim. For jewelry, it should note the size and weight of stones and their settings, as well as clarity, purity and color. Art and antiques should be evaluated for age, condition and any special factors, such as rarity.

Whenever you hire an appraiser, you should engage only one who charges by the hour, by the day or by the job. Most professionals believe that it is unethical to base fees on a percentage of the value of your goods, since there is an obvious temptation to overstate their worth. You also should avoid anyone who offers to appraise your belongings and buy them too. In that case, the appraiser may deliberately underestimate.

The cost of a personal property appraisal depends on how long the job takes, which can be from less than one hour to several days. For simple pieces of jewelry, you may pay $50 to $250 an hour. Even gemologists who are not certified appraisers can charge up to $150 an hour.

When a personal property appraiser comes to your house to evaluate your furniture, silverware and other property for insurance purposes, he or she will check each item's condition. He or she may also photograph your valuables. If not, you should take photos yourself, including close-ups of any significant details.

Keep your appraisals current. The prices of jewelry, antiques and other collectibles fluctuate so sharply that you should have your insurance appraisals updated every two years. Send one copy of your appraisal to your insurance agent. Hold all other copies and photographs of your belongings in a safe-deposit box or in your lawyer's office or another place that is fireproof and theftproof. One appraiser tells of a client who stored in his dining room sideboard a list of the values and locations of his most prized possessions. A thief found the list and neatly checked off the items as he loaded them aboard his truck. He then scrawled on the list, "Thanks for the appraisal." It was just about the only thing he left behind.

# Home Movers

Ever since the Exodus, the act of moving from one place to another has been among life's most stressful events, yet you can avoid the three major hassles of modern moving: delay, damage and overcharging.

How do you find a good mover? Ask friends and co-workers who have moved recently, or your real estate agent or the person who arranges transfers at your company. Consider hiring only those firms that conform to government-regulated standards. If you are relocating to another state, your moving company should be certified by the Interstate Commerce Commission. If you are moving within the same city or state, choose a firm authorized by the appropriate state regulatory agency, usually the Public Utilities Commission or the state Department of Transportation.

Also check the reputation of the moving company's local agent, because that's who you will be dealing with. Call your local Better Business Bureau or consumer-protection agency and ask whether complaints have been filed against the agent. Avoid any agent against whom 10 major complaints have been lodged over the past year.

Then solicit and compare written bids from several reputable agents. Make sure the bids include charges for extras, of which there are many. For example, if the movers do the packing, figure on paying up to $37 a box. Carefully read the mover's contract, or bill of lading, before you sign. The contract should include the total cost of the move, an inventory of goods to be shipped, the amount of liability insurance and the pickup and delivery dates you and the mover have agreed on.

Some movers "lowball" their bids by underestimating the weight of a shipment just to land a job. You can protect yourself by getting a "binding estimate," which guarantees that the mover charges you whatever he agrees to charge you. So it pays to solicit several estimates. It also pays to read the Interstate Commerce Commission's booklet *When You Move: Your Rights and Responsibilities.* Your mover is required by law to give you this booklet. If he doesn't, you can get a free copy by writing to the ICC, Office of Compliance and Enforcement, Room 4133, 12th Street and Constitution Avenue NW, Washington, D.C. 20423 or by calling the ICC at 202-927-5520.

Before the move, make an inventory of your possessions, then check them off one by one as they go into the van. When the movers unload the truck at your new house, unpack dishes and other breakables right away. Note any damages on your inventory list and give one copy to the driver of the van. If the move went well, you probably will want to tip the driver and crew members $10 to $20 each.

If there are damages and you are not satisfied with the mover's offer to repair or replace your damaged goods, look at your contract to see if the company has an informal dispute-resolution system. If you still have questions, call your local branch of the American Arbitration Association, or write to the organization at 140 West 51st Street, New York, New York 10020-1203.

Many movers are reluctant to handle small shipments at all or will charge you as much as $2,000 to do so. One exception is Bekins Van Lines in Hillside, Illinois. It welcomes shipments as small as 300 pounds or 45 cubic feet through its "Bekins-Lite" program. Bekins charges from $200 to $500 for these small shipments anywhere in the continental U.S.; distance determines the exact fee. There are no special packing requirements to get the low rate. If you are shipping breakables, you can pack them yourself or pay the movers to pack for you. One warning about small shipments: They may have to wait for other shipments to fill the van.

## Help When You Relocate

Moving to a new city can be made considerably easier if you use some of the many sources of help. However, you will have to do a fair amount of letter writing, library reading and talking to strangers. And eventually you should visit the place where you think you would like to live.

Anyone contemplating a move would do well to read *Places Rated Almanac* (Macmillan Travel, $20). This useful book compares the climates, crime rates, housing, education, recreation, arts, economic conditions and transportation systems, among many other things, in 343 metropolitan areas. The Bette R. Malone Relocation Service of United Van Lines has free fact sheets, each of which describes any one of 7,000 U.S. and foreign cities. Just call your local United Van Lines agent and he or she will send you the sheets on the cities that interest you. *The Book of the States,* which you can find in most libraries, gives you the tax rates of each state, county and municipality. The local chamber of commerce, of course, is another source of information.

To get a feel for life in a community, subscribe to local newspapers and city or state magazines and talk to people who live there. You can come closest to experiencing life in a strange city by visiting or becoming a paying guest of someone in town. One way is to seek commercial bed-and-breakfast accommodations in private homes.

Once you arrive, walk through the neighborhoods. A stroll past shuttered shops on Main Street and in nearby malls may tell you more about the state of the economy than any chamber of commerce brochure. Seek out real estate agents. They know the virtues of various neighborhoods, and they are willing to spend a lot of time with serious sales prospects.

## When Your Employer Asks You to Relocate

So your employer has asked you to move to another job in another city. Resist saying yes immediately. Instead, find out precisely what's being offered to you — and not just in terms of moving benefits. It is easy to underestimate the adjustment that a move will require. You need to know three things, says Professor Eugene Jennings, formerly of Michigan State University and an authority on relocation.

First, the precise nature of your new assignment. Who, for example, will you be reporting to? Bad chemistry could more than wipe out any points you win by agreeing to relocate.

Second, your new compensation. A raise is the most sincere expression by your bosses that they really want you for this post.

Third, the opportunities for advancement that the new job will open up. The chance to make the first leap up the corporate ladder may come only once or twice in a career. Is the job being dangled before you such an opportunity?

The most serious portion of your analysis consists of exploring the possibilities with your family. If you have a two-career family, you will have to consider the job implications for your partner. You will, of course, want to look at the figures to see how the move would affect the family budget, both for the short and long haul. The company probably will cover the immediate costs of moving. But it may not be willing to cover the difference in housing prices here and there. Your children may also be less than delighted with their prospects. To keep a move from being a childhood trauma, consult with your kids from the start.

# Finding a Good Lawyer

Whether you are buying a house, making a will or filing a suit, sooner or later you will need a lawyer. Discovering the right attorney at the right price can be a trial.

You are probably better off not to search in one of the large, wood-paneled law firms. Most of those partnerships specialize in corporate work, and even if their members agree to defend you in traffic court, the meter could start ticking at $100 an hour, or considerably more. Some large firms are willing to recommend clients to young lawyers who have left the firm to start their own practice — usually at a lower cost. You could also scout for a general practitioner in a moderate-size firm that handles personal and small-business affairs.

To locate one, the best advice is old-fashioned: Ask people whose judgment you trust, such as your banker, insurance agent or a member of your company's legal department. Make sure that the recommended attorneys have dealt with cases similar to yours. Your neighbor may have had a Perry Mason for his auto accident case, but that is probably not the right lawyer for your landlord-tenant dispute.

If you want more recommendations, try your state or local bar association's lawyer-referral service. The number is listed in the Yellow Pages. The referral service will give you the next name up on a list of participating attorneys. The trouble is, quality can vary widely. Some bar associations add the name of any attorney who wants to be included; others charge a fee or require only a minimum amount of experience. So ask the service what screening procedures are used. Also explain what kind of legal help you need, since many services break down their lists by specialties.

You can check the background of almost any attorney by consulting *The Martindale-Hubbell Law Directory,* available at most large public libraries. It describes the lawyers in your community and their educations. Sometimes it also gives evaluations by judges and fellow attorneys. If you need a foreign lawyer — to settle a relative's estate, for instance — write to the Overseas Citizens Services at the Department of State, Room 4817, 2201 C Street NW, Washington, D.C. 20520, or call 202-647-3666.

Lawyers typically charge $50 to $100 for an initial consultation, but many waive the fee if they do not take the case. Do not be shy about inquiring how much time and money your case will cost. Most attorneys charge by the hour; ask for an optimistic and a pessimistic price estimate.

For routine procedures, a lawyer may charge a flat rate — say, $75 to as much as $700 for a simple will. For personal injury and damage cases, you might pay a contingency fee ranging from 25% to 40% of the amount finally collected, depending on how much work is required of your lawyer. Real estate closings are often charged as a percentage of the sales price or mortgage, typically 0.5% to 1%. Remember that the fee is only one factor. Some of the least expensive advice can be as sound as the costliest. But $150 an hour for a tough, experienced specialist may be well spent — if you stand to lose heavily in a property settlement or child-custody battle.

When your problem is relatively simple, you might turn to a cut-rate legal clinic for no-frills assistance. But even clinics offer low prices only on high-volume procedures, such as wills. Handling extras might be charged by the hour — at $75 per hour in some cases.

In shopping malls and storefronts, legal clinics are springing up. A customer who knows what legal clinics can and cannot do, and follows a few simple rules in dealing with them, usually can get a genuine bargain. Legal clinics generally work on routine personal law problems: uncontested divorces, simple wills, real estate closings, bankruptcies, uncomplicated personal injury suits, traffic violations and similar situations. Unlike traditional law firms, the clinics often advertise, and this generates high volume. Since most of the cases are similar, secretaries and paralegals can do the bulk of the paperwork with standardized forms. This lets the clinic's lawyers handle more clients more quickly. Another good alternative is legal assistance offered by law-school law clinics. These clinics are topic- or group-specific, such as Brooklyn Law School's Legal Services Corporation — Senior Citizen Law Office. It offers students supervised by law professors.

Prices at clinics can be much less than those at traditional law firms. For example, at any of the 10 Minnesota Dial Lawyer Network offices in the Minneapolis–St. Paul area, an uncontested divorce starts at around $500 and a simple will at $120. Old-line law firms in the area charge some $150 to $300 an hour and $250 to $800 for uncontested divorces. In general, the fees of conventional lawyers are three or four times greater than those of clinics. Most clinics are open on evenings and weekends, so they also offer convenience. And most get good marks for competence. Yvonne Weight, a Virginia attorney who studied the discounters for three years as a member of a state bar disciplinary committee, says, "I don't recall a single neglect-of-legal-matter case on the part of clinic lawyers. They're efficient. They get their paperwork done." But she gives them lower marks for courtroom work.

Clinic lawyers did even better in a study by the University of Miami's Law and Economics Center. It found that 22 clients of California's Jacoby & Meyers clinics got cheaper, faster and better deals than 52 clients of more traditional Los Angeles law firms.

To locate clinic-style practices, consult the Yellow Pages for ads of law firms that list several offices and boast of low or flat fees for routine services. Then call around to comparison-shop. Unlike many traditional law firms, legal clinics usually will quote fees over the phone. Check out the firm by going in for a quick consultation — usually about $35 for half an hour or so.

Of course, not every clinic delivers high quality for its discount rates. You would be wise to get a referral from someone who has used the clinic. Also check that your case fits into the limitations of the clinic's practice and ask for an estimate of the probable fee.

Another way to save is to use a prepaid legal plan — the legal profession's version of a health maintenance organization. About 95% of the people enrolled in these plans gain membership through a larger organization, like a union. Often a lawyer provides certain basic services free to the members of the group. For more complex problems, the lawyer gives members a 25% discount. Individuals can also join and, by paying a fixed premium, receive basic services for the entire family. The American Bar Association has strongly endorsed the idea, and quite a number of firms offer plans. Prepaid plans can be fine for simple legal matters. A landlord who refused to return the security deposit on an apartment, for example, might change his or her mind if he or she received a letter written by a lawyer on your behalf. Or say your new car turns out to be a lemon. A prepaid service lawyer can help you get the manufacturer to make good on the warranty.

Complex problems such as a liability suit, contested divorce, bankruptcy or sophisticated mortgage arrangement may not be fully covered by prepaid packages. Also, the plans rarely cover court appearances. To make sure a plan suits you, you have to shop warily. Prepaid legal programs differ widely in their range of services. For example, one with a broad reach is Lawphone (4501 Forbes Boulevard, Lanham, Maryland 20706; 800-255-3352). It has member law firms in all 50 states, the District of Columbia, Puerto Rico and Canada. A one-year family membership costs $132 and includes phone consultations, review or preparation of simple documents (including a simple will) and follow-up phone calls and letters on the client's behalf. If court representation is needed, Lawphone has contracted with thousands of private attorneys to give discounts of 25%. Lawphone is available directly to the public as well as through trade and professional associations. Sometimes you may get it as an employee benefit.

If you belong to any organization with at least 200 members in the same location, you may be able to organize your own free legal service plan. A brochure titled "Free Legal Service Plans" can help you get started. Send a stamped, self-addressed envelope to the National Resource Center for Consumers of Legal Services, P.O. Box 340, Gloucester, Virginia, 23061. The center will also send a list of programs in your state that you can join as an individual. Prepaid legal service plans are now available in every state. California has several dozen, many of them small. In other states, including Colorado, New York and Pennsylvania, you can choose from up to 10 services. Usually you have a choice of four to six.

# Settling Out of Court

Americans seem to sue by reflex action when they believe they have been wronged. Yet, as Abraham Lincoln once noted, "The nominal winner is often a real loser — in fees, expenses and waste of time."

When your impulse is to sue, you don't necessarily have to go to court and tell it to a judge. There are better ways to settle legal disputes. For example, you can rent a judge who is sometimes called a "dispute resolver." Or you can go to a so-called dispute mediation center to adjudicate a quarrel. Such innovations are cheaper, faster and simpler than traditional litigation. Basically, they offer third-party mediation — help in resolving differences.

The best-known alternative to going to court is the American Arbitration Association. Its 35 regional offices handle more than 59,000 cases a year. People who seek arbitration submit their dispute to an impartial third party for a final and binding decision.

An increasingly popular device for business people to settle their fights out of court is the mini-trial. Representatives of two disputing companies argue out their case before top executives of both of those companies. If they then cannot reach a compromise, they bring in a third party to help, often a retired judge.

Similar procedures also are well suited for disputes involving, say, a homeowner and a contractor over faulty bathroom plumbing; or the owner of a wrecked auto who is claiming more damages than an insurance company is willing to pay. They hire a retired judge — and often he or she can sit down with both sides and work out a settlement in an afternoon. The fee might run $300 to $4,000, depending on the type of dispute and size of the claim.

The savings are not only in money but also in damage to the disputants' feelings. An added benefit of resolving a case out of court is privacy. So is the fact that the remedy can be flexible, shaped by the plaintiff, the defendant and the dispute resolver. Although courts award money damages, they generally cannot order a contractor to fix a leaky roof.

Most out-of-court settlements involve mediation — that is, an attempt by the persons involved to resolve their dispute with the aid of a neutral third person. The savings can be large. For instance, in Denver, a mediated divorce case with no legal counsel usually costs about $1,200 for a settlement agreement. A court divorce involving lawyers could run well into the thousands for each side. Many of the divorce mediators around the country are lawyers with training in mediation.

To handle everyday disputes such as neighbor-against-neighbor and landlord-tenant disagreements, more than 350 mediation centers have popped up in all 50 states. They are sometimes called neighborhood justice centers, and they are usually state-supported. Not only are they fast, informal and effective, but they also charge nothing to iron out such problems as dogfights, broken windows and loud stereos.

For consumer complaints, state or local courts that hear small-claims cases often serve you well. The maximum claims range from $300 in Arkansas to $25,000 in Georgia. These courts are supposed to be simple, straightforward and designed to make it easier for you to get justice, perhaps even without hiring an attorney. But because most states allow lawyers to represent either side, you might find that your opponent has hired one who outclasses you or ties you up in costly appeals. Even so, you might do very well on your own — and it will cost you only a few dollars to bring your complaint to court.

For more information on how you can get help in settling legal disputes out of court, look in the Yellow Pages under "Mediation Services." Or phone an organization named Endispute, which provides alternative resolution services worldwide, with offices in Cambridge, Massachusetts (800-400-3773); Chicago (312-739-0200); and Washington, D.C. (202-942-9180).

Finally, the Better Business Bureau offers mediation and arbitration services to consumers at most of its 138 offices.

## ENSURING YOUR PERSONAL SECURITY

# Protecting Your Checks and Credit Cards

Every four seconds some American falls victim to personal larceny. When your pocket has been picked, you are left with a purseful of problems. But there are ways to prevent a rip-off or to help your recovery.

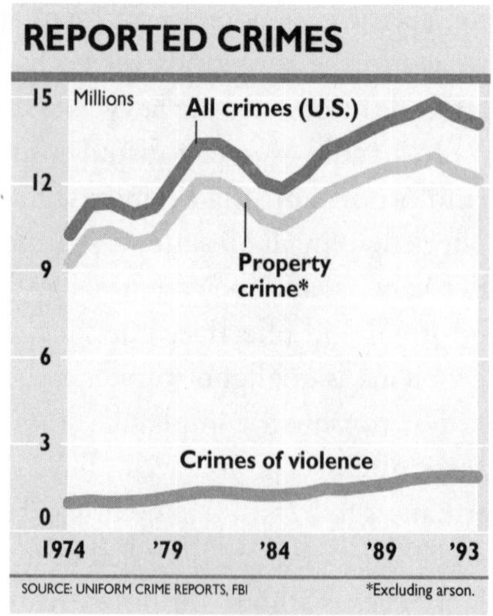


Though chances are slim that your property will ever be recovered, you should quickly inform the police about the theft. You will need a police report to prove your loss to the IRS, to your insurer and perhaps to your bank.

You should also immediately notify your bank and all your credit-card issuers. A thief can swiftly begin using your checks and credit cards, and a few hours' delay increases the chances that he or she will get away with it. If you know the numbers of any stolen checks, your bank can stop payment. If you don't know the numbers, you will probably have to close your account and open a new one. You are not liable for checks written by a thief, but if the signature closely matches your own, you will have to spend time proving to the bank it was a forgery.

Once you report the loss of your credit cards, you are not liable for any subsequent charges. If the thief gets away with using your cards before you report the loss, your liability is limited to $50 a card, but your credit-card issuer may not hold you responsible for that. If you lose a MasterCard, corporate policy forbids issuing banks from holding you liable for even a dollar. Many credit-card issuers have operators available around the clock. They may also provide toll-free numbers or accept collect calls.

New technology is making theft and fraud harder to commit. MasterCard and Visa have designed cards with "neural networks" that learn your spending habits — what geographic area you make most of your purchases in and what your price range is — and can flag uncharacteristic purchases. For instance, if charges were made to your card in Atlanta and Madrid on the same day, the bank might signal the merchant to call before approving the transaction. The neural networks also detect fraud on the merchant side of business by tracking fraud patterns and high-risk merchants. If your transactions intersect too often with these patterns or merchants, your issuing bank may alert you. Running your purchase through the neural network takes seconds. By the year 2000 many cards will incorporate microprocessor chips, making fraudulent use even tougher. MasterCard's planned chip card, called SmartCard, will require you to enter a personal identification number (PIN) every time you make a purchase, thereby preventing someone who doesn't know your PIN from using your card.

*A tip:* If you use an on-line computer service, be very careful

**SALES ON STOLEN CARDS**

Amounts charged worldwide on stolen Visa cards

| | Sales (billions) | Total fraud (millions) | % of sales |
|---|---|---|---|
| **1995(1st q.)** | **$172** | **$157** | **0.09%** |
| **1994** | **631** | **645** | **0.10** |
| **1993** | **515** | **667** | **0.13** |
| **1992** | **444** | **679** | **0.15** |
| **1991** | **396** | **538** | **0.13** |
| **1990** | **340** | **364** | **0.11** |

SOURCE: VISA

about making credit-card purchases on it or about filling out any on-line credit applications. Banks and credit-card issuers are working to develop secure transaction technology and the commercial on-line services, such as America Online and CompuServe, have in place their own encryption software that is intended to protect on-line transactions. But the possibility still exists for on-line users with computer-hacking experience and desires to access files containing credit-card numbers. Many people do order products through on-line services using credit cards. But you must remember that there is no guarantee yet of total security. A number of companies, including Microsoft and Netscape, are working together to develop more sophisticated and standardized encryption software that is intended to make all on-line transactions secure. Naturally, if and when such technology succeeds, you may be able to conduct credit transactions on-line.

To guard your cards today, sign up with a credit-card protection service offered through banks and credit-card firms. For $9 to $18 a year, it will immediately contact all your credit-card issuers after you notify it of the theft. The service pays any liabilities you incur after you call. Some services will even wire you money if you are robbed while traveling. Among the leaders in the field are:

- SafeCard Services (800-468-5463), which charges $15 a year for its notification service, a change-of-address service, access to emergency cash if you are 100 miles away from home (as much as is available on your credit card), a document registry that keeps records of your passport and other legal documents so that they can be replaced in event of loss, auto-rental discounts, a 24-hour toll-free message service and several other benefits.
- Credit Card Sentinel (800-423-5533), which charges $9 a year for credit-card notification and change-of-address service, $100 emergency cash, 24-hour toll-free message service. For $18 you get the basic coverage, plus 11 other benefits, including emergency cash up to $1,000; special registration labels for your luggage, keys and credit cards; a medical emergency card; and car-rental discounts.

What if you lose, or are robbed of, the plastic used to operate your bank's automatic teller machines or your bank-account debit card? Generally, if you notify the bank within two days of losing the card, your liability will be limited to $50. If you wait longer and the bank can prove that it could have stopped someone from using your card if you had told the bank, your loss could be as high as $500. If you don't report the loss within 60 days after the bank sends you your account statement, your exposure could be unlimited — *if* the bank can show that charges to your account after the 60-day period could have been prevented if it had known about the lost card.

If you lose a dual-purpose debit/ATM card, your liability depends on whether the thief uses it to charge purchases or withdraw money from your bank account. If the thief charges a Harley-Davidson, you're liable for the $50 maximum, the same as you would be for a credit card. If he or she extracts $200 from your bank account, the rules for ATMs apply — that is, if you delay reporting that the card is gone, your liability may be higher than $50.

What if your bank or credit union sends you a renewal card and it gets lost in the mail? Even if someone charges up a storm on the card, you wouldn't have to pay a penny. Federal law holds that you have to "accept" the card before you become liable for bad purchases. And if you didn't receive the card, you didn't accept it.

When you have any problems, state your case to your card issuer in writing. If that doesn't clear things up, ask the issuer who its primary regulator is and contact that organization. For most banks, it's the Federal Reserve. If you have a card issued by a credit union, write to the nearest office of the National Credit Union Administration. Credit cards from retailers are governed by the Federal Trade Commission.

## Keeping Records to Reduce Your Loss

To prevent a burglary from leaving you broke, make an inventory of everything you have in your home. Your insurance company probably can give you a form to fill out or you can receive a free brochure, "Taking Inventory," by calling the National Insurance Consumer Helpline (800-942-4242).

Go through each room, opening drawers and cupboards and carefully listing every object of value. Record all identifying information, such as serial numbers of appliances and account numbers of credit cards. For tableware note the manufacturer, pattern and number of place settings. Describe jewelry as fully as possible.

You can simplify the job with Quicken Deluxe ($58) the computer program for tracking finances that also has an inventory feature. Organized by rooms, the program lists likely belongings; you click on the ones that you own and an estimated value is automatically assigned to each item, unless you put in the actual value. There is plenty of room to add items that aren't on the standard list. Later, as you have time and receipts, you can go back and put in purchase dates, prices and serial numbers.

It's also wise to photograph the contents of your house. Do this yourself with self-developing film that does not need to be processed by strangers. You might even videotape your possessions. This lets you zoom in on details of antiques and fine art, highlighting makers' marks and signatures, while commenting on their value. Videotaping services will do the job for you. But before you hire anyone to videotape your belongings, check his or her reputation with the Better Business Bureau and the local police.

For art, antiques and family heirlooms you'll also need to cite estimates of each item's age and value. The best proof is an appraiser's dated statement. Get receipts and appraisals for particularly valuable items. Without these documents, you will have to rely on what the insurance adjuster says your goods are worth. An appraisal must be precise and explicit to back up a claim. Don't accept any that give only highly generalized descriptions of your valuables. Store a copy of all these records in a safe-deposit box or in another secure location away from home. Remember to update your appraisals periodically. Appraisers recommend updates every two or three years, but ask your insurance agent about your situation.

You can find appraisers through the American Society of Appraisers, 535 Herndon Parkway, Herndon, Virginia 22070; 800-272-8258. It publishes a free directory of those members who are personal property appraisers, plus a free pamphlet, "Information on the Appraisal Profession." For $7 you can get its *Directory of Professional Appraisal Services,* which includes appraisers in all fields.

If your home is burglarized, you will need accurate records for both the IRS and the police. These records can help you reduce your losses. After a burglary the criminals often melt down the precious metals and break up the jewelry to prevent its being traced. Most other stolen merchandise winds up back on the market intact. Police sweeps of pawnshops, suspected fences and crooked retailers sometimes turn up stolen property.

You are allowed to deduct only those losses that exceed 10% of your adjusted gross income plus $100 per casualty. For example, if your adjusted gross income is $80,000, your loss would have to exceed $8,100 before you could deduct it. And the loss must be figured as the lower of two amounts: the price paid for the item or its current value. So if you lose something that is worth less today than when you bought it, you can deduct only its current market value. But if an item has grown in value since you bought it, you can deduct only its original, lower cost.

## Protecting Yourself with Locks and Alarms

You can help make your home safe by installing the right locks and alarms, and it need not cost you a fortune or create a fortress. To stop a thief, first call the police — not for a squad car but for a free security checkup. Police departments will often send patrolmen to inspect your property and show you where it is vulnerable. Burglars don't bother to pick the lock — they kick in a door. Most burglars get in that way. Windows are the second-most-common entry point. Still, your primary line of defense is strong locks on *all* doors, not just the front door. Crime-prevention experts recommend replacing ordinary key-cylinder locks with pick-resistant ones, such as those made by Medeco, Multilock and Assa, among others. Your primary door lock should be supplemented by a rigid dead bolt that extends at least one inch into the jamb. A heavy-duty lock won't do much good, though, if it isn't securely installed with three-inch screws into a metal or hardwood door and door frame.

If burglars can't get in your doors, they'll try the windows, so you need to install sturdy locks there as well. The National Burglar and Fire Alarm Association estimates that burglars spend less than a minute trying to break in, but they spend 30 to 45 minutes choosing their target.

For most residences, ultra-sophisticated locks that replace keys with magnetic cards, voice recognition or coded pushbuttons are expensive overkill. Burglar bars, while offering more protection from thieves, can be disastrous in the event of fire. The bars make it harder for you to get out of the house and almost impossible for firefighters to get in. Avoid them.

Homeowners who want more protection than locks provide should install a security system. When you consider buying a security, or alarm, system, you enter a field of bewildering diversity. There are wired and wireless systems, monitored and unmonitored, dealer-installed and do-it-yourself. You can buy a little slice of protection for only $100 or you can automate your entire home, integrating heating, cooling, lighting, security, phones and more through a sophisticated, computer-controlled network for a ducal $10,000.

Wireless systems, which use radio frequencies to connect components, are much simpler and neater for the do-it-yourselfer and are the trend in the security industry. A wired system requires drilling holes into the walls and running wires through them. This job is best left to a professional installer. Years ago, the wired systems were the less bulky of the two, but technology has made the wireless systems almost as unobtrusive.

A basic security system usually comprises a control panel, a siren, door and window sensors, and an interior motion detector. It's suitable for a small house with two doors and a few windows. You can buy it at a home-supply, hardware, discount or consumer-electronics store. At Radio Shack the package is $199. For the same price, ADT Security Systems will install a system for you; but with ADT, you also contract to have it monitored, which will cost $20 a month.

Particularly easy-to-install wireless systems are Linear Corporation's Keepsafer Plus and Defiant, sold at hardware and home-building stores nationwide or by calling 800-221-9362. The Defiant is also sold through Home Depot; $170 for a starter kit. Included in the starter kit are a control panel, a remote control, keypad, siren, two door/window sensors and a video showing you how to install everything. If you don't want to use tools, you can put in the whole system with double-sided tape. Radio Shack's infrared motion alarm, $100, doesn't require any installation: You simply put it on a shelf or table and plug it into an outlet.

For a larger home, or a house with a lot of windows and doors, or with a cache of valuables, you will want something beyond the basic system. Once you begin thinking about adding infra-red-beam sensors, smoke sensors, floor-pad sensors, panic switches to automatically trip the alarm, glass-breakage detectors and strobe lights, you ought to talk to a professional installer. He can help you decide what equipment you actually need for your home.

One good mid-range system is the CareTaker Plus ($800 to $3,000, depending upon the application). Made by Interactive Technologies (800-777-5484), it is a wireless system that can be controlled by homeowners not only from the numeric keypad with a few specialized buttons but also from any Touch-Tone phone on or off the premises. So if you set the alarm while forgetting that the cleaning lady is coming, you can call home and disarm it. The system has, among other features, a digitized voice that tells you how the system is operating and whether or not you need to replace batteries.

Although not new technology, video screening is newly affordable. Linear sells a three-and-a-half-by-three-inch camera, monitor and plug-in cable for about $350 that you can use to watch a baby or a pool. An adapter will connect the monitor to your television, and additional cables will allow you to record the images on your VCR.

You should shop as warily for an alarm system as for a used car. Check out the craftsman who puts in the system, since alarms are only as reliable as the people who install them. Get competitive bids. Ask for and follow through on references from several recent customers. Call your Better Business Bureau or state or local Consumer Affairs Office to see if there have been any complaints about installers whom you are considering.

About 2,500 installers are members of either the National Burglar and Fire Alarm Association (NBFAA) or the Central Station Alarm Association. Both are in Bethesda, Maryland, and the NBFAA (301-907-3208) will put you in touch with your state chapter, which will give you a list of members in your city. It also will send you a free brochure, "Safe and Sound: Your Guide to Home Security," that will help you evaluate security systems.

Expect to spend at least $800 to $2,000 for a contractor-installed alarm system. You can often get discounts of up to 10% on your property insurance if you put one in.

Most professional installers will also want to sell you a monitoring service. When your system is monitored, it is connected to a central control station that is staffed 24 hours a day. If your alarm is triggered, someone at the station will call your home. If there is no answer or the person who answers can't give the correct code word, the monitoring station will summon the police. The charge for this service most often begins around $20 a month and goes up, depending upon the features you add to your system. For example, ADT charges $2 extra a month to monitor a smoke alarm.

The hottest new monitoring technology is two-way voice communication. With it, the monitoring station bypasses the phone lines and communicates directly, using radio waves, through a small transmitter installed on a wall in one room of the home. Highly sensitive, the monitor can hear whispers several rooms away, and someone at the monitoring station can actually talk to the homeowner. It is particularly useful for someone who has contracted for medical monitoring and, in the event of an emergency, may not be able to get to a phone. The price for the equipment begins around $100, but you'll pay another $3 to $10 per month on your monitoring bill.

If you choose a monitored system, find out who is going to monitor it. It may not be the company that sells you the alarm system. Virtually all small companies and some larger companies subcontract with a monitoring firm to handle calls, and that company may not even be in your state. Find out what the monitoring company's response time is; it should be within two minutes. (A monitoring company uses 911 just like everyone else and has no extra clout to get police or fire dispatched.) Ask whether or not it has back-up in case of a power loss and whether it charges for false alarms.

You'll know that your monitoring company is secure if it has an Underwriters Laboratory (UL) rating; but lack of that rating doesn't mean it's a poor monitoring station. Nationwide companies that sell systems with 24-hour monitoring services include ADT of Parsippany, New Jersey (800-238-7870) and Honeywell Protection Services of Minneapolis (612-951-1000).

Brinks Home Security of Dallas, with offices nationwide (800-445-0872), leases, rather than sells, its basic package. You pay an installation price — varying from nothing to $199, depending upon specials being offered — and you must sign a two-year monitoring contract, which begins at $21 a month. You must buy any additional equipment that you want.

A self-installed system can also be monitored. We Monitor America (800-221-9362), a UL-listed central station, will monitor your system for $15 to $20 a month, provided that a dialing mechanism can be plugged into the system.

For those building a new home, a security system can be just one part of what is called home automation — the integration of lighting, security, heating and cooling, telephone, TV and audio. With this technology, for example, when your alarm goes off at 6 A.M., the shades in your bedroom would slowly begin to go up; your shower would turn on, warming up to a predetermined temperature; the heat would be coming up; the coffee would begin perking; and lights would turn on in the rooms you would be most likely to enter. In the evening, you could tell as each child comes home because each would have a separate security code; motion and heat-sensor monitors could tell you which rooms in the house were occupied.

Because the concept is so new, there is no single technology. Rather, there are many ways to integrate the systems of your home. A simplified X-10 application, Radio Shack's Plug-in Power, for example, controls eight lights or appliances anywhere in the house from a single keypad, which costs $13. The corresponding module that you must plug into your appliance is about the same price. For $70 you can get a computer interface (Windows applications only) that will control 256 items, 128 of which can be timed.

A mid-range home-automation product is Interactive Technologies' VuFone, which works in concert with the CareTaker alarm system and retails for around $500. Designed like a telephone with a small screen and keyboard, VuFone incorporates sophisticated security-system programming capabilities. Among other features, it has caller ID capacity, which is a new service by some local telephone companies allowing you to identify the telephone number of the person calling you. VuFone also has a built-in credit-card swipe and a data entry keyboard for the day when you'll be doing your banking, bill paying or home shopping electronically. To receive a brochure about home automation and a list of dealers in your area, contact the Home Automation Association (808 17th Street NW, Suite 200, Washington, D.C. 20006-3910; 202-223-9669). Three reliable companies with home-automation systems are Honeywell (612-951-1000), Smart House (800-759-3344) and ADT (800-238-7870).

# Buying a Safe for Your Home

Since there is often a long wait to acquire safe-deposit boxes in banks, more and more people are searching for a secure place to store their valuables right in their own homes. The biggest weakness of a home safe is its accessibility. If you take a weekend away from home, burglars have plenty of time to find and defeat your safe. So a safe-deposit box in a bank is the most secure place for jewelry, securities, coins and other valuables. But a home safe can be useful for documents and records. Superior safes are made by American Security Products of Fontana, California (800-421-6142) and Fire King International of New Albany, Indiana (800-457-2424).

Make sure that any safe you buy has been rated by the Underwriters Laboratories for fire resistance. Say it is rated a class 350 one-hour safe. That means that temperatures inside will go no higher than 350 degrees Fahrenheit during a one-hour fire. A class 350 one-hour safe is good for protecting savings bonds, passports and other paper documents. For stamps, which have glue on the back, computer tapes or anything protected in plastic, you must have a class 125 one-hour rating, because those things will be destroyed at a lower heat and by moisture that is emitted by a class 350 safe as it heats up.

Underwriters Laboratories also rates safes for burglary and impact resistance. A safe rated RSC (residential security container) will withstand a five-minute attack by normal hand tools. This rating is suitable for many homes. Going up the scale in burglar resistance (and cost) are the TL (tool resistant) and TR (torch resistance) ratings. A TL-30 rating, for example, means a safe would withstand a 30-minute attack by burglars' tools. If the safe is impact rated, that means it can be dropped from 30 feet without the door opening or cracks forming on the surface of the safe. For most homes an RSC safe with an impact rating and a class 350 one-hour fire rating is adequate. It will cost you $300 to $800.

If you insist on keeping not only your documents but also tiaras and gold bullion in your home, forget about a wall safe. A burglar can drill around the metal box and pull it free. You will need a so-called burglary-resistant safe. It should be anchored with bolts or embedded in a concrete floor and concealed by a rug. A floor safe the size of a file-drawer cabinet can cost from $500 to $1,500.

Fancier, stronger safes go for more. You can easily pay over $3,000 for a medium-sized model with inch-thick special alloy walls, and an inch-and-a-half-thick door, a special locking mechanism in the door and an Underwriters Laboratories label marked TL-30. Be sure to check with your insurance company. Most policies will spell out what specifications your safe should have to meet your coverage. If your policy doesn't explain them in detail, insist that your agent put the requirements in writing.

*A tip:* For mail-order shoppers, The Safety Zone (Hanover, Pennsylvania 17333; 800-999-3030) offers a large selection of products for your health, safety and security at home and on the road.

If you don't have a safe, the best protection for your valuables is ingenuity. Avoid the more common hiding places, like the toe of a shoe or the bottom of a sugar canister. Some people have foiled burglars by using false-bottom books, sewing jewelry into stuffed toys or pillows or even freezing diamonds in the ice tray. Just be careful not to gulp them down in a martini.

CHAPTER 22

# Securing Your Retirement

## Strategies to Start Saving Now

As the 21st century approaches, we have an aging America whose people are living longer with every passing year; we have a government that is spending less than before in support of pensioners; we have a Congress that has been steadily cutting away at retirement benefits, notably for affluent people and diligent savers; we have employers who are requiring that employees put up more to fund their own retirement; and we have a population that is not saving nearly enough — 40% are saving nothing at all — to prepare for their senior years. Consequently, more of us will be working later in life, though not at the same jobs.

Against that backdrop, here are the basics to prepare for a secure retirement:

- Because employers and the government are squeezing back on pension contributions, you will have to take on a greater responsibility for financing your retirement. Perhaps as much as half of your retirement money will have to come from your own personal savings and investments.
- Because life spans are lengthening, you probably will have to put away more than you think. More and more people will spend almost as many years in retirement as they did on the job.
- The sooner you start saving and investing for retirement, the better. But it is never too early and seldom too late to begin.

Start at age 21 to put $2,000 a year into an IRA; earn and reinvest an average 9% on the money; and by the time you're age 65, you'll have more than $1 million. Don't overly worry if you're well into your middle years and have not put away enough; you *can* catch up.

- While you want to diversify your investments and savings, probably your best investment will be stocks, or stock mutual funds. Even when you are retired, you will want a good part of your portfolio to be in stocks. You may well live long enough to make good use of the superior returns of stocks. Historically, they offer the highest returns in the long run.
- When your employer offers you any tax-saving or tax-deferring plan — such as a 401(k), a profit-sharing or company savings plan — grab it. Many employers add 50 cents for each dollar that you contribute, and it's hard to find another way that you can make 50% on your money from day one. Also take advantage of IRA, Keogh and other tax-sparing plans.
- At the same time, be careful that you don't accumulate so much in your tax-sheltered "qualified" plans that you will later face a tax penalty. Start now to devise a strategy for withdrawing money from your tax-sheltered plans.

To repeat: You have probably underestimated the amount of money you will need to retire. Remember that you may live for two or three decades after leaving your job. More and more companies are terminating medical benefits for retirees, so you can't count on receiving free health insurance from your employer. Your pension shrinks when you change jobs often, and these days jobs disappear easily.

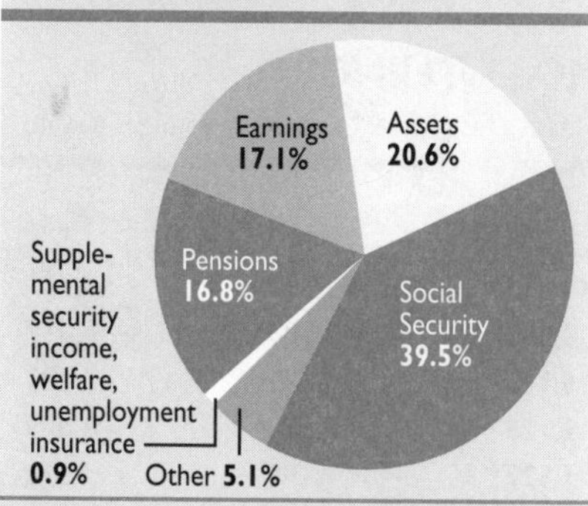


Women should put away even more for their retirement than men should. Unfortunately, women often earn less than men

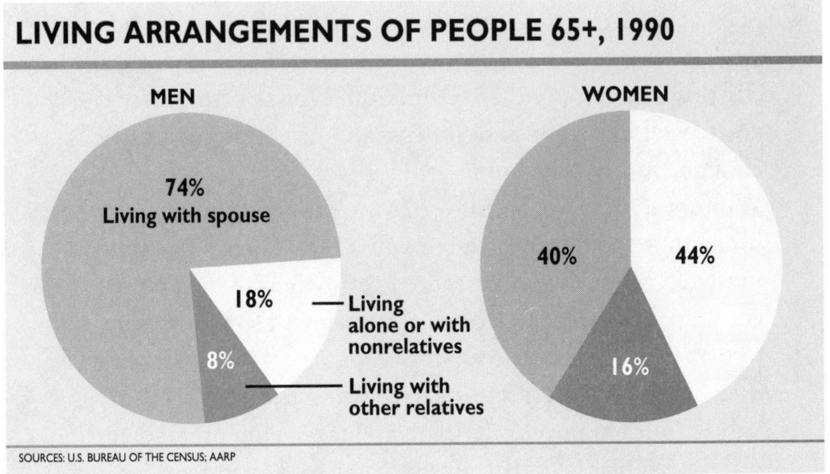


do throughout their careers. They also tend to have less money than men in Social Security, company plans and personal savings. More women than men work in smaller businesses that do not offer pension plans. The numbers of widowed, divorced and always single people have been increasing in America. Women typically outlive men and are less likely to remarry. Again, the message for women is: Save more.

Regardless of your age or gender, *now* is the time to figure out how much you will need to make retirement secure — and where that cash will come from.

First, calculate your anticipated annual income and expenses during your postemployment years. You won't need as much as your final year's pay on the job. Your work-related expenses will disappear, your tax bill

**RETIREES SPEND LESS FOR MOST THINGS**

Because their annual outlays are lower, inflation doesn't hit retirees* as hard as younger people.

| | AGE | | | |
|---|---|---|---|---|
| | 45-54 | 55-64 | 65-74 | 75-plus |
| **Food** | **$5,485** | **$4,638** | **$3,637** | **$2,721** |
| **Housing** | **12,027** | **9,683** | **7,304** | **6,417** |
| **Transportation** | **7,479** | **6,340** | **3,742** | **2,283** |
| **Health care** | **1,817** | **2,176** | **2,610** | **2,883** |
| **Entertainment** | **2,490** | **1,527** | **1,198** | **578** |

SOURCE: U.S. BUREAU OF LABOR STATISTICS

*Figures apply to "consumer units," which can be one or more persons.

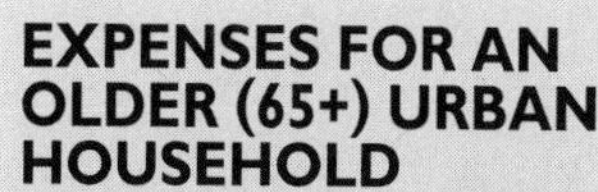


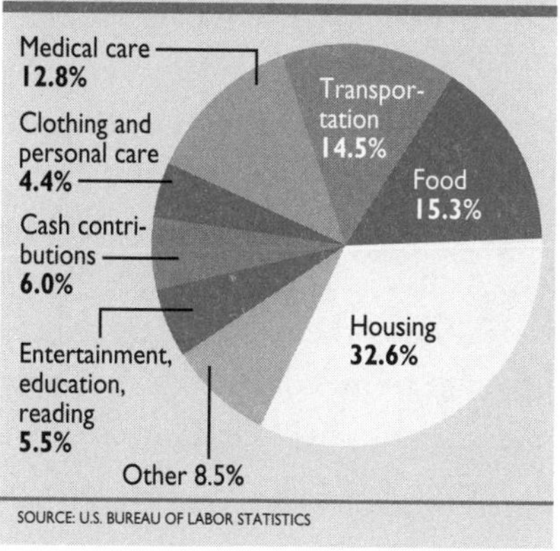


SOURCE: U.S. BUREAU OF LABOR STATISTICS

stands to decline, and you may not be putting part of your income into retirement savings any longer. So, as mentioned, 70% to 80% of your preretirement earnings, before taxes, should suffice. Be aware that traditional pension plans often pay you only 30% of your final five-year average compensation if you retire at age 60. If you have spent your whole career at one company and depart at age 65 you can count on only about 40% to 45% of your income when you retire.

If you have a benefits administrator where you work, ask him or her for a picture of your retirement benefits. How much do you stand to collect, and when? Will you be better off to take the money in a lump sum or in monthly payments for life? Will you be eligible for five-year or 10-year averaging, and will that be beneficial to you? As explained in detail later in this chapter, you can get an estimate of your future Social Security benefits by calling 800-772-1213, the agency's 24-hour automated service line, and ordering a free Personal Earnings and Benefit Estimate Statement (PEBES).

Second, estimate your life expectancy. Use the national mortality tables that you can get from your insurance agent, but add another eight to 10 years to ensure that you don't run out of money — and it's a pleasant thought that should brighten your day.

**EXPECTED NUMBER OF YEARS IN RETIREMENT**

| Expected retirement age or current age if already retired | Life expectancy for... Individual | Surviving spouse of couple |
|---|---|---|
| 55 | 28 YRS. | 34 YRS. |
| 60 | 24 | 30 |
| 65 | 20 | 25 |
| 70 | 16 | 21 |
| 75 | 12 | 16 |

SOURCES: INTERNAL REVENUE SERVICE; T. ROWE PRICE

Almost everyone can look forward to a longer and healthier life than his or her forebears. But if you are younger than 40, what you probably will not be able to do is retire as early as your parents could, quit working completely when you do retire, or count on the government for as much of your support in your great age. Because you will have to do more to take care of yourself when you are old, you will have to start saving and investing while you are reasonably young.

Population trends will strain Social Security and private pensions, but only in the future. In the decade of the 1990s, the Social Security system will enjoy a huge surplus — some estimates run to $1 trillion by the year 2000 — because the people who start retiring and tapping into Social Security benefits in the 1990s will come from the small generation that was born in the 1930s Depression. Meanwhile, the bulging generation of baby boomers born from the mid-1940s to the mid-1960s will be reaching their peak earning years and paying tremendous sums in Social Security taxes. The Social Security system thus will have more than enough cash when today's 60-year-olds retire. It is *after* that, that trouble may set in.

Today, less than 13% of America's population is older than 65. But as the 75 million baby boomers grow older, that figure should swell to almost 14.6% in the year 2015 and to 20% in 2030. Though the primary reason for the aging of America is the increase in births in the years just before 1920 and after World War II, lengthening life spans are also a factor. If a man makes it to the age of 65 in the year 2010, he will have a 50-50 chance of living one to three years into his 80s; women will live even longer — into their mid-80s.

With fewer young people and many more elderly, the few will have to support the many through Social Security taxes. The U.S. probably will have to scale back government-paid retirement benefits. They will be lower in real dollars and will start later in life. Thus, your private pension — from either your employer or your 401(k), your Individual Retirement Account or Keogh plan, or a combination of them— will become relatively more important than such sources are for contemporary retirees.

We have seen that your pension, your investment and savings income, and your Social Security benefits need to add up to 70% to 80% of your final year's salary to maintain your standard of living. Take, for example, a single person who retired in 1995 and requires 75% of a $57,000 income before taxes to live comfortably. Figuring maximum Social Security of $1,199 a month or $14,388 a year, the income from pensions and investments would have to be slightly over $28,000.

Or take a married person who requires 75% of a $120,000 household income; his or her income from pensions and investments — on top of maximum Social Security of $1,798 a month, or $21,576 — would have to be $68,424.

Remember: Even loyal employees who have spent their entire career at one firm get only about 40% to 45% of their income when they retire. The highest private pension coverage is provided to employees in the automotive, chemical, oil, aircraft and public utilities industries. Retailing, food-processing and garment-manufacturing firms tend to have the lowest pensions. Some of the best pensions go to government employees — military people and federal and state civil servants. A cost-of-living escalator makes many of their retirement plans especially generous.

Happily, great new opportunities to save and invest for retirement are opening up. The number of tax-deferred corporate pension and savings plans has more than doubled in the last 20 years. IRAs, which let your savings grow tax-free until you withdraw the money, are now available to everyone who works for money, though not everyone can deduct his or her contributions (see Chapter 8, "How to Play Your IRA").

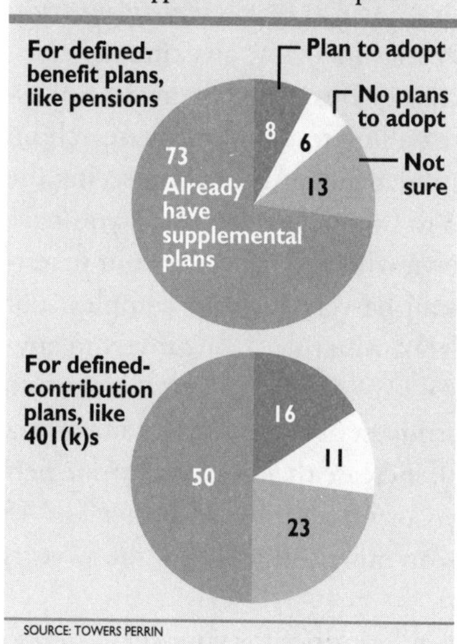


Qualifying for an old-fashioned lifetime pension is easier in some ways now than it once was. You have to work at the same company for only five years to become vested — meaning that you are guaranteed benefits when you retire even if you quit the company before then. Or employers can choose an alternative plan that stretches out the process to seven years, by vesting 20% of your pension benefits after three years and 20% in each of the subsequent four years.

In addition to pensions, many companies offer payroll-deduction savings plans such as

401(k)s. Eighty-one percent of 1,035 major corporations surveyed in 1994 by Hewitt Associates offered both a defined-benefit pension plan and one or more defined-contribution plans for savings and investment. Ninety-seven percent of the employers in the survey offer a 401(k) salary-reduction plan.

If your employer offers you a savings or profit-sharing plan where the company kicks in 50 cents or more for every dollar you invest, that is an offer you can't refuse — with one exception. If the plan invests exclusively in the company's own stock and you are not confident about your employer's future, you might be wise to put your money elsewhere.

Nearly all companies with profit-sharing or savings plans let their vested employees leave with a lump-sum benefit. What comes next can be a real bonanza. The employee can take the employer's contributions plus any money that he or she has earned in the plan and defer paying taxes on the total by depositing all of it in an Individual Retirement Account. This is known as a rollover. There the money can be invested, just like regular IRA contributions, and will compound tax-free until it is withdrawn.

Even if you have only a meager company pension, you can maximize whatever assets you have. You might start investing for retirement by putting money into a growth mutual fund, the type that invests in stocks of solid companies that offer better-than-average opportunities for capital appreciation. You might further diversify by asking your stockbroker or financial planner to seek out real estate *investment trusts* (REITs), which are public companies that invest in apartments, commercial buildings and health-care facilities. But generally avoid real estate *limited partnerships* unless you are willing to do a lot of research on your own. Partnerships don't have an independent board overseeing the assets like REITs do, and if you want to liquidate your assets, you have to go out and find someone on your own who will take over your investment. In addition, the prospectuses can be very big and complex. For most people limited partnerships violate a wise rule: Don't invest in anything you don't understand.

As stated earlier, it's wise to save or invest at least 5% of your pretax income between the ages of 30 and 40; increase that amount by one percentage point a year between the ages of 40 and 45; and after age 45 continue saving and investing 10% or more annually in those years when you don't have college expenses.

Ideally, while in your 30s, start setting priorities for your spending, so that your major expenses will be paid off when you retire. At this age, it is a good time to buy a house or apartment, so your mortgage will also be paid off by the time you quit work.

Once you hit your 50s, your investments should tilt conservatively. Look for blue-chip stocks, conservative mutual funds and fixed-income investments, such as bonds and Government National Mortgage Association mortgage funds. Even with all that, my own inclination would be to keep more than 50% of assets in stocks or stock mutual funds for a lifetime. But I am bullish for the long term. You may be more cautious, and in that case, you might be better advised to take on more fixed-income investments. As stated earlier, nobody can put a price on your ability to sleep peacefully at night.

## How Much Social Security Contributes

When you reach your 60s, you should be aware that:

- The government will not send you a Social Security check until you notify the local Social Security office that you are ready. So be sure to file an application three months before you want the first check to arrive.
- If you are part of a married couple in which only one spouse works for pay, Social Security will send you a monthly check amounting to about 1½ times the worker's entitlement.
- Though Social Security docks your benefits if you earn more than a certain amount from a job, you can earn all the investment income you want and not be docked a dime.

You qualify for Social Security retirement benefits as early as age 62 if you have held a job and paid Social Security taxes for at least 10 years. If you are younger and want an official estimate of your future benefits, call 800-772-1213 and request Form SSA-7004-PC. Its questions are easy to answer; you can ask for estimated retirement amounts at various ages, from 62 to 70, the period during which benefits postponed rise handsomely in terms of monthly income. A few weeks after returning the form, you will receive an eight-page Personal Earnings and Benefit Estimate Statement. Just remember, the figures will be in today's dollars.

The benefit estimate statement will tell you not only what you will receive in retirement benefits but also the monthly amounts that your family would get if you died or that you and your family would get if you were disabled.

The payout for someone who will retire at age 65 depends on that person's income and present age. To qualify for the highest payment, you will have to earn the highest amount of income subject to Social Security tax — and continue to do so over several years. For example, the top amount subject to the tax in 1991 was $53,400 and in 1995 it was $61,200.

So how much can you look forward to? If you were born in 1950 and earned $40,000 in 1994, for example, Social Security's computers estimate that your maximum monthly benefit when you eventually retire will be $1,178. If you were born in 1940 and earned $61,200 or more in 1994, your monthly benefit will be an estimated $1,325. (Those figures are 1994 dollars. Because actual payments are adjusted each year for inflation, you should view your future benefits in terms of their present buying power.)

Social Security almost certainly won't replace most of your income from work, although people who earned low wages most of their working lives might get benefits equal to as much as two-thirds of their final pay. More likely, the Social Security pension will provide one-third or less of your nest egg — and you will have to provide the rest.

Social Security penalizes workers for early retirement. Retiring at the youngest age, 62, will cost you 20% of what you could have claimed at 65, which Social Security currently considers the "full" retirement age. For 1995, the maximum annual benefit at age 62 was $11,508 per worker, or $17,256 for a couple with a non-working spouse also age 62. The age of full retirement, however, is due to rise for people now in their early 50s and younger. If you were born between 1943 and 1954, you'll have to wait until you're 66 years old to get the full benefit. If you were born after 1959, make that age 67.

Unless you postpone this pension until age 70, it probably won't pay to work after your Social Security checks start rolling in. If you do, you will be docked for earning more than a minimal amount. In 1995 a 65-year-old flunked the so-called earnings test if he or she made more than $11,280. For every three dollars above that, you would have received one dollar less in Social Security benefits. If you were younger than age 65, the earnings threshold was a mere $8,160, and the penalty for earning more was one dollar in lost Social Security benefits for every two dollars of pay.

The good news about working beyond age 65 is that the extra income will increase your average earnings once you do retire, so you could wind up ahead in the long run. By staying on the job until age 70, you qualify for benefits as much as 40% higher. In addition, people who delay retirement get a special credit. This credit, which is a percentage added to your Social Security benefit, varies depending on your date of birth. For people turning 65 years old in 1995, the rate is 4.5% per year. For example, if you delay receiving benefits for three years — until age 68 — your benefit then increases by 4.5% times three, or 13.5%. That rate will gradually increase in future years, until it reaches 8% per year for people turning 65 in 2008 or later.

No matter how old you are, you must pay income taxes on part of your Social Security benefits if your other income pushes above fairly modest levels — $32,000 for married couples and $25,000 for singles. If your income is over $44,000 for married couples, and $34,000 for singles, you will be taxed on as much as 85% of your Social Security benefits. For this, the government counts as income half of your Social Security benefits and all your tax-free interest on municipal bonds.

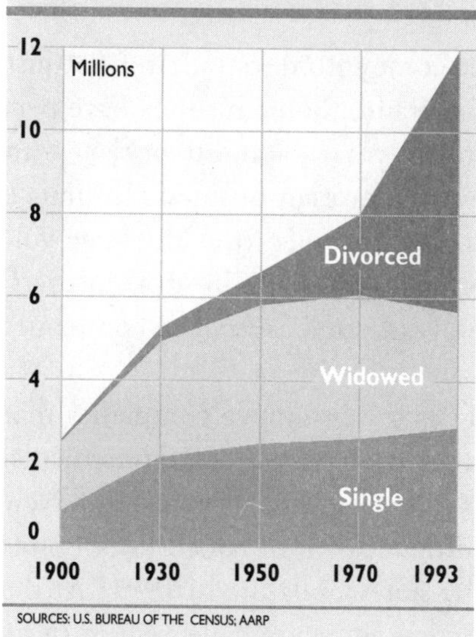


## Those GICs in Your Savings Plan

Few people really understand guaranteed investment contracts, yet employees saving for retirement have poured billions of dollars into them. About 25% of the more than $800 billion in 401(k) savings plans are in GICs. You may well be putting some of your pay into GICs but probably don't know it, because these investments usually carry another name, such as "stable value fund," "guaranteed fund" or "capital preservation fund."

GICs are a type of security issued only by insurance companies, backed only by the insurer's own assets and sold only to large financial institutions such as those that take custody of employee benefit funds. They resemble bank certificates of deposit but have one big advantage over CDs: GICs generally return at least two-thirds of a percentage point more than CDs of comparable maturities. Over the term of the contract, usually one to five years, the insurer promises to pay a stated rate of interest. This guaranteed interest rate will depend on when you buy them and the issuing company, but it is usually about 6.5% for a five-year contract. During that time the value of your investment, including its earnings, does not fluctuate. GIC investors get the peace of mind that goes with owning something with constant value. The trouble is, unlike CDs or Treasuries, GICs are not guaranteed or insured by the U.S. government.

Banks have got into the lucrative act by offering nearly identical bank-investment contracts, or BICs. Initially, BICs were covered by federal deposit insurance, but after the insurance industry cried foul, Congress dumped BICs from the FDIC program.

Lately the safety of some GICs has come into question and not just because of their lack of government insurance. Some insurers have perhaps unwisely boosted the interest rates they pay — and their risk — in the battle for a larger piece of the retirement-plan business. Insurance analysts and rating services have become concerned over the large volume of shaky junk bonds and unprofitable real estate in some insurers' investment portfolios. In the past few years some insurance companies have abandoned the GIC business.

GICs may prove to be only as safe as the insurance companies that issue them, and an insurer is only as safe as its assets and investments. Remember when Executive Life of California, Executive Life of New York and Mutual Benefit Life, loaded down with devalued junk bonds or bad real estate loans, were seized by state regulators in 1991? At the time, the retirement plans of over 20 companies and colleges held more than $1 billion in GICs issued by these insurance companies. A few employers promptly announced they would make good any employee losses, but they were the exceptions. While employees who have investments in those GICs may eventually get their money out, most of it was frozen so that it could not be withdrawn or switched to other investments. Most states have insurance-guaranteed funds that protect policyholders from company bankruptcies to a certain extent; the amount of coverage for GICs varies from state to state. When Executive Life collapsed, only 12 state guarantee associations covered GICs, and many of them capped coverage way below the contracts' value.

Banks, bond funds and some insurers are now promoting the so-called synthetic GIC. Some synthetics give you the fixed rate of a traditional GIC, but others have rates that are reset monthly or quarterly. These are generally called floating-rate synthetic contracts. The other difference with synthetics is that your employer can choose the assets that back the contract; they may include mortgages backed by Fannie Mae — or U.S. Treasuries, which are fail-safe.

On balance, GICs may well deserve a place in your retirement savings and investment portfolio, but it is up to you to make sure that your money is entrusted only to healthy insurance companies. Your corporate benefits office should be able to name the insurers and give you their financial ratings. In case you draw a blank there, ask for the name and phone number of the fund's trustee. Here's what you need to know:

- How is the trustee screening the insurers for safety?
- Is the portfolio well diversified? That is, does it include GIC and BIC contracts from four to six insurers or banks?
- Do all the insurers have a top rating for claims-paying ability? Specialists in GICs sometimes prefer the evaluations of Standard & Poor's, Moody's or Duff & Phelps to those of A. M. Best. Until this year, A. M. Best updated its ratings annually instead of on an ongoing basis, as do other ratings companies. Look for a rating of AAA or AA, nothing less.

## Annuities: Savings with a Tax Shelter

The word *annuity* is a genuine MEGO: Mine eyes glaze over. But consider these words: steady interest payments, all tax-deferred;

guaranteed principal; monthly checks for life. Now do I have your attention?

An annuity is a savings plan sponsored by an insurance company that offers tax benefits. It is a contract promising to pay you a regular income, usually from the day you retire through the rest of your life. Annuities are sold by brokers, bankers, financial planners and insurance agents. Contracts called single-premium annuities generally require a deposit of $5,000 to $10,000 or more, but others called flexible-premium annuities let you start with as little as $250. The earnings on the money compound tax-deferred, just as with an IRA. And if you buy an annuity for your IRA, your contributions — up to $2,000 a year — may be tax-deductible.

The earnings on your annuity grow until some time in the future, usually after you retire. Then you can either take one large lump sum or "annuitize" — that is, start collecting monthly payments that will continue either over a fixed period or for the rest of your life and perhaps your spouse's, too. Each payment is considered to be partly a return of principal that will not be taxed, unless your annuity has been in an IRA, and partly your earnings on that principal (which will be taxed in any case). If you should die before you can begin collecting, the proceeds in most states go to your beneficiary and are not subject to probate.

After you buy a contract, the insurance company may let you withdraw up to 10% of the value of your annuity each year without any penalties. But you do have to pay income tax on your withdrawals, under a last-in, first-out rule that all withdrawals are considered interest until no more earnings are left. If you want to take out more than 10%, the company will also exact a surrender charge in the early years. Often it starts at 5% to 10% of your withdrawal during the contract's first year and declines until it disappears after five to 10 years. In addition, the IRS imposes a 10% penalty if you withdraw money from your annuity before age 59½. Many companies also charge maintenance fees of $12 to $30 a year on fixed-rate and variable contracts.

Annuities are not for you if you are looking for short-term investments. Nor are they sensible for young adults whose financial situations change often and who may need to have access to their capital. But disciplined savers in their mid-30s or older who seek tax relief should seriously consider annuities as part of an investment program for retirement.

Say a man of 45 put a $100,000 inheritance into an annuity that paid an average 7% interest over the years. By the time he reached age 65, the tax-deferred buildup would be $386,968. If he then took payments for life, he might draw $3,000 each month from an insurance company.

Different insurance companies make widely different monthly payments. The lifetime payment for a man of 65 ranges from $7.39 to $9.23 a month for each $1,000 of accumulated capital. For a woman of 65, the range is lower because of a longer life expectancy: $6.77 to $8.98 per $1,000.

When you buy a deferred annuity — that is, one in which to build up retirement funds — the sponsor guarantees to pay you a certain interest rate on your money, generally for a year and sometimes up to 10 years. After that, the rate moves up or down at the sponsor's discretion. Most insurance companies used to guarantee to pay you at least 5.5%, even if rates dip below that in the future, but now the standard is 3.5% a year.

The insurance company also guarantees to pay your heirs back all the money you put into a fixed annuity if you die before you can annuitize. So, you would be wise to deal only with major insurers rated AAA or AA by the insurance ratings agencies. You can find their reports in public libraries or insurance agents' offices. The companies that rate annuities are Moody's, Standard & Poor, Duff & Phelps, A. M. Best, and Weiss Research.

Variable annuities differ from fixed ones in that the principal is not guaranteed, and the benefits you earn directly reflect the earnings of the assets (stocks, bonds or money-market securities) that back the contract. Very important, *you* select where you want your money invested. Variable annuities reflect the performance of the markets and the ups and downs of interest rates, and your returns will vary accordingly. These annuities are designed in part to offer protection against the devastating effects of inflation on fixed incomes.

When shopping for a fixed annuity, fight the temptation to buy the one that promises the highest interest. Many contracts dangle high rates before you but slash the interest in later years. Before you buy any fixed annuity, ask to see the interest rates that the insurance company has paid over the past 10 years. That information will give you an idea of what the company pays over the long term.

Most companies offer an option that lets you pull out your money without paying an early-withdrawal penalty if the interest rate drops below a set level, such as one or two percentage points under the rate paid when you bought the annuity. This bailout clause usually comes at the cost of an initial interest rate of one-half to one full percentage point below those without escape clauses. If you bail out, you can transfer the money to another company and avoid paying taxes. But you're generally better off choosing a no-bailout annuity from a company that has paid consistently high rates.

Some company sponsors consistently outperform others in surveys by Lipper Analytical Services. The leaders for top-rated investment-grade bond fund variable annuities — based on the total reinvested rate of return for five years — have been New England Mutual's Zenith Accumulator Back Bay Bond Income, Northbrook's Dean Witter Variable Annuity Quality Income, Charter National's Variable Annuity Bond and Aetna's Variable Annuity Account Income Shares. Leading the money-fund variable annuity rankings for five-year performance were NW Mutual C, Security Benefit 4 and Aetna C Encore.

One research service that compares different insurers' ratings, interest rates and charges is U.S. Annuities (98 Hoffman Road, Englishtown, New Jersey 07726; 800-872-6684). It provides free quotes by phone and publishes a quarterly, *Annuity & Life Insurance Shopper* (single issue, $20; one-year subscription, $45).

You can have your annuity payments calculated and distributed in any one of four ways. Ranked in order of size of the monthly payments, your choices are:

- *Single life.* You get annuity payments for life, but they stop when you die. Because your spouse would then get nothing, this option is losing favor. Before you can choose it, your spouse has to agree in writing.
- *Fifty percent joint-and-survivor.* You get annuity payments for life, but they are some 7% lower than with a single-life annuity. When you die, your surviving spouse gets half of what you were collecting, until he or she dies. Most retirees choose this option.
- *One hundred percent joint-and-survivor.* You get annuity payments for life, but they are some 20% lower than with a single-life annuity. When you die, your surviving spouse gets all of what you were collecting, until he or she dies.

- *Term-certain.* You and your surviving spouse get annuity payments for a fixed number of years, but after that you collect nothing. If you and your spouse both die before the term ends, the remaining payments go to your heirs.

# How to Check Your Company Pension

To be sure of having something later on, check now into the pension plan that your employer provides.

Pension plans come in two varieties:

*The defined-benefit plan,* which is declining in popularity, promises you a fixed benefit upon retirement. Your pension is related to your salary and the length of your employment, no matter what the cost to the company — meaning you can count on at least a certain minimum payment.

*The defined-contribution plan,* which is rising in popularity, permits you or your employer (or both) to invest a certain sum every year, before taxes, on your behalf. You get this money, and the earnings on it, when you retire. Defined-contribution plans are commonly company thrift or profit-sharing programs. Your employer may agree to match and invest a portion of your savings, or to set aside for you a percentage of profits pegged to your salary. Employee contributions and all earnings are tax-deferred. But if the plan's investments do poorly, the losses eventually come out of your pocket. So it pays to monitor closely the performance of a defined-contribution plan.

Hewitt Associates points out what a little foresight can do: Assume that a 30-year-old man earning $40,000 a year puts only 1% of his pay in a 401(k) plan, and his employer contributes 50 cents for each dollar he invests. If his salary rises 6% each year and his investments earn an average 8% a year, he could retire at age 60 with a nest egg of $129,600. With it he could buy an annuity from an insurance company based on a life expectancy of 79 years; the annuity would pay him $14,500 a year, or 7.5% of his final five-year salary. But if he were to put away a full 6% of his salary, he could quit at age 60 with $777,600. He could then buy an annuity paying him $87,000 a year — the equivalent of 45% of his final five-year pay.

Your pension is probably safer under a defined-benefit plan than under a defined-contribution plan. Even if your company runs into grave financial trouble, the federal Pension Benefit Guaranty Corporation insures defined-benefit plans against termination. You are guaranteed to receive at least some pension. In 1995 the maximum insured benefit was $30,886 a year for a single-life annuity beginning at age 65.

Even if your pension plan is well managed and adequately funded, you may be in for a shock when you retire. Your monthly payments could be much less than your individual benefit statement has led you to expect — because the calculations on most statements are based on a retirement age of 65 and on pension payments as a single life annuity. If you retire before age 65, you will see a reduction in your pension payments. And if you are married when you retire, the law requires that your spouse receive payments after you die, usually according to the 50% joint-and-survivor plan. As stated earlier, this can lower your payments by 7%. You can switch to a single life annuity that will more closely reflect the payments on your benefits statement *if* your spouse agrees to sign a waiver. Another point: Only 3% of the companies surveyed by Hewitt Associates give cost-of-living raises to pensioners.

Remember: You will not get a company pension unless you work for the firm at least five years, after which you are vested. You stand to get a richer pension if you work for the same company for many years than if you move around a lot. Also, employees of big companies often get better pensions than their counterparts at smaller businesses (although the latter sometimes do better in collecting stock options from start-ups). At best, a pension will replace 40% to 45% of your preretirement income, and then only if you have worked for one of the more generous companies for at least three decades. If you retire at age 60 instead of 65, many employers will cut your benefits by a third, and by half if you depart at age 55.

To calculate your pension, read the summary plan description that your employer has to give you once a year. Turn first to the section on Social Security. You may discover that your company reduces your pension benefit by a percentage — as much as 83% — of the amount you will get from Social Security. If you are thinking of taking a leave or quitting and coming back, you had better examine the provisions for interrupted service. Be sure not to jeopardize your vesting.

If you want to know more than what the summary plan description tells, ask your company for the complete plan description, which enlarges on all categories and details the plan's investment strategy. You also can get the pension fund's tax return, Form 5500, by writing to the Department of Labor, PWBA Public Document Facility, 200 Constitution Avenue NW, N5507 Washington, D.C. 20210. Officials will respond more quickly if you include your employer's identification number and the plan number, which your company can provide.

Once you have a copy of Form 5500, give it a careful reading. The first thing you want to know is whether the company has told the IRS that it might terminate the plan. If so, the information will appear in item 9.

Item 21 tells whether the company is up to date on its payments to the fund. If not, the next step could be termination of the plan.

Item 34 lists the fund's assets and liabilities. Notice whether considerable sums languish in non-interest-bearing bank accounts. Look for diversification and degree of risk. More than a third of the assets invested in a single kind of real estate, for example, could be a sign of unnecessary risk.

Your company's employee benefit managers should be happy to answer any questions about Form 5500. But if you get the feeling they are trying to hide something, take that as a warning about the future of your pension. For a free booklet on private pensions, call the Department of Labor at 202-219-8776.

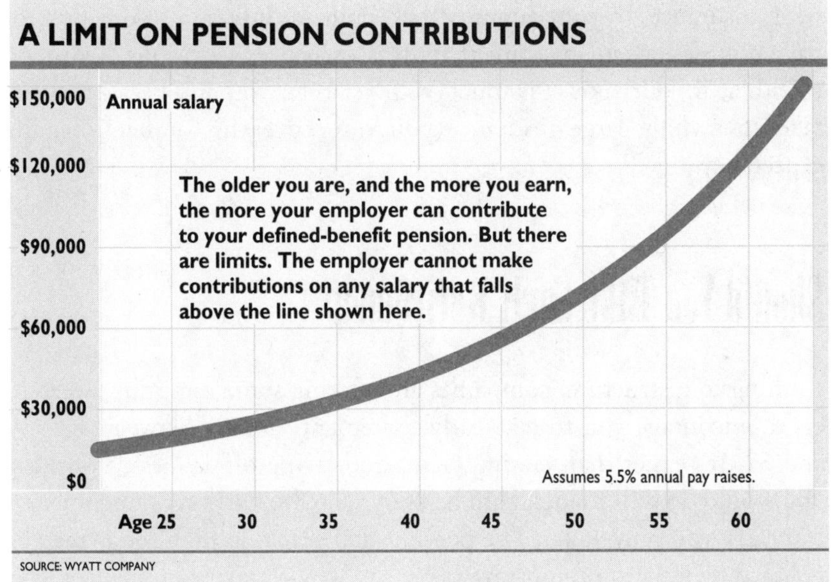

# Should You Insure Your Pension?

If you are married, your pension could well be 20% less than a single employee's, because employers pay insurance companies more for an annuity for a couple than for a single person, and generally pass the cost on to the employee in the form of a smaller pension. But if the married employee dies before his or her spouse, the spouse will collect some pension for the balance of his or her life. Provided you are vested, the law requires companies to give your spouse at least one-half of your pension benefits after you die, unless he or she waives this right. If you and your spouse choose this longer-lasting pension — and that's usually the right decision — your monthly payment will be reduced while you are alive (see pages 766–67).

Insurance agents argue that you should opt for the higher pension, and use the extra income to buy an insurance policy on your life. This is generally not a good strategy. The problem is that you're trading a sure thing for a gamble. If you do die before your spouse, the insurance policy will certainly pay off. The gamble is whether the proceeds will do the job. Will this suddenly-accessible lump of money generate as much income for your spouse as your passed-along pension would have guaranteed? You surely should not replace your spouse's annuity benefit with insurance if your annuity has built-in inflation protection or pays bonuses when investment returns exceed expectations. Don't do it, either, if your spouse is much younger than you are, because it will take an awfully large insurance policy to cover his or her long life expectancy.

# Should You Take Early Retirement?

Rushing to restructure, companies are offering some tempting sweeteners to encourage you to take early retirement, usually between ages 55 and 62. It's easier than closing plants and laying off armies of workers. You would do well to look hard before you leave. Early-retirement extras can carry you only so far. The pension that seems so high today may be gobbled by inflation tomorrow.

Almost every company pension plan provides for early retirement. About 85% of major plans contain terms that reduce early retirees' pensions by less than the actuarial tables would mandate. Yet the difference in payments can be substantial. In some cases, if you quit at age 55 — when your earnings may well be on the rise — you might get only 25% of the monthly pension you would have received had you worked till age 65.

When deciding whether to retire early, figure out what you want to do and whether you can afford to do it. Analyze your expected income and outgo. Your company's personnel department should provide individual or group counseling to help you. But it's wise to beware of the arm-around-the-shoulder manner of some company-paid consultants. They may make retirement seem more flowery than it will be.

As mentioned above, most retirees need 70% to 80% of their preretirement pay to match their standards of living. To figure out how much you'll need, draw up two scenarios — one assuming a modest annual inflation rate of 3% to 4% and one at 6% or more. You can shade toward the lower end of that spectrum if your major outlays — costs of housing, children's education and medical bills — are under control. If not, you will require more. If the combination of your pension and Social Security falls short of your needs, you will have to make up the difference through savings and investments or a second career.

About 70% of pension plans permit you to take your pension in a lump sum, up-front, and it's a good option. Quite often you also have the choice of accepting any severance pay in installments or in a lump sum.

One appealing investment choice is to have the whole lump-sum payout, except for your contribution, transferred into a rollover-type Individual Retirement Account. But if, on the other hand, you accept the lump sum in a check, your company will have to withhold 20% for tax purposes. Having the money transferred directly to an IRA defers taxes on the money and its future earnings until you withdraw it later on. The IRA rollover is particularly attractive for the many early retirees who find that their biggest nest egg is in their company's tax-deferred thrift or 401(k) plan. Unless you need a large chunk of the money, you'll do best to keep it locked up in an IRA and let it compound untaxed even while you are retired.

# Making the Most of Your Nest Egg

Tax-deferred retirement accounts offer several choices of how you can withdraw your money.

Most retirement plans, except IRAs, let you use forward-averaging to calculate your taxes. That is, you take your money in a lump sum, but you can divide the total amount by either five or 10, depending on whether you use five-year or 10-year averaging, and then calculate your taxes based on that amount. Your taxes will be lower because the amount, one-fifth or one-tenth of the total, will be taxed in a lower tax bracket.

If you reached age 50 by January 1, 1986, you can use either five-year or 10-year averaging. For example, if you received $200,000, you would pay a total of $42,775 in taxes with five-year averaging and $36,920 with 10-year averaging. This must be paid in one lump sum in the year in which you receive the distribution. People who were younger than age 50 on January 1, 1986, must use five-year averaging.

You could get an even better tax break on a lump-sum withdrawal if you began participating in the plan before 1974. Before then, lump sums were taxed at low, long-term capital-gains rates. After 1974 you began paying ordinary income tax on the money. But you can divide the money according to how many years you participated in the plan before and after 1974. Say that you started just over 26 or 27 years ago, in 1969. Then about one-fifth of your retirement fund will qualify for capital-gains treatment, and four-fifths for forward-averaging.

For people who were younger than age 50 on January 1, 1986, the low tax rates on your capital gains for the pre-1974 investments started to be phased out in 1987 and were totally eliminated in 1993. But if you were 50 or older by January 1, 1986, you can still take advantage of the capital-gains rate on your pre-1974 portion. For example, take a person who was 50 or older in 1986, started accumulating a pension in 1964 and who will retire in 2001 with $300,000 in a pension plan. He or she would be taxed for the pre-1974 years, which represents 37% of the whole amount of years, at the old capital-gains rate. Thus, 37% of the $300,000, or $110,000, would be taxed at 20%. The rest of the $300,000 would be taxed at the regular income rates.

You have to pay ordinary income taxes on anything you take out from an IRA. If you have retired early, you can sometimes start withdrawing without penalty before age 59½ — provided you take out enough each year to simulate an annuity. That is, you need to take the money evenly over your life expectancy, which can be computed with IRS life-expectancy tables. But starting at age 70½, which is the last deadline for beginning withdrawals, you must stick with a withdrawal schedule based on life expectancy. If your 70th birthday falls within the year, and you are a single man, you would have to withdraw one-fifteenth of your total IRA money; a woman would have to withdraw one-sixteenth. A husband and wife, each 70 years old, would have to take out one-twenty-first. Each year after that, their life expectancy would change and so the fractions would change.

If you're single, you can slow your withdrawals by naming a beneficiary. If possible, choose someone at least 10 years younger than you are. Then the first withdrawal could be no more than 4% of your tax-deferred savings.

## Does It Pay to Work After You Retire?

The word *retirement* no longer conjures up golf carts and golden-years cruises. More and more retirees choose to find another job. But after all the taxes you have to pay and all the Social Security benefits you stand to lose, does that really make economic sense?

Your income after you retire includes your pension, Social Security and any money you collect from IRA, Keogh and other plans and your investments. As long as you don't earn any money from a job, you can keep all of this income, less the taxes you must pay. But if you are younger than 70, the more money you earn from work, the smaller your Social Security check will be. As noted earlier in this chapter, in 1995 retirees 62 to 65 years old could earn up to $8,160 without jeopardizing their payments; people aged 65 to 70 could earn $11,280. And don't forget: Your new salary will be subject to Social Security payroll taxes; it can also throw you into a higher income tax bracket and thus shrink the net return on your investments. Depending upon the amount of your adjusted gross income, you may have to pay income taxes on part of your Social Security benefits. The good news is that after you hit age 70, you collect your full Social Security benefits no matter how much you earn from a job.

If you plan to go on working, ask your company retirement counselor or an accountant to figure out how much you really will earn. Ideally, you should start three years before retirement to investigate the job market, make contacts and take any necessary classes.

One excellent place to begin a postretirement job search is with Forty Plus, a group of self-help cooperatives staffed by job-seeking members in 21 cities. They run placement services, aid you in preparing your résumé and coach you in job interviewing.

If you don't want to work for pay but wish to keep busy, look for volunteer work. Two programs that can help place you are the Retired Senior Volunteer Program and Voluntary Action. You can find them in the phone book or by calling your local Office for Aging. Also, check your city or county agency that directs services for the elderly; it may list volunteer jobs.

## Your Medical Care

One thing is sure about your health insurance after you retire: Medicare, which reimburses no more than $60 out of every $100 of your medical expenses, will not be enough to see you through. You should get a "Medigap" policy to supplement it. A new law says that you have six months after retirement to buy any Medigap policy without having to undergo a medical exam or answer questions about your health.

If your pocketbook permits, buy a plan with at least these features:

- full coverage of doctors' bills
- full coverage of hospital bills after Medicare runs out
- coverage of existing illnesses
- guaranteed renewable coverage
- nursing-home coverage. The first 20 days of post-hospital care in a skilled nursing home are Medicare's complete responsibility. The next 80 days cost the patient $89.50 per day. A Medigap plan should take care of that expense. But don't expect any Medigap plan to pay for care in a custodial nursing home, where people with chronic illnesses spend the rest of their lives. That kind of coverage calls for a special long-term-care policy.
- illnesses while you're out of the country

To help you evaluate the new Medigap policies, United Seniors Health Cooperative has updated its booklet, *Managing Your Health Care Finances* (United Seniors Health Cooperative, 1331 H Street NW, Suite 500, Washington, D.C. 20005; $10). You can also consult the 1993 Medicare Handbook, free at Social Security offices throughout the U.S. (For more information, see Chapter 14, "Cutting Your Health-Care Costs.")

# Your Housing

One of the major financial decisions when you near retirement is what to do with your house. Do you sell it? Or stay in it and tap your home equity?

If you are age 55 or older, you probably can take the once-in-a-lifetime exclusion that exempts you from taxes on the first $125,000 gain from selling your home. But if you don't want to sell, you can dip into the equity that you have built up in your house by getting a so-called reverse mortgage. As long as you remain in your home, you can collect monthly payments, tax-free or, if you prefer, take the money as a lump sum or line of credit, or any combination of these options. Principal and interest are due only when you sell your house or die.

Faced with growing demand for reverse mortgages, private companies are offering an increasing variety of them, including one insured by the federal government. For a list of reverse-mortgage programs, send a stamped, self-addressed envelope and $1 to the National Center for Home Equity Conversion, 1210 East College Drive, Suite 300, Marshall, Minnesota 56258. You can also get a book, *Retirement Income on the House,* for $29.45 from the National Center, or by calling 800-247-6553.

You can sell your house and continue living there by making a sale-leaseback deal. For example, the buyer gives you a 10% down payment and you give him or her a 10- to 15-year mortgage at 9% to 10% interest. You also sign a lease granting you the right to rent the house for the rest of your life. During the term of the lease, your income from the mortgage should pay your rent and leave you with some extra cash, too. The buyer in a sale-leaseback deal is responsible for taxes, insurance and maintenance, which saves you money. Many parents have sold their houses to their grown children and then leased them back.

The American Association of Retired Persons staffs a home-equity-conversion clearinghouse and publishes a free, 43-page *Home-Made Money: Consumer's Guide to Home-Equity Conversion* (AARP, Home Equity Information Center, 601 E Street NW, Washington, D.C. 20049). The publication is updated every two years, and the most recent one was May 1995.

When choosing a place to retire, look at a number of factors, including services from health care to transportation, as well as crime statistics, climate, leisure and cultural activities and cost of living. While Florida still draws the highest number of retirees, the state isn't as popular as it once was. Many retirees are choosing desert and mountain communities, particularly in the West. College towns, such as Oberlin, Ohio; Ithaca, New York; and Bloomington, Indiana are becoming magnets for retirees because they offer relatively inexpensive cultural events and educational opportunities, plus good health care, low crime and a vibrant mix of age groups. Oberlin's biggest draw is the college and its Conservatory of Music. Oberlin College helped start a Learning and Living Institute for retirees, offering courses on topics from great literature to computers.

You may also want to retire in an area where the average household income comes close to your retirement income. Your money is likely to go much further in Oxford, Mississippi, for example, where the average household income is $35,800, or 13.5% below the national average of

## MOST DESIRABLE PLACES TO RETIRE

*Retirement Places Rated,* by David Savageau, published this list based on housing, climate, personal safety, services, work opportunities, leisure and cost of living.

| | | | |
|---|---|---|---|
| 1 | Las Vegas, NV | 11 | Savannah, GA |
| 2 | St. Petersburg/Clearwater, FL | 12 | Daytona Beach, FL |
| 3 | Bellingham, WA | 13 | Fort Myers/Cape Coral, FL |
| 4 | Fort Collins/Loveland, CO | 14 | Fayetteville, AR |
| 5 | Medford/Ashland, OR | 15 | Gainesville, FL |
| 6 | Tucson, AZ | 16 | San Diego, CA |
| 7 | Coeur d'Alene, ID | 17 | San Antonio, TX |
| 8 | Traverse City, MI | 18 | Camden, ME |
| 9 | Phoenix/Mesa/Scottsdale, AZ | 19 | Austin, TX |
| 10 | Melbourne, FL | 20 | Port Angeles/Sequim, WA |

SOURCE: *RETIREMENT PLACES RATED*, DAVID SAVAGEAU

$41,428, than in Laguna Beach, California, where the figure is $81,400. Some states offer you excellent deals on taxes. Seven states have no income tax: Alaska, Florida, Nevada, South Dakota, Texas, Washington and Wyoming. New Hampshire has a 5%, and Tennessee a 6%, tax on dividend and interest income but not on other income. Mississippi waives all state taxes on Social Security and pensions. The best way to learn about a state's taxes is to write for its resident income tax form, fill it out and compare the bottom line with that of your current state. Five states — Alaska, Delaware, Montana, New Hampshire and Oregon — have no sales tax. To a retired couple, this could mean a savings of $300 to $600 a year.

If you plan to buy a home, another way to save is to retire in a state with low property taxes. Two are Louisiana and Alabama, both with a tax of .4% of the property's value. An average-priced home in Guntersville, Alabama, would carry a property tax of $286 a year, compared with $3,661 in Lake Winnepesaukee, New Hampshire, or $3,843 on Cape Cod, Massachusetts. Alaska is the only state where people older than age 65 are completely exempt from property taxes, but ironically Alaska is the state with the lowest proportion of people over 65. A good, comprehensive guide for choosing a retirement location is *Retirement Places Rated* (Macmillan Travel, $19.95).

## COMINGS AND GOINGS

Top 10 states for net elderly net in- and out-migration, 1985-1990

| MOVING OUT | | MOVING IN | |
|---|---|---|---|
| 1. New York | -135,237 | 1. Florida* | 223,089 |
| 2. Illinois | -44,464 | 2. Arizona | 40,443 |
| 3. New Jersey | -39,176 | 3. North Carolina | 23,985 |
| 4. California | -36,815 | 4. Nevada* | 17,641 |
| 5. Michigan | -27,176 | 5. Oregon | 15,281 |
| 6. Massachusetts | -20,928 | 6. Washington* | 12,848 |
| 7. Ohio | -17,355 | 7.Texas | 12,714 |
| 8. Pennsylvania | -16,607 | 8. South Carolina | 11,557 |
| 9. Connecticut | -14,930 | 9. Georgia | 6,695 |
| 10. Indiana | -6,091 | 10. Tennessee* | 6,221 |

SOURCE: WILLIAM H. FREY, UNIVERSITY OF MICHIGAN, ANALYSIS OF 1990 U.S. CENSUS DATA

*No personal income tax

# Continuing-Care Retirement Communities

Imagine yourself as a retired person enjoying safety and independence in comfortable surroundings with few worries about bills for catastrophic illness. A dream? Yes, but one already being realized by thousands of people who live in continuing-care communities.

There are now nearly 900 such communities in the U.S., many of them in Florida, California and Pennsylvania and almost all sponsored by religious or other nonprofit organizations. For a one-time payment plus monthly maintenance, you can get a contract that entitles you to an apartment, meals, medical service and, if necessary, nursing-home care until you die. In 1994, the entrance fees for a one-bedroom unit in a continuing-care retirement community usually ranged from $59,000 to $86,000, plus a monthly fee of $1,000 to $1,400. Costs are lower if you choose a contract that covers less nursing-home care, and still lower if you pay for medical services as needed.

Continuing-care facilities are not new. The four oldest were established before 1900. But most have appeared since 1960, and it's estimated that hundreds more will get started in the next 10 years. Unfortunately, in the 1970s and early 1980s many of these facilities fell into bankruptcy, or suffered severe financial troubles. In the most egregious cases, the operators were con men. Other communities were run by people with the best of intentions but the worst of calculations. Victimized by circumstances beyond their control, elderly residents failed to get the homes and care for life that they had been promised. The money they paid was gone.

Today's picture is far brighter. Thirty-six states have laws regulating continuing-care communities, including how they handle their financial obligations. And the nursing-home industry itself has tackled the job of inspection and accreditation. So far, about 150 communities in 24 states have won approval from the Continuing Care Accreditation Commission, an independent agency sponsored by the American Association of Homes and Services for the Aging. For a list of them, send a stamped, self-addressed business-size envelope to the CCAC at 901 E Street NW, Suite 500, Washington, D.C. 20004-2037.

If you are considering this kind of retirement, carefully check out all aspects. In a sense, you are choosing an insurance policy as well as a home. Restrict yourself to communities whose financial stability has been studied by an actuary. Read a copy of his or her report. If you can't get one, or if it says fees may be raised to cover cash shortfalls, strike the place from your list. Think twice about high up-front fees and lack of escrow accounts for the money you deposit on your entrance fee while you are on the waiting list to move in. Ask for the biographies of the community's principal owners and operators. They should have solid experience in similar developments. Request the names of residents of these communities and make some phone calls to investigate whether the projects are financially sound and deliver what they promise.

If you are thinking about a new project that is financed with state revenue bonds, ask for a copy of the prospectus and study it closely. The developer should allot more than 50% of the bond sale proceeds to land acquisition and construction costs. Spending anything less than 50% on these basics is a clear warning that the developer is skimping — or skimming.

For more information about continuing-care communities, write to AARP, 601 E Street NW, Washington, D.C. 20049, or to the National Consumers League, Suite 928, 815 15th Street NW, Washington, D.C. 20005. The American Association of Homes for the Aging publishes *The Continuing Care Retirement Community: A Guidebook for Consumers.* It includes a consumer checklist and a financial worksheet to help you decide if you should sign a continuing-care contract. You can get it for $5 from AAHA Publications, Suite 500, 901 E Street NW, Washington, D.C. 20004-2037. Other publications are also available from AAHA; for more information, call 202-508-9442.

# Retiring to Foreign Countries

Hoping to live comfortably on a modest income in an ambience of choice, some 400,000 Americans have chosen to retire abroad. But many people are learning that bargains do not come that easily. Fluctuations in the dollar's value make it hard to plan how far your money will go, especially in countries with strong currencies. Rising living standards in a host of nations bring higher living costs. And Mexico has presented another kind of problem with its economic troubles and political unrest. Nonetheless, more than 300,000 Americans have retired to Mexico, the largest concentration being in and around Guadalajara, in the state of Jalisco. South of the Border Tour & Travel publishes a quarterly newsletter titled *Retire in Mexico: Updates and Business News.* It costs $39 a year. The agency also offers retirement and investment seminars in Mexico. The price (except airfare) for five days is $969. South of the Border Tour & Travel is at 40 Fourth Street, Suite 203, Petaluma, California 94592 (707-765-4573).

If you are considering a foreign address, don't cut all home ties until you have tried living temporarily in your chosen spot, at various seasons if necessary. Keep an open mind and be prepared for adjustments that can range from petty annoyances to downright disillusionment.

Pick a country with topflight medical standards, notably Canada, Costa Rica, France, Germany, Britain, Ireland, Sweden or Switzerland. Medicare does not extend beyond U.S. territory, but many private plans, including Blue Cross/Blue Shield, will cover you. Local health insurance is also available. In countries with large expatriate enclaves you will find private health-insurance programs, such as that of the American Society of Jalisco. Your best opportunity in some countries may be a government-sponsored health program. Spain's program, for example, serves Americans living there.

As for taxes, the U.S. Internal Revenue Service takes its cut of your income no matter where you go. You may also be subject to the taxes of the country where you live, though you usually need a substantial income, or business, to owe taxes to your adopted country. One comfort: The U.S. has tax treaties with many countries that let you credit one set of taxes against the other, so you don't pay twice. For information on which countries the U.S. has treaties with and what exemptions are included, you can request publication 901, *U.S. Tax Treaties,* from the IRS by calling 800-TAX-FORM. If you relinquish your citizenship, you must still pay taxes as a non-resident alien on income from U.S. sources, including your pension. The IRS also has laws to tax retirees who shift assets to the Cayman Islands and other tax havens. If you have questions about possible taxation, consult a tax lawyer of the country before you move there.

Should you keep your money in the local currency or in U.S. dollars? As long as the dollar is more vigorous than the local currency, expatriate retirees should hold their money mainly in greenbacks. Some countries allow you to maintain a local bank account denominated in dollars or in another foreign currency of your choice.

Wherever you settle, you should have two wills: one covering property in the U.S., the other for assets in the other country. And each should mention the other.

The monthly *International Living* ($29 a year, $2.50 an issue) often discusses retirement abroad. Each year the January issue rates countries on their quality of life, weighing such factors as health, cost of living, culture and the economy. The editors have also written a book, *The World's Top Retirement Havens* (Agora, Inc., $19.95). Both are available from Agora, Inc., 824 East Baltimore Street, Baltimore, Maryland 21202; 410-234-0691; 800-433-1528.

If you wish a personal contact, write or phone Richard Krueger, Lifestyles Explorations Inc., Suite 1900, 101 Federal Street, Boston, Massachusetts 02110; 617-371-4814. It sets up one- and two-week group trips to countries that are popular with Americans who want to live abroad, particularly Costa Rica, Honduras, Ireland, Portugal, Uruguay and Canada. Each tour includes meetings with and lectures by local real estate brokers, business people and academics as well as transplanted Americans, both retirees and entrepreneurs.

# Help from Software

A variety of software programs can help you plan your retirement. According to the American Association of Individual Investors' magazine, titled *AAII Journal,* these are the top five programs:

- Vanguard's Retirement Planner, version 2.0, is a reasonably priced (about $18) and easy-to-use program that automatically calculates, among many other things, your Social Security benefits. It also allows you to run different scenarios for your taxes and investment returns before and after retirement.
- Retire ASAP by Calypso Software sells for about $103 but is considered worth its hefty price tag. It allows you to determine asset allocations at any stage in life, not just at retirement. And like Vanguard, it allows you to determine how much you might lose in Social Security benefits if you retire early.
- Harvest Time by Computer Lab is $54 and not as user-friendly as Vanguard and Retire ASAP but does have tables that allow you to track your contributions and investment growth in your

retirement plans. You can print out charts displayed on the screen.

- Fidelity's Retirement Planning Thinkware, priced about $18, explains investment strategies. One drawback: It doesn't calculate tax rates before or after retirement.
- T. Rowe Price's Retirement Planning kit is only $15 but is not as good as Vanguard's and Fidelity's fund-family kits. It doesn't offer specific retirement-planning charts or compute your Social Security benefits. But it does include an illuminating three-stage risk/reward drill, followed by portfolio recommendations.

For more information, you can get a free AARP booklet, *Receiving a Lump Sum Distribution: A Guide for Investors Aged 50 and Over,* by calling 800-322-2282, extension 4536. And for a list of publications from the Pension Rights Center, call 202-296-3776.

## RETIREMENT PLAN CHOICES

Here are the choices and limits you have with various types of plans at retirement.

| TYPE OF PLAN | Your choices at retirement | Limits and tax effects |
|---|---|---|
| **Social Security** | You get a monthly check for life. But the longer you wait to collect (up to age 70), the bigger your check. | Payments will be taxed if your taxable income tops $32,000 filing jointly, or $25,000 if you're single. |
| **IRAs** | You can take a lump sum or withdraw in installments. | With some exceptions, you cannot make withdrawals until age 59½ and you must start withdrawing by age 70½ to avoid penalties. You pay regular income tax on withdrawals of all earnings and all pretax dollars you contributed. |
| **Qualified pension or profit-sharing plans, e.g. 401(k)s** | Depending on the plan, you may roll over into an IRA or take a lump sum. Or you may get deferred or installment payments. (If you can take a lump sum, it may be eligible for five- or 10-year averaging.) | You face generally the same limits and penalties as with IRAs. |
| **Keogh plans** | Same as above. | You face generally the same limits and penalties as with IRAs. |
| **Simplified employee pensions (SEPs)** | You get annuity payments for life or take a lump sum, | You face generally the same limits and penalties as with IRAs. |
| **Non-qualified plans for high executives** | You get annuity payments for life or take a lump sum. | You pay regular income tax on payouts. Usually you must start taking them at retirement. |
| **Annuities** | You can get annuity payments for life or make withdrawals. | You pay regular income tax on payments. There is a penalty tax if you withdraw before age 59½. The annuity company will also hit you with a penalty if you withdraw in the early years of the plan. |

SOURCE: JOHN HANCOCK FINANCIAL SERVICES

C H A P T E R 2 3

# Dealing with Wills, Trusts and Estates

## Drafting Your Most Important Document

The prolonged, moderately growing prosperity that many forecasters expect for the U.S. could have one rather unexpected consequence that would be a mixed blessing for you. It could so greatly swell the value of your retirement programs — your company stock purchase, savings and pension plans; your 401(k), IRA, SEP, Keogh and other tax-deferred plans; and your additional investments — as to create both a windfall and an estate tax migraine for you and your heirs. Even if your income is moderate, you may be building up substantial — and eventually highly taxable — retirement and estate benefits.

Here are some historical examples of the impact of estate taxes:

| | *Gross Estate* | *Settlement Costs* | *Net Estate* | *Percent Shrinkage* |
|---|---|---|---|---|
| Walt Disney | $23,004,851 | $6,811,943 | $16,192,908 | 30% |
| Robert Frost | 421,678 | 156,725 | 264,953 | 37% |
| John D. Rockefeller, Sr. | 26,905,182 | 17,124,988 | 9,780,194 | 64% |
| Franklin D. Roosevelt | 1,940,999 | 574,867 | 1,366,132 | 30% |

Listen to the logic of an expert estate planner, John Elbare of Tampa, Florida: "Americans over sixty-five now have approximately ten trillion dollars in wealth, and every bit of that will be transferred over the next thirty years or so. The lack of an estate plan is really a plan to leave as much of your wealth as possible to the IRS."

As noted elsewhere, you don't have to be wealthy to be worried. Even people of modest means will be affected, and even young adults should be starting an estate plan now. Bear in mind the basics:

Any assets that you leave to your spouse will go to him or her tax-free — provided he or she is a U.S. citizen. Any assets you leave to others — for example, to your children — will be hit by the estate tax after the first $600,000. (Congress has been talking about raising the limit, but what follows are the rates as of late 1995.) The federal tax starts at 37% for anything above $600,000 and then steps up to 41% on anything above $1 million, 53% on anything above $2.5 million, and 55% on anything above $3 million.

Now, about your $600,000 exemption:

You may leave all of it to a single child, if you choose, or $300,000 to each of two children, or $200,000 each to a child, a grandchild and a nephew or niece — free of federal estate taxes. In addition, your spouse can also distribute up to $600,000 free of federal taxes.

You may think that your estate is well below the key $600,000 mark and that you and your heirs will escape heavy taxation. But you must add up the value of almost everything you and your spouse possess: your home; your savings and investments; your personal property and collectibles; your life insurance policies; your IRA, 401(k) and other tax-deferred retirement plans; and the appraised value of any farm or vacation home that you may own. Your estate will also swell in value because of inflation and appreciation of your assets.

- An estate worth $500,000 with a growth rate of only 6% per year will rise in 25 years to $2 million.
- An estate worth $1 million with 8% growth will rise in 10 years to more than $2 million.
- An estate worth $1 million with 10% growth will rise in 15 years to $4 million.

Remember also that when you withdraw money from your IRA, your 401(k) and other tax-deferred plans, you generally have to pay income taxes on all of it, except for funds that were after-tax contributions. A considerable number of companies allow you to contribute an additional amount of after-tax dollars. You must pay tax on your employer's contributions, your own pretax contributions and all of the growth. Say that your combined federal, state and local income taxes net out to a total 35%. In that case, a withdrawal of $100,000 would leave you $65,000.

And generally, if you ever withdraw more than $150,000 a year from your tax-deferred retirement plans — such as your 403(b) annuities, 401(k), SEP and IRA accounts — you would have to pay an additional 15% penalty tax. This is the neatly named "excess retirement accumulations tax." It is indexed to inflation so the $150,000 will grow over the years. The primary exception to the tax affects people who qualify for grandfathering — those who accumulated total retirement benefits of at least $562,500 on August 1, 1986, and made a special election on their 1988 tax return — but only the initial amount is exempt, not the growth.

Say that you want to withdraw $200,000 in a year and your total income taxes amount to 35%. A withdrawal of $200,000 would net you $130,000. If your spouse also has an IRA, then the total you may withdraw per year before the 15% excise tax kicks in jumps to $300,000.

State taxes on your estate can also be high. So, even if you still think you will never be worth enough to worry, you had better visit a lawyer anyway to find out how all those taxes stand to reduce your estate — and what you can do to ease the bite.

You may think that estate taxes hit only the rich, but in fact they affect hundreds of thousands of Americans who save diligently and invest wisely. Your estate will be skimmed by federal taxes if it exceeds $600,000 if you are single or $1.2 million if you are married. The surest, simplest way to reduce estate taxes is to give to your heirs while you are still alive the maximum amount that the law allows and that you can afford.

You can give as much as $10,000 a year tax-free to as many people as you want. Married couples jointly may bestow up to $20,000 a year to any individual. For example, if a couple has five children, they can give $20,000 to each of them — a total of $100,000 — every year. You can also pay tuition and medical bills for your children and grandchildren above and beyond the $10,000-per-person limit. But you must pay them directly to the institution or care provider.

In addition, because you will have more than you expected to leave to your heirs, it is increasingly important to put in writing just who will inherit your accumulated wealth. You can do one or more of three things:

- You can write a will, leaving instructions on how you want your wealth to be distributed after your death. Your state officials will then see to it that your intentions are carried out, through probate. That is the process of administering and proving a will under the jurisdiction of a court. Probate costs run from 1% to 8% of the estate, depending on the state in which you live.
- You can declare who will get your various possessions when you die. You designate a beneficiary for financial assets such as life insurance policies, bank and brokerage accounts, and retirement plans. With real estate you do so by sharing the title of ownership jointly with the person who will inherit it by "right of survivorship." In either case, this kind of transfer is not subject to probate.
- You can create one or more trusts to which you turn over the legal ownership of some of your worldly goods. The most common form is a living revocable trust. Its primary benefits may be to avoid probate, to give you the ability to keep your affairs private and to create a user-friendly mechanism to manage the assets of the grantor (the person who established the trust) if that person is unable to do so for himself or herself. The one thing that this kind of trust does *not* do is save any estate taxes beyond what a well-drafted will can save. To do that, you need to establish *irrevocable trusts,* like life insurance trusts, qualified personal residence trusts, charitable trusts, grantor retained annuity trusts, etc. These trusts are described later in this chapter.

By far the *worst* thing you can do is nothing. In the absence of legally binding instructions, the law of your state determines who gets what — quite possibly not the heirs you would have named. Usually the state gives one-third to one-half of your after-tax estate to the surviving widow or widower and the rest to the children. If you have no surviving spouse or children, then your estate goes to your parents, brothers and sisters, and other blood relatives — or if you have none, then to the state itself. Unless you make proper provisions, your legacy will not be passed on to a friend or live-in lover whom you might have preferred to be your heir.

Appallingly, nearly two-thirds of adult Americans abdicate and leave matters to the state; they do not have a valid will. Yet merely by putting the right words on paper and having them properly witnessed, you may save your survivors considerable bitterness among themselves (and in their feelings about you) and spare them much hassling with the probate courts. No family situation brings on more stress than dividing up Dad's or Mom's estate. One academic study shows that where no legally binding instructions were left behind, arguments among the heirs were four times as likely to occur.

Fights over estates often stem more from frustrated expectations than anything else. One top estate lawyer tells the story of a widower who sought to leave 95% of his estate to his impoverished daughter and 5% to his son, who was a wealthy doctor. The son challenged the will and settled out of court for another $5,000. Says the estate lawyer, "I guess he wanted to prove that Daddy loved him as much as his sister."

More than mere wealth may be at stake. If you have young children, two of the most critical decisions that you must make are (1) the naming of a guardian and a backup in your will and (2) choosing the trustees for the children's funds. Only in a properly executed will can you appoint a guardian for your children; you also can make special provisions for an aging relative or a handicapped child. You cannot name a guardian in a trust but you can ensure that similar special provisions are made.

Many people think that writing a will or creating a trust is unnecessary because their surviving spouse will automatically inherit everything. But in most states, the law will make your spouse share your estate with your children or siblings or parents — unless you declare otherwise in a will. And since assets left to anyone other than a spouse face heavy estate taxes if they exceed $600,000, the government can become an unintended heir to your estate.

Dissolution of a marriage cancels any rights your ex-spouse might have to your estate. But should you die before a separation agreement is signed, your soon-to-be ex probably will still inherit. And people will think it was very sporting of you not to hold a grudge.

No matter how much or how little money you have, you should establish a solid and up-to-date will. Here are several tips for doing it right:

- Hire a lawyer to draft your will — and your spouse's. Resist the temptation to write one yourself following the instructions in a how-to book or using forms published by some states. A technical slip could make your homemade testament worthless. Take heed of what attorney Alexander Bove Jr. says in *The Complete Book of Wills & Estates:* "Approach preprinted forms in the same way you would a cheap suit of clothes bought from a mail-order supply house. The price may be right, but you'd be a fool to think it will fit or be fit to wear."

Only a lawyer knows what constitutes a valid document in your state. You're better off to find a lawyer who has special experience in writing wills and trusts than to rely on the general-purpose attorney who handled the sale of your house. Just as with a surgeon who performs many operations during a year, practice makes nearly perfect.

- Seek advice from other professionals — a financial planner, a bank trust officer, an accountant. Their goals should be to prudently maximize your estate's holdings and save taxes.
- Get witnesses. Most states do not accept wills or trusts that have not been vouched for by witnesses. Don't ask a beneficiary to be a witness; the will may be legal, but the beneficiary could lose his or her legacy.

Some lawyers at legal clinics will draw up your will for as little as $75, but $250 is average for a simple document. The cost rises with the complexity of your finances. Don't be shy about interviewing a prospective lawyer and getting the cost in writing.

Lawyers admit that wills are often loss leaders, and they hope to be made executors or trustees, or be hired to help settle the estate. Fees for executors typically are 2% to 5% of the gross estate. But you are under no obligation to do more than pay your lawyer for the will. Once the will is drawn up, sign only one copy, preferably under the supervision and witness of your attorney, and leave it with him or her. You can make minor changes with amendments at any time. Don't put your will in a safe-deposit box. Some states require that safe-deposit boxes be sealed on the holder's death, and it takes time to get the will released.

When drafting a will, people often make the mistake of trying to control their beneficiaries after they themselves have gone. For example, some time ago, one man set up a trust in his will but specified that the trust could hold only assets that yielded 4% to 8%. That was a reasonable return when the will was written — and anything above 8% was considered dangerously speculative. But when interest rates roared up some time ago, the trust manager was forced by the terms of the will to sell off many sound and high-yielding investments.

In making bequests, use a combination of percentages and dollar amounts. If you don't, much can go wrong. Take the sorry case of a man who left all of his $100,000 estate to his beloved sister, except for $10,000 that he willed to his nephew. But when the man died after a long illness, medical bills had shrunk his estate to $12,000. The nephew got his promised $10,000 but the unfortunate sister collected only $2,000. If the man had left his nephew 10% of the estate: he would have been left $1,200 and the sister would have collected $10,800. In the example above, if the estate's assets were to double to $200,000, then the nephew would receive $20,000, twice the amount his uncle intended. To avoid such complications, the bequest could state that the nephew is to receive the lesser of $10,000 or 10% of the estate. This way, if the estate goes up, he still gets the desired $10,000; but if it goes down, he doesn't end up getting a part of his aunt's inheritance.

Review your will at least once every three years, or more often if there is major new tax legislation, and keep it up to date. Be sure to revise your will if you move, particularly from a common-law state to a community-property state, or vice versa. In a community-property state, any assets acquired during marriage are jointly owned by both partners — except for gifts and inheritances. But in a common-law state, assets are owned by whoever buys them.

You do not have to write a new will every time you want to make small changes, such as substituting a beneficiary or changing the amount of a bequest. In these cases, your lawyer will usually write a codicil, which must be witnessed and kept with your will. Whatever you do, don't write on the will itself. Such changes may invalidate it, reducing all your careful planning to ashes.

Finally, you may think a will or trust is a statement of who gets what. But it may be just as important to state explicitly who does not get what — and why. In most of the world, custom and law dictate that children automatically receive most of the wealth when their parents die. That is, unless the kids have committed some awful crime. Only Britain and her former colonies give people the freedom to leave their heirs whatever they deem appropriate. So leaving it to the kids or not leaving it to them is a choice Americans enjoy as a vestige of our colonial past.

Let's say you decide to leave everything to your darling daughter — but you want to cut off entirely your unworthy son. You had better say so in no uncertain terms in your will or trust. If you simply omit any reference to a child, rather than specifically disinheriting him or her, that relative might be able to make a case that the drafting was flawed, that you "lacked testamentary capacity" or that people whom you left your money to exerted "undue influence." Disenfranchised children are frequent will-challengers. If their claim is upheld in court, they stand to gain an inheritance equal to what state law would provide if a parent dies intestate. That's usually one-half to two-thirds of the estate.

Two valuable books on drawing up wills and trusts are *Probate* by Kay Ostberg (Random House, $8.95) and Alexander Bove Jr.'s *The Complete Book of Wills & Estates* (H. Holt & Co., $10.95).

# Trusts That Reduce Your Taxes

You may think that trust funds are only for fabulously wealthy people, but you could easily be wrong. If you have children or substantial investments, you may be able to reduce your taxes by setting up a trust. The basic idea is simple: You transfer ownership of property or money to a trust on behalf of a beneficiary. Your beneficiary can be one or more persons — usually including your spouse or children. Or it can be an institution, such as a college or a church.

Trusts are increasingly being used by the middle class, a large and growing number of whom face the prospect of ultimately paying federal *and* state estate taxes. As noted, those taxes at the federal level run (as of late 1995) from 37% for any estate worth more than $600,000 to 55% for everything over $3 million. Some of the state taxes can be credited against the federal tax. So if, say, the federal tax is 37% and the state tax is 10%, the total tax on the estate is not 47% but somewhat less. You have to check a knowledgeable attorney or accountant for the precise figure in your case. Also, some states do tax estates that are worth *less* than $600,000, so an estate may escape the federal estate tax but *not* necessarily the state tax. (State taxes are explained in detail later in this chapter.)

The person who sets up or creates the trust is called the grantor. This is generally the person who transfers or donates assets to the trust. The grantor sets down instructions for the management of the trust and for passing out its income and principal. The grantor also chooses a trustee: a third party who holds title to the trust property and administers the trust. You can serve as trustee, or manager, of a trust you set up only if it is a revocable living trust (that trust saves no taxes), a qualified personal trust or a grantor retained annuity trust. You cannot be the trustee of your own insurance trust or an irrevocable trust (other than a charitable remainder trust) that you wish to be permanently outside your taxable estate. Of course, you will need to consult a lawyer about the proper way to establish a trust tailored to your needs.

There are two broad kinds of trusts.

*A testamentary trust* is established in your will and starts paying off after you die. It is usually set up so a financially astute relative can manage the inheritances of youthful or potentially spendthrift heirs. Because testamentary trusts are part of your will, they do not avoid probate, the lengthy and sometimes expensive legal process by which estates are inventoried.

*A living trust* is funded while you are still alive. As the grantor, you make provisions as to when both the principal and income is to be distributed. After your death, the trust assets automatically pass to your chosen heirs — or remain in trust for their benefit. The assets escape probate. That can be a big bonus in some states, notably California and Massachusetts. Estate administration can take months or years to complete, and the costs can be high. Attorney fees and probate expenses can slice 5% to 7% off a medium-sized estate that includes a house, some pension benefits and personal cash.

Several computer software programs can help you set up a living trust. One is TrustMaker by Legisoft, which works for both Macintosh and IBM-compatibles. The same company also created WillMaker. It may be worthwhile to use a program for reference and as a double-check, but you are probably better off to engage a lawyer who can tailor a trust to your specific needs.

Married people have a special advantage. Under the unlimited marital deduction, you can transfer an unlimited amount of money and property to your spouse free of gift and estate taxes. Under this provision, the heirs of a married couple can put off paying estate taxes until the second spouse dies.

But if you are married, make sure that *both* you and your spouse fully use your separate $600,000 lifetime gift tax exemptions. (Many couples don't!) You do so by creating a *credit shelter trust,* often called a *bypass trust,* for each of you.

When one of you dies, up to $600,000 of your estate goes in trust — free of federal estate taxes — for your children or other heirs you have named. If you were to leave these assets to your spouse, they would be tax-deferred — but only until he or she dies. By putting the $600,000 in trust you completely bypass the tax. While your surviving spouse may not *own* the assets, you can arrange the trust so he or she can collect all the annual *income* from the $600,000 for life.

For larger estates (those approaching $2 million), you might prefer to make the income discretionary rather than mandatory. This way you don't force more money than your spouse may need out of the trust's estate tax protection, only to be accumulated in his or her own estate for later taxation. With discretionary income payments, the independent trustee (the trustee who is not the surviving spouse) determines each year how much should go to your spouse, your children or other family members — and how much should stay and accumulate in the trust.

The independent trustee can also distribute *principal* to the surviving spouse, children or other heirs. If the trustee is a child or other beneficiary, the amount of principal that can be given is limited by an "ascertainable standard" — this accounts for financial concerns such as health or education. But, with both discretionary income and principal payments, you can give the trustee clear direction — by stating that your spouse's needs are to be considered first.

If you want to ensure that your spouse gets a definite share of the trust's assets, you can give him or her "5-by-5 withdrawal power." This means that your spouse has the unconditional power to take up to $5,000 or 5% of the assets from the trust each year — whichever is greater.

When the second spouse eventually dies, *another* $600,000 goes to the children or other heirs, free of federal estate taxes. The result: You have protected a total of $1.2 million from the federal tax collector.

An example: A husband and wife are both age 60. Together they have accumulated assets in excess of $1.2 million, which is not an unusual amount for couples who bought a home when real estate was cheap and faithfully contributed to tax-sheltered retirement accounts. Since you do not know who will die first, both married partners establish provisions in their respective wills to set up a bypass trust if they are the first to die, naming their spouse as primary beneficiary and the children as contingent beneficiaries. The man dies first at age 75, and then $600,000 from his estate goes into trust. His widow collects the interest, dividends and capital gains on that $600,000 so long as she lives. She then dies at age 90, and that $600,000 from her husband's original estate goes to the couple's heirs, and the whole amount is still tax-free. *In addition,* up to $600,000 from her own estate also goes to her heirs, tax-free.

If the trust were drafted with a discretionary income provision, and the surviving spouse never needed any of the income or principal, the trust would grow from the time of his death at age 75 until her death at age 90. With an annual net growth rate of 6%, the $600,000 in the trust would have grown to over $1.4 million by the time of her death 15 years later. This amount, plus $600,000 from her own estate — a total of $2 million — would be 100% estate tax–free.

Leave the rest of your estate — amounts over $600,000 — to a *Qualified Terminable Interest Property* trust, or Q-TIP. Your surviving spouse gets the annual income plus designated powers to draw additional money from the trust for as long as he or she lives. But when he or she dies, all the money in the trust, after taxes have been paid, goes to the heirs you have named, again, usually your children.

As John Elbare points out, the Q-TIP works particularly well when you (or your spouse) have children from a previous marriage. You probably want to pass your assets on to your own children, but only after you and your spouse have both departed. If you die first, your spouse may need the earnings from your assets to live comfortably, so you may not want to give your wealth to your children at your death. On the other hand, if you leave everything to your spouse, who may marry again, the wealth you wanted to pass to your children could wind up in the hands of total strangers, perhaps the children of the person your spouse marries.

This possibility can be avoided with a Q-TIP trust. It provides support to your spouse for life and then passes the assets to *your* children. Estate taxes on the Q-TIP trust are not paid until the second spouse dies.

Here is a complex but very important point:

When you draft your wills and trusts, make sure that the "titling" (or ownership) and beneficiary designations of your assets coordinates with the design of your wills and trusts. Many couples assume that their assets will automatically flow into their bypass or Q-TIP trusts, but this is not always the case. Most property that is jointly owned by a husband and wife is titled "joint with right of survivorship." It goes directly to the surviving spouse when the other dies, regardless of what the will says. Similarly, property assigned to beneficiaries — like your IRA, 401(k) or Keogh plans, annuity life insurance contract, etc. — goes directly to the beneficiary (usually the surviving spouse) upon the owner's death, again, regardless of the will.

For example, a married man has an estate worth $1 million. His will states that $600,000 is to go into a bypass trust and $400,000 will go into a Q-TIP trust, both primarily for his wife and children's benefit. Whether the assets will actually end up in these trusts depends on the titling and beneficiary designations of his other assets, which include: a $350,000 IRA rollover, half of a $400,000 house that he and his wife own "joint with right of survivorship," a $300,000 life insurance death benefit, and $150,000 of individually owned stocks. His wife is the beneficiary for the IRA and the insurance benefit, so when he dies, they will go directly to her along with his share of the house. This would leave only the $150,000 worth of stocks to fund the $600,000 bypass trust, and *nothing* would end up in the Q-TIP trust. It is also important that your executor select the Q-TIP election on the estate tax return.

To avoid these potential disasters *be sure* that your estate planning considers the ownership of your assets and coordinates it with your wills and trusts.

## The Virtues of Life Insurance

Beyond the bypass, there are other trusts to consider. If you and your spouse have insurance policies, you may want to give away ownership of them to an *irrevocable life insurance trust,* naming your children as beneficiaries. Doing so alleviates estate taxes if you do it right. Giving away your policies will keep them out of your estate only if you live more than three years after you make the gift and let the new owner pay the premiums. You must also be sure not to retain any powers to change the policy or tap into its cash value or exercise any other of what the IRS calls "incidents of ownership." If you are buying a new policy, you can avoid the three-year rule by setting up the trust first and having the *trust* buy the policy. In other words, don't buy and transfer it yourself.

Life insurance pays benefits that are not *income* taxed. An irrevocable trust protects this money against *estate* and *gift* taxes. Thus, putting life insurance into an irrevocable insurance trust lets you hand down your money to your heirs free of all taxes.

Insurance trusts are complex, lengthy documents that can be written in infinite ways. Be sure that you choose an expert lawyer, one well experienced in writing trusts, and that he or she understands your intentions. Be sure he or she explains to you such arcane — but most important — particulars as generation-skipping taxes, Crummey powers and hanging powers. Get a second opinion; after the trust has been drafted, get your lawyer's approval to engage a second, quite independent attorney to study and approve the text.

Also, be sure that you choose a solid trustee, plus a back-up in case your first choice cannot serve for any reason. Remember, the trustee almost certainly will not be called upon to serve until many years from now. It is wise to choose someone at least 10 years younger than you are. You can also name back-up trustees, or the trustee can name his or her own successor.

*A warning:* An irrevocable trust is just what its name implies; once you sign it, you cannot change or revoke it. If you want to control the trust, give up the tax savings and make the trust revocable. Never let a professional adviser talk you into making decisions for tax purposes if they do not coincide with your personal goals and wishes.

Once you have set up an unassailable insurance trust, it's wise to buy enough new insurance to pay a large part of your expected estate taxes. Those taxes must be paid within nine months of your death. Given the volatility of markets, prices for stocks, bonds, real estate and other assets may be depressed during this nine-month period — and the trustees of your estate would have to dump those assets at fire-sale prices.

Life insurance can be particularly helpful if most of your estate consists of a small business or real estate or other large, illiquid assets. To pay the estate taxes, your heirs may be forced to sell the asset — the family business — at distressed sale prices, if you can find a buyer within nine months. If you can't, most business owners will automatically qualify for a loan from the IRS. But even with a portion of it subject to a favorable loan rate, most heirs will not be able to pay the taxes plus interest plus the normal expense of running the business. No wonder so few small businesses are successfully passed on to younger generations.

To avoid such a calamity, you can turn to the charmingly named "second-to-die" life insurance policy. The premium is relatively low because this policy pays off only after *both* spouses have died. The heirs can then use the money to pay the estate taxes, which are due once both spouses have died.

Example: A married couple, ages 65 and 70, buy a $1 million second-to-die life insurance policy from an insurance company that has high grades from the ratings firms, such as A. M. Best or Standard & Poor's. If both spouses get the top health ratings, the annual premium should be about $25,000.

This premium presumes that the policy is a "blend" of approximately 50% whole life and 50% term insurance. Randy Siller, an estate and financial planning expert in Elmsford, New York, says, "You have to understand that when you add term insurance, you're adding risk because the term insurance part of the policy generally doesn't have guarantees. The premium could increase, the death benefit could be reduced if the insurance company encounters problems. The price for these policies is cheaper for a reason — you're accepting more risk. The price can be higher if it's largely a whole life policy, which builds up cash value like a savings account. But you're getting more guarantees, and long-term performance potentially as good as or better than those policies that include term insurance." Naturally, the premiums are lower if the insured husband and wife are younger than our hypothetical 65 and 70 years old, and higher if the insured couple has less-than-sterling health ratings.

Each year the insured couple can make gifts of the $25,000 premium to the trust, and the trustee then pays the premium to the insurance company. But since the $25,000 exceeds the annual gift tax exclusion of $20,000, gift tax would be due on $5,000, or it could be counted against the lifetime $600,000 exemption. Of course, $25,000 is a fistful of money — especially when you have to pay it every year. But remember that it is buying you $1 million worth of protection, and your heirs may need every nickel of it to pay the estate taxes.

*Charitable trusts* are also effective tools for doing well with your estate while doing good for a cause. The two main types:

*Charitable remainder trusts* are irrevocable trusts that are often set up to pay you and your spouse a lifetime income, give you an immediate income tax deduction, permit you to avoid paying capital-gains tax on the sale of appreciated securities or other property, and remove a big asset from your estate. The price for these advantages is that the principal in the trust goes to your chosen charity, or charities, after you and your spouse die.

These trusts work best if you own highly appreciated assets that pay you little or no income. They may be stocks, bonds or real estate that you got for a very low price and that have surged in value but pay little or no dividends or interest.

John Elbare provides an example:

You own 1,000 shares of stock that you bought for $10 a share. It has risen in value to $100 a share but pays you annual dividends of only 2%. If you sell the stock, you get $100,000 — but you have to pay 28% capital-gains tax on your $90,000 profit, thereby reducing your gain by $25,200, to $74,800. If you invest this gain in bonds yielding 8%, you get an annual income of $5,984.

You do much better with a charitable remainder trust. Instead of selling the stock, transfer it to the trust. The trust sells the stock but pays no capital-gains tax because these charitable trusts are tax-exempt. The full $100,000 from the sale is invested by the trustee in 8% bonds, who then pays you annual income of $8,000. That is a lot better than the $5,984 income you get if you sold the stock yourself, or the $2,000 you would collect in dividends if you hung onto the shares.

In addition, when you fund the trust, you get a federal income tax deduction and in most states, a state income tax deduction. The amount varies depending on your age and the amount of income the trust pays you each year. But using this example and assuming both spouses are age 65, the tax deduction will approximate $21,000 — saving about $8,300 in taxes if you're in the 39.6% bracket.

*Charitable lead trusts* work in the opposite manner: They provide a stream of annual payouts to your favorite charity for a fixed number of years, after which your children or grandchildren — not the charity — get the principal. You receive an immediate one-time estate or gift tax deduction for the present value of the income stream to the charity, and this deduction can offset most of the tax you would otherwise pay on the asset that you want to transfer to your children.

Jacqueline Kennedy Onassis planned her estate around a large charitable lead trust. She left us all an excellent lesson on how to write a last will. She spared her heirs from arguing by laying out who would get exactly what material goods — for example, her children got her Manhattan apartment and her stepbrother got her property in Newport, Rhode Island. She knew that it is easier to divide up money than property. Jackie also knew that Uncle Sam taxes everything, so when she gave gifts of cash ranging from $25,000 to $250,000 to various friends, maids and the butler, she designated that the taxes on those gifts be paid by the estate.

Most important, she put the bulk of her estate into the trust. In her will, Ms. Onassis directed her trustees to donate to certain charities an annual amount equal to 8% of the initial fair market value of the assets in the trust. After 24 years, the principal will pass to her grandchildren almost tax-free. A charitable lead trust is a good means to give money to heirs who don't need it immediately, and the donations to charity reduce the trust's taxes.

As journalist Susan Kuhn wrote in *Fortune:* "Charitable lead trusts are a great way to give money to family members and charities and save on estate taxes, provided your heirs don't need the income right away." Then, using calculations provided by Louis Hamel, chairman of the trusts and estates department of Hale and Dorr, a Boston law firm, she added:

> Assume you put $1 million into a 24-year charitable lead trust. You can set the payout rate to charities as high or as low as you wish, but to maximize the tax benefits on a trust of this size, a 4% rate is about right. If you choose to give the charities $40,000 per year, the present value of that gift, discounted at a current federal rate of 8.4%, is $407,000. Your taxable estate is reduced by this amount to $593,000, or just below the $600,000 exemption, so your taxes are zero. If you gave $1 million to an heir outright, on the other hand, the estate taxes would be $153,000. If this gift was for your grandkids, and it was more than $1 million, it would suffer yet another blow from the generation-skipping tax, which reduces the sum by 55%.

All this, admittedly, is pretty complicated stuff for just about anyone. An experienced lawyer can explain in detail how these trusts work and can tell you which of them, if any, make sense for you. Then the lawyer can design your estate accordingly.

## JACQUELINE KENNEDY ONASSIS' ESTATE PLAN

In one of her legacies to us, the President's widow left us a model of intelligent planning.

| ACTIVITY | WHAT JACKIE DID | WHY IT WAS SMART |
|---|---|---|
| **Giving gifts** | Left gifts of cash to friends and specified that taxes be paid out of the rest of her estate. | If the will does not direct the taxes to be paid from the estate, the value of a gift could be cut in half. |
| **Leaving property** | Specified exactly who would inherit each of her real-estate properties. | Homes are laden with emotion and should be disposed of directly, not lumped into total assets. |
| **Creating trusts** | Put the bulk of her estate into a charitable lead trust. The trust gives money to charities for 24 years, then the rest goes to her grandchildren. | A charitable lead trust is a good way to give money to heirs who don't need income immediately. The donations benefit charity and cut the estate's taxes. |
| **Making personal bequests** | Gave her personal property and letters to her children and requested that they respect her wish for privacy. | When giving gifts of valuable personal property, make your wishes known but allow the beneficiaries some flexibility. |

SOURCE: *FORTUNE*

The calculus of estate taxes, and thus of how much estates actually pay, is exquisitely complex. Sometimes I think that the government made it that way in order to confuse people — because so much money is at stake. But bear with me while we look at a few basics. They should inspire you to visit a knowledgeable trust attorney to see if your estate planning needs a tune-up.

If your estate is worth $2 million or more (unlikely as it now seems, smart investing may get you there), you should consider two additional kinds of trusts. They are the Qualified Personal Residence Trust (QPRT) and the Grantor Retained Annuity Trust (GRAT).

The QPRT covers your home and/or your second home. This trust has two advantages: (1) It reduces your gift tax on them by discounting the gift tax value of your home and (2) it removes any future appreciation in the value of your house or houses from your estate.

## WHO GIVES TO CHARITIES

| Sources of Contributions | 1993 (billions) | 1994 (billions) |
|---|---|---|
| **Individuals** | $101.2 | $105.1 |
| **Bequests** | 8.5 | 8.8 |
| **Foundations** | 9.5 | 9.9 |
| **Corporations** | 6.1 | 6.1 |

SOURCE: AMERICAN ASSOCIATION OF FUND-RAISING COUNSEL

In such a trust you transfer ownership of your home (or homes) to your beneficiaries, usually your children. But you retain the right to live in the home, rent-free during the term of the trust. When the trust terminates, the home would be transferred free of gift taxes to your beneficiaries — usually your children. Since your beneficiaries have to wait to receive the property, the IRS considers that the value of the property is reduced. And, consequently, the gift tax is reduced.

An example: Mrs. Jones, age 50, gives her $1 million home in a 15-year QPRT to her children. Mrs. Jones has the right to live in the house for all those 15 years. After that, she will pay rent to her children to continue residing there. What a terrific way to transfer assets without paying gift taxes on them!

When Mrs. Jones transfers title of the house to the trust after 15 years, it is worth not $1 million but only $215,000. And why is that? Answer: Because the IRS figures the beneficiaries had to wait 15 years. So Mrs. Jones winds up giving her children a terrific asset and paying *no* gift tax on it. The reason is that the $215,000 easily fits within Mrs. Jones's $600,000 lifetime exclusion from federal gift taxes.

There is one potential problem: The grantor of the property (Mom, in this case) must be alive when her children eventually inherit it. Otherwise, all bets are off, and the property re-enters the parents' estates and is treated like an ordinary asset. So this gives everybody the incentive for Mom and Dad to live longer.

Now, let's presume that the property rises in value by an average of only 2.5% a year, and Mrs. Jones still lives another 20 years. At that rate, by the time of her death, Mrs. Jones's property is worth $2,370,000. And *all* of it is free of estate taxes. By contrast, if she did not have this trust, then her beneficiaries — meaning her children — would have to pay a federal estate tax of $1,185,000 on the house. So it comes down to simply this: Whom do you want to get the money, Uncle Sam or you?

A GRAT works in a similar way, but it is not limited to a house or houses. For example, it can cover a small business. Example: Mr. Henry, age 50, owns an S corporation that has been appraised as being worth $5 million. He transfers half of it to a 15-year GRAT trust, naming his son as the beneficiary. In return, the GRAT will pay Mr. Henry 5% annually on the $2.5 million.

But because Mr. Henry's son had to wait 15 years to receive the business, the IRS discounts the value of the gift to $600,000. And since Mr.

**SAVE TAXES BY GIVING YOUR HOME AWAY**

Transferring your home to a Qualified Personal Residence Trust (QPRT) can save you thousands in federal and state taxes.

| | Hold | Donate to trust* |
|---|---|---|
| Market value of home today | $1,000,000 | $1,000,000 |
| Value of taxable gift to personal-residence trust today | — | $296,910 |
| Annual appreciation of home | 2.5% | 2.5% |
| Value of property after 15 years | $1,448,300 | $1,448,300 |
| Combined federal and state estate-tax bracket | 55% | 55% |
| Combined estate taxes | $796,565 | $163,300* |
| ESTATE-TAX SAVINGS | — | $633,265 |

*Estate taxes are based on "remainder interest" of $143,975, or taxable value of home given to trust. Appreciation is exempt while home is in trust. Illustration assumes woman dies shortly after trust expires.

SOURCE: TAX FOUNDATION

Henry has a $600,000 total exclusion from gift taxes, he winds up paying *no* federal gift taxes at all. Again, to make this work, Mr. Henry has to outlive the term of the trust, in this case 15 years to age 65. If he dies within that 15-year period, his S corporation assets are included in the estate, and his heirs collect much less.

But what if Mr. Henry not only reaches 65 but then proceeds to surprise everyone and live to age 80? By then, his original $2.5 million gift has grown to an assumed $10.8 million and this appreciated value of $10.8 million is removed from his estate. This saves his heirs roughly $5.6 million in federal estate taxes, assuming that Mr. Henry is in the 55% estate tax bracket.

The short form is simply this: QPRTs and GRATs can be very good deals if you are likely to have a large estate. And to repeat, you should look into them with a lawyer — or accountant or financial planner — who is expert in trusts.

## Wills Versus Living Trusts: The Pros and Cons

In recent years millions of people have traded in their will for a living trust, largely to avoid the sometimes-costly and time-consuming process of probate. That's the legal process by which the state oversees the carrying out of a person's wishes as set down in a will. A living trust is a great supplement to a will, but it should by no means replace it. Such a trust covers only the assets transferred to it, which do not include personal property like, for example, your car. You also cannot name the guardian for your children in a trust as you can in a will. Living trusts can be used for the more complicated aspects of your estate, thus allowing you to make a much simpler will. A will is probated publicly, while a trust is a private matter — unless some disgruntled heir challenges it in court.

In books and do-it-yourself manuals, advocates present trusts as the solution to all the problems of estate planning. It is true that a living trust can carry out your wishes in life and death while usually leaving you in charge of your wealth until the end. But according to its enthusiasts, a living trust can also speed the settlement of estates, liberate cash needed by survivors to pay the household bills, shield family assets from public scrutiny, fend off creditors and save legal fees.

As with all panaceas, the truth about these kinds of trusts falls short of the claims. There's no disputing that they can do the job of a will and circumvent probate. But whether a trust will serve better than a will depends on its purpose, who creates it, where that person lives and what he or she hopes to accomplish. For example, a living trust is the document of choice for putting a professional in charge of your investments during your lifetime, if and when you no longer are competent to manage your own money or interested in doing so. A trust can also continue to handle your investments after your death if you don't want your heirs to take on that responsibility.

A living, or inter vivos, trust used as a substitute for a will should be a revocable trust, one that can be readily changed or terminated by the person who created it. It must be signed, witnessed and notarized to become an effective legal instrument. Typically, you transfer all your assets to the trust and name yourself the beneficiary of its income and principal. Then, as in a will, you specify who will inherit its assets, and under what conditions.

Laws governing living trusts differ markedly from state to state. For example, most states let you act as your own trustee, so you can continue to have full control of your investments. But in at least one state, New York, you cannot be the only trustee. Someone else must be named co-trustee, meaning you must get the other trustee's signature every time you make an investment move or do anything else not specifically authorized in the trust document.

Advertisements soliciting business for lawyers who specialize in living trusts sometimes claim that these trusts will save you money in taxes. That is just plain bunkum. Whether it is controlled by a will or a living trust, your estate is subject to the same taxes. Trusts do erect a privacy screen around your bequests; neighbors and the press cannot gain access to a trust, as they can to a will that has been filed for probate. But wills do not reveal precisely how rich you were, except to the extent that you make large specific bequests.

As money savers, living trusts make better sense in some states than in others. Massachusetts and California permit notoriously high legal fees for probating a will. There, trusts are becoming the document of choice for people of means. In many other states legal fees for settling an estate are the same whether it is controlled by a will or by a trust. In some cases, trust estates have been more expensive to settle than probated estates.

Probate provides protections that trusts do not. The deadline for creditors to file claims against a probated estate and for disappointed heirs or disowned relatives to contest the will is generally three to six months after the will is filed for probate. No such time limit protects a trust. Further, estates governed by a trust can be tied up just as long as probate estates.

The first stumbling block is the Internal Revenue Service. An estate must remain open until all the assets have been evaluated and set down on a federal estate tax form, and the information filed with the IRS. Beyond that, the disposition of an estate depends on the dispatch with which your lawyer and accountant handle the case. Estates often get low priority on law-office calendars.

## Beware of State Taxes

If you are planning to move to another state after you retire, you had better confront the delicate subject of state death taxes. As mentioned above, your estate can escape federal taxes if it is valued at $600,000 or less. But the states levy their own inheritance or estate taxes. Happily, the federal government gives you a credit for your state tax payments. In all, 28 states and the District of Columbia have arranged their estate taxes so that they equal the federal credit. These states are known as "pickup tax" states, since they pick up the federal tax credit. What this means is that in these states, you don't pay more than the federal tax. (Pickup tax states are Alabama, Alaska, Arizona, Arkansas, California, Colorado, Florida, Georgia, Hawaii, Idaho, Maine, Massachusetts, Michigan, Minnesota, Missouri, Nevada, New Mexico, North Dakota, Oregon, Rhode Island, South Carolina, Texas, Utah, Vermont, Washington, West Virginia, Wisconsin, Wyoming — and the District of Columbia.)

The remaining states collect taxes above and beyond the credit allowed by the federal government. They exempt anywhere from $25,000 to $600,000 of the estate, but the remainder is taxed at rates of 1% to 21%, depending on the state and the estate's size (Mississippi is the one with the 1% minimum, New York is the one with the 21% maximum.) It hardly needs to be added: Check with your tax adviser to see if your estate will be hit by state taxes, and how hard.

## STATES TAKE THEIR SHARE OUT OF ESTATES

Net state taxes on a $1 million estate left entirely to your child. The federal tax is $153,000.

|  |  |
|---|---|
| Most states | $33,200 |
| North Carolina | $35,000 |
| Kansas | $41,750 |
| Indiana | $51,900 |
| New York | $53,500 |
| Delaware | $55,250 |
| Ohio | $58,100 |
| Pennsylvania | $60,000 |
| South Dakota | $71,250 |
| Iowa | $71,825 |
| Connecticut | $77,935 |
| Kentucky | $70,000* |

*$70,000 is effective through June 1996. But Kentucky's estate tax for children of the deceased is being phased out in steps, down to zero as of July 1, 1998.

SOURCES: U.S. ADVISORY COMMISSION ON INTERGOVERNMENTAL RELATIONS; *FORTUNE*

Often the amount of the tax depends on whom you leave the money to. If you are a Delaware resident and leave your entire estate directly to your spouse, he or she owes no tax. But your child will pay tax on anything over $25,000.

More than one state can tax your estate. Stocks, bonds and other paper assets are taxed in the state where you legally resided at the time of your death. But real estate, jewelry, furniture and other so-called tangible assets are taxed where they're situated. Most states consider you a resident if you pay income tax there or if you vote, do your banking, register your car, get a driver's license or have your primary home there.

You can cut the bill by taking full advantage of deductions. State laws generally give your spouse, children and grandchildren the most generous exemptions and the lowest tax rates. So, the more you give or leave to your immediate family, the less is owed to the state taxman.

If you want to leave your entire estate to your spouse, you can do it in such a way as to escape part or all of the state tax when he or she dies. To accomplish this feat, bequeath part of your property directly to your spouse and instruct that the rest be placed in an irrevocable trust from which your spouse can draw income after you die.

Most important, before making any estate-planning decisions, call your state tax department for detailed information. And be sure to consult an attorney.

# An Example of Minimizing Taxes

Let me tell you the true story of a millionaire who has set up his estate so that when he dies, his heirs will inherit his wealth without having to pay any taxes. You need not be a millionaire to learn an estate-planning lesson or two from Saul Jacobson.

An engineer from Delaware, who is now retired in Palm Beach, Florida, Jacobson is 82 years old and hopes to live to be at least 90. But just in case he doesn't, he has set up his estate so that his heirs will inherit it all — more than $1 million — without having to pay any taxes. He calls his planning "an enduring act of love."

Jacobson wisely sought advice from professionals — not just one, but four of them: a financial planner, an accountant, a lawyer and a bank trust officer. All this cost him about $10,000, but he estimates that it will save his family at least half a million dollars.

His will states that half of Jacobson's assets will go directly to his son. The son could inherit up to $600,000 tax-free under federal law. To pay the taxes on any amount above that, Jacobson has bought life insurance.

In addition, he has set up a Q-TIP — a qualified terminable interest property — trust. It will provide for Jacobson's wife. If she survives him, she will collect the income from the Q-TIP trust for as long as she lives. When she dies, the money in the trust will go to Jacobson's two grandchildren. Only then will it be subjected to the estate tax. The Q-TIP trust defers the tax until the death of the second spouse.

You might be able to draw a lesson from Saul Jacobson and leave the largest possible tax-free estate for your spouse and any children or grandchildren. Just consult a seasoned lawyer and inquire whether you should set up a Q-TIP, a bypass or some other trust. If you set up a Q-TIP trust like the one described here, however, a federal tax may be imposed because the terms of the trust call for skipping a generation. You should discuss with your tax adviser or lawyer the various legal means to avoid or hold down the generation-skipping tax.

Carefully study the plan, trust or will prepared by your professional advisers. Unless you strongly indicate otherwise, their proper goal will be to minimize your taxes. Only you know your true wishes — and maybe they will include giving an outright bequest to some friend or relative, with no strings attached.

## Picking a Trustee

Any trust needs a trustee who will take responsibility for the money, acting as both a watchdog and a safe-keeper. The trustee protects the assets in the trust, collects any debts or dividends that are due and may pay a regular stipend to the heirs in accordance with the trust.

Very often people who write wills and set up trusts designate banks as the trustees. For honesty, impartiality and continuity, banks are hard to beat. The fees that trustees are entitled to collect vary from state to state and from institution to institution. In New York, for example, the annual fee on assets of $1 million is .69%. Above that amount, the percentage of assets lost to fees is even less. But how well do bank trust departments really do in managing estates and in guiding assets to growth?

In an earlier era of money management, bank trust departments minded the wealth of millionaires' widows and the heirs to great fortunes. The departments placed caution above all else, and so they invested in top-grade bonds and conservative stocks in order to produce annual returns of 3% or so. That hardly seems acceptable today, and most banks have up-to-date trust departments that skillfully handle people's money. Still, if you go to a bank, be aware that its investment policy is almost sure to be more conservative and cautious than another trustee's policy.

Most trusts designed to minimize estate taxes are irrevocable. Unless the trust specifically permits beneficiaries to switch banks, they can do little short of going to court, or threatening to do so, to upgrade performance or dismiss incompetent trustees. State and federal bank regulators are powerless to help. The courts can oust a trustee, but only on proof of fraud, incompetence or misappropriation of funds. So lawyers offer some advice to anyone establishing a trust:

- Give beneficiaries an escape hatch by specifying their right to replace trustees. Don't retain any such rights yourself. You would be taxed under the grantor trust rules of the Internal Revenue Code — effectively defeating your original intentions in establishing the trust.
- Appoint a co-trustee, preferably a friend or relative whom the bank would have to consult before changing investments and who would serve without fee.
- Spell out the trustee's responsibilities; they can range from simple caretaking to complete control.

Above all, investigate now whether your spouse, your children or your other heirs would benefit by your setting up a trust and getting a trustworthy trustee.

## Becoming an Executor

It seems like such an honor. A relative or close friend asks you to be the executor of his or her will. You are flattered to be so trusted. But be warned: Estate administration is tough, time-consuming and sometimes even risky. You could wind up spending months, or even years, worrying about death, taxes — and greed.

The first rule of being the executor is not to be one in the first place. Tell Aunt Sadie to get a lawyer or a seasoned bank officer who knows how to administer an estate. The only problem is that such a professional costs money, and Aunt Sadie didn't get to be rich by spending a cent she didn't have to. If you refuse the job, then the fees for a professional executor will reduce the estate by 2% to 5%. Under most state statutes, the executor (professional or not) will be entitled to a fixed fee unless it is waived. Banks and trust companies may charge more than the amounts provided by statute.

If you do accept the request to become a nonprofessional executor, you will find that the job, for all its drawbacks, can be fascinating. It is like having a person's life suddenly open before you. Of course, you may also find out a lot you didn't want to know.

Don't try to do the job of executor by yourself. Get an expert lawyer to help, unless Aunt Sadie lived in Texas or one of the few other states that have fairly simple probate procedures. If the estate includes land, an ongoing business, a trust, substantial charitable bequests or anything else that could cause a tax problem, then whatever state you live in, hiring a lawyer is a must.

Finding that lawyer is not always easy. Start with the attorney who drafted the will. If he or she is not available, ask at your local bar association for recommendations. Try to find a lawyer who is a fellow of the American College of Probate Counsel. Members have had at least 10 years' experience and are recommended by their peers.

When you become the executor, face up to the fact that you are going to be busy for quite a while. The first thing you must do is find the will and read it. Next, have the lawyer whom you've hired get the will probated, that is, "proved" in the probate court as a valid will. The court will issue to you what's known as letters testamentary that give you authority as executor. You then have to notify all the heirs and any relatives who would have been entitled to inherit under state law if there had not been a will.

Your real chore will be finding and taking possession of the deceased person's property. Tangibles such as the house, car or jewelry should be locked up. An obituary is an advertisement for burglars. Buy or renew the insurance on all the property. If you don't, you could be personally liable for any loss.

Put any cash into a separate checking or savings account for the estate. Pay all the bills out of the estate checking account. Fortunately, it's usually the lawyer's job to pay any taxes, but you will need to give him or her a precise inventory of the assets and their value. And you — the executor — are responsible for seeing that the taxes are paid on time.

When the will has been probated and all taxes and debts have been paid, the executor prepares an accounting for the probate court of all assets received and sold, all claims and expenses paid, and all amounts due to those who are to get the remaining estate. Then he or she is finally ready to distribute what is left to the heirs.

Sometimes the court will allow an executor to make distributions to needy heirs before the final accounting. Otherwise, you allow at least four to six months for creditors to come forward before parceling out, say, the deceased person's pearls or the 300 shares of General Motors. If you do not wait and there is not enough money left in the estate to satisfy creditors, you could be held personally liable.

Probably the most trying aspect of your job as an executor is keeping meticulous records of the estate's expenses and receipts. That means more than just filling up a shoebox with check stubs and random bank statements. It might be worthwhile to pay the minimum annual fee of around $750 to a bank trust department to act as custodian. The bankers will keep the records for you.

If the estate includes a large portfolio of securities, the executor will need astute investment advice to preserve and perhaps increase the assets before he or she hands them over to the heirs. Hiring a professional investment counselor means another fee, but it may save the estate money in the long run.

Executors are held to a high standard of fiduciary responsibility. They run significant legal risks if they act in any way that could be considered contrary to the heirs' interests. So there are a few things not to do. Don't deposit in your personal checking account any checks made out to you as executor, and never make yourself a temporary loan out of the assets of the estate. Also, you shouldn't buy anything from the estate without permission of all the other heirs and possibly the court.

Should you take an executor's fee? In a few states, compensation is set by law — usually a one-time fee of 1% to 5% of the estate. In most states, though, an executor simply puts in for a "reasonable" fee and the court upholds it as long as no one objects.

For years it was traditional for executors who were family members to forgo a fee for their blood, sweat and tears. The fee might reduce the executors' own inheritance, and as ordinary income it would be taxed at higher rates than estate taxes. But now lawyers are urging executors to take the money. Chances are, by the time you have made all the distributions and the court has discharged you from your responsibilities, you will have earned every cent.

## Should You Leave It All to Your Children?

Nowhere but in America do so many parents enjoy the privilege of grappling with the question of what to leave their children. There are about 2 million U.S. households that enjoy a net worth of at least $1 million. Most of the millionaires inherited their wealth or built it on a business they founded. But plenty of corporate careerists also have created seven-figure estates by taking advantage of company profit-sharing, retirement savings and stock purchase plans. In short, estate planning is fast becoming a major concern of the middle class.

And nowhere is the feeling about inherited wealth so ambivalent as in the U.S. Many people worry that Commodore Vanderbilt's grandson was right when he declared that "inherited wealth . . . is as certain death to ambition as cocaine is to morality."

*Fortune* magazine surveyed 30 multimillionaires on the subject of what they plan to leave to their heirs. One-fifth of them said their children would be better off with only minimal inheritances. And almost half plan to leave at least as much to charity as to their heirs.

For example, billionaire Warren Buffett, chairman of Berkshire Hathaway, contents himself with giving his children several thousand dollars each at Christmas. He plans to leave most of his money to his charitable foundation. Buffett says that setting up his heirs with a "lifetime supply of food stamps just because they came out of the right womb" can be "harmful" for them and is "an antisocial act." T. Boone Pickens, the famous oilman, warns, "If you don't watch out, you can set up a situation where a child never has the pleasure of bringing home a paycheck."

Yet there are sensible ways of passing on what you have without depriving the kids of their own feeling of achievement. Estate experts have some tips:

First, don't be so secretive with your heirs. As soon as the children begin to mature, bring the family finances into the daylight, so they will know approximately what they will get some day and have some idea of how to hold on to it. They should also know, of course, if they will not be getting anything. Talks about family money, like those about sex, should begin as early as possible.

Second, shelve the silver spoon. No matter how well off you are, make sure your children go to work. Psychiatrists say that lack of work experience not only alienates heirs from humanity but also contributes to insecurity about their ability to survive without their inheritance.

Third, give later rather than sooner. Most estate advisers agree that the age of 21 is too early for children to reap a windfall. Businessman William Simon, one-time U.S. Secretary of the Treasury, suggests that parents put a reasonable amount in a trust that starts paying interest only when the child reaches age 35 and then allows him or her to tap into the principal in two installments, at ages 40 and 45.

Above all, put child-rearing above estate planning. Psychiatrists say that wealthy parents in particular often pay too little attention to child-rearing. As Buffett advises, "Love is the greatest advantage a parent can give."

## Widows: Managing When Alone

It is sad but true that more than 11 million American women are widows. Those who are in the best financial shape are not necessarily the ones with the largest inheritances. Rather, they are the women who regularly, thoroughly and candidly discussed family finances with their husbands and, more important, what to do with their legacies if their husbands died first.

Because women live much longer than men, widows outnumber widowers by five to one. The median age of widows is about 73. At that point in their lives, quite a few may have been widowed for some years, and unless they have remarried or are still going to remarry, they could be looking forward to a decade or more of life on their own. Up to the time of their husbands' death, many of them had never thought much about how to handle the family's assets or how their own economic needs would be met. Of course, this is true of men, too. People of both genders often do not give enough attention to their financial affairs. But the problem is more acute with widows because there are so many more of them than widowers and because many older women traditionally depended more on their mates for such decisions than younger women do.

By contrast, the widows who cope the best are those who taught themselves — well in advance — how to manage money. The wrong time to start asking about, say, the difference between money-market funds and stock mutual funds is when a woman has to start managing the family assets alone.

Wives should insist on periodically reviewing their family assets and liabilities with their husbands. Lynn Caine, author of the book *Widow,* suggests that a couple set aside an annual "contingency day" to assess what the surviving spouse would inherit and consider what he or she should do with it. They should discuss whether he or she ought to sell the major inherited assets, such as their house or art collection or business. The couple should also re-examine their wills every year and discuss where the widow or widower should seek financial advice.

Every married couple should update and put in writing all the information that can help the survivor and an executor settle the estate, including such basic facts as the names and phone numbers of the family attorney, accountant, stockbroker and insurance agent; the locations of bank accounts and safe-deposit boxes and important documents, such as wills, deeds and partnership agreements; and a list of assets and debts. Of course, all this information should be kept in one secure and convenient place.

Every married woman should regularly read the newspaper business pages and financial magazines. That is a necessary first step in planning for the possibility that someday she may have to direct her own financial affairs. A wife should also handle her own checking account, pay the bills periodically and take an active part in meetings with any of her husband's professional advisers, such as the stockbroker or insurance agent.

The first priority of a widow should be to preserve her inheritance. For instance, it may be foolish to sell off the family house, which is probably the best place for her to live today and may well be worth more tomorrow. She may be able to delay paying some bills so that the money can earn bank or money-fund interest. To guard against mistakes and con men, a new widow would be wise to double-check whether questionable bills have already been paid.

She ought to wait six months or a year before considering investing her inheritance in anything that isn't safe and liquid. Her thinking may be clouded if she makes any immediate decisions. Until the widow seeks advice from professionals to decide how to diversify her investments, any insurance money and other inherited cash can be kept safely in certificates of deposit, money-market funds or mutual funds that invest in conservative stocks.

A new widow or widower can get wise counsel from a booklet titled *What Do You Do Now?* It is available for $4 with a $20 minimum-ordering requirement plus 15% for cost of shipping from LIMRA International Association (Order Department, P.O. Box 208, Hartford, Connecticut 06141) or call 800-235-4672. She or he can also get information on self-help groups in the U.S. and Canada by writing to the International THEOS Foundation, 322 Boulevard of the Allies, Suite 105, Pittsburgh, Pennsylvania 15222. Another source of support and financial information is the Widowed Persons Service, an AARP agency at 601 E Street NW, Washington, D.C. 20049. The service sponsors about 230 programs across the country and encourages widows or widowers to write for the nearest address.

Remember: Eventually, a widow must assume responsibility for financial decisions. The sooner any married woman prepares for widowhood, the better. A much more secure legacy than money is knowing how to manage it.

## Why Everyone Should Write a Living Will

A living will (not to be confused with a living trust, described above) is a document that spells out any medical situations in which you would not want to be kept alive after becoming terminally ill. Everyone older than 21 should consider drafting a living will, says Giles R. Scofield, the director of the Health Law Program of Pace University Law School. "It doesn't matter how old or young you are. My recommendation: If you have ever thought about what you would want done, write it up." Recent Supreme Court decisions have held that a living will or some evidence of your intention regarding life-sustaining methods is necessary in order to allow a physician to stop such treatment .

You don't need a lawyer. Groups such as Choice in Dying (200 Varick Street, New York, New York 10014), a nonprofit educational council, can help you fashion a living will for yourself that will withstand most challenges. Choice in Dying will send you a set of forms at no charge, though it welcomes donations.

The kit includes a form to create a "durable power of attorney for health care," also known as a "health-care proxy." This is a legal document in which you give your next of kin or another trusted person the power to decide, when you cannot, whether you should be kept alive by artificial or heroic means, such as heart resuscitation. Pro-life advocates have strong reservations about living wills. "People signing them often contemplate circumstances far different from those being invoked," cautions David O'Steen, executive director of the National Right to Life Committee.

It is up to each person who writes a living will to make his or her wishes clear and explicit. If you agree with the right-to-life philosophy, you can express your desire to be kept alive under most circumstances. You might, for example, wish to reject only the kind of extraordinary treatment that is risky and therefore elective.

To give your living will maximum authority, sign it in the presence of two witnesses who are not your relatives, and have all signatures notarized. The late Robert Klein, business editor and Certified Financial Planner, sensibly advised taking these other steps to strengthen your position:

- Choose a person to make medical decisions for you if necessary. There is no hard-and-fast rule, but a friend may be more persuasive to a judge than a relative who is also your heir. Discuss your feelings with this representative before signing your living will, and periodically afterward, to make sure you are both in accord. Give this person a copy of your living will.
- Give copies of the documents to members of your family, your physician, attorney and clergyman. Keep them informed of your wishes so that they won't interfere if the time ever comes to invoke your wishes. In particular, make sure that your doctor agrees with your decision and is willing to put a copy of

your living will with your medical records. If he or she refuses, think about finding a more understanding physician.

- When choosing a hospital or nursing home, ask the institution to agree in writing to comply with your living will. If it will not, go elsewhere.
- Put your living will with other important papers or have your attorney put it in his or her files along with your will. Do not keep it in your own safe-deposit box.
- Update your living will regularly. At least every five years sign it again before witnesses and a notary. Not only will a recent reaffirmation of your wishes carry extra weight with doctors, hospitals and judges, but it will also force you to reconsider your position. The idea of clinging to a life you cannot enjoy may be abhorrent to you now, but who knows? In 10 or 20 years, any thread of life may seem precious.

If all this seems challenging, let us offer a piece of wisdom from Katharine Hepburn: "Growing old ain't for sissies."

EPILOGUE

# A 52-Week Plan to Get Your Finances in Shape

You've probably discovered by now that I'm an optimist. How could I be anything else? I've seen that $1 invested in the market back in 1980 is worth almost $10 as of mid-1995. I've seen that people who have earned the most are those who adopted a strategy and stuck with it. When the market plunged, they did not panic, but instead used the opportunity to pick up some bargains.

I believe that as long as our country does well, its economy will do well and, consequently, its markets will do well — over the long term. And all of us should plan our lifetime financial strategy for the long term.

I suggest that, in framing your strategy, you follow certain guiding principles, which are discussed in this book:

Have a bias for action. Build up enough liquid savings to make you secure against an emergency, but favor investing over saving. Favor stocks over bonds, and — particularly if you are young — favor growth stocks over more conservative shares. Favor no-load funds over load funds, discount brokers over full-service brokers — unless you need ongoing investment guidance. Practice dollar-cost averaging, investing a fixed amount from every paycheck. Take advantage of every tax-deferring investment program that you can: IRA, 401(k), 403(b), SEP, Keogh, etc.

I'm convinced that, whatever you have, you can make more of it.

You can make your money grow significantly — by having a plan, a strategy. You work at it steadily. You take some intelligent steps, one at a time.

Let's say you take just one step a week to make or save money now. Do that, and at the end of one year, you will have greatly improved your financial fitness. Here's a 52-week program, re-emphasizing without overly repeating what is discussed throughout this book:

*Week 1:* Start the new year off right by contributing to your IRA as early as possible, as described in Chapter 8. That way, your money can benefit from the most growth — all tax-sheltered. Many people wait to make their contribution until April when they pay their taxes. Wrong! Why waste 1¼ years of your earning potential? And if you or your spouse don't have an IRA, there's no better time to start one than now.

*Week 2:* While you're at it, also start a Keogh if you have any self-employment income. A Keogh lets you shelter much more money than an IRA, and, yes, you can have both plans at the same time. To see if you're eligible, consult Chapter 1.

*Week 3:* Pay off all your credit-card bills — even if you have to borrow from a bank or against your life insurance or some other source. As noted in Chapter 10, it costs you much less to pay off a bank loan than to pay your credit-card bills. Just think: If you're in the 28% tax bracket, you'd have to earn 25% on your money, before taxes, to equal what you would save simply by paying off your balance on a credit card that's charging you 18% interest.

*Week 4:* Pay off your other bills with money you get from a home-equity loan, described in Chapter 10. Your interest payments on home-equity loans as big as $100,000 are tax-deductible, but your interest payments on ordinary consumer loans are not.

*Week 5:* Arrange with your employer to have a fixed amount transferred from every paycheck — or tell your bank to transfer a fixed amount every month from your checking account — into one or more mutual funds. For more on mutual funds, see Chapter 5.

*Week 6:* Buy a software program for your personal finances — and use it. Doing so keeps you constantly up-to-date on the state and shape of your finances and enables you to make better investments and financial decisions. Chapter 18 offers much valuable information about which computers and software will serve you best.

*Week 7:* Buy a tax-software program and use it. Use it even if a tax professional fills out your tax forms. You will find some savings that he or she misses. For specific ways to save on taxes, consult Chapter 9.

*Week 8:* If you got a tax refund on last year's income, have your payroll department increase the number of dependents listed on your W-2 form. This stops you from overwithholding and adds to your take-home pay. Chapter 9 can also be valuable on the subject of tax withholding. You don't want to give interest-free loans to Uncle Sam.

*Week 9:* Shift out of some corporate bonds and into some municipal bonds, a move that will spare you taxes. Buy munis issued by agencies in your own state, and they generally will be triple-tax-free. But do the calculations to make sure that you will collect higher net interest than you're now getting from your ordinary, taxable bonds. For more on bonds, see Chapter 7.

*Week 10:* Examine your life insurance to see that you have both enough coverage and the right kind of policies for your age, income and family responsibilities. As explained in Chapter 13, you might want to shift part of your money out of whole life and into lower-premium term or universal — or vice-versa.

*Week 11:* If you are voluntarily paying for group life insurance where you work, check whether you can get the same coverage for less expense outside the plan.

*Week 12:* Re-examine your health insurance to make sure that you and your family are well covered. If you're not in a group plan, shop around for better coverage at a lower price. Buy a dental care policy, too, unless your employer has you covered. For details, see Chapter 14.

*Week 13:* It's tax preparation time. When you go through all those stubs, checks, monthly bank and brokerage statements, make an inventory of your assets and liabilities, as discussed in Chapter 2. Gather your bank, brokerage and mutual-fund account numbers (include names and telephone/fax numbers) and give a copy of everything to your lawyer and/or accountant.

*Week 14:* Tell your doctor and your pharmacist that you prefer to buy generic drugs if there is no medical difference between them and much costlier brand-name pharmaceuticals. If you're taking the same drug over a long period, buy it from a discount mail-order supplier. For more, see Chapter 14.

*Week 15:* Confirm with your payroll department that you are indeed contributing as much as you can to your 401(k), profit-sharing and other tax-sheltered plans that are discussed in Chapters 3 and 9. Many people think they're putting the maximum into their 401(k) when they really aren't.

*Week 16:* Examine the mix of your investments in tax-sheltered company plans, and consider putting more of your money into one kind of investment (for example, a growth-stock fund) and less into another (for example, an income fund). Most participants in these plans invest too conservatively.

*Week 17:* Shift out of mutual funds that are underperforming and into funds that have the best record over three to five years. Chapter 5 explains more about mutual funds.

*Week 18:* Sign up for dividend-reinvestment programs, if you own stocks in companies that offer them. Your dividends will be used automatically to buy you more shares, with no commission charges and sometimes at a 3% to 5% discount. This is a great — and painless — way to build your stock ownership. For other tips on investing in stocks, see Chapter 6.

*Week 19:* With the vacation season approaching, check your travel agent for any buy-one-get-one-free airline ticket specials, deep-discount cruises, and other travel bargains. You'll find many of them in Chapter 20.

*Week 20:* Instead of spending a king's ransom on a vacation, join a vacation club and swap your residence for one abroad, or in some marvelous domestic destination.

*Week 21:* Move to a discount stockbroker, as discussed in Chapter 6, unless you feel you need ongoing guidance to pick shares. If you choose to stay with a full-service broker, then for the sake of diversification, consider splitting your account between two firms: a nationwide broker and a local, regional broker.

*Week 22:* After interviewing at least three of them and preferably more, select a personal financial planner. Ask him or her the questions and use the selection guidelines detailed in Chapter 2.

*Week 23:* Reread Chapter 4 and determine what asset allocation you want: What percentage of your investments to put into stocks or stock mutual funds, bonds or bond funds, real estate investment trusts, precious metals, etc. Then start steadily shifting your assets until you achieve the desired allocation. Remember: Historically, asset allocation, not what individual stocks or funds you pick, has a greater impact on the success of your investment program.

*Week 24:* The end of the school year is a good time to review your financial planning for your children's education. Check that you are putting away enough — and making the right investments. And for the inside on financial aid you can still get, see Chapter 15.

*Week 25:* School is out, summer is here, and it's the season when Junior's accidents are most likely to happen. In that unhappy event, resolve to check all hospital bills for errors, which are common. And for a guide to finding the best hospitals, look again at Chapter 14.

*Week 26:* Check with an insurance agent to make sure that you have adequate fire and casualty insurance on your house, as well as an "umbrella" policy to protect you against lawsuits and other risks that are mentioned in Chapter 13. Get competing bids from several agents for your business.

*Week 27:* Re-examine your auto insurance and get new, competing bids. Unless your car is quite new and very valuable, you'll probably want to raise your deductible to reduce your premium.

*Week 28:* Make a thorough inventory of everything you own, as discussed in Chapter 21. Take photos of all your rooms or, better yet, videotape them. No, you won't make or save any money right now, but you'll thank me, and yourself, if you're ever burglarized.

*Week 29:* While you're at it, make photocopies of all your credit cards. Leave copies in your office and at home, and carry one in your purse or briefcase at all times. You'll be happy you did if your purse or wallet is ever stolen.

*Week 30:* Buy a "Club" locking device to protect your car against break-ins. Also buy an alarm system or the Safestop Starter Interrupt, which disables the starter each time the ignition is turned off; security devices for your car; and pick-resistant locks or a wireless security system to save your house from illegal entry. These devices, explained in detail in Chapter 21, protect from amateur thieves. They may or may not protect you from professionals, but they will probably lower your insurance premiums.

*Week 31:* Protect the value of your house by scheduling any necessary preventive maintenance, as detailed in Chapter 11. You can save money by repairing your house in stages, from checking the electrical system to fixing the roof. And now may be a good time to do indoor or outdoor painting.

*Week 32:* Visit your banker and — particularly if you carry a high balance in your checking accounts, or conduct other business through the bank — request to be paid a higher interest rate on your savings. The bank should oblige. If it doesn't, consider shifting your savings to a federally insured bank or savings and loan in another state that does pay higher interest.

*Week 33:* Wherever you choose to bank, make sure that your interest is being compounded and credited *daily.* Chapter 3 includes still more on getting your best deals in banking.

*Week 34:* If you're regularly carrying much more of a balance in your checking account than you really need, transfer some of the funds to a money-market deposit account at the bank; it pays you higher interest, as detailed in Chapter 3. If you can afford to tie up some of the money for three months or longer, move it into a still higher-yielding certificate of deposit.

*Week 35:* Take time to re-evaluate your career goals and directions. Consider whether you should get some training to develop a new skill, or sharpen an existing one. Chapter 16 can help.

*Week 36:* Enroll in a nearby university or community college for a course in personal finance, accounting, retirement planning, computer use or some other subject that will help you handle your money.

*Week 37:* Visit your lawyer to update your will if you haven't done so in the past two years or longer. And two years from now, as recommended in Chapter 23, examine your will again.

*Week 38:* Check with a lawyer who is expert in trusts to see whether the time has come for you to start setting up trusts to protect your estate from excessive taxes. When a trust is written, get a second opinion from another lawyer in another firm. Chapter 23 can help you with this subject, too.

*Week 39:* Look into the advantages of leasing a car instead of buying one. Chapter 19 can get you started.

*Week 40:* Open custodial accounts at a bank or brokerage for each of your children or grandchildren. And make gifts to those accounts. The taxes on the earnings will be lower than on your savings or brokerage accounts.

*Week 41:* Consider buying your parents' home from them and renting it to them. Then they can invest the proceeds from the sale in income-yielding securities, and you get the tax benefits of renting out property that you own — deductions for property taxes, mortgage interest and depreciation. You must charge your parents a fair market value rent. But you can forgive the rent and make it a tax-free gift. The limit for annual gifts is $10,000 from a child to one parent, or $20,000 if both parents are still alive. For other guides on gifting, see Chapter 23.

*Week 42:* In a variant of the above, just go out and buy a house or condo, and rent it to your aged parents or to your grown children. This gives them a good deal and enables you to take major tax deductions for renting out your property.

*Week 43:* If you are living with a person of the opposite sex without benefit of marriage, take the steps detailed in Chapter 12 to protect her or him. And consider the financial advantages that marriage would bring; for example, you could leave your whole estate to your spouse, tax-free. Getting married may be the most sensible thing you could ever do to enhance your financial security. For more on love and money, see Chapter 12.

*Week 44:* Put up to $5,000 each year — in *pretax* dollars — into a flexible spending account (FSA) for dependent care, if your employer offers such a plan (about 80% of employers do). Use these tax-free FSAs to pay for care for your dependents, usually your children or a disabled spouse. If you are in the 31% tax bracket and you use all $5,000 per year to which you are entitled, you'll save in federal income taxes. In many cases, these accounts are free of state taxes. You also may put aside $2,000 to $3,000 in a separate FSA to pay your medical bills.

*Week 45:* If you're older than 62, check into all the discounts and bargain rates you can get from hotels, airlines and cruises and for many goods and services. If you're not yet that age, pass this tip on to your parents.

*Week 46:* Call the marketing departments of AT&T, MCI, Sprint and any other long-distance phone company serving your area, and sign up with the one that gives you the best deal on the kind of calls you make most often.

*Week 47:* Give up to $10,000 a year to each of your children and grandchildren. The sum, of course, can be much less than that. In any case, you will not have to pay federal gift tax.

*Week 48:* Take all of the year-end tax deductions you legally can, as outlined in Chapter 9. For example: Send in your January mortgage payment in December. Make next year's charitable contributions in December, perhaps on your credit card (they will be billed in December, but you need not pay them until January). Make early payments of some real estate taxes, state taxes and quarterly estimated taxes. Renew next year's subscriptions to business and professional magazines this year. Pay next year's professional dues this year; consider selling mutual funds on which you have losses, or swap bonds that aren't performing well.

*Week 49:* To take a tax loss, dump a few dogs among your investments. Sell mutual funds on which you have losses. Sell bonds that have been doing poorly and replace them with others in the same investment category. You may do the same with stocks, but it will be harder to find shares almost identical to the ones you already hold. Don't wait until late December to make these swaps; it may be difficult at that time to get just what you want.

*Week 50:* Begin a program of buying U.S. savings bonds. The interest they pay is tax-free if you use it to pay college tuition for your children, grandchildren or spouse — or anyone else. For more on bonds and other investments, consult Chapter 7.

*Week 51:* If you plan to give a substantial sum to a charity, set up a charitable remainder trust. The charity gets the benefit of your contribution, and you get important tax deductions plus a steady stream of income for the rest of your life.

*Week 52:* Critically examine your stock holdings, bite the cannonball, and sell off those that have underperformed.

And on *Day 365,* or *Day 366* during leap year, resolve to follow through and pursue these and other moves every year in the future, as you build your lifetime financial strategy.

Good luck, and good fortune!
M. L.

# Index